Praise for *Pacific Destiny*

"Unlike many investigators, Walker does not claim
that he has found the truth about these and many other
mysteries. He presents the evidence (both pro and con),
and lets his reader draw their own conclusion."

—*The Mail-Star* (Halifax)

"Engrossing . . . a compelling narrative."
—*Publishers Weekly*

Praise for *Bear Flag Rising*

"An electrifying account of the quest for
the Pacific Coast."
—*Booklist*

"An expertly written, well-documented history of the
American seizure of California from Mexico."
—*Kirkus Reviews*

OTHER BOOKS BY DALE L. WALKER

Legends and Lies:
Great Mysteries of the American West

The Boys of '98:
Theodore Roosevelt and the Rough Riders

Eldorado: The California Gold Rush

Westward:
A Fictional History of the American West

Januarius MacGahan:
War Correspondent

Rough Rider: Buckey O'Neill of Arizona

Will Henry's West

In a Far Country

Jack London: No Mentor but Myself

Mavericks: Ten Uncorralled Westerners

PACIFIC DESTINY

AND

BEAR FLAG RISING

DALE L. WALKER

FORGE®

A TOM DOHERTY ASSOCIATES BOOK | NEW YORK

PACIFIC DESTINY AND BEAR FLAG RISING

Pacific Destiny copyright © 2000 by Dale L. Walker

Bear Flag Rising copyright © 1999 by Dale L. Walker

Maps on pages 8–11 by Mark Stein

Map on pages 518–519 © 1999 by Miguel Roces

A Forge Book
Published by Tom Doherty Associates
175 Fifth Avenue
New York, NY 10010

www.tor-forge.com

Forge® is a registered trademark of Macmillan Publishing Group, LLC.

ISBN 978-0-7653-9349-4

Our books may be purchased in bulk for promotional, educational, or business use. Please contact your local bookseller or the Macmillan Corporate and Premium Sales Department at 1-800-221-7945, extension 5442, or by e-mail at MacmillanSpecialMarkets@macmillan.com.

First Mass Market Edition: November 2017

Printed in the United States of America

0 9 8 7 6 5 4 3 2 1

CONTENTS

PACIFIC DESTINY   1

BEAR FLAG RISING   511

PACIFIC
DESTINY

The Three-Century Journey
to the Oregon Country

To my friend of all these years,
Elroy Bode

CONTENTS

Acknowledgments
Introduction
Prologue

PART ONE

1. The Patriot

The Prisoner
2. The Spaces in the Wound
3. The Sphere of Fate
4. The City's Burden

CONTENTS

Maps   8
Introduction   13
Prologue   19

PART ONE: SEA-LANES

1   The Pacific Littoral   23
2   The River of the West   34
3   Nootka Sound   49

PART TWO: ASTORIA

4   Pro Pelle Cutem   75
5   The Voyage of the *Tonquin*   92
6   The Phial of Wrath   109
7   The Overlanders   126

PART THREE: WILDERNESS CROSSINGS

8   To the Tetons   145
9   South Pass   163
10   Fort Vancouver   185
11   Captain Smith   202
12   Kelley's Odyssey   219
13   The Iceman   240

PART FOUR: OUT TO ARCADIA

14	The Macedonian Cry	263
15	Spies	287
16	Champoeg	309
17	Sapling Grove	320
18	Jumping Off	339

PART FIVE: MEDICINE ROAD

19	Toward the Elephant	359
20	The Great Migration	382
21	The Parallel	397
22	The Bostonian	417
23	Waiilatpu	432
24	Last Trails	452

Epilogue	474
Sources	481
Bibliography	485
Index	493

Westward the course of empire takes its way;
The four first Acts already past.
A fifth shall close the Drama of the Day;
Time's noblest offspring is the last.

        —Bishop George Berkeley (1685–1753)

Eastward I go only by force; but westward I go free. . . .
I should not lay so much stress on this fact if I did not
believe that something like this is the prevailing tendency
of my countrymen. I must walk toward Oregon, and not
toward Europe. And that way the nation is moving, and I
may say that mankind progresses from east to west.

        —Henry David Thoreau (1817–1862)

When God made man,
He seemed to think it best
To make him in the East,
And let him travel West.

        —unknown pioneer poet

In my book a pioneer is a man who turned all the grass
upside down, strung bob-wire over the dust that was left,
poisoned the water, cut down the trees, killed the Indian
who owned the land, and called it progress.

        —Charles M. Russell (1864–1926)

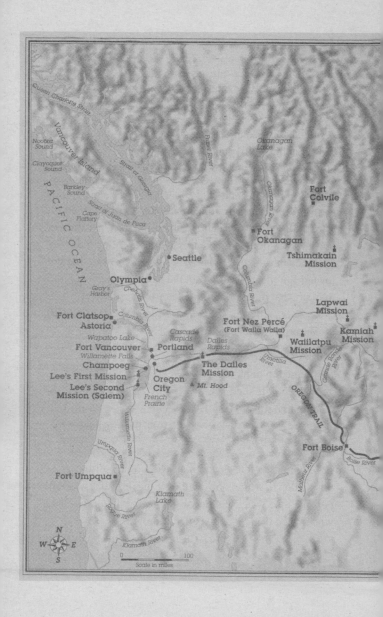

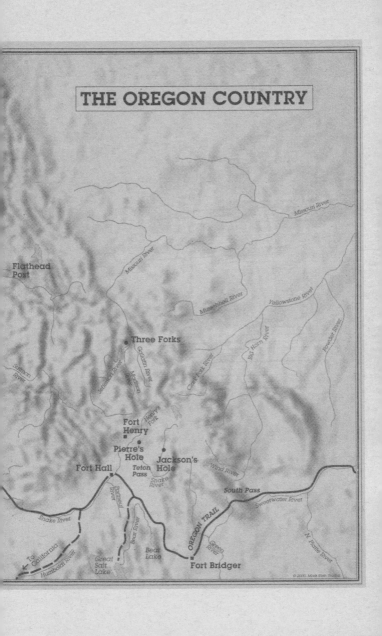

THE OREGON COUNTRY

Missouri River

Flathead Post

Missouri River

Musselshell River

Yellowstone River

Powder River

Big Horn River

Three Forks

Gallatin River

Madison River

Jefferson River

Salmon River

Clark's Fork River

Henry's Fork

Fort Henry

Pierre's Hole

Jackson's Hole

Wind River

Fort Hall

Teton Pass

Snake River

South Pass

Sweetwater River

Snake River

Portneuf River

Bear River

OREGON TRAIL

Green River

N. Platte River

To California

Humboldt River

Great Salt Lake

Bear Lake

Fort Bridger

© 2000 Mark Stein Studios

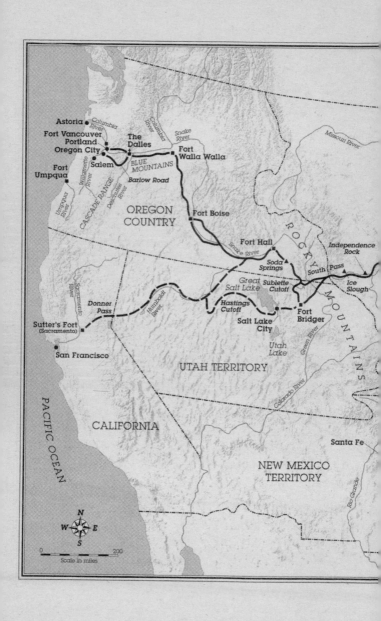

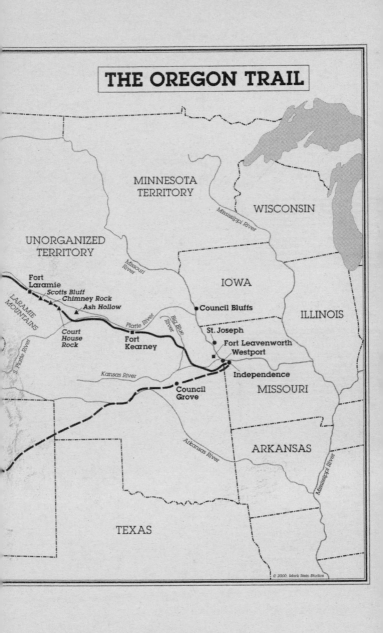

THE OREGON TRAIL

MINNESOTA
TERRITORY

WISCONSIN

UNORGANIZED
TERRITORY

Mississippi River

Missouri River

IOWA

ILLINOIS

Fort
Laramie
Scotts Bluff
Chimney Rock
Ash Hollow

● Council Bluffs

*LARAMIE
MOUNTAINS*

*Court
House
Rock*

Platte River

Big Blue River

St. Joseph

Fort Leavenworth
Westport

N. Platte River

Fort
Kearney

Kansas River

Independence

MISSOURI

● Council
Grove

Arkansas River

ARKANSAS

Mississippi River

TEXAS

© 2000: Mark Stein Studios

INTRODUCTION

Through most of the decade of the 1840s, the Indians of the Great Plains came to the camps along the Platte River in Nebraska to witness the strange migration along what they called the White Man's Medicine Road. They sat their ponies in the noisy dawnings, caught the scent of bacon cooking, watched and listened as the camps broke, heard gunshot signals, the clank of pots and pans, the shouts and curses of teamsters, the wails and shrieks of hungry babies and skylarking children, the babble of people scurrying to their tasks. They heard the pop of white canvas sails billowing and the crack of long bullhide whips over the backs of oxen and mules drawing the creaking prairie schooners westward.

What the Indians saw we still see: trains of covered wagons headed west, the archetypal image of our archetypal American saga, and there can be little wonder why the story has such a grip on us. Those who made that epic journey toward the setting sun had all manner of reasons for going—cheap land, escape from debt, the lure of gold, the craving to teach Christianity to the heathens, the sheer adventure of it all—but whatever their motives, they acted out a dream common to all of us: the dream of a new beginning in a new place.

So captivating is this epic that there is a natural tendency in books on the subject to dwell on the pioneer "experience," to stitch together the journals and diaries of those who actually made the harrowing overland journey. For example, Merrill J. Mattes, whose *The Great Platte River Road* is among the undisputed classic works on the westering emigrants of the 1840s, listed over 1,000 sources for his work, and examined something like 700 eyewitness journal-diary narratives.

But in the research and writing of *Pacific Destiny* I kept imagining what the Indians of the Platte must have wondered: Where were these people *going*, and *why*?, and it seemed natural to me to begin where the emigrant dream really began. In this I was influenced by the lucky circumstance of having visited the end of the trail before traveling over the beginning of it.

During a trip to Portland a few years ago, I was able to visit the Fort Vancouver National Historic Site, drive south along the Willamette River to spend a few hours in Oregon City, and even travel up the Columbia, the fabled "River of the West," on a sternwheeler.

Oregon history is infectious, and I bought books at world-renowned Powell's, collected maps and pamphlets, and caught the spirit of the place—even in the space of a week.

That trip came back to me during an October 1998 drive from Saint Louis to Fort Laramie, Wyoming, roughly following the Oregon Trail route taken by Francis Parkman in 1846.

Parkman did not reach the end of the Oregon Trail—he traveled about 40 percent of it, to a point sixty miles west of Fort Laramie—but he *saw* the trail better than anybody in his time, saw it as a symbol of the westering movement and of what that movement signified for the future. "Great changes are at hand," he wrote, "the buffalo will dwindle away, and the large wandering communities who depend on them for support must be broken and scattered. The Indians will soon be abased by whiskey and overawed by military posts; so that within a few years the traveller may pass in tolerable security through their country. Its dangers and its charms will have disappeared altogether."

With the benefit of 152 years of history and technology behind me, I traveled his route, passing in tolerable security through the Indians' country, the dangers of which are restricted to flat tires or spewing radiators on lonely roads. I had two books with me: Parkman's *The Oregon Trail*, and Gregory M. Franzwa's indispensable guide for the modern traveler, *The Oregon Trail Revisited*. I stopped frequently to consult both, especially to examine the landmarks, sites, and swales described so meticulously by Franzwa. And I daydreamed, from the Museum of Westward Expansion at the Saint Louis Arch through a tour of the Fort Laramie National Historic Site, about the people who pointed their wagons toward the Pacific Rim and rolled free of the rude civilization of Missouri to take the first tentative steps of their 2,000-mile walk to the northwest coast of America.

By the time I dropped away from the trail to the town of Wheatland and made my way south to Cheyenne and home, I was thinking of those who blazed that trail thirty years and more before Parkman traveled it, and the story of that Land of Giants, the Oregon Country, before the name "Oregon" was concocted (a fascinating tale by itself).

In *Pacific Destiny*, by taking a somewhat chronological approach to the story, starting at trail's end and ending with the trail's beginning, my ambition has been to answer the questions I imagined the Platte River natives asking: Where are all these people going and why? and Why Oregon? This book seeks to tell the story of the original Oregon dreamers and pay proper homage to them: sea dogs and explorers; *voyageurs*, trappers, and traders; visionaries and missionaries; adventurers; misfits; opportunists—all pioneers in the purest sense of the word.

In no other episode in western American history is there

a more beguiling assortment of characters than those figuring in the long journey to the lands north of the 42nd parallel and west of the Shining Mountains, the people who made the Oregon Trail not only possible, but inevitable. Only history, never fiction, could give us such figures as Dr. John McLoughlin, the White Eagle laird of Fort Vancouver; Captain Jonathan Thorn, doomed skipper of the frigate *Tonquin*; that "fuming, vainglorious little man," Duncan McDougall, who cowed the Indians with his "phial of wrath"; Wilson Hunt and Robert Stuart, the original Astor overlanders; Hall J. Kelley, the half-mad dreamer who crossed Mexico to get to the Oregon Country after his followers double-crossed him; Nat Wyeth, the Cambridge iceman, and Francis Parkman, the Cambridge scholar. Not even a poet could have invented the adventures of the missionaries Jason Lee, Marcus and Narcissa Whitman, Samuel and Eliza Parker; the mountain men Jedediah Smith, Broken Hand Fitzpatrick, Ewing Young, and Joe Meek; or of such minor players as Miss Jane Barnes, the first woman to visit the Oregon coast, and Reverend Herbert Beaver ("a good name for a fur-trade station," as Peter Skene Ogden dryly observed), who had the misfortune to say something scandalous about John McLoughlin's wife.

Nor is there, to my mind at least, a more compelling tale in our Western history than that of the V-shaped ripples made by certain aquatic animals, especially *Lutra enhydris marina* and *Castor canadensis*, which aimed us toward our Pacific destiny and which bound together this astonishing melange of early dreamers.

A final note: There are necessary anachronisms in the pages that follow. Obviously there was no "Oregon" or "Oregon Country" when Ferrelo and Drake sailed up the Pacific coast of the continent in the sixteenth century; there were no Colorado, Wyoming, Montana, Idaho, Utah, or Nevada when the Astorians crossed the Rocky Mountains, or even during Frémont's early expeditions and, as in the opening paragraph of this introduction, no Nebraska, at least as a state, until 1867. But for easy reader orientation in the often confusing geography of the era of western expansion, I have used out-of-time state and place names to avoid such tedious repetitions as "the future state of Washington" and "what would later become the state of Oregon."

Among generous friends whose assistance of various kinds made it easier to write this book, I want to thank Richard S. Wheeler of Livingston, Montana; James Crutchfield of Franklin, Tennessee; Candy Moulton of Encampment, Wyoming; George Skanse, proprietor of the incomparable Book Gallery in El Paso, Texas; and my friends at the Village Inn, where some of the book was written: Celia Davidson, Evelyn Anderson, Tony Garza, Michelle Garza, Aldo Monterrey, Lisa De Haro, Travis Doctor, Nicole Smith, Julee Morrissy, and Marie Giger.

—DALE L. WALKER
November 18, 1999

PROLOGUE

Westering, Thoreau said, "is the prevailing tendency of my countrymen," and the movement west, inching the frontier toward that "other" great boundary, the Pacific, is as old as America. The original band of Jamestowners who reached Chesapeake Bay in the spring of 1607 were soon pulling out of Tidewater to explore and plow on the Piedmont, and within a hundred years Americans had scattered outposts along the Atlantic from Maine to Carolina.

It took a century and a half for colonists to remove from their striking distance to the sea, but the French and Indian War, proving ground for leaders on both sides of the American Revolution, pushed the frontier to the forks of the Ohio River and began a movement down the Cumberland to the valleys of eastern Kentucky and Tennessee. The Appalachians, running from Québec to the coastal plains of Alabama, proved no obstacle, nor did the escarpments and plateaus of the Allegheny wilderness, which funneled them into Ohio and Kentucky, the Lower Mississippi, and the Old Northwest of Indiana, Illinois, and Michigan.

In March 1803, when Ohio was admitted to the Union, there were seventeen United States, but American territory had not yet crossed the Mississippi. All that changed on October 20 of that year with the ratification of the Louisiana

Purchase. Suddenly the nation's area doubled—$15 million bought 828,000 square miles of land—and jumped its western boundary to the crest of the Rockies.

To the south and west of those unmapped mountains lay New Spain, including its exotic outposts of New Mexico and Alta California; to the northwest, from the Rockies to the Pacific, lay the Oregon Country, strangely alluring, as all hidden places are.

The Lewis and Clark Corps of Discovery reached the sea-slashed coast of the Oregon Country in November 1805, over 250 years after the first white men saw it. Both explorers, and their sponsor, Thomas Jefferson, knew this history, knew that Spaniards, Englishmen, Frenchmen, Russians, a Dane, possibly a Greek, and certainly a handful of Americans had already been there. Fifteen years before the advent of Lewis and Clark, Spain had signed a document that recognized British rights to trade and settle along the northwest coast of America, and in 1792 the Columbia River was named for the first American vessel to anchor there. "Bostons," the Yankee merchant captains from Massachusetts seaports, and Englishmen, and Russians, among others, had established a sea otter fur trade among the coastal Indians.

Jefferson's explorers were therefore not altogether surprised, once they reached the coast and began the work on their fort, to learn that the Indians in the vicinity had already experienced a certain level of "commercial intercourse" with whites. The Clatsops and other tribes the explorers encountered had in their vocabularies a supply of common European profanities, and knew such bartering words as *musket*, *powder*, *shot*, and *knife*.

The Corps of Discovery, stunning in its accomplishment, as "perfect" an exploration as has been recorded in history, made no claim of "discovering" Oregon, only of discovering an overland route to the Pacific, of being the first party of white men to cross the western half of North America.

PART ONE

• •

SEA-LANES

■

1

The Pacific Littoral

■

"... TOO MUCH CONFIDENCE AND UNARM'D."

1

The first trails to Oregon were sea-lanes, the wakes left by Spanish caravels and *fragatos* with lateen sails bulging in ferocious winds and masts bent perilously as they blundered along the Pacific coast of North America in pursuit of obscure missions approved by the viceroy of Mexico.

A Portuguese soldier in the service of Mexico, Juan Rodríguez Cabrillo, led a two-ship expedition from the Pacific port of Natividad in June 1542, searching for fables: the "Coast of Cathay," believed to be a large island somewhere in the north; the seaport of Quivira and its Seven Cities of Gold; and the Strait of Anián, a northwest passage across North America to the Atlantic. Cabrillo's flagship *Victoria,* a stout and sizable vessel, and the smaller *San Salvador*, a frigate, sighted the California coast in July and in the same month sailed into a "closed and very good harbor" he named San Miguel, subsequently known as San Diego.

The bold soldier-sailor sailed on in October, threading through the Santa Barbara Channel Islands. He avoided the terrifying seas off Big Sur and led his ships north past the Farralon Islands and past the great headlands, shrouded in fog, that hid inside them a magnificent bay, to an

anchorage at 38 degrees north latitude, just above the entrance to the Golden Gate. He named this cove Los Pinos
for the great green mantle of pines that surrounded it, and
spent some days there before sailing a short distance north
to Bodega Bay.

Cabrillo hoped to proceed north along the coast but battering seas off Bodega forced him to direct his ships south
to a winter anchorage at San Miguel Island in the Santa Barbara Channel. In January 1543 the former crossbowman in
Hernán Cortés's conquest of Mexico died after a shipboard
accident, and it fell to his handpicked successor, an Italian
Levantine named Bartolome Ferrelo, to continue the voyage.

Ferrelo led the *Victoria* and the *San Salvador* past Cape
Mendocino—the westernmost point on the California
coast—and north at least as far as latitude 41 degrees 30
minutes off Klamath, California. He may have sighted the
Oregon coast above 42 degrees before gales drove him back,
to return to Natividad in April.

Insofar as finding gold and silver, the Seven Cities, or the
Strait of Anián, the expedition was a failure, but Cabrillo and
Ferrelo had charted a real seacoast as fabulous as any Qui-
vira of the imagination.

Francis Drake, the bold son of Devonshire and corsair of the
Spanish Main, may have exceeded the *Victoria* and *San Salvador*'s northernmost mark when he brought his *Golden
Hind* along the California coast thirty-six years after Ferrelo
returned to Mexico.

Drake sailed from Plymouth in December 1577, with a
syndicate sponsoring him as captain-general of a six-ship expedition. His backers expected him to sail through the
Strait of Magellan into the Pacific and seek the Northwest
Passage, the all-water route connecting the two great oceans,
a lodestone that lured mariners and trade-minded politicians
for more than four centuries.

Exploration, however, was incidental to Drake's work as a privateer, a pirate with governmental sanction, so he plundered Spanish ports at Valparaiso, Chile, and Callao, Peru, as he made his way up the Pacific coast. By his own account, the *Hind* approached land between 42 and 48 degrees north latitude before retreating downcoast. In *Hakluyt's Voyages*, published in 1589, Drake is credited with a northern limit of 42 degrees (the latitude of the California-Oregon boundary), which he reached on June 5, 1579. Historian Hubert Howe Bancroft, who studied the sources on Drake's voyage, concluded that the privateer "was probably, though not certainly, the first discoverer of the western coast from Cape Mendocino to the region of Cape Blanco, including fifty or sixty miles of the Oregon coast."

Drake spent five weeks in June and July on the western coast and, like Cabrillo, missed sighting the foggy entrance to San Francisco Bay as he proceeded to an anchorage north of the Golden Gate—Cabrillo's Los Pinos—subsequently named Drake's Bay.

Somewhere, at Drake's Bay, Bodega Bay, or farther north, perhaps near Cape Mendocino, the *Hind* was beached and careened, and in the process the captain-general and his men were visited by a number of Miwok Indians. The naked "sauvages" were presented with gifts of trinkets and in return brought broiled fish; a supply of a lily root they dried, ground into a meal, and ate; and such gifts as shells, sea-otter and gopher skins, and bird feathers.

Drake named the country New Albion (Albion being the Greek name for England) after passing an area of white cliffs that reminded him of the south coast of his home country.

On July 23, Reverend Francis Fletcher, a member of the expedition, said the Miwoks "tooke a sorrowfull farewell of us" and the *Hind* sailed west to Mindanao, the Indian Ocean, and home to Plymouth, arriving there, after nearly three years' absence, in September 1580, completing the first English circumnavigation of the world.

2

In 1596, a letter was published in Europe purportedly written by a Greek explorer in the service of Spain. Apostolos Valerianos, who adopted the name Juan de Fuca, claimed to have sailed a small caravel into the Pacific for the viceroy of Mexico in 1592 and to have found the western opening of the Northwest Passage, a broad inlet on the northern coast between 47 and 48 degrees north latitude. He told of "sailing inland" for more than twenty days and of finding a people who wore the skins of beasts and a land rich in silver, gold, and pearls.

His story was probably a fiction, common enough in the day, but mapmakers put his "opening" in the latitude he described. Two hundred years later, the Juan de Fuca Strait, separating Vancouver Island from the Washington mainland and leading into Puget Sound, was discovered not many sea miles distant from de Fuca's 48 degrees north.

Visions of the Northwest Passage continued to draw mariners along the Oregon coast of America. In 1602, the Spaniard Sebastián Vizcaíno led the *San Diego* and the *Tres Reyes* out of Monterey on the California coast as far north as the 43rd parallel, searching for Quivira and the Strait of Anián.

Nor were all the explorers Spaniards and Englishmen. Peter the Great of Russia had conquered Siberia by 1639 and reached the Pacific, and in 1741 Vitus Bering, a Dane, sailed in the *St. Peter* from Kamchatka to the coast of North America near Sitka. In the 1765–68 era, the Russians were on the move south along the coast, slaughtering sea otters and coastal Indians with equal rapacity.

In 1774, at the time when the First Continental Congress was meeting in Philadelphia, Spain sent an expedition to the

Oregon coast. Among other accomplishments, it discovered Nootka Sound, on the west coast of what became Vancouver Island.

By 1812, with the consent of Spain, Russian hunters out of Sitka founded Fort Ross on Bodega Bay in California and later another fort in the Sandwich Islands. American politicians considered these outposts dangerous in their implications, especially due to their proximity to San Francisco Bay, and in 1816 James Monroe proposed a treaty of amity in North America with the 49th parallel as the boundary between the interests of the two countries. Monroe did not mention England in his proposal, but in any event the idea was not pushed to fruition.

The Spaniards interpreted the Russian incursions as threats to her claims in the Pacific and sent new expeditions out to expand explorations of the coast of Alta California and establish missions and presidios from San Diego to Sonoma, north of the Golden Gate.

But Spain did not pursue its discoveries and, after it seemed clear that the Russians were more interested in the fur trade than in permanent settlement, it was the British who rose to challenge Spain's claims.

In 1778, in his third and final voyage to the Antipodes, Captain James Cook, England's greatest navigator, came to the Oregon coast with his flagship *Resolution* and the sloop *Discovery*. His mission was to conduct a thorough search for the Northwest Passage (for which Parliament was offering a £20,000 prize) by sailing above the northernmost latitude of Ferrelo and Vizcaíno, and above the latitude of Drake's New Albion exploration 200 years before. His cautionary instructions from the Admiralty were to avoid any encounters with foreigners and to respect Spanish dominions on the American coast. His orders stated, "You are also, with the consent of the natives, to take possession in the name of the king of

Great Britain, of convenient situations in such countries as you may discover, that have not already been discovered or visited by any other European power, and to distribute among the inhabitants such things as will remain as traces and testimonies of your having been there."

The world had no more experienced explorer than James Cook. He had helped chart the Saint Lawrence River, surveyed the Newfoundland coast, made two previous epic voyages, that of 1772–1775 his greatest legacy: In three years he had sailed over 20,000 leagues on the southern seas—three times the circumference of the globe—with a loss of only four men (defeating scurvy with sauerkraut and meat broths), and charted the coasts of Antarctica and Australia.

In 1776, when Cook sailed from England for the last time on his square-rigged flagship *Resolution* (his sailing master was a twenty-one-year-old navigator from Plymouth named William Bligh), his orders were almost too specific. He was to proceed around the Cape of Good Hope into the Pacific, cross from Tahiti in the Windward Group of the Society Islands to the coast of North America, and proceed northward to determine the value, if any, of the theory that in arctic waters would be found the western entrance to the Northwest Passage. Failing to find it there, he was to continue through the Bering Strait and search for an open-water polar passage. Such confidence was placed in his success that the Admiralty dispatched naval vessels to meet him in Baffin Bay on the Atlantic side of the continent.

He reached and rediscovered Hawaii (which he named the Sandwich Islands after the First Lord of the Admiralty, the Earl of Sandwich), and on March 7, 1778, sighted the coast of Drake's New Albion at the 43rd parallel and charted and named such features as Capes Arago, Foulweather, and Perpetua as he sailed upcoast. He missed seeing the tumultuous mouth of the Columbia River, but on March 22 the *Resolution* and the *Discovery* stood at a cape on the edge of a strait Cook denied existed. He named the promontory Cape Flattery and wrote in his journal, "There appeared to be a small opening, which flattered us with the hopes of finding a harbor . . . . It is in this very latitude where we now were, that geographers have placed the pretended strait of Juan de Fuca . . . . But we saw nothing like it; nor is there the least probability that ever any such thing existed."

Cook's ships made their first landing at Nootka Sound, and the explorer wrote about the desolate, windblown place in his journals, which were eagerly published in England and the United States and widely read. He wrote about the furs secured from Indians at Nootka, which fetched handsome prices in the China trade (sea otter pelts, purchased for a handful of beads, sold in Canton for as much as $200 each); of savages paddling canoes, some of them forty feet long and seven wide, made from a single cedar trunk, and throwing feathers and red dust in their wake. He saw men dressed in fur-edged blankets of dog hair mixed with cedar bark and decorated with scenes of whale hunts, over which were draped capes of sea otter skins; people whose bodies were smeared with red clay mixed with whale oil, their hair long and soaked in fish oil sprinkled with bird down, their ear-lobes and noses decorated with bone and bits of metal, wearing wooden masks painted into grotesque visages. These amazing people had articles of iron and copper, leftovers from Spanish landings, and one native wore two silver spoons as ear ornaments. Their houses, "filthy as hogsties, everything in and about them stinking of fish," Cook said, were surrounded by racks of drying fish, piles of excrement, and strange totems.

In spring of 1779, soon after he returned to the Sandwich Islands from the northwest coast, Captain Cook, age fifty, was killed by natives at Kealakekua Bay. One of six marines from the *Discovery* and the *Resolution* fighting hand-to-hand the natives who stabbed Cook to death was an American named John Ledyard.

3

The lure of the Pacific Northwest in the last decade of the eighteenth century and the first of the nineteenth had nothing to do with its potential for settlement, or with its vast timber and fishery potential—which were obvious from the starboard rail of any ship headed north—or even with that ancient, chimerical idea of a Northwest Passage. The great enticement in those two decades was *Lutra enhydris marina*, which the Russians knew as *Bobri morski,* "sea beaver," and which American and English sailors called the sea otter.

These gregarious, aquatic animals lived and bore their pups in their favorite habitats, the reefs and rocks and floating kelp beds of coastal California, British Columbia, and Alaska. The animal was prized for its thick, fine underfur, perfect for sewing into royal robes, and for the tails, which were used for decorating hats and gown borders. Like the beaver, next on the list for extermination, sea otters were "harvested" recklessly. Between 1790 and 1812 an average of 12,000 a year were clubbed to death. In fact, the animal was all but extinct on the northern coast by 1800.

English mariners to the Northwest knew the value of the sea otter from Drake's time, and the Russians were slaughtering them on Alaskan shores even before they began their poaching sorties out of Sitka down to Fort Ross. Coastal Indians had known the animals' worth from time immemorial: Two sea otter pelts would buy a slave, and when the first white explorers came, the furs could be traded for any number of iron tools, beads, and gewgaws.

In 1785 the French sent an expedition to the Oregon coast and, not surprisingly, one of its objectives was to obtain reliable information on the fur trade there. Since 1600 France had worked to establish a fur monopoly in the New World, and by 1750 its *coureurs de bois* (runners of the woods) and brigades of trappers had penetrated the continent as far west as the Mandan villages of the Missouri River and south to Santa Fé in Spanish New Mexico.

Louis XVI personally had a hand in planning the 1785 Pacific expedition. Like other European monarchs, he was interested in the China trade and therefore captivated by the idea of "some river or narrow gulf" that might communicate between the two great oceans—a Northwest Passage. He also wrote of "the possibility of a colony or at least a factory [trading post] in a region not yet occupied" on the Pacific coast of America.

A nobleman and celebrated navigator named Jean de Galaup, Comte de La Pérouse, led the expedition, commanding two vessels, the *Boussole* and the *Astrolabe*. At age forty-four he had already spent thirty years at sea, starting his career as a midshipman during the Seven Years' War. In addition to a full complement of officers and seamen, La Pérouse had aboard his ships a remarkable assortment of scientists, interpreters, and "observers" who were to gather data on the country, its people and "products," the extent of Spanish establishments ashore, and the latitude at which furs might be obtained without giving offense to Spain.

La Pérouse's ships found the northwest coast on June 23, 1786, and spent six weeks in Alaskan waters as far north as latitude 59 degrees 37 minutes, then sailed down past Nootka and the Oregon coast to California. The *Boussole* and *Astrolabe* made frequent anchorages and lowered boats, the shore parties conducting a brisk trade with Indians. The fur-shrewd Frenchmen had bartered for over a thousand sea otter "pieces" before crossing the Pacific to Macao, the Portuguese port on the China coast. There the scraps, tails, and hides were sold and the profits divided among the crews of the two ships.

"I believe there is no country in the world where the sea-otter is more common than in this part of America," La Pérouse wrote in his log, "and I should be little surprised if a factory extending its operations only forty or fifty leagues along the sea-shore might collect each year ten thousand skins of this animal." He cautioned, however, that a French factory on the northwest coast of America might cause problems with the courts at Madrid and Saint Petersburg.

In September 1787 the navigator put his Russian interpreter ashore at Kamchatka to make his way to Paris with reports and maps, then sailed south. In January 1788, now two and one half years out of Brest, the French ships battered their way into Botany Bay, the harbor on the eastern shore of Australia discovered eight years earlier by Captain Cook. There was a historical coincidence in La Pérouse's appearance there. Watching him maneuver his vessels into the bay were the crews of two British warships and nine merchant transports, which had just landed over 700 British convicts ashore after a voyage of 15,000 miles from Plymouth. This was the "first fleet" of the criminal population of Australia.

The French explorers spent six weeks at Botany Bay among the Englishmen and their prisoner-colonists before setting sail and disappearing into the maw of the Pacific. Thirty years would pass before it was determined that La Pérouse and all hands had perished when the *Boussole* and the *Astrolabe* went down among the Coral Sea reefs of the New Hebrides, 1,200 miles east of the Australian coast.

In the same year as the La Pérouse expedition, Captain Charles Barkley (or Barclay or Berkeley), an Englishman, sailing from Ostende in the merchant vessel *Imperial Eagle* under the flag of a fictitious "Austrian East India Company," entered Nootka Sound, and began a trade with the Indians of Vancouver Island. His notable contribution to the history of the American Northwest occurred in July 1787, when he found the "lost" Strait of Juan de Fuca. Barkley did not venture far into it; instead, he continued south to trade with the natives.

The sailors of the *Imperial Eagle* were among the first to learn that native naïveté and docility could not always be depended upon. Four of Barkley's crew were killed after going ashore with "too much confidence and unarm'd," and the captain's report established that the attack took place at 47 degrees 46 minutes north, at a place he appropriately named Destruction Island. He ordered the burning of a village in retribution and established a pattern of violence that would last a half century.

Despite the conflict with the natives, the origin of which was not reported, Barkley's expedition made a trade bonanza among the coastal tribes, departing the coast with 4,000 sea otter pelts, which were taken to Macao in the winter of 1787 and sold at an immense profit.

2

· · · · · · · · · · · · · · · ·

The River of the West

■

1

From the interior of what became the Oregon Country to its thundering coast lived a diverse people who had occupied the land for centuries before Ferrelo and Drake saw it. Some of the native clans were given French or English names such as Nez Percé, Flathead, Coeur d'Alêne; and there were also such tribes and subtribes as the Cayuse, Colville, Kalispell, Spokane, Yakima, Walla Walla, and Wishram; and the coastal Chinook, Chehalem, Salish, Clatsop, Puyallap, Tillamook, Coos, and Umpqua. Their cultures have been called by anthropologists the most elaborate in the world among nonagricultural native people.

All the tribes, land-bound and coastal, had a common riches: the land's lush abundance. Fish, salmon in particular, and timber for boats and homes distinguished them. Many of the coastal folk, those first encountered by Europeans, were fish-rich, status-conscious slaveholders. Their social structure was sharply divided among autocrats and commoners with a hereditary chief at the center who owned huge tracts of village lands, hunting and fishing grounds, and was served by slaves captured in raids on other tribes. This chief's status among his people and his renown among peers

in neighboring clans was to a degree dependent on the elabo-
rateness of his periodic *potlatch* (a Chinook word essentially
meaning "giving away"). In this religious ceremony, after
much speechmaking and feasting, to demonstrate his riches
the chief would distribute gifts—from caches of dried fish
to parcels of land—according to the social status of the re-
cipients.

Among the coastal clans were accomplished artisans
much admired (and soon feared) by the explorers and navigators who visited their sea-wracked shores from Nootka
Sound to Alta California. In ships' logs and explorers' journals are descriptions of their longhouses and carved and
painted totems, of delicately carved bowls made of alder-
wood, blankets of animal hair, weirs—basket-traps—of
woven willow, fish lines and nets made of twisted wood
fibers and grasses, hooks and harpoons made of wood,
bone, and shell. They wrote of dances and rituals with much
noisemaking with rattles and bells, the participants wearing
wooden masks and long cloaks made of shredded cedar bark
dyed with berry juices.

White chroniclers admired the native watercraft, especially the great flat-bottomed, cedarwood dugouts, some of
them thirty or forty feet long, capable of carrying a crew of
five and a ton of weight. Chinooks and Nootkas, among others, made such boats—rough-shaping them with stone
adzes, firing them for hardness, sanding and polishing them
with sharkskin—and paddled them from Vancouver Island
to California waters and up the Columbia to the Indian commerce center at The Dalles rapids. They harpooned whales
in them, caught sharks and seals and sea otters, netted fish,
and pulled the boats ashore to collect mollusks along the
beaches.

Another artistic and functional craft of the coastal tribes
was the canoe. This vessel—unlike those familiar to the
voyageur, made from birch bark and hide lashings—the Pacific Northwest Indian made his from a split log, chipped

with adzes until the walls were thin and pliable, the bottom
burn-hardened with heapings of hot coals, the skin painted,
and the wooden prow carved into animal figureheads.

William Clark described these canoes as "butiful . . .
neeter made than any I have ever Seen and calculated to ride
the waves, and carry emence burthens."

The culture of the sea and river people, and even important features of their religion, were founded on fish. The
Nootkas honored Salmon Beings, and the first fish caught
each year was eaten ritually at an altar and its bones thrown
back into the water to reincarnate. Even the inland Colvilles
had a Fish Guardian Spirit. They used fish oil, which they
preserved in fish- or animal-gut bags, in cooking, for flavor-
ing, for mixing with berries, and for rubbing in their hair
and on their skin.

Many, perhaps most, of the Northwest tribes were, to use
the white man's word, "peaceable," avoiding wars with their
neighbors and even mediating family and intertribal quar-
rels. Some had communal food-gathering practices and
tribal assemblies in which all adults, male and female, had
their say.

But there were some tribes who had waged war before the
white man came and remained warlike thereafter.

2

The river rises in southeastern British Columbia and
flows northwest, then south, in the Rocky Mountain
trench for 465 miles before crossing the 49th line of latitude.
Just below the mouth of the Spokane River lava beds force
it to make a bend westward, then it veers south again, running swiftly through a narrow valley where it is joined by
its chief tributary, the Snake. Now on a westward course, the
river flows through the magnificent gorges it created over the

millennia, through the Cascades and the Coast Ranges, reaching the Pacific, 1,210 miles from its source.

The Spanish explorer Bruno de Heçeta, probably the first European to observe its fearsome estuary, named it the San Roque. Early geographers and cartographers, who knew of its existence before learning anything specific about it, called it the River of the West. And in 1778, an explorer who had come no closer to it than the headwaters of the Mississippi called it the Oregon River.

Jonathan Carver of Weymouth, Massachusetts, was nearly fifty years old when he had his brush with history. A shoemaker, and married, he enlisted in the British army in 1757 to fight the French, and was wounded during the siege of Fort William Henry in the foothills of the Adirondacks of New York.

His service must have been exemplary. After nine years in the army he had risen from the ranks to a captaincy, and in 1766 he had an important rendezvous at Mackinac Island in the strait between the upper and lower peninsulas of northern Michigan. There Carver met with Major Robert Rogers, the celebrated founder of Rogers' Rangers, the militia force he raised during the French and Indian War. Rogers had an ambition to explore. He had written a book, *Concise Account of North America,* and during a trip to England had submitted a proposal to King George that he would lead an expedition to find a route from the Mississippi to the Pacific. The "sanction," or sponsorship, of the plan was denied, but Rogers was at least given a command in upper Michigan and there determined to launch the expedition himself.

Why he chose Captain Jonathan Carver to lead it is unknown, but the two met at Mackinac, and soon thereafter Carver began what was to become the first English expedition to explore and survey the Upper Mississippi and Great

Lakes region. He was specifically assigned to map the
rivers of Wisconsin and Minnesota, and to determine the
feasibility of an all-water passage to the Pacific.

In the summer of 1766, Carver led a small band of frontiersmen to Green Bay, at the mouth of the Fox River in
northeast Wisconsin, then followed the Fox to the Wisconsin River and down to the Mississippi. He wintered at the
Falls of Saint Anthony, near Saint Paul, Minnesota, and
there refined his maps and journals and anticipated continuing his journey westward.

In this, for reasons never adequately explained, he was
thwarted. During the spring thaws of 1767, Carver and his
crew traveled to Grand Portage on the north shore of Lake
Superior. He expected to find reinforcements and supplies
awaiting him there that would enable him to push west to
the Pacific, but when the manpower and materiél were not
forthcoming, he disbanded his men and in 1768 returned to
Boston.

In London in 1774 Carver joined in a scheme with Richard Wentworth, a wealthy member of Parliament, to take
fifty or sixty men up the Missouri River, explore the "Shining Mountains" (the Rockies), find the source of the River
of the West, sail down it to its exit in the Pacific, and build
a fort at its mouth. The plan appears to have had the sanction of the British colonial government but was buried by the
intervention of the American Revolution.

Carver remained in England, married again (without di-
vorcing his first wife in America), and died in poverty in
1780. He had one success after his Mississippi expedition, the
publication in 1778 of his mixture of fact and fantasy, *Carver's Travels Through the Interior Parts of North America in
the years 1766, 1767, and 1768,* which sustained a reader-
ship through thirty editions.

In the book, Carver told of his explorations of the headwaters of the Mississippi, his talks with an Indian tribe he
designated the Naudowessie, and his learning of the coun-

try to the west, in particular of the Shining Mountains, a range he said began in Mexico and continued northward on a line east of Spanish California. These mountains were rich in gold, he wrote; indeed, the metal was so plentiful the Indians there made their commonest utensils from it. "Probably in future ages," he said, "they [the mountains] may be found to contain more riches in their bowels than those of Indostan and Malabar, or that are produced on the Golden Coast of Guinea; nor will I except even the Peruvian Mines." He also learned that the natives of the Shining Mountains dressed in the soft, warm covering of beasts "which skipped upon the surface" (presumably beavers), and that these natives were white.

From the Shining Mountains, Carver said, rivers flowed in every direction, these including the River of the West, which he said "falls into the Pacific Ocean at the straits of Anián."

(Of these claims H. H. Bancroft says wryly, "Brave words for one who might as well have been speaking of the Mountains of the Moon so far as actual knowledge or even probability was concerned.")

Carver wrote that the Indian name for the River of the West was the "Oregon," or as he sometimes spelled it, "Origan," and in so saying created a puzzle unsolved to this day: the source of the word *Oregon*.

He claimed he heard the name from the Naudowessie Indians near the headwaters of the Mississippi. His sponsor, Robert Rogers, may have used it—as "Ouragon" and "Ourigon"—in the unpublished "memorial" he wrote to King George asking for governmental sponsorship of an exploration of the trans-Mississippi region.

Wherever the word originated, it does not appear in any of the several dialects of the Oregon Country, and several theories on its provenance have been advanced. One of these has it that the word derives from *Origanum*, or sweet marjoram, a useful plant believed to have had medicinal properties.

But it is not explained how Indians would know the Latin name of the plant, or indeed if they even knew of the plant to begin with. A writer in an 1871 issue of the *New York Ethnological Journal* proposed the more plausible idea that "Oregon" might derive from the Spanish *huricán* (hurricane), describing the shrieking winds of the northwest coast in certain months remarked on by all early-day explorers.

The word does not appear in Lewis and Clark's journals, although Jefferson used it in his instructions to the explorers. It appeared in print for the first time in Carver's 1778 book of travels, and for the second time in the 1817 poem "Thanatopsis" by William Cullen Bryant ("Or lose thyself in the continuous woods/ Where rolls the Oregon, and hears no sound"). Bancroft wrote that Jefferson and Bryant had read Carver's book and that the poet "seized upon the word that fitted best his meter, and in his 'Thanatopsis' made that word immortal."

The historian said it is doubtful that Carver understood the natives who allegedly uttered the word, but admitted, "There could have been no object, apparent to us, for him to misrepresent; he could never have dreamed that this probably meaningless sound, caught up from the wind by his too attentive ear, should ever be applied to the designation of a great, progressive state."

3

Fourteen years after Jonathan Carver's fanciful naming of the River of the West, a company of six Boston merchants financed a fur-trading enterprise to the northern Pacific, the first such American venture. The sponsors were apparently inspired by publication of Captain James Cook's journals of his 1778 voyage, especially those passages dealing with the "sea beaver" furs to be found there and their worth in the China trade. They put up $50,000 to dispatch two trade vessels from Nantucket Roads in September 1787.

In command of the expedition was the veteran privateer and trader John Kendrick of Harwich, Massachusetts, sailing on the *Columbia Rediviva* ("America Reborn"), a 212-ton, 83-foot merchantman with a thirty-man crew and armed with ten cannons. Kendrick's second was a thirty-two-year-old Rhode Islander named Robert Gray, another privateer in the American Revolution and a self-styled "sea-peddler." Gray, who commanded the *Lady Washington*, a ninety-ton merchant sloop, had a reputation as a rough and ruthless seaman with none of Kendrick's diplomacy and kindliness of character.

The ships carried a $25,000 cargo: scrap iron, 135 barrels of beef, 60 of pork, 1,500 pounds of gunpowder, 5 hogsheads of New England and West Indian rum, 2,000 bricks, tea, chocolate, copper sheets, "Barr iron," "Iron Hoops," "Chissells," and gimcracks and utensils for trade with coastal natives. These included snuffboxes, jew's harps, mirrors, buttons, cloth remnants, iron tools, cookpots, and pewter medals to be awarded to tribal dignitaries. The ships managed to maintain visual contact on the voyage from Nantucket to the Cape Verde and Falkland Islands, but lost sight of each other in a Cape Horn gale. Gray sailed on and reached "New Albion," perhaps near Cape Mendocino, on August 2, 1788. He continued upcoast to the vicinity of Tillamook Bay, above the 45th parallel, and there occurred a lamentable incident that caused Gray to call Tillamook Murderer's Harbor.

The Indians who greeted the *Lady Washington*'s shore parties were friendly and traded enthusiastically, bringing baskets of berries and crabs to Gray's famished and scurvy-ridden crewmen, exchanging furs for iron implements, assisting in gathering wood and fresh water. On August 16, nine seamen rowed ashore to gather a load of grass and shrubs for the ship's livestock. The trouble began when an Indian onlooker seized a cutlass that Gray's servant, a Cape Verde Islander named Marcos López, had left stuck in the sand. López and three others pursued the thief and caught him but in the melee López was killed and the other sailors, after slashing one attacker to death with cutlasses, succeeded in getting into a boat and to the sloop offshore. Captain Gray then directed the *Lady Washington*'s swivel gun at the pursuing canoes and drove them back to shore.

A month after the Tillamook fight and with the help of two British traders already at anchor there, Gray brought his sloop into Nootka Sound. Within a few days Captain Kendrick arrived in the *Columbia Rediviva* after a rough passage around the Horn.

The traders spent a successful winter bartering for sea otter and other skins, and in the spring of 1789 Kendrick ordered the furs loaded on the *Columbia* and turned the sloop over to Gray to sail to Canton. At Whampoa, the great traders' anchorage in the Canton River, the *Columbia* threaded its way among East India Company merchantmen, tea boats, and sampans, and in the bustling warehouses Gray sold the furs for more than $20,000—half of which he paid out in fees, bribes, and ship repairs. He took on a cargo of 21,462 pounds of tea with the remainder of the money and sailed home to Boston. On August 10, 1790, after a three-year absence, the *Columbia* anchored off Nantucket, the first American ship to circumnavigate the globe.

After less than two months ashore, Gray was rehired by the company of Boston merchants and now, as part owner of the *Columbia*, fitted his ship out for a return to the Pacific. In June 1791, after an uneventful voyage, Gray navigated his ship to its anchorage in Clayoquot Sound on the island above the Strait of Juan de Fuca and again began searching for Indians willing to trade sea otter pelts. And he was not alone. That year no fewer than twenty-eight vessels, flying the flags of France, Portugal, England, and the

United States, visited the northwest coast, more than half of the number engaged in the fur trade.

Little is known of Gray's activities after he reached Clayoquot Sound except that his volcanic temper created deadly conflicts with the natives. He lost his chief mate and several seamen to Haida tribesmen in the Queen Charlotte Islands soon after he arrived, and in January 1792 one of his trading outposts ashore—its whereabouts are not precisely known—was attacked by a large force of Indians. The assault was beaten back and resulted in Gray's seamen burning a large native village.

In April 1792 Gray sailed the *Columbia* on a trade mission downcoast and in returning north on April 29 encountered the exploring ship *Discovery,* commanded by the English navigator George Vancouver. This brilliant young seaman had sailed from Falmouth, England, rounded the Cape of Good Hope to make the passage to Australia, then sailed across the Pacific. He had made a survey and mapping of the coast from San Diego to Alaska and would soon become the first explorer to circumnavigate the big island subsequently named for him.

Vancouver and his officers boarded the *Columbia* and exchanged information with Gray. On April 27, the master mariner said he had sighted the mouth of a river but, "not considering this opening worthy of more attention," had sailed on north. The *Columbia* was the first ship he had seen in eight months. Gray in turn told Vancouver that he had recently "been off the mouth of a river," in the latitude of 46 degrees 10 minutes, "where the outset, or reflux, was so strong as to prevent my entering." On that occasion the *Columbia* apparently stood out to sea and did not attempt to enter the mouth of the river first sighted by Bruno de Heçeta seventeen years before.

On May 11, 1792, Gray brought his ship back to the estuary, braved the whipping seas, and after eleven days found a passage through, crossed the bar, and anchored ten miles within the entrance. A party of thirty men sailed a cutter thirty miles upstream, found a Chinook village, and thereafter the ship was visited by numerous Indian canoes bringing furs to trade. Bad weather prevented the *Columbia* from escaping the estuary until May 20, by which time Gray named the river after his ship and claimed the territory around it in the name of the United States.

After breaking through the river's mouth in May, he took the *Columbia* to Nootka Sound and continued to trade for furs so that by the time he sailed for Canton in the fall of 1792 he had 700 sea otter skins and 1,500 other furs on board, which he traded for tea, nankeens (garments made of a natural yellow cotton), sugar, and porcelain.

George Vancouver's expedition was no less successful. His *Discovery* and armed tender *Chatham* made eighteen anchorages on the northwest coast and named such sites as Puget Sound (for its chief explorer, Lieutenant Peter Puget), Cape Dungeness, Admiralty Inlet, Port Orchard, Port Discovery, Whidbey and Vashon Islands, Bellingham Bay, and the Gulf of Georgia.

Vancouver's report to the Admiralty was lavish in its description of the lands he visited or saw through his spyglass. He wrote, "The serenity of the climate, the innumerable pleasing landscapes, and the abundant fertility that unassisted nature puts forth, require only to be enriched by the industry of man with villages, mansions, cottages, and other buildings, to render it the most lovely country that can be imagined."

On June 4, 1792, the birthday of George III, Vancouver took possession of the land from Puget Sound to 50 degrees north and named it New Georgia.

After Gray's departure, his commander John Kendrick took the *Lady Washington* to the Sandwich Islands, where he dreamed of developing a trade in sandalwood and pearls, then continued on to China, remaining there fourteen months. He returned to the Pacific coast in 1791, visiting Japan en route, *Lady Washington* being the first American ship to drop anchor in the waters of that forbidden land.

In December 1794 Kendrick was killed in a bizarre accident as his ship lay at anchor off Honolulu. The British trader *Jackal,* anchored adjacent to the American vessel, fired its saluting cannon to honor Kendrick, but the gun had been inadvertently "shotted"—loaded with round- and grapeshot—which pierced the side of the *Washington* and decapitated Kendrick as he sat at a mess table.

Robert Gray died of yellow fever during a voyage along the Atlantic coast in 1806. Of his accomplishments, historian Samuel Eliot Morison wrote: "On her first voyage, the *Columbia* solved the riddle of the China trade. On her second, empire followed in her wake."

4

Alexander Mackenzie of Lewis Island, the northernmost point of the Outer Hebrides of Scotland, has the distinction of being the first European to reach the Pacific Northwest coast from the interior of the continent, preceding Meriwether Lewis and William Clark by twelve years.

He seems to have had the heart of an explorer from the onset of his career when in 1779, at age fifteen, he became a clerk in a fur-trading company in Montreal. Possessed of "a vigorous mind and a fine physique," as Bancroft put it, he devoted all his free time to poring over the primitive maps of North America available to him, made a trip to London to study astronomy and navigation, and read assiduously the literature of New World explorations, including Jonathan Carver's book, and particularly the journals of Captain Cook's third voyage in 1778.

Mackenzie was also greatly influenced by the American-born North West Company fur trader Peter Pond, a former soldier and seaman whose adventures had taken him from fights at Fort Ticonderoga and the siege of Montreal to the West Indies; who had fought at least one duel (and killed his opponent), explored the Upper Mississippi country, and had traded among the Yankton Sioux and the Lake Superior Ojibway. Pond spent two years as a trader in Saskatchewan and was credited with the 1780 discovery of the Peace River, one of the chief headstreams of what was to become the Mackenzie River.

Pond and Mackenzie seem to have met at Fort Chipewyan on Lake Athabaska in northern Alberta in 1787, and there Mackenzie saw a map Pond had drawn, based on his own explorations and from what he had learned from Indian friends. The map depicted a river flowing out of Lake Athabaska to Great Slave Lake, 250 miles to the northwest. Pond believed this river flowed on to the Pacific and that its mouth was an inlet on the Alaskan coast described in Cook's journals.

In 1788 Pond quit the fur trade, sold his interest in the North West Company for £800, and returned to his home in Connecticut. Mackenzie, adopting Pond's river theory, set out from Fort Chipewyan on June 3, 1789, to prove it.

With a party of four *voyageurs*, a German friend, and an Indian named English Chief serving as hunter and interpreter, Mackenzie reached Great Slave Lake and made swift progress down the river Pond had described. The Scotchman soon realized that the river, which turned out to be 1,120 miles in length, would not reach the Pacific, but instead flowed northwest and debouched into the Arctic Ocean. He reached its mouth on the Beaufort Sea and, after chasing whales and paddling among the icebergs "under the starless summer sky and never setting summer sun of the hyperborean sea," he returned by the same route, investigating along the way any tributary that might take him west to the Pacific. He arrived at Fort Chipewyan on September 12, after 102 days on the river that would henceforth bear his name.

The river passage to the Pacific never strayed far from Mackenzie's mind, but three years were to pass before he could undertake a new expedition to find it. On October 10, 1792, he again embarked from Fort Chipewyan and proceeded up the Peace River to the foothills of the northern Rocky Mountains, where stood the farthest-flung western trading post of the North West Company. He outfitted there and chose a trusted (and ill-fated) friend, Alexander McKay, as his second-in-command. With a twenty-five-foot birchbark canoe loaded with 3,000 pounds of supplies, Mackenzie and his ten-member party pushed off a place called Fork Fort on May 9, 1793, and made a heroic portage around the Peace River canyon. In his search for a waterway that would carry him west to the ocean, Mackenzie often acted on information given to him by Indians and often on his own instinct, the latter taking him on a difficult and mistaken detour down the Fraser River. In mid-July the party crossed a 6,000-foot defile in the subsequently named Mackenzie Range, and descended the Fraser (which the explorer mistakenly thought was the Columbia) to the Bella Coola River and to its discharge into a narrow canal. This waterway emptied into Queen Charlotte Sound just north of Vancouver Island and by negotiating it, Mackenzie and his party reached Pacific tidewater on July 20, 1793.

He returned along the same route to caches of buried pemmican along the Fraser, reached Fork Fort on August 24, and a month later was back at Fort Chipewyan to resume his work as a fur trader. He made no further explorations.

Mackenzie's *Voyages from Montreal Through the Continent of North America,* published in 1801, was widely read and esteemed for its modesty and felicity of language. Thomas Jefferson was among the book's ardent admirers, as were the president's transcontinental agents, Messrs. Lewis and Clark, who carried the book to the Pacific on their own expedition in 1804.

For his services to the crown, Mackenzie was knighted in 1802 by King George III. Sir Alexander retired to Scotland in 1805, married, enjoyed his children, and died at his home at Mulinearn on March 12, 1820, at the age of fifty-six.

3

Nootka Sound

■

1

John Ledyard seemed destined to make his mark in the crowded exploration decade of 1778–1788 when Cook, La Pérouse, Barkley, Gray, and Mackenzie were finding, re-finding, and defining the northwestern Pacific coast. No man of his time, with the exception of his patron Thomas Jefferson, had a greater vision of what the region could mean to the United States than this half-mad seeker of a "passage to glory."

Ledyard was born in Groton, Connecticut, in 1751, the eldest of six children of a sea captain in the West Indies trade. After his father's death in 1762, he lived with his grandparents and at age twenty-one, acting on an ill-defined ambition to "minister to the Indians," undertook mission-ary training at Dartmouth. Not long after he began his theo-logical studies, however, he ran afoul of certain stringent rules, and for his insolence and disobedience obliged the college by leaving it. Now disinherited by his family, he signed aboard a merchant ship out of New London bound for the Barbary Coast of North Africa, but deserted when the ship reached Falmouth, England. He was arrested in Bristol, jailed, and eventually given the choice of sailing

aboard a ship departing for the Guinea coast or "taking
the King's shilling"—enlisting in the army. Ledyard chose
the army, transferred to the Royal Marines, and, in July
1776, as his home country launched its Revolutionary War,
he learned of Captain Cook's preparations to launch his
third voyage to the Great South Sea. With typical brash-
ness, he sought an audience with Cook to ask for a billet,
and the eminent navigator was sufficiently curious about
the tall, powerfully built American at his doorstep to permit him across the threshold. Ledyard, an intelligent, excitable talker, explained his mission and told his history. Cook
was impressed with his visitor's "ardent nature," and the
Connecticut Yankee in King Cook's court left the lodging
with the rank of corporal of marines on the *Resolution*, the
only American in the expedition.

The *Discovery* and the *Resolution* sailed from Plymouth
on July 12, 1776, and Ledyard kept a journal of the expedition's progress to the Cape of Good Hope, the outer waters
of Antarctica, Van Diemen's Land (Tasmania), Australia,
New Zealand, Tahiti, the Sandwich Islands, and of the voyage along the North American coast, which was reached in
March 1778. At Nootka Sound on the western shore of Vancouver Island Ledyard studied the island's natives and reflected on his long absence from home. He wrote, "This
was the first fair opportunity I had of examining the appearance of those unknown aborigines of North America. It
was the first time too that I had been so near the western
shores of that continent which gave me birth; and though
more than 2000 miles distant from the nearest part of New
England I felt myself painfully affected."

One of the American's notable adventures occurred when
Cook guided his ships northward and anchored off Unalaska,
one of the largest of the Aleutian chain. Ledyard was among
the shore party that found traces of other "civilized"
visitors—campfires, rusted iron traps, a black waistcoat—
and he volunteered to conduct a search of the island for the

white men who had abandoned the belongings. With native guides he located a camp of Russian trappers who greeted him warmly and invited him to share their meal of whale meat and broiled salmon. Using sign language and drawings, he learned that the Russians came to the Alaskan coast every year from Kamchatka to trap sable, fox, ermine, beaver, and sea otter and to trade for these skins among the natives. Ledyard learned of the Siberian and Chinese markets for the furs and the enormous profits to be made from them.

After Cook's death in the Sandwich Islands in 1779, his officers continued the expedition, returned north, sailed along the Russian Asiatic coast, called at Macao and Canton, and returned to Plymouth in October 1780 after a voyage of four years and three months.

In 1782 Ledyard returned to the United States and made his way to Groton a few weeks after the British surrender at Yorktown.

With publication of his *A Journal of Captain Cook's Last Voyage to the Pacific* in 1783, Ledyard became something of a celebrity, with newspapers referring to him as "the Great American Traveler." He was afire with schemes born from his Pacific adventures. He wanted to captain a ship that would round the Horn and sail to Nootka Sound, proceed to Alaska, and there trade in furs to take to China to exchange for tea, silks, and spices. With the profits from this venture he proposed to mount an expedition to cross the continent east to west and establish an American fur-trading post at Nootka, thus anticipating accomplishments by Lewis and Clark, and the German-born fur entrepreneur John Jacob Astor.

Supremely self-confident, vigorous, and possessing an infectious enthusiasm and the enviable history of having James Cook as his mentor and the *Resolution* as his classroom, Ledyard carried his visonary ideas to New England financiers. He earned their interest—who would not be interested, at least, in hearing the Great American Traveler recount his adventures and ideas?—but not their backing, and decided to try his luck in Europe.

Dependent on the income from his *Journal* and loans from his brother for his daily expenses, the "mad, romantic, dreaming Ledyard," as he called himself, took a room in a Paris hostelry. As a celebrated American expatriate he managed to meet such sympathetic compatriots as the American minister to France Benjamin Franklin, his successor Thomas Jefferson, the Marquis de Lafayette, and the naval hero Captain John Paul Jones. All were impressed by Ledyard's exploits, and Jefferson later wrote of him as "a man of genius, of some science, of fearless courage and enterprise."

At this time, John Paul Jones happened to be in Paris and became so ignited by Ledyard's ideas that he engaged in planning to fit out a trade ship, which he would master, to take his partner to the Pacific. Perhaps even two ships, the two decided, might be necessary, one of which would be left with Ledyard at Nootka Sound while the other carried furs to Canton and returned with a cargo of Chinese luxuries.

This scheme fell apart when Jones learned from the American charge d'affaires in Madrid that Spain was "too jealous to permit any commercial speculation" in its Pacific lands. Ledyard also failed to interest French authorities in forming a mercantile company to engage in the fur trade in the Pacific Northwest.

Dismayed and all but penniless but still brimming with ideas and ardor, Ledyard paid a visit to Thomas Jefferson, now American minister to France, in the summer of 1786. The two had met before—it was Jefferson who introduced Ledyard to Jones—and had corresponded regularly. The future president had noted in his diary that in past talks with Ledyard, "I suggested to him the enterprise of exploring the western part of our continent, by passing through St. Petersburg, then across Russia to Kamchatka, and procuring a passage thence in some of the Russian vessels to Nootka Sound, whence he might make his way across the continent."

Now Ledyard eagerly seized on this grandiose idea and in his perfervid talks about it, Jefferson noted, "only asked to be assured of the permission of the Russian Government . . . . I undertook to have the permission [from Empress Catherine II] solicited. He [Ledyard] eagerly embraced the proposition."

The Great American Traveler departed London for Saint Petersburg in December 1786 with a letter of introduction from Jefferson (describing the bearer as a man of "much singularity of character") and ten guineas in his pocket. He traveled to Hamburg and to Stockholm, and after walking halfway across the frozen Gulf of Bothnia before finding open water blocking him, he returned to Stockholm. After a brief recuperation, he set out north through Swedish Finland and Lapland on the 1,200-mile journey to the Russian capital. Sheltered, and sustained by a diet of salt herring, milk, and bread given him by strangers in hamlets and farms along his route, Ledyard arrived in Saint Petersburg in March 1787.

Upon learning of this astonishing perambulation, Jefferson wrote a friend, "I had a letter from Ledyard lately. He had but two shirts, and yet more shirts than shillings. Still he was determined to obtain the palm of being the first circumnambulator of the earth."

In his several weeks in Saint Petersburg, Ledyard managed to obtain a paper permitting him to proceed across Siberia to the Russian maritime provinces. Somehow—perhaps because he was an oddity, an American carrying a letter from Jefferson, and the author of a book about Cook's last voyage—he was able to travel the first 3,000 miles across the steppes, to Novosibirsk, in a *kibitka,* a three-horse carriage-sleigh, accompanied part of the way by a Scottish physician employed by Empress Catherine. From the Ural Mountain town of Barnaul, he joined a party of government couriers to Irkutsk on Lake Baikal, "driving with wild Tartar horses over a wild and ragged country," and after a few days' rest traveled with another governmental party down the Lena River to the fur-trading outpost of Yakutsk. They reached the forbidding place in September 1787, with dropping temperatures and winter winds preventing his continuing east to the Sea of Okhotsk and his goal, the peninsula of Kamchatka, the jumping-off spot for a crossing of the North Pacific to Nootka Sound.

Ledyard wrote in his journal at Yakutsk, "This is the third time I have been overtaken and arrested by winter; and both the others, by giving time for my evil genius to rally hosts about me, have defeated the enterprise. Fortune, thou hast humbled me at last."

But then he had an experience awaiting him more humbling than the Siberian winter. In the spring of 1788, as he prepared to continue eastward, Ledyard was arrested on orders from Empress Catherine and accused, inexplicably, of being "a French spy." The accusation was in fact a ruse. The French ambassador to Russia investigated the matter at the request of Ledyard's friend from his Paris days, the Marquis de Lafayette, and reported that the empress's actions probably "disguised her unwillingness to have the new possessions of Russia on the western coast of America seen by an enlightened citizen of the United States."

Ledyard, of course, did not know this as he was hurried under armed escort to the Polish frontier. "The royal dame has taken me out of my way," he wrote as he made his way back to London, there to report his harrowing tale to the author of his journey.

Jefferson noted in his autobiography, "Thus failed the first attempt to explore the western part of our northern continent."

Ledyard was driven by the conviction that he was destined to make an indelible mark in history and was thus able to bear his misadventures gracefully and with honest, self-

deprecating humor. His utter confidence that he would succeed in some great enterprise had an infectious quality. He
was eager, daring, inexhaustible—he had proven it—and he
was believed.

In London, even while he was regaining his health and
strength, Ledyard cast about for some new endeavor. He visited the eminent botanist and promoter of explorations Sir
Joseph Banks, who proposed that the Great Traveler's future
lay not in America but in Africa. Banks told of an exploration of the sources of the Niger River being sponsored by
the Association for Promoting the Discovery of the Interior
Parts of Africa, and Ledyard fairly leaped on the idea.

"When can you be ready?" Sir Joseph asked.

"Tomorrow morning," his guest said.

Banks advanced him the funds to travel to Cairo, where
the expedition was to be launched. There, in Turkish-
controlled Egypt, Ledyard wrote apologetically to Thomas
Jefferson, who had expressed disappointment that the Traveler seemed to have abandoned his ideas of exploring the
American West. Jefferson later wrote James Madison that
Ledyard "promises me, if he escapes his [present] journey,
he will go to Kentucky, and endeavor to penetrate westwardly to the South Sea [the Pacific]."

Compared to Ledyard's incomparable crossing of Russia
and Siberia, such a transcontinental journey might well have
been accomplished with relative ease. Certainly no single
man of his time had better credentials to attempt it.

But in Cairo in January 1789 Ledyard's impatience grew
to fury at repeated postponements of the caravan that was
to take him into the African interior, and he died suddenly
on the tenth of the month.

Jefferson, who apparently investigated the details behind
the loss of his "man of genius," explained that "Mr. Ledyard
took offense at the delay and threw himself into a violent
rage with his conductors, which deranged something in his
system that he thought to cure by an emetic, but he took the

dose so strong as at the first or second effect of its operation to burst a blood vessel—in three days he was suffocated and died."

The Traveler, Jefferson later remarked, "was a person of ingenuity" who "unfortunately had too much imagination," an extraordinary thing for a man of such ingenuity and imagination to say. Ledyard was Jefferson's agent of action, the man who saw the Pacific littoral with his own eyes, envisioned it as America's *mare nostrum* of the future, and shared his vision with the future president.

The ingenious and imaginative idea of an exploration of the western American continent with which Thomas Jefferson had inspired John Ledyard, and which he so mightily tried to accomplish, would have to wait another fifteen years.

2

Spanish claims of sovereignty over the coastal lands of western North America originated with a papal bull in 1494, fifty years before Juan Rodriguez Cabrillo's expedition actually set out from La Natividad. Subsequently, Spain sent other expeditions from Mexican ports, and galleons from the Philippines, their holds laden with silks, damasks, spices, porcelains, wax, and other exotic goods of the Far East. These vessels followed the Great Circle from Manila northeast toward Japan, then due east along the 41st parallel to the vicinity of Cape Mendocino and down the California coast.

With such voyages and its first actual land-based foothold, the *presidio* of San Diego, which was established in 1769, Spain made its presence known from Baja California to Cape Mendocino and sent occasional expeditions as far north as Vancouver Island and even into the Bay of Alaska. But in the fifteen years between Cook's voyage in 1778 and the beginning of their war with Napoleonic France, the

British were preeminent in breaking the shaky grasp the Spanish held in the sea-lanes along and above the Oregon coast.

Furs, the sea otter in particular, and the riches they represented in the China trade drove the English as they had Russians and Frenchmen before them, and the Americans soon to come. The fur trade gave a new and perfect meaning to the old Spanish phrase for the mythical lands of the Pacific Northwest—the "Coast of Cathay"—and at the center of it was an obscure dimple on the ragged western shore of Vancouver Island named for the principal Indian clan inhabitating its shores.

Nootka Sound, discovered by the Spaniards, charted by Barkley and Cook, was a small detour on the sea trails to Old Oregon, but it had a significant role in the story. The place was known to Northwest explorers and fur traders for two centuries; the Indians inhabiting Nootka Island and the fringes of the Sound surrounding it posed "problems" for British and American traders that often erupted into violence, and it became the arena where contending nations fought over the sea otter, the China trade, and rights to settlement on the Pacific coast of America.

All these matters—exploration, exploitation, Indian problems, international conflict—were exemplified by the 1788 adventure of a British seaman-entrepreneur named John Meares.

The historical verdict on Meares is mixed: To some of his contemporaries he was a tireless, driven, intrepid figure like Ledyard, anxious to make a contribution to his nation as well as to history. To others, and to virtually all modern historians, he was an egoistic, relatively talentless rogue, full of high-sounding rhetoric but fundamentally little more than a self-promoting fortune-seeker who happened to trigger, as such frenetic blunderers often do, an international incident.

Born in 1756, Meares served as a lieutenant in the British navy and after the Peace of Paris of 1783, which settled the American Revolutionary War, entered the merchant service. He took command of a ship bound for India and in Calcutta organized a commercial house to trade on the Pacific Rim of North America. In this enterprise he was much influenced by the publication of Cook's *Voyages to the Pacific Ocean* in 1784, and by the reports of Cook's successor in command of the *Discovery* on the great value placed on sea otter skins in the Orient.

Meares learned of other voyages between England, Nootka, and the trading emporiums at Macao and Canton that resulted in immense profits for their sponsors. He acted on the information with his customary zeal. He gathered the funds to outfit two trade ships, named them after his destination and quarry—*Nootka,* a 200-ton vessel, and *Sea Otter*, at 100 tons—and put to sea in February 1786 with a consignment of opium to be delivered to Malacca on the Malay Peninsula before setting a course for the north Pacific.

Meares, commanding the *Nootka,* arrived in the Aleutian Islands in August and island-hopped around the misty shores from Attu to Unalaska, where he found a good anchorage and discovered a Russian trappers' camp. He and his crew were treated cordially by these bearded, fur-bedecked, Cossack-like hunters, and Meares, thirsty for information on the sea otter potential of the region, seems to have found ways to question the Russians at length. Like Ledyard, he was an excellent interrogator and observer.

The Russians, he wrote, came to Alaska from Kamchatka in "galleots" (small oar-and-sail galleys), each carrying from sixty to eighty men. "They heave their vessels up the same convenient station here," he said, and "hunt sea-otters and other animals whom nature has cloathed in furs. The natives of the different districts are also employed in the same occupation, and are obliged to give the fruits of their toil, as a tribute to the Empress of Russia, to whom the trade exclusively belongs." He discovered that the natives received "small quantities of snuff, of which they are immoderately fond" for their furs, "and obtaining that favorite article, they are content with their wretched condition, from whence, as far as respects any exertions of their own, they will never emerge."

Anxious to find his own fur-trade below the Russian outposts in the Aleutians, Meares took the *Nootka* into the Bay of Alaska that summer and anchored in Prince William Sound to await the *Sea Otter*'s arrival. The sister ship never came; indeed she was never seen again, presumably lost at sea.

Meares gave some thought to making a run for the Sandwich Islands to spend the winter but decided that his men, restless, some ill with scurvy, and all dreaming of loading the *Nootka* with furs and making their fortunes in Canton, might desert the ship. He preferred the rigors of a winter at latitude 60 degrees north to the possible ruination of his mission.

By January 1787 twenty-three of the *Nootka* crew had contracted scurvy (Captain Cook carried kegs of sauerkraut on his ships and thus defeated this ancient sailors' scourge) and eight men, including the ship surgeon and pilot, died. In April, with warm weather returning, local natives brought fish and game to Meares' camp and in that month another trade ship, the *Queen Charlotte*, entered the sound and, although Meares had to pay for provisions, the ship was welcomed "as a guardian angel."

With the help of crewmen and the ship's carpenter from the *Charlotte*, the *Nootka* sailors spent a month refitting their ship, caulking seams, and mending shredded sails and rigging. Meares paid for services with his trade goods and in June set sail for Honolulu. There, after more refitting and the recuperation of his crew, he continued on to Macao with the meager collection of furs he had bartered for among the natives at Prince William Sound.

By now he had a new scheme in mind. Despite his disastrous experiences in Alaskan waters, the loss of crewmen from scurvy, and the disappearance of the *Sea Otter*, Meares was aflame with the notion of establishing a British fur-trading post at Nootka Sound and building a small fleet of trade vessels to ply coastal waters from Vancouver Island down along the Oregon coast bartering for furs. He seems to have had little concern about the excellent chance that his enterprise would meet opposition from the Spaniards, who claimed the territory by right of discovery, and he knew his home country would not sanction his activities. To avoid such conflicts, he flew the Portuguese flag from his mainmast, thereby using, also without permission, the port of Macao as a front for his activities.

In Macao, through some never-explained financial prestidigitation, Meares managed to get rid of the decrepit *Nootka* and purchase a 230-ton brig, the *Felice*. At Canton he employed several Chinese "artisans" (actually carpenters) to build his factory and trade schooner. He also took aboard the *Felice* a young Vancouver Island native named Comekela, who had been taken to China the year before as a crewmen on another trade vessel. Comekela was the brother of Maquinna, chief of the Nootka people, and a compelling, if not sinister, figure in events to come.

In April 1788, nearly four months out of Canton, the *Felice* anchored in Friendly Cove, abreast of the village of Nootka, on the southern tip of Nootka Island, at the entrance to Nootka Sound. The *hetman* Maquinna came out to greet the ship with a great war-canoe assemblage. "They moved with great parade round the ship," Meares wrote. "There were twelve of these canoes, each of which contained about eighteen men, the greater part of whom were cloathed in dresses of the most beautiful skins of sea otter, which covered them from their neck to their ancles." He said Maquinna and his entourage wore white bird down in their hair, "and there faces bedaubed with red and black ochre, in the form of a shark's jaw, and a kind of spiral line, which rendered their appearance extremely savage."

The Nootkans fascinated Meares. They lived in sturdy wooden houses, hunted whales with bone-headed harpoons, fished for salmon and herring—their staple diet—and highly prized *olachen* oil, which was extracted from candlefish and used in cooking. They were adept with harpoons and knives in sea otter hunts, a dangerous business at close quarters when some of the animals measured six feet from nose to tip of tail and were ferocious when cornered.

Maquinna, he said, wore a royal otter-fur dress and a high, conical cap feathered at the point, and "appeared to be about thirty years, of a middle size, but extremely well made, and possessing a countenance that was formed to interest all who saw him."

That chameleonic countenance, before which traders in years to come would cringe in fear, seemed to smile on Meares. The chief was no doubt more pleased that his brother Comekela had been delivered home than by the gifts the Englishman presented to him—"copper, iron, and other gratifying articles." On the *Felice*, Meares wrote, Maquinna shrugged out of his otter garments "and threw them, in the most graceful manner, at our feet, and remained in the unattired garb of nature on the deck."

Meares negotiated with Maquinna for a parcel of land to build his factory and schooner and said the chief "not only most readily consented to grant us a spot of ground . . . but promised us also his assistance in forwarding our works." The two-story log structure was completed on the Nootka shore at the end of April. Meares would later say he "purchased" the land for a brace of pistols, a claim denied by Maquinna.

While the fort and ship were under construction, Meares took the *Felice* southward to the entrance of the Strait of

Juan de Fuca and continued to Cape Flattery, the Columbia River estuary (which Spanish charts designated as San Roque but which Meares did not rediscover, that distinction going to Robert Gray three years later). They sailed down as far as Tillamook Head on the north Oregon coast, taking a jollyboat crew ashore periodically to trade among the natives. On the return voyage along the southwestern edge of Vancouver Island, the *Felice*'s crew enjoyed such a brisk sea otter trade that Meares dispatched his first officer, Robert Duffin, and several sailors in a longboat to penetrate the Strait of Juan de Fuca to investigate the trade potential east of Cape Flattery. Instead of finding compliant Indians eager to exchange furs for bits of iron and copper and cheap beads, Duffin's boat was attacked by native canoes. Four of his sailors received arrow wounds, and, said Meares, "the rest of the people were bruised in a terrible manner by the stones and clubs of the enemy; even the boat itself was pierced in a thousand places by arrows."

Now the natives were the "enemy," and when Meares returned to Nootka to supervise the building of his log fort, he "explained his power" by ordering the throwing up of a breastwork in front of the structure with a small ship's cannon mounted atop it.

In September, after the completion of the palisaded fort as well as the schooner *North West America*—"the first bottom [keel] ever built and launched in this part of the globe"—Meares sailed the *Felice* to Canton with a hefty cargo of furs, leaving the Nootka operation to be supervised by his partner, a Captain Douglas, master of the merchantman *Iphigenia*.

To Meares, his scheme was working perfectly. His experiment with the Chinese "artisans" had resulted in the building of the fort and schooner, he had located many profitable trading locations, he had lorded it over Maquinna of the Nootkas, and had purchased for a brace of pistols a factory site that would be the epicenter of a great fur-trading monopoly.

But Meares had underestimated the Spanish resolve to protect their interests on the Pacific Rim, and during his absence in China his nascent fur empire fell to pieces.

During the building of the fort, a Spanish expedition returning from investigating Russian activities on the Alaskan coast reported to the viceroy of Mexico that the Russians were contemplating a trading post in the south to take advantage of the "commerce which the English from Canton are carrying on at Nootka." The commander of this expedition urged immediate action, and in February 1789 the viceroy dispatched two warships with a complement of soldiers "to occupy said port [Nootka] and garrison it." Several missionaries accompanied the expedition to win the goodwill of the Indians and proselytize among them. Meantime, the soldiery were to deal "with prudent firmness" with the anticipated advent of Russian traders and any English, American, or other foreign intruders.

The Spanish ships reached Nootka Sound in May. The *Iphigenia,* commanded by Meares' partner, and the newly launched *North West America* were seized. The former was later released and Douglas was permitted to sail away—which he did, to Honolulu and on to Macao. But the Spaniards claimed the *North West America* as a "prize ship," appropriated the 215 sea otter skins in its hold, placed a crew on board, changed its name to *Gertrudis,* and put it into service. Meares' factory and outbuildings were also confiscated in the name of King Carlos III.

At the time of these seizures, the American ships *Columbia Rediviva* and *Lady Washington* were also anchored in Nootka Sound but were not interned, and their skippers, John Kendrick and Robert Gray, were permitted to come and go at will. Kendrick was even allowed to take some of the *North West America* sailors on board the *Columbia* as crew members. The Americans, after all, were not forming a permanent settlement in Spanish lands while the British stood as a symbol of invidious trespassing in Spanish territory.

In China, Meares learned of the events at Nootka Sound in November 1789, four months after the fact, found a berth on a trader, and returned to England in April 1790. There he presented a report to the government on his activities in America and on Spain's "illegal" seizure of his assets.

As it happened, Meares' document came to his government's attention at a propitious time: England was attempting to negotiate with Spain for certain rights in the fur trade in the North Pacific but had reached a stalemate. The Court of Spain, according to a report made to King George III, was maintaining "exclusive rights of sovereignty, navigation and commerce in the territories, coasts and seas in that part of the world," and Spain was said to be sending armed expeditions to reinforce its claims. Parliament urged His Majesty to "act with vigor" and approved an expenditure, if necessary, of £1,000,000 to enable the king to act "as the exigency of affairs might require."

This meant England was prepared to go to war with Spain over the rights to trade and settle the northwest coast of North America and, among other, more important matters, the British government insisted that Spain indemnify Captain Meares for his seized property at Nootka Sound.

Meares was eventually paid a large restitution—said to be, in American terms, "two hundred and ten thousand hard dollars in Specie"—and with this considerable fortune he appears to have retired. His final years are difficult to trace. His book, *Voyages Made in the Years 1788 and 1789 From China to the Northwest Coast of America,* appeared in 1790, and although he had no further active service for England, he received a promotion to commander in the Royal Navy in 1795.

Meares died in 1809 at age fifty-three.

3

On August 9, 1790, the year following Ledyard's death and four months after Meares returned to England, Captain Robert Gray and his *Columbia* crew returned to Boston from their voyage around the world. They arrived in time to witness a development bothersome to all Yankee skippers and to their government: an agreement that gave England certain trading rights in the Pacific Northwest that were denied, at least on paper, to other nations.

The Meares incident at Nootka Sound was a coincidental but pivotal event in the dispute between England and Spain over territorial rights-of-way in the north Pacific. Spain's claim of discovery had been ill-attended, its realization of the value of the fur trade in the region belated. England had its own claims of discovery—Cook's voyage in particular— and had in fact rights by virtue of occupancy of Nootka Sound, where British subject John Meares purchased land from Chief Maquinna, and south along the Oregon coast to Spanish California, where British vessels had conducted trade for a decade. The stalemate between the two countries had about it the alarming potential of a call to arms, a matter that concerned the newly elected first president of the United States. George Washington worried that if England went to war it might seek access across American territory to strike at Spanish possessions in Louisiana and Florida. To refuse such access might embroil America in the conflict. Alexander Hamilton, Washington's pro-British secretary of the treasury, favored granting the right-of-way; Secretary of State Thomas Jefferson proposed to ignore such a request if it were made.

The issue never materialized. Spain could not stand alone against England and turned to Louis XVI for assistance, but France was convulsed in revolution and unable to render aid. With no alternative but to capitulate, in October 1790

Spanish ministers signed the Nootka Sound Convention, recognizing England's right to navigate, trade, and settle along the Pacific Northwest coast above San Francisco. Each nation was to have free access to the establishments of the other in those regions.

The convention strengthened British interests in the region and signaled the end of two centuries of Spanish claims.

Of course, the natives of Nootka Sound were not consulted in the international debate over the lands they had inhabited for untold centuries, but the Nootkans were by now familiar with the white men who came to their island. It made no matter if they were Russian, English, Spanish, French, or American; they were all of the same template. Their despicable habits had grown intolerable. The traders had always sneered at the Indians' religious rites, trampled on village customs, threatened their chiefs, and treated the coastal people as vassals. The whites were belligerent, cheated in their trading, made a show of force at the least provocation, stole, brutalized, and murdered, all without redress.

Within a few years after their first contact with the seaborne barbarians, the Indians were regarding the trespassers as useful enemies. They were not fooled by being invited aboard the traders' "floating cities," or by the strained amity as they displayed their furs on the deck to trade for bits of metal, beads, mirrors, pots, and knives. They had learned quickly the white man's wiles and had raised the ante for their otter skins; they began to barter rather than accept any gewgaw for the wares the intruders so obviously lusted after.

Magellan had been killed by natives in the Philippines in 1521; Captain Cook underestimated the Sandwich Islanders and at Kealakekua Bay in 1779 had paid for the error with his life. Countless other intruders had tried to construct native alliances for selfish gain—territorial expansion and trade being the principal motives—without understanding or respecting the natives. It seemed to be the white man's way.

Some of the trespassers on the northwest coast of America did not see Cook's or the other historical examples as instructive, but thirteen years after the Nootka Sound Convention they were taught an abrupt and bloody lesson.

4

The man who fatally exasperated Chief Maquinna of the Nootkas was Captain John Salter, and we know little about him before he brought his trading vessel to Vancouver Island in the spring of 1803. Judging from what appears to be his chronic exasperation with the natives, he was probably a veteran of the North Pacific sea-lanes and may have known Maquinna from a previous voyage.

Salter sailed from Dover in September 1802 with a crew of twenty-nine on the *Boston*, laden with trade goods. The merchantman doubled the Horn and on March 12, 1803, anchored five miles inside Nootka Sound just beyond the notch on the shore called Friendly Cove. While crew members were busy filling water casks and gathering wood for galley fires, canoes were pushed off from the beach and Maquinna and a dozen of his men made the first of several visits to the ship, bringing their furs and haggling over the trade items displayed on the *Boston*'s deck. Salter, following the tradition of presenting the chief with a special gift, gave Maquinna an old double-barreled fowling piece.

Trouble erupted on the twenty-first as Salter and his crew were preparing the ship to proceed downcoast to trade among the other coastal people. Maquinna's canoes paid a farewell visit and he and his courtiers clambered aboard. The chief brought a gift of a string of wild ducks for Salter, but he also brought the old gun with him, complaining that it didn't work, was *peshak*—bad. An armorer on the *Boston*, a twenty-year-old blacksmith's son named John Jewitt who had shipped aboard the trader at Hull and who kept a diary of the voyage, witnessed the exchange between the captain and the chief.

"Captain Salter was very much offended at this observation," Jewitt wrote, "and considering it as a mark of contempt for his present, he called the king a liar, adding other opprobrious terms, and taking the gun from him tossed it indignantly into the cabin." Maquinna "said not a word in reply, but his countenance sufficiently expressed the rage he felt, though he exerted himself to suppress it, and I observed him while the Captain was speaking repeatedly put his hand to his throat and rub it upon his bosom, which he afterwards told me was to keep down his heart, which was rising into his throat and choking him."

Maquinna knew enough English to understand Salter's words and left the trader in a rage. The next day, just hours before the *Boston* was to set sail, the chief returned to the ship amidst a small convoy of war canoes. He and twenty of his men were permitted aboard while the other canoes circled the *Boston*'s hull. Maquinna presented Salter with a bundle of salmon and suggested the captain might send some men out on a seining expedition and store the fish in the larder. Salter liked this idea and dispatched nine men in a yawl and a jollyboat to Friendly Cove, where the *hetman* said salmon were plentiful.

Despite these ominous events—the number of natives on board his ship, the number circling it in canoes, the dividing of his crew—Salter seems to have had no suspicion of impending trouble. Maquinna, wearing what Jewitt called "a very ugly mask of wood representing the head of some wild beast," appeared to be in good humor, and with his people capered and danced on the deck while Salter waited for his fishermen to return.

Jewitt, meantime, had gone below deck to work at his vise-bench, where he was accustomed to fashioning knives and hatchets for the Indians, sharpening cutlasses, repairing and cleaning pistols and muskets (of which there were 3,000 on board). He was attempting to repair Maquinna's *peshak* shotgun.

"I had not been there more than an hour," he wrote later in his journal, "when I heard the men hoisting in the long boat, which, in a few minutes after, was succeeded by a great bustle and confusion on deck. I immediately ran up the steerage stairs, but scarcely was my head above deck, when I was caught by the hair by one of the savages, and lifted from my feet; fortunately for me, my hair being short, and the ribbon with which it was tied slipping, I fell from his hold into the steerage."

Still, he was stuck by an ax and gashed in the forehead and fell senseless to the floor. On the main deck, while the yawl and jollyboat were being pulled aboard, Maquinna shouted a signal and his men sprang on the sailors, clubbed them down, and cut their throats. Maquinna himself grappled with Salter and threw the captain over the rail, where he was killed by those in the canoes.

Groggy and covered with blood from his scalp wound, Jewitt struggled up the steerage ladder to the deck and was taken prisoner. Maquinna then led him to a grisly display. Along the *Boston*'s rail were arranged twenty-seven heads, those of Salter and his crew, including the nine men who had returned from the salmon expedition. The chief demanded that the armorer identify each and describe his own work on the ship. Jewitt fully expected that his head would be added to the others, but Maquinna offered to let him live providing he was willing to become the chief's slave and serve as his master's blacksmith. Jewitt ecstatically agreed.

The only other survivor of the *Boston* massacre was a Philadelphia-born sailmaker named John Thompson, who is described as "a powerful, fearless, violent sailor of about forty years of age"; he was found hiding in the hold, his face slashed and bloodied. When he was dragged before

Maquinna his life was also spared when Jewitt claimed that Thompson was his father.

Under the two survivors' rudimentary seamanship the *Boston* was maneuvered and towed into Friendly Cove and beached so that it could be stripped of its sails, rigging, and cargo. Soon a great crowd of natives flocked to the cove to see the ship and the loot taken from it and to deck themselves out in sailcloth and the clothing found in the slopchest. Hogsheads of rum were stove in and during the feast ashore, one drunken native, rummaging in the *Boston*'s hold, set the ship afire. It burned to the waterline.

Word of the fate of the *Boston* spread quickly, and for many months traders gave Nootka Sound a wide berth. During his three years' captivity, Jewitt managed to smuggle out some letters, written, like his diary, in boiled blackberry juice. In his waiting for rescue, he took a native wife, did blacksmithing, repaired weapons, and learned the Nootka tongue. John Thompson also went native, even to the point of joining his captors in their raiding parties against neighboring tribes.

Maquinna told Jewitt he had several times been ill-treated by foreigners, that English sea captains had entered his home and stolen furs, frightened his women, and killed many of his people. This accumulation of grievances, and Captain Salter's insults, had led to the massacre.

In July 1805 the brig *Lydia* out of Boston appeared off Friendly Cove. Her captain, Samuel Hill, had come across one of Jewitt's letters appealing for rescue and decided to investigate the fate of Salter and his ship. It appears that Maquinna agreed to meet with Hill, for Jewitt was ordered to write a letter that would absolve the chief of any blame for the massacre. The armorer wrote the letter but included in it some damning words. Maquinna took the letter aboard the *Lydia,* and Hill read it and had the chief clapped in irons. Although Captain Hill intended executing his prisoner, Jewitt interceded and spoke of his own rescue by Maquinna and subsequent kindnesses. The appeal worked: The Nootka *het-man* was released.

In the winter, the *Lydia* set sail, crossed the Columbia bar, and anchored on its north shore. After a trading cruise and the accumulation of a valuable cache of furs, Hill proceeded to the Whampoa trading center, in the Canton River. Jewitt stayed with the *Lydia* until it returned to Boston in June 1807. He published his journal, *A Narrative of the Adventures and Sufferings of John R. Jewitt; Only Survivor of the Ship*, Boston, *during a Captivity of nearly three years among the Savages of Nootka Sound*, that year and thereafter disappeared from the historical record.

While the *Lydia* stood at anchor in the Columbia estuary in November 1805, a group of Clatsop Indians visited the ship and proudly displayed to Captain Hill some medals recently given to them. The bronze pieces were stamped with the likeness of President Jefferson and the natives said they had gotten them from two white men who had recently come downriver leading several other men. Jewitt, who understood enough of their language to serve as translator, learned that the two leaders, Lewis and Clark, had just departed the area to return home on their overland route.

Jewitt must have mistranslated. In truth, on November 25, 1805, only a few days before the Indians' representations, Meriwether Lewis and William Clark and their Corps of Discovery left the exposed northern shore of the Columbia for the more protected woods on the south bank. At the moment the Indians were talking to Captain Hill, the explorers were camped just out of the *Lydia*'s view, in the dense forest, surveying a site for the winter quarters they would name Fort Clatsop.

They all might have returned home in the *Lydia,* might at least have benefited from the ship's supplies, but neither the explorers nor the *Lydia*'s party knew the other's proximity when Captain Hill put to sea for Canton.

PART TWO

ASTORIA

4

Pro Pelle Cutem

■

"PERSEVERANCE"

1

Among his many professions—planter, magistrate, chancery court judge, sheriff, militiaman—Colonel Peter Jefferson was a surveyor and mapmaker, and good at both. He helped mark the boundary between Virginia and Carolina in 1749, and with another man made a map of Virginia in 1751 that was regarded as definitive for its time. He died when his son was but fourteen, but by then the gangly, red-haired boy was already poring over maps, his protean mind always exploring. He studied astronomy, navigation, shipbuilding, and the journals of the world's explorers, and held a high regard for the maxim of Henry the Navigator of Portugal: "You cannot find a peril so great that the hope of reward will not be greater."

He would never stray far west of his native Virginia, but twenty years before he became president, Thomas Jefferson had fixed his map-filled imagination on the great blank space between the Mississippi and the Pacific and was encouraging its exploration. While governor of Virginia and a delegate to the Continental Congress in the 1780s, he asked his friend George Rogers Clark, the renowned frontiersman and Indian fighter, to lead an expedition west of the Mississippi.

This plan did not materialize, but Jefferson's pursuit of it continued. In 1786, when minister to France, he met John Ledyard and proposed to that fellow visionary "the enterprise of exploring the western part of our continent." Ledyard's heroic effort ended in Siberia in September 1787, but even when the frustrated Traveler turned his attention to Africa, Jefferson held out the hope that he would eventually "endeavor to penetrate westwardly" to the Pacific. In 1793, while serving as George Washington's secretary of state, Jefferson gave advice and support to the French botanist André Michaud, who was preparing to lead a party of scientists to the Pacific under the sponsorship of the American Philosophical Society. Apart from the scientific work, Jefferson urged, Michaud should concentrate on finding "the shortest and most convenient route of communication between the U.S. and the Pacific ocean." But when Napoleonic France declared war on England, Michaud's plans had to be terminated.

A decade passed before Jefferson, now president, was able to strike an epochal bargain that made his ambition for western exploration a necessity. On April 30, 1803, the president's negotiators in Paris signed a treaty, the most consequential state paper in American history excepting only the Declaration of Independence and the Constitution, by which the United States paid $15 million for the Louisiana Territory, more than a half-billion acres of wilderness five times the size of France. Although the territorial boundary would not be clarified for another sixteen years, the Louisiana Purchase roughly doubled the area of the United States, adding to the Republic the lands between the Mississippi and the Rocky Mountains and encompassing the later states of Louisiana, Arkansas, Oklahoma, Missouri, Kansas, Iowa, Nebraska and South Dakota, most of Wyoming and Montana plus portions of southwestern Minnesota and South Dakota, northeastern New Mexico, and eastern Colorado.

Three months before the Paris treaty, Jefferson, supremely confident of gaining the great and largely unexplored tract and electrified, as he had always been, by its potential, sent a secret message to Congress. The letter detailed plans to explore the lands west of the Mississippi "even to the Western Ocean, having conferences with the natives on the subject of commercial intercourse." He asked for an appropriation of $2,500 to finance a military expedition to assert American claims to the territory and to explore a route "across the continent, for the purpose of commerce." The president also wanted to know about any foreign activity in the new territory and beyond it, on the Pacific coast.

Just over a year from the signing, Meriwether Lewis, Jefferson's private secretary and a captain of infantry, and William Clark, younger brother of George Rogers Clark and a veteran artillery officer, launched their Corps of Discovery into the wilderness.

The expedition headed out from Saint Louis on May 14, 1804, traveling up the Missouri in a fifty-five-foot keelboat and two flat-bottomed pirogues. In addition to the co-leaders, the party consisted of twenty-seven young, unmarried soldiers, a hunter-interpreter, and Clark's black slave, a man named York. The exploring party crawled up the river in the cloying heat and humidity at the rate of fifteen miles a day and wintered among the Mandan Indian villages of the Upper Missouri. In mid-autumn they reached the mouth of the Knife River in North Dakota and there constructed a triangular log stockade, which they named Fort Mandan.

That winter temperatures fell to 45 degrees below zero, but the Corps commanders made good use of their time. Hunting and wood-cutting parties were sent out; boats, equipment, and clothing were mended; drawings and journal entries made. Clark found a Mandan chief who claimed to know the lands to the west and with the expedition interpreter

worked on the making of tentative maps. Both Lewis and
Clark met with delegations of Mandans, Minatarees, and
Arikaras who came in curiosity to the strange log fort on the
Missouri to see the white men and to marvel over the black
skin of Clark's slave.

The expedition departed Fort Mandan on April 7, 1805, to
continue its journey up the Missouri, the explorers distributed among six small canoes and two large pirogues. A
grueling monthlong portage around the Great Falls led
the expedition into the high country; in July, they reached
the headwaters of the Missouri, pushed on toward a pass
in the Bitterroot Mountains, and crossed the Continental
Divide into Idaho. They traveled on, down the Clearwater,
Snake, and Columbia Rivers, and reached the Pacific—
"that ocean, the object of all our labors, the reward of all
our anxieties," Lewis said, on November 8, 1805, after a
journey of more than 4,000 miles. A few miles inland from
the beach they built a stockade, Fort Clatsop, named for
a friendly Indian tribe of the area, and settled down for
the winter.

The explorers learned that the Clatsops and other native
tribesmen who came to see them and their fort had become
considerably familiar with white fur traders over the years
and had in their vocabularies a number of common profanities and words such as *musket, powder, shot, knife, iron,
copper*, and *file*. Lewis told of their bartering skills: "They
begin by asking double or treble the value of their merchandise, and lower the demand in proportion to the ardor or experience in trade of the purchaser; if he expresses any
anxiety, the smallest article, perhaps a handful of roots, will
furnish a whole morning's negotiation." (He also took time
to state that a Chinook or Clatsop "beauty" was "one of
the most disgusting objects in nature," and said that in
all the tribes, "a man will lend his wife or daughter for a
fish-hook or a strand of beads.")

The return journey began on March 23, 1806, and in a

little over three months the expedition reached the mouth of the Flathead River (Bitterroot today) at a point called Traveler's Rest. Here the commanders split up, Lewis exploring along the Missouri to probe the Maria's River, Clark south along the Yellowstone.

They rendezvoused at the juncture of the Yellowstone and Missouri, about 200 miles west of their 1805 winter quarters, and on September 23 reached Saint Louis, completing one of the most momentous explorations in history. Lewis hurried off a letter to his sponsor and benefactor: "In obedience to your orders we have penitrated the Continent of North America to the Pacific Ocean. . . ."

2

Lewis and Clark had been unable to report discovery of an all-water route from the Missouri to the Columbia, and the trail they blazed was impossible for all but the hardiest of wilderness hands, but they had begun the serious work of filling in the great blank space west of the Mississippi.

In the first decades of the nineteenth century that space was marked on maps as "Unknown" and indeed, much of what was thought to be known about it was wrong. The Great Plains—that immense tilted upland formed by the streams flowing eastward out of the Rockies toward the Mississippi—were depicted in school primers as a desert. Army explorer Zebulon Montgomery Pike, who set out from Saint Louis in 1805 searching for the source of the Mississippi, said the region had been put there by Providence "to keep the American people from a thin diffusion and ruin." He said the country was fit only for Indians, who grew no crops and lived off the buffalo who shared the plains with them.

Fifteen years later, this notion had the endorsement of Major Stephen Harriman Long of the newly created Army

Topographical Engineers, sent out on an exploratory mission from Belle Fontaine, Missouri. Long and his party traveled up to the falls of Saint Anthony with orders to chart the course of the Upper Mississippi and "to exhibit the general topography of the shores, and to designate such sites as were suitable for military purposes."

The American Philosophical Society provided Long with a riverboat, the *Western Engineer*, constructed expressly to frighten hostile Indians: The vessel had a prow in the shape of a black sea serpent's head which blew steam from its mouth. (The muddy waters of the Mississippi clogged its boilers, however, and the attempt to explore the West with it failed early.)

In his 1820 exploration, Long traveled along the Platte River to the Rockies searching for a source of the Red River. He failed to find it but in his five expeditions, no explorer between Lewis and Clark and John C. Frémont was more influential, and none brought back more a mixture of solid scientific work and wrongheaded speculation. On returning from his Red River search, Long expanded prolifically on Pike's speculations by delineating a strip of land six hundred miles wide, beginning in Texas and running to the Canadian border and from the 100th meridian to the Rocky Mountains, as "the Great American Desert." He said this region "bore a manifest resemblance to the deserts of Siberia" and his report to his superiors in Washington contained this observation: "In regard to this extensive section of country between the Missouri River and the Rocky Mountains, we do not hesitate in giving the opinion that it is almost wholly unfit for cultivation, and of course uninhabitable by a people depending upon agriculture for their subsistence."

This myth of the Great Plains as a desert lasted fifty years and decorated maps of the region up to the opening of the Civil War.

As for the formidable Rockies, those sprawling, ill-defined

masses of north-south ranges and valleys cut by ancient glaciers at the Continental Divide, Long and others before him believed them to be five miles high and a bastion as unbreachable as the Himalayas. They, too, seemed to represent a providential dead-end sign, something reflected in a congressional report of the era that warned, "Nature has fixed limits to our nation; she has kindly interposed as our Western barrier, mountains almost inaccessible. . . . This barrier our population can never pass."

But the barrier could be passed, indeed had been passed, by the time of the warning, by trappers traveling up the Missouri River to its headwaters and beyond, into the Oregon Country. French-Canadian trappers who saw the Rockies' snowy flanks and peaks called them *les montagnes dont la pierre luit la jour et la nuit*, which early American fur traders translated as the Shining Mountains.

Among the curious features of the long story of the American journey to Old Oregon is the fact that so many of the earliest venturers there were lured along and bound together not by any lofty motives of exploration and discovery or by adding to knowledge, but by the value of certain aquatic animals. *Lutra enhydris marina,* the sea otter, drew the trade ships from New England around the Horn to the Northwest Pacific coast; *Castor canadensis*, the beaver, lured trappers overland from Saint Louis westward and incidentally made explorers of them.

On its journey to the Pacific, the Corps of Discovery had encountered small parties of French-Canadians who knew the Rocky Mountain country well as a fur hunter's paradise, and on the Corps' return, descending the Missouri, it had encountered eleven separate trapping parties on the river. These men had twenty boats loaded with trade goods, and they were planning to winter among the Arikara, Sioux,

Pawnee, Crow, and other tribes and trade for furs. Meriwether Lewis speculated on the beaver riches of the Upper
Missouri in his journal, even recognizing the dangers of
the trade once the Indians of the region learned the value of
the furs.

The commerce in furs in North America was already over
two *centuries* old by the time of the Lewis and Clark expedition. It had begun with the French explorations of Jacques
Cartier, which established the trade with Indian tribes in the
Saint Lawrence River valley around Montreal. In 1603,
Henry IV of France sent Samuel de Champlain to the gulf
of the Saint Lawrence for the express purpose of establishing a fur market, and until their expulsion from North America in 1763, the French were the most successful of all
nations in the trade. They built outposts from Maine to the
Great Lakes and north into the Canadian wilderness, sending *coureurs de bois* out among the Hurons, Ottawa, Miami,
and other tribes to barter, moving the hundred-pound packs
of pelts in canoes (some so large—these called *canotes de
maître*—it took a dozen men to paddle them), pirogues
(hollowed-out cottonwood tree trunks, some seventy feet
long and four wide), and huge keelboats capable of carrying
up to twenty tons of goods along the waterways from Montreal to the Great Lakes and the Mississippi.

After navigator Henry Hudson's search for the Northwest
Passage resulted in the discovery of an immense inland sea
in northeast Canada in 1610, the British entered the North
American fur trade with King Charles II's chartering of
"The Governor and Company of Adventurers Trading in
Hudson's Bay" in 1670. The Hudson's Bay Company, with a
governor and seventeen noblemen as partners, was instructed
to establish and maintain all the fur trade and traffic "to and
from all havens, bays, creeks, rivers, lakes and seas into
which they shall find entrance or passage by water or land

out of the territories, limits or places aforesaid." In brief, the Company was to monopolize the fur traffic around all the lands watered by the rivers and streams emptying into Hudson Bay—a territory of about 1.5 million square miles.

The Company had as its insignia a crest depicting a moose rampant, a fox and four beavers, a Christian cross on a shield, and the scrolled motto *Pro Pelle Cutem*—"A skin for a skin."

After founding its first settlement in Prince Rupert's Land (which the Hudson's Bay territory was then called) the Company's progress was stifled by the decades of conflict between Britain and France that followed. Only after the Treaty of Paris in 1763, under which all of France's North American possessions (except Louisiana) were ceded to England, did the Company begin its true era of progress. It expanded its influence then, swarming out of Fort Garry (Winnipeg today), Mackinac, and Prairie du Chien to barter with Indians as far west as the Mandan people of the Upper Missouri, and soon into the Rocky Mountains and west to Oregon.

The Hudson's Bay Company's fur monopoly experienced its most serious challenge in 1784 when competing traders organized the North West Company—the "Nor'westers" as they were called—at Montreal. They took their coat of arms and their motto, "Perseverance," to such trading posts as Fort Chipewyan on the Peace River in British Columbia and Fort William on Lake Superior and fought a trade war with the "Honourable Company" in Alberta and the Lake Athabasca region of Saskatchewan.

The war ended in 1820 when the rivals merged, retaining the name Hudson's Bay Company and representing British fur interests in North America.

All trappers, no matter their nationality, who ventured into Canada, roamed the shores of the Great Lakes, journeyed the continental backbone of the Rockies, or followed the Snake and Columbia Rivers into the Oregon Country eventually encountered the agents of this tightly organized and relentlessly opportunistic society, the Hudson's Bay Company.

By the beginning of the eighteenth century, while such furs as mink, otter, marten, sable, silver fox, weasel (or ermine as it was called when its coat turned white in the winter) were still trapped, the trade had centered on the beaver. There was a northern European–Asian variety of this aquatic rodent, *Castor fiber*, but *Castor canadensis*, teeming in the waterways of Canada and America, became especially valued in European markets. The animal had a brown, silkily rich waterproof fur prized in making felt hats, coats, muffs, linings, and other adornments; its scaly tail serving as a meat substitute in Catholic Europe, and its musky glandular secretion, *castoreum*, was extracted for perfumes and for fever and headache nostrums.

To find them and kill them, trappers had to learn the beavers' habits and history. They are social, mainly nocturnal, animals subsisting on a tree-bark diet supplemented by aquatic plants, thistles, meadow-sweet, leaves, twigs, seeds, and roots in summer. In full growth they range from two to three feet in length and weigh twenty-five to sixty-five pounds. They mate for life and live in family groups with the female birthing up to eight "kits" in each litter. The young, fully coated, can swim within hours of birth. Their tail is used for propulsion and steers like a rudder, their hind feet are large and webbed, their nose and ears seal shut when diving, and membranes protect their eyes underwater. Their life span is fifteen to twenty years.

The beaver's incisor teeth are coated with a hard orangish enamel, and a pair of the animals can gnaw through a four-inch tree or branch in fifteen minutes; a beaver family can fell 300 trees each winter. The cut logs and branches are towed underwater as stored food sources; the dams they build are reservoirs for their dome-shaped lodges of branches and mud, which have underwater entrances and a living chamber above the waterline.

They were killed by drowning. Heavy iron traps weighing five pounds each were baited with a twig smeared with the beaver's own castoreum. The trapping was ideally done in winter months, when the furs were prime, with the traps placed in the streambed at dusk and raised at dawn, and the animal was skinned on the spot. The castoreum glands and tail, a delicacy when fried, were saved, and the "peltries"— undressed hides—were scraped and stretched on a frame for drying, then folded fur side in and bundled.

The dressed hides, called "plews" (from the French *plus*, more), each weighing up to two pounds, at the peak of the trade were worth four to six dollars per pound in Saint Louis, and a bale of plews might weigh as much as 100 pounds.

Average-grade beaver furs were used by European hatters to make the surface of the tall-crowned "stovepipe" hats that were fashionable (especially after the English dandy Beau Brummell fancied them in the early 1800s) for decades on both sides of the Atlantic, and also for other hats, from tricorns to ladies' riding helmets. The long, stiff guard hairs of the pelts were picked clean and the hatter shaved the soft underfur and twanged the string of a huge bow through it, the vibrations making the hairs hook together, to mat or "felt." This matted pile was flattened, covered with wet linen, kneaded into a conical hood that was shrunken and thickened by boiling, treated with acid, and, while hot, molded into a hat shape on a wooden block. After drying and ironing, the nap was raised by brushing with a wire paddle.

The finest beaver skins were sold to furriers for capes and coats and other luxuries for the wealthy.

The French in Canada in the seventeenth and eighteenth centuries were the first to exploit and export beaver furs, followed by Spaniards, Englishmen, and Americans. The epic slaughter of this engaging animal—at the peak of the trade 100,000 beaver furs were harvested annually—would endure for 130 years.

3

The American era of the fur trade—the gaudy thirty-year adventure of mountain men—might be said to have begun when the Corps of Discovery neared the mouth of the Yellowstone River on its return from the Oregon coast. There, on August 12, 1806, the explorers, their chronometer broken and their coordinates only to be guessed at, stumbled across the camp of two Americans heading up the Yellowstone to trap beaver.

The trail-weary trappers, Illinois men named Forrest Hancock and Joseph Dickson, were as startled and delighted as Captains Lewis and Clark to see white men in the wilderness 1,500 miles from Saint Louis, and spent several days with the explorers exchanging tales and information. When the Corps departed toward the Mandan villages one of the men, a thirty-two-year-old private from Staunton, Virginia, named John Colter, was granted permission to stay behind to join the Illinoisians in their beaver hunt. By the end of the year, the three mountain men had trapped their way along the Yellowstone and taken shelter in a Rocky Mountain valley.

Hancock and Dickson endured the winter blizzards, but when the snow cleared in the spring they took their share of plews and followed Lewis and Clark's trail toward civilization. Colter stayed on alone in the mountains.

The story of this born-to-the-wilderness mountain man, a trusted hunter with Lewis and Clark, the first "free trapper" of the American fur-trade era, and a bridge between the era of Daniel Boone and the establishment of Astoria, is worth following.

* * *

Colter had become what French trappers called a *hivernant* (hibernator), having spent his first winter in the Shining Mountains. He had $180 in gold, his mustering-out pay for three years' service with the Corps of Discovery; he had a small cache of furs in his canoe, and in the summer of 1807, some months after Hancock and Dickson departed for Saint Louis, he headed downriver toward civilization.

On the Platte River that June he encountered two keel-boats and a fifty-man expedition out of Saint Charles heading up the Missouri to trade among the tribes. Leading this enterprise was Saint Louis businessman Manuel Lisa, the thirty-five-year-old New Orleans–born entrepreneur who had been among the suppliers of the Lewis and Clark party. Colter had met the man at the Corps' camp on the Illinois side of the Mississippi and was impressed enough with that recollection, and with the manpower and provisions of Lisa's expedition, to sign on as hunter and guide. Lisa saw in Colter a potentially valuable employee—a fine hunter and an experienced mountain man who had made friendly visits among the Crow during his winter in the mountains and had picked up sign language and a smattering of Indian dialects.

Meriwether Lewis, among others, despised Lisa for his rapacity and wrote of him and his partner, a man named Benoit, "Damn Manuel and triply damn Mr. B . . . . they give me more vexation . . . than their lives are worth." A Lisa employee in Saint Louis said, "Rascality sat on every feature of his dark-complexioned Mexican face." Others saw him as a "bold and daring character, with an energy and spirit of enterprise like that of Cortez or Pizarro."

Few denied that Lisa was ruthless in his consuming ambition and search for the dollar above expenses, but he was also courageously creative. As an intinerant trader on the Mississippi and Ohio Rivers in the 1790s and barely out of

his teens, he built a mercantile post at the old French settlement of Vincennes on the Wabash River in southwestern Indiana and by 1802 had established a thriving commerce
with the Osage people. Following settlement of the Louisiana Purchase, Lisa set up an operation in Saint Louis to begin trading on the Missouri, particularly in its fur-rich
upper country.

The Lisa-Colter party moved up the Missouri, encountering minor problems with an Arikara band that required a
show of weaponry before they could continue, and they
faced similar threats in Mandan and Assiniboine country
farther upriver. At the confluence of the Yellowstone and Big
Horn Rivers, in the midst of some of the richest beaver
streams in North America, they built a timbered blockhouse
and named it Fort Raymond, after Lisa's son. (It also became
known as Manuel's Fort.)

The entrepreneur planned to have his men strewn among
the Absaroka—Crow—villages of the Yellowstone and
hoped, by displaying goods coveted by the Indians, to persuade them to bring their furs to the new fort. The Crow
were adept trappers and Lisa hoped to win their loyalty first,
followed by that of other tribes, including the Blackfeet, ancient enemies of the Absaroka, and build a string of outposts
to establish his trade empire in the Upper Missouri country.

With his experience among the Crow, Colter was the
linchpin of this plan and in the winter of 1807 he began a
solitary odyssey on foot into the wilderness, traveling in a
great circle south from Fort Manuel via the Big Horn, up the
Wind River and its mountain range to a place later called
Jackson Hole, across the Tetons, north to Yellowstone Lake,
and back to Fort Raymond.

Wearing deerskins over the remnants of his "civilized"
clothing from Corps of Discovery days, Colter carried a
fifty-caliber musket, buffalo horns of black powder, blankets, snowshoes, a thirty-pound pack, and a "possibles"
bag—a buffalo-hide sack containing such necessities as lead

balls, flint, a steel striker, an awl for mending and stitching, and a folding lancet for opening abscesses and extracting arrowheads and bullets. He also carried iron traps and steel butcher knives to skin and dress hides. He lived on the meat he killed and slept in brush lean-tos under the stars wrapped in his blankets. He seems to have been welcomed into the Crow villages and was fed and sheltered there, sharing his meat as they shared theirs. He seems never to have hesitated to move on no matter how tempting it must have been to stay with Indian friends, nor does he seem to have doubted his ability to survive.

Colter wrote nothing of his journey and made no maps, but at some undetermined time, perhaps in the spring of 1808, he entered a foreboding valley of the Yellowstone, a place the Crow warned him was bewitched, inhabited by baleful spirits. He was the first white man to see, feel, and smell what they meant. There were bubbling, sulphurous tar pits all about, and steaming springs of water too hot to touch, rumblings under his moccasined feet that exploded in geysers vaulting from holes in the earth that created a scalding mist and shimmering rainbows. When he reported these things to Lisa and the men at Fort Raymond, they howled with laughter at "Colter's Hell"—what we know today as Yellowstone National Park.

On subsequent journeys into the wild, Colter explored the Green River, the valley of the Big Horn, and the headwaters of the Missouri—the Three Forks, where the Jefferson, Madison, and Gallatin conjoin—and at least three times escaped capture and torture by Blackfeet, or "Bug's Boys," as they were known to mountaineers who considered them spawn of Satan. Near the Three Forks he found himself in the midst of a battle between his Crow allies and the Blackfeet, and he took an arrow in the thigh but managed to escape. In the fall of 1808, Colter and John Potts, another Lewis and Clark expedition veteran, hunting with a party of Crow and Flatheads, ran into a Blackfeet band on the Jefferson fork of the Missouri. Potts was killed and his body chopped to pieces, but Colter was spared, stripped naked, and told to run for his life while a score of warriors chased him. He ran barefoot over brambles, stones, and pine needles, toward the Madison fork, six miles distant. In a desperate move, he stopped suddenly, turned and fought his lead pursuer, killed the man with his own spear, and reached the river. He dove in and hid for hours under a tangle of tree branches and mats of leaves and moss in the water. He made his way back to Fort Raymond, a 250-mile trek, in eleven days, appearing at the gate bleeding from a hundred cuts and shivering under a blanket he had taken from the slain Indian.

In April 1810, after again escaping a war party of Blackfeet, which killed five of his companions, Colter decided to quit the mountain country. He was a *hivernant* six times over and had the wounds, if little else, to prove it. He resigned from Lisa's service and reached Saint Louis in the summer with enough of a grubstake to start a new life.

Colter visited William Clark, provided his old chief with a wealth of information on the Yellowstone country, and learned of the tragic end of his other captain, Meriwether Lewis, dead from gunshot wounds at age thirty-five in the Natchez Trace of Tennessee. Clark thought his partner a suicide, as did their sponsor, Thomas Jefferson. Others thought Lewis had been murdered.

In the fall after Colter reached the Mississippi, he was visited by a delegation from an expedition sponsored by the New York fur magnate John Jacob Astor. The company of sixty-three men, headed by a man named Wilson Price Hunt of New Jersey, intended following the Lewis and Clark route up the Missouri to the Yellowstone, and Colter was happy to share his firsthand knowledge with them. He was probably offered a billet as hunter and guide with the Astorians, but declined.

He bought a piece of land at Charette, Missouri, close on the Mississippi. Not many miles away lived seventy-six-year-old Daniel Boone, the very embodiment of American pioneering, who had come to Missouri in 1799. Whether he and Colter met is not recorded, but one hopes they did and that these two frontiersmen spun many yarns telling what they witnessed in their years in the hinterlands. Boone was dreaming of pushing west to the Pacific when he died in 1820 at the age of eighty-five. Those last dreams might have been fortified by what Colter told him of what lay beyond the Shining Mountains.

John Colter died of "jaundice"—perhaps liver disease—at his homestead in Missouri seven years before Boone, in November 1813, age about forty. He was the original "free trapper," the link between Lewis and Clark and the fabulous era to come when mountain men would re-explore the Yellowstone country Colter knew so well, and South Pass on the Continental Divide, the Great Salt Lake, and the overland routes—the White Man's Great Medicine Roads—to Oregon and California. That era gave work and a certain fame to such men as Jedediah Smith, James Clyman, Jim Bridger, Tom Fitzpatrick, Ewing Young, Kit Carson, and Joseph Reddeford Walker, the men who followed Meriwether Lewis, William Clark, and John Colter to match the mountains and rivers of the West.

5

The Voyage of the *Tonquin*

■

"... A GUNPOWDER FELLOW."

1

On the sunny afternoon of August 4, 1810, onlookers on both sides of the Narrows separating the upper and lower bays of New York witnessed what celebrated New York author Washington Irving called "a nautical apparition." Down the mouth of the Hudson River and through the Narrows, heading for Rockaway Point on Long Island, slid a splendid flotilla of birch-bark canoes and *bateaux* filled with merrily whooping, halooing crews of French-Canadian *voyageurs* chanting boat-songs in an old patois of French and Indian tongues only they understood. Oblivious to the muggy weather and their sweaty work at the paddles, the variegated band wore beaded deerskins and blanket capotes, striped cotton shirts, moccasins and leggings; some had fur-trimmed, feather-bedecked caps on their heads, others wore feathers in their braided hair and paint on their faces. Dutch farmers along the Hudson naturally mistook them for a crew of savages. To the *voyageur* the gawkers on the riverbanks were, among kinder epithets, *mangeurs de lard* (pork-eaters).

H. H. Bancroft, in one of his flights of romantic fantasy, described the *voyageur*'s life as "wild, unfettered, buoyant, joyous, revelling, rollicking . . . full of beauty, with ever fresh and recurring fascination." He pictured them "as they sit at night eating, smoking, and chatting round the ruddy camp-fire, with weary limbs and soiled clothes, after a day of many portages, or perhaps after a wreck in a rapid, or a beating storm, their dark, luxuriant hair falling in tangled masses round their bronzed faces, and their uncouth figures casting weird shadows on the background foliage." On a frosty, hyperborean morning, he wrote, "See them as they rise from their hard though welcome bed, at the first faint streak of dawn . . . to the guide's harsh, leathern-voiced call of *'Lève! Lève!'* [wake up!] joking good-humor gradually arising out of the wheezes, sneezes, grunts, and grumbles of their somnolence. See them now, merry and musical as larks, throwing themselves with their luggage into the boats, and shoving off from a bank out upon the placid, polished water, striking up their morning song to the soft, low, rhythmic dip of their paddles, which rise and fall in unison as if moved by one hand."

These men, the backbone trappers of the Great Lakes, had come to New York from Lachine, their settlement near Montreal. They had transported their watercraft by wagon from the Saint Lawrence to Lake Champlain, crossed the lake, hoisted the boats on wagons again to travel to Lansingburgh, there pushing off on the Hudson toward the New York bays for what promised to be a grand adventure: They had enlisted as *engagés* for five years' service with John Jacob Astor's new Pacific Fur Company and were to sail from New York on the 290-ton frigate *Tonquin* to build a trading post at the mouth of the Columbia River, gateway to the fur riches of the Oregon Country.

Mr. Astor had no notions of "adventure" in launching his expedition to the Pacific. The scheme was purely a business matter; indeed, *he* was pure business, a financial genius all his adult life. He was a butcher's son, born in Waldorf, Germany, near Heidelberg, in 1763, who emigrated with his family to England when he was seventeen, and to America in 1784. He had an entrepreneurial gift, selling musical instruments for a time, then, discovering the profits to be made in furs, tramping the New York countryside to buy pelts from farmers and independent trappers and from the Iroquois and other tribes. He started an import-export business and in a few years had agents trading furs in China for nankings, silks, tea, fans, cloves, and nutmegs.

After twenty years in America, Astor had his own ships in the China trade and had become the foremost fur trader in New York and one of its richest merchants. He organized the American Fur Company in 1808 and made it dominant in the Great Lakes trade, then, as Bancroft put it, "pregnant with purposes of wealth and power, Astor's mind now labored with a great conception," setting up the Pacific Fur Company for a massive assault on the fur trade of the American West. He aspired to build a chain of forts westward from Saint Louis to the Pacific with a headquarters entrepôt, to be named Astoria, near the Columbia River estuary. And he devised an overland expedition, to depart soon after the *Tonquin* set sail, which would follow Lewis and Clark's route westward and which would survey sites for forts and trading posts and blaze a trail for a migration of Americans to the Pacific coast.

Astor foresaw Astoria as the soaring American presence in the Pacific Northwest, the monopolistic center of the fur trade west of the Rocky Mountains, a place where beaver, sea otter, and other skins would be shipped to Canton, where they would fetch the highest prices.

Astoria and its satellite posts would form a commercial emporium that would strike a mighty blow against England's puissant Hudson's Bay Company and especially against Astor's greatest rival, the North West Company, which for a quarter century had dominated the Saint Lawrence valley trade.

Astor hobnobbed with the elite at the North West Company headquarters in Montreal and at the exclusive Beaver Club in the city. There he heard the stories of the rivalry between the Nor'westers and the Company and the impossibility of either to engage in the China trade because of the monopoly there held by the British East India Company. The nabob of New York had no such restraints, and the acquisition of the Louisiana Territory and the overland pathmaking of Lewis and Clark convinced him he could construct an American fur cartel on the north Pacific Rim while the British companies were busy warring against each other.

To this end, Astor recruited seasoned agents and business partners from the discontented ranks of the North West Company to help put his plan into motion. He launched his Pacific Fur establishment on March 10, 1810, with nine partners, five of them Scotch veterans of the Nor'westers: Alexander McKay, who had been a clerk accompanying Mackenzie on his explorations to the Pacific Coast in 1793; Donald Mackenzie, who had spent ten of his twenty-seven years in the service of the Nor'westers; David Stuart, born in Perthshire in 1753, a fisherman and fur trader; Robert Stuart, David Stuart's nephew, who migrated to Canada in 1807; and Duncan McDougall a former Nor'wester described by Washington Irving as "an active, irritable, fuming, vainglorious little man, and elevated in his own opinion, by being the proxy for Mr. Astor."

The nabob signed an agreement with these men, put up $400,000 of his own money, named himself as chief stockholder and president of Pacific Fur, and agreed to bear all losses in the company's first five years of business.

McDougall and McKay were selected to lead the seaward expedition to the Pacific on the *Tonquin*, a frigate built in 1808 expressly as a trader, which had already made two

successful voyages to the Pacific and which Astor purchased for $40,000 two weeks before it sailed. Donald
Mackenzie and Wilson Price Hunt of Asbury, New Jersey,
would lead the land-bound party. At age twenty-seven,
Hunt was an established merchant in Saint Louis when he
first met with Astor and learned of the Pacific plan. He became such an enthusiastic backer of it that he was selected
as leader of the "Overland Astorians" with orders to take
charge of the Columbia River post.

As laborers—woodsmen, carpenters, hunters, wheelwrights, packers, and the like—Astor hired many Americans "of respectable connections and of good moral character
as possible" but he knew he needed the *hommes du nord* for
his boats and traps. His agents were instructed to begin hiring these northmen immediately and found them in the taverns and warehouses at Lachine in the months before the
Tonquin was due to hoist anchor and sail for the Falklands.

In June 1810 Alexander McKay led the first of three
parties of fourteen *voyageurs* and several clerks to join Mc-
Dougall in New York. Between June and the end of August
these men had gathered and stowed their canoes and *bateaux*
aboard the frigate and were ready to sail on a far greater
body of water than they had known before.

2

As sole financier of the Oregon undertaking and a meticulous planner, Astor tried to cover all details and
contingencies of the *Tonquin* voyage. A few days before the
frigate spread its canvas, he addressed a letter to his four
partners aboard the frigate, enjoining them to "cultivate harmony and unanimity" among themselves and the *Tonquin*
crew and to take special care in creating good relations with
"the wild people of the Oregon coast." He said, "If you find
them kind, as I hope you will, be so to them. If otherwise,

act with caution and forbearance, and convince them that you come as friends."

To ensure these good relations, he had financed certain precautions on the *Tonquin*. The frigate, manned by a crew of twenty sailors, carried not only the Astor partners, a number of *voyageurs*, twelve clerks, a party of workmen to build the fort on the Columbia, $50,000 in trade goods, plus tools, provisions, and even a small, dismantled coastal vessel, it also carried nearly a ton of gunpowder in its hold, was armed with ten cannon, and was "pierced" (had gunports available) for ten more.

Astor's powder-and-ball insurance, influenced by the massacre of the *Boston* crew at Nootka Sound in 1803 and rising tensions between the United States and Britain, extended to his selection of the *Tonquin*'s captain. Five years after Nelson's victory at Trafalgar, at a time when Napoleon was at his zenith but Wellington was fighting and winning battles against French generals in Portugal and Spain and William Henry Harrison was defeating Tecumseh at Tippecanoe in Indiana, the financier told friends he wanted "a gunpowder fellow" to command his ship "in fine style." He found the fellow, if not the style, in a thirty-one-year-old salt named Jonathan Thorn of Schenectady, New York. Astor was impressed by Thorn's history: He had been appointed a midshipman in the navy in 1800, served on men-of-war in the Mediterranean and on frigates against Tripolitan pirates in the Barbary Wars. So valorous was his service in these engagements, in particular the memorable expedition under Stephen Decatur to destroy the captured *Philadelphia* in Tripoli harbor on February 16, 1804, that the New Yorker had been commended by Commodore Decatur in dispatches and promoted to lieutenant. Thorn had also commanded the New York Navy Yard and its gunboats in 1806 and 1807, during which service he may have been introduced to Astor. In any event, the navy granted him a two-year leave, beginning in May 1810, to command the *Tonquin*.

Thorn had, no doubt, earned Decatur's wartime commendations, but between wars, in all the navy of the United States no worse choice could have been made to command a merchant ship than this surly, stern-visaged, acid-tongued autocrat. Even the attribute Astor must have found attractive, Thorn's sycophantic loyalty toward his employer, would prove catastrophic. In truth, Thorn had no interest in Astor's expansive, expensive fur cartel scheme. Washington Irving, Astor's hired amanuensis, wrote, "He [Thorn] evidently had but a narrow idea of the scope and nature of the enterprise, limiting his views merely to his part of it; everything beyond the concerns of his ship was out of his sphere; and anything that interfered with the routine of his nautical duties put him in a passion."

Astor saw none of the man's potential for folly when he wrote Captain Thorn a letter on the eve of the *Tonquin*'s departure urging his "strictest attention" to the health of himself and crew and the "promotion of good humor and harmony aboard the ship." The nabob's closing paragraph to Thorn would yield a bitter irony: "I must recommend you to be particularly careful on the coast, and not to rely too much on the friendly disposition of the natives. All accidents which have as yet happened there arose from too much confidence in the Indians."

Irving noted that these final admonitions were particularly pregnant and asked his readers "to bear these instructions in mind as events will prove their wisdom and importance, and the disasters which ensued in consequence of the neglect of them."

On September 8, 1810, the *Tonquin* and its thirty-three passengers ran down to Staten Island for a brief anchorage off Sandy Hook Lighthouse before proceeding south into the Atlantic. The presence of an escort ship, the USS *Constitution*, had been arranged by Astor. Royal Navy vessels out of

Halifax, Nova Scotia, were cruising nearby and he feared that his ship, with its Canadian subjects aboard, might be boarded by press gangs. The presence of Old Ironsides also illustrated the government's interest in the Astor enterprise in the midst of growing tensions between the two powers. Two years past, Astor had written to President Jefferson of his scheme, seeking governmental sanction for it because of its "great public utility." To this appeal the president took a middle course: He made it known that while he encouraged private merchant vessels to trade in the Pacific Northwest, he opposed any official "partnership" in these expeditions. Newly elected President James Madison followed his predecessor's wishes but did extend to Astor the government's "full approbation and best wishes" for the Oregon experiment.

After striking the trade winds, on October 5 the *Tonquin* sighted the Cape Verde Islands off the West African coast and, while stores and water were low, Captain Thorn decided against an anchorage and shore party. He remained worried about British warships lurking nearby, and indeed one unidentified brigantine, mounting twenty guns, approached the *Tonquin* in what Thorn believed to be a hostile manner and followed for three days in a cat-and-mouse game until the merchantman caught a racing wind and lost its pursuer.

The sea chase was a diversion from serious problems aboard the Astor frigate. Captain Thorn's proclivity for petty tyranny seems to have surfaced the instant he climbed the boarding ladder into his floating fiefdom. From that moment he was oblivious to his civilian passengers, including Astor's partners, except as victims of his wrath. He made it known that he regarded these landsmen as "live lumber, continually in the way," and had no sympathy for their cramped quarters or their tendency to suffer *mal de mer*. "Lubberly" was his favorite word for them, including the *voyageurs*, the rivermen, who suffered as much as the partners, clerks, and workmen "the doleful rigors and retchings of sea-sickness."

Throughout the voyage, Irving wrote, Thorn found it intolerable to discover the French-Canadians "lurking below in their berths in squalid state, or emerging now and then like spectres from the hatchways, in capotes and blankets, with dirty nightcaps, grizzly beard, lantern visage and unhappy eye, shivering about the deck, and ever and anon crawing to the sides of the vessel, and offering up their tributes to the windward."

Gabriel Franchére, a clerk aboard the *Tonquin* who somehow managed to keep a journal, said that Thorn, when he first addressed his passengers, "laid the foundation of rankling hatred between the partners and himself which ended only with the voyage." The captain's Bligh-like pronouncements included the news that he intended enforcing a ship-of-war discipline and therefore all cabin lanterns would be extinguished punctually at eight o'clock each night and any man proving "refractory" would be manacled. Moreover, Thorn added, he would shoot any man challenging his authority.

These decrees were clearly aimed at Astor's partners and clerks, who were accustomed to burning midnight oil as they pored over their charts, plans, and correspondence, but Thorn, described by Bancroft as "as thoroughly disagreeable a Yankee as ever crossed the path of Scotchmen," underestimated Scotch mettle. The "irritable, fuming," Duncan Mc-Dougall was having none of Thorn's insolence and after a later confrontation with the captain he seized a pistol and swore he would kill Thorn if he ever subjected him to further indignity.

After a month at sea and now approaching the equator, the skipper's annoyance with his passengers deteriorated further. He was suspicious of the Canadian passengers from the start, wondering about their national loyalties, and he now made a habit of scowling at them as they bent over the rail wracked with sea sickness, blaspheming over the squalid, stinking state of their berths, calling them the worst "lubberly scoundrels that ever broke a sea-biscuit." And now, with no reprovisioning stores and fresh water for over a month, he grew especially irritated at the civilians' "keenness of appetite" and "daintiness" at the mess table.

At first, the ship's stores and galley served up what would be sumptuous meals for a sailing ship: fresh pork loins, hams, tongue, smoked beef haunches, sweetened puddings made of flour, rice, tapioca, and raisins. But the passengers complained incessantly at this fare and the furious Thorn called them "effeminate" and wrote to Astor that he would never take to sea again with such a group "without having a Fly-market on the forecastle, Covent-garden on the poop, and a cool spring from Canada in the maintop."

In the stifling heat of the slow passage below the equator, he rationed water to a quart a day—soon reduced to a pint and a half plus a half-pint of Souchong tea—and reduced the food allowance per man to fourteen ounces of hardtack, a pound and a quarter of salt pork or beef, a small portion of rice, beans, and cornmeal pudding with molasses. Even this still-considerable ration was not enough for them, he said, and he claimed that the Canadians had to be restrained from raiding the stores.

He was also irritated by the camaraderie among the Astor partners, clerks, and *voyageurs*, at their grouping together to tell tales of their lives—David Stuart was particularly loquacious in recalling his halcyon days as a fisherman off the coast of Labrador—as they cackled and sucked their pipes and sang old boat-songs. Thorn regarded such badinage as idleness, shocking to naval etiquette in general and his quarter-deck authority in particular, and beneath the dignity of Astor agents. He also regarded it highly suspicious that the clerks were incessantly scribbling in their journals, "showing literary pretensions."

The passengers were forever clamoring to find an anchorage so they could go ashore, Thorn wrote. They "insisted on my stopping at the Cape de Verds. Next they said the ship should stop on the coast of Patagonia, for they must see the large and uncommon inhabitants of that place. Then they must go to the island where Robinson Crusoe had so long lived. And lastly they were determined to see the handsome inhabitants of Easter Island."

Naturally, Thorn wrote to Astor, he turned down such requests peremptorily as "contrary to instructions." Washington Irving gave Thorn the benefit of the doubt in his dealings with the "lubberly" civilians on the *Tonquin*, admitting that the crusty seaman had some sound reasons to have "seaman-like impatience" toward the landsmen and that at least he had an "honest, trusty concern for the interests of his employer." Irving wrote that Thorn "pictured to himself the anxious protector of the enterprise, who had disbursed so munificently in its outfit, calculating on the zeal, fidelity and singleness of purpose of his associates and agents; while they, on the other hand, having a good ship at their disposal and a deep pocket at home to bear them out, seemed ready to loiter on every coast, and amuse themselves in every port."

Down the Torrid Zone, through the Tropic of Capricorn, and into cold and rainy weather as they lost the trades in advancing south, the *Tonquin* saw a few distant sails and only one up close, a Portuguese brig out of Recife on the Pernambuco coast of Brazil. In early December a lookout in the shrouds sighted the barren, reef-scattered outline of the Falklands, 300 miles east of the Strait of Magellan, and Thorn ordered his helmsman to follow a corridor through the maze of small islets and rocks to a small bay, there to take soundings, anchor, and fill water casks. The Canadians were overjoyed to set foot on dry land, and explored the bleak moorlands, visited the ancient graves of mariners who died there, swam, chased penguins and killed them by the dozens (their flesh, black and leathery, carried a strong fishy odor even when thoroughly cooked), and stole their eggs.

Thorn meantime had determined the anchorage unsafe and fresh water scarce, and stood out to sea after signaling the shore for the civilians to return to ship. To his fury, they straggled back in the jollyboats and it was nine at night before all were aboard. The next morning, after assurances from the Canadians that they would return on a moment's notice, they were again taken ashore with the water party. With the wind up favorably, Thorn was anxious to find a new anchorage and had signals made to the shore. After a half-hour with no boat seen pulling away from the beach, the captain reconnoitered with his glass and, as Irving wrote, "to his infinite vexation, saw the loiterers in the full enjoyment of their 'wild-goose chase.'" He ordered the *Tonquin* to set sail and when the Canadians saw the ship under way they jumped into the boats and pulled hard at the oars before coming alongside and aboard.

On December 7, the last act of this absurd melodrama occurred when Thorn took the ship to another Falklands bay that promised a better source of water and wood for galley fires and a safer sanctuary for repairs. The *Tonquin* remained at the place, called "Fort Egmont" on the charts, for four days, during which time the Canadians were given a boat to themselves, pitched a tent on the beach, and resumed their rambling explorations, chasing and butchering sea lions, geese, penguins, foxes, and any animal life that waddled, ran, flew, or swam.

As before, the captain warned his detested civilian supercargo not to wander far and to remain within hailing distance, for he would not detain the ship this time waiting for them to react to his signal to reboard; the Astor men, true to their custom, ignored him.

On the morning of the eleventh, the *Tonquin* signaled the shore that it was time to embark, but the civilians were scattered, some inspecting tombstone legends, others hunting and exploring, and two of the partners, David Stuart and Duncan McDougall, pursuing penguins on the south end of the island. Those closest to the anchorage heard the report of the gunshot signal and scurried about to locate the missing

members of the shore party while the skipper angrily
paced the deck of his ship. The landsmen had thrice defied
him and he could bear it no longer: He ordered the sails
spread and the ship put to sea.

The eight Canadians on the beach saw their ship stand out
of the bay, and by the time they were all aboard their twenty-
foot longboat the *Tonquin* was three miles offshore in surging
seas. For three hours the boat tried to close the gap, thrown
high on the waves as its occupants bent to the oars and
bailed the water shipped by every roller. Aboard the frigate
the other Canadians and crewmen implored Thorn to heave
to and await the longboat, but he refused. Finally, Robert
Stuart, nephew of David, "a young man of spirit and resolution," Irving said, went below and grabbed a brace of pistols
"and in a paroxysm of wrath swore he would blow out the
captain's brains unless he put about or shortened sail."

Stuart's proposed mutiny died out with the wind, which
suddenly abated and allowed the longboat to come alongside
and its sopping, exhausted passengers to board. In his account of the incident, Irving put the best face on it by allowing, "We can hardly believe that the captain really intended
to carry his threat into full effect, and rather think he meant
to let the laggards off for a long pull and a hearty fright."
But in a letter to Astor Thorn made it clear that if not for the
wind hauling, "I should positively have left them." In his
blind constancy to his employer he apparently thought he
would have done Astor a favor by abandoning the partners
and clerks. "I cannot but think it an unfortunate circumstance for you that it so happened, for the first loss in this
instance would, in my opinion, have proved the best, as they
seem to have no idea of the value of property, not any ap-
parant regard for your interest, although interwoven with
their own."

The "property" Thorn referred to was certain articles of
spare clothing in the ship's slopchest, which the partners
asked be distributed among them. Naturally, Thorn refused

to consider the request and posted the ship's mastiff to guard the chest. This pettifoggery Thorn dutifully described in his letters to Astor, as he did the feuds among the partners themselves—with unalloyed delight. Alexander McKay and Duncan McDougall, Thorn said, were particularly argumentative over their "rank" in the Astor scheme. They drew plans for the fort on the Columbia, he said, and disputed over placement of doors and windows until McDougall would produce a letter in which Astor named him his main representative and proxy, whereupon the word-contest ended and the two men "would be caressing each other like children."

On December 15, the mountains of Tierra del Fuego hove into view and on the eighteenth the ship, fifteen leagues from Cape Horn, encountered a lucky calm in the wind and a good current that carried it to the cape's stupendous rocks and seas. Thorn, excellent seaman that he was, managed to breech the Horn in a wild gale and reach the Diego Ramirez Islands—9,165 miles from New York—for a final water-and-repair stop. Six of the ship's cannons had broken loose from their carriages in the Horn gale and careened about the deck, splintering railings and tangling lines before being wrestled down and secured, and the ship was leaking and had damaged canvas and rigging, but there was time to patch and mend before the run north to the Sandwich Islands.

3

The *Tonquin* spotted the snowcapped peak of the Mauna Loa volcano on the island of Owhyee (Hawaii) on February 11, 1811, and sailed into Kamehameha Bay two days later. At anchor, the ship was surrounded by canoes filled with islanders clamoring to come aboard and exchange their yams, taro, plantains, coconuts, cabbages, and breadfruit for beads, needles and cloth, and other such treasures the vessel carried.

Great changes had occurred in the islands in the thirty-
two years since Captain Cook had been murdered there upon
his return from exploring the northwest coast of America.
The archipelago had been unified in 1810 by King Kamehameha, a crafty bargainer who knew the value to his
people of Western technology and welcomed foreign ships
to his shores. The islands had already become a trade cross-
roads, linking Canton with Boston, Bristol, Marseilles, and
other foreign ports.

The *Tonquin* remained in the islands two weeks, cultivating good relations with the natives and purchasing livestock
and provisions with trade items and silver coins. In planning
his North Pacific sovereignty, Astor had not neglected the
importance of the islands as a place for his ships to reprovi-
sion en route to Astoria and in their comings and goings to
China. Washington Irving said Astor "even had a vague idea
of, some time or other, getting possession of one of their islands as a rendezvous for his ships, and a link in the chain
of his commercial establishments."

As he took the *Tonquin* to Maui and back to the big island of Hawaii, Thorn grew increasingly unhinged over what
he considered the scandalous conduct of the civilians. They
all stayed ashore, dazzled by the snow-white beaches, warm
waters for swimming, the splendid hospitality afforded them,
and the singing and dancing of the native women, whose
dress exposed them in a manner he described as "very revolting to a civilized eye," but which did not seem to injure
Scotch sensibilities. Far from it, Irving said; the Canadians
"were delighted with the charms and graces of the dancing
damsels."

While at Hawaii, the Astor men and a number of crew
members hiked to Kealakekua Bay on the Kona Coast for a
pilgrimage to the spot where Cook had fallen under native
knives in 1779. An old islander served as their guide and
pointed out the spot on the beach where the greatest of English navigators died and where the rocks and coconut palms

still bore the marks of musket balls fired by the marines—
including John Ledyard—who formed Cook's escort, and
from boats offshore. The Canadians took pieces of palm
bark and rock as precious relics back to the ship.

Thorn was unimpressed by this holy mission; indeed he
threw a fit at the unauthorized shore leave by his crewmen.
Alexander Ross, a twenty-eight-year-old Astor man on the
Tonquin, wrote in his journal of Thorn "storming and stomp-
ing the deck," and how "the captain called up all hands; he
swore, he threatened, and abused the whole ship's company."
The crewmen, whom the captain labeled "deserters," were
rounded up and brutally flogged, Ross said. He wrote that
Thorn was exceedingly angry at the Scotchmen for fomenting the desertions, for speaking in Gaelic and "making gestures toward him he construed as mutinous."

Before departing the islands, the *Tonquin* paid a visit to
the village at Waikiki on Oahu, the royal residence of King
Kamehameha, whose two-story "palace" of stone and wood
was guarded by two dozen men dressed in long blue coats,
each armed with a musket. The corpulent king, dressed in a
tight regimental uniform complete with ceremonial sword,
came out to the frigate in his royal barge accompanied by a
large retinue that included three of his wives. Thorn permitted a three-gun greeting for the king, and while the Canadian partners appeared on deck in tartans and kilts to present
greetings from Mr. Astor and engage in diplomatic talk,
Thorn, ever the practical man, sought to buy hogs from the
sovereign of the Sandwich Islands.

Kamehameha, Irving said, "was a magnanimous monarch
but a shrewd pork merchant. . . . Several interviews were
requisite, and much bargaining, before he could be brought
to part with a bristle of bacon, and then he insisted on being
paid in hard Spanish dollars; giving as a reason that he
wanted money to purchase a frigate from his brother George,
as he affectionately terms the king of England."

At length Thorn managed to buy a hundred hogs, a number

of goats, two sheep, and a coop of chickens, adding these to an abundance of island vegetables.

The Astor partners were greatly impressed by the Hawaiians' singular skills at canoeing, swimming, and diving and said they had not seen their equal even among the *voyageurs* of Canada. They talked to the king about recruiting thirty or forty of these fine "watermen," but Thorn objected to the number. Eventually, with royal authorization, twenty-four natives were signed for three years' service with the Pacific Fur Company, during which time they were guaranteed food and clothing and, at the end of their service, $100 "in merchandise."

On the last day of February the *Tonquin* sailed from the warm and placid bay off Waikiki toward the sterner waters of the North Pacific. In Hawaii, Thorn had left a large packet of seething letters to his employer to be forwarded to New York on the next ship bound for the New England coast. Now, heading toward the Columbia, he wrote Astor again to describe the disgusting conduct of the agents' fraternizing with the natives, dressing in Highland plaids, loosening tongues and probably the morals of the Hawaiian women with gifts of rum and wine, making a great show of visiting the site of Cook's murder, and similar "ridiculously contemptible" acts. "To enumerate the thousands of instances of ignorance, filth, &c., or to particularize all the frantic gambols that are daily practiced, would require volumes," he said.

6

The Phial of Wrath

■

"I HAVE BUT TO DRAW THE CORK."

1

In the three-week voyage from the Sandwich Islands to the Oregon coast, Jonathan Thorn's enmity toward the Astor agents on the *Tonquin* deepened. He may have, as Washington Irving speculated, "picked up some information at Owyhee, possibly of war between the United States and England" and begun suspecting that the Canadians were plotting to take over the ship and alter its destination. He detected clues of conspiracy: The civilians held long conversations in Gaelic "of a mysterious and unwarranted nature," he wrote to Astor; they had their own store of firearms and distributed them among their party; they seemed furtive and silent when he made a sudden appearance among them. He saw their every utterance and act as evidence of mutinous conduct and believed that it was only his stalwart defiance of them, made clear by word and deed, that overawed them and kept them from enacting their despicable plans.

One example Thorn cited to Astor of his fortitude in dealing with this gang of disloyal Gaels was the occasion when the *Tonquin* struck a violent storm in the North Pacific, one that washed much of the penned livestock overboard. During the squall the Canadians, without seeking his permission, attempted to procure rain gear from a storage locker. Thorn proudly reported that he drove them off with a pistol.

The real test of the *Tonquin*, its captain, and crew began on March 22, 1811, when the ship approached the Oregon coast and the surging mouth of the Columbia River. The estuary was four miles wide with a low sandy spit of land on the south called Point Adams, a peninsula and promontory on the north side crowned with a forest of pines and connected to the mainland by a narrow land neck. Within the cape opened a wide inlet, Baker's Bay, the entrance to which was guarded by numerous sandbars and a chain of crashing breakers. Captain Robert Gray had described the river's mouth in 1792 as perhaps the most perilous passage along the northwest coast and Thorn saw the evidence of the assertion before him. On the tossing quarterdeck of the Astor frigate he examined the hellish gate through his glass and determined that he could not attempt to penetrate it without a sounding and a close-up survey by whaleboat.

Selected to lead this perilous if not suicidal mission was Thorn's first mate, a man named John Fox. The captain ordered that he take John Martin, an old sea hand who had visited the Oregon coast before, and three of the *voyageurs* with him in the boat to sound the channel and discover a safe passage to the beach while the *Tonquin* stood three miles offshore. Fox made a mild protest over the Canadians, asking for more experienced deepwater sailors to accompany him, but Thorn refused this patently prudent request, saying that he needed his crew to help guide the *Tonquin* to anchorage. He told Fox that the Canadians were supposed to be expert small-boat men and ought to serve admirably under the guidance of two veterans like Fox and Martin.

Nothing is known of John Fox's history except that he was an experienced sailor who had a premonition that he would never return to the *Tonquin*. He sought sympathy from the Astorians, telling them pitifully, "I am sent off without seamen to man my boat, in boisterous weather, and on the most dangerous part of the northwest coast. My uncle was lost a few years ago on this same bar and now I am going to lay my bones with his." But when he protested that the mission was ill-conceived, Thorn answered, "Mr. Fox, if you are afraid of water, you should have remained in Boston."

The whaleboat was lowered at one o'clock that afternoon, and the five men rowed into the foaming breakers and disappeared in the foggy mist. The *Tonquin* searched for them all day and the next, lowering boats, which stayed on the seaward side of the bar, but no sign of them was ever found.

At the end of the second day of waiting and with the wind abating, Thorn took his ship closer to shore and anchored at a fourteen-fathom sounding north of the long peninsula forming the north side of the river entrance that was aptly named Cape Disappointment. Here a boat was lowered carrying several sailors and the Astor partners Alexander McKay and David Stuart, who hoped to find some trace of Fox and his men. But the crashing surf drove them back to the ship. Another boat, carrying an experienced crew and two of the Hawaiian outrigger experts signed aboard at Oahu, clawed its way to within a league of the shore before being tossed high on a ferocious breaker that nearly capsized it. It too limped back to the ship.

By now the *Tonquin* itself was in serious danger, riding perilously at anchor in shallow water in a roaring wind and smashing surf that threatened to splinter the ship to oak kindling on the rocks despite the extra anchors thrown overboard. Thorn had a final plan: He turned to three of his most experienced hands to guide the frigate through the passage. An old tar named Aiken, who had signed on to command the disassembled schooner on board the *Tonquin*, commanded the escort boat, with a sailmaker named John Coles; an armorer, Stephen Weekes; and two Hawaiians as crew. The plan called for Aiken to steer the boat and take soundings while the *Tonquin* followed under shortened sails.

When Aiken had found the channel he was to signal with a pistol shot and return to the ship.

For a time the plan seemed to be working, but eventually Aiken's boat broached broadside to the twenty-foot waves crashing inland and was carried away. On the *Tonquin*, crewmen climbed the quaking mizzentop and saw the boat desperately trying to reach the ship, then saw it vanish in the surf. The frigate meantime had entered shallow water, scraped its hull against the rocks, and ploughed across sandbars, until at nightfall, with the help of a tidal surge, it was pushed into Baker's Bay and, at a depth of seven fathoms and with the wind lulling, cast anchor.

At daybreak, with lookouts on the masthead peering out over the wild coast for signs of the missing boat parties, Thorn sent searchers ashore. On the beach some natives who had been watching the *Tonquin* struggle into Baker's Bay came out to the ship in canoes, and were questioned with sign language about the missing sailors, but they seemed to have no information. Thorn himself led one of the search parties and a short distance along the beach he found Stephen Weekes, the armorer who had been with Aiken's whaleboat. He told a harrowing tale of the boat being swamped, of Coles, the sailmaker, and Aiken disappearing in the boiling surf. Weekes and the two Sandwich Islanders had managed to turn the boat on its keel and retrieve its oars. One of the Hawaiians died, presumably of exposure in the numbing cold before the boat beached itself; the other was found by *Tonquin* crewmen later on the morning of March 25, half dead from cold and fatigue.

The armorer and the Hawaiian were the only survivors of the ten men sent into the channel, an event, Irving wrote, "that cast a gloom over the spirits of the whole party, and was regarded by some of the superstitious as an omen that boded no good to the enterprise."

* * *

The natives of the lower Columbia, principally Chinook and Clatsop people, had dealt with white traders for many years and knew what they sought, and thus swarmed to the *Tonquin*'s anchorage from its first day in Baker's Bay, their canoes carrying sea otter skins and other furs. These fisherfolk were waterway artisans, and the *voyageurs* especially admired their craft, some of which were fifty feet in length, hewn from a single fir or white cedar and capable of carrying thirty men. The thwarts were thick and the gunwales flared outward, features that enabled them to stay upright in the most treacherous of waters; the bows and sterns of the boats were intricately carved into grotesque figures of men and animals, some of the prow-pieces as tall and stately as any Viking ship. The canoers sat on their haunches to paddle; one man in the stern with a paddle serving as rudder. Women were not excluded from canoe-work and were as expert as any paddler and often took the important tiller position aft. Irving, who gathered descriptions from those who saw the natives at work, wrote, "It is surprising to see with what fearless unconcern these savages venture in their light barks upon the roughest and most tempestuous seas. They seem to ride upon the waves like sea-fowl." He compared the Columbia River people with the horseback Indians of the Great Plains and said that while the buffalo-hunting tribes were "generally tall, sinewy, meagre but well-formed, and of bold and fierce deportment," the Oregon coastal tribes, "lounging about the river banks, or squatting and curved up in their canoes, are generally low in stature, ill-shaped, with crooked legs, thick ankles, and broad flat feet. They are inferior also in muscular power and activity . . . to their hard-riding brethren of the prairies."

While the natives came to the *Tonquin* camp ashore and out to the ship in their canoes, some bringing otter skins to trade, many just to gawk, and some to pilfer, Captain Thorn and a number of the Astor partners explored the Columbia estuary searching for a suitable site for the trading post. As

ever, Thorn was angry. He had lost eight men in his haphazard attempt to find an entrance to the Columbia estuary,
and he was anxious to be rid of his insubordinate Canadian
passengers and their sinister Gaelic babble. He was particularly infuriated at Duncan McDougall, the vain and sple-
netic little man who made so much of being Mr. Astor's
proxy. It had not escaped Thorn's notice that McDougall
seemed to have a covetous eye toward the wives and daugh-
ters of the Chinook chief Comcomly, a tendency the captain found as disgusting as the women themselves. Irving
admitted that McDougall "seems to have had a heart susceptible to the influence of the gentler sex," and of the Chinook women reported that they "painted their bodies with
red clay, and anointed themselves with fish oil, to give additional lustre to their charms." According to H. H. Bancroft, McDougall later "took to wife a dreamy daughter of
the Chinook chief."

Thorn was particularly incensed that McDougall had invited Comcomly aboard the *Tonquin* with his many wives
and large retinue without so much as a by-your-leave, an
event that, one of the partners later wrote, "stirred the spleen
of the captain, who had a sovereign contempt for the one-
eyed chieftain and all his crew."

Above all, Thorn was impatient to move on, to leave the
lubberly managers and fort builders on the beach and take
the ship upcoast to fulfill what he considered the most important of Mr. Astor's assignments, the investigation of
the fur-trade potential of the entire Oregon coast. He ordered the building of a shed on the shore of Baker's Bay to
receive the supplies, tools, and equipment needed for building the trading post, and the dismantled schooner and its rigging. He intended to relieve the *Tonquin* of this cargo and
the supernumerary civilians as well and take his leave of the
entire land enterprise.

Meantime, McDougall and David Stuart set out in a boat
to find a site for the fort and in the first week of April se-

lected a densely wooded point of land on the south shore of the bay. Point George, as they named it, lay opposite the site of Lewis and Clark's Fort Clatsop, twelve miles from the Columbia entrance channel and above a good harbor where trade vessels of average size could anchor within fifty yards of shore.

Work began on the fort on April 12 with axmen on scaffolds topping the biggest trees and cutting down the firs and alders. In heavy rains, laborers chopped underbrush, moved rocks, blew up stumps with gunpowder, and landed goods and livestock. Others worked to erect a twenty-by-sixty-two-foot warehouse, a powder magazine, and a "residence" of barked logs surrounded by gardens, the plots hoed and sewn with vegetable seeds brought on the ship. As this work proceeded, two shipwrights Astor had employed began laying the keel of the trade schooner brought crated on the *Tonquin*.

At last Captain Thorn was free to take his ship to sea and search for furs along the northern coast. Aboard were twenty-nine men, including the only civilians, Alexander McKay, listed as "supercargo," with one James Lewis serving as his clerk. A Chehalem Indian named Lamanse, who had picked up some English and served vessels as interpreter to tribes along the northwest coast, was taken aboard at Gray's Harbor, after which the *Tonquin* sailed north to Vancouver Island.

Of Captain Thorn's freedom from the Astor men, Bancroft asks rhetorically if "our most sturdy captain" might not now "shake from his feet the dust of Scotch fur-traders and filthy French *voyageurs* and on the *Tonquin*'s cleanly scrubbed deck, laugh at the discordant past, laugh as with his own crew only on board she flew before the breeze, and swept gayly into the coves and estuaries of the admiring savages?" His answer: "Alas! no; with his evil temper, evil times forever attended him. Doomed to destruction, the gods had long since made him mad."

2

J onathan Thorn, relieved of his burden of Gaelic-gabbling
civilians and the detested cargo for building and provisioning of Fort Astoria, proceeded northward to Vancouver
Island on June 5, 1811. He had a specific mission to fulfill:
Mr. Astor wanted him to trade for furs among the coastal
tribes and, having gathered a sufficient number of sea otter
and other skins, to return to Astoria, check on the needs of the
fort builders, and then proceed to China to sell the furs and
sail back to New York. According to Astor's plan, the *Tonquin*
would become one of several trade ships making a periodic
run to the Oregon coast, thence to Canton and back, with
Astoria as the epicenter of the Astor-Pacific emporium.

For his anchorage Thorn selected an inlet—called New-
eetie by Irving, Clayoquot or Kyuquot by the natives—
opposite a large Indian village thirty-odd miles above
Nootka Sound. Lamanse, the Indian interpreter on board,
warned the captain that the people of the village were "of a
perfidious character," but Thorn ignored the warning.

Late in the first day of the anchorage, a group of natives
came out to the ship bringing bundles of sea otter hides in
their canoes and were welcomed on deck. Among the visitors were emissaries of the village chief, one Wicananish,
who invited the white leaders to his lodge. Thorn declined
the offer, but Alexander McKay went ashore with the interpreter and was received hospitably by Wicananish and spent
the night in the chief's home, sleeping in a warm bed of otter skins. As assurance of his amity toward the traders, the
chief left six of his men—Irving called them "hostages"—
aboard the *Tonquin*.

The next morning (the date is unknown but is believed to
be about June 15), Thorn, without waiting for McKay's return to the ship, had his crewmen spread the trade goods on
deck: blankets, cloths, knives, beads, fishhooks, odd pieces

of iron. The captain expected a prompt and profitable sale,
but as the natives boarded the ship with their packets of furs,
Irving says, Thorn quickly learned that they "were not so
eager and simple as he had supposed, having learned the art
of bargaining and the value of merchandise from the casual
traders along the coast."

The negotiations were guided by an old subchief named
Nookamis, a wily bargainer with a long history of haggling
with the Bostons and King George's agents and "who had
grown gray in traffic . . . and prided himself upon his acute-
ness." Thorn, in contrast, Irving said, "was a plain, straightforward sailor, who never had two minds, nor two prices in
his dealings, was deficient in patience and pliancy, and to-
tally wanting in the chicanery of traffic."

The day's trade did not begin well, but then it got worse.
Thorn pointed to the furs Nookamis' people had brought on
board, pointed to the goods he would trade for them, and the
old chief laughed and shook his head merrily and made a
counteroffer. The captain, sorely offended from the start,
sullenly paced the deck, hands thrust in his pockets, followed
by Nookamis holding out a sea otter skin and pestering him
to make an offer. After a few minutes of Nookamis' hector-
ing chatter, Thorn, "never remarkable for relishing a joke,
especially when at his own expense," exploded. He snatched
the pelt and rubbed Nookamis' face with it, then strode
about the deck swearing, kicking the furs about, his face an
ugly mask. He grabbed Nookamis by his hair and shoved
the old man to the rail, grabbed another—named Shewish,
one of Wicananish's sons—and booted him toward the
sallyport, and shouted to the others to leave the ship instantly.
The Indians ran to the rail, "as one might recoil from a pestilence," Bancroft said, and jumped into the sea or down the
boarding ladder to their canoes, Nookamis and Shewish
shouting imprecations at Thorn as their men scurried to the
paddles.

When McKay returned to the ship later in the morning

and learned of the incident, he and Lamanse warned of the danger and urged Thorn to make sail, as there would surely be reprisals. The captain scoffed at the panicky agent and interpreter and pointed to the *Tonquin*'s cannon and small arms locker, saying, "Do you think I would run before a lot of naked redskins so long as I had a knife or handspike?" Bancroft observed that the captain "loved to triumph, not less over those about him, than over the barbarians ashore. . . . After all, it would not sound well in polite circles to have it said that a lieutenant in the navy sailed a peddling-ship all the way round Cape Horn, and then thrashed the savages with his own hand because they were more skillful traders than he."

Accounts vary on the events that followed Thorn's tirade, but it appears that a day or two elapsed in an odd calm, as if the eye of a storm were passing over the *Tonquin* as it swung at anchor in Clayoquot Sound. During this lull the natives returned to the ship with their furs, a canoe at a time, and, as before, were invited aboard. Thorn appears to have kept to his cabin in these days, perhaps letting McKay conduct the negotiations.

The eye passed over just after dawn one morning when a large pirogue-sized canoe carrying twenty native traders and their bundles of furs came alongside the *Tonquin*. The canoe was commanded by Shewish, the chief's son Thorn had banished from the ship. He and the others held up their otter skins and the officer of the watch, determining the visitors to be unarmed, permitted them to board while Thorn and McKay slept in their quarters below the main deck. Soon other canoes appeared from shore, and more of Wicananish's villagers climbed the ladder and scattered around the deck displaying their bundled goods. The watch officer eventually sent a man below to wake the captain and the Astor partner, and by the time these sleepy gentlemen appeared on deck the *Tonquin* was swarming with Indians. McKay, with one quick glance around, told Thorn he must abandon the harbor in all haste and the captain, standing on the quarter-deck, saw the number of canoes surrounding the ship and others shoving off from shore and barked orders to his officers to weigh anchor and send men aloft to make sail, and ordered others to clear the Indians from the deck.

As hands manned the capstan and crewmen began un-reefing sails, one of the natives—perhaps Shewish—gave a yelled signal and in an instant knives, hatchets, and war clubs hidden in the fur bundles were produced and the *Tonquin*'s deck turned into a killing ground. James Lewis, McKay's clerk, was standing by a bale of trade blankets, arms folded across his chest, when he was stabbed in the back; McKay himself, seated at the taffrail, was knocked overboard, where he was clubbed to death by the Indian women in the canoes; Thorn, armed only with a clasp-knife, slashed at his attackers, is said to have killed Shewish with it, and, according to Irving's unlikely account, dealt crippling blows left and right, "strewing the quarter deck with the slain and wounded" before being hemmed in, smashed down, and stabbed to death and his body heaved overboard. James Thorn, the captain's sixteen-year-old brother, a "ship's boy," was also slain.

Of the seven sailors sent aloft to work the sails, three were killed as they descended from the rigging, the four remaining, including armorer Stephen Weekes, who was mortally wounded, fighting with knives and handspikes down the steerage hatchway to a cabin where they barricaded the door. They smashed open the arms locker, loaded muskets, and came up to the main deck firing volleys at the clots of natives looting the dead and managing to force the Indians to flee over the rails to their canoes below. The four crewmen loaded the light shipboard cannon and fired grapeshot, "which did great execution among the canoes, and drove all the savages to shore," Irving claimed.

The melee had lasted only a few minutes, but the attack caught the crew unarmed and outnumbered, and Thorn, McKay, and twenty-four crewmen, half of them Hawaiians, were killed. Most of their corpses were thrown overboard, where they floated about the ship's keel.

That night, three of the four surviving sailors lowered a longboat and rowed away from the ship, intending to make their way south along the Oregon coast to Fort Astoria. They were unable to manhandle their boat beyond the wall of surf of Clayoquot Sound, however, and were forced to beach the craft in a small cove. During the night, they were captured and tortured to death.

Weekes, dying from loss of blood, stayed aboard the *Tonquin* and survived the night. At first light the Indians returned to the ship and circled it. With them was Lamanse, the Gray's Harbor interpreter whose life had been spared and who had been taken prisoner. He recognized Weekes, who stood at the rail waving at the canoes, but the armorer quickly disappeared and was forgotten as the Indians boarded and roamed the deck, looting the blankets and trade goods. By mid-morning at least thirty canoes had reached the ship, the Indians swarming over the rails in search of plunder.

Before the first of them boarded, Weekes found the strength to get below decks to the powder magazine and there he waited, listening to the whoops and shouts and the thud of running feet above him. He poured a train of gunpowder to the magazine and, before he lost the last of his strength, lit it. The explosion blew the *Tonquin* into scraps of oak and human flesh. Lamanse, in the main-chains, was thrown from the deck into the bay and survived. He later said that "arms, legs, and heads were flying in all directions," and for days afterward the limbs and torsos of the dead were washing up on the beach.

Irving described the scene: "The ship had disappeared, but the bay was covered with fragments of the wreck, with shattered canoes, and Indians swimming for their lives, or struggling in the agonies of death; while those who had escaped the danger remained aghast and stupefied, or made with frantic panic for the shore."

(Astor's author asserted that James Lewis, the clerk who was among the first men attacked on the *Tonquin*, lit the fuse, and that on the voyage out Lewis had "expressed a presentiment that he would die by his own hands; thinking it highly probable that he should be engaged in some contest with the natives, and being resolved, in case of extremity, to commit suicide rather than be made a prisoner." Gabriel Franchére, one of the Astor agents on the *Tonquin* who stayed at Fort Astoria when the ship departed north, stated that the magazine was blown up by Stephen Weekes. It seems likely that a ship's armorer, in charge of all the small arms on the vessel, would know more about the powder magazine and how to detonate it than a civilian clerk.)

As to Captain Thorn, Irving—who appears to have known him personally—wrote of him as "a frank, manly, sound-hearted sailor . . . loyal, single-minded, straightforward, and fearless" and said, "With all his faults and foibles, we cannot but speak of him with esteem, and deplore his untimely fate; for we remember him well in early life, as a companion in pleasant scenes and joyous hours."

Many months later John Jacob Astor learned of the fate of the *Tonquin* in New York and took the news stoically, although, as Irving said, he "felt it with all its force, and was aware that it must cripple, if not entirely defeat, the great scheme of his ambition." While attending a play not long after receiving the terrible news, a friend asked the financier how he could remain so calm while in possession of such dreadful information. "What would you have me do?" Astor wondered. "Would you have me stay at home and weep for what I cannot help?"

3

Six weeks passed before the first rumors of the *Tonquin* massacre reached Duncan McDougall, David and Robert Stuart, and the other Astorians preoccupied in the building of their factory and fort on the Columbia. But news of another sort reached them in July from upriver that a party of thirty white men had appeared out of nowhere and were hastily erecting buildings on the riverbank. David Stuart and eight men prepared to set out to investigate the report but were held back when, on July 15, a canoe came sliding down the river, a Union Jack fluttering at its stern and bearing a party of *voyageurs* and a distinguished passenger, David Thompson, astronomer, explorer, cartographer, and a partner of the North West Company. He was a formidable wilderness man, only thirty-one years old but already with seventeen years' experience in the Canadian back country, where he had opened trade with several Indian tribes and explored and mapped routes between far-flung Canadian forts and factories. He had crossed the Rockies in 1807, blazing a trail south of that of Alexander Mackenzie, and built a fort at Windermere Lake, the first on the Upper Columbia.

Thompson's visit to the fort seems to have been the result of his own failure to reach the vicinity before the Astorians and, in Washington Irving's words, "anticipate Mr. Astor in his intention of effecting a settlement at the mouth of the Columbia River." In crossing the Rockies with a sizable party, all but eight of his men had deserted and Thompson was now reduced to seeing firsthand his company's competition. To Irving, Thompson was "little more than a spy in camp," although welcomed by McDougall, who, the author said, "had a lurking feeling of companionship and goodwill for all of the Northwest Company."

It appears that Thompson freely shared information with the Astorians on the upriver country for, on July 23, 1811,

David Stuart set out for the interior with four clerks, two *voyageurs,* and two Hawaiians in three canoes loaded with provisions. During this expedition Stuart explored the Columbia River valley and the Willamette, the 300-mile-long navigable river that issued from the Cascade Range and flowed north to the Columbia. He found the Willamette valley a region of luxuriant beauty with lakes and pools and green meadows shaded by noble copses of trees. Before returning to Astoria, he and his men made their way as far north as the Okanogan River, a Columbia tributary in the Colville Indian region, and built a fort on the east bank of the river.

Early in August, some sparse information on the fate of the *Tonquin* at last reached Fort Astoria, brought by a wandering band of Indians from the Juan de Fuca Strait. At first the partners treated the story dubiously, but it was soon substantiated by other natives who came south to the unfinished fort to trade and fish. Details of the massacre were eventually filled out by the interpreter Lamanse, who somehow contrived to be freed by his captors and make his way back to Gray's Harbor.

Duncan McDougall treated even the scantiest first information with gravity, and as details of the killings and loss of the ship arrived, he was devastated. There had been rumors from the time the *Tonquin* departed Baker's Bay of a conspiracy among the coastal tribes to attack white traders, and they had alarmed Mr. Astor's proxy, the more so after the dire news from Clayoquot Sound reached him. He even suspected his future father-in-law, Comcomly of the Chinooks, of complicity in the gossiped plot. In answer, the chief made repeated professions of peace and pointed to his people's history of friendly relations with white men since the time they welcomed Lewis and Clark in 1805. The chief had even saved McDougall's life in the first weeks after the

Tonquin's landing when a longboat had overturned in the Columbia estuary and Comcomly had plucked the terrified agent from the water and pulled him aboard the royal canoe.

To McDougall, the Astorians were now a handful of helpless men clinging to a savage coast surrounded by hostile tribes, with no means of escape by sea. Moreover, it would be months before the fort could be reinforced by the men of Astor's overland expedition, which was supposed to have started out from Saint Louis shortly after the *Tonquin* sailed. For all McDougall knew, the party may not yet have begun its ascent of the Missouri.

During this unsettling time, the Astorians set to work throwing up a primitive siege works around the still uncompleted fort—a "palisades" consisting of little more than a high picket fence and bastion-like platforms to hold the four four-pounder cannon brought on the *Tonquin* expressly to protect the fort—and posting round-the-clock vedettes and sentinels.

Still they worried. Their feeble little enclave could not long withstand any concentrated attack by a native force, even though it would be armed with only spears, knives, and clubs. No sound evidence existed that a confederation of tribes was planning a war against the whites, but the rumors alone created terror and to counter even a dim possibility of a native rising, McDougall created an ingenious stratagem.

The Astorians and all who traded among the coastal tribes knew of the Indians' greatest fear: the scourge of smallpox. Epidemics of the disease, first brought by the whites in decades past, had swept away entire tribes. The bringers of the disease seemed to survive it, but the Indians inevitably died. The specter of smallpox haunted the native people.

McDougall's design involved assembling several tribal chiefs, Comcomly among them, whose domains lay in the vicinity of Fort Astoria. These were the leaders whispered to be involved in the conspiracy against the traders, and when he managed to bring them together at Fort Astoria he told them he had heard of their treachery and that he and his men were prepared to deal with it.

"The white men among you," he said (according to Irving), "are few in number, it is true, but they are mighty in medicine. See here." At this he dramatically drew forth a small flask. "In this bottle," he said, "I hold the small-pox, safely corked up; I have but to draw the cork, and let loose the pestilence, to sweep man, woman and child from the face of the earth!" He said that so long as the whites were unmolested he would keep the "phial of wrath" sealed, but at the least hostility the fatal cork would be drawn.

Whether or not there ever was a conspiracy, the ruse had its effect; the rumors died out and thereafter the Indians called McDougall "the Great Small-Pox Chief."

(Ironically, Comcomly died in a smallpox epidemic in 1830. In his days of glory, according to the Jesuit missionary Pierre-Jean De Smet, the Chinook chief's retinue included 300 slaves and "he used to carpet the ground that he had to traverse . . . with beaver and otter skins." Father De Smet said Comcomly "had sight in only one eye, but that proved sufficient for he was all-seeing, sagacious and, in the view of some whites, unduly mercenary.")

On October 26, 1811, the Fort Astoria factory building, a structure of timber, clay, and unmortared stone, was completed and the schooner, whose frame had been carried on the *Tonquin*, assembled and given its first sea trials. Named *Dolly*, it was the first American vessel built and launched on the Pacific coast.

Now the little factory, center and symbol of John Jacob Astor's great experiment, settled down and waited for the overland expedition to join them.

7

The Overlanders

■

"... THE WANDERINGS OF SINBAD."

1

In October 1810, as the *Tonquin* sailed down from the Cape Verde Islands toward the equator, the overland Astorians broke camp and, with maps based on the trail followed by Lewis and Clark just seven years past, began their ascent of the Missouri River.

Astor's choice as commander of this expedition was not, as might have been expected, an experienced wilderness hand; indeed Wilson Price Hunt was "born to mercantile pursuits," his milieu the stockroom and bank, his custom to read ledgers, not maps. But the nabob of New York had cast his crafty eye on this twenty-eight-year-old businessman from Trenton, New Jersey, and saw in him an organizer, an administrator, a diplomat, a leader of men, "scrupulously upright and faithful in his dealings, amicable in his disposition, and of most accommodating manners," as Irving said. These attributes came to Astor's attention in 1809, when the two men met for the first time in Manhattan. Hunt had removed from New Jersey counting houses to Saint Louis when he was twenty-one and had built a profitable commerce there in the Indian trade. Astor liked the man, perhaps saw in him the same ambition and scrappiness that had estab-

lished the financier's fortune, and recruited him as a partner in the Pacific Fur Company. Hunt's assignment was to
supersede the Scotch-Canadians who had sailed on the *Tonquin* and take over as chief factor of Fort Astoria. In that
role he was to negotiate a contract for furs with the Russians
at Sitka and placate the North West Company and Hudson's
Bay Company traders on the coast. Astor's confidence in
Hunt had a single limitation: The man had no trail experience, and this deficit had to be made up by the men selected
to follow him to the Oregon Country.

While Hunt was the titular leader of the expedition, he
was fortunate in having as his chief associate a keen veteran
of the woods named Donald Mackenzie. This hulking former Nor'wester—by far the biggest, at over 300 pounds, of
the Scotch-Canadian fraternity of "Macs" who figured in the
financier's plan—was so energetic that he was nicknamed
"Perpetual Motion" Mackenzie, and he had been roaming
the Canadian wilds from age seventeen. While he would
later be suspected of intrigue and perhaps even treachery in
the Astor camp, in June 1810, when he met Hunt in Montreal, the ancient emporium of the fur trade, Mackenzie was
a trusted Pacific Fur lieutenant. If he resented Hunt's superiority in command he gave no sign of it, and he fell to work
with his customary energy in recruiting others for the expedition.

Since much of the journey west, would be by the Lewis
and Clark designated waterways, or so it was guessed, the
first men recruited were *voyageurs*, and at Montreal and Ottawa, probably through Mackenzie's knowledge of them,
forty *hommes du nord* were signed on. These were the same
wild breed of woods- and rivermen who called the Astor
agents and clerks and all men softened by indoor luxury
"pork-eaters"; the same French-Canadian brotherhood who
would soon be paddling down the Hudson to Long Island in
their birch-bark canoes and *bateaux* to ship out on the
Tonquin. By late July, after stopovers at Mackinaw, the old

trading post on Michilimackinac Island in the strait between Lakes Michigan and Huron at Green Bay and Prairie du Chien, most of the expedition members were in
place. In Saint Louis on September 3, 1810, and on a return
visit the following January after the expedition had reached
its winter quarters, Hunt had sixty men to outfit and provision. He also had command of four boats, two keelboats,
one barge-like flatboat, and an outsized vessel known as a
Schenectady barge, which had been purchased at the old
French trading post at Mackinac. All the vessels were
equipped with masts and sails, and the keelboats were
armed with a swivel gun and two howitzers.

In addition to the forty *engagés*, Hunt and Mackenzie had
enlisted an interpreter, Pierre Dorion, son of the Pierre
Dorion who had served in the same capacity with Lewis and
Clark. Dorion's love of liquor, Irving said, "in which he had
been nurtured and brought up, would occasionally break out,
and with it the savage side of his character." Dorion was accompanied by his pregnant Iowa Indian wife and their two
children. In Saint Louis another young (age twenty-three)
Astor associate and Hunt acquaintance, a Glasgow-born fur
trader named Ramsey Crooks, joined the party, as did
Crooks' former business partner. This man, Robert McClellan, a Pennsylvania frontiersman and Indian fighter and
scout, was lean and athletic, fearless and dependable, but
with an ungovernable temper. Crooks had for several years
worked for the North West Company among Missouri River
tribes. McClellan, a one-time partisan serving with General
"Mad Anthony" Wayne in his Indian campaigns in the Ohio
Valley, had spent twelve years in Louisiana Territory ranging the Mississippi between New Orleans and Saint Louis
as one of the earliest American fur traders in the region.
Joining the Hunt expedition with these veterans came Joseph
Miller of Baltimore, once an infantry lieutenant and a capable trapper and hunter on the Missouri; John Day, a tall
mountain man out of Culpeper County, Virginia, thirteen of

whose forty-one years had been spent in the Missouri woods where he earned a living as trapper, hunter, and gunpowder-maker; and John Reed, an Irishman whose history is lost but who, while signing on as a "clerk," had trail experience and would serve the expedition as scout.

Perhaps because of the scientific precedent set by the Corps of Discovery, and at Astor's and Thomas Jefferson's urging, two botanists were assigned to travel with the Hunt party. These were John Bradbury, a Scotchman who had come to the United States in 1809, sponsored by the Linnaean Society of Liverpool to collect American plants, had been a guest of Jefferson's in the White House and thereafter made Saint Louis his base of explorations for studying the flora of the Missouri River; and Thomas Nuttall, a Yorkshireman who had emigrated to Philadelphia in 1808 and joined Bradbury in his Missouri studies in 1810. While neither scientist would travel with the Astorians farther than the Mandan villages of the Missouri, Nuttall would return to the trail and make a journey all the way to Oregon in 1834.

On October 21, 1810, six weeks after the *Tonquin* sailed from Long Island, Hunt, Mackenzie, and their fifty-eight men began their long journey, launching their boats on the Missouri to head west and north to winter camp at the mouth of the Nodaway River.

The river work was backbreaking, the progress agonizingly slow. The boats often had to be drawn up the Missouri with grappling hooks, using roots and overhanging tree limbs for purchase, or towed by long cordelles, barge ropes, when the riverbank was clear enough of trees and brush thickets to permit men to pull along the shore. Special dangers were floating logs and "sawyers," sunken trees with sharp, jagged limbs lurking just underwater to snag and pierce the vessels. Another danger, of which the expedition leaders had been warned by Manuel Lisa, John Colter, and others in Saint Louis before they set out, were the menacing bands of Indians, Sioux in particular, who, it was said, would be watching them from the forested banks waiting to pounce on them.

The brutal work and the fear of Indian ambush caused several men to desert during the first few weeks of the journey, but others were enlisted en route to replace them. These were wandering hunters and trappers, some of them familiar with the country beyond the Nodaway. These recruits advised Hunt against following the Lewis and Clark route in favor of one more southerly for an easier crossing of the mountains ahead. This trail, they said, led to the headwaters of the Platte and Yellowstone and avoided the murderous Blackfeet, whose domain lay in the northern reaches of the Missouri. This advice seemed critically important to Hunt and he acted on it, deciding to leave the river at the Arikara villages in the Dakota country, purchase packhorses, and proceed south to the Yellowstone, the route William Clark had followed on returning from the Pacific.

The expedition reached the Nodaway River in mid-November, 450 winding Missouri River miles from their embarkation point, and settled down to camp for the winter. Hunters found ample game for the cookpots and beaver traps were set in the slushy streams, the furs baled to await the spring thaw and the move west.

In January 1811 Hunt and eight men returned to Saint Louis on horseback, with a stopover at Fort Osage, a government outpost founded in 1808 by William Clark on the south bank of the Missouri, to collect the last of his expedition members, including the two botanists. On the return trip he stopped at the village of Charette and spent some enjoyable hours with Daniel Boone, then in his seventy-sixth year, and also visited John Colter's nearby homestead. The Lewis and Clark corpsman rode several miles alongside the Astor lieutenant, providing valuable information on the Missouri and Rocky Mountain tribes, before returning home.

Hunt rejoined his party at their Nodaway River camp on April 17.

At the time Hunt and his men departed Saint Louis, Manuel Lisa, practical ruler of the Missouri River fur traffic, mounted a trapping expedition, and nineteen days after Hunt's departure led his twenty-five men upriver in a barge with a swivel-gun mounted at the bow. The two parties intersected at the Arikaras' domain, a scattering of lodges above the mouth of the Grand River that Lisa considered his domain as well—and were instantly at loggerheads. Vague old feuds resurfaced. Pierre Dorion, who appears to have departed Saint Louis a few steps ahead of his debtors and the law, was plied with liquor and urged to quit Hunt and join Lisa's party but grew incensed at Lisa's threats to have him arrested. Irving says Dorion "snatched up a pair of pistols belonging to Mr. Hunt, and placed himself in battle array." Robert McClellan, who held a grudge against Lisa over some unhappy past business dealings, also threatened violence against his former employer, and Ramsey Crooks announced that he was prepared to help McClellan. Hunt tried to act as intermediary and calm tempers, but "an impression was made use of by Lisa derogatory to his honor," and the Astorian, normally the most sanguine of men, was driven to challenge Lisa to a duel.

Somehow the disputes were salved over and Lisa, who well knew the "Rees" (as the Arikaras were known by mountain men), assisted Hunt in purchasing horses from the tribesmen. He also exchanged fifty animals of his own, sent down from his fort near the Mandan villages 180 miles upriver, for the boats Hunt had decided he must abandon. In the spring and early summer the Astorians camped among the Rees, hunted and trapped and pieced together a herd of eighty-two horses to serve as pack animals excepting riding mounts for the partners and Pierre Dorion's pregnant wife and their two children.

On July 18, 1811, Hunt, now with sixty-five men, broke camp and left the Missouri, bound south and west for the Grand River and thence to the Little Missouri. Upon their leaving, according to Washington Irving, "the veteran trappers and voyageurs of Lisa's party shook their heads as their comrades set out, and took leave of them as of doomed men; and even Lisa himself gave it as his opinion, after the travelers had departed, that they would never reach the shores of the Pacific, but would perish with hunger in the wilderness, or be cut off by the savages."

2

One of the Lisa men who joined Hunt's party and who would serve as guide into the Absaroka country west of the Black Hills was Edward Rose, mulatto son of a white father and a Cherokee-Black mother. He was about twenty-five, had grown up in Kentucky, and had roamed the Missouri River country since age eighteen. In some obscure Indian fight he received a face wound and the name "Cut Nose," and in his trapping forays into the Big Horn Mountains had earned the friendship of the Crow, had fought with them against the Sioux, and was said to have collected five scalps in one battle. He was a colorful, reckless character with a shady past, but came highly recommended by Lisa, who shared many of Rose's wilder attributes. Hunt, who had learned something of Rose's unsavory history in Saint Louis, was nonetheless grateful to have such a knowledgeable pilot to take him through the dangerous lands ahead.

(Irving speaks of a "plot" by Rose "to rob and abandon his countrymen when in the heart of the wilderness, and to throw himself into the hands of the savages." The author described Rose as "one of those desperadoes of the frontier, outlawed by their crimes, who combine the vices of civilized and savage life, and are ten times more barbarous than the Indians with whom they consort.")

In August Hunt's party skirted the Black Hills and struck

westward along the arid divide to the Big Horns and crossed
Crow lands, during which time Rose stayed behind with Indian friends. Proceeding to the Wind River, Hunt and his
men crossed the Continental Divide to the Green (called then
the Spanish) River. In camp on the Green, a band of Snake—
Shoshoni—Indians sold Hunt a large supply of buffalo
jerky and through sign language and dirt-drawn maps provided help for the next leg of the journey.

The party crossed the Big Horn River and the lower Wind
River Range in September and reached the headwaters of the
westward-flowing Snake, which the trappers accurately called
the Mad River. Known from Lewis and Clark reports to be a
tributary of the mighty Columbia but unknown to Hunt and
his party, the Snake was a writhing, death-dealing 1,038-mile
waterway filled with narrow, rock-walled canyons and deep,
timber-choked gorges with miles of churning rapids between.
It was a mad river in every respect, and Hunt intended to
negotiate it to the Columbia and Fort Astoria. The partners
voted unanimously to attempt the river route and in early October turned most of their horses over to their Shoshoni
guides, presumably in exchange for labor in constructing the
fifteen canoes and pirogues required to carry downriver the
party, their supplies, and the furs they had gathered. The necessary trees, big cottonwoods, were found at Henry's Fort in
Idaho, a deserted trappers' stockade where a deceptively tranquil bend of the Snake widened to 150 yards.

Joseph Miller, the Marylander, could not go on, due to
what Irving mysteriously called a "bodily malady," and
stayed behind at the fort with a group of trappers detached
from the party. These men, provided with some of the remaining horses, were to occupy the fort, continue to trap
beaver that fall and winter, and bring their furs on to Fort
Astoria in the spring.

Hunt and the fifty-four members of his expedition remaining pushed off the banks of the Snake on October 19

and spent the rest of the month and the first week of November attacking the river and losing the battle. One
voyageur drowned; several canoe-loads of provisions and
furs were lost in the seething, bitter-cold water; and progress was agonizingly slow, every yard of advance gained in
peril and exhaustion. At night, hunkered at their campfires,
they made plans for the dawning: Detachments were sent out
under various partners and by the clerk John Reed to hunt
game, explore ahead, find possible new routes along the
Snake's banks, find Indians who might serve as guides, and
barter for horses.

At one point near what became Twin Falls in south-central
Idaho, the river was abandoned and the expedition split into
two parties. Hunt led the main force of thirty men and
Dorion's wife and children; Ramsey Crooks took charge of
the others. Furs and other impediments to fast travel were
cached, and the detachments set out on opposite sides of the
Snake on November 9, still 700 miles from Fort Astoria,
hoping to find Shoshoni camps, horses, and food. Both parties suffered as they trudged northwestward along the general
course of the Snake in blizzard weather. Game was scarce,
and all were reduced to eating roots and berries. One of
Crooks' party said that during one nine-day period the men
subsisted on "one beaver, one dog, a few wild cherries and
some old mockason soles." Another of Crooks' contingent,
a *voyageur* named Jean Baptiste Prevost, went insane from
starvation and drowned in the river. In Hunt's camp, Marguerite Dorion gave birth and although her baby died after a
few days, she managed to keep up with the line of march.

On December 15, Hunt and his people stumbled on a Shoshoni village of a dozen lodges near the merging of the
Snake and Boisé Rivers, where the Hudson's Bay Company
would subsequently erect a trading post. By the end of December, with three Shoshoni guides and with segments of
the parties now rejoined, the expedition proceeded north-

westerly, crossed the Grande Ronde valley and the Blue Mountains, and on January 6, 1812, struck the Umatilla River and located a large Indian camp. The party rested there six days before proceeding to the banks of the Columbia and following the river on purchased horses to The Dalles rapids, where they obtained canoes for the last miles of the journey. They arrived at Fort Astoria on February 15 with the stragglers coming in over a period of several weeks, each with a harrowing tale to tell. Crooks and John Day, wandering west from the banks of the Snake, would not be found and rescued until April.

Upriver from the fort, Hunt had received sketchy information from Chinook informants on the *Tonquin* disaster, now eight months past, and in conference with the other Astorians learned the chilling details. As dismayed as he was at the news and while still recovering from the privations of the sixteen-month trek from Saint Louis, Hunt undertook his duties as factor-in-chief at Fort Astoria. He sought to follow Astor's instructions on negotiating with the Russians and cementing friendly relations with the British fur traders on the coast, dispatched trappers upriver, assigned duties at the post, and took the resignations of partners Ramsey Crooks and Robert McClellan, who joined Robert Stuart in the summer for an overland journey back to Saint Louis.

The opportunity to begin Astor's diplomatic work came in May with the arrival in Baker's Bay of the *Beaver*, a 490-ton brigantine commanded by Captain Cornelius Sowle of Rhode Island and carrying reinforcements and tons of foodstuffs, supplies, and trade merchandise, some of which was transferred to the fort's warehouses. In the fall, Hunt boarded the ship and sailed with Sowle to Sitka, the flourishing capital of Russian America, 600 miles north of Vancouver Island. Sitka, and the island on which it lay, was ruled by

the fierce, erratic, vodka-loving Count Alexandr Andreevich
Baranov, and at Hunt's advent in his miniature kingdom the
nobleman had spent forty of his sixty-five years in the fur
trade in Siberia and Alaskan waters. He was as tough a
customer as any Astor man was likely to encounter, but the
New York financier's confidence in Hunt, and Hunt's te-
nacity, paid dividends as the Astorian traded to Baranov all
the *Beaver*'s cargo of food, arms, powder, and trade merchandise, except for the portion that had been necessary to
provision Astoria, in exchange for 75,000 seal skins. In
Canton, by Hunt's calculations, the furs were worth four or
five times the value of the cargo exchanged for them.

Baranov's furs were stored in a fishery in the Pribilof Islands, and Hunt remained aboard the *Beaver* as it sailed to
the Bering Sea for the six-week detour required to get there,
load the skins, and return to Astoria to pick up the baled furs
awaiting the China trade. Hunt decided to omit the Astoria
stopover and instructed Captain Sowle to drop him off at
Oahu, then to sail on to China with the Baranov furs. It was
now early in 1813, and the chief factor hoped to make passage back to the Oregon coast in the spring on the *Lark*, the
resupply ship Astor had dispatched to the Pacific.

News of the American war with Britain reached the Sandwich Islands shortly after Hunt's arrival there, and all his
plans—and those of his employer—went awry. The *Lark* arrived in the islands on schedule, but she was wrecked in a
gale off Maui in March, at a cost of seven men drowned. The
surviving crew members and their captain were rescued after a harrowing twelve days in the splintered and dismasted
hulk of the vessel, living on a small ration of salt pork and
wine that had been saved. Hunt was forced to purchase a
Boston brig, the *Pedlar*, to return him to Astoria. He arrived
there on August 20, just in time to witness the sale and abandonment of the fort.

3

Astor's proprietors had witnessed signs of deteriorating relations between the United States and England even before the *Tonquin* sailed in September 1810. The ship had been escorted from Long Island into the open sea by the *Constitution* to prevent its being boarded by British press gangs ostensibly searching for deserters from their navy— but, lost to the world in their tiny enclave on the Oregon coast, the Astorians knew virtually nothing of the war's cause and progress. What little news seeped into the fort told nothing of Britain's seizure of American merchant ships in European waters; President James Madison's trade embargo against England; the fall of Forts Michilimackinac, Detroit, and Dearborn to the Americans; the battle at Queenston in the Niagara campaign; the capture of York, capital of Upper Canada; or Perry's defeat of the British fleet at Lake Erie.

To John Jacob Astor, the war meant potential ruin for his Pacific enterprise, and he begged the Madison administration for protection. He sent urgent letters asking for a minimal force of forty soldiers to be dispatched to Astoria to protect his interests, which he felt were American interests, but his entreaties to Secretary of State James Monroe were ignored. In March 1813 he sent the supply ship *Lark* to the Columbia, but it was lost at sea. And, fearing that a blockade of New York Harbor would prevent departure of a second supply vessel that autumn, he managed to get a dispatch to Captain Sowle of the *Beaver*, then at Canton selling the Baranov furs, to return to Astoria with his ship's hold filled with supplies.

While these measures were being taken, the partners at Astoria were measuring their anomalous situation: They had learned of the war in January 1813, probably via North West Company trappers who came visiting, and now they were British subjects trading under the flag of the United States, unable to bear arms against their own country. They were isolated on a wild coast with a warehouse full of furs, cut off from Astor supply vessels, faced with dwindling food reserves and the imminent possibility of takeover by any armed British ship arriving on the coast or any British land force traveling down the Columbia.

The threats were real. While the Astor agents were nervously conferring on their plight, their great rival, the North West Company, "clearly perceiving this to be their time to strike, and plant thorns beneath Astor's pillows," Bancroft says, dispatched the twenty-gun man-of-war *Isaac Todd* to the Columbia to "plant a fort and dominate the region." Many months would pass before this ship reached the Oregon coast, but the North West Company paid a visit in the meantime, and the Astorians saw no recourse but to make terms with them.

Wilson Hunt was still at Oahu on April 11, 1813, when his fort was confronted by a convoy of canoes and pirogues led by a Nor'wester named John George McTavish. This man was welcomed, somewhat too warmly, some thought, by Duncan McDougall, senior partner at Astoria and now both Astor's and Hunt's "proxy." McTavish notified McDougall, Donald Mackenzie, and the others that the war now presented certain "difficulties" for the Americans. He told of the expected advent of the *Isaac Todd* and notified the Astorians that since the Oregon coast was now in British hands he was authorized to take control of the fort and purchase its stores, buildings, and furs. At some point in the discussions McTavish appears to have made certain other representations and incentives to those Astorians who were former North West Company men.

In August, Hunt returned at last to Astoria on the *Pedlar*. He argued against selling or quitting the fort but was voted down by the other partners.

After the negotiations that summer, the Astorians agreed to sell the fort's goods "at cost" and the furs housed there at

the current London market price. The sale was completed
on October 12, 1813, with McTavish presenting bills of exchange in the name of the North West Company. The selling price was $58,191.01, a fraction of Astor's investment and
of the value of the property and goods.

There was a tense moment during the negotiations, reported by Alexander Ross, one of Jonathan Thorn's hated
"scribbling clerks" who kept a journal on the voyage to the
Columbia. A twenty-eight-year-old Nairnshire, Scotland,
native, Ross had been fortunate in staying with the fort-
building party while the man who had hired him, Alexander
McKay, sailed north to his death on the *Tonquin*. Ross witnessed the sale of Astoria to the North West Company
agents and wrote that near the conclusion of the negotiations,
McTavish seemed to be buying time: He had learned that the
Isaac Todd and perhaps other British warships were due to
arrive on the coast at any moment, whereupon the American fort and property would "be seized as a prize," costing
his company nothing. McDougall and Mackenzie, Ross said,
"saw through this piece of artifice" and insisted that the bills
of exchange be signed immediately. While McTavish stalled,
"full of commercial wiles," the partners summoned all
seventy-two of the Astorians and ordered the fort manned,
the cannons shotted and pointed—presumably at McTavish's
camp, which was situated a short distance from the fort—
and slow matches lit. "In an instant," Ross said, "every man
was at his post, and the gates shut. At eight o'clock a message was sent to McTavish, giving him two hours, and no
more, either to sign the bills or break off the negotiation altogether and remove to some other quarters." This offensive
move seems to have convinced McTavish not to wait for his
warships: He signed the bills and the fort was delivered up.

One month later, the Nor'westers formally took possession of Fort Astoria, raised the Union Jack over its factory
building, and christened the place Fort George. Many of Astor's Pacific Fur Company employees, including some of

the *voyageurs*, who had come out to Oregon on the *Tonquin*, entered the service of the Nor'westers. McDougall, suspiciously, some of the Astor faithful thought, accepted a partnership with the British company. A few of the Astor overlanders decided to stay in Oregon, thus becoming among the first permanent settlers in the Willamette River valley.

In April 1814 Wilson Price Hunt sailed out of Baker's Bay in the *Pedlar*, which he had purchased for Astor in the Sandwich Islands, and spent two years in the Pacific coast trade trying to recoup some of his employer's investment. He ended his tour with a voyage to Canton and sailed home with the *Pedlar* loaded with chinaware, silks, and tea. He reached New York in October 1816, after a seafaring adventure "that might have furnished a chapter in the wanderings of Sinbad," Irving said.

Hunt resumed his former life as a merchant in Saint Louis, prospered in his business ventures, married a widow with three children, and died peacefully on April 13, 1842, on the eve of a great migration to the Oregon Country.

On November 29, the British sloop-of-war *Raccoon* anchored in Baker's Bay and its main passenger, another of the ubiquitous Macs of the Astoria saga, one John McDonald, a senior partner in the North West Company, assumed command of Fort George and the entire Columbia River fur enterprise. The skipper of the *Raccoon* took one look at the fort's split-board "palisades," pitiful bastions, and earthworks and said to McDonald, "This, then, was your enemy's stronghold, requiring a navy to conquer? Damn me! With a single four-pounder I would have battered it down in two hours!"

And, in April 1814, the long-awaited *Isaac Todd* crossed the Columbia bar and anchored before Fort George, thirteen months out of England, bringing with it another North West Company eminence, another Mac, another McTavish, another Donald, all in the person of Donald McTavish. Another noteworthy passenger on the warship was a certain Miss Jane Barnes, and H. H. Bancroft found it a pity "that the first European woman to stand upon the banks of the Columbia should have been of so questionable a character."

According to the historian, "One of the Macs [presumably Donald McTavish], doomed to the perils of western life yet loath all at once to relinquish every creature comfort, had brought with him some bottled porter, canned beef, cheese, and a blue-eyed, flaxen-haired female companion." Miss Barnes was a "daughter of Albion," who, "at the solicitations of this Mac had resigned her position as bar-maid in a Portsmouth hotel, and had come to this land of doubtful pleasures and profits, where at once she became an object of deepest interest to all." The more carnal-minded on the wild coast, the historian said in an abundance of superfluous language, "were scandalized that this lecherous Mac should so far break the laws of God and of the Honorable Northwest Company, as to form an unholy alliance with a frail fair one whose father was no chief, when fur-trading interests demanded duskier relationships. Make as many unmarried wives as you please of native maidens, and the great interests of commerce shall guard your good name, but to bring hither a white mistress—what will the savages say?"

Duncan McDougall's Chinook wife was envious, Bancroft said, "for pretty Miss Barnes flaunted a new frock almost every day," and McDougall's father-in-law, Chief Comcomly, was "curious, and one of his sons who had now but four wives, was amorous, wishing immediately to marry her." This young warrior, arrayed "in the richest robes, well painted, and redolent of grease, came and laid at her feet the offering of his heart. One hundred sea otter skins her owner should have, and she should never carry or dig. She should be queen of the Chinooks, and all his other wives should humble themselves before her. Elk, anchovies, and fat salmon should be heaped upon her lap, and all the livelong day she should sun herself and smoke."

But Miss Barnes declined these royal overtures and, indeed, found the society of the Columbia unsuited to her taste. She quickly determined to return to England and bartending by the ship that brought her out "but at Canton where the vessel touched, she fell in love with a wealthy English gentleman of the Honorable East India Company, and consented to grace a splendid establishment which he offered her."

Donald McTavish, however, had little time to enjoy the company of Miss Jane. His factorship at Fort George lasted barely a month. On May 22, as he crossed the river in a longboat, a sudden squall struck the channel and the boat filled and sank in a few minutes. McTavish and five other men from the *Isaac Todd* drowned.

PART THREE

· ·

WILDERNESS
CROSSINGS

■

8

To the Tetons

■

1

Among the heroes of John Jacob Astor's little band of Scotch fur traders at Fort Astoria, none stood taller than the Perthshireman Robert Stuart. He was born on his father's small farm in 1785, of a lineage that seems to have been more affluent than the ordinary crofter family of the southern highlands. The family had a crest bearing the legend *Nobilis ira est leonis* ("Noble is the anger of lions") and his father, John Stuart, known locally as *Ian Mair na Coille*, "Big John of the Woods," saw to it that his nine children were well educated. In his youth, "Little Robert of the Woods" made plans to join the Honorable East India Company as a clerk, sailing to Calcutta and seeing the world beyond the Stuart farm. He probably shared this dream with his uncle David. Twenty years older than Robert, David Stuart had emigrated to Canada in 1800 with no special prospects, had worked as a fisherman and trapper, and soon became a trusted North West Company trader. He saw promise in Robert, understood the lad's need to quit the farm and make his own life, and urged him to come to Montreal, where employment in the Nor'westers awaited him. Robert sailed and in 1807 joined the company as a clerk, and in 1810

followed his uncle to New York where John Jacob Astor's
new Pacific Fur Company was organizing a ship to carry the
enterprise to the Columbia River.

We have a photograph of Robert Stuart taken thirty-five
years after he sailed on the *Tonquin* to the Oregon coast as
a raw "junior partner" in Astor's magnificent scheme. The
carte de viste, although taken in about 1845, when he was
sixty, corroborates certain contemporary impressions of him
in the early years of his quarter-century career as Astor's
ablest lieutenant. In that time, when he received a salary of
$500 or $600 a year from Astor, Stuart was the best of bar-
gains. In the daguerreotype he gives the impression of a man
who has fulfilled the promise in Bancroft's phrase for him:
"a most promising young man." He seems tall even though
the image is of him from the waist up, his arms folded across
his chest, stern and statesmanlike in a frock coat with velvet lapels and a stock-like collar. He is high of forehead and
clean-shaven, his curly hair (which one imagines was a rusty,
maybe fiery, red in his youth) graying at the temples, and he
is the living representation of *Nobilis ira est leonis*, leonine
and fiercely handsome—and impatient if not angry. His
flared nostrils and clamped jaw give the sense of a man unaccustomed to waiting, certainly of one unused to smiling.
He seems to have required no instructions on freezing for
the moment it took for the daguerreotypist to capture him
on film; indeed, one has the sense that he scarcely flinched
when the powder flashed. He stares at the lens with irasci-
bility, resoluteness, and utter self-confidence. Many saw and
remembered Robert Stuart's dour and grimly purposeful aspect: the starving, fever-stricken, hope-abandoned men he
led through the western wilderness; the natives of over
twenty tribes and bands, from Walla Wallas to Missouris,
he encountered on his expedition from Astoria to Saint
Louis; businessmen in boardrooms, politicians in legisla-
tures, Presbyterian ministers in their pulpits.

One who had cause to remember those deep-set blue eyes

and unblinking gaze, and the coiled ferocity lying within the tall, thin, clerkly frame hovering over him, was Captain Jonathan Thorn of the *Tonquin*. In December 1810, as the Astor brig bobbed at anchor off an island in the Falklands, Stuart had taken a stand, a flintlock pistol in one hand, the other a fist shaking in the choleric captain's face as he threatened to blow Thorn's brains over the compass box. The would-be Bligh looked into this Covenanter's eyes and had enough of his sanity remaining to realize that there were some men he could not tyrannize.

After Wilson Hunt reached Fort Astoria in February 1812 and took command of the post, he had the urgent duty of sending dispatches to Mr. Astor in New York to apprise the financier of the details he had gathered on the *Tonquin* calamity and the state of affairs on the Columbia. With no ship to carry the papers home, he arranged an overland expedition back to Missouri that would follow the rough and meandering trail he had blazed to the Pacific.

The original expedition, a two-month fiasco, consisted of three small parties under Stuart's generalship that set out late in March 1812. One of the detachments was to proceed east to the Snake River to salvage the furs, traps, and provisions cached by Hunt the previous November. The second group, which included Hunt's Irish clerk John Reed and five other men, would carry the important dispatches to Mr. Astor and locate and assist two of Hunt's men who had as yet not reached Fort Astoria. Before starting east the third group, headed by Stuart, was to take two *bateaux* loaded with supplies to a subsidiary trading post established by his uncle on the Okanogan River, a tributary of the Columbia 250 miles northeast.

The three parties, seventeen men in all, paddled upstream from Astoria to rapids of The Dalles (from the French for "flagstones," the name deriving from the basaltic rocks of

the canyon walls), the site of an old Indian commerce center and a "notorious plundering place," Irving said. There the
parties unloaded their canoes and recruited a number of
Cathlasko natives—a small band related to the Chinooks—
whose village lay nearby to provide horses and assist in the
portage around the rapids. In a rocky defile, several of the
Cathlaskos bolted up a narrow path, taking with them two
bundles of provisions. When Stuart, who was riding behind,
heard of the theft, he moved to the front of the column to
keep an eye on the "impudent villains."

After passing the rapids, Stuart and his men and Indian
portagers reached the fishing village of the Wishram people and, Irving says, "found themselves benighted in a
strange place, and surrounded by savages bent on pilfering."
Guards were posted, and at dawn the party pushed off from
shore in their reloaded canoes to "gladly bid adieu to this
abominable den of robbers," Stuart said. But his problems
had just begun. Along the banks above The Dalles the Wishrams were gathered in force, whooping and brandishing
their spears and war clubs and with arrows nocked and ready.
The Indians pretended to offer help in the next portage, but
Stuart believed they were bent on further plunder and when
the canoes came ashore below the Great Falls (so named by
Lewis and Clark), they were surrounded by several hundred
of the "river ruffians." Stuart promised to employ them as
portagers next day if they conducted themselves peaceably.

During the night, Stuart attempted to steal a march on
the Indians. He roused his men in the moonlight, gathered
the canoes, gear, and provisions, and led the portage afoot
while the natives slept. Reed and Robert McClellan, the
temperamental Ohio Valley Indian fighter, brought up the
rear.

The ruse lasted until dawn, when some of the Wishrams
on the opposite bank of the river pushed their canoes off and
paddled toward Stuart and his portagers. They were quickly
joined by others, and by the time they struck the shore num-

The Seattle Public Library

Columbia Branch

Visit us on the Web: www.spl.org

Checked Out Items 10/27/2018 16:09

XXXXXXXX2343

Item Title	Due Date
0010092762326	11/17/2018
Pacific destiny ; and Bear flag rising	

# of Items: 1

Balance Due: $7.98

Renewals: 206-386-4190

TeleCirc: 206-386-9015 / 24 hours a day

Online: myaccount.spl.org

Pay your fines/fees online at pay.spl.org

bered at least a hundred. Reed, with his dispatch case on his back, seems to have been a special attraction. "Shining afar," Irving said, "like the brilliant helmet of Euryalus," the tin box became a glittering prize. The Indians fell on McClellan first, throwing a buffalo robe over his head while attempting to stab him. He wrestled free, raised his musket, and shot one of his attackers through the heart. Reed, meantime, was also under attack. As he fumbled for his rifle he was clubbed senseless and stripped of his weapons and the dispatch case. McClellan ran forward, killed one of Reed's assailants with a pistol, and then was wounded by a tomahawk blow. Stuart and the other men now came forward to the fight, firing their weapons into the Indian force and scattering it into the woods.

Later in the day, as Reed's and McClellan's wounds were being tended, a Wishram chief approached Stuart's camp. This elder announced, apparently through sign language, that his people demanded vengeance for the deaths of two of their brothers. Stuart stood his ground and made it clear that his guns would kill many more warriors if he and his men were attacked again. Eventually, after much awkward diplomacy, an agreement was negotiated. Stuart said the compromise cost "3 Blankets to cover the dead, and some Tobacco to fill the Calumet of Peace, on condition they should immediately cross the River and leave our passage free, which was Soon complied with and we saw no more of them."

The tin dispatch box was never recovered, but Stuart allowed no time to search for it. He led his party back to the Okanogan and was returning downriver toward Fort Astoria when at least one of the missions of the original three parties was fulfilled. Below the forks of the Columbia, Stuart's canoes were hailed from shore by two wraith-like figures. They were white men, thin, long-bearded, and entirely naked, and when the canoes reached the shore, Ramsey Crooks and John Day, the "lost" members of Wilson Price

Hunt's expedition who had been left on the banks of the Snake River in December last, fell at their feet.

The entire party reached the fort on May 11, and by the end of June Stuart was ready to restart his expedition to Saint Louis.

2

The Astor brigantine *Beaver* rammed into Baker's Bay a few days before Stuart and his men reached the fort after their near disaster at The Dalles rapids. The ship brought supplies and reinforcements, and since as yet there was no news of war with Britain, Astoria rejoiced in its new prosperity. Among the newcomers were five clerks, fifteen American laborers, six Canadian *voyageurs*, and twelve Hawaiians who signed on for service on the Columbia during the ship's stopover in the Sandwich Islands. In charge of the civilian contingent aboard the *Beaver* was a new partner and distant relative of Astor's, John Clarke, an American with long service in the fur trade, including six years with the North West Company.

The reinforcements breathed new life into the Pacific outpost and six weeks after they were landed, the senior partners launched four new expeditions to extend the fort's operations up the river and one to carry dispatches east. Two of the parties set out on foot, led by Donald "Perpetual Motion" Mackenzie and John Clarke, to locate sites and establish new trade posts above the forks of the Columbia; a third headed north for Fort Okanogan with supplies; and the fourth, "one of peril and hardship," which "required a man of nerve and vigor," Irving said, was designated to convey dispatches to Saint Louis, thence to New York for Mr. Astor, replacing those carried by John Reed in the tin box recently lost to the Wishrams. This mission was confided to Robert Stuart, who, Irving said, "though he had never been across the mountains, and a very young man, had given proofs of his competency to the task."

Bancroft provided a prose poem to describe the leave-taking of the parties:

> It was a beautiful sight and one which would have warmed the blood of Astor . . . see these sixty-two men on the Thirtieth of June, 1812, set out in ten canoes and two barges from the fort which was now to become the Mother of Forts and a great city on these broad Western waters, and with paddles flying, with shout and song, and the ringing of artillery, strike boldly from their several posts.

Stuart had six men with him when he departed Fort Astoria with the other parties. Ramsey Crooks and Robert McClellan, both having resigned from Astor's service, were eager to return to Saint Louis, as were François LeClairc and André Vallé, both Canadian *engagés*, and Benjamin Jones, a Virginia backwoodsman. This latter valuable man had left home at age sixteen, spent time in Kentucky, and drifted to Saint Louis in 1802, where he and a partner, Alexander Carson (a distant relative of Christopher "Kit" Carson), began trapping along the Upper Missouri. Although his history is sketchy, Jones, and Carson as well, may have served with Lewis and Clark in 1804, at least as far as the Mandan villages. The Virginian had been canoeing down the Missouri when he encountered Wilson Hunt's westbound expedition and joined it to Astoria. He was an excellent hunter and a crack shot, had been in the thick of the fight with the Wishrams at The Dalles, and had Stuart's complete trust.

The sixth man was John Day. He had barely survived the privations of Hunt's party and with Crooks had been rescued by Stuart less than two months past. Irving described him as about forty years old, six-foot-two in height, and "straight as an Indian; with an elastic step as if he trod on springs, and a handsome, open, manly countenance." But his vigorous step and strong physique dated back to the time he joined Hunt's overlanders in their winter camp on the Nodaway River at the end of 1810. The seven months he and Crooks had wandered the country between the Snake and Columbia—sick, starving, and lost—had beaten Day down. Now he was thin, tired, and delusional, and it became clear soon after the departure from Astoria that he would not survive the journey ahead. Stuart, who had no experience with trail fevers and no patience with sick men, observed Day's babbling and noted in his journal that the man "spoke in the most incoherent, absurd and unconnected sentences." After four days on the river, Day put a pair of loaded pistols to his head and pulled the triggers but fired high and was wrestled to the ground, bound, and placed under guard. Stuart had him escorted back to the fort.*

Most of July was occupied in portages and slow advances in ascending the river to the mouth of the Walla Walla, a shallow stream that debouched into the Columbia. The natives of the region were a hospitable horseback tribe and greeted the Astorians with a huge bonfire on the riverbank and, after camp was established, conducted a dance in their honor. Stuart purchased twenty horses from the Walla Wallas, most of them to be used as pack animals, and on the last day of July he and his men set out with their string of ponies to the southeast over the open plains toward the Blue Mountains.

The trail they blazed roughly followed Wilson Hunt's route, but Stuart hoped that traveling it in summer would avoid the privations Hunt and his men had experienced. Game ought to be plentiful now, the weather agreeable for a fast passage of the mountains and the approach to the Snake

---

*He recovered enough to join the North West Company's service but seems never to have conquered his infirmities and died, "infirm of body," in a defile in the Salmon River Mountains of Idaho in February 1820. One of his trapper companions wrote, "He appeared to die the good death of a good man."

TO THE TETONS   153

River. But as the little party entered the arid wastes, naked
and sandy hills, and crossed sunbaked and cracked ravines
and streambeds, the search for water consumed them and
slowed their pace to a crawl. The waterskins they carried
were too soon exhausted, and horse and man became tortured by thirst, trudging forward in stifling, dust-bearing
winds on sunburned sand and clay "without the least appearance of having experienced any share of the dews of heaven
since the time of Noahs Flood," Stuart wrote.

They were four days crossing forty-five miles of desert before spying a fringe of forest in the distance and, upon approaching it, heard the water. The horses needed no goading
and led the party to the bank of the Umatilla River, the same
lifesaving stream Hunt and his men had fallen on after crossing the Blue Mountains seven months past.

After a camp on the gravelly beach and a skimpy meal,
and with the skins filled and the horses watered and fed, Stuart and his men left the Umatilla on August 1. They followed a
grassy plain to another stream, which Stuart identified as
the "Glaise" (Clay) River (subsequently called the Grande
Ronde), and on the seventh entered the dense forests at the
foot of the Blues. They led their horses in crossing and re-
crossing rocky streambeds, through wooded defiles and
narrow paths shouldered by great promontories and drop-
aways. On August 12 the party broached the mountains,
crossed a fertile meadowland, and arrived on the shore of
the tumultuous Snake, 400 yards wide, its frothing waters
running below high, shrubby sandbanks.

The men recuperated on the riverbank for two days, and
on the evening before they pushed on they were visited by a
solitary Shoshoni who rode into the camp and through laborious signing told of a white man living with his band a
day's journey upriver. Stuart figured that the man was probably one of Wilson Hunt's trappers who had remained at Fort
Henry to hunt beaver and had vanished into the wilderness.
Finding one of them would be the key to learning the fate

of the others, as well as the location of the several caches of furs, saddles, and supplies left behind by Hunt's Astorians.

After two days' travel upstream with no sighting of the mysterious straggler, the journeyers reached what Stuart called "a renowned Fishing place," a junction where another large waterway, apparently the Boisé River, flowed into the Snake and where Shoshonis in great numbers gathered to collect the salmon teeming in the confluence. At a stream-side village inquiries were made about any white men seen in the vicinity, and the party was directed to another Indian camp on the opposite shore. Stuart found a Shoshoni willing to canoe across to seek out any white men and bring them across the river.

The Astorians spent a miserable night in the Indian camp, galled by clouds of mosquitoes, which, Stuart wrote, "assailed us in innumerable hosts, and completely deprived our eyelids of their usual functions; even after the dew had fallen those infernal Pests Still continued their music to our no small annoyance." In the morning they were disappointed to learn that the Indian messenger had returned alone in his canoe. There were no white men across the river or, so far as could be determined, anywhere else in the vicinity. As the morning wore on, disquieting news came to them when an elderly Shoshoni rode into their camp, dismounted, ran directly to Stuart's horse, flung his arms around the animal's neck, and hugged and kissed it. The horse, purchased from the Walla Wallas, Stuart had so grown to love as a "noble animal, admirably shaped, of free and generous spirit" that he intended taking it to New York as a gift for Mr. Astor. Now he learned from the Indian elder that the beast had been stolen from him and that he wanted it back.

While this uncomfortable sign-and-word conversation was proceeding, Crooks, McClellan, Ben Jones, and others who had been in Wilson Hunt's party came forward and recognized the old man as one of the "trusty Snakes" who had served as guide the preceding autumn when they all reached Fort Henry. They questioned the elder closely and learned much bad news: The horses Hunt had left in the care of the Shoshoni guides had been stolen by an Absaroka war party; all of Hunt's caches had been plundered; and the missing trappers had been attacked by the Crow marauders, stripped of their weapons, horses, and goods, and left to wander along the river.

One piece of intelligence that had great implications for the future was given to Stuart that August 16, 1812. The Snake elder told the Astorians that he knew a shorter and safer route across the Rocky Mountains than that taken by Wilson Hunt. Stuart noted in his diary that upon "learning that this Indian was perfectly acquainted with the route, I without loss of time offered him a Pistol a Blanket of Blue Cloth—an Axe—a Knife—an awl—a Fathom of Beads, a looking glass and a little Powder & Ball if he would guide us from this to the other side, which he immediately accepted." The Indian, who had seemingly forgotten the matter of the stolen horse, said he was tired of eating salmon and longed to hunt buffalo and so rode off to retrieve his arms and equipment for the journey across the Rockies— the shorter "trace," as Stuart called it, which lay south of the Wind River Mountains.

He rejoined the Astorians the next morning and after the horses were collected, all tormented during the night by flies and mosquitoes clouding up from the river, the party "journeyed quite harmoniously together," Irving said, "though now and then, the Snake would regard his quondam steed with a wistful eye." They had made a late start and had traveled only about nine miles when they came to a great bend in the river. The Shoshoni guide advised that they make camp there and get an early start for the next full day's travel. That day, he said, would take them across a hilly stretch of country that would save many miles in the approach to the western foothills of the Rocky Mountains.

At the dawn muster of his party, Stuart discovered the

guide and the noble horse missing. Tracks showed that the Shoshoni had ridden off, and taken his other horse as well. Irving wrote, "It was plain the Snake had taken an Indian mode of recovering his horse, having quietly decamped with him in the night . . . . New vows were made never more to trust in Snakes, or any other Indians." Sentries, three each night, were assigned to watch the remuda.

The march proceeded in sultry weather across the prairie lands paralleling the Snake, with "Mosquitoe Serenades" and hordes of sand flies—"Imps of Darkness," Stuart called them—continuing to devour the party during the day and thirst driving them again and again to the willow-rimmed edge of the river, where they fell in its cooling waters to drink and wash away trail grime.

On August 20, during one of these respites, they stumbled upon a gaunt white man in ragged clothing fishing at the river's edge. It turned out to be John Hoback, one of the missing Hunt men. After Stuart and his men greeted this specter of the forest, three other of the missing trappers emerged from the willows—Joseph Miller, Jacob Reznor, and Edward Robinson. All had served in Andrew Henry's fur brigade before joining Hunt's overlanders and were among those who, the previous autumn, had elected to remain at Fort Henry to trap. Miller was the former infantry lieutenant from Pennsylvania; of Hoback, Reznor, and Robinson nothing is known except that they were Kentuckians and that Robinson, who may have been the oldest of the group, had been scalped in some past Indian fight and wore a handkerchief knotted about his head.

The men told of their desperate experiences over the past ten months. They had twice been robbed—by Arapahoes, not Crow—of their furs, horses, provisions, and most of their weapons, and had wandered hundreds of miles, not straying far from the Snake, where they could at least subsist on fish. "Nothing could exceed their joy on thus meeting with their old comrades," Irving wrote, "or the heartiness with which they were welcomed. All hands immediately encamped; and the slender stores of the party were ransacked to furnish out a suitable regale." Stuart jotted in his diary, "After regaling our half famished friends with the best our small pittance of luxuries could afford, we proceeded along the banks of the river, for 3 miles, to a good fishing and grazing place, where we took up our lodgings for the night."

3

The expedition, now numbering ten men, continued to follow the course of the Snake for several days, encountering small Shoshoni fishing camps en route and a large one of over 100 lodges at a falls on August 25, where they gorged on salmon and purchased a quantity of dried fish before moving on. Soon after, they reached the vicinity of Hunt's caches and located nine of them. Six had been dug up from ground covered with wolf tracks. Stuart concluded that the ripe buried beaver hides had brought the scavengers and that Indian scavengers followed, taking everything remaining except the books, which lay scattered about. The three unmolested caches contained some clothing articles, ammunition, and beaver traps. With clothing, arms, and traps, and with their strength returned, Robinson, Reznor, and Hoback decided to stay on in the Snake River country. Thus, Irving said, "fitted out for a campaign of beaver-trapping," the men "forgot all that they had suffered, and determined upon another trial of their fortunes; preferring to take their chances in the wilderness, rather than return home ragged and penniless."*

---

*In January 1814, all three were killed by Shoshonis at the mouth of the Boisé River, together with the Irishman John Reed (who had lost the Astor dispatch box at The Dalles rapids) and Pierre Dorion, the liquor-loving interpreter with Wilson Hunt's party. The only survivors

On September 7, the seven-man party left the banks of the Snake to head for the Teton Range in western Wyoming, still following Wilson Hunt's route. Joseph Miller, who had had enough of Indian country and stayed with Stuart "to return to the bosom of civilized society," volunteered to serve as guide but proved "indifferent," Irving said, and the travelers were soon lost on the game-barren plains and, having used up their supply of dried salmon, had to eat roots and serviceberries mashed into cakes and a dog purchased from a forlorn Shoshoni lodge. They struck the Bear River after five days' travel, averaging twenty to twenty-five miles a day, and on the last day of their rest, while fishing the stream discovered a dozen Absarokas prowling their camp. The Crow chief, whom Irving described as "a dark Herculean fellow, fully six feet four inches in height, with a mingled air of ruffian and rogue," was at first friendly, even sending some of his people to their nearby village to bring buffalo meat for the white men. But by midnight, with over twenty of the native band around the camp, Stuart and his men grew apprehensive, more over "the adroitness of these fellows in stealing Horses," Stuart said, than for their own safety.

Watches were doubled, and after an uneasy night the Astorians repacked their animals and prepared to push on. The Crow signed and pointed to Stuart's muskets and indicated that they wanted to trade horses for powder. Stuart declined and the big Crow leader grew belligerent, slapped himself on the chest, and announced his power as a great chief. He signed that it was customary for chiefs to give each other gifts. He pointed to Stuart's horse and when it was denied him he grasped Stuart and shook him as if to pull him out of the saddle. Irving reported, "Mr. Stuart instantly drew forth a pistol and presented it at the head of the bully-ruffian.

---

of the massacre were Dorion's Indian wife, Marguerite, and their two children. Marguerite married thrice again and died in 1850, at age eighty, at her home on the Willamette River.

In a twinkling his swaggering was at an end, and he dodged behind his horse to escape the expected shot." Stuart ordered his men to level their rifles at the others but not to fire unless he gave the order. The ploy worked. The Crow scrambled into the brush. Not long after, the chief emerged from cover affecting to laugh off the affair, and Stuart gave him twenty charges of powder as a gift.

They moved on uneasily, heading east over a chain of hills, watching columns of smoke in the mountain foothills around them, and made a hard twenty-five-mile march before setting up a closely guarded camp, hobbling their horses, setting the sentries, and sleeping fitfully with their rifles.

On September 18, six days and 150 miles from the Bear River confrontation, the party reached the "Mad River," Henry's Fork of the Snake, just west of the Tetons. At dawn, as an antelope-meat breakfast was cooking, Stuart was standing at the riverbank when he heard the cry "Indians! Indians! To arms!" at the camp. A Crow raiding party swooped down on the small horse herd and proceeded to drive them off, and as the Astorians ran to their rifles the main body of raiders, about twenty men, crashed out of the brush and began carrying off the packs of provisions and supplies lying about the campfire. The leader of the Crow party rode past the panicking Astorians—he was the same bulky leader Stuart had encountered the week past—and, rising from his horse's back, slapped himself on the buttocks ("clapping his hands on the most insulting part of his body" in Washington Irving's delicate phrase) and yelled some jeering words.

Lapsing into a style adopted by dime-novelists many decades later, Irving re-created the scene that followed:

Sharpshooter Ben Jones leveled his rifle and caught the big chief in his sights.

Stuart shouted, "Not for your life! not for your life! You will bring destruction on us all!"

Jones replied, "O, Mr. Stuart, only let me have one
crack at the infernal rascal, and you may keep all the pay
that is due me."

"By heaven, if you fire," cried Mr. Stuart, "I'll blow
your brains out!"

Jones was angry to be prevented from making his clear
shot, but Stuart knew instinctively what the consequences
would be had he permitted it: He told Irving that the Indians
believed in a life for a life and the whole Crow nation would
have risen in vengeance. He said signal fires would have directed war parties to their camp to slaughter them; they
were but seven men, now afoot, at the mercy of the Indians—
Crow, Blackfeet, even the ostensibly friendly Snakes—the
land, and the elements. He had to admire the savages and
their leader and wrote in his journal, "On the whole it was
one of the most daring and intrepid actions I ever heard of
among Indians, and convinced me how determined they
were on having our Horses, for which they would unques-
tionably have followed us any distance."

The party was now in desperate straits, heading toward
unmapped mountain passages and unknown hazards, without pack animals and able to carry only what they could
mount on their backs, facing the coming winter and the necessity of finding a camp and game to sustain them for the
months of immobile isolation. But they had little time to
despair and spent the day after the raid making their back-
packs, burning in a bonfire the goods they could not carry,
and cooking a scanty meal from a beaver Ben Jones had
trapped in the river.

They followed the Mad River through a mountain defile
to a point below Fort Henry where it emptied back into the
Snake. They lived on fish, built two crude rafts, and floated
on the Snake's currents for six days, poling ashore at each
dusk to set up camp, hunt, and fish. Jones eventually killed
a deer and they gorged on the meat, jerked what remained,

and made moccasins of the hide to reinforce their tattered boots.

Stuart hoped to find a Shoshoni village where he might barter for at least one packhorse, but none were found. They were now on dangerous ground—Blackfeet territory—and grew fearful of hunting since a gunshot might attract these intractable white-hating warriors. The nights turned bitter, a sharp reminder of the need to find a winter hideaway, and after floating over ninety miles on the south fork of the Snake, Stuart took his men ashore. They quit their rafts and struck east toward what Stuart called the "Pilot Knobs," the Tetons (which French *voyageurs* had named *Trois Tetons* for their perceived resemblance to three female breasts). They tramped over an alluvial bottom thick with cotton-woods, hawthorns, and willows and across a series of stony hills and ravines, skirting sulphurous hot springs.

Ramsey Crooks took a fever in this stretch of the march but struggled on with the others, after a day's rest, to the foothills of the Snake River Range. Here, on the last days of September, near a place under the Tetons later called Pierre's Hole, Stuart consulted with his men on the question of climb-ing the low chain of mountains or detouring around them to the south. Since it was decided that the longer route might put them among Blackfeet hunters, six of the seven Astori-ans decided to climb. The dissenter was Robert McClellan, the forty-two-year-old Indian fighter, "hot-headed and impatient at all times," Irving said, who "had been ren-dered irascible by the fatigues of the journey, and the condi-tions of his feet, which were chafed and sore." He swore he would rather face the Blackfeet than climb another mountain and soon fell back, deriding the others, and disappeared— "a braggart spirit, that took a pride in doing desperate and hare-brained things," in Irving's estimation.

Crooks' fever flared violently during the crossing and a willow bower was thrown up for him to lie in. He was dosed with castor oil and made to endure an "Indian Sweat," made with hot coals in water. Some of the members thought he was dying and apparently talked of leaving him behind. Stuart would not hear of it and noted in his diary that such an idea was "too repugnant to my feelings to require long deliberation." He used the occasion to write philosophically of men daring the "unknown and untravelled wilderness." The artificial solitude of parks and gardens, he said, is apt to give humans "a flattering notion of self-sufficiency" but "the phantoms which haunt a desert are want, misery, and danger," and the wilderness reminds that "man is unwillingly acquainted with his own weakness, and meditations shew him only how little he can sustain, and how little he can perform."

9

South Pass

■

"... HARBINGERS OF THE WISHED-FOR LAND."

1

Robert Stuart's party crossed the low hills west of the Teton Range on October 1, 1812, the passage made difficult by snowdrifts and the weakened state of Ramsey Crooks, who was still suffering the effects of his fever. He could not eat, but there was little to eat for any of them, and Stuart said they were all "reduced to their last extremity, nor had they strength to make use of their rifles, although now and then some deer were seen."

From the summit of the hills could be sighted a grassy plain stretching at least twenty miles in width with a meandering river bordered by willows at its edge. Those who had traveled with Wilson Hunt recognized the place and pointed out to Stuart the route they must take to Henry's Fort, the deserted trappers' post where Hunt had abandoned his horses and proceeded on the Snake in canoes. As they descended to the plain, Robert McClellan was spotted in the distance making his solitary, sullen way toward the stream. They halloo'd to him but he did not respond.

They camped in the willows on the edge of the river. Crooks was so weak and despaired that some of the party again spoke of leaving him behind. They were in Blackfeet country, winter was approaching fast, the Tetons were probably snowbound, they were starving, and no game had been seen in many days. But Stuart was aghast at such a suggestion, said they must give the ailing man time to recuperate, and sent Ben Jones out along the river with a beaver trap and rifle despite the continuing fear that a gunshot might attract hostiles to their camp. Jones shot but only wounded a grizzly bear, which vanished into the brush, but six miles from the camp he came upon a number of grazing elk and was able to kill five of them. The camp was moved to the meat, with Crooks supported between two of the party, and by the end of three days his fever had eased and he was able to eat and regain some of his strength. The elk meat that remained was smoked and dried, and later a grizzly was killed and added to the larder. The fat on its rump, Stuart said, was three inches thick.

They pushed on, with Crooks now able to walk alone and carry his rifle, and crossed Teton Pass through nine inches of snow, bending their course eastward as much as possible through a succession of rocky heights, deep valleys, and rapid streams. Their path lay along the margins of perpendicular precipices several hundred feet in height with the rocky bed of the river roaring below. Their food supply, the elk and bear meat they were able to smoke and pack, disappeared even after careful rationing, and they found no game and only a few trout in the Teton River. When a small deer was killed, Stuart eked out a three-day meat allowance from it.

On October 11 they stumbled upon a camp McClellan had made, found the remains of a wolf he had eaten, and the next day spotted a plume of smoke in the distance, which François LeClairc was sent out to investigate. Stuart and his men were starving and had forgotten their fear of the Blackfeet, and they hoped the smoke was issuing from an Indian camp. Stuart wrote that he and his men "sat up late waiting his

[LeClairc's] return in expectation of getting something to eat, but at last despairing of his coming we went to bed about 11 o'Clock, again supperless."

In the morning they resumed their march and en route were hailed by LeClairc as he made his way back to the night's camp. He reported that the smoke had risen from McClellan's campfire on the banks of the river, where he had tried and failed to find fish. They reached the Pennsylvanian in an hour and as Stuart dispassionately described the scene, "We found him lying on a parcel of straw, emaciated and worn to a perfect skeleton & hardly able to raise his head or speak from extreme debility."

In the twelve days since he had angrily struck out on his own, McClellan had fared worse in finding game or fish than the others, and while Stuart said "our presence seemed to revive him considerably," the older man said he would as soon die on his pallet than go on. Nevertheless, they dragged him to his feet, distributed his pitiful belongings into their packs, and were able to proceed to a new riverbank camp after plodding on seventeen miles.

Weak with hunger, three days since the last scrap of jerky had been consumed, Stuart and those who could summon the energy to hunt spent the afternoon of October 14 foraging for anything edible. They found no fish, and the few antelope they saw were too far away to kill. They returned to the camp, Stuart said, "with heavy hearts but I must confess we could not enter the same complaints against our stomachs." He wrote in his journal that "one of the Canadians" (Irving said it was LeClairc) came to him that evening and suggested they drew lots, proposing, "It is better one should die than that all should perish." Stuart wrote, without mentioning the cannibalistic implications of the proposal, "I shuddered at the idea & used every endeavor to create an abhorrence in his mind against such an act, urging also the probability of falling in with some animal on the morrow but, finding that every argument failed and that he was on the point of converting some others to his purpose, I snatched up my Rifle, cocked and leveled it at him with the firm resolution to fire if he persisted." He said, "This affair so terrified him that he fell upon his knees and asked the whole party's pardon, swearing he should never again suggest such a thought—after this affair was settled I felt so agitated and weak that I could scarcely crawl to bed."

The day after this incident, eleven miles along their route they found an old buffalo bull wandering alone and succeeded in killing it. They were so ravenous they ate some of the meat raw, then butchered and carried the remainder to the camp, where Stuart instructed they boil some of it and drink the broth before gorging on the steaks.

Now "somewhat recruited and refreshed," they moved on, left the river, and traveled another fifteen miles, heading toward the foot of the Wind River Range, a bulking, unbroken wall of snowcapped mountains running toward the northwest and forcing the Astorians southward. After fording a tributary of the Green River they came upon an abandoned Indian camp strewn with buffalo bones and lying within a copse of pines. They stopped to examine it and found at its center an enormous lodge 150 feet across. The tepee-shaped structure was composed of twenty pine logs, each twelve inches in diameter and forty feet long, the whole covered with pine and willow boughs. Inside it, opposite the entrance, three bodies lay on pallets, at their heads a branch of red cedar and at their feet a large black-painted buffalo skull. From the conical ceiling were suspended "numerous ornaments" and many children's moccasins. While Stuart gave only a clinician's description of the sacred place, he knew its significance. The time and labor taken to assemble it, he said, gave a hint "that the personages on whose account it was constructed were not of the common order."

On the eighteenth, the men crossed a ridge of the Wind River Mountains, waded a branch of the Green River, and

coming up from the bank encountered six Shoshonis in a
hunting party who escorted them to their streamside encampment. There were four pine-branch huts in the camp
and Stuart found the people "poor but hospitable in the
Extreme," and traded a pistol, an ax, a knife, a cup, two
awls, and some beads for the single horse they had with
them, some deerskin for moccasins and a bit of buffalo
meat. The natives explained that they had been ravaged by
Crow raiders who had stolen all but one of their horses and
most of their food and effects and had abducted several of
their women. Stuart told them that "the day was not far
distant when we would take signal vengeance on the perpe-
trators of those deeds," and smoked a pipe with them.

On October 19 the seven Astorians packed their horse
with enough buffalo jerky to last six days and left the Snake
camp to follow the river branch southeast. They were grateful
to the Indians, and justly so: They had a horse to ease their
burdens, they were reasonably fit now and well fed, and even
McClellan and Crooks had revived their strength and were
anxious to push on. They found a beaten path, which Stuart
surmised was a trail the Crow used in their forays along
the river, and followed it all day. LeClairc and André Vallé,
hunting ahead of the others, killed a buffalo calf toward
dusk and they had a camp feast that night, with a kettle full
of meat on a roaring fire as the wind whistled and snow fell
around them.

The next day they quit the Crow trace, which seemed to
wind too far north for their purpose and was too dangerous
in any event. Keeping to it, Irving said, "they might be described by some scouts and spies of that race of Ishmaelites,
whose predatory life required them to be constantly on
alert." Instead of taking such a chance, they tramped southeast through new-fallen snow, across undulating country
with the ridges of the lower Wind River Range on their front
and left, and crossed a salt plain to camp in a cutting wind on
another stream bank. At twilight, as they sat huddled before

their fire, McClellan set out with his rifle and killed a buffalo, which they would skin and slaughter the next morning.

October 21, 1812, had no special significance to Stuart or his
men beyond the fact that on that day they were able to cover
only a paltry fifteen miles of ground in the face of a wind
driving needles of snow. The expedition leader noted the
snowfall and biting cold in his diary "soon after we left the
drain which compelled us to encamp at the end of 15 miles
ENE on the side of a Hill [which he later called "a handsome low gap"] which we must inevitably traverse where we
found a sufficiency of dry Aspen for firewood, but not a drop
of water." Washington Irving, writing from Stuart's notes
and journals and presumably from interviews with Stuart,
Crooks, and others of the expedition, said the seven men "set
forward on their bleak and toilsome way" on the twenty-first
"towards the lofty summit of a mountain, which was necessary for them to cross."

The camp that day was made on a hillside at the approximate latitude 42 degrees 26 minutes, not far above the line
that would later establish the California-Oregon border,
and the "handsome low gap" was the western entrance to a
twenty-nine-mile-wide, gently sloping saddle of the Wind
River Range. Stuart and his party of seven had discovered,
without their slightest knowledge of it, the corridor through
the Rocky Mountains that thirty years hence would enable
the American settlement of Oregon and California.

The gateway, located where the Continental Divide debouched into a wide, arid plain of sage and sand forming
the eastern boundary of the Oregon Country, would come
to be called South Pass ("south" because it was south of the
mountain passes followed by Lewis and Clark). The Astorians' camp lay two miles southwest of the 7,412-foot-high
summit of the pass, squarely on its western terminus.

2

At daybreak on the twenty-second the Astorians ascended the pass three miles, found a spring, and made a fire beside it to cook breakfast. After five more miles they scrambled upward to a level ground strewn with pumice stones and strange shells—"evidently the production of the sea," Stuart noted, "and which doubtless must have been deposited by the waters of the deluge." This "top of the mountain . . . in the midst of the principal chain" lay at the Continental Divide, the North American backbone running from northern Alaska to Mexico and in the Rocky Mountains marking the point separating westward- and eastward-flowing rivers.

Over the next five days winter closed on them as they descended the pass, a northeast wind harrying them as they plodded on through intermittent but blinding snowstorms, making tortuously slow progress and early bivouacs. There was little grass, and time had to be spent searching for forage for the faithful packhorse as well as for hunting for meat and wood for the campfire. Two bighorn sheep were shot and the men feasted on the "mountain mutton," but as often they rested huddled together with no meat and no fire. They followed an eastward-bearing stream and drank from it; Stuart was convinced of its "great similarity of taste to the muddy waters of the Missouri." They found a great supply of dried "Buffaloe dung," which solved their campfire problem for a time, and on October 28 entered what Stuart called "a handsome Plain" with a meandering river sixty feet wide running through it. This was the river that came to be called the Sweetwater, one of the headwaters of the Platte River, which flowed in turn into the Missouri.

Winter now barred their progress, and the need to find a place to survive it preoccupied the Astorians. They were less

than 900 miles from Saint Louis, but six months would pass
before they reached it.

They followed the Sweetwater, camping in the willows along
its banks. One of their bivouacs was set up four miles east
of a 128-foot-high turtle-shaped granite boulder overlooking the river. This was an unremarkable formation from their
vantage point, but to the emigrants who would see it coming from the east, it would have a special significance. The
boulder lay 814 miles from the Missouri frontier and came
to be called Independence Rock.

For the first time in many weeks, game and water were
plentiful. Three buffalo cows were shot one morning ("the
hump meat is by far the most delicious I have ever tasted,"
Stuart said), and bighorns, black-tailed deer, and elk were
often seen feeding at the base of the mountain or at the water's edge.

On November first the Astorians crossed the Platte and
on a bend found a low point of land covered with willows,
firs, aspens, cedars, and cottonwoods. It seemed a perfect
place for winter habitation: plenty of wood for fuel and constructing a hut, game abounding, and water nearby. Stuart's
only apprehension was a visit by the "villainous and rascally
Poncas." They were a small band of Missouri River Indians
normally on friendly terms with whites but whose propensity for thievery had been witnessed by Crooks, McClellan,
and the other Wilson Hunt veterans.

With their winter site selected and their camp established,
Ben Jones and the two *engagés,* LeClairc and Vallé, set out
to hunt. In three days they had killed twelve buffalo and
stored the meat in a frozen cache near the river. By the tenth,
the Astorians had killed, butchered, and cached the meat of
thirty-two buffalo, twenty-eight deer and bighorn sheep.
After Ramsey Crooks had a dangerous encounter with a
grizzly that he found whuffling in a pile of buffalo guts,

Ben Jones bagged the animal and added the meat to the cache.

When not hunting and transporting the meat and hides to the campsite, all hands worked at constructing their winter quarters, an eight-by-eighteen-foot hut six feet high made of cottonwood logs and buffalo hides with a fire pit in the middle and a hole in the roof over it, Indian style. The party now reveled in abundance. They had a snug cabin, plenty of meat, water, forage for their packhorse, and deerskins to scrape and soak and soften to replace tattered shirts, trousers, leggings, and moccasins. They "looked forward to a winter of peace and quietness," Irving wrote in a poetical reverie:

> . . . a time of roasting, and boiling, and boiling, and feasting upon venison, and mountain mutton, and bear's meat, and marrow bones, and buffalo humps, and other hunter's dainties, and of dozing and reposing round their fire, and gossiping over past dangers and adventures, and telling long hunting stories, until spring should return; when they would make canoes of buffalo skins and float themselves down the river.

But these dreams were rudely interrupted a few days after the hut was completed, its log walls chinked with river clay, its fire pit dug and fueled, the communal kettle cooking meat. At daybreak on December 10, "savage yelps" woke the men and they sprang up and grabbed their weapons. From the low entrance to the cabin they saw Indians, armed and painted, in the fringe of trees and brush bordering the camp. Joseph Miller, the one-time infantryman from Wilson Hunt's party, was first to speak. "We are in trouble," he said to Stuart. "These are some of the rascally Arapahays that robbed me last year."

The seven men slung their powder horns and ball pouches. McClellan, who had taken his rifle apart to clean it during the night, now fumbled to reassemble it and proposed to Stuart that they knock the chinking from the walls for loopholes to fire on the Indians. Stuart cautioned for the moment against bringing any weapons into play. "We must first hold a parley," he said, and, accompanied by one of the Canadians, walked from the hut, rifle in hand, the other held palm-out to signify peaceful intent.

The leader of the Indian band emerged from the brush thicket and shook hands with Stuart. Through signing, pointing, and what few words the *engagé* could translate, Stuart picked up their errand. The Arapahos were from a village several days to the east that had been attacked by Absaroka raiders who had made off with most of their horses and had taken some of their women captive. The warriors facing the Astorians' camp were of a war party, armed with bows, arrows, war clubs, skinning knives, and a few ancient firearms, and had been sixteen days trailing the Crow. They had heard the gunshots of Stuart's hunters, found the remains of the deer and buffalo killed, and followed the tracks to the white men's camp.

The Indians were hungry, and Stuart invited the "chief" and another warrior, seemingly a "lieutenant" in the band, into the hut to help themselves to the haunches of meat hanging from the roof-beams over the smoking fire pit. The chief and his aide needed no urging, and the venison and buffalo quarters quickly disappeared, being passed out the doorway to those waiting outside. There were twenty-three warriors in the Arapaho band and Irving wrote that "a scene of gormandizing commenced, of which few can have an idea, who have not witnessed the gastronomic powers of an Indian, after an interval of fasting."

The Astorians soon realized that the Arapahos were in no hurry to pursue the hated Crow raiders and for two days were content to raid the white man's meat supply. They threw up what Irving called "breastworks," into which they "retired at a tolerably early hour, and slept like overfed hounds" while the chief and his lieutenant stayed in the hut, getting up two or three times at night to carve meat and eat. Irving maintained that it was Stuart's policy to overfeed his rapacious hut-guests and keep the chief and his aide as unknowing "captives" to ensure the "good conduct" of those outside.

At last, on the third day since their encounter, the Arapaho party prepared to leave. They had a six-day journey, the chief said, before they would find the Absarokas, and since they would be traveling through country lean of game asked for provisions for the journey. Stuart complied, noting in his diary that they "departed peaceably about 10 A.M. carrying with them a great proportion of our best meat." The chief also requested powder and ball but, the Astorian wrote, "a peremptory refusal soon convinced them that all demands of that nature were unavailing and they laughingly relinquished their entreaties."

(Irving's story had the chief saying, "We are poor now, and are obliged to go on foot, but we shall soon come back laden with booty, and all mounted on horseback, with scalps hanging from our bridles. We will give each of you a horse to keep you from being tired on your journey." To this Stuart replied, "Well, when you bring the horses, you shall have the ammunition, but not before." The author does not explain how the Arapaho was able to convey all this in such courtly language, nor, apparently, does he think it strange that Stuart, with six men in his command, would speak so rudely to a chief with twenty-two well-armed warriors behind him.)

They were relieved to be rid of the Arapahos but knew their meat-hungry guests would return and so held a council. They were in a vise, caught between freebooters and freeloaders, the Crow within a six-day ride on stolen Arapaho ponies, the Arapahos bound to come again, probably with more people from their village and this time probably not amused to be refused ammunition. Stuart and his men agreed on their only course of action and he entered in his journal that "we determined to abandon our Chateau of Indolence" after dressing enough deer and buffalo skins "for Mogasins etc." and "extricate ourselves out of the paws of our rascally neighbors by going a very considerable distance down the river." He hoped to make their next cantonment on the Missouri River.

On December 13 they set out in the crusted snow, their bony packhorse laden with as much frozen meat as it could carry, and managed to travel twenty-five to thirty miles a day. The country turned barren after the first few days; the horse had to be fed cottonwood bark and willow twigs, and finding fuel for their fires required tedious work. Footsore from breaking through miles of frozen ground, Stuart early on noted that they were so anxious to find new winter quarters that they were willing to face hostile Indians and "rather than die on the march, fall valiently on the field of Mars."

On the thirty-first they set up their second winter quarters on the North Platte River in far eastern Wyoming in a grove of big cottonwoods and devoted the early days of 1813 "solely to the gratification of our appetites." Buffalo were so plentiful that seven were killed in one day, and the Astorians "destroyed an immoderate quantity" of hump meat and tongue. Stuart also described exhausting the party's tobacco supply, "but in commemoration of the new year we cut up as a substitute and smoked Mr. Miller's Tobacco Pouch."

They completed their cabin on January 6, dug their fire pit, laid in the meat as they had six weeks before, and felled two trees to hollow for a trip down the river in the spring.

The two months they spent in their cabin passed uneventfully. They were troglodytes but they had plenty to eat, plenty of work, and no Indian visitors.

3

On March 8, with the river running free of ice, the Astorians launched their rough canoes. Two men were left behind to follow the Platte bank with the packhorse while the canoe experiment got underway. After only a few miles of labored travel it became clear that boat travel, at least on this segment of the Platte, was impossible. The river ran so shallow, was laced with so many sandbars, sinuous, sandy channels, fallen trees, "sawyers," and boulders that the canoes had to be dragged downstream as often as floated. They were soon given up and after a camp to wait out a sudden reversal of weather—a terrible wind that froze any foot progress—the party resumed its march on the twentieth, following the river as it wound a mile wide and knee-deep east by northeast across the undulant prairie. The nights remained bitter and they shivered at their bivouac fires, but buffalo, wild geese, ducks, and grouse abounded. The flatlands, sparse of trees even at the riverbanks, grew rich in grass and the lovable horse fattened on it. The grass was of a variety the Hunt veterans recognized as being native to a region close to the bottoms of the Missouri. As well, some of the driftwood gathered for their fires bore ax marks, another tantalizing clue that they were nearing the white man's habitat. "Thus they went on," Irving wrote, "like sailors at sea, who perceive in every floating weed and wandering bird, harbingers of the wished-for land."

Toward the end of March they passed through three deserted hunting camps, Pawnee or Oto, it was guessed, littered with buffalo skulls, bones, and forlorn, hide-denuded tepee poles. A day or two later they discovered a hut in the midst of another Indian camp in which three old women were waiting to die. "It is a common practice with the Pawnees, and probably with other roving tribes," Irving said, "when departing on a distant expedition, which will not admit any encumbrance or delay, to leave their aged and infirm with a supply of provisions sufficient for a temporary subsistence. When this is exhausted, they must perish."

Stuart made gifts of buffalo meat to the women, but they were so terror-stricken at the sight of the white men that no information could be gleaned from them, and they had to continue overland another day before coming upon the first landmark that gave them their bearings. This was an enormous island on the Wood River near its junction with the Platte, its features recognized by the Hunt veterans as a mere 150 miles from the Missouri. Soon after this comforting sighting, the Astorians encountered a solitary Oto hunter on the riverbank and the man greeted them warmly and escorted them to his Platte-side village. There they found two white men, the first they had seen since plunging into the wilderness nearly ten months past. The men, François Derouin and Jean Baptiste Antoine Roi, were trappers and Indian traders out of Saint Louis and they were brimming with news and had an audience voracious for it. From the traders Stuart and the others learned of the war with Britain, now a year old and begun before they had pushed off the banks of the Columbia to begin their wilderness sepulture.

Stuart struck a bargain with Derouin. He provided a sound canoe in exchange for their venerable and much-loved packhorse and after a few days of convivial information exchange, the Astorians set out on April 16 for the penultimate fragment of their march.

The Indian-constructed canoe, actually a canoe-shaped bull-boat, was a godsend: Twenty feet long, four wide, and eighteen inches deep, it was a sturdy vessel with a willow frame covered by sewn and stretched elk and buffalo hides, the seams caulked with "unctuous mud." They paddled it effortlessly down the Platte thirty miles from the Oto camp to reach the swiftly flowing Missouri, then were borne along briskly another hundred miles where they beached at an old trappers' camp. There they found a larger, wood-and-bark

canoe, transferred their gear and provisions into it, and
rode the river another fifty miles to a bend and a glorious
scene on the south bank: the ramparts of Fort Osage. There
Wilson Hunt and his eight companions had been cordially
received before their return to their winter camp on the
Nodaway River.

Lieutenant John Brownson was still in charge of the post
and was delighted to welcome the ragged Astorians and treat
them to a meal including pork and bread, the first they had
tasted since leaving the Columbia.

They set out again on the twenty-seventh in good spirits
and with "a sufficiency of Pork & flour," compliments of Fort
Osage. At just before sunset on April 30, Stuart wrote, "we
reached the Town of St. Louis all in the most perfect health
after a voyage of ten months from Astoria during which time
we underwent many dangers, hardships, & fatigues, in short
I may say, all the privations human nature is capable of."

He calculated that the journey covered 3,768 miles counting all the numerous detours and wanderings, and estimated that he and his men had encountered thirty Indian
tribes, bands, and hunting parties, including Cathlamet, Chinook, Walla Walla, Clatsop, Absaroka, Arapaho, Pawnee,
Ponca, Oto, and Shoshoni.

Stuart spent three weeks in Saint Louis before embarking
for New York for an audience with Mr. Astor, but except for
the details of his overland adventure he had no news not already known to his employer. The war with England had
begun on June 19, 1812, ten days before he and his party
embarked on their mission, and by journey's end Fort Astoria was an isolated American enclave in the midst of the
enemy—the North West Company—and was destined to fall
as a casualty of the war. Many months were to pass before
either man learned of it, but as Stuart reached Saint Louis
that spring of 1813, a convoy of Nor'wester canoes was

already headed downriver to begin the takeover of Astor's
Pacific Fur emporium.

The New Yorker had a high regard for the Perthshireman
and had employment for him. Beginning soon after his marriage in New York to Elizabeth Emma Sullivan in July
1813, Stuart became Astor's fur-trade representative in Montreal. In 1817 he joined his overland partner Ramsey Crooks
as a co-agent at the Michilimackinac post, the center of Astor's Great Lakes and Upper Mississippi operations, where
he supervised 200 clerks and 2,000 *voyageurs*. (One of his
employees said he was "one of those Scotchmen who gave
his orders abruptly and expected them obeyed to the letter,
yet a man of a deal of humor and fond of fun.") He held this
post until 1834, when Astor sold his northern fur enterprise
to Crooks and other investors.

The other five members of the Stuart expedition scattered
once they reached Saint Louis.

Robert McClellan, the irascible old Indian fighter, was imprisoned briefly for debt, opened a store in Saint Louis, and
died there after a brief illness on November 22, 1815, at the
age of forty-five. He was buried on the farm of his friend
William Clark.

Benjamin Jones bought land on the Mississippi after he
returned from Astoria but became restless and went to Santa
Fé in 1825 and remained in the Southwest four years. When
he returned to Missouri he settled on a tract of land on Gra-
vois Creek near Wilson Hunt's homestead. Jones died of
cholera in 1835, leaving a wife, five children, fourteen slaves,
fifty-four books, and considerable property.

There is no record of the lives of former army lieutenant
Joseph Miller of Baltimore, and the two *engagés,* François
LeClairc and André Vallé, after they reached Saint Louis.

In 1856, three years before his death in New York at age
seventy-two, Ramsey Crooks took exception to certain newspaper stories lauding the western explorations of John
Charles Frémont, then the Republican Party presidential

candidate. Crooks was particularly disturbed by claims (which Frémont himself did not make) that the explorer-politician had "discovered" South Pass. In a letter to a friend that was subsequently published in the *Detroit Free Press,* Crooks wrote that "even if the Colonel *had* discovered the 'South Pass,' it does not show any more fitness for the exalted station he covets than the numerous beaver hunters and traders who passed and repassed through the noted place full twenty years before Col. Frémont had attained a legal right to vote." These men, he said, "were fully his equals in enterprise, energy, and indomitable perseverance, with this somewhat important difference, that he was backed by the United States Treasury, while other explorers had to rely on their own resources." He stated, as if to make a formal record of it, that he was among the seven men "who left Astoria toward the end of June, 1812, crossed the main chain of the Rocky Mountains, and through the celebrated 'South Pass' . . . reaching St. Louis the following April."

In a splendid stew of metaphors, the *Free Press* editor preceded Crooks' letter with his own comments, saying that the letter "quite dissipates the halo of glory sought to be woven around Col. Frémont's brow as the alleged discoverer of the 'South Pass,' and plucks the stolen plume with which his supporters have adorned him."

Robert Stuart lived to witness the Great Migration to Oregon and California along the trail he helped blaze and over South Pass, which he and his little expedition stumbled upon on October 21, 1812. After retiring from Astor's service he purchased land in Detroit and built a home, became an elder in the Presbyterian Church, a bank director, state treasurer of Michigan, and the United States superintendent of Indian affairs for Michigan.

He died in Detroit on October 29, 1848, leaving an estate valued at over $78,000, and upon his death, his widow, Elizabeth Sullivan Stuart, wrote in his Bible, "He leaveth the incense of a good name."

4

When the news reached him in New York of the fate of his beloved fort on the Columbia, Astor said, "Had our place and our property been fairly captured, I should have preferred it; I should not feel as if I were disgraced . . . . The very idea is like a dagger in my heart."

His dream of empire ended with a financial loss estimated at $150,000* and while at first he blamed the war for the failure of Pacific Fur, he later adopted the idea that he had been betrayed by certain of his partners, chief among them Duncan McDougall, who had, Washington Irving said, received the Nor'westers "with uncalled for hospitality, as though they were friends and allies," and supplied them with stores from the fort. In Astor's view, were it not for McDougall's largesse, Donald McTavish and his North West Company minions would have been starved off for want of provisions, or driven off by the Chinooks "who only wanted a signal from the factory to treat them as intruders and enemies."

In 1823, at the request of John Quincy Adams, then secretary of state in the James Monroe administration, Astor gave an account of his lamented enterprise and of the sale of Fort Astoria. Of McDougall he wrote, "From the price obtained for the goods, etc., and he himself having become interested in the purchase, and made a partner in the North West Company, some idea may be formed of this man's correctness of dealings." Another view was held by Alexander Ross, one of the Scotch partners who had sailed

---

*And the lives of sixty-one men, according to Alexander Ross, who listed eight men lost "on the bar" of the Columbia, five in Hunt's overland expedition, twenty-seven on the *Tonquin,* eight on the *Lark,* and another thirteen in miscellaneous mishaps between Astoria and the Snake River country.

to Oregon on the *Tonquin*. He maintained that "M'Dougall
had been with the nabobs of the North West before, and did
not leave them without tasting of the bitter cup of disappointment; he could, therefore, have had no predilection
in their favour." On the other hand, Ross also had transferred *his* allegiance back to the Nor'westers after the sale of
Astoria.

The loss of his investment meant less to Astor than the
loss of his dream, and he drew little comfort in viewing the
establishment of Astoria as strengthening American claims
to the Oregon Country. He wrote to Wilson Hunt that his
spirit had been "aroused" by the conduct of the North West
Company. "After their treatment of me," he said, "I have no
idea of remaining quiet and idle." In fact, he said, he was
determined to resume his Pacific enterprise upon the end of
the war with Britain.

In the summer of 1814, that opportunity seemed in the
offing with the news that Adams, Henry Clay, and other
American commissioners were conferring with their British
counterparts in the Flemish town of Ghent to reach a peace
accord. Five months passed before the document emerged
that ended the war, and not until February 11, 1815, did details of the agreement reach New York. Of principal interest to Astor was the provision of *status quo ante bellum*
under which all pre-war territorial claims were restored.
This meant that Fort Astoria and the adjacent Columbia
River lands were once again American property. Moreover,
in the winter of 1815, Congress passed a law prohibiting all
traffic of British traders within the United States' claims.

But all this diplomatic and legal paper lay 3,000 miles
from the Columbia, where the facts were quite different. The
withdrawal of the Astorians had left the Pacific Northwest
in the hands of the well-armed and belligerent agents of the
North West Company who were already engaged in a trade
war with the Hudson's Bay Company, and to dispossess them
would require more than a cadre of Scotch partners, clerks,

and *voyageurs*. Astor above all was aware of this and made an "informal overture" to President James Madison, through his Treasury Secretary Albert Gallatin, offering to renew his Oregon enterprise and reestablish Fort Astoria providing it would be militarily protected by the American flag. He estimated that the force required for its protection "would not exceed a lieutenant's command."

Gallatin approved the idea and recommended it to the president, but Madison chose not to respond to it. Said Irving, "Discouraged by this supineness on the part of the government, Mr. Astor did not think fit to renew his overtures in a more formal manner, and the favorable moment for the re-occupation of Astoria was suffered to pass unimproved."

The failure of Astor's scheme, Irving said, was ascribable to a series of "cross purposes, disasterous to the establishment." These included the loss of the *Tonquin* ("which clearly would not have happened had Mr. Astor's earnest injunctions with regard to the natives been attended to"); Wilson Hunt's long detainment in the Sandwich Islands, during which Astoria was sold to the Nor'westers; the loss of the supply ship *Lark* off the island of Maui; the War of 1812, which "multiplied the hazards and embarrassments of the enterprise"; and the failure of President Madison to support the idea of a military reoccupation and protection of Astoria.

And so the financier turned his brilliant business mind to more profitable, settled, matters—his fur business in the Upper Mississippi and Great Lakes—and watched discontentedly while certain diplomatic efforts surfaced that affected his late Oregon dream. In 1818 President James Monroe's secretaries of state, Richard Rush and John Quincy Adams, negotiated an agreement with Britain that established the Canadian-American border at the 49th parallel between Lake of the Woods, in the pine forests of northern Minnesota, southern Manitoba and Ontario, and the Rocky Mountains. Both nations claimed the lands west of the

Rockies, the Oregon Country, and since no boundary could be agreed upon, a compromise was reached: That territory was declared "free and open" to both England and the United States, a quasi-solution called "joint occupation." Meantime, Adams sought to pressure Spain to relinquish its claims on lands north of its province of Alta California, this part of the sweeping Adams-Onís Treaty signed in February 1819. In it Spain, weakened by its colonial problems in South America, ceded the Floridas to the United States and defined the western limits of the Louisiana Purchase. The 42nd parallel became the boundary separating northern California from the Oregon Country, to which Spain relinquished its claims.

Two years later Russia gave way. In the late eighteenth and early nineteenth centuries Russian traders had moved south of Alaska and established outposts as far down the Pacific Rim as San Francisco. In 1821 Czar Alexander I rattled a saber by issuing a proclamation prohibiting the ships of foreign nations from coming within 100 miles of the 51st parallel of the North Pacific coast of America. Since this latitude encompassed lands claimed by Britain that were still a subject of dispute with the United States, both nations pressured the czar. As a result, in 1825 Russia disclaimed all territories below the latitude of 54 degrees 40 minutes, a pairing of numbers that would reverberate in years to come.

John Quincy Adams, one of many political figures who viewed the United States and North America as synonymous, saw these developments as leading to a time when "the remainder of the continent should ultimately be ours" and, citing the Monroe Doctrine, considered the entire hemisphere "closed to any new European colonial establishments."

Thus by the mid-1820s, only the old establishments—England and the United States—remained to contest the territory between 42 degrees north and 54 degrees 40 minutes. Britain's claims rested on the Nootka Sound Convention of

1790 and various explorations from the time of Captain James Cook and the establishment of fur-trading posts by its Hudson's Bay Company. The United States had its own declarations: explorations by Robert Gray, discoverer of the Columbia River, and by Lewis and Clark; the acquisition of Spanish claims in the Adams-Onís Treaty; and the fact that Oregon was contiguous to American lands gained in the Louisiana Purchase.

The joint occupancy accord between the vying nations was renewable as long as each signee agreed to renew it. Either signee had the right to renounce it, giving the other a one-year notice.

Twenty years would pass before the "Oregon question" was finally settled.

10

Fort Vancouver

■

"... THE OARS BRIGHT FLASHING LIKE TOLEDO BLADES."

1

George Simpson preferred to travel in a big, white birch-bark *canot du maître*—master's canoe—paddled by six or eight black-bearded *voyageurs,* and at a fur-trade out-station have a bagpiper in full tartan regalia announce his arrival. On such occasions he would wear a tall beaver hat to improve his 5½-foot height, a scarlet-lined black cloak over a buttoned-up, expensively cut frock coat with matching trousers and waistcoat, a boiled white shirt and black cravat. This outfit, severe against the filthy but brightly beaded deerskin shirts, leggings, and moccasins of his oarsmen, was purposeful: He would never be mistaken for a mere trader, factor, or petty bureaucrat but would be instantly recognized as possessor of the impressive and sonorous title of governor of the Northern Department and Columbia River District of the Honourable Hudson's Bay Company.

There were times when Simpson's ostentation had the reverse effect, when onlookers greeting him on the beach at some far-flung Company factory gathered from his show and ceremony, and from his dark raiment and dour visage, that he was precisely what he looked like: a vainglorious politician, or a porer over ledgers, more at home among pallid boardroom colleagues or barricaded behind a tower of paperwork than in the wilderness amongst trappers and traders and bales of beaver furs.

If the "Little Governor," as he was called, gave these impressions when he stepped ashore at Fort George, formerly Fort Astoria, on November 8, 1824, they did not last long. He *was* a politician and ledger man, but in its history of a century and a half the Hudson's Bay Company never had a high-ranking officer to match Simpson's physical vitality. His stature belied a strength and endurance that matched that of any of his *voyageurs,* and he proved it in pushing these woods-wise roughnecks overland from the Company's headquarters at the York Factory on Hudson's Bay to the Pacific. In eighty-four days they crossed Manitoba, Saskatchewan, Alberta, the Rocky Mountains, and the Selkirk range and paddled down to the mouth of the Columbia. The linear distance was about 1,500 miles, but the actual miles traveled, on winding, wandering waterways, in portaging, walking, and climbing, may have been a thousand miles more.

Simpson did not yet have a piper to skirl notice of his coming—that fine touch would be added when he began his inspection tours—but the unheralded occasion of his arrival at Fort George on that crisp winter forenoon had great portent for the future of British-American relations in the Oregon Country. Simpson was only thirty-seven and had risen swiftly in the Company's service since he ventured to Canada from his birthplace of Ross-shire, Scotland. He was a well-knit, broad-chested man with blazing blue eyes, an imposing mode of speech, and an affable manner. He possessed other qualities, including something called "redundant animal spirits," that his superiors adored: He had an educated, orderly mind, a driving ambition, a work ethic that shamed the most tireless of his colleagues, and a penny-pinching profit philosophy. He had, a contemporary said, "the imagination of a Clive," the reference, electrifying to

Englishmen of the era, being to Robert Clive of Plassey, the soldier-founder of the British empire in India. Simpson was regarded as such a pragmatic visionary and was sent to the Pacific Northwest to take advantage of the fall of Astoria and Astor's failure to persuade his government to provide military support for reopening his fort on the Columbia. The governor was to consolidate Fort George's strength and wage a campaign to solidify the Company's fur empire: send trapping brigades east into the Snake River and Rocky Mountain country, north into Canada, and south to Mexican California; prosecute the fur trade vigorously; monopolize it by fending off American trappers venturing across the Rockies; and make a profit for the directors and stockholders in London. He was also authorized to abandon Fort George and build a new trade center on the north bank of the Columbia.

This intimidating mission was made possible by the merger, after thirty-seven years of vicious rivalry, of the North West Company with the Hudson's Bay Company. The Nor'westers had been organized in 1784 specifically to compete for a fur monopoly in Canada and fought—often literally—for trapping rights throughout "Rupert's Land" (named for King Charles II's cousin Prince Rupert, first governor of the Honourable Company), that is, all the lands that drained into Hudson's Bay, 1.5 million square miles of North America. The competition turned brutal in the second decade of the nineteenth century in the Red River country of Manitoba and in what later became northern Minnesota and North Dakota. In these rich trapping grounds the rival companies built well-armed forts, broke up traplines, stole each other's furs, and conducted guerrilla warfare in the rivers and forests around the frontier town of Winnipeg. In this region occurred a particularly destructive episode that sealed the fate of the warring competitors.

In 1811, Thomas Douglas, the Fifth Earl of Selkirk and a major stockholder in the Company, was granted 116,000 square miles of territory in the valley of the Red River. Lord Selkirk intended to set up an agricultural colony in his wind-scoured wilderness and succeeded in attracting his first settlers there in 1812. The titular governor of Selkirk's colony soon alienated the local descendants of *voyageur* fathers and Indian mothers—who were called métis—and the Nor'westers joined in the conflict with these families. The factions engaged in outright battle in 1816, with twenty white settlers killed by the métis at Fort Douglas in the colony. After the failure of Selkirk's struggling domain the Hudson's Bay Company transferred his territory back to their control and in 1820, the year his lordship died, the British colonial secretary launched negotiations for the merger of the adversarial companies.

The result of these negotiations was the issuance in 1821 of a "deed of co-partnership" amalgamating the two companies under the Hudson's Bay Company name and extending the Company's fur-trade hegemony. The area covered was no longer limited to the territory prescribed in the 1670 charter—all the territory draining into Hudson's Bay—but now embraced the entire Canadian west, including the Oregon Country, "Westward of the Stony Mountains."

While the British were thus consolidating in the Pacific Northwest, American influence there seemed waning despite certain ominous stirrings between the fall of Fort Astoria and George Simpson's arrival there in the winter of 1824. These portents, recognized by the politically astute and American-wary governor and his associates, began surfacing in February 1815 with the treaty that ended the Anglo-American war. The nettlesome *status quo ante bellum* stipulation of the Ghent diplomacy and the subsequent agreement between the nations for "free and open access" to and "joint occupancy of" the Oregon Country would eventually have to be confronted.

After Astoria, the Hudson's Bay Company had an almost exclusive Columbia River fur-trade foothold, one that would

endure fifteen years. The Americans, however, had not forgotten the Oregon Country and while the march back began
slowly, it gained momentum every year of those fifteen.

2

A week or so before he set out from York Factory for the
Pacific, Governor Simpson sent ahead his appointee as
chief factor for the Columbia District, John McLoughlin, a
man who needed no beaver hat to tower over his employees
nor London cut of clothes to impress them. He was formidable in stature, physical strength, and endurance, protean
in intellect and temperament, one of those singular men who
seemed born to be a liege lord of some great remote domain.
Through the sheer, blunt force of his presence he left an
impression, not always positive but always indelible, on everyone who came in contact with him. "Once seen, he was
never forgotten," H. H. Bancroft said of him.

Simpson, who would quarrel often with his colleague and
eventually scheme against him, stood in awe of McLoughlin, never quite knowing what to make of the man. On September 26, 1824, the governor and his *voyageurs* caught up
with McLoughlin's Columbia-bound vanguard party near
the Athabaska River north of the future town of Edmonton,
Alberta. At this rendezvous Simpson recorded in his diary
an impression of the man whose character he would recognize, from the beginning of their relationship and over
twenty years to come, as bearing no resemblance to his own.
"He was such a figure as I should not like to meet in a dark
Night in one of the bye lanes in the neighborhood of London," he wrote with an amusing hyperbole that barely hid
his condescension, "dressed in Clothes that had once been
fashionable, but now covered with a thousand patches of different Colors; his beard would do honor to the chin of a
Grizzly Bear, his face and hands evidently Shewing that he

had not lost much time at his Toilette, loaded with arms and his own herculean dimensions forming a *tout ensemble* that would convey a good idea of the highway men of former days."

Bancroft wrote that McLoughlin "was of an altogether different order of humanity from any who had hitherto appeared on these shores. Before or after him, his like was unknown; for he was far above the mercenary fur-trader, or the coarse, illiterate immigrant."

He was born Jean Baptiste McLoughlin in 1784 in the parish of Rivière du Loup, 120 miles down the south shore of the Saint Lawrence from Québec, his father an Irish farmer, his mother a Fraser of the great Scotch clan. In 1803, when he was nineteen and after a period of study with a Québec surgeon, McLoughlin received his certification as a physician and joined the North West Company, rising from post surgeon to chief trader in the Sault Sainte Marie area of Ontario. At some point in his service there he married a Cree Indian woman who bore him a son but died in childbirth.

In Ontario, McLoughlin became acquainted with Alexander McKay, the Nor'wester trader who had accompanied Alexander Mackenzie on his explorations to the Pacific Coast in 1793 and, as one of the original Astor partners, sailed for the Columbia on the *Tonquin* in September 1810. McKay was murdered by Indians at Clayoquot Sound on Vancouver Island the following June and soon after this McLoughlin married McKay's widow, Marguérite Wadin McKay, the half-Cree daughter of a Swiss trader. She was nine years the young physician-trader's senior, had four children fathered by McKay, and would bear another four by her utterly devoted second husband.

At the time he reached Fort George with Governor Simpson in November 1824, McLoughlin was forty years old and, says Bancroft, "as he appeared among his pygmy associates, white or red, there was an almost unearthly grandeur in his presence. Body, mind, and heart were all carved in gigantic proportions." Everything about him did seem majestic. Six and a half feet tall, a full foot taller than Simpson, McLoughlin was lean and tough as a lath, wide-chested, long-limbed, and thick-necked, with a massive head crowned by an unruly mass of shoulder-length white hair, mid-parted and swept back behind his ears. When he shaved the grizzly bear's beard Simpson had noted, he uncovered a squarish, handsome face with a hawk's nose, a wide mouth, and deep-set, palely luminous blue eyes.

From his mane of white hair, Columbia River natives gave him the name White Eagle and in the years ahead he became their personal King George. To others, including the Americans he befriended, the names for him were always regal—"Emperor of the West," and "King of Old Oregon"—befitting the benevolent autocrat of a 670,000-square-mile wilderness realm.

Bancroft, given to few panegyrics in his massive histories, was captivated by the man: "His life should be written by the recording angel and pillared at the crossing of the two chief highways of the universe. Search these shores from Darien to Alaska, and you will find none such . . . . His life though quiet and untrumpeted was full of glory."

Governor Simpson's plans for construction of a new factory on the Columbia River and installing McLoughlin there to run it were elements of a scheme aimed at warding off any American interference in the Hudson's Bay Company's fur monopoly in the Northwest. The new fort would serve as the hub of the Company's commerce in the Oregon Country and from it and other, smaller, posts in the region Simpson intended having his brigades fanning out west to the Rocky Mountains and south to Mexican territory to trap beaver to extinction. The idea was to create a "fur desert" between American lands and the southern approaches to the Columbia

that would discourage American traders and, as a consequence, discourage American emigrants.

To implement this brutal strategy, Simpson selected as his
chief brigade leader for the Columbia district Peter Skene
Ogden, age thirty when he came down from the Spokane
post and joined Simpson and McLoughlin at Fort George in
the winter of 1824.

A contemporary described Ogden as "humorous, honest,
eccentric, law-defying, short, dark and exceedingly tough,"
and it was said that he had "a taste for violence." He was born
in Québec City, the son of a Canadian admiralty court judge,
and ran away from legal studies to join the North West Company as a clerk. He was a prodigious, ambitious worker and
by age twenty-four, after commanding a fur post at Lake
Athabasca, he earned a transfer to the Columbia, which in
1818 was the remotest of the Nor'wester's many remote fur
interests. There, in two years' time, he had led trapping parties from Fort George to Puget Sound and all the waterways
of the Columbia and was promoted to brigade leader. He had
a single black mark on his record, a time when his meteoric
career plummeted to earth. In 1821 Ogden was among the
most outspoken opponents of the merger of the North West
Company with Hudson's Bay and proved such an irritant that
his name was excluded from the list of Nor'westers to be retained in service. During this period of unemployment he
traveled to London to appeal to Hudson's Bay officials and
apparently made a good impression on the Company sirs and
lords. They saw the value of his experience in the raw Columbia River country, as did the new governor of the district, George Simpson, who reinstated Ogden as clerk of the
first class and brigade leader at the Columbia factory.

Ogden's return to the Oregon Country did not begin aus-
piciously. From his headquarters at the Spokane fort he
followed Simpson's orders to begin the campaign to "trap
out" the competition by sending a brigade east into the

Snake River beaver streams. The leader of this expedition
was Alexander Ross, one of the former Nor'westers who
had come to the Columbia on the *Tonquin*. He was a capable
administrator but proved overcautious in Blackfeet territory and returned with an unsatisfactory cache of furs.
Simpson was not happy at the outcome of this first foray
and wrote Ogden: "The Snake River Expedition has hitherto been considered a forlorn hope [a British army term for
a suicidal mission], the management of it the most hazardous and disagreeable office in the Indian country . . . . This
important duty should not be left to a self-sufficient and
empty-headed man like Ross who feels no further interest
therein than that it secures to him a Saly [salary] of £120 p.
Annum and whose reports are so full of bombast and mar-
vellous nonsense that it is impossible to get any information
that can be depended on from him."

A month after he arrived at Fort George, Simpson fixed
the problem: He saw in Ogden a man who could best serve
the Company on the trail, Ross best in a clerkly capacity, and
so appointed Ogden to command the Snake River brigades
and Ross to take over Ogden's duties at the Spokane post.

In his first expedition east, Ogden set out in December
1824 with a heavy brigade of over 70 trappers, each with five
heavy, iron-jawed and chained traps, plus 372 horses, 80
guns, and an unwieldy party of camp followers—wives and
children of the trappers, clerks, and interpreters. He also had
seven Americans in his company who had returned with
Ross to Spokane after being separated on the Green River
from a band of traders organized by William Henry Ashley.
Among the seven was a twenty-five-year-old New Yorker,
Jedediah Smith, a name soon to be familiar to Hudson's Bay
authorities in Oregon.

This cumbersome company miraculously crossed the
Continental Divide to the headwaters of the Missouri, doing so in the dead of winter without serious incident. Near

the Three Forks of the Missouri they found a region rich in beaver and buffalo but one also haunted by Blackfeet and the clear realization that they were trespassers in American territory. Ogden led them west again and they spent much of the winter trapping, hunting, and camping on Salmon River streams and byways in Idaho and, in April 1825, on the Salmon's juncture with the Snake. The fur hunt that month was "tolerable," Ogden scrawled in his journal, but of "short duration"; the principal hindrance, as it had been with Ross and countless other expeditions, was again the Blackfeet. (The enmity of these natives began, some said, after two Piegans—a Blackfeet band—were killed by Meriwether Lewis and his men on their return journey from the Columbia in 1806.) A small band of these nomadic buffalo hunters killed and scalped one of Ogden's trappers and caused "unrest" among the others; this event was followed by an encounter with Americans that came close to a territorial battle and the near ruination of his first expedition.

In May Ogden led his party southward along the foothills of the Wasatch Mountains of Utah to the Bear River and a point where, Ogden noted, it "discharged into a large Lake of 100 miles in length." (The Great Salt Lake had first been seen by white men only the year before, by the twenty-year-old Virginian James Bridger and his trapping party.) The Bear River and its streams and feeders swarmed with beaver, so many that Ogden's men dressed 600 skins in under two weeks—then lost them.

This disaster began on May 25, 1825, while Ogden's party camped on the Weber River, east of the Salt Lake. He was working on papers in his command tent when he was paid an unfriendly visit by an American named Johnson Gardner who coolly informed the brigade leader that Hudson's Bay men had no business on United States soil and said they must "return from whence they came without delay." Ogden left no record of his reaction to this abrupt command, but it can be assumed that he greeted it with less diplomacy than he reported.* He informed Gardner that he and his brigade were on lands "jointly owned" by Britain and the United States and that therefore he was no trespasser. The American was adamant, ordering Ogden to collect his men and depart, Ogden countering that only upon receiving orders from his government would he do so.

During this edgy colloquy Ogden's trappers were mixing with Gardner's and were being educated on the difference between "free" trapping and working for the Company: The Americans were being paid significantly more for their furs than the British paid. This lesson learned, twenty-three of Ogden's men decamped to Gardner's side and took with them 600 beaver skins—most of the catch to date.

With his brigade depleted by a third, Ogden took his remaining men north and west before he lost more of them. By the time he brought the remnant into Fort Nez Percé in November he had only 400 furs on his packhorses, a trifling number for an expedition so well manned and mounted.

No one was more furious over the outcome of his first Snake River expedition than Ogden, nor more unwilling to admit to failure. He rested twelve days before starting out again, this time with a compact company of thirty-seven seasoned *engagés* and "freemen" (trappers contracted for a single season). The demi-brigade struck out across the Blue Mountains to the Snake in November and by the end of March 1826 had 1,000 furs, and 3,800 by the time it returned to Fort Vancouver in July.

"M'sieu Pete," as his men called him, led four other trapping-exploring parties through 1830 searching out new fur territories for the Company. In 1826 he marched south from Fort Nez Percé to Klamath Lake, just above the border of Mexican California; in 1828 he returned to Utah, ex-

---

*Nor did Gardner make a record of the encounter. Nothing is known about him except that in 1831 he was killed by Arikaras on the Yellowstone River.

plored the northern shores of the Great Salt Lake, and upon his return became the first white man to trace the Humboldt River (then variously called the Mary's, the Unknown, the Swampy, and Ogden's River) to its sink in northern Nevada and to put to rest the long-standing notion of the "Bonaventura River," a mythical waterway believed to flow from the Salt Lake to the Pacific.

On his sixth and final expedition in 1829, Ogden led a brigade south out of Fort Vancouver through the Great Basin to the Colorado River and down through Mexican territory to the Gulf of California, fighting one pitched battle with Mojave Indians en route. He returned up the length of the San Joaquin and Sacramento valleys of Alta California, having heard stories of the trapping opportunities in the region spun by Jedediah Smith, who came through them in 1828. Another informant was a Tennesseean named Ewing Young, whom Ogden met near Yerba Buena, the town subsequently named San Francisco, who was on his way to the Oregon Country.

Ogden went on to serve the Company in British Columbia and in the fastnesses of the Canadian Northwest Territories, but as a factor rather than an explorer-trapper. That life, he said, "makes a man sixty in a few years," and he managed to live only four years beyond that age. It is said that he "mellowed with age," developing a certain tact and charm that were not noticeable in his early years with Hudson's Bay brigades.

3

As Ogden's first brigade worked its way toward the beaver streams of the Snake, Governor George Simpson and Chief Factor John McLoughlin were supervising the construction of Fort Vancouver on Belle Vue Point, ninety miles southeast of Fort George on the north bank of the Co-

lumbia near the mouth of the Willamette River. The new
"grand mart and rendezvous for the Company's trade and
servants on the Pacific" lay in territory claimed by both the
United States and Britain. It was trapezoidal-shaped, 750 by
450 feet in size, surrounded by hewn-log palisades twenty
feet high with a bastion at its northeast corner armed with
twelve-pounder cannons. There were several eighteen-
pounders inside the compound as well, and the massive log
gates of the main stockade were manned by armed sentries.

All of Fort George's supplies, furniture, furs, and men
were ferried upriver early in 1825, and the new fort was officially opened and christened with a bottle of rum on March
19 by Governor Simpson. He paid honor to its namesake,
explorer George Vancouver (who died in 1798) and claimed
the site "on behalf of the Honorable Hudson's Bay Company
and King George IV." After the ceremonies Simpson departed for York Factory headquarters and left Fort Vancouver in his chief factor's charge.

Over the twenty years that McLoughlin had its command,
the fort would evolve into a true "nerve center of British
trade west of the Rockies," eventually housing a bakery, a
chemist's shop (pharmacy), warehouses and fur stores; workshops for mechanics, carpenters, blacksmiths, coopers, tanners, tinners, and wheelwrights; houses for officers and
their families; a chapel, a schoolhouse, a powder magazine of brick and stone, and a governor's house with dining hall and public sitting room. This "veritable hive of
industry" was surrounded by saw- and gristmills, orchards,
gardens, cultivated fields—cleared by idle trappers in summer
months—which eventually produced wheat, oats, peas,
corn, barley, buckwheat, and potatoes, and maintained
herds of cattle and horses from California, sheep from Canada, and hogs from the Sandwich Islands. When Lieutenant
Charles Wilkes, the American naval explorer, visited Fort
Vancouver at the peak of McLoughlin's stewardship, the
officer remarked on the industriousness of this "large

manufacturing, agricultural, and commercial depot," and said he found "few, if any idlers, except the sick. Everybody seems to be in a hurry, whilst there appears to be no reason for it." He and many others before and after him recalled the big fort bell calling cooks, teachers, and shop and field hands to work, calling people to church and school, heralding the arrival of Company boats and ships and, like a bo'sun's pipe, welcoming visiting Company dignitaries aboard Fort Vancouver.

The fort gates were thrown open in the summer months to receive the trappers with the year's fur harvest, their boat-songs heard two miles from the fort. The canoes and *bateaux*—some of the latter pine-constructed, thirty-two feet long, and seven feet amidships—each bearing the Company's crest and *Pro Pelle Cutem* motto, came down-stream, "the oars bright flashing like Toledo blades" Bancroft said. The big boats, carrying fifteen or twenty tons of furs, swept down the current in perfect order amidst the shouting and cheering from the shore and the clanging of the fort's big bell. The *voyageurs*, "in gala dress, ribbons fluttering from Canadian caps and deerskin suits orna-mented with beads and fringes," contracted trappers, and brigade leaders came ashore where the big Union Jack flut-tered in the breeze above the fort's ramparts. There they off-loaded their cargos and filed into the huge dining hall where Kanaka (Sandwich Islander) cooks and servers laid out steaming platters of meat and bread.

McLoughlin rose before dawn and did not quit his work-day until after dark. He supervised all trapping operations at the Company's headquarters, which annually shipped out furs valued at $150,000, and managed all the fort's subsidiary businesses: selling smoked meat and salmon, lumber, hard-ware, vegetables, and grains to the Sandwich Islands, Rus-sian Alaska, China, and even England. He was also responsible for opening new trade centers in the Columbia Department: Fort Walla Walla (also known as Fort Nez

Percé) north of the Umatilla River, Forts Okanogan and
Colville in British Columbia, Forts Boisé and Hall in the
Snake River country, and even a post at Yerba Buena in
Mexican California. He once described his territorial responsibility as running "from San Francisco . . . to Latitude Fifty-Four North [Russian Alaska] and the Interior as
bounded by the Rocky Mountains."

The factor and his family had a fine nine-room white
home at Fort Vancouver surrounded by grapevine trellises
and with an outbuilding for laundry and cooking. He became
famous for his hospitality at the "Big House" and at the fort's
great dining hall, where dinner was always a dignified social affair, the men and their ladies in their best finery and
military visitors in full uniform ablaze with medals and orders. Sumptuous meals were served during which McLoughlin relaxed his own abstemiousness, permitting wine to be
served (but no liquors) and even taking a glass himself while
he led the after-dinner talk. There were mariner's tales of
beating around Cape Horn and circumnavigating the globe,
of battles and travels in exotic lands, and of wilderness
adventures where fights with savages contended with the
catastrophic whims of Mother Nature. McLoughlin loved
books and talked about them, and spoke as well of his studies in botany and anthropology and other natural sciences.

During these memorable times glasses were filled and
pipes were lit. McLoughlin, who did not smoke, did allow
himself a pinch of snuff now and then and shared his snuff-
box with his guests. One who shared one of these banquets
with him recalled, "The doctor at the head of the table suddenly pulled the bell-tassel. 'Bruce!' and in a few minutes
Bruce would be on hand with an open mull, from which a
pinch would be taken, without a word on either side." (The
fort did stock and sell tobacco, most of it from Brazil, which
was twisted into a cord an inch in diameter, coiled, and
sold by the foot. American settlers in the area called it
"trail-rope.")

Marguérite McLoughlin shared her husband's love for
these social occasions and always appeared at the table resplendent in her scarlet shawl, blue broadcloth petticoat,
beaded and quilled leggings, and mocassins decorated with
tiny bells, her hat trimmed in gay ribbons. Bancroft said "she
presented a picture, if not as elegant as that of a lady of the
sixteenth century at a hawking party, yet quite as striking
and brilliant." And another favorite at the table was Eloisa,
the McLoughlins' only daughter residing at the Big House,
who often joined her father on his inspections. Many kept a
fond image of her: a tall, pretty blond girl on a beautiful tan
mare riding alongside her hulking father in his dark blue
cloak, their manes, white and blond, flowing in the wind.

Yankee trade ships continued to come to the Oregon
coast periodically after the abandonment of Astoria, and
an occasional Yankee trapper appeared out of nowhere to
find succor at Fort Vancouver. The New Yorker, Jedediah
Smith, for example, stumbled into the fort in the summer of
1827, his trapping party having been massacred by Indians
on the Umpqua River, his furs and horses stolen.

Americans supposedly "shared" the riches of the Oregon
Country under the 1827 joint occupancy agreement, but the
Company gave no sign that they were pleased with the arrangement and forbade all but rudimentary assistance to the
Americans who wandered into their Columbia River domain. McLoughlin was realistic, perhaps even fatalistic, on
the subject, but he was also of a practical mind. As chief
factor for the Hudson's Bay fur enterprise in the Oregon
Country, his responsibility lay in protecting that interest,
widening it, and making a profit. Even though he built Company forts to the south on the Umpqua and, with Mexican
sanction, even at Yerba Buena, and Fort Walla Walla and Fort
Hall to the east, he became convinced that the future of the
Company's business lay north of the river. Thus, while he

saw the American push toward Oregon as inevitable—they would come, to trap and trade, to preach and teach among the Indians, to settle and to farm—he would shrewdly point the settlers toward the Willamette Valley south of the Columbia, and the missionaries to the east.

In truth, the Americans vexed him: He liked most he met, treated them hospitably, helped those in need, and in return, too often, they showed no gratitude.

11

....

Captain Smith

■

1

In January 1822, Jedediah Strong Smith of Jericho, New York, landed in Saint Louis with a few coins in his pocket and everything he owned on his back. His treasured possessions were the two books that inspired him: the Bible and the heavy 1814 edition of the Lewis and Clark journals.

He had come to the Gateway to the West aimlessly, but he seemed to be have been making his way there from childhood.

Jedediah was the fourth of eleven children of Sally Strong, who was from a pioneering Massachusetts family, and Jedediah Smith, Sr., of New Hampshire, and was born on January 6, 1799, in the Susquehanna valley of southern New York. His and his father's given name had significance among strict Methodist farm folk: In Samuel II of the Old Testament, Solomon, the second son of David and Bathsheba, who would become the last king of Israel, was called at birth Jedediah, "beloved of the Lord."

The Smiths moved to Erie County in northwestern Pennsylvania in the early 1800s, and at about the age of twelve the boy was taken under the tutorial wing of a local physician and received a good frontier education.

In 1812 the family occupied farmland on the southern shore of Lake Erie, and Jedediah, now a gangly, God-fearing lad of thirteen, found work as a clerk on a Lake Erie freighter. In this period his mentor introduced him to the newly published journals of the Lewis and Clark expedition, and he pored over this book almost as assiduously as he read his Scriptures.

His movements between 1814 and 1822 are uncertain. The Smith family had permanently settled in the farm country of the Western Reserve of Ohio by 1817, and Jedediah apparently continued to work on Lake Erie while hinting to his family of his ambition to travel somewhere west and become a geographer. Sometime in the spring of 1821 he made his way to Illinois, spent the winter near the Rock Spring rapids of the Mississippi, and after the New Year crossed the river.

His appearance in Saint Louis, population about 5,000, was weirdly propitious for a yearner to walk the wilderness steps of Meriwether Lewis and William Clark. He scarcely had time to find cheap lodgings in the teeming town when he read a notice in the *Missouri Gazette & Public Advertiser* that seemed to have been written with Jedediah Smith in mind:

TO
Enterprising Young Men

The subscriber wishes to engage ONE HUNDRED MEN, to ascend the river Missouri to its source, there to be employed for one, two, or three years. For particulars enquire of Maj. Andrew Henry, near the Lead Mines, in the county of Washington, (who will ascend with, and command the party) or to the subscriber at St. Louis.

The subscriber was William Henry Ashley, a forty-four-year-old Virginian who had migrated to Missouri in 1802 and become a mine operator, a colonel in the War of 1812, and a brigadier general of militia. His hasty life knew few disappointments and many triumphs, the latest his election as lieutenant governor of the new, twenty-fourth, state of Missouri.

Smith, at age twenty-three a rangy six-footer with soft blue eyes and a self-possessed, somewhat pious manner, found his way to the entrepreneur's busy office. "I called on Gen'l Ashley to make an engagement to go with him as a hunter," he later wrote of the encounter. "I found no difficulty in making a bargain on as good terms as I had reason to expect."

Smith and the other men recruited as "hunters," a varied, scruffy lot, a good many of them Saint Louis waterfront toughs and sweepings from the taverns and mean alleys of the town, were to be paid $200 per annum to trap beaver in the Rocky Mountains.

Manuel Lisa, the man Wilson Hunt met on the Missouri River in 1811 and challenged to a duel, had led the first organized American trapping party up the Missouri River in 1807, and mounted thirteen expeditions between that year and his death, in his forty-seventh year, in August 1820. His brigades ranged as far upriver as the merging of the Yellowstone and Big Horn Rivers, and his Missouri Fur Company trappers, while few in number, had scattered along the rivers, making peace and trade with the Mandans, Assiniboines, and Arikaras (but not the Blackfeet) and building forts in their territories. One of Lisa's partners in the Missouri Fur Company was Andrew Henry, a Pennsylvanian who served as Lisa's field captain and took his trappers as far afield as the Snake River in the Idaho wilderness. The fort he built on a bend of the Snake had been useful to both Wilson Hunt's and Robert Stuart's Astorians in their journeys out to the Columbia and back to Saint Louis.

Andrew Henry and William Ashley were neighbors,

veterans of the late war with England, comrades in the Missouri militia, and after Lisa's death they pooled their money to invest in the Missouri beaver trade. Ashley began with the recruiting effort, hoping to engage 100 men for an expedition to the Upper Missouri country that would depart from Saint Louis in the fall.

The *Missouri Gazette* notice turned up a good number of likely men—some of them more likely than either organizer could realize. Among the first of the Ashley-Henry contingent were Jedediah Smith, James Bridger, and Thomas Fitzpatrick, who would have consequential connections with the Oregon Country.

The Ashley-Henry plan borrowed and modified Hudson's Bay Company tactics. The partners intended to move a trapping brigade into beaver country, build a fort, and stock it with goods that would attract the native trade. Ideally the Indians would do most of the trapping and exchange their catches for such inexpensive commodities as gunpowder, scarlet cloth, traps, alcohol (illegal in the Indian trade but much in demand), vermillion powder, knives, tobacco, beads, mirrors, and the like. The hunters were at first salaried but later contracted for a season's hunt, emulating and improving on a system devised by Donald Mackenzie, the former Astorian who had traveled overland to the Pacific with Wilson Hunt in 1811. "Perpetual Motion" Mackenzie, in the years before the Nor'westers and Hudson's Bay Company merged, was instrumental in opening up the rich Snake River country to the fur trade and in this work took his brigades into the mountains, supplied them with horses, equipment, and provisions, and arranged to meet them at a prescribed rendezvous in the summer where he would buy their furs.

Ashley and Henry combined their resources to do much the same thing: supply their trappers with a string of packhorses and outfit and provision them for half of the plews they brought back, agreeing to purchase the balance of the furs at the market price. The money paid the "free trappers" would finance them another year in the mountains and another fur catch. And the harder they worked, the farther they journeyed to explore richer beaver streams, the more cash they would earn.

Another Ashley innovation was the "rendezvous," a prescribed place—the Siskadee (later Green) River valley, Bear Lake, the Cache Valley of northern Utah—where the hunters would gather in the summer (off-season for beaver trapping) and meet with the trade wagons out of Saint Louis or Independence. These caravans were loaded with traps, guns, ammunition, knives, tobacco, and liquor, useful to the white as well as the Indian, and "foofuraws"—cheap goods attractive to Indian women, such as mirrors, needles, bells, beads, ribbons, and cloth.

The first rendezvous was held in midsummer 1825 on the Green River in Wyoming, and they continued for fifteen years thereafter. At the peak of the trade, when beaver furs fetched five dollars a pound in Saint Louis, hundreds of mountain men, traders, and Indians at rendezvous held horse races, wrestling contests, duels, and buffalo chases before heading back into the mountains or another year of working their traplines. Called by Bernard De Voto "the mountain man's Christmas, county fair, harvest festival, and crowned-slave carnival of Saturn," the rendezvous came to exemplify the unfettered life of the free trapper, spending his time living off the land and coming down from the mountains for a few summer days of roistering with his comrades. Bancroft called the rendezvous "Olympia, with Dionysius enthroned," "a fair in the wilderness . . . the tournament of the prairies" where "Extravagant and depraved habits were pandered to . . . with whiskey at three dollars a pint, and gunpowder at six, with tobacco at five dollars a pound, and fancy articles at fancy prices." The gathering of moun-

taineers, he wrote, was "as motley in character as it was
numerous, embracing every class and race. The Indian was
represented in all stages, from the degraded, root-eating, naked Bannock, with humble yet cunning mien, to the chival-
rous Nez Percé in gaudy trappings, dashing to and fro on
caparisoned steed . . . . The half-breed was there, the connecting link between Indian and white man, despised by the
one for his blood, admired by the other for his superior intelligence and appearance." The Mexicans, the *voyageurs,*
the free trappers in attendance, he said, were "independent
of all save his horse and rifle."

Nathaniel Wyeth, a New England ice merchant who came
west in 1832 and attended a rendezvous that year, had a less
romanticized view. He took one look at the filthy, loud,
frightening crowd of drunks gnawing buffalo meat around
a roaring fire and pronounced them "a great majority of
scoundrels."

2

In his first year as an Ashley-Henry trapper, Jedediah
Smith distinguished himself in a fight with Arikaras and
disfigured himself in a fight with a bear.

The Ree incident took place on June 1, 1823, when something like 500 Indians battled an Ashley brigade between
two of their Missouri River villages in the Dakotas. Concentrated fusil fire by the Arikaras killed thirteen Ashley men
and wounded another dozen in a quarter-hour before the
Americans could escape in keelboats and canoes.

After reaching the safety of a wooded shore some distance
downriver, the two dead men they had managed to wrestle
aboard the boats were buried and, with sentries posted,
the party bedded down for a few hours of uneasy sleep. At
dawn, Smith volunteered to take a canoe north through the
Arikara pincer to the Yellowstone fort to notify Andrew

Henry of the attack and bring back reinforcements. A French-Canadian boatman accompanied him, and after they departed Ashley had the other dead and wounded loaded on the keelboat *Yellowstone Packet* and dispatched it down to Fort Atkinson on the Nebraska-Iowa border, the administrative center and fur-trade base for the Upper Missouri.

Two months passed before a sufficient punitive force could be gathered for a counterattack on the Rees. From Fort Atkinson, Colonel Henry Leavenworth brought 230 of the Sixth U.S. Infantry in three keelboats and on foot and horseback upriver. Andrew Henry, after receiving the dispatch carried by Jed Smith, left twenty men to protect the Yellowstone fort and took the balance of his force down the Missouri to join Ashley, giving them eighty men between them (forty of Ashley's crew, mostly *voyageurs,* had deserted). The Missouri Fur Company contributed another fifty men led by Joshua Pilcher, who had become president of the company after Manuel Lisa's death, and eventually over 300 Sioux—Yanktons, Tetons, and Hunkpapas, all long-time enemies of the Arikaras—joined the expedition after being promised all the plunder they could gather at the villages.

Leavenworth's force reached Ashley on July 30, and in two days the Sioux and other stragglers arrived to join the "Missouri Legion." The attack on the lower Ree village began on August 9 with Jed Smith, whom Ashley had appointed a captain at the head of a company, in the midst of the fight, but the Sioux volunteers outdistanced all the others, charging impetuously into the village, killing anything that moved, cutting up the dead, and dragging dismembered arms and legs over the ground behind their horses.

After a five-day battle, thirty Arikaras were killed, with but a small number of American casualties. The Indians abandoned both villages during the night of August 13, stealing off into the woods without alerting Leavenworth's pickets. Joshua Pilcher said the only living things found in the

two villages were the aged mother of a Ree chief, forty or
fifty dogs, and a single rooster.

In September 1823, a month after the Arikara fight, Captain Smith led a crew of Ashley-Henry men in a venture
across the plains south of the Yellowstone in search of new
beaver grounds. Among the fourteen men with him were
James Clyman of Fauquier County, Virginia, hired as a
"clerk" by Ashley; Thomas Fitzpatrick of County Cavan,
Ireland, who had trade experience among midwestern Indians before enlisting with Ashley; James Bridger, another
Virginian, son of a surveyor and innkeeper, who came west
in 1818 with his family and apprenticed to a blacksmith in
Saint Louis; and Etienne Provost, a Québec-born trapper
who, on a trade venture to Santa Fé, had been arrested as a
foreign interloper and jailed by Spanish authorities.

After about a month of trapping, Smith had an encounter
with a grizzly west of the Black Hills and in a few desperate seconds of the mauling had his ribs broken and his scalp
torn away at the hairline, exposing the bone of his skull and
leaving his ear hanging loose at the side. Clyman sewed the
scalp and ear back in place and later wrote, "The bear had
taken nearly all his head in his capacious mouth close to his
left eye on one side and close to his right ear on the other
and laid the skull bare to near the crown of the head, leaving a white streak where his teeth had passed. One of the
captains ears was torn from his head out to the outer rim. . . .
Then I put my needle stitching it through and through over
and over, laying the lacerated parts together as nice as I could
with my hands."

Smith recovered after a few painful days in camp, although
he carried the scars from his injury the rest of his life and
thereafter wore his hair long to cover the mutilated ear.

He and his crew worked and wintered on the Wind River
and in the early spring moved on, drifting north, setting their
traps and searching for fresh beaver country. In March 1824
they crossed South Pass, by September reached Hudson's

Bay territory in northwestern Montana, and spent the winter of 1824–25 at the Company's Flathead post just before Peter Ogden arrived to take over the Company's trapping operations there.

They rejoined the other Ashley-Henry men on the Green River in July 1825 for the first of the annual rendezvous. Smith's personal take from the season's hunt was 668 beaver furs, a record catch for a single trapper at the time.

At the end of the rendezvous he had become a partner with Ashley and when the two departed for Saint Louis they took with them nearly 9,000 pounds of furs worth $50,000.

In August 1826 Smith set out from Cache Valley, Utah, heading south of the Great Salt Lake with seventeen trappers. He led his party south to the Sevier River, then on to the Colorado, crossing it into the Black Mountains of northwestern Arizona. Two of his party deserted, half his horses died, and Smith and the fifteen others were starved and nearly out of water when they emerged from the mountains into a broad valley and made their way to a Mojave village where they rested for two weeks. In November they moved on westward across the Mojave Desert and the San Bernardino valley and arrived in the San Gabriel Mission near Los Angeles, completing the first overland crossing of the southwestern route to Alta California.

They were at first welcomed by Mexican authorities but trappers were unknown in California at the time and Smith, who traveled on south to San Diego to meet the governor-general of the province, had difficulty explaining his mission and profession. The governor ended up listing him as a *pescador* (fisherman) and considered imprisoning him in Mexico until they could figure out what he and his ruffian-like crew were up to, coming uninvited to their country. Only the intervention of Captain William H. Cunningham, master of the Boston trade ship *Courier* anchored in the harbor of San Diego, prevented this, but the Mexicans had seen enough of the American *pescadores* and in the spring of 1827 Smith and his men were ordered to leave California.

Captain Cunningham took Smith north to San Pedro Bay, where he was reunited with his fourteen-man trapper party and, equipped with new provisions and horses, retraced his route over the San Bernardino Mountains, fulfilling the governor's orders. But instead of returning to American territory, he led his men north along the Mojave Desert to the southern margin of the San Joaquin River valley, which proved to be rich beaver grounds, and wintered there.

In May, after trapping along the Stanislaus River and amassing a season's haul of 1,500 pounds of furs, Smith and his men tried to cross the Sierra Nevada via the American River but were turned back, losing five horses along the way, by heavy snow in the passes. Leaving his main party behind, Jedediah and two others made a second attempt and succeeded in crossing the range, becoming the first white men to traverse the Sierra Nevada range and adding another record by completing a passage through the Great Salt Desert. Their journey of 600 miles ended in July 1827, in time for the rendezvous at Bear Lake.

After the summer gathering and with a party of eighteen other trappers, Smith headed south, picked up their California trail, and on August 15, 1827, reached the Mojave village on the Colorado. This time they were not welcomed. The Mojaves, tired of being victimized by white hunters who had found them easy marks for theft and abuse, attacked the Americans as they crossed the river and killed ten of them, capturing their horses and supplies. Smith and the eight survivors managed to escape, making their way across the desert on foot.

In mid-September, Smith, who had traveled alone to the San José Mission to buy provisions, was arrested and jailed briefly before posting bond and agreeing, again, to vacate

Mexican territory. As before, he did not leave—his righteousness did not, apparently, apply in keeping his word with Mexican authorities—but rejoined his men and spent the winter of 1827–28 in southern California. The deaths of ten comrades had not dampened their trapping ardor, and the furs gathered in his absence, and those accumulated in the winter season, were sold to a sea captain and the proceeds used to buy 250 horses and mules. Smith and his men planned to sell the animals at a profit at the 1828 rendezvous.

But instead of riding eastward across the Sierra Nevada, the trappers, including new recruits gathered along the way, moved north along the California coast through unmapped country and reached the Klamath River in July 1828. This expedition, the first to travel California south to north into the wilds of Oregon, resulted in the third of Smith's four Indian fights—Arikaras in 1823, Mojaves in '27, and now the Kalawatsets on the Umpqua River.

With two other men, Smith set out by canoe on July 14 to discover a route northward to the Willamette River, and during his absence, about 100 Indians entered the American camp and butchered eighteen trappers. Only one man, Arthur Black, described as a "Scotchman," escaped wounded into the woods and made his way to the coast and north 100 miles to Fort Vancouver. When Smith and his two companions returned to the Umpqua camp on August 10, they were fired upon from the shore and beat a retreat to a high point on the opposite bank, where the deserted camp could be seen in full view. Smith sadly—and correctly—concluded that his men were dead. He had also lost 780 beaver, 50 sea otter, and miscellaneous other skins valued at over $20,000.

With his companion and after much suffering, Smith made his way to Fort Vancouver.

When John McLoughlin heard the story of the Kalawatset ambush from Smith, he took off his spectacles, threw them on the mess-hall table, snatched his cane, and marched to the mess-building porch shouting for his stepson, "Mr.

McKay! Thomas McKay! Tom! where the devil is McKay?"
McKay, a tall, dark-skinned, powerful man of noted courage
who had commanded many trapping parties into Blackfeet
country for the Hudson's Bay Company, at last made his
appearance. According to Bancroft's re-creation of the
moment, McLoughlin quit his angry pacing and said, "Here,
Tom, this American has been robbed, his party massacred.
Take fifty men. Have the horses driven in. Where is La
Framboise, Michel, Baptiste, Jacques; where are all the men?
Take twenty pack-horses; those who have no saddles ride on
blankets; two blankets to each man; go light, take some
salmon, pease, grease, potatoes—now be off, cross the river
tonight; and if there be one of you here at sunset I will tie
him to the twelve-pounder and give him a dozen lashes."

During the bustle of preparations for the punitive raid,
McLoughlin dictated instructions to his clerk and handed
them to McKay at the door. "Take this paper and be off," he
said, clapping his devoted stepson on the back. "Read it on
the way; you'll observe the place is beyond the Umpqua.
Good-by, Thomas; God bless you. Be off! be off!" He later
wrote angrily of the Kalawatsets in his diary, "such barbarians . . . have no horror or compunction of Conscience at de-
priving a fellow Man of Life."

(It appears the expedition was commanded by long-time
Nor'wester and Hudson's Bay Company brigade leader Al-
exander McLeod, who had led a similar raid against Puget
Sound Indians. It is possible that Thomas McKay asked
McLeod, fourteen years his senior, to lead the party, or to
serve as co-commander.*)

---

*However, Oregon historian Horace S. Lyman states, "Thomas McKay
was the military leader of these expeditions, and was naturally disposed to treat the Indians with severity, saying he would revenge his
father (Alexander McKay, killed in the *Tonquin* massacre) upon the
red race—although perhaps expressing more ferocity in his language
than he actually felt, as he is not known to have killed Indians wan-
tonly or without orders."

The expedition set out along the Willamette early in October 1828, with twenty-two *engagés,* fourteen Indians, Jed Smith and his three surviving party members, and a string of packhorses. At the Umpqua River the pitiful remains of the American camp were found. McLeod wrote in his journal of the traps, kettles, shirts, lead pencils, and similar oddments the Indians had left behind, and of the dead found scattered about the camp. It was, he said, "a sad spectacle of Indian barbarity," with "the skeletons of eleven of those Miserable Sufferers lying bleaching in the sun." By the end of the month they returned safely to Fort Vancouver. Twenty-six horses and mules and most of the stolen furs had been recovered without a fight. For the Company's services McLoughlin charged Smith a modest four dollars each for the horses lost during the mission and prorated the *engagés'* time at the rate of sixty dollars per annum. Governor George Simpson, who during the expedition was visiting Fort Vancouver, paid Smith £486.18s.5d. Sterling—$2,369.60 American—for the recaptured furs.

3

A year after the Arikara misadventure the Ashley-Henry partnership dissolved. Andrew Henry, after bringing in a good fur catch to Saint Louis in the fall of 1824, retired to his home in Washington County, Missouri, and died there in 1832. Ashley continued to direct trapping operations on the Upper Missouri for another year, but at the end of the 1826 rendezvous in the Cache Valley he gave his farewell speech and sold out to Jedediah Smith, William Sublette of Kentucky, and David Jackson, an older man said to have fought with Andrew Jackson at the battle of New Orleans in 1814. All three of the new partners had fought in the Ari-

kara battle. Between 1823 and 1827 Ashley is believed to
have brought to Saint Louis 500 bales of beaver furs and
made an average profit of $50,000 for each year. In Saint
Louis he continued for a time to serve as a *bourgeois* (agent
and outfitter, called a "bushway" by mountain men) until reentering politics. He was twice elected to Congress, twice
defeated for the governorship of Missouri, thrice married,
and when he died on March 26, 1838, at age sixty, he left a
substantial estate.

He was, as a contemporary said, "a thoroughly honest and
good-natured man, and to his Yankee shrewdness, with one
eye ever on the main chance, he united thoughtful intelligence engendering independent action."

Hudson's Bay governor George Simpson's plan to fend off
fur trade competition with his Columbia River Department
was something his superiors in the Hudson's Bay Company
must have admired as a model of ruthless simplicity. Trapping beaver to extinction, creating "a fur desert" buffer zone
between American territory and the southern approaches to
the Columbia, would preserve the Oregon Country for the
Company and eliminate Yankee traders and the immigrants
who followed in their tracks.

This scheme, as it happened, was both too ambitious
and too late. By the time Peter Ogden's brigades made
their first forays in Snake River lands to implement the
governor's orders, the detested competition was already in
place. Ogden met Johnson Gardner's trapping crew in
northern Utah in March 1825, and that rude encounter
served notice that no number of Hudson's Bay trappers
could stop the American march. In little more than a generation the Americans, in an unwitting partnership with
the British and with the unforeseen assistance of Chinese
silk merchants, would accomplish what Simpson's people

could not have done alone: create a fur desert vaster than
either competitor ever imagined.

The thirteenth rendezvous, the last memorable one, took
place in the summer of 1837 in the Green River valley, a favored site remembered as the place where a pack of rabid
wolves attacked the trappers' camp in '33, where Kit Carson fought (and won) a duel with a French-Canadian bully
named Shunar in '35, and where that same year a New York
physician-missionary named Marcus Whitman dug an old
Blackfoot arrowhead from Jim Bridger's back. In 1837 fur
profits were down, but 100 trappers congregated to welcome
the American Fur Company's wagon caravan with its cargo
of trade goods and whiskey. Among visitors to the Green
that year were the soldier-hunter-adventurer William Drummond Stewart of Scotland, who had become a familiar figure at rendezvous, usually traveling with Tom Fitzpatrick's
men. This time he brought a guest, Alfred Miller, a Baltimore
artist. Stewart met Miller in New Orleans and commissioned him to produce sketches and paintings of the 1837
hunt and rendezvous to be displayed in Murthly Castle, the
Stewarts' ancestral home in Perthshire. Miller kept busy. Besides the mountain men, the Astor supply train, and its traders, there were hundreds of Indian lodges along the looping
river and throughout the valley, and the largest of the Indian
contingents, the Shoshoni, filled Miller's sketchbooks.

But for all the flashing color and carefree carousing Miller
witnessed, the end was in sight and the last rendezvous, in
1840, produced a sadly low number of trappers, traders,
and Indians; the beaver pelt that fetched five or six dollars
in 1832 was now valued at a dollar. Shiny silk hats were
now the fashion and, fortunately for the beaver, the demand
for its hide was disappearing quicker than its slide toward
extinction.

For the American mountain man, the fur trade had

endured a generation, and at the end its vestiges were confined to a desultory business at Fort Laramie and a scattering of other old posts on the eastern edge of the Rocky Mountains. The old trappers still trapped, but there was no wage in it and they had to turn to other sources of income born of their wilderness skills. They had broken the trails, the Oregon Trail among them, to and across the Rockies, prepared the way for others looking westward. Now they would guide the others.

Jedediah Smith, who had stood above and apart from his comrades from the beginning of the mountain-man era, who had seen more of the western wilderness than any man of his time and filled in more of its blank spaces in his journeys, did not live to see the era end.

After his deadly experience with the Kalawatsets in Oregon in 1828, he rejoined his partners and continued to trap the Upper Missouri and the Yellowstone. In August 1830, seemingly tired of the hardships of life on the trail and stating that he "missed the care of the Christian Church," he sold his trapping interests and, now a man of moderate wealth and but thirty-one years old, returned to Saint Louis in retirement.

But he chafed at inactivity and, within a few months, with his former partners William Sublette and David Jackson pooled funds for a venture in the booming Santa Fé trade. The men bought twenty-four wagons of trade goods and in April 1831 Smith, his old crony Tom Fitzpatrick, and seventy-four men departed Saint Louis bound for New Mexico.

In late May, after several days' travel in the arid country between the Arkansas and Cimarron Rivers, Smith and Fitzpatrick rode ahead of the caravan to find a streambed in which to dig for water. The two men took separate trails and, as later evidence indicated, on May 27, 1831, Smith found a water pocket in an old buffalo wallow in the Cimarron. What

he could not know was that the wallow was closely watched
by a band of Comanches. Legend has it that Smith was able
to get a single shot off from his Hawken rifle, killing the
leader of the Comanche band, before he was overwhelmed
and probably stabbed to death with lances.

His body was never found.

Josiah Gregg, who wrote a book titled *The Commerce of
the Prairies* in 1844 about his experience as a Santa Fé
trader, first set out with a trade caravan in May 1831 from
Missouri to seek relief for his lifelong frail health. On that
journey, a Mexican *cibolero* (buffalo hunter) rode up to his
caravan and brought news that a famous *Americano* had
been killed by Indians on the Cimarron. Later Gregg learned
that the American was the celebrated mountain man and explorer Jedediah Smith, a man who, Gregg said, "would surely
be entitled to one of the most exalted seats in the Olympus
of prairie mythology."

The eulogy that appeared in the *Illinois Monthly Magazine* in 1832 described Smith as "modest, never obtrusive,
charitable, and without guile . . . a man whom none could
approach without respect or know without esteem." Others
spoke in similar terms. Jed Smith was a prototypical Yankee puritan—grim, celibate (his biographer Dale L. Morgan
points out that Smith was never known to have had an interest in women, least of all in taking an Indian wife or mistress
as so many of his trapping cohorts did), high-minded, and
without fear. He was "a bold, outspoken, professing and
consistent Christian," a trapper friend named William Waldo
said.

A modern historian of the mountain men, Win Blevins,
wrote of Smith's "Love of wild places," which "had rooted
into him and become a deeper religion." Blevins says Jed
Smith's "altar was the mountaintop, his place of meditation
not the pew but the wilderness, his sacraments his mountain
skills."

12

Kelley's Odyssey

∎

". . . A GREAT AND CRAZY VISION."

1

In the winter of 1820, while Stephen Harriman Long of the Army Corps of Topographical Engineers was mapping the Great American Desert and describing it as a retardant to westward migration, Congressman John Floyd, M.D., of Virginia, took up the Oregon question. He said England was stealing the Pacific Northwest from America and advocated annexation of it and filling it with settlers.

Dr. Floyd had grown up in Kentucky, and Bancroft wrote that he "understood the character of the Western states," where everyone was "a pioneer of the Alexandrian type, sighing for more worlds to conquer, more wilderness to redeem to civilization by the sheer strength of brawny arm and independent will." The congressman counted among his friends several prominent Astorians and the explorer William Clark. (Floyd's cousin, Charles Floyd, had served as a sergeant in the Lewis and Clark party and died of a ruptured appendix in August 1804, the only casualty of the expedition.) The idea of Oregon inspired the Virginian, and the British presence there as the sole occupant of the "joint occupancy" angered him. "With two oceans washing our shores," he liked to say, presaging the tenets of Manifest

Destiny, "commercial wealth is ours and imagination can hardly conceive the greatness, the grandeur, the power that await us."

On December 19, 1820, Dr. Floyd presented to his colleagues in the House of Representatives a petition for the appointment of a select committee to "inquire into the situation of the settlements upon the Pacific Ocean and the expediency of occupying the Columbia River." The document was adopted and Floyd named chairman of the panel. The committee's report, introduced on January 25, 1821, was praised by Senator Thomas Hart Benton of Missouri, one of the most influential expansionists in Washington, who said that with it "the first blow was struck; public attention was awakened, and the geographical, historical and statistical facts set forth . . . [the report] made a lodgment in the public mind." But the report carried with it a bill, considered overly radical, which authorized the president to occupy "the Origon country," extinguish whatever Indian title to the lands existed, and provide for the establishment of a government there. The measure failed but Floyd reintroduced it in 1822, revised to provide that when the settlement in the region reached a population of 2,000 it should become "the Territory of Origon," and a possession of the United States.

Floyd made an impassioned speech on his bill on December 17, 1822, but it aroused little interest other than a discussion of the northwest coast as a fur and whaling station, a fishery and timberland. Some congressmen dreaded the potential of war with England over the region and wondered whether such remote lands were worth such a danger.

Still, the Virginia legislator did not yield. On January 19, 1824, he presented yet another bill—another revision of the old one—that would authorize occupation of the Columbia River by the United States, establish a military post and a territorial government there, and hold out as an enticement a section of land to each new settler.

The War Department reported that transportation by the

Missouri and Columbia Rivers of sufficient numbers of troops and horses to man a military post in the Pacific Northwest would cost $30,000, and transportation by sea of the heavy baggage, ordnance, and supplies would amount to another $14,000.

The issue was debated and, while no questions were raised on the validity of the American claims to the region, Floyd repeatedly tried to refute claims that mountain barriers made colonization of the Oregon Country impossible, that the lands west of the mountains were "bleak and inhospitable" with "impenetrable forests" and a climate so forbidding as to "preclude cereal crops." Some said that the Columbia was too distant to attract settlers, but Floyd reminded his fellow representatives that in 1775, Kentucky was considered "too far away to be a part of the Union." He found supporters such as Congressman Baylies of Massachusetts (who assailed the "Gentlemen who are talking of natural boundaries" by asserting, "Sirs, the natural boundary is the Pacific Ocean") and others among New England's merchants. These monied men saw the potential for fishing and whaling in North Pacific waters and for a timber industry in the forests stretching from the 42nd parallel to Russian Alaska and inland from the Pacific to the Cascade Range; there were fortunes to be made in pine, spruce, hemlock, fir, and cedar.

On December 23, 1824, after four years of effort and in defiance of such influential opposition as that of Representative John Quincy Adams (who damned the proposal as a "tissue of errors; there was nothing could purify it but fire"), Floyd saw his bill for the occupation of the Columbia River and establishment of the Territory of Oregon pass the House by a vote of 113–57.

In February 1825 the bill arose in the Senate, where it was batted down by Senator Mahlon Dickerson of New Jersey, who contended that the military occupation of Oregon would lead to war with Britain, and that it would never become a state of the Union or accrue to any advantage to the United

States. He said the proposed $50,000 for implementing the bill was a bagatelle, that a sum ten times that amount would actually be needed. He ridiculed the idea of a territorial representative coming to Washington and returning to Oregon via an overland route or around Cape Horn in under a year's travel time. Moreover, he said, in a clear echo of the Long expedition report, the region between Council Bluffs and the Rocky Mountains, which would have to be traversed by the military party and by any settlers venturing to the Oregon Country, was sterile, without wood or water, its mountains inhospitable—fit only as "a retreat for red men."

Floyd's colleagues were clearly not yet ready to share his dream of a Pacific commonwealth and his bill was tabled, consigned to Congress's paperwork perdition. In Bancroft's words, the subject of the occupation of the Columbia "was suffered to lie perdu in the minds of the people of the United States, except as attention was called to it by the writings of Hall J. Kelley, or by some more obscure person."

"In the long story of our nation's westering there are few adventures more curious or difficult to assess," historian David Lavender wrote of Hall J. Kelley's half-century-long Oregon obsession.

"He is neither a great hero nor a great rascal," Bancroft said of Kelley. "He is great at nothing, and is remarkable rather for his lack of strength, and in staggering for fifty years under an idea too big for his brain. He was a born enthusiast and partisan, one of a class of projectors more capable of forming grand schemes than of carrying them to a successful issue."

Bernard De Voto said Kelley was "a man of a great and crazy vision."

Of his contributions to the 300-year journey to the Pacific Northwest Kelley himself said plainly, "The colonization of Oregon was both conceived and achieved by me, and all for the hope of laying a foundation for the advancement of religion and the kingdom of Christ." And the prolix titles of the abundant books and tracts he published (works Bancroft said were "no less voluminous than peculiar") told his faithful armchair adventurer–readers precisely whose single-handed travails and triumphs were responsible for the American presence in the North Pacific littoral. One example: *A History of the Settlement of Oregon and the Interior of Upper California, and of Persecutions and Afflictions of Forty Years' Continuance, Endured by the Author, Hall J. Kelley.*

One hundred and sixty years after he made his mad hegira to the land of his dreams, Hall Jackson Kelley remains the most vexatious character in the story of the Oregon Country. While he annoyed his contemporaries by making too much of his contributions, his contemporaries annoy us by making too little of them. In David Lavender's memorable phrase, Kelley was "cursed with the unfortunate propensity for getting on the nerves of everyone with whom he came in contact"—a propensity that still lingers. He was precisely what his peers said of him: a waspish, humorless, pious, self-aggrandizing, overbearing pest, and a likely lunatic. But even his cruelest critics had to admit he saw things and did things beyond their dreams, and even beyond his own.

Before he clasped to his heart the notion that he had been selected by God to lead a great congregation to the banks of the Columbia, Kelley had other obsessions, among them Christian religion and educating himself and others. Born in New Hampshire in 1789, his family had the resources to see that he received a fine formal education. He earned an undergraduate degree at a Middlebury, Connecticut, college, and a master's degree at Harvard, where he is said to have ruined his eyesight by studying Virgil by moonlight in the Cambridge hills, and he became a surveyor and a proficient teacher of mathematics. Until 1824 he seems to have been content in the worthy, if mundane, life of a Massachusetts grammar-school teacher (during which tenure he may have introduced the first schoolroom slate blackboard), dedicated churchgoer (he is credited with the founding of the first Sunday school in Boston), and active and probably vociferous member of the Boston Young Men's Education Society and the Penitent Female Refuge Society. He had a facility with the pen even in these early years, publishing in 1820 a book on elementary education titled *The American Instructor.*

The precise moment Kelley caught the Oregon fever is not known, but he caught it early, before most people had heard of the place, even before the name "Oregon" caught on. As had Jedediah Smith, Kelley became mesmerized by the Lewis and Clark journals. He studied accounts of Astor's failed venture on the Columbia, collected clippings on the renewal of the joint occupancy agreement with England, and seems to have followed assiduously the debates in Congress over Congressman Floyd's bill. Bancroft states that by 1824, Kelley had given himself over to study of the Columbia River country: "Nor did he cease writing and raving, until at the ripe age of eighty-five he was transferred from his New England hermitage, where after his fruitless excursions he had retired to brood in poverty over the wrongs inflicted by a soulless corporation and an ungrateful republic."

He devoured exploration journals, tracts, pamphlets, newspaper stories, and congressional publications, and pored over the pathetic maps then existing of the lands beyond the Rocky Mountains, most drawn by cartographers who had never been close to them. Slowly accreting in his brain, a plan took shape, "the first thin strands of Manifest Destiny did twine together in his frantic, half-crazed hands," as Lavender wrote. This scheme, devised by a man who never led anybody anywhere, who had traveled out of New England no farther than Washington, was curiously premonitory. He threw himself fanatically into the idea of American settlement of the Oregon Country, envisioning the formation of an emigration society and taking 3,000 New England farmers to the banks of the Columbia River.

After throwing over his teaching duties, Kelley began the work God had assigned him by composing broadsides and making speeches to anyone willing to listen. Churchgoers were inspired by his ardor, as he put it, to "promote the propagation of Christianity in the dark and cruel places about the shores of the Pacific," and it was impossible not to be impressed with his encyclopedic knowledge of these places he had never seen. He made a good appearance: He was handsome, with a squarish, clean-shaven face, high forehead, dark hair cropped short and brushed forward in Napoleonic style, and expressive eyes; he was dignified and well dressed. His screeds and tracts, his voluminous letters to Boston newspapers, and his impassioned speeches gave the impression that he had tramped over all of the dark and cruel places and the sun-dappled and friendly ones of the Oregon Country. He dwelled on the positive, wrote and spoke of the land out there as an Eden, a pristine, fecund region of farmlands so rich they would require "but little labor" to raise grain, vegetables, and cattle; a place teeming with beaver and other precious fur-bearing animals and game of every known species and many unrecorded ones; and a trove of fish and timber beyond mortal calculation. As for getting there, he said, warming to the real heart of his plan, the journey would not be taxing: People would ride comfortably in wagons, and the materials needed to set up a colony would precede them in ships sailing out of Boston Harbor and following the Cape Horn route to the Pacific. Congress would underwrite most of the expenses. Each emigrant might need as little as fifty dollars for incidental expenses on the trail, and perhaps five dollars for each accompanying child.

He gathered money in small donations wherever he spoke and, like citizens of the late twentieth century signing on to colonize a space station, his listeners placed their names on

his petitions as they dreamed of a place as remote then as
the moon, the Eden awaiting them on the lush and friendly
banks of the Columbia.

In 1828, Kelley began petitioning Congress, each paper
submitted carrying new numbers, longer and more ambitious
blueprints for his settlement, and new proposals and bud-
getary requests to carry them out. The original document
he drafted outlined the general Kelley plan and stated that
the undersigned and 3,000 others were prepared to start west
on short notice. A year later, he refined his congressional request, asking that a modest twenty-five square miles of the
Columbia valley be granted him for colonization. He listed
500 members of his American Society for Encouraging the
Settlement of Oregon Territory, and in 1831 incorporated
the group under the laws of Massachusetts. Among his
original members were some influential citizens, such as
the impatient Cambridge ice merchant, Nathaniel Wyeth,
but, as Bancroft summed up the matter, "This society was
Hall J. Kelley. He was the body and brains, the fingers
and tongue of it."

While awaiting favorable response from Washington, Kelley and his society members met in Boston churches and
lecture halls, debated, drew up bylaws, recruited new members, collected funds, and scrapped over the details of
founding a town in Oregon, to be built in New England
style, which would "repeat, with appropriate variations, the
history of the Puritan Colony of Massachusettes Bay."

The thrill of all the meeting, debating, planning, and
petitioning waned early, and Kelley was faced with the inevitable duty of setting a date when the vanguard of the
society membership would actually start west. He had no
congressional commitment but he had some funds, a host of
anxious emigrants-to-be, and a handful of associates willing to join him in taking the first real steps toward the
Pacific.

He appears to have traveled to Saint Louis in 1828,

perhaps alone, or more likely with a few close society advisers, to investigate an overland route to the Columbia. In this mission he failed and returned angrily to Boston with vague threats against the minions of the Hudson's Bay Company and certain American fur traders, who he said had thwarted him. By now he was confident that powerful enemies were arrayed against him, some of them identifiable, others unseen but no less mighty, and all devoted to causing him to fail.

He took comfort in pinning his reverses on them.

2

For another four years there were fits and starts—mostly fits—while Kelley proceeded to make maps, write his copious and strident letters to newspapers, hold society meetings, cadge donations, and besiege the Jacksonian-era Congress for land allotments and official sanction for his scheme. Kelley's plans for an emigrant invasion of the Oregon Country were ever-changing. He seems to have realized that an overland trek to the Columbia River would probably be taxing after all, especially for a Boston congregation for whom a trip to Cape Cod or Poughkeepsie was a long haul, and that the answer was to travel by merchant ship along with the cargo necessary for setting up the colony. Astor had set up his Columbia River enterprise by sending his first agents out there by sea, and American traders had been sailing out of Massachusetts Bay for the Pacific for fifty years. To be sure, the voyage would be tedious, and even occasionally uncomfortable—Cape Horn and all that—but these were minor considerations.

In 1832, by now the nation's chief Oregon boomer, Kelley made a frenetic effort to get his expedition underway. He increased the tempo of his fund-raising—adding to his familiar appeal the idea of taking missionaries with him to work among the Oregon "savages"—and actually chartered a ship as proof that his was no armchair dreamer's scheme, something a good many of his supporters had begun to suspect. But he was arrested that summer, probably for nonpayment of debts, before he and a handful of his faithful could sail. He used the occasion of his brief tussle with the law to rail at his "wicked adversaries," notably the Hudson's Bay Company and Astor's American Fur Company, whose hirelings "watched every movement of mine, pursuing me from city to city, laying every plan to vex and worry me." The falsehoods, calumnies, and "vile sayings" of these shadowy nemeses "panic-struck my followers and turned them back," he said.

The arrest, and the furor he made of it, seems to have revived Kelley's faltering campaign. In some miraculous way he paid his debts and in the winter of 1832 made his way out of Boston to New York. There he found new converts waiting and obtained contributions of cash and credit sufficient to engage a merchant vessel to carry himself and a few of the society elite to New Orleans—where they promptly deserted him.

There are many possible motives behind the exodus of Kelley's people. Thrust in with him in a confined space, they must have grown weary of his nagging, irascible self-absorption. In New Orleans they must have realized at last that only a shore-to-ship gangway separated them from the start of a crack-brained undertaking from which there might be no return. Perhaps the passage to the mouth of the Mississippi wrung from them in its first installment the dream of a pioneering adventure. Very likely, the idea of continuing on, six weeks or more to Rio de Janeiro, another two months via the Horn to Valparaiso, untold months crawling northward along the Pacific coasts of South America and Mexico, Baja and Alta California, in a stinking, wallowing, merchant sailing ship chased them back to their New England comforts.

Under the protection of whatever spiritual force is in charge of lunatics, Kelley was undaunted by the mutineers who fled his ship. He proceeded alone in the spring of 1833 to Vera Cruz, experiencing "incredible hardships," he said vaguely, and overland to the Mexican capital, where he somehow gained an audience with President Antonio López de Santa Anna. At the time of Kelley's visit, this august personage, then newly elected in the first of his five scattered administrations, was facing civil war in his country and unrest among the American settlers in Mexican Texas. While Kelley was permitted to proceed in his journey across Mexico, much of his baggage was seized. Americans were anathema in Mexico, and Kelley no doubt made of himself a particular nuisance. The baggage may have been taken as payment for having to put up with him, the permission to travel given in the belief that he would die en route to the Pacific.

He added Mexico to his list of thwarters and set out across the country, joining a pack train part of the way, traveling alone much of the time. In a month or two (everything is vague about this journey) he struggled into San Bias near the eastern shore of the Gulf of California, presumably made his way north to the Sonoran capital of Hermosillo, thence to Puebla, a town near San Diego in Alta California. What battles he fought against the elements, fever, hunger, thirst, hostile Indians, and Yankee-suspicious Mexicans are not recorded. He may have had a rudimentary command of the Spanish language, but how this vociferous, cantankerous man got across Mexico alive is a question that Kelley, for all his voluminous writings, left unanswered.

In the spring of 1834, in San Diego, Kelley contrived to meet with the governor of Alta California, José Figueroa, perhaps seeking permission to travel upcountry to Monterey, Yerba Buena, and on north. His eyes were trained on the Oregon Country, and he must have assured the governor that he did not intend to remain in the Mexican province.

Permission was granted. He then offered his services to survey the Sacramento River valley and after this strange overture was politely declined, Kelley moved on north to the Los Angeles pueblo, and there had the first of three encounters with an American trapper named Ewing Young. This burly frontiersman had twice before ventured to Alta California on trapping expeditions and had a firsthand knowledge of the country from tramping it from San Diego to Klamath Lake on beaver hunts. At the time Kelley met the man, subsequently so troublesome not only to Kelley but to John McLoughlin and the entire Hudson's Bay enclave at Fort Vancouver, Young was already among the most seasoned of mountain men.

Born about 1792 in the wilderness near Jonesboro, Tennessee, he had training as a carpenter and cabinetmaker but, according to Bancroft, was "a man of fine intelligence and nerve united to a grand physique, and too restless and fond of new experience to remain beside a turning-lathe all his life." He moved to Missouri in 1822 and accompanied one of the first American commercial caravans to reach Santa Fé, a year after Mexico's independence from Spain and the opening of New Mexico (and Alta California) to a trickle of American traders. After this profitable enterprise, Young recruited a few partners and trapped beaver on the Pecos and San Juan Rivers, dealt in Missouri produce and Mexican mules, and survived fights with Osage, Papago, Yuma, Apache, and Mojave war parties.

In 1829, just a year after Jedediah Smith's adventure in California and on the Umpqua River in Oregon, Young led a trapping party (which included "Kit" Carson, a nineteen-year-old runaway from a Missouri saddle shop) out of Taos, New Mexico, to the San Gabriel River, a few miles northeast of Pueblo de los Ángeles. He returned to California in 1832 with ten trappers and again in 1834 by the Gila River route.

In Los Angeles, Kelley collared Young and belabored him

on the wonders of Oregon, among which were its beaver riches, and seems to have been lobbying for a billet in Young's party, which was then preparing to march north to Monterey. Young was wary, Kelley overinsistent. The two proceeded separately.

In June Kelley arrived in Monterey, the most cosmopolitan town on the Pacific Seaboard, and tarried, basking in the beauty of the place, investigating taking passage on a trader headed for the Columbia River estuary. He was in no hurry. He had survived, or so he thought, all the worst of his journey, had crossed Mexico on foot, arriving unconquered in this semblance of civilization, a mere 600 miles from the Columbia. He was practically home.

The capital of Alta California was situated on a commanding headland south of a magnificent bay first seen by Portuguese explorers 300 years before. Its whitewashed and red-roofed adobes were scattered between piney hills and a wide strip of white beach, the town and its setting as invigorating as the sea breezes that cooled it. In 1834, scarcely a decade before American annexation, Monterey thrummed and jostled with trade. (Alta California's greatest export treasures were its cowhides, sought for shoemaking and other leather goods, and tallow, sold in rawhide bags, twenty-five pounds for two dollars, for soap and candles; it imported everything, including the shoes, soap, and candles made from its hides and tallow.) The waterfront swarmed with a heterogeneous collection of foreigners—mostly trade-ship captains and their crews, trappers, and hunters—and Mexican soldiery, customs officials, and clerks. Monterey Bay was forested by the masts of merchant vessels from seaports as distant as Genoa, Marseilles, Rio, and Boston, and by visiting ships-of-war, mostly British, that cruised Mexican waters from Acapulco and Mazatlán to Yerba Buena and on to the Oregon and Alaskan coasts.

It must have been a relief for Kelley to discover that there were other "Bostons" among the brigantine and schooner crews lounging near the Customs House and wandering the dirt streets of the town. No doubt he harangued them with his grand plan to reclaim Astoria and populate the Oregon Country with righteous American emigrants. He may have paid a visit to the most eminent American residing in Monterey, Thomas O. Larkin (from Charlestown, Massachusetts), who had come to Monterey in 1832 and with a capital of $500 opened a a flour mill and a small store dealing in such things as furs, horses, and lumber. He had married a widow on shipboard en route from the Sandwich Islands, and Rachel Hobson Holmes Larkin was said to be the first American woman to reside in Mexican California and their child, Thomas, Jr., the first American baby born there. Larkin had political connections in New England and Washington and in a few years would become United States consul in Monterey.

Kelley and Ewing Young talked again in the seacoast town. This time Young listened as Kelley extemporized. The trapper knew there was some truth in the stories of Oregon's untapped fur riches—he had seen the potential when wandering the upper reaches of the Sacramento River in '33—and finally agreed to take Kelley along with him.

Young's plan was to buy horses and mules en route north and take the herd into Oregon to sell, grubstaking himself and his sixteen men—"adventurers, deserted seamen and others," Bancroft said of them—to a season in the beaver streams. A hundred of the animals were collected in Monterey and San José, and on the journey to Yerba Buena the party was joined by nine other men with their own herd of fifty-six horses. At least two of these suspicious newcomers were Americans. Kelley later called them "marauders" and he suspected, as did Young, that their animals had been stolen.

In August, Young, Kelley, and the others reached the Umpqua River valley, near the site of the massacre of Jedediah Smith's party in '28. In camp near the river, while the

other men were rounding up strayed animals, Kelley fell desperately ill with malaria and was unable to walk a step or
mount a horse. While Young ministered to him as best he
could, the expedition was stalled several days. Then, in a
lucky circumstance, a band of Hudson's Bay trappers, returning from Sacramento River hunting grounds, came
upon Young's camp. The leader of the party was the French-
Canadian Michel Laframboise, who had been among the
voyageurs who had sailed from New York to the Columbia
on the *Tonquin* in 1810. His employment as an intrepid "utility man" in the Company, meaning that he was assigned
dangerous missions to uncover new fur grounds, was accompanied by a reputation as a thief and "womanizer"—George
Simpson, Hudson's Bay governor of the Pacific Northwest,
called him "a lying, worthless blackguard." His checkered
history notwithstanding, Laframboise saved Hall Kelley's
life by agreeing to take him on to Fort Vancouver, where he
could receive medical care and assistance from Dr. John
McLoughlin.

Thus assisted by representatives of the entity that topped
his list of enemies in all his Oregon schemes, traveling by
Hudson's Bay mule and Hudson's Bay canoe, Kelley saw for
the first time the land of his letters, tracts, petitions, and fan-
tasies. At the same time others who knew of his obsession
saw him. In the Willamette valley, after Ewing Young and
his motley group of horse herders caught up with the Laframboise party, Kelley met Québec-born Jason Lee and his
nephew Daniel Lee, who had come out to do Methodist religious work among the Flathead Indians. While there is no
record of their conversation, Kelley certainly took the opportunity to preach to them on his Oregon dream and his
original idea of taking missionaries to this Eden. The Lees
no doubt listened patiently. Daniel later recalled Kelley as "a
New England man, who entertained some very extravagant
notions in regard to Oregon."

Laframboise brought Kelley into Fort Vancouver in late

October, and his party was followed a few days later by Ewing Young's and its horse herd.

They were not welcomed; indeed, the gates of the customarily hospitable place were closed to them.

3

Six weeks before Young and Kelley appeared in Fort Vancouver, the Hudson's Bay schooner *Cadboro* returned to the Columbia from a trade voyage to Monterey and delivered to John McLoughlin an angry communique from Governor José Figueroa of Alta California. The letter denounced the two Americans as horse thieves and cautioned the factor to have nothing to do with these outlaws, least of all to buy the horses and mules stolen from Mexican ranchos.

Confronted with the charges, both men protested their innocence. Young admitted he had allowed some suspicious characters to join him north of Yerba Buena but said he paid for every animal he had brought in. Moreover, he said the Mexicans were the real thieves, claiming that he had been "plundered" of thousands of dollars in furs by California customs authorities in payment of fines for unauthorized trapping in the province.

McLoughlin remained dubious of this upstart American, and when Young tried to trade some beaver skins collected on the journey to Oregon the factor refused them, although he sent the supplies Young requested to his camp. This charity infuriated the trapper and he ordered the goods returned. In effect, McLoughlin was saying the furs were as tainted as the horses, to Young a choice example of hypocrisy since the Company was also poaching furs in Mexican territory. He rode to the factor's headquarters to demand an explanation. McLoughlin listened patiently—he was never a man to be cowed by another's anger—and invited Young to ad-

dress a protest to Governor Figueroa, which would be sent
to Monterey in the *Cadboro,* soon to depart for Mexican
waters, with the factor's own request for details and proof
of the horse-thievery charges.

Young wrote a letter but was not mollified by McLoughlin's suggestion and left Fort Vancouver sullenly, taking his
horses and mules with him. He eventually settled near
Champoeg, an old Indian camp on an open, sandy peninsula on the east side of the Willamette River. He built a cabin
there, hired workers to erect a sawmill, and within two years
was also proprietor of a whiskey distillery—an immensely
disturbing development to teetotaling McLoughlin—and a
cattle company, and was claiming over fifty square miles of
territory for his enterprises.

A few months after McLoughlin received the damaging
letter, Young and Kelley were exculpated of the horse-theft
charges, but Young never forgave the factor for treating him
as an outcast. In 1836 William A. Slacum, an American "private merchant" on a tour of Oregon, reported a conversation with Young at Champoeg in which the Tennesseean
claimed that "a cloud hung over him so long through Dr.
McLoughlin's influence, that he was almost maddened by
the harsh treatment of that gentleman."

These words might have been written by Hall Kelley;
indeed, in slightly different language, were so written,
countless times. While Ewing Young was taking the brunt
of the punishment for the crimes alleged by the California
governor, Kelley had his own stories of "maltreatment" at
the hands of McLoughlin, and they dovetailed perfectly
with the theories he devised before he ever set foot in Oregon: that the Hudson's Bay Company had contrived to
ruin him.

In the beginning of his barrage of letters to newspapers
back east, and in personal correspondence, Kelley wrote of
arriving in Oregon "much depressed in spirits and under
great bodily weakness, then recovering from a violent attack

of fever and ague." He said he was received in Fort Vancouver as "an unwelcome guest" and without being specific about the horse-thievery charges said "calumnies and slander were propagated" against him, and that "bloody men" had more than once threatened his life.

In fact, Kelley was the author of all his problems. He had fallen in with outlaws but was as innocent of any crime as Ewing Young—and probably more innocent. But his reputation as a haranguer of the Hudson's Bay Company had preceded him. From reports in eastern newspapers and from such Americans as Jason and Daniel Lee and Nathaniel Wyeth, who had preceded him to Oregon, McLoughlin knew of Kelley's intemperate and irrational accusations against the Company, and his grandiose ideas of "driving the British out of Oregon."

Even the handful of Americans coming in and out at Fort Vancouver shunned him. Wyeth, who had been inspired to come to Oregon by Kelley's writings and oratory, paid him only a perfunctory visit. (Kelley surmised that Wyeth had "crossed over" to the Hudson's Bay intriguers, even to embracing their policies of discouraging emigrants.)

McLoughlin, exasperated at having this difficult and foolish man at his fort, remained great-hearted. Kelley was shaken by fever, gaunt and weak, and "out of humanity" the factor assigned him a servant's hut, saw to it that he was attended by the post surgeon and that food was delivered to him regularly as he recovered his strength. Kelley, while spending the winter of 1834–35 at Fort Vancouver, demonstrated his gratitude for McLoughlin's largesse by demanding his "rights" as "an American on American soil . . . pursuing the avowed purpose of opening the trade of the territory to general competition."

One visitor to the fort who saw Kelley that winter described him as "five feet nine inches high, wearing a slouched hat, blanket capote, leather pants, with a red stripe down the seam, rather *outré* even for Vancouver . . . penniless, and ill-clad, and considered rather too rough for close companionship, and was not invited to the mess."

Kelley appears to have recovered enough from his debilitations that winter to write voluminous journals and make extensive notes on his surroundings. In an 1839 publication, he claimed to have surveyed the Columbia from Fort Vancouver to its Pacific estuary and provided convincing proof of his wanderings with data on the topography, climate, and soil conditions of his surroundings and observations on the Columbia bar and entrance, harbors and mountain ranges, timber and mineral potentials. He even claimed to have discovered deposits of gold, silver, copper, and coal in the vicinity of Fort Vancouver.

But for all his activity that winter, Kelley was anxious to return home. He was without funds or friends, at the mercy of the charity of his enemy, and his health was weakened. He still believed passionately in his Oregon dream, saw all his research and sumptuous descriptions, written in the comforts of Massachusetts, beggared by the actual place. For all the despair he experienced in getting there, his meager five months at Fort Vancouver steeled him. Now he could say out of experience and observation that Oregon must be American territory; he could use the personal pronoun in the lecture hall and in his writings: I have been there and this is what I saw.

McLoughlin, no doubt delighted to be rid of his resident ingrate, made him a gift of £7 and passage to the Sandwich Islands on the Company ship *Dryad,* and Kelley departed the Oregon coast in March 11, 1835, never to return. Bancroft says he remained true to his propensities to bite the hand that fed him: "The rude manners of the sailors with whom he was forced to associate in his feeble state of health were a sore annoyance to him, operating yet more to prejudice his diseased imagination against the company to whom he was indebted for this means of getting out of the country of his misfortunes."

McLoughlin wrote later that he had provided Kelley with shelter and victuals "until he left . . . when I gave him passage to Oahu. On his return to the states, he published a narrative of his voyage, in which, instead of being grateful for the kindness shown him, he abused me, and falsely stated I had been so alarmed with the dread that he would destroy the Hudson's Bay Company's trade, that I kept a constant watch over him."

From Oahu, Kelley was able to take passage to Boston on an American whaling vessel and arrived home early in 1836. He was then forty-six years old and had a long life yet to live. He wrote even more voluminously than before his Oregon odyssey, "planned and prayed, and blessed his friends, and cursed his enemies by the hundreds of pages," Bancroft wrote. "Besides pamphlets and newspapers, he wrote letters literally by the bushel." His books and treatises bore such titles as *A Geographical Sketch of that Part of North America called Oregon, A General Circular to all Persons of Good Character who Wish to Emigrate to the Oregon Territory; Embracing some Account of the Character and Advantages of the Country, the Right and the Means and the Operations by which it is to be Settled; and all Necessary Directions for Becoming an Emigrant,* and *History of the Colonization of the Oregon Territory.*

While he wrote often of his struggles and persecutions and took credit for not only the settlement of Oregon but also of California, not all his writings were foolish. Among influential politicians who were educated by Kelley's work were Senator Lewis Linn of Missouri, who subsequently introduced bills to extend American laws to Oregonian settlers and to give generous land grants to emigrant families; Senator Thomas Hart Benton, also of Missouri and a powerful expansionist voice in Congress; and Senator Daniel Webster of Massachusetts, who upon reading Kelley's *Geographical Sketch of Oregon* wrote the author, "I think much of your project; I will do all I can to sustain it."

Not long after his return to Boston, Kelley married and hoped to have a career as a respectable businessman. He enlisted some partners and built a cotton mill in Three Rivers, Massachusetts, counting on his share of the income from the business to finance his continuing Oregon work. But the mill failed and he lost what remained of his meager finances—and his sanity. Thereafter, he thought, talked, and wrote of nothing but his Oregon expedition and the oppression and inhumanity of the Hudson's Bay Company, imagining that every annoyance of whatever kind he suffered was attributable to its "hirelings." Bancroft wrote, "So great was his suspicion of every one, and so irritable had he become, that he drove his wife and children from him, and afterwards resided alone on a small piece of land heavily mortgaged, at Three Rivers . . . where he was designated as The Hermit, and from which the entreaties of his friends were unable to draw him."

Kelley died "of paralysis" on January 20, 1874, at the age of eighty-five.

"To the very last he remained the warm friend of Oregon," Bancroft said, "indignantly denying that he had ever entertained 'extravagant notions' of that country, which he still contended was 'the finest on which the sun shines.'" The historian was saddened by the end of Kelley's life, as were many of the old man's contemporaries. "Had I been in Congress," Bancroft said, "I would have given the old schoolmaster something to sweeten his second childhood's cup withal, and I would have praised and petted him somewhat in an official way, for he did more than many a well paid officer of the government."

13

The Iceman

■

"...A PERFECT INFIDEL."

1

Among the 500 members of Hall Kelley's American Society for Encouraging the Settlement of Oregon Territory was an outspoken Bostonian named Nathaniel Jarvis Wyeth, an impressive businessman with broad shoulders, thick chest, and an open, clever face, the lower portion framed in straggly chin whiskers, the middle of it unmasked even by a mustache. He was big-nosed and large-headed, and his mouth was shaped into a perpetual grin—not a smirk or affectation but the slight smile that success, and the prospect of more of it, brings. He was dynamic, brim full of ideas, and impatient to shake Kelley from his perpetual dreams. Wyeth's tenure as a Kelley man would be brief; after all, how much oratory, tract-writing, and planning would it take to make a start for the Columbia?

Patience was no virtue to Nat Wyeth, nor did he profess any lofty motives in his own plans to get to the Oregon Country. No patriotic or spiritual needs haunted him; indeed, one of his religious-minded acquaintances called him "a perfect infidel." He wanted to make a fortune in the Pacific Northwest fur trade and the fact that he knew nothing of the fur business from experience was no deterrent. He had known nothing of the ice business, either, when he got into it in his early twenties and accumulated a modest wealth from the frozen ponds around his native Cambridge, Massachusetts.

Nat Wyeth's love of ice had no poetry in it. He looked upon the beauty of ice with a clear commercial vision, just as John Jacob Astor looked upon the beauty of furs. Ice was seasonal, and thus not everyday common; it was free for the taking; there was an eager market for it in places where it was treated as a luxury. While working for the Frederick Tudor Ice Company in Boston, Wyeth acted on these alluring facts by inventing a horse-drawn machine that grooved pond ice so that it could be cut into huge blocks to be hoisted upon wagons and stored under mounds of sawdust in warehouses. Tudor's ice was sold locally and shipped everywhere, including an especially lucrative market in the West Indies and eventually as far away as Calcutta.

Wyeth saw no great leap from the ice business to the fur trade. Beaver were seasonal, free for the taking, luxury items fetching handsome profits. But he could not wait for Hall Kelley to start walking, and so, late in 1831, he launched his own Oregon-bound organization by putting up $3,000 of his own money and raising another $5,000 by mortgaging his ice patents. With this cash backing he formed the joint-stock, imposingly named Pacific Trading Company and enlisted twenty-four "industrious and temperate men" who anted up forty dollars each to join him. Among these "investors," most of them interested in making their fortunes in Oregon in other endeavors than trapping beaver, were his brother, Jacob Wyeth, M.D., who agreed to serve as the company physician; a nineteen-year-old cousin, John B. Wyeth; a gunsmith; a blacksmith; two carpenters; two fishermen; a cooper; a founder; and an assortment of farmers and tradesmen.

Wyeth planned as carefully as his chronic impatience permitted. His was to be an overland expedition, not across

Mexico in the Kelley mode but a plunge from the Missouri frontier across the Rocky Mountains to the Columbia. Faced with a 2,000-mile journey, most of it on foot, some of it on horseback, and some by boat crossings of rivers, he determined that his company would travel light, buying the necessary provisions, horses, and mules en route. He bought space on the merchant brig *Sultana,* which was sailing from Boston early in 1832 for the Pacific, and loaded the hold with foodstuffs, traps and supplies, and a consignment of goods from Boston merchants to be used in trading with Indians for furs. The ship would rendezvous at the Columbia bar with Wyeth's overland party.

Some of his ideas were more imaginative than practical. He outfitted his recruits in spiffy uniforms—woolen jackets, canvas-like pantaloons, striped cotton shirts, brogans—and armed them with muskets, bayonets, knives, and axes. He hired a bugler to call the men to parades and mess, and to blow tattoo and reveille. He upset his own "travel light" plans by buying heavy, cumbersome tents. He devised and had constructed a thirteen-foot-long "amphibious machine" consisting of three small wagons in tandem, their gondola-like boxes to serve both for mule-drawn cargo and as boats to cross any waterways on the trail west. This contraption was dubbed the "Nat-wyethium" by Cambridge wags who saw it, and much else in the iceman's preparations, as "extremely notional."

On March 11, 1832, at a time when Hall Kelley was under arrest as a debtor, Wyeth got his two-dozen-man "Band of Oregon Adventurers," as the local press called them, aboard a merchant steamer, each man paying his own way, and out of Boston Harbor for the passage to Baltimore, Pittsburgh, Cincinnati and Saint Louis.

In the Mississippi metropolis, old trailsmen told Wyeth that the boat-wagon was too flimsy and awkward to portage across the Rockies, that in any event it wouldn't work even on the Platte, the least problematical of the rivers he would be crossing, much less on the Sweetwater, the savage Snake, and the Columbia. He considered this advice and got rid of the Nat-wyethium, finding a buyer interested in trying it out and who paid half of what it cost to construct.

A much more serious disappointment was the defection of six of his company, men who decided they had more of the pioneer-adventurer in them in the planning than in the actuality. They apparently found, after taking in a day or two of the riotous, stinking, mud-filthy Saint Louis water-front, that their Cambridge comforts beckoned them too strongly to resist. Wyeth bid them farewell and good rid-dance and trooped the others aboard the steamer *Otter* for the 300-mile drift up the serpentine Missouri to Indepen-dence. This settlement, scattered across high ground in rocky, well-timbered country about three miles from the boat land-ing, lay only a few miles inside settled territory. In 1832, five years after its founding, it was a ramshackle congeries of log huts, tent-taverns, and outfitting shops, but for all its forlorn appearance was already a principal staging area for trade caravans outward bound to Mexican lands on the Santa Fé Trail, and for fur traders provisioning for the summer rendezvous in the Rockies.

Wyeth and his company spent ten days in Independence. He bought three horses for each of his men, fifteen sheep, two yoke of oxen, and reached an agreement with Kentuckians William and Milton Sublette, who had been among Ash-ley's original "enterprising young men" of the 1823 expedi-tion up the Missouri. The Sublettes were partners with Jim Bridger, Tom Fitzpatrick, and others in the Rocky Mountain Fur Company and were taking a sixty-two-man fur brigade to the trappers' rendezvous at Pierre's Hole in eastern Idaho. The brothers permitted Wyeth to attach his Oregon Adventurers to their company.

The trail to the rendezvous was a trial, with a signal error of Wyeth's authorship. Under the Sublette brothers' steady and knowledgeable guidance, the brigade, with the tenderfoot component bringing up the rear, made good progress, averaging twenty-five miles a day, to the Platte River, conduit to the fur country. There the trappers set about fashioning bull boats of buffalo hides sewn over willow frames and caulked with a mixture of elk tallow and campfire ashes, to ferry men and supplies across the shallow but swift river. Wyeth observed this activity, and Bill Sublette urged him to get his men busy building their own boats but, as one of the Cambridge tenderfeet observed, "Captain Wyeth was not a man easily diverted by the advice of others." This stubbornness proved costly: Wyeth and his party built a raft, and as it was being poled across the Platte's unpredictable current, valuable stores, the blacksmith's equipment, and several kegs of gunpowder were washed overboard and lost.

One incident scarier even than the Platte crossing was a night raid on the brigade's horse-string by a Blackfeet band. Five horses were lost but no human casualties resulted.

The only other memorable experience en route to the rendezvous occurred near South Pass when the Sublette party encountered twenty wagons loaded with trade items, the train led by Benjamin Louis Eulalie Bonneville, a Paris-born army captain on leave to trap and explore the Rockies and the Oregon Country. Bonneville's wagons were making history as the first to cross the Continental Divide and to reach the Green River valley. Later the captain would give serious thought to an American occupation of Oregon, and in a letter to Army Adjutant General Roger Jones on July 29, 1833, he wrote, "The information I have already obtained authorizes me to say that if the Government ever intend taking possession of Oregon the sooner it shall be done, the better." He said the Hudson's Bay Company "are too much exposed by their numerous small posts even to offer the least violence to the smallest force."

The brigade reached Pierre's Hole on July 8, and within a few days Wyeth lost another seven men, including his physician brother Jacob and nephew John. All had experienced quite enough of the wilderness and arranged to turn back to Independence with Bill Sublette, who was returning to Missouri with pack animals loaded with beaver plews. Nat Wyeth, now with eleven men remaining in his company, joined with Milton, who was preparing to move on into the Snake River country. On July 18, a short distance west of the rendezvous, Wyeth and his remnant found themselves on the fringe of a bitter fight against a Gros Ventre war party. The New Englander and his men suffered no casualties but five white trappers were killed in the battle.

By contrast at least, the rest of the journey was uneventful. Wyeth and his men were able to do some amateur beaver trapping, and on October 29, 1832, eight months after departing Boston, he brought his tenderfeet into Fort Vancouver, making them the first westbound party of Americans to travel along what came to be called the Oregon Trail. But Wyeth was not a man looking at the historical record; bringing the first emigrants overland to Oregon was incidental to his real mission—to make a fortune in the fur trade—and in this, struggling with his forlorn and foreshortened party into Fort Vancouver that fall day, he had failed. The crowning blow was the news trickling into the fort of the fate of the *Sultana,* the merchant vessel he had commissioned to precede his overland party and carry his traps, trade goods, and equipment for his Columbia River scheme. The ship, he learned, had sunk in a gale after striking a reef east of Tahiti. The ship's captain and most of its crew had survived, making a miraculous sixty-eight-day voyage in a launch to Valparaiso.

As would be the case with Hall Kelley two years hence, Wyeth and his men had to depend upon the generosity of John McLoughlin to survive the winter.

Being beholden to the man representing the company he intended to compete with was not what Wyeth had in mind. Nor were those who came with him overjoyed at their prospects for the future: In the spring, eight of them, with

McLoughlin's assistance, found passage to return to Boston. Of the three who remained to become among the first Americans to settle in the Oregon Country, one became a teacher to the Indian wives and half-breed children of the French-Canadian trappers at the fort, and two took up farming in the Willamette valley, where a small vanguard of retired Hudson's Bay men and their families were clearing land and planting crops.

Wyeth returned to the Rockies in March 1833, traveling with a Company pack train to the Portneuf River in southeastern Idaho, where he retrieved a cache of furs left there the previous summer. His mind boiled with ideas for a second expedition to the Oregon Country to reverse the bad luck that dogged him. He proposed to McLoughlin a plan whereby the Company would outfit him and a party of trappers to hunt beaver south of the Columbia, in exchange for which he would sell his furs exclusively to the factor at Fort Vancouver. He sought out Benjamin Bonneville for a partnership. And before returning home he made arrangements with Milton Sublette and Tom Fitzpatrick to supply their Rocky Mountain Fur Company with $3,000 in trade goods from Boston at less cost than they would pay for them in Saint Louis. He also harbored an idea of shipping kegged salmon from the Columbia to Boston at a handsome profit, and proposed to build a trading post on the Portneuf that would become the center of an American fur monopoly in the northern Rockies.

Wyeth had never experienced failure and had no space in his mind for such a concept. He was certain something in his grab bag of ideas to conquer the Oregon Country would succeed. He had monied friends in the East who would help finance such costly matters as hiring cargo space on another merchant ship bound for the North Pacific; buying trade goods to be shipped to Saint Louis and Independence; hiring trappers, teamsters, laborers, fishermen, and stevedores; and financing construction of a fort. He had his own resources to draw on, such as his ice-cutting and storage patents, which he leased to his employers. He had his reputation as a sound man of commerce and, unlike some Oregon boomers, he had *been* there; he knew the country and its resources.

2

In 1832, the precise date unknown, four native chiefs from the Oregon Country appeared in Saint Louis with a fur caravan and found their way to the home of General William Clark, superintendent of Indian Affairs for the city. The chiefs, Spokanes, Nez Percé, Flatheads—it is not clear—explained that their fathers had told them of Clark's visit to their nation a quarter century past with Mr. Lewis and a great party of other whites. From travelers and trappers they had learned of the white man's God and holy book, and they had a hunger to know more about this "Great Spirit." They had journeyed 2,000 miles to ask the White Chief Clark to send religious men to their country to point the way to Heaven.

There are various accounts of the fates of these Indian emissaries. Two are said to have sickened and died in Saint Louis soon after their meeting with Clark, one may have died on returning to his tribe, and one is said to have reached home and spread the news that white men of God were coming. Clark appears to have summoned three Methodist elders to his home and reported on the Indians' visit. According to John W. York, one of those present, Clark explained that while he was a Roman Catholic, "Methodist traveling preachers were the most indefatigable laborers, and made the greatest sacrifices of any men in the world" and that while "Catholic priests could teach the mysteries of religion . . .

Methodist ministers taught practical piety and husbandry, and the two united would be the best arrangement he could think of." The elders agreed and promised, if possible, to send a missionary to Oregon.

To the Indians, it did not matter whether the missionaries were Protestant or Catholic, since they probably did not know the difference. They had learned about the "black robes"—Jesuit priests—from French-Canadian trappers and from Catholic Iroquois who worked for the North West Company and taught some of the Flatheads and Nez Percé about prayer.

The Indians who visited Clark may have represented a very practical idea among their people: "To the Indian mind it was quite clear that the white man's guns, knives, cloth, burning glasses, and talking paper were the product of extra powerful medicine," David Lavender wrote. "Mastering the white man's medicine, it followed, would lead to mastery of the white man's power."

Of course, no such speculation was made when a highly wrought version of the Clark visitation story appeared in a letter published in the March 1, 1833, issue of the New York–based *Christian Advocate and Journal*. The Methodist convert who wrote the letter described the Indians as "three Nez Perces and one Flathead" and said that no sooner had they arrived at General Clark's doorstep than two of them dropped dead from exhaustion and privation, the first martyrs to the cause of spreading the Word of God to the heathens of the Pacific Northwest. The letter was accompanied by a drawing by an educated Wyandot Indian named William Walker showing the manner in which Flatheads deformed the shape of their children's heads in infancy by lashing them to a cradle-board. (Actually none of the Indians visiting Clark had this deformity; nor, for that matter, did the Nez Percé have pierced noses. The name came from a clumsy French translation of Indian sign language.)

The inspiring letter and the editorial peroration in the

same issue of the *Christian Advocate* ("Let the Church awake from her slumbers and go forth in her strength to the salvation of these wandering sons of our native forests") created a small sensation among churchly New Englanders. The Missionary Board of the Methodist Episcopal Church was galvanized to call for a mission "among the Flatheads," and the celebrated Oregon fanatic Hall J. Kelley, then still stumping around New England trying to get a start toward his imagined Eden, was aided by the clarion call. "His schemes multiplied," Bancroft wrote, "his pen worked with new vigor; he urged the preachers of the Word not to confine their efforts to the mountains, but to descend the broad River of the West to the Canaan there awaiting them, and unite earthly empire with heavenly enlightenment."

With uncommon alacrity, the Missionary Board chose a thirty-year-old newly ordained Methodist minister named Jason Lee as its candidate to lead the church into the wilds beyond the Rockies. He had been among the first to step forward and volunteer, and he had perfect credentials: He was a former farmer; he was a native of Stranstead, Québec, which gave him something in common with many of the Hudson's Bay agents in Oregon, including John McLoughlin; he had an impeccable record as a church deacon and elder. Lee possessed other striking qualities as well. He *looked* as if he could survive any of the vicissitudes of the trail, clear a forest and build a mission house with his bare hands, and convert Indians to Christianity by the sheer strength of his character and physical bulk.

Lee was a brawny, shambling man, six-foot-three in height, powerfully chested and shouldered, with a massively jawed face featuring a shaggy black beard, a prominent nose, and eyes described as of a "superlative, spiritualistic blue." He carried himself awkwardly, as if his brain's instructions took an extra millisecond to reach his faraway limbs, but still he had a certain sureness, was frank, affable, and inspired confidence. "Strong in his possession of himself," Bancroft said, "there was nothing intrusive in his nature . . . . Some would have said he lacked refinement; others that his brusque straight-forwardness was but simple honesty, unalloyed with clerical cant, and stripped of university gown and sectarian straitlace."

Daniel Lee, who had joined his uncle Jason in volunteering for the Flathead mission, was hardly identifiable as a Lee relative. He was thin and bony, in Bancroft's words, "a pious Pierrot, a man in stature, but a child in mind and manners," and possessed of a face "beaming in happy, good-natured unconsciousness of his lack of knowledge, particularly of knowledge of the things of this world."

Two lay preachers and a schoolteacher were selected to accompany the Lees, and in October 1833 the Missionary Board came up with $3,000 to finance the expedition. The expectation was that additional funds would be raised as the men made their way to Saint Louis, there to join a fur caravan heading to Independence and the Rocky Mountains.

By perfect happenstance, as the Lee party was preparing to leave New York news reached the city that Nathaniel Wyeth had arrived home after a journey to the Oregon Country and was preparing to return. Jason Lee hurried down to Boston to meet with the iceman. The "perfect infidel" may have cringed at the notion of shepherding Lee's divines through the wilderness, but he needed the money to help finance his new venture and Lee needed Wyeth's expertise to get him, his followers, and his baggage to the Columbia. By the end of their meeting, they had made a business arrangement: Lee would send his mission supplies ahead on the *May Dacre,* the merchant vessel Wyeth had commissioned to precede him to the Pacific, and Lee would rendezvous with Wyeth in Saint Louis in the spring.

The expedition got underway at the end of April 1834, with Wyeth and Milton Sublette in the lead, and 70 trappers and

250 horses loaded with the supplies Wyeth hoped to sell at the Pierre's Hole rendezvous. Jason Lee's party brought up the rear with their own horses and a small cattle herd.

For Wyeth the rendezvous was a financial disaster. William Sublette had beaten him there with a pack train out of Independence and by the time the iceman arrived with his, the trappers had already purchased their winter's supplies from Milton's brother. Wyeth, in a fury, decided to push on to the Portneuf River and build a cottonwood-log trading post, from which he hoped to sell his surplus goods. Lee and his followers went along, and in July, as Wyeth's men cleared some ground for building the fort, the minister held his first Sunday service. He had a strange congregation: Wyeth and his trappers ("the most profane company I think I was ever in," Lee later said of them); a number of Hudson's Bay fur traders and *voyageurs* under Thomas McKay; some Nez Percé and Flathead Indians, all of whom had drifted down to the grassy meadow along the Portneuf to investigate the goings-on at the place Wyeth was calling Fort Hall (after one of his prime backers). Bancroft painted a memorable word picture of Jason Lee's sermon in the wildwood: "It was a grand and solemn sight, these rough and reckless children of the forest, gathered from widely remote quarters, with varied tongues and customs, here in the heart of the mighty wilderness, the eternal hills their temple-walls, and for roof the sky." He added, "What these same devout worshippers were doing an hour afterward, drinking, trafficking, swearing, and stabbing, it is needless to detail. Man is oft an irrational animal, and we are least of all to look for reason in religion."

On July 30, with Wyeth and his men remaining behind to complete Fort Hall, Lee and his party pushed on to the west with McKay. After some tribulations, including the loss of much of their baggage at The Dalles rapids, Lee brought his bedraggled party into Fort Vancouver on September 16, 1834.

John McLoughlin treated the Americans with great cordiality, opened his home to them, and even provided Lee with a temporary place to preach. His first Sunday sermon was expounded to a motley flock, stranger even than the one gathered at Fort Hall, consisting of Englishmen, Irishmen, Scotchmen, French-Canadians, Indians of several tribes, Sandwich Islanders, and three Japanese shipwreck survivors.

McLoughlin also slyly redirected Jason Lee's plans to erect a mission house some distance south of the Hudson's Bay headquarters. The Flatheads, he told Lee, were not disposed to religious conversion. Their tribal lands were an exceedingly wild and dangerous country hundreds of miles to the east. They had an ancient tradition of warring against the Blackfeet. They were a nomadic people, difficult to pin down, impossible to gather up and funnel toward any mission church. He suggested that Lee settle in the nearby Willamette valley and proselytize among the natives in that region, the Calapooyas, Umpquas, Clackamas, and Tualatins, among others.

With horses, provisions, and men provided by McLoughlin, the Lees explored the valley and fell in love with it. Along the river they found a dozen French-Canadian families. The men, retired Company fur hunters working new farms, generously welcomed the Americans to stay over. One man, Joseph Gervais, even set up a tent for the Lees in the midst of his melon and cucumber garden. Jason Lee was reminded of the passage in the first chapter of Isaiah about "a lodge in a garden of cucumbers."

He selected for his mission house a tract of richly grassed alluvial plain on the east side of the Willamette, sixty miles below its mouth. The site, two miles above the Gervais farm, was bordered by copses of oak, fir, cottonwood, white maple, and ash trees.

Lee returned to Fort Vancouver full of hope and plans and ready to work. The *May Dacre,* Wyeth's brig, had survived the Horn passage and South Pacific storms and arrived on the Columbia, and McLoughlin supplied boats and crews to transport the American's mission goods ashore; horses, ox teams, and canoes to transport the supplies to the Willamette, and teamsters to drive the mission stock to their new home. By October 6, six weeks after the Lee party arrived at Fort Vancouver, they were sleeping in tents among the oaks and firs along the river. Some of the Canadians farming nearby, together with a Calapooya boy, a Kanaka volunteer, and later several of the horse-drovers who came to Fort Vancouver with Ewing Young and Hall Kelley, helped the Lees saw planks and split shingles for cabin building and stake out thirty acres of rich ground for spring planting of wheat, oats, corn, and garden vegetables.

3

In February 1835 Jason Lee wrote to his Mission Board and told of the progress he had made in the Willamette valley. He made a lengthy appeal to the board to send more men, with their families, to the Columbia. He said female schoolteachers were especially needed, and other "White females" because he had learned they "would have more influence among Indians than males," and could relieve the menfolk who he said were "doing too much household work."

The mission grew in direct ratio to the number of able-bodied men and women who planted and tilled the fields; built cabins, a schoolhouse, and outbuildings; and found time to teach and proselytize among the Indians. In the latter effort they had limited success. Most of the Indians in the region were reluctant to leave their children at the mission school, and those who did come were mostly orphans. The prospect of laboring in the fields while receiving religious instruction was also unappealing to the natives, who were unaccustomed to any kind of regularized labor. An attempt to locate a branch mission among the Calapooya people failed, Lee reported, because of the indolence and apathy of the natives.

Over two years passed before his letter home had the effect Lee hoped for, but in July 1836 the merchant brig *Hamilton* sailed from Boston Harbor bound for the Sandwich Islands with a "reinforcement" for the Willamette mission of thirteen Methodist men, women (three of them unmarried), and children. This small contingent arrived on the Columbia in June 1837, after a long delay in Honolulu, and within two months Jason Lee married Miss Anne Maria Pitman of New York, described as a "prepossessing woman," in the first Methodist wedding ceremony in Oregon. Additional church people arrived on the *Sumatra* that fall, giving the Willamette mission a population of sixty, about half of that number native children.

By then Lee was spending more time at his administrative duties and less at his religious ones. He had explored the whole region south of the Columbia and found no prospect of success working with or teaching, much less converting, the natives. Many of the tribes he regarded as hopelessly depraved and diseased, others—such as those of The Dalles, Umpqua, and Rogue River valleys—as unredeemable banditti. It was impossible for Lee to think the Lord intended him to minister to a handful of orphans. His personal mission had to be bigger: Perhaps it was that of a colonizer.

In the winter of 1837 Lee paid a visit to the handful of pioneers in the Umpqua River valley. They, like all the Americans in the Oregon Country, were eager to talk about encouraging settlers to come west. They wanted "good people"—hardworking, God-fearing folk. All were fearful of an influx of unprincipled adventurers, deserting seamen, and other flotsam washing ashore from such refuse dumps of humanity as Botany Bay.

Lee began thinking of the Willamette valley as the perfect place to draw respectable, God-loving Americans, a colony that would enjoy the guidance of the Methodist Church and the protection of the United States government. In March 1838 he recruited a few men and started out on an overland journey home. He hoped to collect funds and enlist new settlers en route and then meet with the Missionary Board and seek its assistance to deliver a "memorial," signed by fifty colonists, to the Congress of the United States. The petition gave the history of the Willamette settlement from 1832 to the present and stated that the American people were ignorant of the riches of the lands beyond the Rocky Mountains and its limitless potential for commerce with China, India, and the islands of the Pacific. The paper urged that the United States take immediate formal possession of the Oregon Country south of the Columbia River for the benefit of the nation at large and the protection of the settlers already there, who regarded themselves as the nucleus of a great new state of the Union.

Faced with such mighty responsibilities, Lee could not be deterred, not even by the crushing blow he received while resting at Pawnee Mission, near Council Bluffs, Iowa. There an express rider delivered a letter sent out from Fort Vancouver by John McLoughlin notifying Lee that his wife Anne Maria had died on June 26 past, three weeks after the birth and death of their son. She had been buried near the mission house, the grave site shaded by fir tree.*

---

*Later her remains were reinterred in the mission cemetery in Salem, where a marker told her story: "Beneath this sod, the first ever broken in Oregon for the reception of a white mother and child, lie buried the remains of Anne Maria Pitman, wife of Rev. Jason Lee, and infant son. She sailed from New York in July 1836, landed in Oregon June 1837, was married in July 1837, and died June 26, 1838, in full enjoyment of that love which constrained her to leave all for Christ and heathen souls. So we have left all, and followed Thee; what shall we have therefore."

Nothing could be gained by going back, so Lee went on and began lecturing in churches from Independence to New York, often to large audiences but more often to small ones, on the subject of Oregon, its riches and opportunities, and its certain future as a territory of the United States. He was a persuasive orator, filled with ardor and righteousness, presenting to his audiences his unromanticized views of the potential of the great land in which he had labored, experienced joys and sorrows, and had grown to love. Elijah White, a physician from Tompkins County, New York, who had been among the first reinforcements at the Willamette mission, said that Reverend Lee's only concern was that his heated oratory might draw to Oregon an undesirable element, men "from the western frontier of the states, of a restless, aspiring disposition."

In New York in November 1838, Lee appeared before the Board of Managers of the Methodist Episcopal Missionary Society and was so persuasive that a "call" was published in the *Christian Advocate and Journal* for missionaries, church laymen, physicians, farmers, mechanics, and young women to serve as teachers. Lee's petition was turned over to Congressman Caleb Cushing of Massachusetts and presented to the House of Representatives together with Lee's voluminous correspondence and supporting papers from Nathaniel Wyeth, Hall Kelley, and other notable Oregon enthusiasts. One of the newest of these was a government agent named William A. Slacum who had just returned from Oregon, where he spent time with Lee at the Willamette mission. His voluminous report to Congress merged perfectly with Lee's petition.

All the submissions were published as a Report of the Twenty-Fifth Congress in a printing of 10,000 copies and were widely distributed.

In all, thirty-six adults and sixteen children sailed from New York for the Oregon coast on the *Lausanne*, a ship chartered by the society and carrying $42,000 in supplies and equipment. Lee, who had by now remarried, joined the contingent with his new wife, and they all reached the Columbia in May 1840. The new colonizers, called the Great Reinforcement, firmly established the permanent American presence in the Oregon Country.

Over the next five years, Lee continued his labors for federal recognition of the Methodist settlement in the Willamette. In that time he also weathered the repeated frustrations of ministering to the Indians, the peak moment of which was a camp meeting in 1841 where he reported 130 baptisms. But, he admitted, most of the conversions to Christianity would likely not be permanent. He said many of the Indians asked to be paid for attending services.

In 1844 he returned to New York to visit the missionary board and to work on soliciting funds. Two months before his forty-second birthday he died, on March 2, 1845, at Lake Memphremagog in the province of Lower Canada. His remains were reinterred in Salem in 1906.

Lee had lived to see the first stirrings of an American colonial government in Oregon and the first organized emigrant wagon trains reach the Willamette valley. He died in the month and year of the inauguration of President James K. Polk and the push to settle the Oregon boundary question.

"He certainly saw how grand a work it was to lay the foundation of a new empire on the shores of the Pacific," Bancroft wrote of Lee, "and how discouraging the prospect of raising a doomed race to a momentary recognition of its lost condition, which was all that ever could be hoped for the Indians of western Oregon. There is much credit to be imputed to him as the man who carried to successful completion the dream of Hall J. Kelley and the purpose of Ewing Young."

Except for guiding Lee's party to the gateway to the Oregon Country, Nat Wyeth's second Oregon expedition failed miserably; his confidence, fall-back schemes, and superhuman efforts arrived at nothing but frustration. The arrangement he had proposed to McLoughlin, for the Hudson's Bay Company to outfit him and his trappers in exchange for exclusive rights to all the furs he brought in, was turned down by Governor George Simpson. The partnership he suggested to Captain Benjamin Bonneville did not advance beyond the discussion stage. By the time Wyeth arrived at the summer 1834 rendezvous, the Rocky Mountain Fur Company had gone under. Worse, Bill Sublette had beaten him to Pierre's Hole with a pack train of supplies, and those Wyeth brought so laboriously from Boston to sell to the Rocky Mountain outfit were no longer wanted. He wrestled them by pack train to his Fort Hall site but was able to collect only $500 for them, a small fraction of their cost.

The salmon scheme proved to be an even greater financial disaster, and the crowning blow came when he was forced to sell Fort Hall to the Hudson's Bay Company, again at a huge loss.

Wyeth returned to Boston in the fall of 1836, having devoted five years of his life and $20,000 of his own money (a substantial fortune in the era) to his Oregon labors. He had no regrets; he let others blame the Hudson's Bay people for thwarting his designs on the Oregon Country. (One of his prolix contemporaries wrote that the Company "preceded him, followed him, surrounded him everywhere and cut the throat of his prosperity with such kindness and politeness that Wyeth was induced to sell his whole interest, existent and prospective, in Oregon, to his generous, but too indefatigable, skillful and powerful antagonist.")

Wyeth returned to the Tudor Company at triple his former salary and patented new devices for ice gathering, and when he struck out on his own in 1840 he made a new fortune shipping refrigerated fruit and vegetables to the tropics.

His beloved Oregon remained in his thoughts. For congressional reports he wrote accounts of his Northwest ventures, provided his observations on the potential for commerce there, and urged governmental support of American efforts to settle the Pacific Northwest. Like Jason Lee, Wyeth lived to witness the emigrant migrations to the Oregon Country, but he also lived to see it declared a territory of the United States.

He died in Cambridge on August 31, 1856.

Bancroft memorialized Wyeth by writing that "The flag of the United States was planted by him simultaneously in the heart of the continent and on the seaboard of the Pacific. He it was who, more directly than any other man, marked the way for the ox-teams which were so shortly to bring the Americanized civilization of Europe across the roadless continent."

· ·

PART FOUR

OUT TO ARCADIA

■

14

The Macedonian Cry

■

"WATCHMAN, TELL US OF THE NIGHT . . ."

1

The story of the Indians who came to William Clark's home in Saint Louis to find out about the white man's Book of Heaven created many an armchair dream among readers of the *Christian Advocate and Journal*. Pious imaginings of taking leave of cozy hearthfires and braving the rigors of the wilderness were commonplace, many listened when the *Advocate* editor wrote "Hear! Hear! Who will respond to the call from beyond the Rocky Mountains?", and many read every stirring word of the *Advocate* article by Dr. Wilbur Fisk, the celebrated divine, educator, and founder of Wesleyan College in Middletown, Connecticut. He wrote: "Let two suitable men, unincumbered with families, possessing the spirit of martyrs, throw themselves into the [Indian] nation—live with them—learn their language—preach Christ to them . . . . Who will go? Who? Were I young, healthy, and unincumbered, how joyfully I would go! But the honor is for another. Bright will be his crown, glorious his reward."

Marcus Whitman, like Jason Lee, never seems to have hesitated to respond; indeed, when the idea came to him, probably through the writings of Fisk, Hall Kelley, and Lee, he would not be denied. In 1834, when he made a fervent application to the American Board of Foreign Missions in Boston for an assignment in the Oregon Country, he was thirty-two years old and still searching for his life's niche. His parents, descendants of colonial New Englanders, were citizens of Rushville, New York, where Marcus was born, and provided him with a comfortable Congregationalist up-bringing and a good education. In his twenties he turned to medicine, riding the lumber camps of western New York state as a physician's apprentice. He studied for two sixteen-week terms at a medical school in Ohio and received an M.D. degree in 1831, but he was not fulfilled by buggy travel over the back roads of New York state lancing boils, splint-ing broken limbs, and tending to sick, wounded, and dying farm folk. Nor was he satisfied by Sunday school and tem-perence teaching or the sweaty labor at the sawmill he op-erated with his brother in Rushville. All he learned seemed destined for some higher purpose, and when he asked to be sent to Oregon he listed his qualifications—"physician, teacher, or agriculturist"—and hoped one or more of these valuable skills would earn him an assignment.

The Mission Board clearly liked his application. Here was a man in the prime of his life, from a good and Godly fam-ily, a physician and a teacher. He had an excellent church record. He was unmarried. If Whitman made a personal appearance before the committee he would have impressed them the more. He fairly radiated energy, enthusiasm, and *bonhomie*. He was of medium height, thin but sinewy, with big but not unhandsome facial features, iron-gray short-cropped hair, muttonchop whiskers, and deep-blue, soul-searching eyes. His habitual slovenliness of dress and outspokenness the members would have dismissed as the products of an outdoorsman's life. This was a man who had bent his back in physical labor, not in hovering over a desk and paperwork. He had what the Boston mission people imagined were the characteristics of a real "Western man," no actual specimen of which they had ever really seen.

He had but one serious drawback, his lack of divinity training, and on this basis he was initially rejected as a missionary. Formal Christian religious training, it was felt, was absolutely necessary if one were to preach, teach, and proselytize among savage races. But Whitman's application came at a propitious time: The Mission Board had been studying the feasibility of opening an Oregon mission and had commissioned a seasoned Presbyterian divine, Reverend Samuel Parker, to make an overland tour of the "Flathead country" beyond the Rocky Mountains and report on potential mission sites. Parker had been to Saint Louis once before, in the spring of 1834, six weeks after Jason Lee and his Methodists had departed with a fur caravan for the frontier. He ran out of money and was forced to return home, but he was regarded as a veteran trailsman, and Whitman, distressed at his rejection, was thrilled when he received notification from the board that he could accompany Parker to the Oregon Country as physician-missionary.

Theirs was a strange pairing; they seemed to have only their religious zeal in common. Parker, born in Ashfield, Massachusetts, held degrees in theology from Williams College and the Andover Theological Seminary and had been ordained a Congregational minister in 1812. At the time of his commission, the fifty-five-year-old church wheelhorse was working as a teacher in a girls' school in Ithaca, and had a reputation for erudite oratory and a much-appreciated talent for fund-raising. He was handsome, prim, mannered, fastidious, and authoritarian—never a man to be called "Sam"—the very picture of the studious, sedentary preacher. He was perceived as having forceful leadership qualities, a physical vitality, a scientific and linguistic bent, and a churchly dignity and flintiness that would serve well in a wilderness setting.

For all their differences, Whitman was beholden to Reverend Parker for speaking on his behalf to the board—and for being the instrument by which Marcus met the woman of his dreams.

In November 1834 Parker made a speech at a small Congregational church in Amity, in Allegany County, New York, on the need for missionaries to serve among the savage tribes of the far West. In the audience sat a particularly enthralled young woman named Narcissa Prentiss who, after hearing his sermon, sought out the visiting theologian. She was twenty-six at the time, tall, golden-haired, "buxom," a contemporary said of her, and "symetrically formed," with a strikingly pretty oval face. She made a good impression on Parker, especially after he learned her unusual history.

The third of nine children of Stephen and Clarissa Ward Prentiss, Narcissa (named after the amaryllis-like flower) was born in Prattsburg and afforded a formal education unusual for a young female of the era. Her father, a fourth-generation descendant of a Massachusetts Bay colonizer, had made a prosperous business as a builder and was respectfully called "Judge" Prentiss for the single term he served as a probate court magistrate. He and his wife were devout in their Congregational religion and devoted to the idea that a good education leavened, rather than diminished, the Christian faith. As a teenager, Narcissa, third of the nine Prentiss children, was sent off to the Academy for Women in Troy, and later came home to Prattsburg to attend Franklin Academy, a coeducational religious school her father had helped endow.

(In the course of her studies at Franklin, Narcissa met a polite, broodingly serious theology student named Henry Harmon Spalding, who was bowled over by her good looks and vivacity and startled by her honest humor. Some of these attributes were considered suspect by the gravely pious of the 1830s, people who, in Henry L. Mencken's definition of Puritanism, seemed to have "the haunting fear that someone, somewhere, is happy." Spalding was smitten but mistook Narcissa's naturally gregarious, friendly nature for affection, and when he made a sudden proposal of marriage she gently turned him down.)

After graduating from Franklin Academy, Narcissa and one of her sisters opened a kindergarten in the town of Bath, but she felt she was merely marking time and must have conveyed her frustration to Samuel Parker, a man preparing to embark on a great, meaningful journey of faith, one she had dreamed of all her life, to Christianize Indians. She had studied assiduously the *Missionary Herald,* organ of the Presbyterian Congregational and Dutch Reformed Churches, and the Methodist *Christian Advocate.* She had been utterly captivated by the story of the Flathead and Nez Percé supplicants in Saint Louis, the accounts of Jason Lee's mission to the Columbia, and had what the religious journals called "the Macedonian Cry"* echoing in her brain.

Samuel Parker was won over by Narcissa's ardor to be of service "among the savage races" and in a communication to the Mission Board wrote, "Are females wanted? A Miss Prentiss . . . is very anxious to go to the heathen. . . . Her education is good, her piety conspicuous, her influence good. She will offer herself if needed." He understood that she could not accompany his quick exploratory journey but hoped she might be a part of some actual mission party in the future.

Having performed one signal service each to Marcus

---

*The reference is apparently to the passages in Acts 16, in which the Apostle Paul has a vision of a Macedonian coming in the night asking for prayer and saying, "Come over into Macedonia, and help us." In biblical times, Macedonia, a land often visited by Paul, lay north of Greece in the Balkans and had been ruled, three centuries before Christ, by Philip II, and later by his son, Alexander the Great.

Whitman and Miss Prentiss, Parker may have even brought the two anxious evangelists together.

Toward the end of 1834, Whitman, then practicing medicine in the town of Wheeler, a short distance south of Prattsburg, met Narcissa Prentiss. He doubtlessly learned of her ambition to serve in the Oregon Country through Parker. Whatever the occasion of their meeting, he fell in love with her in the moment and let her know his feelings. She no doubt was gracious and appreciative of the sentiment, but sudden professions of love, as in the case of Henry Spalding of sad and recent memory, made her cautious. She found Whitman curiously attractive—rugged, honest, forthright, rather charming in his awkwardness—and could imagine their doing God's work together in the wilderness. He was a man a woman could learn to love.

In January 1835 Whitman presented himself to the Prentiss family, then living in Amity, and there he and Narcissa made a pact before he set out for Saint Louis ahead of Samuel Parker. The arrangement seems to have been a betrothal of sorts.

In February, as Whitman was en route to the Mississippi, Narcissa made a formal application to the Mission Board for service among the Indians of the far West. Her bid was enthusiastically endorsed by the pastor of her church in Amity. Reverend Oliver S. Powell and his wife were making plans of their own for a mission in the Flathead country and hoped to have Miss Prentiss accompany them. He wrote to the board, "I am happy in the prospect of having so efficient a fellow-laborer in the missionary service," then gave a clue as to the arrangement his parishioner had recently made: "As it is probable that Miss Prentiss will hereafter become the companion of Doctor Marcus Whitman (should he be established as missionary beyond the Rocky Mountains), it may be proper to add that he expressed a desire that she might accompany us on our mission."

Narcissa's application was accepted by the board in March

1835, but because the Powells were unable to carry out their expedition plans, she had to wait. Marcus had departed for Saint Louis ahead of Reverend Parker, and it would be many months, perhaps a year or more, before he returned for her.

2

Samuel Parker left Ithaca on March 14, 1835, and reached Saint Louis three weeks later via Buffalo, Pittsburgh, Wheeling, Cincinnati, and Louisville, staying with church families, distributing tracts, holding services in the ladies' cabins of steamers, talking to whoever would listen about his forthcoming journey.

Whitman was awaiting him and had made preliminary arrangements with the help of local churchmen to attach Parker and himself to a party of trappers heading up the Missouri to the summer rendezvous on the Green River. Leading the brigade was a capable if somewhat boozy trader named Lucien Fontenelle. This man, a Louisianan, had twenty years' experience trapping along the Missouri and in the Rockies; skirmishing with Blackfeet, Snake and Crow horse raiders; and confronting Hudson's Bay agents over "rights" to certain rich beaver streams. He was not enamored of the idea of escorting church folk to rendezvous, but he was persuaded, probably by Whitman, who could be quite persuasive.

They traveled upriver by steamer to Liberty, the Missouri frontier town just above Independence, and were delayed there three weeks. Fontenelle used the time to enlarge his trapping party to fifty men and put together a pack train of horses and mules, three yoke of oxen, and six light wagons. The wagons were to carry trade goods and supplies to rendezvous and furs and buffalo hides (which were fetching more on the market than beaver hides) back to Missouri. Parker and Whitman occupied themselves by visiting a nearby Mormon settlement and riding "twenty miles out of the United States" to Cantonment Leavenworth in Kansas, where Parker preached to the garrison.

At first, Fontenelle and his rough-hewn mountaineers treated both New Yorkers with contempt. Parker in particular seemed an easy target for their sneers. To the filthy, foul-mouthed, buckskinned trappers sucking their pipes at the campfires the reverend cut a comic figure in his plug hat, black suit, white neck stock, and nose-in-the-air manner. He seemed to think he was in charge of the expedition, and it was galling to watch him standing aloof and unhelpful, never bending his back to any camp labor, parceling out chores to his companion then finding fault with everything done, including the doctor's "unskillful management" of their horses and the single mule they had purchased in Liberty. Whitman took everything in stride. He felt fortunate to be at the brigade camp waiting to jump off into savage lands, soon to see the Indian country of the Upper Missouri, the great Shining Mountains, and the mysteries that lay beyond them. He was learning from Fontenelle and his men, felt he was fulfilling his destiny, knew that he would be useful.

Whitman's utility was proven sooner than he expected. The caravan departed Liberty on May 15 and made its way upriver to Council Bluffs, crossed the Missouri in bull boats, and camped at Bellevue, a few miles below Omaha. There in the rain-soaked bottomlands Fontenelle and several of his men fell ill with cholera. The Asiatic strain of the disease had ravaged Europe in the 1830s and came to America on passenger ships, struck the Eastern Seaboard (killing 3,000 people in New York City alone), and spread inland, thriving in crowded campgrounds amid fetid sloughs of garbage and the excrement of men and animals. Whitman knew the awful symptoms of the disease: the clayey appearance of the skin, bluing of fingernails and face, the violent diarrhetic attacks, ceaseless vomiting and sweating (cholera killed by dehydrating its victims), and had treated it with the accepted remedies of the day and with the same mixed results. Many died of it, some recovered, some never contracted it even in the most plagued areas.

He took charge of the stricken, administered the recommended apothecary doses of sixty drops of laudanum in half a glass of cold water followed by thirty more drops every half hour. He prepared clysters (medicinal enemas) by mixing three teaspoonfuls of laudanum in a thin, warm gruel, and mustard poultices, and cold cloths to bathe foreheads and limbs. He bled his patients, and purged them with tepid water and salt, or with ipecacuanha. He also recommended that the camp be moved from riverside to higher ground, and this was done. Three men died of the disease but Fontenelle and several others recovered, and Whitman's labors earned him the respect of the brigade, a reputation that preceded him as the caravan moved west to Grand Island to pick up the Platte and follow it across Nebraska.

At Fort Laramie, Fontenelle turned over the brigade to his partner Tom Fitzpatrick, who would lead it to the rendezvous. From the white-haired, Irish-born mountain man Samuel Parker and especially Marcus Whitman got a wilderness education. "Broken Hand" had twenty years in the Indian trade. He had been with Ashley in 1823 and, of more interest to the New Yorkers, had traded among the Flathead people northwest of the Rockies. He was wise, patient, and admired; the churchmen questioned him incessantly. Whitman had heard of Captain Bonneville's party taking a number of freight wagons across the Continental Divide and South Pass to the Green River just three years past and quizzed the guide on the feasibility of emigrant wagons making their way across the mountains to the Oregon Country. On this matter Fitzpatrick was not sanguine, but his doubts did not dampen Whitman's enthusiasm on the subject. He studied the fur traders' wagons and felt that similar conveyances were the key to success in establishing missions in the far West, and to attracting families of settlers who would set up their households in the wilderness.

Samuel Parker had a moment of triumph at Fort Laramie in late July when a band of Oglala stood in silence while he, with his plug hat clapped across his heart, preached to them and sang "Watchman, Tell Us of the Night." He told Whitman the Indians had asked for an encore and noted in his journal that "the expression on their countenances seemed to say, we want to know what all this means."

Fitzpatrick, true to his wagon doubts, left them behind at Fort Laramie and had all the equipment, provisions, and trade goods packed on horses and mules. Thus unencumbered, he led his party westward to the Wind River Range and South Pass, arriving there on August 10, and a week later at the Green River rendezvous.

The churchmen were wide-eyed in wonderment during the week they spent with the traders and trappers, and particularly among the Indian lodges crowding the hillsides along the river. Parker expressed disappointment that the Flatheads and Nez Percé appeared to have neither flat heads nor pierced noses, but his wanderings among them, and among the Arapaho and Sioux camps, convinced him that they were all conducive, if not eager, to receive the Word. Whitman, naturally sociable, enjoyed the friendship of Fitzpatrick's trapper-trader comrades, many of whom had heard of his good work among the cholera victims at Bellevue camp and sought him out for medical advice. One who came forward was the mountain man Jim Bridger, who was bothered by a Blackfeet arrowhead he had carried in his back for many years, the point now embedded in bone with cartilage grown around it. Whitman deftly extracted it without anesthetic (except for whatever whiskey Bridger took internally beforehand) in front of a crowd of mountaineers and Indians, and when he expressed amazement that the wound had not festered, Bridger opined, "Meat don't spoil in the Rockies."

The missionaries picked up heartening news from soldier-hunter William Drummond Stewart of Perthshire, Scotland, who was traveling with Fitzpatrick's trappers. He was an experienced rendezvous hand who had shot game all the way to Fort Vancouver with Jason Lee's party the previous year and told Whitman and Parker that Lee had set up his mission on the Willamette and had thus bypassed Flathead country. The field among this tribe was still open.

Whitman also met Bridger's friend Kit Carson at the rendezvous and may have witnessed, or at least been nearby during, one of the most celebrated episodes in Carson's colorful career, a favorite of dime-novel writers ever after. Fitzpatrick, Bridger, and other traders had set up their camp adjacent to an Arapaho village, and as the days passed Kit's eye is said to have fallen on an Arapaho girl named Waa-nibe and he went so far as to make a preliminary courtship present of powder and ball to her father. Accounts vary widely on precisely what happened after this, but it appears that in the camp was a French trapper named Shunar (or Chouinard or Shunan), a huge, bullying drunk much disposed to ragging and threatening the Americans. One of Carson's biographers claims that Shunar insulted or tried to rape the Arapaho girl and that Kit confronted the Frenchman, a foot taller and a hundred pounds heavier, in his lair.

Most sources agree on the result of the challenge. Both men fetched their sidearms and horses and rode up to one another. Both guns were fired simultaneously; Shunar's wrist was shattered by Kit's bullet, and Kit's hair was "parted" by Shunar's shot and his face burned by the powder.

Carson "married" Waa-nibe before the rendezvous ended.

3

The Green River turned out to be the temporary end of the trail for Marcus Whitman. While Parker was to proceed to the Columbia River with a number of Flathead and Nez Percé guides to scout mission sites, Whitman would return east for "reinforcements," Narcissa Prentiss among them. A year hence, he would return to the rendezvous and reunite with Parker, who would come out from Fort Vancouver to the Green to intercept him. The plan may have been agreed upon during the course of the journey out of Saint Louis, but the clear motive for it was that the two men were becoming alienated. The minister was not a compatible companion for Whitman or anyone else, and Parker's conduct at their separation makes Bancroft's assessment—"it is most probable that the want of congeniality made it acceptable to both of them"—seem excessively euphemistic: The reverend appropriated their mule and the others purchased en route and gave Whitman five dollars to buy a horse for himself. Since horses were selling for a minimum of seventy-five dollars at the rendezvous, Whitman dug deep and scraped up enough to buy a scrawny animal—"a disgrace to any man to pack on account of his extreme sore back," he said—and hired two men, one to act as interpreter and guide, the other to cook and mind the horse, each to be paid eighteen dollars for the two months they were to serve him.

On August 22, 1835, Parker accompanied Jim Bridger and sixty men riding out from the Green River to Pierre's Hole at the headwaters of the Snake. There the trappers took a course toward Blackfeet country and left Parker with his escort of ten Nez Percé to proceed to the Oregon Country. The reverend suffered greatly in the Salmon River mountains, weakened and dizzy with fever, but heroically pushed on, falling from his saddle at day's end, often unable to eat and with barely enough strength to bleed himself, as he'd been taught by Doctor Whitman, add new pages in shaky hand in his journal by campfire light, and crawl into his blankets. By late September, when he and his Nez Percé escort crossed the Salmon and climbed the Kooskooskie (Clearwater) range, he found his health improving in the "wild, cold mountains" and his strength regained by the time he reached Fort Walla Walla on October 6.

Parker rested two days among Hudson's Bay people, then with three husky Walla Walla Indians embarked by Company canoe on the Columbia. He visited a Cayuse village on the south side of the river, and on the twelfth, near The Dalles rapids, met Nathaniel Wyeth, the one-time ice merchant then en route to his fort on the Portneuf River, and home.

Parker reached Fort Vancouver on October 29, 1835, and spent the winter enjoying John McLoughlin's hospitality and "the society of gentlemen, enlightened, polished, and sociable." He was provided half of a newly built and furnished house, dined with the factor, was given books from McLoughlin's library and horses to explore the Oregon coast and Willamette valley. He met and was greatly impressed by Jason Lee and the Methodist minister's mission house and gardens on the east side of the Willamette River. He especially admired Lee's work in setting up a temperance society, and if he experienced any disappointment as Lee's guest, it was upon learning that the sheer physical labors of building and maintaining a mission had kept the minister from attending to his spiritual work. In any event, Lee told the chagrined Parker, Christianizing the savages was exasperating, impossible work, and he had written his superiors that "we have no evidence that we have been instrumental in the conversion of one soul."

Parker shared with Lee the conviction that more women were needed in the Oregon Country and endorsed the idea contained in a letter Lee had written home in March 1835: "I have requested the Board not to send any more *single men*, but to send men with families . . . . A greater favor could not be bestowed upon this country than to send to it pious, industrious, intelligent females." Parker later wrote, "Christian white women are very much needed to exert influence over Indian families." Clearly they had differences on the issue: Lee wrote more as a settler than a missionary; Parker's only interest was Christianizing Indians.

On April 14, 1836, the reverend bade farewell to McLoughlin and Fort Vancouver. He planned to explore the Upper Columbia, scout sites for mission stations, then, with his Nez Percé as guides, move on to the Green River for the summer rendezvous. There he expected to meet with Marcus Whitman and whatever party his erstwhile partner was able to organize in the East.

Parker reached Walla Walla on the twenty-sixth and remained there two weeks, preaching to a number of Nez Percé and Cayuse Indians who came to the fort and learning firsthand what Jason Lee meant about the frustrations of converting the savages. The Cayuse chief could not accept that doctrine of monogamous marriage as the Nez Percé people seemed willing to do, explaining to the missionary that he could not dispense with any of his wives, was too old to turn away from the ways of his people, and preferred "the place of burning" if that was the only recourse.

On May 9 Parker set out for the Green with his Nez Percé faithful. He dreaded taking the terrible Salmon River Mountain route to the rendezvous site—he had narrowly escaped dying there the year before. He tried to persuade his escort to take the Grande Ronde and Snake River route, but the Indians preferred the Salmon since it avoided hostile Blackfeet country, and they could not be persuaded otherwise. Parker may have fallen ill again on the trail, or he may have had a change of heart about returning east over such arduous country, for he sent letters ahead addressed to Whitman, then turned back to the Columbia to await a merchant ship that would take him home.

He scouted mission station sites on the return to Fort Vancouver and was particularly enamored of a spot twenty-two miles from Fort Walla Walla near the mouth of a small stream and in a pretty valley amidst high rolling hills covered with dark green grass. The Cayuse people, in whose country it was located, called it Waiilatpu, "Place of the Rye Grass."

He traveled as far north as Fort Colville, the northernmost Company post on the Walla Walla River, and preached among the Palouses, a people related to the Nez Percé, and the Spokanes. He explored the Spokane River and made extensive notes in his journal in which he envisioned a mission that would minister to the Nez Percé, Palouse, Spokane, Coeur d'Alêne, Pend d'Oreille, and Shuyelpi tribes.

Parker returned to Fort Vancouver in early June and found the Hudson's Bay Company's new steamship *Beaver* recently arrived on the coast from England. A sidewheeler of 110 tons with a crew of thirty and armed with four six-pounder cannons, the *Beaver* was the first steam-powered vessel to reach the Pacific coast. Parker booked passage on the steamer and on June 18, 1836, embarked for Honolulu and New York.

He reached home on May 23, 1837, and calculated that he had traveled 28,000 miles, counting his sea voyage, in the twenty-six months that had passed since he set out for Saint Louis. In 1838 he published in Ithaca his *Journal of an Exploring Tour Beyond the Rocky Mountains*, the first detailed account of the Oregon Country and its Indian tribes since Lewis and Clark's journals and the miscellaneous writings of Hall Kelley. The volume was immensely popular, selling 10,000 copies.

In the book Parker mused "upon the probable changes which would take place in these remote regions in a very few years" and told of his dream of "a new empire to be added to the kingdoms of the earth."

4

His unhappy experiences with Samuel Parker forgotten, Marcus Whitman returned to New York anxious to tell of his adventures on the trail from the Missouri frontier to the trappers' rendezvous on the Green River. He wanted nothing more than to marry Miss Prentiss and return west and conveyed both these ambitions to the Board of Missions. The board members were impressed by the report he made to them and by the two Nez Percé boys, Tackitooits and Ais—their Christianized names Richard and John—he brought home with him. There remained a stumbling block. The board was satisfied with Whitman's plans for the return journey: using wagons at least as far as Fort Laramie, having a small cattle herd to supplement whatever game they were able to kill en route, purchasing horses, pack animals, flour, and similar stores from Missouri outfitters. But the unresolved question had to do with the non-negotiable requirement that an ordained minister must accompany his party. Whitman was a mere physician, after all, and did not have the requisite training to elevate the heathen heavenward.

For the doctor, everything hung in the balance. If a certified church servant did not accompany him, there would be no mission; if there was to be no mission, Miss Prentiss would not marry him—such was their agreement—and his life would fall in a shambles. He sought her out in Amity and learned that she was aware of the problem, and had even thought about prospective ministerial candidates for the mission. She had reluctantly landed on the name Henry Harmon Spalding, a man she suspected was embittered and probably vindictive over her rebuffing his marriage proposal when they were classmates at Franklin Academy in Prattsburg in 1828.

Spalding, now thirty-two and as gloomily pensive as ever, was only recently returned to New York from Missouri, where he and his wife had conducted mission work among the Osage Indians. He had not forgotten Narcissa's rejection; indeed he seemed still to be nursing the wound and wondering about her motives in declining the offer of such a prize catch, as he wrote the board that he did not wish to travel to Oregon with her: "I do not want to go into the same mission with Narcissa," he said cryptically, "as I question her judgement."

But after receiving certain assurances from the board, perhaps that he would be "senior" in the expedition, perhaps that in Oregon he would have a separate station from the Whitmans, he was persuaded to reconsider and even paid a courtesy call to the Prentiss family in Angelica a few days before Narcissa's wedding.

Soon after his rebuff by Miss Prentiss, Spalding had married Eliza Hart, the daughter of an Oneida County, New York, farmer. She was described by Bancroft as "a tall, slender, plain, dark woman, sympathizing, and faithful" who "won the confidence of all about her." What she lacked in personal charms, he said, "she made up in the excellence of her character, taking for her own standard that of the highest in pious life." She was a talented artist and linguist, a frail and shy spinster when she fell in love with Spalding and his missionary dreams through the correspondence they conducted during his theological studies. She waited patiently while he completed his preliminary degree work, and the two married while he was attending a seminary in Cincinnati, she taking in boarders to supplement their meager income. Spalding, in his limitless capacity for caddish expression, wrote the Mission Board that he had married Eliza "for the express purpose of giving my wife the opportunity of pursuing the same Theological studies as myself."

After completing his studies, the couple returned to Utica to await the birth of their first child and a response from the Mission Board to Spalding's application for a "foreign" appointment. He was ordained a Presbyterian minister in the summer of 1835, and in October Eliza's baby was stillborn. Spalding's reaction to the tragedy was that "the Lord most righteously chastised us for our sins." In this he might best have spoken only for himself, for in recommending the couple to the board for a mission appointment, one reference stated that Eliza was beloved by a large circle of friends and was "one of the best women for a missionary wife with whom I am acquainted." The writer also seemed to know her husband well, stating that Henry Spalding "can turn his hand to almost any kind of handy work, is not remarkable for his judgment and common sense . . . is sometimes too much inclined to denounce and censure those who are not as zealous and ardent as himself." The correspondent also used the word *jealous* to describe the man "so fortunate as to have married Eliza Hart."

Eliza and Narcissa were to become friends, but of Spalding Narcissa wrote her father during their journey, "The man who came with us is one who ought never to have come. . . . My dear husband has suffered more from him in consequence of his wicked jealousy, and great pique towards me, than can be known in this world."

They arranged to join forces in Cincinnati.

Marcus Whitman and Narcissa Prentiss married in Angelica, Allegany County, New York, on February 18, 1836, two months after his return from the Rocky Mountains.

Since much of the courtship had taken place before he left the state the previous year, Whitman had only to make certain she wanted to accompany him to the Oregon Country. He described the rigors of the trail, much of it arduous and dangerous, and reminded her that she would be separated from her family for an indefinite period; indeed, she might never see them again.

"It is God's will," she said. "I will go."

She wore a handmade black bombazine dress at the wedding where the minister led the party in a hymn by Reverend Samuel F. Smith, author of "America," the last stanza of which, it was reported, "was sung by the sweet voice of Mrs. Whitman alone—clear, musical and unwavering":

In the deserts let me labor
  On the mountains let me tell
How he died—the blessed Savior—
  To redeem a world from hell!
Let me hasten,
  Far in heathen lands to dwell.
Yes, my native land, I love thee,
  All thy scenes I love them well.
Friends, connections, happy country,
  Can I bid you all farewell?

Narcissa made other dresses of gaily colored calico for the journey and purchased a pair of small "gentleman's riding boots" to wear while, she anticipated, riding sidesaddle to Oregon. She bought an inflatable life preserver for crossing the streams and rivers her husband had mentioned, and for the two of them made a spacious conical tent of mattress ticking waterproofed with oil. She also packed a considerable trunk with clothing, books, and similar necessities.

The day after the wedding, the Whitmans and the two Nez Percé boys set out by wagon and sleigh from Elmira to Hollidaysburg, Pennsylvania, where they would board a canal boat bound for Pittsburgh and Cincinnati. In these earliest days of the long journey ahead, Narcissa sustained a loss that would become commonplace on the Oregon Trail: She wrote home that her trunk fell off the sleigh into a creek, ruined her books, and had to be abandoned. On her honeymoon, long before passing the last outposts of civilization, she had arrived at a sad emigrant truth: "The custom of the country is to possess nothing, and then you will lose nothing while traveling."

The Spaldings had gone ahead and in Pittsburgh had a meeting with the artist George Catlin, who in 1832 had traveled to the mouth of the Yellowstone River and along the way made sketches and paintings of Mandans, Assiniboines, Sioux, and Blackfeet. He regarded himself as an authority on the far West and told Spalding bluntly that it was a mistake to take a white woman into that unforgiving wilderness.

The four missionaries came together for the first time in Cincinnati, where the Spaldings tarried several days while Henry visited his former classmates and professors at the seminary. Narcissa said nothing about seeing him again but wrote of Eliza, whom she met there for the first time, "I like her very much. She wears well upon acquaintance. She is a very suitable person for Mr. Spalding—has the right temperament to match him. I think we shall get on well together."

Since they planned to travel to the Green River rendezvous with Tom Fitzpatrick's trade caravan, which was jumping off from the Missouri border in mid-May, Spalding made the arrangements for the party to travel by steamer to Liberty, and in that frontier town their party expanded in numbers and encumbrances. Whitman took charge of a third Nez Percé lad who was waiting to return to his home country in Idaho, and assigned the three to take charge of the livestock he and Spalding purchased. Two white teenagers were hired for camp chores. The final member of the party who joined them in Liberty was William H. Gray, appointed by the Mission Board as "secular agent" for the Oregon missions. He was a cabinetmaker from Utica, age twenty-six, described somewhat ominously by Bancroft as a "good-looking young fellow, tall of stature, with fine black eyes . . . having pronounced natural abilities, of quick feelings, and a good hater where his jealousy was aroused." Gray had applied to the board for missionary service but his sponsor, who said he was a skilled craftsman, and abstinent, stated bluntly that Gray had "a confidence in his own abilities *to a fault*" and described him as "a slow scholar."

On the basis of Captain Bonneville's example and his own limited experiences in traveling from Liberty to the Green River, Whitman was convinced, despite Fitzpatrick's doubts, that wagons could negotiate the tortured trails and mountain paths and be floated across the waterways to Oregon. Wagons seemed especially essential to convey the women, providing them with at least some comfort and protection in bad weather. Eliza Spalding was "sickly," so Henry had purchased and sent ahead a light Dearborn wagon for her and their possessions. Since Narcissa insisted that she preferred to ride horseback beside her husband, a heavy farm wagon was obtained in Liberty for the party's belongings, and the trade goods, camp gear, medicines, blacksmithing tools, plow, grain, seeds, and provisions purchased from Liberty outfitters. In all, with the thirteen-head beef herd, six mules, fourteen horses, and equipage, Spalding and Whitman spent nearly $3,000 in Mission Board funds to launch themselves toward the Rockies.

After sending the wagons ahead, they crawled up the Missouri by ferry to Fort Leavenworth, then afoot and on horseback followed the North Platte, broke a church rule by traveling on Sunday, and reached the Loup Fork of the Platte. There they overtook Fitzpatrick's caravan, an immense column of 400 horses and mules, seven big freight wagons each drawn by six-mule teams, and seventy men.

The missionaries fell into the caravan's daily routine. In her journal Narcissa wrote: "We encamp in a large ring— baggage and men, tents and wagons on the outside and all the animals except the cows fastened to pickets inside the circle . . . . In the morn as soon as the day breaks that first that we hear is the word 'arise, arise'; then the mules set up as much noise as you never heard, which puts the whole camp in action . . . . You must think it very hard to have to get up so early after sleeping on the soft ground. When you find it hard work to open your eyes at seven o'clock, just think of me." While the horses and stock were feeding, she said, "we get our breakfast in a hurry and eat it. By this time the word 'Catch up, catch up' rings through the camp, for moving. We are ready to start usually at six, travel till eleven, encamp, rest and feed; start again about two, travel until

six, or before if we come to a good tavern [her word for
campsite], then camp for the night."

In the scheme of the caravan, her party ate dust. She wrote
on June 3, 1836, "The fur Com[pany] is large this year. We
are really a moving village . . . . If you wish to see the camp
in motion, just look ahead and see first the pilot and the Captain, Fitzpatrick, just before him; next the pack animals, all
mules loaded with great packs. Soon after you will see the
wagons, and in the rear our company. We all cover quite a
space."

She adapted, learned to "dine" on the ground on an
India-rubber tablecloth that doubled as a cloak when it rained;
scrubbed tin dishes, cups, knives, and spoons with sand; gathered buffalo chips for fuel. Of this latter chore she noted in
her journal, "Our fuel for cooking since we left timber (no
timber except on rivers) has been dried buffalo dung. . . . I
supposed Harriet [one of Narcissa's sisters] will make a face
at this, but if she was here she would be glad to have her sup-
per cooked at any rate, in this scarce timber country."

Crossing the Platte and any other waterway on the route
tested everybody's patience and endurance. Wagons had to
be converted into boats by covering the box with waterproof
hides and worrying them across with towlines; the women
crossed in bull boats or on horseback; the cattle were swum
across tended by their drovers, who stripped naked and tied
their shirts around their heads.

At Fort Laramie, to Whitman's disappointment, the heavy
freight wagon had to be left behind with all the other fur
company rolling stock. Fitzpatrick insisted on it but gave
in to the physician's insistence on proceeding with Spalding's wagon, the little Dearborn, which would carry Eliza
Spalding and, after jettisoning what was agreed to be non-
necessities, the missionaries' combined gear. One other
wagon in the caravan, actually a two-wheel cart, carried
Broken Hand's partner Milton Sublette, whose leg had been
amputated the year before and whose cork substitute allowed

him to stand and walk on flat ground but not to negotiate mountain trails. To help move the two wagons across the Laramie Mountains, an old buffalo trail was cleared of boulders and cottonwoods to create a rude roadway. Even so, the Dearborn spilled over once, and Sublette's cart twice, before they cleared the passes. Spalding was depressed over their agonizingly slow progress and in his letter to the board wrote, "Never send another mission over these mountains if you value life and money." Whitman, even though enslaved by the Dearborn, was more optimistic. "I see no reason to regret our choice of a journey by land," he wrote.

Eight hundred miles out from Liberty, the caravan camped at Independence Rock, a granite formation on which the names of passersby were scratched or daubed in axle grease. Fitzpatrick sent a rider ahead to the Green River to let the trappers know his party was coming in, and the express apparently also reported that the caravan was bringing along some missionaries, including two white women. A wild celebration awaited them after they crossed South Pass on Independence Day 1836, and as they pushed through the sagebrush along Little Sandy Creek, a Green River tributary, the travelers were greeted by an advance party of trappers, Nez Percé, and Flathead Indians from the rendezvous encampment. "Their approach was like the rush of a tornado down a mountain side," Bancroft wrote of these welcomers, "the cracking of their rifles and their terrifying yells like the snapping off of the branches of trees before the wind, and the fierce howlings of a tempest."

The raucous greeters were led by a barrel-chested, black-bearded mountain man and bear hunter from Virginia named Joseph Lafayette "Joe" Meek. He wanted to catch an early glimpse of the first white women to cross the Continental Divide and also deliver a message to the missionaries that some Indians had brought to the rendezvous from Oregon. The letter was from Samuel Parker and in it he informed Whitman that he would not be joining them as planned. He

was worn out and could not even consider making the overland journey from Fort Vancouver. He said he had explored
the Oregon Country from Jason Lee's spread on the Willamette to Spokane and Fort Colville on the north, and gave a
rambling discourse on potential mission sites.

This was devastating news. Spalding and Whitman, and
indeed the Mission Board in New York, had counted on
Parker to lay the groundwork for establishing their mission,
gather information, not only locate ideal sites but begin the
clearing and building work, and serve as guide from the
Green River to the Oregon Country. Now they learned that
he had spent a comfortable winter at Fort Vancouver, and
he hinted that he would return home by sea. He had left them
stranded with no place to go but ahead, likely to reach Oregon in the winter with no prospects except to accept, like
mendicants, whatever charity was available from the Hudson's Bay Company.

15

Spies

■

"... TO CONTROL THE DESTINIES OF THE PACIFIC."

1

In his letter to the Whitmans, Samuel Parker dilated excitedly on the explorations he had made out of Fort Vancouver but failed to say what these ramblings meant to the missionaries he left stranded on the Green River. Marcus Whitman was angered at Parker's unexplained and inexplicable reversal of their plan and wrote, "We cannot say how much good Mr. Parker's tour will do others. It has done us none, for instead of meeting us at the Rendezvous as he agreed, he neglected to write a single letter containing any information concerning the country, company, Indians, prospects or advice whatever."

The Whitmans had faith that the Lord and Tom Fitzpatrick would solve their problem of getting on to the Columbia; meantime, there was nothing to do but wait for the solution and enjoy the spectacle around them.

Nothing in their lives, before or after, would surpass the experience of the twelve days the missionaries spent among the 400 fur traders and 1,500 Indians scattered in the camps and lodges along the lush banks of the Green that July of 1836. The women were special celebrities, and Narcissa was ecstatic over the blunt stares and crude chivalric attention paid her as she mingled, wearing her bright calicos, with the rough crews, chatting, shaking hands, hugging, and passing out church tracts. The Indians, mostly Nez Percé, Flatheads, Shoshoni, and Bannocks, were stunning in their paint, feathers, beads, breechcloths, and moccasins, carrying their lances, shields, and war clubs and dancing to chants, drums, and rattles. They staged a wild horseback show for the newcomers, then came forward to inspect the ladies, hoping for a kiss, a foreign practice they heard was commonplace among white men and women. The trappers, the trail-filthy, shag-bearded Sons of Saturn whose drunken "sprees," knife fights, and horseback and marksmanship contests were standard rendezvous fare, came shyly to have a close look at the "Bible-toters." Some even asked for the Good Book and any Christian literature available to take on the trail for any literate comrade to read aloud. Narcissa wrote home excitedly that she and Eliza could have dispensed two mule-loads of books and tracts had they been available.

Eliza, who had a gift for languages, began learning the Nez Percé tongue and compiling a vocabulary. Narcissa helped, but William Gray, the Utica woodworker and would-be missionary who was ever alert for any faint sign of what he considered inappropriate conduct, said Mrs. Whitman spent too much time flirting with Fitzpatrick, Joe Meek, and the Scotsman Stewart. "In consequence of these attentions or interruptions," he wrote, "she did not acquire the native language as fast as Mrs. Spalding."

Narcissa, in fact, drank in the spectacle of the rendezvous precisely as might be expected of a woman cloistered all her life, and saw in the savages—Indian and mountain man alike—the quintessence of her Christianizing dreams. "This is a cause worth living for!" she wrote in her journal, and her exuberance continued until they departed their roistering company to continue their journey into the grim and rocky sage-lands to the west.

Midway in their stay at the rendezvous, the missionaries

were heartened by the arrival of Nathaniel Wyeth, on his way to the states after his failed enterprises in Oregon. He rode into camp with a brigade of Hudson's Bay men led by Thomas McKay and brought additional news from the lately unrevered Samuel Parker. The reverend urged his colleagues to come directly to Fort Walla Walla under the Company's protection, and before they could ponder how they were expected to get there, McKay and his partners graciously offered to escort them. Their hope now was to reach Oregon before Parker departed for home and obtain from him first-hand, specific, critical information on where they should build their missions and how they would sustain themselves through the winter.

They followed McKay's brigade out of their camp on July 18, bound for Wyeth's fort on the Portneuf River. Narcissa was in the early stages of pregnancy, the baby probably conceived at Fort Laramie in June when the couple found some rare privacy. Although she never mentioned her condition in her journal (it would have been unthinkable to do so), she probably suffered from morning sickness—the odor of sagebrush nauseated her—yet she did not seek Eliza Spalding's company in the Dearborn. Instead, she continued to ride the "excellent sidesaddle and very easy horse" with the Nez Percé boys, the "cow column," and the man she called "Husband" at the rear of the column.

She did not complain, but Marcus' bullheaded coaxing of the wagon down along the Bear River sorely tested her. "Husband had a tedious time with the waggon today," she wrote. "Waggon was upset twice. I do not wonder at all at this. It was a greater wonder that it was not turning a somerset continually. It is not very grateful to my feelings to see him wear out with such excessive fatigue. . . . All the most difficult part of the way he has walked, in his laborious attempt to take the wagon over." On one occasion the wagon was stuck fast in creek mud and Whitman spent most of a day waist-deep in water levering and muscling it free. Narcissa had a momentary hope that Marcus would relinquish the wagon when at Soda Springs the axle broke, but he managed to dismantle the forward wheels and rig it as a cart so he could belabor it on toward Fort Hall.

She noticed her Job-like mate "not as fleshy" as when they'd started out from Missouri. In truth, none of them were. On the wicked trail and under cloudless skies and the pitiless sun, the party endured a diet of buffalo jerky and little else. She wrote in a letter home, "I can scarce eat it, it appears so filthy, but it will keep us alive & we ought to be thankful for it." She said to her sisters, "Girls do not waste bread, if you know how well I should relish even the dryest morsal you would save every piece carefully."

But she bore up. "Do not think I regret coming," she wrote. "No, far from it. I would not go back for the world. I am contented and happy notwithstanding I get very hungry & weary. Have six weeks steady journeying before us. Will the Lord give me patience to endure it . . . . Long for rest, but must not murmur."

Wyeth's Fort Hall provided them with a rest and a chance for laundering and to add turnips and fried bread to their buffalo-jerky diet. When they departed the fort and crossed the Portneuf, heading for the Hudson's Bay post at the confluence of the Snake and Boisé Rivers, the misery started again. McKay's hunters brought in some elk meat and fresh salmon, but such delicacies could not divert them long from the oppressive heat, the incessant stink—to Narcissa at least—of sagebrush, "so stif and hard as to be much in the way of our animals and waggon," and the clouds of mosquitoes that nearly drove them, their pack animals, and cows mad.

Marcus continued to heave the wagon-cart forward, even after it turned over in the mud of the Boisé taking its mule team down with it, tangling cart, harness, and drowning animals in a frothing mass that required two horse teams and two men to help turn it aright. Only when they reached Fort

Boisé on August 19, after 1,500 miles of tribulations, was Whitman persuaded by McKay and his men to surrender the infernal wagon at long last.

As they forded the Snake on horseback and on rope-towed rafts made of willows and rushes toward the Burnt River and the Blue Mountains beyond, the missionaries decided they must split up. The Whitmans and William Gray were to push on with some of McKay's men to reach Fort Vancouver before Reverend Parker shipped out for home. The Spaldings and the Nez Percé wards were to follow, bringing along the cattle and pack animals, with the balance the Company's brigade.

On August 29, the advance party reached the western slopes of the Blue Mountains—which reminded Narcissa of the Catskills—and glimpsed the great white cone of Mount Hood in the hazy distance. Three days later they sighted the timber palisades of Fort Walla Walla, the eighteen-year-old Hudson's Bay post on the east bank of the Columbia and at the mouth of the river from which it derived its name. That night Narcissa wrote in a letter home, "You can better imagine our feelings than I can describe them. I could not realize that the end of our journey was so near. We arose as soon as it was light, then dressed for Walla Walla . . . . If you could have seen us now you would have been surprised, for both man and beast appeared alike propelled by the same force. The whole company galloped almost all the way to the Fort."

They reached it at rooster's crow on September 1, 1836, six months and thirteen days after Narcissa packed her black bombazine dress, her calicos and books, and embarked with her husband by sleigh for Pennsylvania.

The post factor, Pierre Pambrun, a Québec veteran of the War of 1812 and one of John McLoughlin's most trusted agents, welcomed the Americans into his drift-log stockade's inner gallery and led them to guest quarters where they could bathe and ready for breakfast. Narcissa breathed in the fort's civilized trappings—clean water, soap, a soft bed, chinaware, cutlery. "No one knows the feelings occasioned by seeing objects once familiar after long privation," she wrote.

The Spaldings and their escort joined the Whitmans two days later. Together they were the first emigrant families to travel overland to the Pacific, more than 3,000 miles from home.

Nothing had been accomplished by the Whitmans' rush across the Blue Mountains to Fort Walla Walla, since the Spaldings, who had been expected to arrive at a later date after inspecting potential mission sites en route, had also proceeded apace without inspecting anything. None of them as yet knew if Samuel Parker had departed the Columbia, but the urgency of determining that fell below resting and gaining lost strength under the hospitable care of Factor Pambrun.

They lingered several days at the fort before embarking for the Company's great fortress on the lower river. Pambrun personally escorted them downstream in a thirty-foot *bateau,* the oars pulled by Company *voyageurs.* The only discomforts of the journey were the high winds, which forced the boat ashore to wait until they abated, and an incident that occurred during a portage around The Dalles rapids. In a Chinook village Narcissa, apparently inspecting it too closely, became infested with fleas. Her hair and dress, she said, were "black with these creatures, making all possible speed to lay siege to my neck and ears." She fled to Husband, who brushed her off as best he could and set up a protective arbor so she could wash and change her clothing.

In the forenoon of September 12, with the *voyageurs* singing and with a bite of fall in the air, the *bateau* swung around a piney point of land and the missionaries caught their first view of what Narcissa called "the New York of the Pacific Ocean." On the Fort Vancouver landing stood Dr. McLoughlin with his second-in-command, James Douglas, to greet them.

They learned at once that they were too late to interdict
Samuel Parker. He had sailed on the steamship *Beaver* for
the Sandwich Islands three months past, about the time his
colleagues had reached Fort Laramie, and had left no messages or instructions. After the earlier Parker disappointments, the Whitmans and the Spaldings seem not to have
been overwhelmed by the news and fell quickly to planning
the exploration of mission sites—plural. At some point in
their travels, probably long before they reached the Columbia, they agreed to separate, ostensibly to spread the Gospel
farther by establishing two missions but as much because
they were never comfortable together. Parker, in the letter
from him received at the rendezvous, advised that a site
might be established among the Nez Percé, perhaps near the
junction of the Clearwater and Snake Rivers in Idaho, and
suggested also a station among the Cayuse people east of
Fort Walla Walla.

These ideas seemed sensible to both families, both eager
to put miles between themselves, and they were probably endorsed by McLoughlin as well, who saw such stations as
pleasingly remote from the Hudson's Bay main theater of operations. He urged that while the menfolk set out on their
explorations the ladies be left in his care; then, when the sites
were selected, the men would gather their wives, the building materials, and the laborers they would require. This was
agreed upon, and Whitman, Spalding, and William Gray set
out on September 21 with some Nez Percé helpers and a few
other men on loan from McLoughlin, promising to return
within a month.

The wives were treated royally at the fort during their husbands' explorations; Narcissa became especially close to the
half-breed Cree wives of McLoughlin and Douglas. Two
other white women were residing at the fort, one married to
a Hudson's Bay agent, the other the wife of Reverend Herbert Beaver, the post's recently arrived chaplain. A special
attraction for the Americans was meeting Jason Lee, up from

his Willamette mission to visit McLoughlin and welcome the newcomers to Oregon.

Meantime, following Samuel Parker's suggestions, Whitman found what he considered an ideal mission site on the north bank of the Walla Walla River, twenty-two miles east of Pambrun's fort in a lush meadow the Indians called Waiilatpu. William Gray and some workers were left behind to bring in tools and supplies purchased at Fort Vancouver while Whitman, Spalding and their escort rode on 100 miles northeast of Waiilatpu to the juncture of the Clearwater and the Snake, a place Parker had recommended. There they met a party of Nez Percé who, when told of the mission plans, led the white men another ten miles east to Lapwai Creek. Spalding had found his site.

While Whitman, Gray, and their workers began the labor of cutting timber for a cabin at Waiilatpu, Spalding returned to Fort Vancouver, arriving there on October 18, to fetch the wives, load two *bateaux* with a winter's supply of provisions, and, with a Company escort, return upriver. Narcissa, now four months into her pregnancy, was landed at Fort Walla Walla to await completion of the Whitman cabin while Spalding and Eliza, with the help of a force of 100 Indians, loaded twenty horses with supplies and set out for Lapwai Creek. They would live in a tent until better shelter could be erected.

The 110 miles separating the missions seemed a perfect distance. The men were frequently at odds; the wives, so different in temperament to begin with, were so wedded to their husbands' views on their work among the natives that their own relations were strained. Spalding, trained and ordained, hoped to change the pattern of Indian lives to make them more susceptible to Christian teachings. He regarded Whitman as an upstart, not even a minister, who seemed to take his lead from Jason Lee's approach, acting as a promoter more of settlement than of Christ and believing that the way to convert Indians was by submerging them among a large white, preferably white American, population.

2

With a few exceptions, John McLoughlin liked Americans and even broke some of the Hudson's Bay regulations in assisting them. His brigade leaders helped Jason Lee, Nat Wyeth, the Whitmans and the Spaldings in their journeys from rendezvous to the Columbia, and he was always a generous host when such Americans, and such troublesome ones as Hall Kelley, reached his domain. His magnanimity extended to the missionaries, though he was wary of them and dubious of their chances of success in Christianizing the native tribes. He had, in fact, no great regard for churchmen, and even less after a particularly hateful episode involving one sent out to him to serve as chaplain at Fort Vancouver.

Herbert Beaver—"an appropriate name for the fur trade," Peter Ogden dryly observed—crossed the Columbia bar on the *Nereid,* out of England via Cape Horn and the Sandwich Islands, early in 1836. He stepped up on the landing below the fort, surveyed its primitive surroundings, shook hands with McLoughlin and his welcoming delegation, and thereafter fell afoul of almost all who came in contact with him. Reverend Beaver was a Church of England divine who had served as a regimental chaplain at Saint Lucia and must have viewed his new assignment as similarly beneath his station as the West Indies. He began his tenure by demanding better quarters and agonizing over the log cottage that was set aside to serve as his parsonage. Worse than the lodgings was his realization that here he was thrust among several hundred French-Canadian *voyageurs* who were Roman Catholics and surrounded by Indian tribes whose heathenish "religions" perplexed and angered him.

Beaver fancied himself a great maker of humorous *mots* and a greater orator, but contemporaries at Fort Vancouver described him as a small, pale man with a high-pitched "feminine" voice, an air of pretension, and an undisguised disdain for all he saw and all he met. Bancroft said, "He was of the fox-hunting type of English clergyman, and had been much diverted by the manners of his fellow passenger from Honolulu, especially Mr. Jason Lee, whom he was constantly in the habit of quizzing." As to the "inmates of the fort," Bancroft said, these grave, dignified, disciplined men, "accustomed to respect, did not always escape the reverend gentleman's sallies of wit." Indeed, "his ideas of clerical dignity were such that he felt himself defiled by association with the gentlemen at Fort Vancouver. McLoughlin was un-civil, the clerks boors, the women savages. Here was a fine beginning of English missionary work!"

Beaver found many of the Hudson's Bay "practices" among the Indians reprehensible and dutifully reported these to the Aborigines Protection Society in London, saying that his work among the savages and his attempts to introduce civi-lization and Christianity to them were constantly thwarted by the Company. He found a special abomination in the practice among "the gentlemen of the fort" of consorting with native women, and in this discovery he made a terrible mistake.

To his horror, Beaver learned that many of the traders at Fort Vancouver were married to Indians without the bless-ing of clergy, and then he discovered, through some species of moccasin telegraph never disclosed, that John McLough-lin and his half-Cree wife Marguérite had cohabited before the death of her first husband, Alexander McKay, in 1811. In a letter home, Beaver referred to Marguerite as "a female of notoriously loose character . . . the kept Mistress of the highest personage in your service at this station."

In his moral certitude and God-given abstruseness, Her-bert Beaver did not count on the chief factor having so many Hudson's Bay friends in England and at the York Factory, and thus had no concern that the contents of his letter might come back to McLoughlin. But they did, and, predictably, the chief factor exploded. It was dangerous enough to spread rumors about McLoughlin, but it was positively suicidal to involve his beloved Marguérite in them.

When the White Eagle got the news, he marched out into the fort's courtyard, found Beaver, and braced him. The scene must have been delectable for any onlooker: Here stood the man whom Governor George Simpson said was "such a figure as I should not like to meet in a dark Night," his formidable six-and-a-half-foot height looming and rigid as an old oak, his great expanse of chest working like a bellows, his white mane of hair flowing, his face suffused with wrath, his icy eyes narrowed, one fist clenched at his side, the other strangling a stout cane. And here stood poor, cringing Herbert Beaver, paler than usual, looking up, snared in a trap sprung by his own folly and from which there was no escape.

McLoughlin demanded an explanation of the vile rumors contained in his worship's letter.

Beaver, nervously searching his mind for a *mot* by which he might wrench his foot from the snare, replied, "Sir, if you wish to know why a cow's tail grows downward, I cannot tell you; I can only cite the fact."

At this astonishing response, Bancroft reports, "Up went the cane of its own volition, and before McLoughlin was aware of it, he had bestowed a good sound blow upon the shoulders of the impudent divine."

Beaver made a full, if quite preposterous, record of what ensued in his encounter with "this monster in human shape." He wrote that McLoughlin "came behind me, kicked me several times, and struck me repeatedly with his fists on the back of the neck. Unable to cope with him from the immense disparity of our relative size and strength, I could not prevent him from wrenching out of my hand a stout stick with which I was walking, and which he . . . inflicted several severe blows on my shoulders." Beaver reported that the factor then "seized me from behind, round my waist, attempted to dash me on the ground, exclaiming 'You scoundrel, I will have your life.' In the meantime, the stick had fallen to the ground; my wife, on impulse . . . picked it up; he took it . . . very viciously from her hands and again struck me with it severely. We were then separated by the intervention of other persons."

If McLoughlin was ever reprimanded for his conduct toward the chaplain, it was done verbally by Governor Simpson and, one imagines, quite diplomatically.

Reverend Beaver, apparently concluding that his salary of £400 per annum was insufficient to include canings, decamped from the Columbia soon after the incident and in 1838 returned to England.

The Hudson's Bay Company sent no more chaplains to Fort Vancouver.

The trickle of American missionaries into Oregon did not go unnoticed by McLoughlin's superiors, and in June 1836, three months before the arrival of the Whitmans and the Spaldings and about the time Samuel Parker was sailing home, the factor received a warning from the Company's headquarters at York. "Were we satisfied that the sole object of those Missionaries were the civilization of the Natives and the diffusion of moral and religious instruction, we should be happy to render them our most cordial support and assistance," the minute read, "but we have all along foreseen that . . . the formation of a Colony of United States citizens on the banks of the Columbia was the main or fundamental part of their plan, which, if successful, might be attended with material injury, not only to the fur trade, but in a national point of view."

The suspicion that these Americans were more interested in colonization than converts to Christianity came as no news to McLoughlin. Missionaries were historically precursors of colonizers, and he viewed all the Americans who

came to Oregon as the vanguard of a settler invasion and
held that belief even before the arrival of Hall Jackson Kelley, as blatant a stumper for American "occupation" of the
Pacific Northwest as Fort Vancouver ever endured. He followed reports in the American press, knew of the congressional work of Dr. John Floyd of Virginia and his bills to
claim Oregon for the United States; he knew of Hall Kelley
and his agitations before that peculiar man ever reached the
Columbia; he had talks with such Americans as Jedediah
Smith, Ewing Young, Nat Wyeth, Jason Lee, and Samuel
Parker.

McLoughlin's hospitable treatment of the Americans who
came to Fort Vancouver was the product of his shrewdly
realistic assessment of his and Hudson's Bay's presence in
Oregon. By 1836 he had twelve years in the Pacific Northwest. He enjoyed a virtual monopoly in the fur trade and had
expanded the Company's enterprises to the north, south, and
east, making good profits for his employer. But he knew that
the British foothold was fragile, the 1827 joint occupancy
treaty toothless, the fur business precarious and already
showing signs of playing out. He was alert to the changes
on the wind. The Americans were returning to the river they
had discovered and never relinquished—the missionaries
were harbingers of a great migration of them—and those
who had arrived, the churchmen among them, were talking of farms, industry, settlements, and of pushing the British out.

McLoughlin dealt with them cleverly. He had an honest
affection for most Americans and assisted them, at times beyond the boundaries of Hudson's Bay policies. He was hospitable and generous, at times to a fault; and would later
reminisce woefully about how certain of the beneficiaries of
his largesse thanked him by stabbing him in the back. He
also did the best he could to protect the Company's interests.
When possible, he shunted the missionaries off to the
Willamette valley and other locations remote from Fort

Vancouver; he loaned and sold, but did not give, supplies and labor to those intending to stay; he was aggressive in keeping the Company paramount in the fur trade—this, after all, being his chief responsibility.

An example of McLoughlin's acumen toward the Americans who sought him out at Fort Vancouver was his use of a man named William A. Slacum.

This gentleman arrived on the Columbia in the last week of December 1836, the single passenger on the American brig *Loriot*, which he had chartered for $700 a month at Honolulu. He identified himself as a "private merchant" who had traveled from Washington via Cape Horn, Guaymas in Baja California, and the Sandwich Islands, to investigate trade possibilities on the Pacific coast. McLoughlin, who learned that Slacum had been an obscure purser in the United States Navy, suspected from the moment he met his overly inquisitive guest that he was neither merchant nor gentleman traveler but an intelligence agent of some kind, and in this he was correct. The visitor had been commissioned by John A. Forsyth, President Andrew Jackson's secretary of state, to visit Oregon to ascertain the truth of Hall Kelley's vituperations that American settlers were being "oppressed" by Hudson's Bay agents, and that the British were thus in flagrant violation of the Anglo-American agreement.

Slacum expressed an interest in meeting Jason Lee and other Americans who had preceded him to Fort Vancouver, and in this request McLoughlin saw the opportunity to utilize the spy in his midst. He told Slacum of the case of the American Ewing Young, who had come to Oregon more than two years past with a horse herd said, by no less an authority than Governor José Figueroa of Alta California, to have been stolen in his province. McLoughlin had banished Young from the fort and refused him trade; then, a few months later, Governor Figueroa exculpated the trapper from the charges. McLoughlin had been instrumental in urging Young to seek redress from Figueroa, but Young had become an enemy, refusing to trade at the fort after McLoughlin lifted the ban, and with a partner had established a farm and sawmill in the Chehalem Valley north of the Columbia.

None of this bothered the factor; what did were the reports that Young had built a still on his farm and was brewing alcohol, using a huge copper salmon-pickling cauldron salvaged from Nat Wyeth's Fort Hall. This was a disturbing development with a high potential for mischief, and McLoughlin asked Slacum to serve as an emissary to entreat Young to abandon the still in exchange for open privileges to trade at the fort stores. Slacum must have thought this a reasonable request and an appropriate assignment for one American to negotiate with another. He remained with McLoughlin until January 10, then, with six *voyageurs* as escort, began his tour by visiting the old Indian camp called Champoeg on the east side of the river, where McLoughlin had a warehouse. There he met with Jason Lee and several others eager to tell him, or any other visiting American, their problems, especially their complaints of subservience to the Company's monopoly on foodstuffs, seeds, supplies, tools, building materials, and virtually everything else needed to build and settle.

While spending two weeks with Lee at his Willamette valley station, Slacum learned that Lee's temperance society had already visited Ewing Young on the whiskey issue. The Methodists had offered sixty dollars and twelve bushels of wheat to offset what Young had already invested in the still if he would tear it down. The trapper rejected the missionaries' offer and that of McLoughlin as well, but he told Slacum he had abandoned the distillery for the present. He said he had turned his attention to a sawmill he had recently built.

Bancroft's assessment of the whiskey issue was that

"Young's distillery speculation had been like the labor of Cleanthes, who supported himself by drawing water at night in order that he might indulge in plucking the flowers of philosophy during the day; it was not appreciated by the Willamette Areopagus."

3

The more-or-less secret agent William Slacum crammed as much travel and talk as he could into his brief visit to the Oregon Country. Probably before he reached Fort Vancouver, the *Loriot* had taken him as far north as Juan de Fuca Strait. He was awed by the great sound that connected to the Pacific, named in 1792 by its discoverer, Captain George Vancouver, for his aide, Peter Puget; he met with delegations of Canadians and assured them that they would not lose their farms when (not if) the United States took possession of Oregon, and cheered them further by saying that under American protection they would receive as much as three times more than the fifty cents a bushel Fort Vancouver was paying for their wheat.

During Slacum's visits with Jason Lee and Ewing Young, the Americans dwelled on beef cattle—their scarcity in Oregon, their importance for colonization—and Young, who had tramped Alta California from San Diego to Klamath Lake as a trapper, daydreamed about the abundance of cheap cattle there. The issue so impressed Slacum that he offered his chartered *Loriot* when Young said he wanted to mount an expedition to buy and bring a beef herd back to the Willamette.

In a report he wrote later the agent said, "I found that nothing was wanting to insure comfort, wealth, and every happiness to the people of this most beautiful country, but the possession of neat-cattle, all of those in the country being owned by the Hudson's Bay Company, who refused to

sell them under any circumstances whatever."* The idea
gained such momentum that even McLoughlin participated
when the Willamette Cattle Company was organized in a
meeting at Champoeg. In all, about $2,500 was gathered to
float the enterprise. Slacum loaned Jason Lee $624 for the
mission's share and put in another $100 of his own;
McLoughlin anted up $558 of his own money and $300 more
in the name of two of his traders. (His contributions were
never mentioned by the Americans.) Young gathered up thirteen men, two of them Indian guides; Slacum packed his
kit, intending to return home after disembarking the cattle
hunters, and they all boarded the *Loriot* on January 21, eager to reach California.

However, from the first day to the last in what became a
tortured nine-month expedition, nothing went smoothly.
First, the Columbia threatened to scuttle them before they
could cross the bar. In Baker's Bay they found that two Hudson's Bay fur vessels had been detained nearly a month by
high seas, and the *Loriot* had to join them. Tossed and battered in the estuary, the brig's mooring cables parted, its sails
were shredded to rags, and its decks and bilges were awash
before it could batter a path into the open sea on February
10. They reached Fort Ross, the Russian trading post fifty
miles north of San Francisco Bay, nine days later, and on
March 1, 1838, Young and some of his men were disembarked at Yerba Buena, after which Slacum sailed south
toward the Horn and home.

Young met with Mexican officials at the tiny settlement
and learned that it was illegal for foreigners to remove live

_____

*Actually, there were so few head to begin with that they went un-
slaughtered in order to multiply, and McLoughlin refused to sell them
not only to Americans but to anyone, including the British. This simple explanation did not prevent the cattle issue from becoming one of
the many bones of contention between the missionary-settlers and
Hudson's Bay agents.

cattle from the province. Three months were lost shuttling
on horseback from the bay to San José, Monterey, and even
as far south as Santa Barbara and north to Sonoma before
the rules were slackened and Young was permitted to buy
800 head of cattle at three dollars each. The stock was anything but prime; the Mexicans fobbed off wild, skinny animals hazed out of the brush and into corrals.

Young spent the last of his Willamette Cattle Company
startup funds by buying forty horses and hiring five foot-
loose Americans found wandering about Monterey to help
the others put the cattle into a semblance of a trail herd. The
drive began by skirting the animals around San Francisco
Bay on the south toward the San Joaquin River. There were
no cowboys in Young's party, and no one had experience in
moving cattle across land, much less water. The terrified animals, already maddened by the flies and mosquitoes infest-
ing the river bottoms, refused to budge from the San Joaquin
banks; even when calves were dragged across the river by
horse and rope their mothers bawled and dug their hooves
into the mud or ran off into the brush. Pens were rigged to
contain them but were quickly reduced to rubble as the animals stampeded, and days were devoted to hunting them
down and dragging them back to the crossing. Then, when
a sizable number were cursed and goaded into the river, they
ignored the far shore and swam out in all directions. Seventeen drowned in one such sortie. Finally, Young and his exhausted, exasperated drovers built rafts of bulrushes and
with a rope strung across the river ferried the cattle one at a
time to the opposite bank.

Toward the end of August they reached the mountains at
the head of the Sacramento valley and on September 12 arrived on the Rogue River (also called Les Coquins and sometimes the Rascal River, after the "rascally," unpredictable
Indians living on its banks) in southern Oregon. This was
dangerous country. Not far to the north, on the Umpqua,
Jedediah Smith's trapping party had been attacked by a

Kalawatset war party ten years past, and some of Ewing Young's men had been in fights with Rogue River raiders and had learned to hate the sight of any Indian in the vicinity. Trouble was assured when one drover shot and wounded a native boy shortly after the herd splashed across a shallow river fording. Each day afterward, arrows flew into the cattle camp and gunshots rang out, and on September 18 there was a fleeting massed attack on the drovers that resulted in the wounding of one white man, several cows, and Young's horse before the Indians were driven off by gunfire.

The cattle company straggled into Jason Lee's Willamette Mission grounds in mid-October, nine months after boarding the *Loriot* and having traveled 700 miles in eighteen weeks from San Francisco Bay, with 600 of the original 800 head of stock still alive, still skinny, and still wild. The drovers were paid off in cattle at the rate of twenty dollars a month, and the remaining stock was prorated among the investors.

William A. Slacum sailed from Alta California on February 10, 1837, arrived in New York that summer, and submitted a report to the Twenty-fifth Congress in December of the year. The document became influential for its strategic recommendations, its lengthy description of Fort Vancouver, and its condemnation of the Hudson's Bay Company. The document also contained random remarks on the Indians and the physical features of the country; firsthand glimpses into the lives, and problems, of the missionary-settlers of the Willamette valley; and recommendations on what was being called "the Oregon Question," the issue of extending American hegemony from the Rocky Mountains to the Pacific.

Slacum wrote of the importance of Puget Sound as a deepwater port and sea-lane into the Pacific, writing, "In a military point of view, [Puget Sound] is of the highest importance to the United States." So important, in fact, that he urged the government to insist upon the 49th parallel as the northern boundary in any settlement with England in order to bring the sound into American control. He added the notion that a large colony of American settlers in Oregon might assist if there should be resistance in obtaining it.

As to the state of the missionaries and other Americans already in Oregon, Slacum had brought their woes, real and imagined, home with him. "Some steps must be taken by our government," he wrote, "to protect the settlers and traders, not from the hostility of the Indians, but from a much more formidable enemy . . . the Hudson's Bay Company."

Slacum's work was perfectly timed with that of his missionary friend Jason Lee who, within weeks of the agent's submission to Congress, arrived in New York with his memorial, signed by fifty settlers describing themselves as the nucleus of a great new state of the Union and urging the United States to take formal possession of the lands south of the Columbia River.

4

A year after Slacum reached Washington, the six-ship United States Exploring Expedition sailed from Norfolk, Virginia, for the Pacific under the command of navy lieutenant Charles Wilkes, a forty-three-year-old New Yorker. With him were an impressive scientific contingent that included naturalists, botanists, mineralogists, a philologist, and even taxidermists. The expedition was to make extensive scientific, commercial, and strategic studies from the South Seas to Alta California and what his orders called "the territory of the United States on the seaboard," the Columbia River country.

The ships made stopovers on the South American coast, at the Paumotus, Samoa, New South Wales, the Antarctic coast, Fiji and the Sandwich Islands, and lingered several weeks in Mexican California before some of them reached the mouth of the Columbia in April 1841.

Wilkes was an imperious naval officer with scientific pretensions ("His impudence was greater than his talents," Bancroft said) who had inexplicably been given the command over many senior officers desiring it. He spent several months exploring the country from Puget Sound to the Willamette valley, from Fort Vancouver as far east as the Spaldings' Lapwai Mission, and was unimpressed by the handful of American settlers he met and dismissed the missionaries as more interested in money than in converting Indians. After he lost one of his vessels, the sloop-of-war *Peacock,* on a sandbar at the entrance of the Columbia (its crew was rescued by Chinook Indians), he wrote, "Mere description can give little idea of the terrors of the bar of the Columbia; all who have seen it have spoken of the wildness of the scene, and the incessant roar of the waters, representing it as one of the most fearful sights that can possibly meet the eye of the sailor," and encouraged the occupation of the coast above forty-nine degrees where safer harbors could be found.

Of the anchorages farther north Wilkes said, "Nothing can exceed the beauty of these waters, and their safety; not a shoal exists within the Straits of Juan de Fuca, Admiralty Inlet, Puget Sound, or Hood's Canal, that can in any way interrupt the navigation by a seventy-four-gun ship. I venture nothing in saying there is no country in the world that possesses waters equal to these."

Later, after he visited Alta California, Wilkes predicted that within a few years that province would probably be separated from Mexico and united with Oregon and "will perhaps form a state that is destined to control the destinies of the Pacific." This future state, he wrote, "is admirably suited to become a powerful maritime nation, with two of the finest ports in the world—that within the Straits of Juan de Fuca and San Francisco."

In October 1841, about a month before he departed

Oregon to sail to Japan before returning home, Wilkes met
with Hudson's Bay governor George Simpson at Fort Vancouver. Sir George (he had been knighted that year) learned
from Wilkes that he intended recommending to his superiors in Washington that the United States should claim the
Oregon Country to the line of 54 degrees, 40 minutes north
latitude. Simpson, upon the American's departure, wrote a
memorandum to the British Foreign Office stating that the
lands south of the Columbia were not worth fighting for,
that the dangers of the Columbia estuary and the "unhealth-
fulness" of the south augured against British interests in
that region. But he urged the government "not to consent to
any boundary which would give the United States any portion of the Territory north of the Columbia River."

The four-year expedition resulted in an eighteen-volume
Narrative under Wilkes' name, which the *North American
Review* described as "a work of oppressive dimensions . . .
crushed under the weight of irrelevant matter." Even so, as
Bancroft wrote, "Meagre as was the knowledge gathered by
this expedition, its influence upon the affairs of the Pacific
territory of the United States in their then incipient state was
important."

In the period of 1838—41, Slacum, Lee, and Wilkes, two
spies and a missionary in John McLoughlin's thinking, were
the new reigning Oregon authorities, supplanting if not replacing such old ones as Hall Kelley, who was still writing
and bemoaning his fate in Three Rivers, Massachusetts, and
Nat Wyeth, still working for the Tudor Ice Company in Boston. Kelley and Wyeth shared platforms occasionally to
speak on the glories of the Arcadia of the Pacific Northwest,
and their orations and writings, and the work by Slacum and
Wilkes, oiled the engine moving the government, and trains
of certain citizens seeking a new life, to provide answers to
the "Oregon Question."

16

. . . .

Champoeg

■

". . . FREE CITIZENS OF OREGON."

1

The annexation petition Jason Lee delivered to Washington anticipated the need for governance in the growing American colony in the Willamette and had influential support in Congress. Massachusetts Representative Caleb Cushing, perhaps inspired by the voices from the wilderness, wrote a combative, twenty-seven-page discourse on the Oregon question for the *North American Review* in January 1840. The congressman questioned the "blindness and supineness of the Federal Government" toward the Hudson's Bay Company's "monopoly of commerce of that wide-spread and noble domain of the United States situated on the Pacific Ocean." He said that "this foul blot on our national honor" must be wiped out "if there is one spark of true patriotic feeling left in the breasts of Congress or the Federal Administration" and urged that the government would be "impelled forward by the irresistible voice of the people."

Senator Linn of Missouri, in 1838, 1841, and annually until his death in 1843, introduced bills to extend American laws to Oregon settlers and to give generous land grants to families who would risk the journey out there. He proposed grants of 640 acres to every male citizen over eighteen years of age, and 160 acres more for each wife and child, this in a time when a subsistence-sized patch of farmland east of the Mississippi cost $200 or more. Linn's bills were invariably voted down or tabled as too severe an affront to the British, and while the Oregon colonists waited for congressional legislation to guide them, they banded together to make some of their own.

The lawmaking occasion was the death of Ewing Young, that "excellent old captain" and "audacious pioneer" Bancroft admired, in early February 1841, after he fell into a delirium at his Chehalem Valley homestead. He had long suffered from some undiagnosed ailment, probably peritonitis from a stomach ulcer, and gave up at the age of forty-nine. At the fevered end of his life Young may have been dreaming of how far he had come from his native Tennessee in his allotted half century; of trapping, wandering, and fighting Indians along the Santa Fé Trail and along western rivers from the Gila to the Rogue. To the end he smarted over the accusation that he was a horse thief, still held John McLoughlin and the Hudson's Bay Company in contempt, and remained proud of the great cattle drive he led out of Mexican California to the Willamette in '37, his 137-head share of which had grown to 600 when he died. He was a cantankerous, lonely figure to the end, never married, and had few friends, but he managed in less than a decade in the Northwest to become wealthy, at least by Oregon standards, with land holdings, cattle, a sawmill, and a homestead.

Since Young died intestate, with no heirs or legal claimants,* the American settlers south of the Columbia

---

*At least until 1854 when a young man named Joaquín Young came out to Oregon from Taos, New Mexico, with papers seeming to prove that he was the son of Ewing Young and María Josefa Tafoya of Taos. Kit Carson was among those who provided paper testimony on the authenticity of the young man's parentage, and others swore that Ewing Young spoke of having a son in New Mexico. The Oregon

decided to gather to liquidate his property and other assets. The process began with a series of public auctions conducted by one of Young's few friends, Joe Meek, "his splendid figure clad in the ragged habiliments common to the improvident mountain man," Bancroft said. The auctions netted a healthy $4,000 (Young's prized, and pristine, two-volume set of Shakespeare, brought $3.50), but the property presented a more complex problem, and to deal with it a call was issued for all Americans in the Oregon Country, and any interested Canadians, to congregate at the Methodist mission on February 17, 1841, to serve as an ad hoc probate court.

Beginning with the matter of Young's estate, this meeting and the others following at Champoeg, in a grassy, timbered place on a bend of the Willamette called French Prairie, gave rise to the first series of "wolf meetings" dealing with predators—wolves, coyotes, mountain lions, even bears—killing the settlers' stock. The attendees also formed a committee to draw up a legal code and constitution, and a miniature provisional government that would press for annexation of the Oregon Country by the United States.

A few months into this process, Lee and others instrumental in the Champoeg meetings approached the naval explorer Charles Wilkes for advice. If the settlers hoped for his endorsement of their efforts they were sorely disappointed, for Wilkes, who had the highest regard for his own importance, worked hard to dampen their ardor. He suggested that the whole governmental scheme was unnecessary, that it was a poor and uninforceable substitute for a moral code such as that preached by the missionaries. He said it would be wise to wait and not to disturb the Hudson's Bay people until the United States officially extended its jurisdiction over the Pacific Northwest. He assured the Americans that

---

Territorial legislature found Joaquín Young's claim to have merit and awarded him nearly $5,000 in settlement of his claim.

he intended to recommend this course in his report to his superiors in Washington.

The settlers pressed on, regardless of Wilkes' admonitions, and created their constitution, calling it their "First Organic Laws" of the "free citizens of Oregon." The document contained a religious freedom article; others on habeas corpus, the right of trial by jury; and a prohibition against cruel and unusual punishment and against slavery. A "voluntary subscription" of funds was to take the place of taxation. As to the natives of the country, the signers pledged that the "utmost good faith shall always be observed towards the Indians. Their lands and property shall never be taken from them without their consent." Voting rights were granted to those age twenty-one and older (males only), and those eligible to vote were also eligible for public office. Provisions were made for a legislative body, a supreme court, a treasurer and "recorder"—a clerk to make records of governmental proceedings. Rights of marriage were reserved to male persons age sixteen and older and females fourteen years and older.

The preamble of the constitution employed the name "Oregon Territory" to describe the lands south of the Columbia even though, when it was signed and adopted by the American enclave on July 5, 1843, there would be a five-year wait before territorial status became federal law. In the meantime, two years after its creation, John McLoughlin, acting on behalf of the Hudson's Bay Company, recognized the Americans' provisional government "for the security of the Company's property and the protection of its rights."

2

In March 1841, a month after Ewing Young died in Oregon, William Henry Harrison became the ninth president of the United States. He was a frail sixty-eight—the last president to have been born before the Revolution. He rode

horseback to his inauguration without a coat or hat in cold
and stormy weather, spent an hour and forty-five minutes
reading his 8,500-word address, and, a month later, at thirty
minutes after midnight on Sunday, April 4, died, of "pleu-
risy fever"—pneumonia—in the White House.

During the administration of John Tyler, Harrison's vice
president and fellow Virginian, the United States and Great
Britain signed a boundary agreement. It fixed the border between Maine and Canadian New Brunswick, added 7,000
miles of disputed land to the United States, and made minor adjustments to the U.S.–Canadian boundary from the
Atlantic to the Rocky Mountains. This "settlement" seemed
an excellent opportunity to reconcile the Oregon boundary
matter, but neither nation was as yet ready for anything so
radical, and left the question unresolved.

In 1841 the American nation of 17 million citizens was
still reeling from the effects of the financial collapse of '37,
the greatest economic depression ever experienced, that followed the end of the Jackson administration. Bad banking
policies and feverish speculation in public lands during the
Jacksonian era lay at the root of the disaster, but among the
hardest hit were those who had no money in banks nor any
interest in land other than what they could grow on it. Farmers, who had to scrabble hard to eke out a living in the best
of times, were devastated by falling prices for their agricultural products and the surpluses clogging the marketplace.
Farms were foreclosed and families rendered homeless and
impoverished as surely, and in some instances as fatally, as
the cholera epidemic that was creeping westward.

The anthem of the dispossessed—"There *has* to be something better out there"—in many cases referred to free land.
All the best farmlands east of the Mississippi had been
claimed; even in Missouri, with its 400,000 settlers in 1841,
an acre of mediocre land was selling at a dollar and a quarter, and a foreclosed dirt-farm family couldn't afford a tract
big enough to subsist on.

The far West propagandists made an impression on such desperate people in the first half of the decade of the forties, the tub-thumpers ranging from those who had been to the Pacific—trappers, traders, travelers, government agents—to those like Linn of Missouri and Cushing of Massachusetts who had not seen, nor would ever see, the places west of Independence about which they wrote and orated.

They all talked about free land—that they had in common, and there was no greater lure for westering than free land—and most spoke of a second chance, a new life for those willing to work for it. They also extolled the salubriousness of the climate, the pure air and freedom from the epidemics of typhoid, dysentery, tuberculosis, scarlet fever, yellow fever, malaria, and particularly Asiatic cholera, which in the two decades to follow would kill 30,000 Americans.

One charming and often quoted story told of a Missourian asking a man just returned from California if there were fevers and "ague" out there. The man said that there was but one man in all of California who ever got a chill there, and he was the subject of so much wonderment that people in Monterey went eighteen miles out into the country just to see him shake.

3

To Marcus and Narcissa Whitman and Henry and Eliza Spalding, 1841 meant they were entering their fifth year of work at their missions, the Whitmans at the "Place of the Rye Grass" on Mill Creek on the north bank of the Walla Walla River, and the Spaldings a comfortable 110 miles northeast, among the Nez Percé at Lapwai.

The first years of their "Call" to minister to the Indians were devoted more to the physical labor required to make their missions self-sustaining—building, planting, fencing, tending to stock—than to teaching and preaching, giving such a visitor as Lieutenant Charles Wilkes the impression that they were more interested in making money than converts.

This notion was entirely specious, for these families made neither money nor converts. Both missionary families suffered frustrations and failures unforeseen in the days when they dreamed of delegations of savages arriving on their doorstep eager to learn the Christian way of life. Henry Spalding wrote Elijah White, a physician who came out to Oregon in 1836, "I have no evidence to suppose but a vast majority of them [the Nez Percé] would look on with indifference and see our dwelling burned to the ground, and our heads severed from our bodies." This fatalistic thinking was echoed by Congregational missionaries among the Spokane Indians near Fort Colville. Elkanah Walker of Maine and Cushing Eells of Massachusetts were of the opinion that the natives were more interested in tobacco than in the Testaments. (In 1847, Mrs. Eells wrote home, "We have been here almost nine years and have not yet been permitted to hear the rites of one penitent or the songs of one redeemed soul.")

The mission families did their best against crushing odds. The Lapwai station was commodious and warmed by eleven fireplaces. It had a reception room, a spinning and weaving room, a dining room and bedrooms, and a schoolhouse, all under one roof. The Spaldings had planned and supervised the building of a church, mill, blacksmith shop, granary, warehouses, and farm buildings. They strove for self-sufficiency, the Board of Foreign Missions' *sine qua non,* and worked, taught, and preached tirelessly, in isolation and, at times, in fear. The Nez Percé, even those who sent their children to the mission school and attended the mission church, were fickle in their relationships with the Spaldings, and unpredictable. They pulled down the sawmill on one occasion, with no known motive, threatened Spalding, at least once carrying guns, and repeatedly insulted his wife.

At Waiilatpu, the Whitmans experienced a similar pattern of progress, frustration, and signals of danger in their efforts among the Cayuse's people. With Indian workers and hired hands they planted wheat and potato fields, built a gristmill and a sawmill, and fenced pasturage for a small herd of cattle, some horses, and hogs and sheep imported from the Sandwich Islands. Their story-and-a-half adobe mission house was sixty feet long by eighteen wide with a library, bedrooms, dining and sitting rooms, a kitchen, and schoolrooms where Narcissa taught reading and singing. A second house, forty by thirty feet in size and occupied by the Utica woodworker and "secular agent" for the Oregon missions, William H. Gray, stood a short distance away. The Walla Walla River and a millpond formed one side of the mission grounds, an irrigation ditch the other. Toward the west stretched a pretty meadow and copses of apple trees. The mission sawmill lay twenty miles up Mill Creek.

The Cayuse, the principal natives of the Waiilatpu area, shared a similar language with the Nez Percé, were related to them through intermarriage, and, like the Nez Percé, were master horsemen.* But the two tribes distrusted each other and the Cayuse were reputedly more erratic in their behavior and more "savage," this perhaps growing out of battles with their traditional enemies, the Shoshoni, whose lands lay on the eastern slopes of the Blue Mountains and in Snake River country.

(In a report he sent east, Elijah White said that the insolence of the Cayuse had been growing since the visit of Captain Benjamin Bonneville, who in 1834 paid the Indians for their furs far more than Hudson's Bay agents and that the Indians began making demands ever after.)

Some Nez Percé who visited the Whitmans early upon their settling at the Waiilatpu station warned them that the Cayuse "were not good people," were "morose and treach-

---

*Hence "cayuse," an Old West word for an Indian pony.

erous." This signal, perhaps dismissed as intertribal bitterness, seemed much more alarming and premonitory after a series of incidents the Whitmans endured that were even more unnerving than those experienced by the Spaldings. From the outset, the Whitmans had to contend with the Cayuse's peculiar notion that they were owed by the missionaries and not vice versa: They demanded to be paid for receiving religious instruction and for use of the land being cultivated. Split-Lip, chief of the Cayuse of the Waiilatpu area, was a particularly demanding and insulting *bête noir* of the missionaries, so much so that on several occasions Whitman had to seek help from Pierre Pambrun, the factor at Fort Walla Walla, in dealing with him. The natives were careful not to anger the Hudson's Bay Company agents, fearing that they might withdraw their trading posts from the country, and Pambrun was generally able to assist Whitman and manage the menacing natives.

Nonetheless, there were confrontations, and the direst of these occurred in 1840 when a band of Cayuse rode through the mission wheat field and trampled it flat. When Marcus Whitman attempted to reprove them, several of the band threw mud at him, while others dismounted and stood face-to-face with the terrified man, pulling at his beard and ears, cocking and snapping an unloaded pistol at his head, threatening him with an ax, and shouting that they would tear down the mission house and burn it. Whitman, shaken by the confrontation, reported it to John McLoughlin. The factor, who had never trusted the Cayuse and was dubious of any missionary efforts among them, strongly counseled the Whitmans to quit Waiilatpu forthwith.

But they stayed on, and in 1841 withstood another menacing incident, this one involving Gray, the volatile cabinetmaker residing on the mission grounds, who struck an Indian boy for some unknown offense. The boy's uncle was the Cayuse chief Tiloukaikt—described by Bancroft as "a haughty and irascible man"—who sought out Whitman in the mission yard and avenged the insult by striking at the missionary and knocking off his hat.

Narcissa, too, had suffered the insults and ingratitude of the Indians but bore them more stoically than her husband. She had learned to bear the vicissitudes of wilderness life by surrounding herself with children. She had arrived in Oregon pregnant, and on her birthday, March 4, 1837, gave birth to their daughter, Alice Clarissa, the first white American child born in the Oregon Country. The girl, the light of the Whitmans' lives, drowned in the Walla Walla River in June 1838, and Narcissa never recovered from her death nor bore another child. She did persuade Marcus to adopt Helen Meek and Mary Ann Bridger, the half-Indian children of the mountain men Joe Meek and James Bridger. In 1842 she took in an orphaned three-year-old "Spanish-Indian" boy, and when her husband returned from a trip east in 1843, he brought with him his thirteen-year-old nephew to join the household. Finally, in 1844, the Whitmans adopted the seven children of Henry and Naomi Sager, both of whom had died on the Oregon Trail.

For all the reverses in their proselytizing, both the Whitmans and the Spaldings were sustained by their faith and the harsh realization that their Christianizing work would require a lifetime or more to produce a healthy number of converts. They were at least making a start in a noble endeavor. They were also learning that their work not only involved battering down centuries of heathenish spiritual beliefs and teaching the path to righteousness, but overcoming secular hindrances as well. The Indians had been despoiled by the white men who had preceded the missionaries, had been taught the *value* of things, a concept foreign to them before their intercourse with whites. Both the Cayuse and Nez Percé complained often that the missions and fields had been appropriated without permission and that the crops were raised and sold to others with the Indians receiving no part of the profits; that mission gristmills even charged the

Indians for grinding their grain. Both tribes wanted the missionaries to share their cattle, hogs, and sheep.

To the Indians these were simple matters. The whites, after all, were intruders—and by 1841 there were nearly 500 of them in the Oregon Country and the number was swelling. To the missionaries and other settlers, the natives were shiftless, intractable, and insolent ingrates, owing much to the whites for teaching them English, the Bible, the value of planting, of livestock, of trading in furs, of *money*. To the whites the Indians were owed nothing, least of all for the land they claimed. The land was American land, there for the taking for those who would "improve" it, and the land claimers and improvers were on the march.

One secular issue that more than any other burdened the missionaries and distracted them from their teaching and religious work was the notion of self-sufficiency. This lodestone seemed so rational and possible in New York, where policies were formulated by men who could not locate the Continental Divide much less divine what obstacles lay beyond it, but in actual practice the idea was chimerical. For the missions to become independent of home support, more churchly people, missionary families, were needed, and above all, more time was needed.

17

Sapling Grove

■

1

In early May 1841, at a place called Sapling Grove, west of Independence, Missouri, a frontier schoolteacher named John Bidwell paced his camp, waiting for other members of the Western Emigration Society to rendezvous and begin their plunge westward to the Pacific. He was headed for Mexican California; others of the society were interested in the Oregon Country. None knew anything about getting to either place ("The ignorance of the route was complete," Bidwell later wrote), and the only maps of the Rocky Mountain country and beyond were filled with blank spaces and purported but unproven lakes and rivers.

Bidwell seemed an incongruous candidate to lead, or even follow, an overland party of emigrants. He was twenty-two, fit and handsome, but except for a brief stint as a farmer had spent his adult life studying and teaching. Still, he had always been drifting westward. He was a Chautauqua County New Yorker, attended schools in Ohio, and ventured to Missouri in 1839 with seventy-five dollars in cash and "nothing more formidable than a pocketknife" to protect himself.

He was teaching school in Platte County when he caught the westering fever after hearing of the glories of California

from a Santa Fé trader who had been there. Toward the end
of 1840, Bidwell and a few like-minded enthusiasts organized the ambitiously named Western Emigration Society.
A month after it was publicized, 500 people, most of them
from Missouri, Illinois, Arkansas, and Kentucky, responded
and signed a pledge to buy a suitable "outfit" and come to
the Sapling Grove rendezvous in the first week of May 1841
"armed and equipped to cross the Rocky Mountains to
California."

Bidwell himself scraped up enough money to buy a gun,
a wagon, and some basic provisions. An associate who said
he would supply horses backed out at the last moment, and
the schoolmaster had to search Independence and Westport
Landing (the future Kansas City) to find another partner.
This man owned a good horse and had a few dollars in cash,
traded the horse for a yoke of oxen to pull the wagon, and
also bought a "sorry-looking one-eyed mule."

When Bidwell reached Sapling Grove a week or so before
the departure time, only one wagon had preceded him; indeed, until a few days ago before heading out, the whole
scheme seemed to have disintegrated. Some attributed the
dampening of enthusiasm among Bidwell's followers to letters appearing in the press written by one Thomas Jefferson
Farnham, a Vermont lawyer who had settled in Illinois and
attended a Jason Lee appearance at the Main Street Presbyterian Church in Peoria in September 1838. Farnham was
enthralled by Lee's tales of the Oregon Country and even
more so by the stories told by one of Lee's Chinook boys
about the salmon runs of the Columbia and how easily the
fish could be caught, dried, and sold. The lawyer began having Nat Wyeth–like visions of a fortune to be made in
salmon-pickling, and in the spring of 1839 he put together a
party of fifteen wilderness-raw adventurers calling themselves the Oregon Dragoons. Mrs. Farnham even stitched
them a flag bearing the legend "Oregon or the Grave." They
set out from Independence for the Pacific with the vaulting

ambition to plant the flag—the Stars and Stripes, not Mrs. Farnham's banner—in the Oregon Country. They intended claiming sovereignty in the name of the United States, repelling any contrariness by the British and their Hudson's Bay agents, pickling a lot of fish, and returning home with shiploads of kegged salmon and their pockets lined with gold.

Not surprisingly, none of this worked out. The Peorians added several men and two missionary couples to their party in Independence, but others defected en route. They missed the outward-bound caravan carrying supplies and trade goods to the Green River rendezvous and were forced to tag along with traders on the Santa Fé Trail to Bent's Fort on the Arkansas River, arriving there on July 5, where more men deserted. Those remaining bickered over "Captain" Farnham's military strictness. One man was badly wounded in a firearms accident and had to be carried in a wagon and at times in a makeshift litter. Farnham accused some of the Oregon Dragoons of planning to abandon the wounded man on the Colorado prairie, resigned his captaincy, and hired a guide at Bent's Fort to take him and four loyalists west across the Rockies. By the time he reached the Walla Walla River in late September 1839, the lawyer was down to two companions and an Indian guide.

He visited the Whitmans at Waiilatpu and Jason and Daniel Lee in the Willamette valley, and there received from a delegation of settlers a memorial signed by sixty-seven citizens of the United States, which he promised to deliver to the appropriate authorities in Washington. The petition contained familiar grievances, demands, and questions: American traders had been driven from Oregon by the British; they were unprotected and beholden to foreigners even for such necessities as clothing; there was an alarming increase in the crimes of theft, murder, even infanticide, which they were helpless to arrest since they had no legal recourses of any kind. The paper also included an alarming reference to being at the mercy not only of the savages around them but of "others" who would do them harm, the "others" a transparent reference to the agents of the Hudson's Bay Company.

On October 15, accompanied by Daniel Lee, Farnham departed for Fort Vancouver, and at The Dalles, where Lee maintained a small satellite mission station, the two had a run-in with a band of Indians that clearly illustrated the problems the missionaries were having with the "savages." Farnham, in his 1841 book, *Travels to the Rocky Mountains,* described how he and Daniel Lee encountered a party of about forty Dalles natives and tried to recover from them a bridle and some saddle leather that had been stolen from Lee's workshop. The Indians took umbrage at the suggestion of thievery and the chief of the tribe drew a pistol while Farnham raised a rifle. No blood was shed, but the natives were greatly agitated and refused to assist the white men in loading their canoes to continue their journey downriver.

At Fort Vancouver, Farnham paid a call on McLoughlin but cut his visit short, planted no flag and pickled no fish— these ideas seemed to have vanished along with most of his Oregon Dragoons. Alexander Simpson, a clerk at the fort related to Governor George Simpson, described Farnham as possessing much dry humor but added that he "talked grandiloquently and acted shabbily."

Eighteen of Farnham's followers, a few of them members of the original Oregon Dragoons, stayed on in Oregon but their disappointed captain departed on the Hudson's Bay ship *Nereid* on December 3 bound for Oahu. Once there, he dispatched the first of his letters to the secretary of war on the nefarious and monopolistic practices of the British and its Hudson's Bay agents. In this he followed the custom of many Americans before him in partaking of the Company's hospitality, sailing on a Company ship, and, once free of its charity, slandering the Company with a will.

From the Sandwich Islands Farnham proceeded to Monterey, spent a few weeks in California—during one of the

province's periodic rebellions against Mexican authority—
and returned home after crossing Mexico from San Blas to
the Gulf of Mexico and New Orleans.

2

U nlike most who visited the Pacific Northwest before
him, Farnham was not impressed with the place. The
Willamette valley, which Jason Lee and others had oversold
as a wilderness Arcadia, the lawyer found unattractive:
unbearably hot in summer, unbearably wet and cold in winter, plagued with mosquitoes and flies and the fevers they
carried. Oregon as a whole was too dry in the east, too wet
in the west; the forests were too heavy in some places, too
sparse in others; the mouth of the Columbia was unfit for
commercial use. He wrote even more scathingly of Alta California and its turbulent governance and warned would-be
emigrants that the province was no Eden and that life there
was harsh. Bancroft took severe issue with Farnham's California views, writing that "in all those parts resting upon his
own observations it is worthless trash, and in all that relates
to the California people a tissue of falsehoods," but the
Peorian's perorations, published as open letters, were influential.

What impact Farnham's work had on the Pacific-bound,
specifically those of John Bidwell's Emigration Society, is
unknown, but it had some negative effect, along with the
cholera epidemic raging through the Missouri countryside,
rumors of Indian depredations and associated miseries of
overland travel, and the economic gloom in Missouri, where
farm prices were still disastrously low. Many of Bidwell's
500 pledge signers were too ill, broke, or scared to go anywhere.

Even so, by the departure date, sixty-nine emigrants,
including five women and several children, gathered at

Sapling Grove with thirteen mule- and ox-drawn wagons. Among the latecomers was one John Bartleson from Jackson County, Missouri, who fourteen years earlier had helped plan the town of Independence. He brought seven men with him and announced to the others that if he were not named captain of the train, he and his associates would stay behind, presumably to wait for another emigrant group willing to let him lead them.

Bartleson was elected, but he had no more idea of how to get wagons and people to the Pacific coast than any of the others. This realization, and his insufferable self-importance, caused frictions among the fragile, fearful neophytes and were factors in the eventual splitting of the party at Soda Springs in Idaho. There, half the party decided to proceed to Oregon rather than accompany their captain to California.

For the present, the pressing problem was how to get to the Pacific with more specificity than following the sun. The answer fell into their laps when a horseman came into the Sapling Grove camp and announced that three Jesuit priests, five teamsters, and two French-Canadian trappers would be arriving soon in the vicinity. The messenger said the priests were headed for the Oregon Country and that they were being escorted by Thomas Fitzpatrick.

This was heaven-sent news. Broken Hand Fitzpatrick! Who had not heard of this Nimrod of the far West? And who knew the route to the Pacific better than he, who had crossed and recrossed South Pass with such peers as Jedediah Smith and Jim Bridger, who had guided the Whitmans and Spaldings to the Oregon Country?

Some in the Bartleson group "thought we could not afford to wait for a slow missionary party," John Bidwell wrote. "But when we found that no one knew which way to go, we sobered down and waited for them to come up. And it was well that we did for otherwise probably not one of us would ever have reached California because of our inexperience."

The three missionaries who had hired Fitzpatrick to guide

them to the Oregon Country, specifically to the Bitterroot
valley of Montana, were led by Father Jean-Pierre De Smet,
a forty-year-old Belgian who had emigrated to the United
States in 1821, entered the novitiate of the Jesuit order near
Baltimore, and in 1827 was ordained. He had worked as a
missionary among the Potawatomis in Iowa, and in 1840
joined a fur-trade caravan to the Green River and spent two
months among the Flatheads in the Three Forks region of
Montana. Now he was returning, with two fellow priests,
Nicholas Point and Gregory Mengarini, to build the Jesuit
Mission of Saint Mary's among the Flathead people.

De Smet was a good-natured Friar Tuck who stood at five
feet seven, weighed over 200 pounds and impressed all who
met him, including the Protestant missionaries who hated
"Romanism" in all its manifestations. Bidwell said, "He was
genial, of fine presence, and one of the saintliest men I have
ever known, and I cannot wonder that the Indians were made
to believe he was divinely protected."

This assessment was correct. De Smet and his Jesuits
were to have a success among the natives of the Oregon
Country that contrasted sharply with the frustrations of
the Lees, Whitmans, and Spaldings. The Jesuits were genuinely sympathetic to the hardships the Indians endured and
found them apt pupils, so eager to learn that when the Flatheads set out in their late-fall buffalo hunt they expressly
asked for a "Black Robe" to accompany them and continue
their religious instruction. This assignment De Smet delegated
to Father Point, who spent six years with the Flatheads, the
neighboring Coeur d'Alênes, and the dreaded Blackfeet. He
followed their hunting parties, lived with them in their winter
camps, made numerous converts (which some said was due
to colorful Catholic symbolism, trappings, and rituals), and
fought what he called "the avarice and cupidity of civilized
man," the "abominable influence of frontier vices," and the
"Apostles of Protestantism."

De Smet had identical attitudes and successes. By 1847

he had three missions in the Oregon Country and by 1850 five Jesuit and two Oblate missions serving in the Pacific Northwest.

3

On May 10, 1841, the first emigrant train to set out from the Missouri frontier for the Pacific rolled northeasterly toward the Platte River on a route soon to bear a heavy traffic. The Bartleson-Bidwell party's thirteen wagons followed Fitzpatrick and the Jesuits with their five two-wheeled carts drawn by mules in tandem hitches. In all, there were close to eighty people in the caravan and, as the true pioneers of what became known as the Oregon Trail, they had to work ceaselessly to make a trail out of a dim trapper's path. Wagons* had to be wrestled along at an agonizingly slow pace, boulders rolled away, giant sinkholes spaded over, brush chopped, and trees felled.

Father Point mirrored the relief of the whole party in having Fitzpatrick riding ahead of the caravan, directing the work and doing his share of it, and taking command of every aspect of their passage west. "In these immense solitudes it was necessary to have an experienced guide," Point wrote. "The choice fell not on the colonel [Bartleson], who had never crossed the mountains, but on the captain Father De Smet engaged. He was a courageous Irishman known to

---

*These were common farm wagons and not, as often depicted, the big (and expensive) Conestogas built in Pennsylvania, which weighed a ton and a half when empty, carried five-ton loads over eastern roads, and hauled the first settlers over the Appalachians. They were too massive for the rain-sodden prairies, river crossings, and mountain defiles of the Oregon Trail. Nor did the 1841 emigrants carry their possessions and foodstuffs in "prairie schooners," although use of this memorable conveyance, perhaps the most enduring single symbol of the Old West, lay just ahead.

most of the Indian tribes as Tet Blanch [White Head] or Broken Hand. He had spent fully two-thirds of his life crossing the plains." The one dissenting voice in the praise for Fitzpatrick was that of Reverend Joseph Williams, a Methodist preacher who caught up with the caravan on May 21, riding up alone, unarmed, and uninvited and attaching himself to the party. "Our leader, Fitzpatrick," Williams later wrote, "is a wicked, worldly man, and much opposed to missionaries going among the Indians. He has some intelligence, but is deistical in his principles." The reverend suspected that nearly all the others in the party were "deists," his favorite word for non-Christians, blasphemers, and those not comporting to his ideas of "Godliness." While his attitude toward the Jesuits is unknown, he no doubt kept his distance from them and all others of Papist inclinations. Fitzpatrick's biographer, Leroy Hafen, said that Williams' statements "may be classed as amusing rather than important."

Father Point recorded in his diary the daily schedule of the caravan under Broken Hand's captaincy: He signaled the departures, ordered the line of march, selected the rest and meal stops and the camps for the night; he set the sentries (the priests did their stint along with every other adult male) and maintained discipline. When possible the camps were made in wooded areas close to water. The wagons and carts were drawn together in a hollow square, "more or less according to the nature of the terraine," Point said, the tongue of one wagon fastened to the rear of the next, the horses, oxen, and pack animals picketed inside. No cookfires were permitted after nightfall so as to prevent alerting Indians in the camp vicinity.

Fear of "red savages" was a palpable feature of all overland emigrant parties, and while there were few instances of Indian hostility against wagon trains, two weeks after the Bartleson-Bidwell party departed Sapling Grove there was a scare that seemed to justify all the campfire qualms and cautions.

One of the young men in the party, Nicholas Dawson, rode a mule out some distance ahead of the wagons as they neared the Platte River in Nebraska. He was a hunter and hoped to find an antelope or two to bring back for the cookfires. But when he ran back to the camp afoot he told Fitzpatrick that he had been assaulted by an Indian war party and robbed of his mule, guns, and even some of his clothing. The captain immediately ordered the wagons into a square and this was completed just as about fifty Indians rode into view and, to the astonishment of the white onlookers, nonchalantly began setting up their lodge poles and making camp. Fitzpatrick and one of his men rode over cautiously for a parley. The Indians were Cheyenne and told Broken Hand that they had been forced to disarm the white boy after he saw them approach, appeared terrorized, and waved his firearms in their direction. They readily turned over the mule and guns they had confiscated.

Nicholas Dawson never heard the end of it, and the story of "Cheyenne Dawson," festooned with elaborate exaggerations, was told around western campfires for years afterward.

Between the South Platte and Sweetwater Rivers, buffalo were in such abundance that the emigrants, few of whom had seen the great beasts before, gorged on them trapper-style, finding the tongue, hump meat, and bone marrow, thumbed out from the split bones in strips, special delicacies. "There is no better beef in the world than that of the buffalo," Bidwell said, but he added plaintively that the animals were slaughtered randomly and needlessly by white hunters who left many untouched carcasses on the prairie for wolves and ravens. He observed the Cheyenne, still traveling two or three miles ahead of the caravan, taking all the meat, the hide, horns, and hooves, wasting nothing.

The animals' numbers were frightening. "I think I can truly say that I saw in that region in one day more buffaloes than

I have seen of cattle in all my life," Bidwell wrote. "They seemed to be coming northward continually from the distant plains to the Platte to get water, and would plunge in and swim across by the thousands—so numerous were they that they changed not only the color of the water, but its taste, until it was unfit to drink; but we had to use it."

The prohibition against night fires that might attract Indians gave way in buffalo country to bonfires and men periodically firing their rifles into the night sky to prevent the herds from trampling the camp. "We could hear them thundering all night long," Bidwell said, "the ground fairly trembled with vast approaching bands; and if they had not been diverted, wagons, animals, and emigrants would have been trodden under their feet. One cannot describe the rush and wildness of the thing."

Perhaps second only to the scary grandeur of the buffalo herds, which were often described as an immense brown blanket on the prairie stretching to the horizon, the journeyers were awed by the sudden and spectacular lightning fireworks of the violent thunderstorms that soaked their camps, turned the trail to a muddy gumbo, sank wagon wheels to their hubs, and caused horses, mules, and oxen to bolt and scatter. The storms usually formed in the afternoon sunlight with the tops of billowing western clouds flattening, followed by light breezes popping the wagon covers and thunder rolling across the prairie. The wind then began screaming at them, frequently reaching eighty miles an hour in force, pummeling man and beast off their feet, upsetting wagons, and driving uprooted trees and brush along in dense clouds of dirt. Often the storms produced hailstones as big as turkey eggs—big enough to knock a man unconscious—and created a panicky run for cover under wagons or in whatever trees were available. Animals in the open were always injured by the plummeting stones.

The caravan forded the South Platte at what was called the Old California Crossing, near Brule, Nebraska, and fol-

lowed the North Platte to Fort Laramie, arriving there on
June 22. The course was now westerly and the party crossed
the North Platte near Casper, Wyoming, and South Pass, descended to the Green River, thence to Soda Springs, in
Idaho, at the northernmost bend of the Bear River.

By now, the Bartleson-Bidwell group, sixty-nine in number at Sapling Grove, had been reduced by five men. One
man (mordantly named Shotwell) accidentally killed himself, presumably while cleaning his rifle; another left the
party at Fort Laramie; and three others turned back after
crossing South Pass. Those remaining divided evenly at
Soda Springs. Thirty-two elected to follow Fitzpatrick and
the Jesuits to Fort Hall, about forty miles distant, and move
on via the Snake and Columbia to Fort Vancouver. The other
thirty-two, Bartleson and Bidwell among them, plunged into
the terra incognita toward California.

The California-bound remnant of the Western Emigration
Society struggled across the Utah and Nevada deserts, their
draft and pack animals dropping in the waterless, grassless
wastes, their wagons left behind as grim sentinels for those
who dared to follow. In the middle of October the travelers
reached the eastern escarpments of the Sierra Nevadas. They
had eaten the last of their mules and oxen and were progress-
ing little more than ten miles in a day when they stumbled
across the mountains just ahead of the worst of the killing
winter snows. They walked into the San Joaquin valley ranch
of an American squatter named John Marsh on November
1, 1841.

Those Oregon-bound from Fort Hall, guided by Nez
Percé, also surrendered their wagons but came safely into
the Willamette valley in the fall of 1841, the first organized
emigrant party to travel the 2,000-mile Oregon Trail. After
they made a stop at Waiilatpu, Marcus Whitman, the veteran
wagon wrestler, wrote, "They have left their wagons at Fort
Hall, but very soon others will discover that they can bring
them through to the Columbia." He saw the newcomers

heralding a great American migration to Oregon. "Lapwai and Waiilatpu will become supply stations to thousands of travellers," he wrote, "and the objectives of the committee [the American Board of Foreign Missions] will be removed. Help can be obtained from the immigrants; a settlement can be formed and a strong Protestant influence brought to counter the efforts of the Catholics."

Holding Romanism in check was a strong argument and one used forceably by Whitman and Spalding in their correspondence with the eastern supervisors. Above all, they said, they needed time to attain the persistently stated aspirations of the Mission Board: self-sufficiency and a record of success in Christianizing Indians. Five years in the Oregon Country was not time enough to accomplish either of these purposes. They were still building and planting, and they needed more people, more funds, more time.

In Boston, the board's commissioners were deaf to these appeals; indeed, in the summer of 1842 they were preparing a plan to dismantle the Oregon stations and recall several missionaries. This drastic departure from the bright and hopeful days of the Macedonian Cry resulted from too-high expectations and inevitable disappointments. Their correspondence revealed that the missionaries seemed more occupied with bickering among themselves than with doing God's work (Elkanah Walker's wife, Mary, wrote that "None of them love one another well enough to live in peace together"); the stations were far more expensive to build and maintain than had been anticipated; and for five years there had been no optimistic word from Waiilatpu, Lapwai, or the smaller mission at Kamiah, opened in 1839 sixty miles up the Clearwater above Lapwai, that the natives were interested in learning of Jesus and the Scriptures.

No matter how loathsome the incursions being made by the Papists in Oregon, the board could not afford to continue its high-minded experiment there. They decided to close the missions at Waiilatpu, Lapwai, and Kamiah, recall the

Spaldings and William Gray, and send the Whitmans to
Chemakane, the station among the Spokanes operated by
Cushing Eells and Elkanah Walker. With this consolidation
and house-cleaning, Chemakane would become the sole
Presbyterian-Congregationalist outpost in Oregon.

4

These devastating orders were to be hand-delivered to
Marcus Whitman and Henry Spalding by Dr. Elijah
White of Tompkins County, New York. Bancroft described
this singular man as having manners that "were of that oblig-
ing kind which made him popular, especially among women,
but which men often called sycophantish and insincere." He
gained a reputation as a busybody, was greatly "fond of or-
atorical display and of society, affectedly rather than truly
pious, not altogether a bad man, though a weak one. He had
no talent, as Heinrich Heine would declare, but yet a character. And strange to say, the longer he dwelt upon this [the
Oregon] coast, the more he became smooth and slippery
like glass, and flat withal, yet he could be round and cutting on occasions, particularly when broken on the wheel
of adversity."

White, about thirty-three, had originally gone out to the
Pacific coast on the brig *Hamilton* in 1836 among Jason
Lee's first reinforcement. The characteristics Bancroft described, and his penchant toward argumentativeness, were
not found to be helpful by the volatile Lee and his Willamette flock. Inevitably, the two men clashed and White had
returned home in 1840 aboard the *Lausanne,* the vessel that
had carried Lee, his new wife, and his "Great Reinforcement" to the Columbia in 1840.

The *Lausanne* was commanded by Josiah Spaulding, with
whom White struck up a friendship. The captain had trans-
muted from a merchant skipper to an Oregon specialist in

his voyages. He seems to have shared his views with Dr. White, who found them so compelling he offered to assist Spaulding in writing them down for the purpose of delivering them to Congress. The lengthy document born of this collaboration was a compendium of rumor and purplish prose describing Indian depredations and massacres and, among other libels, accusations that the Hudson's Bay Company had incited the Oregon tribes to attack American settlers and missionaries.

Spaulding's scuttlebutt-filled report found an audience in Washington, as all anti-British opinions did. It was among the testimonials employed by Senator Linn of Missouri in his 1841 Oregon bill. That document proposed American military occupation of Oregon and contained a recommendation that an "agent" be appointed to monitor Indian activities in the Northwest and keep an eye on the Hudson's Bay Company.

The bill died aborning, but the Indian-agent idea survived and Elijah White, who was in Washington and therefore handiest of the Oregon veterans, got the job, as "subagent," at a $750 annual salary and the promise that the stipend would be doubled upon the resubmission and passage of Linn's bill. His duties were as vaguely stated as his title, but this did not hamper Dr. White, who was quite capable of filling in the blanks. Historian David Lavender wrote that the missionary-physician believed that "Every person there [Oregon], from McLoughlin on down, would have to heed him. By the time the doctor reached the Willamette, indeed, he would consider himself vested with as many powers as a full-fledged territorial governor."

Before departing for Independence, White, a Methodist, apparently paid a courtesy call at the Presbyterian-Congregationalist Mission Board in Boston, no doubt offering to be of service in his new role as Indian subagent in Oregon. As a result he was asked to deliver a sealed directive to Spalding at Lapwai and Whitman at Waiilatpu. White was not privy to the contents of the letter.

Since he divined that his assignment included encouraging westward emigration, when he made his way to Missouri in the spring of 1842 White launched a publicity campaign, made countless speeches, and wrote newspaper letters drumming up a party to accompany him to the Oregon Country. Over 100 people responded, better than half men over eighteen years of age stirred by his tales that the United States would soon be acting on the Oregon question and his assurance that Senator Linn's bill, with its magnanimous land allotments, would become the law of the land.

On May 16, 1842, White led (there was no question, at first, that he would lead) a train of 100 men, women, and children; eighteen wagons; a hundred horses and pack-mules; and a cattle herd west out of Elm Grove, twenty miles southwest of Independence.

At first those who accompanied him suffered the numerous rules their petulant pilot cobbled together, but they soon broke them as they saw fit. They had not gone far when they booted him out as captain of the train altogether, this after he ordered all dogs to be slain lest their barking attract hostile Indians. Of this incident, Bancroft wrote, "King Herod's edict anent the slaughter of the innocents could scarcely have called forth a louder wail of lamentation from the mothers of Judea than was evoked from the women and children of White's party."

The man who replaced White as wagon master and captain, Lansford W. Hastings, a callow twenty-four-year-old out of Knox County, Ohio, did little better. What harmony remained from White's brief regime vanished under Hastings' guidance, so much so that the column broke into two factions, each marching separately until they reached Fort Laramie on June 23.

With the always dependable Tom Fitzpatrick now their

guide to Fort Hall, the Hastings group reached the Sweetwater River on July 13 and, though harassed by a band of
Sioux who stole some of their horses, they pushed on. At
Fort Hall, on Fitzpatrick's long-standing advice, the Oregon-
bound agreed to give up their wagons and trade them for
flour and provisions.

Elijah White went ahead with a group of horsemen to Fort
Boisé and reached Whitman's mission on September 20,
where he delivered the notice of the American board on the
mission closings. He told of the hundred emigrants toiling
behind him and of the more that would come in '43 dependent on the missions for succor. Then, after dispatching the
board's directive to Spalding, he pushed on to Fort Vancouver, with "some feeling of self-importance and exultation on
returning as the first officer of the United States appointed
in that country," Bancroft said.

There is no record of Marcus Whitman's reaction as he read
the startling news, but one can imagine him trembling
with fury at the officious lines on a sheet of foolscap. A
supervisory board 3,000 miles away had expressed a blithe
willingness to throw over five years of incessant work, hu-
miliation, and frustration to establish a Christian station
in the wilderness among a hateful native people. Until now,
he had held out the hope that, given time and resources, the
Indians would come in and that the mission would become
the haven for the heathen they had envisioned when he and
Narcissa first saw Waiilatpu in the winter of '36. Did the
commissioners, in the comfort of their Boston boardroom,
imagine that they could perform miracles? Did they not realize that five years was a tick of the clock when compared
to the centuries the Cayuse and other Northwest tribes had
been mired in savage idolatry?

The Spaldings can have felt little differently about their
work with the Nez Percé or the Eells and Walkers about

theirs among the Spokanes when Whitman met with them
to ask their support. He planned to travel east immediately to
convince the board to reverse their decision to close the
missions.

There were objections: The trip east and back would take
a year and the mission would have to make do without its
only physician, and it was too late in the year to undertake
such a journey. But these arguments could not change Whitman's mind, and he started out on October 3, 1842, with
fast horses, a minimum of supplies, a guide, and a newcomer
to Waiilatpu, A. L. Lovejoy, who had come in with Elijah
White's party. They reached Fort Hall without incident but
with winter closing in, and upon learning that Sioux war parties were abroad along the Platte, they swung south into
Mexican territory and in Santa Fé joined a trade caravan
bound for Bent's Fort, the outfitting oasis on the Arkansas
River. The journey south was an awful ordeal in which the
two men wandered lost, nearly starved, and fought snowstorms, frostbite, and and fatigue. Lovejoy gave out at Bent's
Fort and Whitman went on alone to overtake a fur brigade
bound for the Missouri frontier.

He reached the Eastern Seaboard on March 30, 1843, and
paused in Washington, where he had a brief audience with
President John Tyler, conferred with Secretary of State Daniel Webster on establishing emigrant supply stations along
the Oregon Trail, and talked with editor Horace Greeley of
the *New York Tribune*.

Whitman then proceeded to Boston, and of the Mission
Board's reaction to his unexpected visit Bancroft says it "was
not cordial or even kind; it was frigid. They disapproved of
his leaving his station, of the unnecessary expense of the
journey, and of its object, especially as it asked for more
money and missionaries." Whitman, he wrote, spoke against
closing the stations at a time when emigrant numbers were
increasing by the year—the Oregon contingent of the
Bartleson-Bidwell party being the latest example. He said

the stations needed more than ever to be ministering to the Indians, who would be greatly affected by the increased white presence in their ancestral lands. To these arguments, even to those on the dreaded Catholic advances, the board was cold—"the savages of the inhospitable north-west were not just then in favor with the Sunday-schools," Bancroft wrote acidly. Nevertheless, the board consented to allow the doctor to return to Waiilatpu and continue his work there, providing he was willing to do so without further support of the board, and even without board payment of his return-journey expenses. The Spaldings could stay put as well, but without board funds.

Whitman, burdened with his failure before the commissioners and with apprehension on returning to Oregon empty-handed, resolved to make the best of it. He paid a visit to his New York home and, with a young nephew accompanying him, reached the western Missouri border on June 1, 1843. There he joined a large emigrant train and returned to what Bancroft called a "smouldering volcano" in Oregon.

18

Jumping Off

■

"BEHOLD, THE PLACE WHICH IS NOW
CALLED INDEPENDENCE."

1

On April 13, 1842, at the time when Dr. Elijah White was orating across Missouri to Elm Grove where he would undertake to "lead" a party of emigrants to Oregon, the man who blazed much of the trail White would follow died in Saint Louis.

Wilson Price Hunt, John Jacob Astor's field marshal, had commanded the grueling and adventuresome nine-month trek of the Astor Overlanders from Saint Louis to the Columbia in 1811, and it had been adventure enough for his lifetime. He had reached home, after a detour to China, in 1816, and devoted the rest of his life, twenty-six years, to his merchant enterprises. Those who knew his history must have sought him out to recount the story of that five-year epic when he radically recast his career from that of New Jersey businessman to wilderness journeyer, leading sixty-nine other Astorians to the Pacific just a few years after Lewis and Clark's continental crossing.

Like his employer in New York, Hunt was a businessman and had no interest in the settlement of the Oregon Country except as it might have abetted the fur trade. Yet he lived long enough to witness the death of the fur trade and be

honored as a pioneer in breaking the ground for the overland migration to the Oregon Country. Even his mishaps
and failures had pointed the way. In the fall of 1811, after he
and his footsore and starving party had attempted to negotiate the Snake River in dugout canoes but were battered
into surrender, he found a route to the Columbia that filled
in a blank: the far western segment of the Oregon Trail.

By the time of his death there *was* an Oregon Trail, a mad-
dening route of zigs and zags, detours and wanderings, but
it was becoming defined through the hard-earned work of
an Olympian roll call of trailbreakers: Robert Stuart (first
to travel it west to east; discoverer of South Pass), Manuel
Lisa, the Ashley-Henry brigades, Jedediah Smith, Jim
Bridger, Thomas Fitzpatrick, Nathaniel Wyeth, Benjamin
Bonneville, Jason Lee, the Whitmans and the Spaldings,
the Bartleson-Bidwell party, and Elijah White.

All of these brush cutters, boulder movers, river forders,
and mountain climbers crossed the path, almost literally, that
led to Wilson Hunt's counting house in Saint Louis, and
justly so: The Oregon Trail began there.

In 1842, the year Hunt died, Charles Dickens, the thirty-
year-old author of *The Pickwick Papers, Oliver Twist,
Nicholas Nickleby, Barnaby Rudge,* and *The Old Curiosity
Shop,* came to Saint Louis at the end of his six-month American lecture tour. He landed in New York in January with
two enormous portmanteaux and a mission: to talk about the
detestable habit of American publishers of pirating the work
of European authors and the crying need for an international
copyright law. This was not a particularly inspiring theme
for the man Daniel Webster said had "done more to amelio-
rate the condition of the English poor than all the statesmen
that Great Britain has sent into Parliament." Dickens spoke
poignantly of Sir Walter Scott, whose last days of indebtedness, the lecturer said, would have been lightened if the

thieves of his work had paid a tithe of what was due him.
But on his book-buccaneering exertions the Hartford
Times spoke for many in editorializing, "It happens we want
no advice on this subject." This attitude convinced Dickens, as it had Alexis de Tocqueville before him, that America had far less freedom of expression than the Americans
boasted. He also found too little sympathy for his privately expressed views on slavery—"that most hideous
blot and foul disgrace."

No matter his message, Dickens was a crowd-pleaser, especially so when he gave his brilliant readings from his
works, each character coming alive through the theatrical
quality of his voice. Three months into his tour, in every city
he visited his admirers came out in enormous levees; he
shook 600 hands every day and so enthusiastic were his auditors that they grabbed at his topper and cane and pulled
the fur from his coat for souvenirs. After a great ball at the
Carlton Hotel in New York he was so exhausted that he spent
four days in bed to gather strength to move on.

When Dickens sailed for England in June, he had a six-month journal* of opinions on America and Americans,
much of it negative, written in a dubious, seriocomic tone
giving the reader the impression that these were the memoirs of a hapless victim of circumstance on a hellish junket
of discovery. In truth, he had quickly sickened of America
and Americans; he was revolted by the way men bolted their
food and spit tobacco; thought it fatuous that women attended so many elevating lectures (presumably including
his own); saw nearly every site as dreary and monotonous.

---

*The book based on it, *American Notes* (arrangements for which he
had made before he sailed), went through four quick printings in a
year and earned him £40,000. In this book and in the novel *Martin
Chuzzlewit* (1844) Dickens took a literary revenge on the United
States for ignoring his copyright pleas. His friend, William Makepeace Thackeray, refused to review *American Notes,* considering it
"vulgar and flippant."

Upon returning, after a more comfortable time among Englishmen in Toronto and Montreal, he wrote a friend, "I
would not condemn you to a year's residence on this side of
the Atlantic for any money," and to another who asked about
a particular American acquaintance Dickens wrote, "I do not
know the American gentleman, God forgive me for putting
two such words together."

He traveled as far west as Saint Louis and as his steamer
neared the Mississippi what minute traces of beauty and civilization he had seen in New England gave way to an envel-
oping primeval ugliness: "The trees were stunted in their
growth," he wrote, "the banks were low and flat; the settlements and log-cabins fewer in number; their inhabitants
more wan and wretched than any we had encountered before. No songs or birds were in the air, no pleasant scents,
no moving lights and shadows from swift-passing clouds."

The juncture of the Missouri and Mississippi he found to
be "A dismal swamp . . . teeming with rank, unwholesome
vegetation, in whose baleful shade the wretched wanderers
who are tempted hither droop and die, and lay their bones;
the hateful Mississippi circling and eddying before it . . . a
slimy monster hideous to behold; a hotbed of disease, an
ugly sepulchre, a grave uncheered by any gleam of promise,
a place without one single quality, in earth or air or water, to
commend it; such is this dismal Cairo." To Dickens, the
Father of Waters suffered from an appalling disease, and
probably its bank-dwellers as well. He called it "an enormous
ditch, sometimes two or three miles wide, running liquid
mud, six miles an hour . . . the banks low, the trees dwarf-
ish, the marshes swarming with frogs," and said "the
wretched cabins" were few and far apart, "their inmates
hollow-cheeked and pale, the weather very hot, mosquitos
penetrating into every crack and crevice of the boat, mud and
slime on everything."

In Saint Louis he stayed at Planter's House and observed
the town's "crazy old tenements with blinking casements,

such as may be seen in Flanders." He mentioned its wharves, warehouses, and shops, and found them wanting in comparison even to those in Cincinnati, found its heat and humidity unbearable and its vast tracts of undrained swampland giving off the vapors from which awful fevers were born.

"No man ever admits the unhealthiness of the place he dwells in (unless he is going away from it)," he said, "and I shall therefore, I have no doubt, be at issue with the inhabitants of St. Louis in questioning the perfect salubrity of its climate, and in hinting that I think it must rather dispose to fever in the summer and autumnal seasons."

When Dickens saw it, Saint Louis had been incorporated as a city for only twenty years, and barely eighty years had passed since a primitive fur-trading post was raised on the site by Pierre de Laclède Liguest and named for the sainted thirteenth-century king Louis IX. From those muddy origins in 1764 and thereafter, Saint Louis was to the American fur trade what Michilimackinac, the Grand Portage, and Fort William were to the Canadian fur trade, a frontier entrepôt where trapping brigades were fitted out to venture to the Rocky Mountains and beyond, where furs were received and shipped out and supplies and goods were received.

In Astor's time, the decade of the Louisiana Purchase, when Saint Louis fell into the American sphere, the town was "the centre of rude bustle and business activity," Bancroft wrote. Its original Creole population, descendants of French colonists, were mixed with "keen, trafficking New Englanders; brawny backwoodsmen of the western frontier; tall, big-boned specimens of the unwashed and untaught corn-bread-and-bacon-fed of Tennessee, Kentucky, Illinois, and Missouri." With these were *coureurs de bois* and *voyageurs* from Canada, Indians of many tribes and half-breeds from the prairies, and some who drifted down from the Rocky Mountains; keen traders from the Atlantic states; vagrants, shopkeepers, speculators, and extravagant, bragging boatmen as well as "lavish, loud-joking, royal American

pedlers" who "were then beginning to practice their pis-
tolings, knife exercises, and card-waxing for the forty years
of commercial throat-cutting, highway blackguardism,
and unique boat-racing and boiler-bursting which were
to follow."

This motley populace, which Washington Irving said was
prone to pass its time "in idleness and revelry about the trading posts or settlements; squandering their hard earnings in
heedless conviviality, and rivaling their neighbors, the Indians, in indolent indulgence and an impudent disregard of
the morrow," had changed but little when Dickens' bile rose
upon visiting the town. The Canadian woods runners and
canoemen had departed, but most of the others were still
there, following their several bents, among these a new profession for the old trapper-explorer of the western frontier.
By 1842, Bancroft's "leathern-frocked frontiersmen" were
now guiding emigrant parties out of the Saint Louis gateway and into the air and elbowroom of the far West.

2

Once inside the gateway to the West, commonly at Saint
Louis or its environs on the west bank of the Mississippi, the typical Pacific-bound emigrant followed the Missouri River 250 miles westward to Independence, a log
hamlet on a nicely timbered bluff three miles inland from
the Big Muddy's great northward bend, forty miles downstream from Fort Leavenworth, and just inside the border of
the United States.

The first cabins at Independence had been thrown up in
1827 and grew into a helter-skelter collection of low-roofed
log and adobe huts, taverns, and stores. The area then became the chief staging area for trade caravans setting out on
the 780-mile-long Santa Fé Trail and the departure point for
fur brigades heading for the Rockies and beyond. In 1833

its main steamboat landing washed away and pilots had to find a new one a few miles upstream, at Westport Landing, and the time would come when Saint Joseph, fifty miles to the northwest, would become the favored launching place for overland caravans. But Independence had a running start, and by 1841 it had a permanent population of perhaps 800 and a transient one of 7,000 to 10,000 in the peak spring season. There were dry-goods stores there, and barbershops, saloons, a church or two, harness-making, wheelwright, and blacksmith shops—all booming businesses. There were even a few refined homes above the riverbank and a plain where the canvas tents of the emigrant trains gave off their lantern glow at night.

Nathan Boone, Daniel's youngest son, visited the town early in its history and called it "Eden," and Joseph Smith, the founding father of Mormonism, spoke of it in 1831. God had revealed to him "The land of Missouri," he said, "the land which I have appointed and consecrated for the gathering of the Saints." He had found the land of promise and the place for the city of Zion: "Behold, the place which is now called Independence." (Joseph Smith was murdered in Carthage, Illinois, in 1844, and Missouri turned out to be an earthly hell to Mormons. The Zion he sought became the city founded on the Great Salt Lake of Utah by his successor, Brigham Young.)

No one who passed through Independence in the 1830s forgot its *noise*. Saint Louis had its din, too, but was big enough for it to thin out and even had genteel places where the loudest sounds were the click of billiard balls and the tinkling of a piano. Not so in the tiny Bedlam on the fringe of the immense solitude and stillness of the western prairies. Independence seemed to have been born in a cacophony that never let up.

The racket began at the steamboat slips at Independence Landing, where the tall-stacked paddle wheelers offloaded their complements of traders, trappers, and emigrant parties and the encumbrances of each amid the raucous hooting of steam-whistles, clanging of bells, and slamming down of landing ramps. The trail to Independence was a pandemonium of braying mules and squawking chickens, quarreling emigrants, blaspheming stevedores and teamsters, the hiss and pop of bullwhips, gunshots announcing pack-train arrivals, the rattle of buckets and tinware hanging on creaking wagons—the din rising in volume and tempo in the town itself.

Francis Parkman, a handsome, long-nosed twenty-three-year-old Bostonian and Harvard man, came through the town in May 1846, en route to Fort Laramie and the writing of his enduring classic, *The Oregon Trail*. He had taken passage on a steamer out of Saint Louis, in a throng, he said, of "Santa Fe traders, gamblers, speculators, and adventurers of various descriptions," the boat's steerage "crowded with Oregon emigrants, mountain men, negroes, and a party of Kansas Indians." Thus laden, the steamer struggled upriver for seven or eight days* against the rapid current of the Missouri, "grating upon snags, and hanging for two or three hours at a time upon sandbars." Close to the landing place he began to see "signs of the great western movement that was taking place. Parties of emigrants with their tents and wagons were encamped on open spots near the bank, on their way to the common rendezvous at Independence."

Parkman watched a train of emigrant wagons from Illinois pass through, saw children's faces peeping out from under the wagon covers, and "Here and there a buxom damsel was seated on horseback, holding over her sunburnt face an old umbrella or a parasol, once gaudy enough, but now miserably faded." He allowed, however, that not all the emigrants were of such innocent stamp. "Among them are some of the vilest outcasts in the country," he said.

---

*The trip normally took five days or less, depending on the river's height above the mud that gave it its nickname.

He, too, made note of the noise: "A multitude of shops had
sprung up to furnish the emigrants and Santa Fe travelers
with necessaries for their journey and there was an incessant
hammering and banging from a dozen backsmiths' sheds,
where the heavy wagons were being repaired, and the horses
and oxen shod."

Added to the anvil and animal sounds, the red-clay streets
of Independence pulsed with the shouts, curses, buzz, and
laughter of its swarming transient populace. J. Quinn Thornton, an observer there at the height of the Oregon Trail migration, called the town "a great Babel of African slaves
[probably black stevedores], indolent dark-skinned Spaniards
[Mexicans], profane and dust-laden bullwhackers going to
and from Santa Fe with their immense wagons, and emigrant
families bound for the Pacific, all cheerful and intent in their
embarkation upon the great prairie wilderness." He omitted
to mention the Indians, mostly Kaws and Shawnee, but also
wanderers from other tribes from all points of the compass;
and Mormons, soldiers out of Fort Leavenworth, mountain
men searching for guide work, and a miscellany of drifters,
drunks, and gamblers hanging around the groggeries and
camps looking for somebody to rob. Some of the transients,
Bernard De Voto said, had as their only motive in being on
the edge of nowhere "was to see the elephant* wherever the
elephant might be."

There were plenty of idlers in Independence, but not
among those who intended having a pretty fair and linger-
ing view of the elephant. The emigrants, many of them farmers who had scraped together every dime they could find for

---

*This was a popular phrase for the westering adventure. In the 1840s,
few Americans had actually seen an elephant and fewer in the country beyond the Missouri frontier. The trails west were thus "paths to
the elephant." The "turnarounds," those who went as far as they
dared then turned back to civilization, were said to have "seen
enough of the elephant." A recently published emigrant memoir by C.
G. Hinman is titled *A Pretty Fair View of the Elephant*.

the journey, had no time to waste. They unloaded their dismantled wagons, their animals, chicken coops, plows, furniture, bales, and boxes of supplies at the steamer landing, then reassembled the wagons, hitched their teams, and snaked them to the high ground three miles south of the Independence town square. Some brought their precious cash and sparse belongings and bought their rigs in the town; some, satisfied that they had everything they needed, avoided the town and searched out the rendezvous points, camps with names like Fitzhugh's Mill, Indian Creek, Elm Grove, and Sapling Grove, to await others coming in. At these places the trains were organized, captains and other "officers" elected (often with heated debate), and guides and emigrant leaders pored over their maps and inspected the wagons, ensuring that the draft animals were shod and fed.

Independence and its neighboring outfitting places had their busiest season in April, May, and early June, and for a distinct and critical purpose. The idea was to await the greening of the prairie grass before kicking off the wagon brakes and lurching northwest toward the Platte River. The journey to the Pacific was a 2,000-mile treadmill on which the pioneer family and its ox- and mule-drawn wagon averaged fifteen miles a day—barring disasters. Five months out of Independence to Oregon or California was an excellent pace and leaving later than the first week of June was perilous: There were mountains to cross, and winter closed suddenly and with a vengeance in the passes.

3

While the general outline of the Oregon Trail had been emerging for thirty years before John C. Frémont made his first expedition to the Rocky Mountains, he clarified it, popularized it, and dispensed with certain tenacious myths about it.

When he set out from Saint Louis with his exploring and mapping party in June 1842, he was but twenty-nine years old, a barely tested army topographical engineer yet to inspire poets such as Whittier, Longfellow, and Joaquin Miller as Daniel Boone had inspired Lord Byron. Yet even at twenty-nine he had a record of accomplishment, and he now had powerful forces behind him. For one thing, maybe the main thing for his present purposes, he had married well.

The son of a French adventurer and a pretty American teacher, Frémont's unmarried parents moved from his birthplace in Savannah, Georgia, to Nashville, Tennessee, in 1813, and within days of their arrival there occurred one of our history's momentous coincidences: Within a few days of taking rooms in Nashville's City Hotel, baby John Charles received a pistol-shot introduction to a future president of the United States, to his future father-in-law, and to his future wife's namesake.

In the lobby of the hotel that September day, General Andrew Jackson, fresh from his battles against Creek Indians, and the Benton brothers, Jesse and Thomas Hart, both Tennessee soldiers who had fought with Jackson in the late war with Britain, engaged in a gunfight. The origin of the fracas remains obscure, but Jackson had recently served as "second" for a close friend in a duel with Jesse Benton and while neither duelist had been seriously injured, the Benton brothers saw Jackson's participation as a personal affront and betrayal. In the City Hotel lobby, after some insults and challenges were issued, guns were drawn and Jackson took a ball in the shoulder, following which the general's retinue got into the fight, as did former militia colonel and Tennessee state senator Thomas Hart Benton. More wild shots were exchanged, but somehow order was restored and there were no further casualties.

In the Frémonts' upstairs room, a stray bullet is said to have knocked plaster off the wall where the baby, John Charles, lay sleeping. His mother fainted.

The affair was a splendidly bizarre curtain-raiser for an adventurer's life.

The elder Frémont died in Charleston, South Carolina, in 1818, leaving the family in poverty. John Charles, exceptionally bright, managed to attend Charleston College briefly at age fifteen (he was expelled for "incorrigible negligence") and through the efforts of a family friend, the botanist and statesman Joel Poinsett, won appointment in 1838 as lieutenant in the army's newly organized Corps of Topographical Engineers. In Washington three years later, Frémont was introduced to Senator Thomas Hart Benton, one-time Tennessee politician, soldier, and hotel-lobby fighter. Now representing Missouri, he was among the most persuasive voices in Congress for the exploration of the trans-Mississippi West, known for bellowing "The *facts*! What are the *facts*?" when he rose to challenge what he considered a dubious senatorial issue. He had another noteworthy feature: his towering egocentrism, so pronounced that a journalist described it as "so part and parcel of the man, that it is not at all offensive, but a sort of national institution in which every patriotic American could take a just pride."

Whether the two men exchanged notes on the matter of their peculiar 1813 propinquity is not known, but they became friends, Benton seeing in the dashing lieutenant the pattern of youth, boldness, intelligence, and ambition ideal for an agent of expansionism.

Their long association and friendship faltered seriously only once, when Frémont fell in love with Benton's tomboyish daughter Jessie, second of his six children. She was seventeen and Frémont twenty-eight when the two eloped and married on October 18, 1841. Jessie soothed her father's anger and John Charles was welcomed into the family.

In Washington, the Frémonts met and charmed the capital elite—Senator Lewis Linn, Benton's expansionist partner; Senator Daniel Webster; General Winfield Scott; and President John Tyler among them. At the time, Tyler was not friendly toward the idea of any government-sponsored move into the Oregon Country; he wanted no confrontation with England to interfere with the matters receiving his closest attention, such as the issue of annexing Texas. Even so, he did not oppose a bill sponsored by Benton, which appropriated $30,000 for a topographical party to be led by the brilliant mathematician and cartographer Joseph Nicollet. The expedition's mission was to reconnoiter the opening stretch of the overland route for Oregon-bound emigrants from western Missouri through South Pass in the Rocky Mountains.

Nicollet had been Frémont's mentor in 1839 during a survey of the Minnesota and Dakota territories, and when the frail scientist's health failed on the eve of his departure to South Pass, his protege was given the command.

In June 1842 Frémont set out from Saint Louis with twenty-eight men, twenty of them listed as *voyageurs,* together with a German cartographer, Charles Preuss, and, as guide, the Kentuckian Christopher Houston Carson, who in his thirty-two years had tramped and trapped the West from Santa Fé to California, from the Gila River to the northern Rockies. The Frémont-Carson partnership, which would be sustained through many more expeditions and tribulations in the future, would be compared to that of Lewis and Clark, Burton and Speke, Stanley and Livingstone.

The explorers followed the Kansas River and moved northwest to the Platte, thence up the North Platte toward the Rocky Mountains. On August 8, averaging twenty miles a day, they reached South Pass. Frémont was disappointed in this unprepossessing saddle at the Continental Divide, comparing its ascent to climbing Capitol Hill, and hastened on. His instructions from his superiors at Topographical Corps headquarters in Washington called for him to turn back after reaching and mapping the pass, but, not for the last time, he ignored orders. The party pushed on northwest and set up camp in the Wind River Mountains.

On the return trip, Frémont gathered six of his men in a rubber boat to shoot some Platte River rapids, a foolish venture that came to near disaster when the boat hit a submerged rock and flipped over, taking all his scientific papers to the bottom. Fortunately, duplicates of the journals and maps were carried by the main party.

The expedition reached Fort Laramie at the end of August and Saint Louis in October. In Washington, with Preuss turning out a map and meteorological table, Frémont collaborated with his wife in writing a hefty report to Congress. When it was published and offered to the public, it became a sensation, thanks to Jessie Benton Frémont's literary gifts and her husband's voluminous and meticulous observations and eye for poetic detail. Instead of the customary dusty, officious, fact-foundered explorer narratives of the past, Frémont's *A Report of an Exploration of the Country Lying Between the Missouri River and the Rocky Mountains on the Line of the Kansas and Great Platte Rivers* gave the Twenty-seventh Congress something no Congress had received before: a *book,* beautifully organized and written. It contained lovely descriptive passages such as the rendering of the Wind River Range as "a gigantic disorder of enormous masses, and a savage sublimity of naked rock, in a wonderful contrast with innumerable green spots of rich floral beauty, shut up in their stern recesses." Even the text's data on terrain, weather, soil and water, vegetation and wildlife were lively, as was its advice on where forts should be built, and where good campsites might be located. The book also disproved the "Great American Desert" myth of the Great Plains favored by Major Stephen H. Long in 1819–20.

By the time the *Report* was published in March 1843, Frémont had packed his telescope, sextant, and pocket chronometer and was deep in preparations for a return to South Pass, this time to push on to the Oregon Country. He had

thirty-nine men, including Kit Carson again as guide and
Charles Preuss again as cartographer, and they started west
in May 1843, on what became a fourteen-month milestone
in American exploration, the most significant expedition
since Lewis and Clark.

Frémont's party followed the footsteps of the 1842 journey to South Pass, then turned south and east toward the
Great Salt Lake, arriving there on September 9. After a stopover at Fort Hall, they followed the Snake River to Fort
Boisé and reached Fort Vancouver on November 8, 1843,
where they observed a small but steady stream of emigrants
arriving on the Columbia and moving south to the verdant
valley of the Willamette.

As was his often near-fatal habit, Frémont ignored orders
to lead his men home after reaching the Pacific. In mid-
January 1844, he and his men reached an enormous (188
square miles in size, it turned out) and stunningly pristine
lake in western Nevada, which he named Pyramid Lake for
the rock formations around it, and there planned to cross the
mountains into Mexican California. Whether this decision
was his own alone or inspired by his father-in-law and the
public clamor for information on California, it was a dangerous idea that must have bothered even such a loyalist as
Kit Carson. It was winter, and the Sierra Nevada's cold sav-
agery nearly cost them their lives. Their horses slipped on
the icy trails, many died of hunger or were slaughtered for
food (of their 104 mules and horses, thirty-three survived);
their Indian guides wisely deserted them; they suffered from
starvation, snowblindness, and frostbite. They were fortunate: That Sierra winter was a mild one, and on February 6,
1844, Frémont and a scouting party climbed on snowshoes
to the top of a promontory south of Lake Tahoe. "Far below
us, dimmed by the distance," the explorer wrote, "was a large
snowless valley, bounded on the western side, at a distance
of about a hundred miles, by a low range of mountains,

which Carson recognized with delight as the mountains bordering the coast."

The overlook gave them a panoramic view of the Sacramento valley and they reached Sutter's Fort, the oasis at the juncture of the American and Sacramento Rivers, in early March. John Augustus Sutter, the Swiss emigré who had built the fort on the land granted him by the Mexican government, welcomed Frémont and his men, as he did all Americans. Of their arrival, he recorded, "The starvation and fatigue they had endured rendered them truly deplorable objects."

Among the expedition's accomplishments was the exploration and the Preuss map of what Frémont named the "Great Basin," the vast tract of mountains, deserts, and plains between the Wasatch Mountains of Utah and the Sierra Nevadas; the navigation of the "magnificent object," as Frémont called the Great Salt Lake (explored in a leaky rubber boat at a time when the party was reduced to eating stewed skunk); and the first dependable map and description of the surrounding Bear River basin.* They had mapped the waterways, vital to California-bound pioneers, that rose in the desert and then vanished in the sand before ever reaching the ocean: the Humboldt, which meandered across southern Utah before disappearing into a swampy lake bed Frémont named the Humboldt Sink; and the river that flowed easterly from the Sierras to its terminus in the Carson Sink, named for the expedition's scout.

(Frémont *named* the Humboldt—formerly called Mary's River—but only rediscovered it. In 1833, Joseph Reddeford Walker, another of the Tennessee brotherhood of mountain men and at the time an associate of Benjamin Bonneville, led a trapping party of forty men to the river and made an

---

*Charles Preuss's maps were used by Brigham Young, and Frémont's narrative prompted the Mormon leader to move his followers to the Salt Lake valley in 1847.

arduous three-week crossing of the Sierra Nevada, descending between the Merced and Tuolumne Rivers. In the same expedition, Walker and his men discovered Yosemite Valley and were the first Americans to see the giant sequoia trees. Frémont was aware of the accomplishments of those who had gone before him and did not claim the "Pathfinder" title overly romantic writers bestowed on him.)

The expedition reached Saint Louis in August 1844.

Frémont would make many westward journeys in his tumultuous life, but his second expedition remained the most momentous, and his second *Report* even more widely read and admired than the first. For the Oregon-bound, Frémont's new book, published in 1845, added an immense amount of data on the emigrant route there: topography, Indian inhabitants, game and plant life, and an optimistic view for the country. "Commercially, the value of the Oregon Country must be great," he wrote, "washed as it is by the north Pacific Ocean—fronting Asia—producing many of the elements of commerce—mild and healthy in its climate—and becoming, as it naturally will, a thoroughfare for the East India and China trade."

He had not discovered the Oregon Trail, but for the westering folk gathering in camps and rendezvous places around Independence and Westport Landing, he had mapped it, fixed on paper its waterways and landmarks, and made a perilous journey safer by telling everything he had learned about it.

PART FIVE

MEDICINE ROAD

■

19

Toward the Elephant

■

"NOTHING IS WISE THAT DOES NOT HELP YOU ALONG. . . ."

1

Getting to Oregon took more than a route, a guide, grit, and work; it took money, and by 1840s standards, and the wage of the average emigrant, a lot of it. Sailing-ship passage was out of the question for most people. It was too expensive, too inaccessible, and too nightmarish for a farm family to contemplate. A thousand dollars was not an unusual fare for the 13,000-mile voyage out of New York or Boston, and the price was not much less from New Orleans. Either way, it was going to take five or six months on a converted merchantman butting the terrifying seas off Cape Horn to the Pacific. In 1846 a treaty opened a shortcut across the Isthmus of Panama, cutting the journey by two months' time but adding new horrors: Passengers had to travel the malarial Chagres River by dugout canoes, the last miles by muleback or on foot to Panama City on the Pacific side, and then wait and hope to catch passage on a vessel heading for the Sandwich Islands, or the Alta California or Oregon coast.

Walking the 2,000 miles or so from Independence or the other frontier settlements to the Columbia was cheaper, even though everything but the walking cost cash.

Bernard De Voto estimated that the average family

"outfit"—wagon, draft animals, tools, food, and supplies—
was worth from $700 to $1,500, the money deriving from
selling a farm, liquidating a small business, borrowing, pool-
ing, scraping together. The really poor man with nothing to
liquidate had to hire out as a laborer, camp helper, hunter,
or teamster, carrying his kit on his back and working for his
meals. Many men, and some families, started out on foot
with no wagon or even a horse, toting survival essentials and
hoping to attach themselves to an emigrant train. One man
became an Oregon Trail celebrity of sorts as he made his
way west pushing a wheelbarrow containing a few tools,
some spare clothing, and food.

For the farm-seller and family with the money to invest,
the immediate matters to attend to, before or after reaching
Saint Louis, involved wagons, what to put in them, and the
animals to pull them.

By 1843 there were guidebooks, memoirs, and advice
aplenty from those who had made the journey (and a great
deal of advice from those who hadn't). All these authorities
were in general agreement on the ideal of a light load in a
light wagon drawn by strong, healthy animals. Like all ide-
als, this one was easily stated and difficult to practice. Of
course dependable authority Marcus Whitman, despite his
own failure to take one beyond Fort Hall, believed that wagons were essential for families to reach the Columbia River
valley.

Wagon wisdom, refined over the years since the Whitmans and the Spaldings made their overland journey in
1836, drifted toward the ideal. Few of the Oregon Trail wagons of the 1840s resembled the ponderous, big-wheeled,
boat-curved Conestogas used by freighting outfits. Whether
set aside when farms were sold, or custom built (at a cost of
$60–$100), the typical overland wagon was generally light,
made of hickory or maple as often as oak, springless and
straight-bedded, the wagon box ten to twelve feet long, four
feet wide, and two deep. The box, generally overloaded at

the start of the journey with 3,000 pounds or more of goods and belongings, was packed four feet deep with a narrow passage down the middle. At the bottom were the big, heavy items, like plows, bedsteads, stoves, chests, and bags of seeds; then a layer of kitchen utensils and clothing; and on top the immediate necessities: water kegs, cooking pots, axes, firearms, bags of flour, salt and coffee beans, blankets, and the like. False bottoms provided extra storage for spare wagon parts, and a jockey box up front or mounted on the side of the bed held tools for repairs.

Wagon wheels were complex structures of carefully fitted components: curved oaken or bois d'arc felloes pegged or clamped together on which the iron tires were bolted; heavy spokes socketed into the felloes; massive hubs; all, excepting the tires, bolts, and supporting strap iron, fashioned of wood, since metal was too heavy and too difficult to repair in the wilderness. The rear wheels were commonly five to six feet in diameter and the front ones smaller, four feet or so, to permit sharp turns and to prevent them from jamming against the wagon box. The wheels were dished outward for stabilization and removed by cranking up the bed with a jack.

The wagon undercarriage was a cunning arrangement keyed to a kingpin, the main front pivot, running through a wooden "box bolster," a support on which the wagon box rested. Brakes consisted of hardwood blocks levered against the rear wheels. The running gear was greased from a bucket suspended from the rear axle.

Wagon covers were made of double thicknesses of canvas (often made of hemp, an important cash crop in Missouri and the deep South), drill, or sailcloth, waterproofed with paint or linseed oil and fixed to hickory bows and puckered with ropes rove through their hems. The grimy white covers, billowing and popping in the wind as the wagons crawled across the grasslands, inspired the image of the "prairie schooner," but the name took on a decidedly unromantic

meaning at certain river crossings where timber was un-
available for raft building. On such occasions the wagon
boxes were caulked and sheathed in rawhide or tarpaulin
coated with oakum and tallow, the running gear removed
and placed inside the box, and the box floated across swollen waterways with cursing, sputtering men handling the
guide ropes.

On the downhill side of steep mountain slopes, the wheels
had to be locked in place by chains threaded through the
spokes and fastened to the bed, the wagon then skidded
downhill with curved iron shoes attached to the motionless
wheels to prevent them from developing flat spots.

People walked alongside their wagons, occasionally taking a rest on a "lazy board," a seat projecting from the side
of the box, or on horseback or mule-back. In camp in bad
weather a family would sleep on top of the load under the
canvas; otherwise, they lived outside the wagon and walked
alongside it.

The enduring debate among outfitters, teamsters, and overland travelers had to do with the critical matter of the best
animals to pull the wagon. Horses were seldom a part of the
argument. They were needed by outriders and hunters, but
were not practical as draft animals. They were too expensive ($200 for a good one), they did not forage well on the
dry grass of the plains so their feed had to be supplemented
by grain carried along in the train, they were prone to dis-
temper from drinking alkaline water, too easily plagued by
flies and mosquitoes, and they lacked the strength required
to pull a heavy wagon.

Both mules and oxen had strong adherents. Oxen covered
less ground in a day but were "easy keepers" and cost
less: forty to sixty-five dollars for an ox three to five years
old, ninety or a hundred dollars for a five-year-old Missouri
mule. The ox required no expensive harness, collars, or

trees, only a double hickory yoke about four feet long with up-and-over curves at each end, holes bored in it to receive the ends of the oxbow, and a croquet wicket–shaped loop that ran under the animal's neck, kept in place by wooden "keys," wedges, or cotter pins. A swinging iron ring carried the wagon pole.

Oxen worked in pairs, or yokes, with a minimum of two but usually three yokes for each wagon, plus a spare or two. The biggest animals would be yoked just ahead of the wagon for the hardest work.

Some emigrants with enough pooled money hired teamsters, but most managed their wagons on their own. Oxen trained to the yoke as calves were driven by a bullwhacker walking alongside them with an eighteen-foot braided rawhide whip with a "popper" at the end. The bullwhip was held by its two-foot-long handle, and was swung backward, then in a circle over the driver's head, then forward to crack over the animals' ears. Goads, long sticks with a spike at the end, were also used, but sparingly—no good teamster injured his animals with whip or goad—and occasionally the lead ox would have a rope hooked over his horns and jerked to get his attention.

Oxen were controlled with the standard shouts of "Gee!", "Haw!", and "Whoa!" but they were often unresponsive to such orders. A familiar Oregon Trail tableau was that of ox teams straining against their yokes, heads low, snorting and blowing the dust and burned-over prairie grass from their nostrils, heaving their overloaded wagons forward with chains rattling, axles shrieking, and whips popping loud as pistol shots—all this as the grimy, sun-scoured drivers cursed above the din.

Oxen had disadvantages: They tended to recklessness when thirsty or overheated and would sometimes stampede to a water hole or stream. On such occasions nothing could be done to stop them until they were sated and bogged down in mud. In this characteristic they differed from the other animals in the train, including the humans, only in their bulk and corresponding water requirements and capacity.

The greatest problem oxen presented as draft animals was the tendency for their hooves to wear and split on rocky ground. Cracked hooves were "cured" by drawing a string soaked in hot tar through the split. They were shod with small parenthesis-shaped iron shoes nailed on each side of the cloven hoof, but the average ox was uncooperative in this operation and when his hooves needed examining often lay down with his feet tucked under him. Ox-shoeing was a difficult procedure even in a blacksmith's shop, where the animal had to be driven headfirst into a timbered stall, canvas slings placed under its belly so the beast could be hoisted by a windlass, and its feet tied to a rail for shoeing. On the prairie, the whole thing was hellish: A trench was dug and the terrified ox wrestled into it upside down, the kicking feet lashed together and held while the shoes were tacked on. If spare shoes had been used up between outposts on the trail pieces of thick leather were used as substitutes, or the hooves were smeared with tar and grease and buffalo-hide booties fastened on. Some teamsters were able to rope, tie, and shoe the animals without the trench method, but it was a dangerous business either way.

An emigrant wagon required a minimum of six mules to draw 2,000 pounds and in addition to costing more per animal and requiring relatively expensive harness, they had to be driven, meaning relays of men had to sit on the jouncing wagon for hours on end. Mules were faster than oxen and endured the heat better, but they were sulkier too, shying at sudden noises, and even at shadows, and bolting for no apparent reason—"much given to mayhem," in Merrill J. Mattes' felicitous phrase. Mules were tough and durable, and if a wagon broke down beyond repair mules became pack animals, which oxen did not; on the other hand, Indians would steal a mule but not an ox, and a dead ox made better eating than a dead mule.

Peter Burnett of Indiana, who made his Oregon Trail journey in 1843, said, "The ox is the most noble animal, patient, thrifty, durable, gentle. Those who come to this country will be in love with their oxen by the time they get here."

That nobility struck many a westering family on the Oregon Trail as with rags soaked in camphor clapped to their noses they passed the rotting carcasses of hundreds of oxen that had been shot for food or perished from hunger, thirst, and overwork. One such witness wrote, "There ought to be a Heaven for all ox that perish under the yoke, where they could roam in the fields of sweet clover and timothy."

Early travelers on the Oregon Trail offered valuable advice to the emigrants moving out from the rendezvous places around Independence: For families with children, take a milk cow (and hang a bucket of milk from the wagon undercarriage—it'll bounce and make butter); take a few head of cattle if possible, and maybe some chickens in a coop lashed to the tailgate. They can be let out in camp to forage on bugs and worms and kids can be given the chore of chicken-wrangler to gather them up before the dawn departure. Above all, take spares and extras: spare horse; spare draft animals; extra shoes, yokes, chains and harness; and wagon parts—axles, tongues, wheels, spokes, oxbows, kingbolts and tongue-bolts. Take good water kegs and plenty of rope, light for picketing animals and general chores, heavy for lowering wagons down slopes and towing wagon boxes across water. Take whiskey for dosing animals poisoned by bad water, and a medicine chest for sick humans; take rifles and shotguns, powder, lead and bullet molds, lanterns, extra boots and socks. Take duck trousers, flannel shirts and woolen long johns; ladies take gingham and sunbonnets.

As to provender, experience said to go light on rice and beans—they take too long to cook—and heavy on cornmeal, for johnnycakes, biscuits, and the like. Take flour, dried fruit and vegetables (anti-scorbutics), hardtack, salt, coffee, tea, sugar, molasses, vinegar, saleratus (baking soda), wrapped bacon sunk in a barrel of bran or cornmeal to keep it from spoiling, eggs treated the same way. Take matches sealed in corked bottles and gutta-percha or painted canvas cloths for sleeping on wet ground. Follow Doctor Marcus Whitman's dictum—"Nothing is wise that does not help you along; nothing is good for you that causes a moment's delay" — and take nothing except what is absolutely essential to getting to your destination.

Randolph Barnes Marcy of Greenwich, Massachusetts, an army officer who led emigrant caravans to California in gold rush years, listed in his popular *Prairie Traveller* the minimum "allowance of provisions for each grown person" heading to the Pacific from Missouri, good for four months: 150 pounds of flour or its equivalent in hard bread (hardtack); twenty-five pounds of bacon or pork, and "enough fresh beef to be driven on the hoof to make up the meat component of the ration," fifteen pounds of coffee, twenty-five pounds of sugar, "plus saleratus or yeast powders for making bread, and salt and pepper."

No matter the advice and voices of experience, the wagons crawling west were packed to the sideboards and four or more feet deep with the very superfluities Doctor Whitman and Marcy warned against. Some of these, such as the tools of a farmer's trade—plows, axes, hoes, hammers, kegs of nails, bucksaws, spades, augurs, and whetstones—seemed absolute essentials for one expecting to build a cabin and cultivate a subsistence crop in the wilderness. Other things were carried along because they brought a remnant of civilized life to a savage land: claw-footed tables, heirloom chiffoniers, cast-iron skillets and cookpots, "thunder mugs" (chamber pots), washbowls, rocking chairs, books, churns, bedsteads, feather mattresses, quilts, and bundled clothing.

The opening shake-down miles of the journey determined what the real necessities were and what had to be sacrificed as the ox and mule teams reached rough country and the first serious water crossings. The jettisoning process began a few miles out from the Missouri frontier, took a serious turn near the head of Grand Island, Nebraska, and became more serious by the time Fort Laramie was reached. All along the Oregon Trail load-lightening relics were strewn among the carcasses of oxen and mules: stacks of bacon rotting in the sun—as much as a half-ton in some places—trunks, mattresses, carpenter tools, saddles, sawmill equipment, mining augurs, anvils, bellows, crowbars, scythes, gold washers, plows, grindstones, baking ovens, harness, kegs and barrels, books and furniture, and fatally broken wagons.

Passersby scavaged among these pickings, finding needed wagon parts, tools, and miscellaneous treasures. One posted sign urged HELP YOURSELF, and one pioneer wrote home: "Don't bother to bring cooking stoves. I could pick up one anywhere."

2

Oregon Trail journeyers were a freewheeling lot who were apt to turn their wagons off the roadway with no notice to see the sights or take a rest from eating dust. They wore down their stock, threw up hasty camp corrals that let their animals wander, were late making camp, dallied at starting out in the morning, groused at taking their sentry-duty turn or at doing any other communal chore, argued and fought among themselves, occasionally with real violence. What discipline could be imposed came from their elected train captain and his subordinates or from their guide, but the emigrant trains never abided the rigid marching orders and military order of the Santa Fé trade trains or Brigham Young's Mormons.

They did work assiduously once a campground was selected by the guide, usually on the basis of water, grass, and firewood availability, all three of which were abundant in the early miles of the journey and in the first months of Oregon Trail traffic but became more precious later on.

The Platte River had lush grass along its banks and, early on, plenty of trees on its islands. Its water, brown with suspended silt, had to be filtered through cloth or with a handful of meal in a bucket to settle the mud. Some emigrants boiled their water, not to kill bacteria, which were then unknown, but to get rid of the minnows, "wiggletails"—mosquito larvae—and whatever else was swimming in it. Francis Parkman, in his 1846 journey on the trail, wrote of dipping a tin cup in the Platte after a long ride in the scorching sun and discovering "a troop of young tadpoles sporting in the bottom of my cup." Platte water, called a "Platte River cocktail" when taken straight, warm, brackish, and muddy, had an additional quality: One emigrant wrote home that it "partakes of the same laxative qualities of the Missouri and Mississippi." Where water was scarce clothing could not be washed; when water was found there was great rejoicing, not only to replenish the casks but to bathe, wash clothes, and boil diapers, which in waterless days had to be scraped, dampened, dried, and reused. Unknown to the emigrants, the boiling of water helped check the spread of infectious diseases.

Before the Platte islands were denuded of their trees, willow, poplar, and cottonwood were chopped and gathered by the armload. In tall-grass country, children were dispatched from camp to make twists of prairie grass, slough grass, or hay called "cats," which burned well when dry and burned smokily when green or wet. A better fuel—hotter, slower burning, and odorless—was what the French called *bois de vache,* buffalo "wood," the chips of dried dung gathered by women in their aprons and by kids in large sacks. The gatherers did not at first relish the idea of handling the dung—a trail song said,

> *Look at her now with a pout on her lips*
> > *As daintily with her fingertips*
> > *She picks for the fire some buffalo chips*

—but the pout soon disappeared of necessity. With the rule that "three bushels make a good fire," the chips were collected, placed in a shallow firehole, lit using dry grass as tinder, and the cookpots were then suspended over the fire. (An extra benefit: One or two smoldering chips brought inside a wagon chased mosquitoes away.)

As the trains moved beyond the Platte to the Sweetwater and buffalo thinned and disappeared, the chips were genuinely missed, being far preferable to knotty chunks of pungent sagebrush, which burned too quickly.

In buffalo country, along the succulent grasslands of the Platte where they thrived, where as late as 1850 emigrants were seeing them in a solid phalanx of so many thousands they took two hours or more to pass, the herds were so frighteningly immense that guns had to be fired to prevent the camp from being trampled. The signal of their advent was always a low, distant thunder-like rumbling followed by clouds of dust on the horizon. Then the ground shook as they passed, 2,000 or 10,000 at a time, so closely bunched their horns clacked and rattled against each other.

Buffalo were easily, and therefore cruelly and wastefully, killed. Shot and wounded, lurching about with broken backs and on mangled legs, blinded by shotgun blasts, spouting blood, they were fallen on by hunters with long throat-slitting knives and often butchered before their hearts were still. Buffalo tongues, rib, and hump meat were prized by most, although not by all. Some found the meat inedible even after hours of boiling or roasting, creating an unswallowable bolus when chewed. Jerky, made by soaking strips of meat in brine and drying them over fires or in the sun, was to many the only way to eat buffalo. In truth, however it was cooked, little of the animal was eaten, usually no more than a few pounds of a beast weighing 800 to 1,200 pounds (full-grown bulls could weigh two tons and more). The rest was left to the wolves and coyotes who always haunted the herds awaiting the chance to hamstring a calf or feast on the bloating carcasses left behind by human slaughterers.

The Platte River valley offered a variety of other game for the hunters, and for a time cookpots and skillets steamed and sizzled not only with the customary daily fare of bacon, cornmeal johnnycakes, stewed apples, and coffee, but with the meat of pronghorn antelope, sage hens, rabbits, plover, pigeons, marsh quails, snipe, and even black bears near the Platte forks. There were also edible greens to be gathered, including onions, which were good for protection against scurvy, and berries—goose, black, blue, serviceberries, purple and black chokeberries—to add to the diet.

On the Oregon Trail, as at home, women carried as much of the workload as the men—and sometimes more. They not only gathered fuel, picked greens and fruit, cooked, and tended the children, but they also helped herd the animals and often marched alongside their wagons with bullwhip at the ready. To perform such work, womenfolk discovered early that the trail required modification of their clothing. Their long cotton or linsey-woolsey skirts dragged on the ground, became tattered by brush and rock, were rendered drab by soaking rains and river crossings, and were scorched by cookfires. Some wives wore their husbands' spare trousers,* flannel shirts, brogans, and floppy wide-brimmed

---

*In 1851 Amelia Bloomer's skirt-and-trouser outfit was introduced, but few emigrant women ever wore them.

hats, but most were guided by the admonition in Deuteronomy 22:5: "The woman shall not wear that which pertaineth
unto a man." (But apparently not by 22:11: "Thou shall not
wear a garment of divers sorts, as of woollen and linen together".) They pinched the wings of their sunbonnets together, sewed rocks along hemlines to keep skirts down in
the wind, and went about their never-ending work.

To the emigrant family or individual starting out on the Oregon Trail, everything seemed conquerable except Indians
and disease. Storms and bugs (mosquitoes, buffalo gnats,
grasshoppers, flies, something called a "black gallinipper")
were hated, but injuries, sickness, and Indians (the latter the
subject of the direst warnings in the overland "guides" read
so assiduously in the 1840s, of overheated columns in eastern newspapers, and of word-of-mouth horror stories told in
the Missouri camps) were truly feared.

But in reality the Indian scare, perhaps the deepest dread
of overland families in the early years of the migration
west, turned out to be the least worrisome. The Indians of
the plains and mountain country of the Trail had been
warring against one another since before recorded history,
and fur traders—often the source of the bloodiest of camp-
told Indian tales—had battled with many tribes, bands, and
horse-stealing parties on the Missouri, Platte, Snake, Columbia, and virtually in every nook and cranny between.
Most emigrants, however, saw the Indians as beggers, not
warriors, coming to the camps trading trinkets and looking for food, occasionally helping in river fordings and
other labors, and stealing some horses and cattle at night—
the Pawnee were particularly adept at this. The emigrant
trains were always overarmed for Indian threats; the Indians almost never approached an emigrant caravan with
hostility.

While the overlanders learned that they would probably

not have to combat Indians, they fought injuries and disease—often before they departed the Missouri border. An estimated 20,000 people died on the Oregon Trail in the decade of 1841–50, most by accidents and Asiatic cholera. This strain of the cholera reached epidemic proportions during the California gold rush years, in 1848 to 1850, but it struck western Missouri camps and emigrant trains moving along the Kansas-Nebraska prairies in the early 1840s, the fatal bacteria thriving in garbage and in springs polluted by latrines built too near them.

Occasionally the cholera-stricken miraculously survived. An emigrant named M. L. Wisner wrote in his diary that he "passed a man by the side of the road who had been attacked by cholera, when his company, panic struck, inhumanly left him to die one hundred and fifty miles from any house. He had a sack of provisions by his side, and lying on the ground, could hardly speak . . . . He could not be moved . . . . All I could do for him was to bring him one of my pint tin cups of water . . . . We learned by a man on horseback the next day, that he had recovered."

But such cases were rare, and as a rule no clyster, poultice, or dose of laudanum helped.

While cholera killed more overlanders than all other diseases combined, others also took a toll: measles, typhoid, whooping cough, smallpox, chickenpox, diphtheria (called "Putrid Sore Throat"), grippe, rheumatism, scurvy, malaria and many nameless "mountain fevers," "slough fevers," and agues. Emigrant diaries are filled with mysterious "bilious complaints," "inflammation of the bowels," "congestion of the brain," "intestinal inertia," "excessive vomiting," "childbed fever," "lung fever," and "bloody flux." These homemade diagnoses covered everything from cholera to ulcers, blocked bowels, food poisoning, puerperal fever, peritonitis, strokes, appendicitis, tuberculosis, pneumonia (common from sleeping in wet bedding, enduring freezing winds and sudden temperature changes), and dysentery, which killed the weak and malnourished.

There were also references to hydrophobia (rabies, always fatal), vertigo, "died of exertion" (probably heart attack), trachoma (endemic among the Indians), alkali poisoning, delirium tremens, and gangrene.

After disease, accidents and mishaps of every description took the most lives on the Trail. Drownings were commonplace, as were broken bones and mashed flesh, and frostbite turned gangrenous. There were accidental (and occasionally purposeful) gunshots; a few homicides;* countless falls from heights, horses, and wagons with attendant broken spines and necks; snakebites; lacerations; infections; blood poisoning; and shock from field amputations.

Edwin Bryant, a Kentucky newspaperman who ventured west on the Oregon Trail in 1846, wrote of a boy who developed gangrene from a compound leg fracture. A drover with the boy's party had been a hospital orderly, and after whetting some butcher knives served as surgeon. The boy was dosed with laudanum and camphor held to his nose as the incision was made above the knee. A gush of foul-smelling pus burst from the swollen flesh and the drover cut the bone through with a common handsaw. The boy died as the stump was cauterized and the flap sewn shut.

The emigrant medicine chest, even the sophisticated ones carried by physicians, were filled with nostrums and dubious "cures" mixed with genuinely useful substances: "physicking pills," rum and peppermint "essences," hartshorn, tartar emetic, belladonna, zinc sulphate, Peruna, beef

---

*There were twelve murders recorded on the Oregon Trail and several executions, by hanging or firing squad. Merrill Mattes wrote of a drumhead trial and execution of a Missouri teenager found guilty of an ax murder. According to an eyewitness, the boy "was hyung on the limb of a basswood tree."

tonics, turpentine, sulphur, camphor, calomel, cayenne pepper, tincture of rhubarb, tamarack syrup, bitters, asafetida,
ipecac, Seidlitz and Dover's Powders, Jayne's Car-minitive
Balsam, Ayer's Pain-Killer, and Epsom and Glauber's Salts.

3

In a Christian journal review of Reverend Samuel Parker's
*Journal of an Exploring Tour beyond the Rocky Moun-
tains,* the writer called the Oregon Trail a road "excavated
by the finger of God," the Indians called it "the White Man's
Medicine Road," and those who made the journey and survived it had good reason to think they had accomplished
something epic, even biblical, in its testing of human will
and endurance. In an 1885 address to the annual reunion of
the Oregon Pioneers Association in Salem, Oregon, a Trail
veteran named E. L. Eastham said:

Where else in the history of man, civilized or not, do you
read the story of a 2,500-mile march through hostile country, over unexplored desert and mountain? The host led
by Moses and Aaron wandered for years, but only accomplished a direct journey of a few hundred miles. Xenophon in his famous retreat from the Euphrates had a less
distance to go before he reached safe harbor at home. No
crusade ever extended over so great a distance, and most
of the way through Christian and friendly countries. Napoleon on his disastrous trip to Moscow only essayed a
march of 1,500 miles.

The Trail, which started at Saint Louis for those east of
the Mississippi, began again in the camps around Independence, Westport Landing, Saint Joseph, and even farther
north, at Council Bluffs, Iowa, or Omaha, Nebraska. What
had been a trappers' path and road to Astoria carried only

small numbers of emigrants and missionaries up to 1841, when the sixty-nine-member Bartleson-Bidwell company followed it from Sapling Grove to Soda Springs in Idaho, and there split up, half heading on to Oregon, half to California. In 1842, when Frémont and his first expedition were examining South Pass, close to 200 people were trudging along the Trail, and upwards of 1,000 made the trek the next year, during the "Great Migration." In the twenty-five busiest years of its history, when it had evolved into a true route— actually a series of routes—to the Pacific, the Oregon Trail was the longest thoroughfare in America. And until 1846, when the United States and Great Britain settled the Oregon boundary, its travelers defined the word *emigrant*—people traveling out of their native country into a foreign land—as surely as those sailing from Europe to America.

The first few miles of the journey followed the Santa Fé Trail into Kansas, the caravans following the Little Blue River into Nebraska until it made a southward bend, then making their way across the prairie to a ridge of sandhills from which the Platte River, their conduit for the next 600 miles, could be seen.

Among rivers, Bernard De Voto said, the Platte was "one of the most preposterous in the world," for its width, a mile or more, and its frivolous nature. In spring rains and with plenty of snowmelt from the mountains to the west, the river ran high and crashed and tumbled about its braid of islands; but it was most often little more than a mile-wide trickle so muddy it was said to flow from the bottom up, its quicksand so deep it could swallow a wagon and the ox team pulling it.

After a week following the south bank of the river the caravans had to ford the south branch to follow the North Platte drainage, a crossing that often occupied four or more toilsome days of fashioning bull boats from green buffalo hides stretched over willow frames, dismantling the wagons, and ferrying them and countless tons of goods, people, and animals across.

Once across, the wagons were scaled up a rise called California Hill to a wide, high benchland that dropped off to the North Platte valley. Another twenty miles or so from the fording lay Windlass Hill, where the teams had to be unhitched, the animals led down a forty-five-degree grade, and the wagons with their brakes locked scooted down at the end of guy-ropes into Ash Hollow, which lay 500 miles out and was the first shady place the pioneers had seen in weeks. Of the descent one emigrant wrote, "I cannot say at what angle we descend but . . . some go as far as to say, 'the road hangs a little past the perpendicular!' "

The nights were growing colder as the trains followed the packed-sand riverbanks into higher altitudes and began encountering celebrated Oregon Trail landmarks: Ancient Bluff Ruins; Courthouse Rock, a tall volcanic mound said to resemble a municipal building in Saint Louis; Jail House Rock, four miles off the main trail but so interesting that many rode or hiked to it and climbed to its summit to catch a glimpse of yet another odd formation, a great inverted funnel on the western horizon fourteen miles away. This was the 500-foot-high Chimney Rock, mentioned in pioneer diaries more often than any other site on the Medicine Road. A Dr. A. H. Thomasson (his doctorate clearly not in English composition) saw it in 1850 and noted in his journal, "We went up it about 4 hundred feet then it became so steep they was feet holts cut in so we could clime up about 25 feet further then we could see where some had cut noches and drove little sticks to clime abot 20 feet further but did not venture up that. I suppose that there is not less than 2 thousand names riten in difrin plases."

Thirty-five miles west of Chimney Rock lay Scotts Bluff, another of the Platte's geological curiosities, a Nebraskan Gibraltar looming over the western horizon and hugging the river so closely that wagons had to detour to the south over what became known as Robidoux Pass. Journalist Edwin Bryant, who saw the formation in the mid-1940s, described it as the "ruins of some vast city erected by a race of giants, contemporaries of the Megatherii and the Icthyosaurii." Nile explorer and traveler Richard Burton called it "a massive medieval city . . . round a colossal fortress."

The caravans now entered Wyoming and, ideally in mid-July, reached Fort Laramie, 650 miles from the Missouri border and a point where one overland guide informed his charges, "It is discouraging to tell you that you have not yet travelled one-third of the long road to Oregon."

The fort lay at the junction of the Laramie River with the North Platte, and had been named for an early French-Canadian trapper, Jacques LaRamee, said to have been killed by Indians on the site and his corpse thrown into the river. A hollow square of whitewashed adobe walls six feet thick, fifteen feet high, and about 130 feet on each side, the fort had blockhouses at opposite corners and inside were apartments, storage rooms, corrals, a trading post where supplies were sold at outrageous prices, a blacksmith shop, and even a post office. An old trapper named James Bordeaux, a veteran of the Upper Missouri trade who was married to a Brulé Sioux woman, ran the place and kept peace with the Indians. Laramie was located in prime buffalo country, and there were often as many as 600 Oglala and Brulé lodges—and 2,000 Indians—in the vicinity. A green meadow east of Laramie served as a favorite wagon campsite and there the journeyers rested, mingled with the Indians, reshod their animals, and bought needed supplies. There, too, the travelers, especially those heading for California by the round-about detours west of South Pass, became mindful of falling behind schedule and being shut out of the mountain passes by winter snows.

Eight miles west of Fort Laramie the trail passed a tall sandstone-and-white-chalk bank called Register Cliff, which

required only a nail or knifepoint to inscribe a name and date
on it, and for several miles beyond it the wagons left tracks
in the sandstone hills that so deepened over the years they
would be visible a century and a half afterward.

The steeper westward tilt of the continent toward the
Rockies tried man and beast, and the heavy cargo items—
anvils, chiffoniers, sheet-iron stoves, and the like—became
daily roadside casualties as the wagons rejoined the North
Platte near Casper, heading due west, fording the river again
near where Brigham Young's Mormons would build a ferry
in 1847. The Trail took them over Emigrant Gap, past Poison Springs, identifiable from the animal carcasses surrounding it, to Willow Springs, an excellent campsite with
good water, and on to Independence Rock overlooking the
Sweetwater. This landmark, named by fur traders who discovered it on July 4, 1824, and called it the "Register of the
Desert," was an oval-shaped granite boulder 128 feet high.
Messages were scratched or painted on it, and names and
dates, by nearly all who reached it. Some indicated their relief that they were "half-way" to the Pacific when in fact
they were but 815 miles out from Independence and had
1,200 miles or more to travel.

After passing Independence Rock, the caravans made the
first of no less than nine crossings of the maddeningly meandering Sweetwater, bypassed the awesome 400-foot gash
through the rocks known as Devil's Gate, reached "Three
Crossings," where the wagons thrice crossed the Sweetwater in a gate-like canyon, and came upon Ice Slough. Here
water collected beneath an insulating layer of peat moss and
froze in the harsh winters, remaining frozen through the
summer when travelers could dig it out and use slabs of ice
to cool water barrels.

The wagons negotiated South Pass, 914 miles out, with
little effort, the grassy gap in the Wind River Range at the
Continental Divide sloping so gently "that the traveler would
scarcely perceive that he was ascending were it not for the

great change in the atmosphere," one traveler wrote. The air continued thinning to its summit at 7,412 feet, the Trail then emerging into Oregon Country near Little Sandy Creek and continuing on through desert country to Pacific Springs, a memorable place in that it was the first water the pioneers encountered that flowed toward the western ocean.

Upon reaching the Green River there was a choice of routes to follow. Some took the Sublette Cutoff, named for one of the fur-trading brothers, which cut straight across a fifty-mile alkaline lake bed and grassless, gravelly benchland with the only water available at its far western side. This scary path was eighty-five miles shorter than the drop southeast to Fort Bridger, the trading post on the Green built by mountain immortal Jim Bridger and his partner Lewis Vasquez in 1843, but most were unwilling to chance the Sublette and took the detour, with its ample water and grass.

Joel Palmer, an Indiana legislator who joined an 1844 wagon train to Oregon, described Bridger's post as "a shabby concern built of poles and daubed with mud," but it was a place where a few supplies could be purchased and where "recruited" oxen, ones whose health and strength had been restored by rest and good pasturage, could be obtained by trading in footsore and weary ones and paying a fee.

It was at Fort Bridger, a thousand miles out of Independence, that the Mormons following the Oregon Trail veered off to the southwest into Utah.

From Bridger, the Trail returned northwest to Soda Springs, one of a series of iron-laden carbonated waters, which some travelers said tasted like small beer and made an excellent lemonade when mixed with citrus syrup and sugar. Fifty-five miles beyond the springs lay Fort Hall, the Hudson's Bay post originally built by Nathaniel Wyeth in 1834. Here many wagons had been abandoned over the years and were cannibalized to repair the ones now heading toward Oregon and California.

The Trail out of Fort Hall followed the left bank of the

Snake River, tributary of the Columbia, through "a melancholy and strange looking country," Frémont said, "one of fracture, and violence, and fire," the crossing of the Snake eased somewhat by two islands, which enabled wagons to cross in three laborious stages.

A few miles west of Fort Hall, at the American Falls of the Snake, those heading for California left their wagons and mounted horses and mules. Now, with a train of pack animals they followed their pilot southwestward toward the Great Basin of Utah and Nevada, a known killer of man and beast, 200,000 square miles of white salt beds, sand, lava, alkali, sage, and clay wastes circled by mountains that reflected the sun's heat like a mirror. The Hudson's Bay factor at Fort Hall recommended that emigrants take the California route, hoping to delay the time when Oregon could be invaded by Americans. While playing down the dangers of the southward journey, he warned the Oregon-bound about ravaging Indians, the likelihood of famine, how the Snake River threw itself and its passengers suicidally down its yawning gorges, and how mountain blizzards lay waiting in the Blue Mountains. Much of what he described required no exaggeration.

The Oregonians listened to the stories and moved on anyway, down the Snake to Salmon Falls, across the sage plains to Fort Boisé, and on to the Grand Ronde valley, a gorgeous campground of piney hills, rich pasturage, and abundant watercourses just east of the snow-shrouded Blue Mountains. They crossed the mountains, often in blizzards, visited the Whitmans' mission at Waiilatpu, and continued west to Fort Walla Walla with only the Cascades and sixty-odd miles separating them from the Willamette valley but no wagon road to reach it.*

---

*At least until 1846, when Illinois emigrant Samuel Barlow and workers completed a ninety-mile road over the Cascades to a point south of Mount Hood, which became the standard route into western Oregon.

The more cautious of the emigrants completed their journey down the Columbia banks on horseback. Many took their wagons and struggling animals the 250 miles across the Cascade Range into the forests around Mount Hood, to stagger into the Willamette on their literal last legs. Many more traveled in *bateaux,* dugouts, and canoes on the Walla Walla and Columbia to The Dalles, where they felled trees, made rafts, dismantled their wagons and placed them aboard, and faced the worst stretch of their 2,000-mile journey. The sixty miles of the Columbia to the mouth of the Willamette River rocketed down a basalt gutter that breached the Cascades, a mountain chain sixty to eighty miles wide with canyons 3,000 feet deep, a roller-coaster ride in icy winds blowing upstream that killed many so near the end of their journey and the beginning of their new lives.

After recovering from their Columbia passage, the newcomers crossed the river to the mouth of the Willamette. They hugged the shore for about twenty miles to Oregon City, a village on the east bank just below the falls of the Willamette.*

Most of the emigrants eventually paid a visit to Fort Vancouver, where John McLoughlin received them courteously and at no charge provided them with rooms to rest, salmon, potatoes, firewood, and whatever they required—within reason and usually within the rules of the Hudson's Bay Company—before they left his domain to travel on south to the land they were claiming.

---

*By 1846 Oregon City had a population of 1,000; flour mills and sawmills; a foundary; a circulating library; a temperance society; a debating club; Catholic and Methodist churches; two saloons; a weekly newspaper, the *Oregon Spectator;* and had become the center of the American populace of the Oregon Country, ten times the size of Portland, which lay fifteen miles downstream.

20

The Great Migration

■

1

By 1843, even the European press took notice of the Oregon Trail "movers," the pioneer families who were pointing their wagons west. British papers and journals, protective of their interests in the Pacific Northwest, saw the whole business as inexplicable. In a July 1843 editorial, the venerable *Edinburgh Review* informed its readers that for six months of the year the territory between the western boundary of the United States and the Oregon Country was "a howling wilderness of snow and tempests" and the remaining six months a wasteland "of hopeless sterility" infested with Indians "of more than Sythian savageness and endurance, who cannot be tracked, overtaken, or conciliated." The writer praised the energy of the American emigrants but predicted that "Oregon will never be colonized overland from the United States."

The view was shared by many influential Americans, among them Horace Greeley, editor of the *New York Daily Tribune*, the very man who urged, "Go west, young man, and grow up with the country!" (by which he meant west to the far country of Erie County, Pennsylvania). In 1843 he was in his "Stay east" mode, in which, receiving reports of the extraordinary gathering of wagons and pioneer families on the Missouri frontier he railed, "This migration of more than a thousand persons in a body to Oregon wears an aspect of insanity." He acknowledged that the United States had a rightful claim to Oregon but cautioned against making unnecessary trouble with the British by an emigrant invasion of the Northwest. The place was too distant, he said, and not nearly as fertile and rich in resources as the paeans of the propagandists would have it.

He urged caution. The Oregon boom was a sickness, infecting otherwise sensible folk into febrile acts, such as leaving comfortable homes, good farmlands, and markets, leaving their churches and friends and responsibilities. He wrote in his paper on July 19, 1843, "For what, then, do they brave the desert, the wilderness, the savage, snowy precipices of the Rocky Mountains, the weary summer march, the storm-drenched bivouac, and the gnawings of famine? Only to fulfill their destiny! There is probably not one among them whose outward circumstances will be improved by this perilous pilgrimage."

Nor was that all. Greeley wrote of starvation and savages, warning would-be pioneers who were so accustomed to the comforts and safety of their civilized lives that they could expect Indian attacks, perhaps several, during their journey between Missouri and Oregon, as well as other dangers and privations. He attempted to soften his panicky editorializing by assuring his readers that he was actually in favor of American settlement of the lands beyond Missouri, and looked in favor at the American pioneer spirit. But, he said, a *mass* movement to Oregon was too extreme, and he called upon all prudent men to "stop this side of the woods"—meaning at the Missouri boundary—because it was "palpable homicide to tempt or send women and children over this thousand miles of precipice and volcanic sterility to Oregon."

Greeley's shaky sense of distance and topography improved in 1859, when he made an overland trip to California and en route invented the Q&A newspaper interview after having a chat with Brigham Young in Salt Lake City. However, even as late as 1845, when 10,000 overlanders were clogging the Medicine Road, he was still calling the enterprise "foolhardy," still warning against Indian depredations and famine. He cautioned on the consequences of depending upon the Hudson's Bay Company to be of assistance if the emigrant miraculously got to Oregon, sick, shrunken to a skeleton, with his belongings strewn along the trail and his animals done in or dead. The Hudson's Bay people, he said, could not be expected to provide succor to "a horde."

While Greeley was among the most persistent and eloquent of the lemmings-to-the-sea school of observers of the Great Migration, he had company in his views. The *North American Review* compared Oregon to Siberia and said the roads to each were similarly perilous. The *New Orleans Picayune* advised in 1846, after the Oregon Trail had conveyed thousands to the Pacific, that emigrants, if they insisted on hazarding the journey west, do so via the Isthmus of Panama "to divert the travels to Oregon by the long, dangerous and expensive route across the prairies and Rocky Mountains." Even the *Daily Missouri Republican* in Saint Louis counseled menfolk to "stay home and earn an honest living."

In Congress, reactions to the growing traffic on the Trail were mixed. In January 1843 Senator George McDuffie of South Carolina thanked God "for placing the Rocky Mountains in such a way as to thwart Americans from reaching the Pacific." That same month, Lewis Linn of Missouri, surgeon in the War of 1812, Jacksonian Democrat, and party warhorse, died, indefatigable to the end in introducing bills for the settlement of Oregon. In one of his last addresses to the Senate he spoke of the "easy" passes across McDuffie's thwarting Rockies and expressed envy at the "wild and strange rapture" Daniel Boone must have felt when he penetrated the forests and first cast his eye upon Kentucky. The Oregon pioneer would experience such a rapture, he promised, and, never at a loss for biblical precedent, said the journey of the westward pioneers recalled those going "to the wilderness, like our first parents, when God sent them forth from the Garden of Eden to subdue the earth." Representative Orlando Bell Ficklin of Illinois took this a step further, speaking of the emigrants of the 1840s in allusions to Abraham and Lot, Moses and Aaron, and said he dreamed of the day he could climb the mountains to see and hear "with wild delight" the roar of the mighty Columbia as it crashed into the western sea.

Those whose dreaming had turned to doing were propelled west in 1843 for practical reasons. The residue of the economic Panic of '37 lingered; prices for farm goods remained depressed, as did those who raised the goods, who scratched out a meager subsistence from their Mississippi valley or Ohio valley acreage. Fresh reports from witnesses as reliable as Marcus Whitman, Jason Lee, Elijah White, and John C. Frémont told of open markets, fertile land, and limitless opportunity for "industry" and the industrious in Oregon.

"Hurry on," many who had seen the elephant were writing home, and warnings filtered eastward that the journey was becoming most costly for those who tarried and who did not provision themselves adequately. Post traders, capitalizing on the surge of traffic on the Trail, were charging exorbitantly for supplies. Frémont's cartographer Charles Preuss wrote in his diary in 1843 that "Carson [Kit Carson] was sent ahead to Fort Hall to secure provisions for us. If the emigrants get ahead of us, we shall not find much there." Marcus Whitman, who served as a guide for many of the Oregon-bound that year, wrote of the booming business and high prices at the four principal Oregon Trail posts—Forts Laramie, Bridger, Hall, and Boisé.

(The pitiless scalping escalated: At Fort Laramie in 1846 Francis Parkman seethed that the traders had become the "natural enemies" of the overlanders who, he wrote, "were

plundered and cheated without mercy." He told of "one bargain, concluded in my presence," in which "I calculated the
profits that accrued to the fort, and found that at the lowest
estimate they exceeded *eighteen hundred per cent.*")

On May 18, 1843, at Elm Grove, the rendezvous place
twelve miles out of Independence, recognizable for its one
large elm tree and one small one, a concourse of wagons,
ox and mule teams, horse and cattle herds, and people from
every part of Missouri, Iowa, Illinois, Indiana, Ohio, Kentucky, Tennessee, and farther-flung hamlets and towns
awaited the signal to begin the long walk to the Pacific.
They had trickled in for weeks, "relying only on the fertility of their invention." One notable man among them, Jesse
Applegate, later wrote, "Always ready and equal to the occasion and always conquerors. May we not call them men
of destiny?"

The men, women, and children of destiny numbered between 875 and 1,000 with 150 wagons, an immense cattle
herd, and a collection of spare horses, mules, and oxen—all
told as many as 5,000 animals. The assemblage was late in
starting—a cold spring had kept the bluestem grass in
hibernation—and impatient. They were oblivious to the
stragglers pouring into their bustling camp every day who
jockeyed for lead spots in the line of march. There was much
quarreling over the cow herd, which the cowless felt would
drag them all down and delay them reaching the mountains
before winter.

At the head of the caravan, which moved west on May 22,
was Captain John Gantt, a Marylander and former army officer in his early fifties. A tough, no-nonsense guide, he had
found his own second chance and a new life in the West after being court-martialed and dismissed from the service in
1829 for falsification of pay accounts, and he had close to
twenty years' experience in Indian country. He had been

recruited as pilot at the rate of one dollar per emigrant and agreed to lead the caravan as far as Fort Hall, where he would then continue on to California.

Another experienced hand who signed on to assist Gantt, Joseph Ballinger Chiles of Kentucky, had gone to California in '41 with the Bartleson-Bidwell train and had returned home with permission to build a grain mill in the Napa valley north of San Francisco Bay. He had recruited thirty men and had eight wagons loaded with mill equipment.

News arrived at Elm Grove that Dr. Marcus Whitman would be joining the caravan after he finished some business at Shawnee Mission, the Methodist Indian school at Westport Landing. He had returned to Boston the year past to convince the Board of Foreign Missions to save Waiilatpu and the Spaldings' mission at Lapwai.

When Whitman caught up with the Gantt train on the Platte, he calmed such anxieties as those created by many Trail veterans who warned the party that their wagons could not be taken beyond Fort Hall. Whitman said they could be taken all the way to the Columbia because the caravan had the combined manpower, which he lacked in '36, to get them there.

Also hurrying along toward the Missouri border was Lieutenant John C. Frémont, with a new expedition of forty men, pack animals, carts, and even a twelve-pounder cannon to impress any belligerent Indians on his line of march. He was heading toward South Pass again, but this time he intended pushing on to Oregon.

Notable among the tyros in the 1843 caravan was Peter Hardeman Burnett, one-time storekeeper in Weston, Missouri, a self-taught lawyer who was hopelessly in debt and had an ailing wife and six children. Taken down with Oregon fever, he had spent a year lecturing in western Missouri, calling for the other fever-stricken comrades to join him in Independence to start the journey. He had patched together the funds to buy two wagons and the oxen to pull them and by the time he arrived in Independence he had many followers and seemed a natural leader.*

Also eager and impressive were the Applegate brothers, Jesse, Lindsey, and Charles, from the Osage valley of Missouri. The Applegates were originally Kentuckians, having moved to Missouri when the boys were young to farm corn and cotton and raise hogs and cattle. Jesse had studied surveying and was known to have walked up to sixty miles a day in his work. He was tall, rawboned, and "so homely," David Lavender wrote, "he avoided mirrors all his life." He had gone broke farming and surveying, sold his property, and enlisted his brothers, who were little better off, to sell out. They all brought their wagons, cows, and families to Independence.

2

The train rolled out of Elm Grove on May 22, 1843, heading southwest along an old trace that intersected the Santa Fé Trail, by now a broad roadway pounded flat from two decades of heavy trade-wagon traffic. A day out of Fitzhugh's Mill, near Gardner, Kansas, they turned due west to the Wakarusa River, the first of many river obstacles that would try the patience and endurance of the tenderfeet, a steep-banked stream that required a path to be spaded down for the wagons' passage. The next crossing, the Kaw (or Kansas) River, was far worse. Gantt led the caravan thirty miles along its banks before finding a suitable fording place, then

---

*As he turned out to be. In 1849 Burnett left Oregon, where he had been appointed a territorial judge, for the California gold fields, and in 1850 he was elected the first governor of the state. James M. Nesmith, Burnett's orderly sergeant in the 1843 journey, became a judge, a brigadier general of militia, and, in 1860, a United States Senator from Oregon.

supervised the building of cross-timbered rafts to ferry the wagons, and people, across. The operation, including swimming the horses, draft animals, and cattle herd to the far bank, occupied five days.

Meantime, stragglers continued coming up. On May 31 Frémont and his expedition reached Elm Grove, where he observed ragged files of wagons bumping along toward the Kaw nine days behind the main train. Among the others who caught up were two Jesuit missionaries bound for the Flathead villages of the Bitterroot valley, and William Drummond Stewart, the Waterloo and Fifteenth King's Hussars veteran. Sir William had been hunting and taking part in the fur traders' rendezvous for a decade and was now returning to his beloved American West for the last time, accompanied by a party of sportsmen friends, heading for the Green River. Stewart was popular for his stories of Wellington in the Iberian Peninsula and fighting Napoleon's Grand Armée at Waterloo. Stewart's guide, Bill Sublette, had endless campfire tales of his experiences as one of Ashley's "enterprising young men" in '23: his narrow escape in the Arikara fight on the Upper Missouri, his journey with Jedediah Smith into Crow country and all the way to Hudson's Bay territory in Oregon, recollections of Nat Wyeth in 1832, and his wound in the Blackfoot battle at Pierre's Hole on July 18 that year. Sublette, now ailing and with only two years to live, was, like his employer, making his last journey into the mountains.

Past the Kaw and into rolling hills covered with wildflowers the train crawled northwest amidst daily thunderstorms and whipping winds that blew the rain horizontally into their faces, scattered tents and camp gear, and chased the terrified stock into the brush.

The long passage of the Kaw signaled the need for a better organization of the caravan, one along military lines for better discipline and order. This probably resulted from Captain Gantt's counsel and, perhaps because he brought the most people to the Elm Grove rendezvous, Peter Burnett was elected captain and James M. Nesmith, a bachelor, "orderly sergeant" for the train. Burnett lasted eight days before resigning due to "ill health," but he more than likely succumbed to the squabbles between the cattle haves and have-nots. The big cow herd, ponderously slow crossing the waterways, spooking and scattering in thunderstorms, was delaying the entire party, the have-nots said, and they clamored to have the column split, with those owning only a few head of stock to move ahead while the big herd followed with its drovers in the rear. The Applegate brothers, majority cow owners, undertook to mind the "cow column" with Jesse in overall command.

Jesse Applegate, of whom James Nesmith would write, "As a frontiersman, in courage, sagacity, and natural intelligence he is the equal of Daniel Boone," managed to keep a colorful record of the journey west and in *A Day with the Cow Column,* 1843, described one eighteen-hour day that advanced his party twenty miles toward Oregon.

At four A.M., Applegate wrote, "sentinels on duty fire their rifles in the air and every wagon and tent pours forth its occupants; 60 men spread out to form the cattle in a semicircle around the camp; corral formed by wagons connected to each other by tongue and ox-chains, entrenchment against Indians and impenetrable by a maddened ox or cattle stampede."

From six to seven, breakfast fires were extinguished, tents struck, wagons loaded, teams yoked and brought forward to be attached to their wagons. At seven a bugler signaled the march to begin and "those unready," Applegate said, "have to take their place at the rear of the column and eat dust."

He described how the wagons were divided into platoons of four abreast, each platoon moving forward at the start of each day's march so that all took a turn in the lead. The pilot (John Gantt) and a squad of men struck out ahead of the lead wagons with picks and shovels to "prepare the trail," filling in chuckholes and moving boulders, while a party of hunters rode out in search of game.

Toward midday, Gantt would "measure the ground," judge the speed of the wagons, and walk his horse along to select a "nooning" place, as close as possible to good graze and water, for the party to rest after five hours of travel.

At one, the bugler announced the march to resume. The day wore on tediously with the wagons bumping along old buffalo paths and wallows, the oxen lamed by the needles of burned grass stubble, some wagons straggling out of the line for a brief respite from the choking dust.

With the sun low in the west, Gantt would find a good campsite, whereupon wagons were circled, cookfires lit, and tents pitched. All adult men were formed into companies and divided into watches, with each company standing guard duty every third night.

Applegate wrote of fiddle music and impromptu dances among "the youths and maidens" before the deepening night called the travelers to their tents and bedrolls to a bone-weary sleep after "a prosperous day" of twenty miles' progress.

In July they reached the Platte, always wide, generally shallow and murky, with its notorious shifting beds of quicksand, "an infernal liar," as some Oregon Trail veteran called it, "hardly able to float a canoe." The 1843 emigrants had heard the tales of times when eighteen yoke of oxen were required to drag a single wagon across its mud, but they were faced with a high Platte, swirling with currents, that required ferrying by bull boats made of caulked wagon boxes before they could reform and swing along its southern bank through prickly pear, yucca, prairie-dog towns, and dry grass in the hammering heat of the prairie summer.

Ash Hollow . . . Courthouse Rock . . . Chimney Rock . . . Scotts Bluff . . . rafting across the Laramie River to the adobe fort, 640 miles out of Independence, 1,400 miles to the Columbia . . . the awful last fording of the Platte and the alkali plains beyond it that gave the cattle "scours" (diarrhea) until the trail broke toward the clear, cold Sweetwater.

The days blended into one ceaseless crawl. "Groaning, they fell once more into their dusty line," David Lavender wrote memorably of the awful daily desuetude of the Oregon Trail. "That was the heroics of the migration: not Indian scares or thrilling buffalo hunts or flooded stream crossings but rather this remorseless, unending, weather-scoured, nerve-rasping plod on and on and on and on, foot by aching foot."

At turtle-backed Independence Rock they climbed and painted on its granite face their names and a record of having plodded to this spot:

The Oregon Co.
arrived
July 26, 1843

The 400-foot slit in the rocks called Devil's Gate they detoured via a trail to the south; they surveyed the Wind River Range running north beyond their eyesight, left the Sweetwater for a twenty-mile-wide sagebrush plain, crossed South Pass into Oregon Country, and reached Fort Hall on the Portneuf River of Idaho. There, the Hudson's Bay Company trader in charge, Richard Grant, a burly six-foot-tall Canadian with thirty years' wilderness experience, said it would be impossible for them to take their wagons on to the Columbia and urged them to turn south to Mexican California with Captain Gantt and Mr. Chiles. But the Oregon people had been hearing the wagon warning since gathering at Elm Grove and were assured, again, by Dr. Whitman that they had the muscle of hundreds of men to push the wagons on.

At Fort Hall, John Gantt, having fulfilled his contract, and Joe Chiles collected their partners and wagons laden with grain-mill equipment and departed toward the Humboldt River, the Sierra Nevada, and California. Gantt had done good work and was much respected by his 875 wards. Nesmith spoke of him as "our respected pilot," and Jesse Applegate wrote that the captain "has spent his life on the verge of civilization" and had been chosen to lead the 1843 caravan "from his knowledge of the savage and his experience in travel through the roadless wastes."*

The Oregonians took up a collection and offered Marcus Whitman $400 if he would guide them to the Columbia and to this he readily agreed, and no doubt would have done so without the welcome offer of cash. He led the train down the Snake to Salmon Falls and across the sage plains to Fort Boisé, arriving there on September 20, 1843. After a brief rest he guided the wagons on to the Grand Ronde valley on October 1, and crossed the Blue Mountains in mounting snowstorms to camp, on October 10, within three miles of Waiilatpu.

The Applegate brothers left their cattle at Fort Walla Walla; whipsawed driftwood and timber into rafts; climbed into dugouts, canoes, and *bateaux;* floated to the Celilo Falls; and portaged across to The Dalles. During the harrowing trip through the rapids Jesse and Lindsey Applegate both lost ten-year-old sons to drowning, and Charles Applegate's son was crippled when a boat overturned in the current.

In all, of the approximately 875 men, women, and children of the Great Migration caravan headed for Oregon, sixteen died en route to the Willamette.

---

*Gantt died in California on February 14, 1849, of a heart ailment, at age fifty-nine. He had crossed the Rockies eight times in various trapping journeys and was said to have explored every river between the western settlements of Missouri and the Pacific. Among his other accomplishments, he was the first to see the opportunity for a prosperous trading post on the Arkansas River in southeastern Colorado, a project carried out with immense success by William Bent and his Bent's Fort.

3

In 1844, three new groups of Oregon-bound emigrants formed up on the Missouri frontier, between 700 and 800 people with 150 wagons and 1,500 head of cattle; in 1845, the number westering was about 3,000, and there were fewer in 1846 because of the threats of war against both England and Mexico. The figure rose in 1847, to 4,500 emigrants.

Among the 1845 emigrants was a high-domed, self-styled "intelligent farmer" named Joel Palmer. Born in Canada in 1810 of Quaker parents, he had lived in Pennsylvania before settling in Laurel, Indiana, where he had some success as a canal contractor and farmer. He served a term in the state legislature, but after reading up on the Oregon boundary dispute decided to try his hand at something new in a new place. He left his wife and children behind in Laurel "with a truly melancholy heart" and took a steamer to Independence "with a view of satisfying myself whether Oregon's advantages were sufficient to make it my future home."

He had a magnetic personality and a politician's polish and employed both in getting elected captain of a twenty-five-wagon train that reached Fort Laramie on June 24. There his party made a layover to mend wagons and harness, shoe animals, write letters, and replenish supplies at the outrageous prices then prevalent and going up by the day—fifteen dollars for a hundredweight of flour, a dollar for two cups of sugar or coffee beans. Palmer, a meticulous chronicler of the 1845 migration, recorded counting 145 wagons in four separate trains camped within a few miles of each other on the Platte.

He had an interest in Indians, too, and wanted to know what they had to say of the whites coming into their country in such rising numbers. With the blessing of the people of his party and after enlisting an interpreter, he arranged a banquet for the hundred or so Oglalas camped near the fort on the bank of the Laramie River. Each emigrant family provided two dishes of food and the feast was arranged on buffalo robes at the edge of the village. The Indians seated themselves in two concentric semicircles, the pioneers making up a single one opposite. The Oglala chief was asked to speak and did so, bluntly: "This country belongs to the red man but his white brethren travels through, shooting the game and scaring it away. Thus the Indian loses all that he depends upon to support his wives and children. The children of the red man cry out for food, but there is no food." He asked for guns to kill game like the white man since the game that survived the whites' incursions were now too skittish for bows and arrows.

Palmer later wrote, "As it devolved upon me to play the part of the white chief, I told my red brethren that we were journeying to the great waters of the west. Our great father owned a large country there and we were going to settle upon it. For this purpose we brought with us our wives and little ones. We traveled as friends, not as enemies." He said he and his companions were farmers and had no guns to trade. He urged the Oglalas to feast on the meat, rice mush, cakes, bread, and coffee spread out before them. The eating went well; Palmer's words, which would be repeated countless times, with countless variations, in the years ahead, often with howitzer and rocket displays and peace pipe sharing, were unsatisfactory to the "red brethren."

On November 1, 1845, after 200 days on the Oregon Trail, the Palmer train reached Oregon City. The intelligent farmer recalled in his *Journal of Travels Over the Rocky Mountains* that the town had among its civilized establishments "a neat Methodist church, a splendid Catholic chapel, two grist mills, two sawmills, four stores, two taverns, one hatter, one tannery, three tailor shops, two cabinet makers, two silversmiths, one cooper, two blacksmiths, one physician, three lawyers, one printing office, and a good brick yard."

Palmer returned to Indiana in 1846, satisfied that Oregon

indeed had sufficient advantages to make a home, collected his family, and returned. Among his accomplishments as an Oregon pioneer, he became superintendent of Indian Affairs where he was directed to prevent the Cayuse and Nez Percé tribes from joining forces for hostile purposes. Bancroft said wryly that he "bent his enormous energy and personal magnetism to the difficult task of obtaining all their lands from the Indians without creating enough dissatisfaction among them to cause a war." Even so, Palmer was genuinely sympathetic toward the Indians and respectful of their rights to the point that he came under severe censure by white Oregonians.

He negotiated treaties with the Umpquas, Shastas, Walla Wallas, Cayuse, and Nez Percé, and is said to have diligently sought and found good reservation lands for the dispossessed tribes. Bancroft, conceding that Palmer made "some errors," judged his efforts on the whole to be "humane and just." His faults, the historian said, "were those of an over-sanguine man, driven somewhat by public clamor, and eager to accomplish his work in the shortest time. . . . He succeeded in his undertaking of removing to the border of the Willamette Valley about 4,000 Indians, [and] for his honesty and eminent services, he is entitled to the respect and gratitude of all good men."

Palmer was removed from office in 1857 because of white impatience with his solicitude toward his Indian charges. After his discharge, he opened a route to the British Columbia gold fields, engaged in many business enterprises, and served as a state representative and state senator. He died at Dayton, a town he founded southwest of Oregon City, in June 1881.

21

The Parallel

■

1

The man who would at last answer the Oregon question, James Knox Polk, came to the presidency by a fluke, announced early that he would serve but a single term, set forth a number of goals for his administration, and left office after accomplishing all of them, something remarked on 100 years later by Harry S. Truman: "James K. Polk, a great president; said what he intended to do and did it."

Born on the family farm in Mecklenburg County, North Carolina, in 1795 and the eldest of ten children of a prosperous planter, Polk came to Tennessee with his family in 1806 and received a university education in classical studies—Latin, Greek, mathematics, philosophy—as well as law. He served in the Tennessee legislature, was admitted to the state bar in 1825, and began his rise in national politics that year as a congressman from Tennessee and a staunch supporter of Andrew Jackson, with whom he had a close personal friendship. Polk served as Old Hickory's floor leader in the House of Representatives, and became Speaker in 1835, serving two years in the office before returning to Tennessee to campaign for, and win, the governorship.

"Young Hickory," as his adherents called him, actually

had none of Jackson's charisma, daring, physical stature, or stamina, but the two men shared other characteristics: a combative nature, a thin skin, an obduracy, and a passion for politics.

Polk was short, slender, high-browed, and thin-lipped, with deep-set gray eyes, his unruly graying hair brushed behind his ears. He had a dignified carriage and was always scrupulously dressed. He suffered ill health most of his life, a delicacy worsened by living in Washington amid the Potomac swamps and their disease-laden miasmas, and he tired easily. He was exceedingly ambitious, and for the most part well liked, although he had few close friends and only one confidante, his wife, Sara Childress Polk, a lively and charming adjunct to her dour mate.

Many, even Polk's admirers, regarded him as historian Bernard De Voto did: "rigid, narrow, obstinate . . . pompous, suspicious, and secretive." Abraham Lincoln, in his single term in the House of Representatives, said in 1848 that Polk "is a bewildered, confounded, and miserably perplexed man." But others saw beneath his granitic exterior and humorlessness a thoroughly honest and incorruptible man, a better man than Jackson in many respects, and while "in no sense a man of brilliant parts," as Woodrow Wilson would say of him, he was "a sturdy, upright, straightforward party man."

Polk sprang from party-workhorse obscurity to national prominence at the 1844 Democratic Party convention. What happened in the Odd Fellows' Hall in Baltimore between May 27 and 30 that year surprised the most acute prognosticators among the party faithful.

The frontrunner nominee of the Democrats was Martin Van Buren of Kinderhook, New York, who had served as Jackson's secretary of state and vice president and had succeeded Old Hickory as president in 1836, serving one term. As expected, he won a majority in the first ballot voting in Baltimore. But he failed to win the necessary two-thirds

majority of the delegate votes for the nomination, and after
the first ballot other party hopefuls—Lewis Cass of Michigan, Richard M. Johnson of Kentucky, and James Buchanan
of Pennsylvania—eroded the Van Buren margin. The former
president's cause was doomed by his opposition to one of the
party platform's strongest planks, the annexation of Texas, at
a time when the American people (or so said their representatives in Washington) were ardently "expansionist," lusting
after Texas, California, Oregon, and whatever else was occupied by foreigners west of the Mississippi. Van Buren had
opposed Texas annexation, over the slavery issue, when he
was president, alienating southern Democrats, the heart of
Jackson's party, and continued to oppose the proposition in
1844 just as the southerners continued to oppose him.

Polk stayed home in Nashville during the Baltimore convention. He had been mentioned as potential vice presidential timber for whoever was selected to head the ticket, but
he had no inkling that he might be placed in nomination. His
name appeared on the eighth ballot and he won the nomina-
tion, with 233 votes, on the ninth, becoming the first "dark
horse" in American political history.

He accepted by letter, thanking Jackson for his endorsement and the convention delegates for their confidence in
him. He pledged a one-term presidency (which he believed
was implicit in Jacksonian ideology, although Jackson served
two terms) and set out to win the general election.

Polk's Whig opponent, Henry Clay of Kentucky, who had
thrice before been a presidential candidate and had been
thrice rejected, now had to endure a final, failed, hurrah. He
sought to appease all factions of his party by equivocating
on the Texas and Oregon questions while Polk advocated
both the annexation of Texas and the assertion of American
"rights" to the "whole of Oregon," from the 42nd parallel, the
border with Mexican California, and the 54th, considerably
north of Edmonton, Canada, and taking in all of Vancouver
Island.

Polk narrowly won the election, becoming the eleventh, and at age forty-nine, the youngest, president, carrying fifteen states to Clay's eleven (including Polk and Jackson's Tennessee), and the popular vote by 37,000 votes out of the 1.7 million cast.

He had a remarkably clear and deceptively simple vision of what he wanted to accomplish as president: revision of the protective tariff, acquisition of California, and settling the Oregon question. In foreign affairs he hoped to avoid war, but in his inaugural address on March 4, 1845, he pugnaciously embraced the Monroe Doctrine: "The people of this continent alone have the right to decide their own destiny. . . . No future European colony or dominion shall with our consent be planted or established on any part of the North American continent." And he reasserted American rights to Oregon in his first annual message to Congress the following December, when he recommended that measures be taken to protect American claims to the "whole of Oregon" and proposed abrogation of the joint occupation agreement.

Polk's enduring distrust of the British he confided in his diary in this period: "The only way to treat John Bull," he wrote, "was to look him straight in the eye."

2

Before 1845, Americans had no name for the precept they believed was inscribed on some heavenly scroll: that the United States (twenty-six of them in Polk's era)—that is the white portion of its population of 20 million—was destined by God's decree to occupy the continent.

The idea, an article of faith dating from the dawn of civilization when one state desired the territory of another and found a providential inspiration in taking it, received a memorable designation four months after James K. Polk took office.

In the July–August 1845 issue of the New York–based *United States Magazine and Democratic Review,* lawyer-editor John Louis O'Sullivan wrote a lengthy editorial favoring the annexation of Texas. This joining to the Union, he wrote, would serve as a warning against foreign interference and would have the effect of "checking the fulfillment of our manifest destiny to overspread the continent allotted by Providence for the free development of our yearly multiplying millions."

What the editor wrote of Texas and California applied to Oregon as well: "The Anglo-Saxon foot is already on its borders. Already the advance guard of the irresistible army of the Anglo-Saxon emigration has begun to pour down upon it, armed with the plough and the rifle," and this admirably matched the new president's pronouncement that "our title to the whole of Oregon is clear and unquestionable."

In Polk's day, Manifest Destiny was no idle slogan; it was an operating principle, especially when combined, as Polk combined it, with certain tenets of the Monroe Doctrine of 1823: that the United States would not countenance further occupation by European powers, and that it would regard as dangerous to its peace and safety any attempt at colonization in the Western Hemisphere. The one point of the doctrine expansionists studiously ignored was the part that said the United States would not interfere with existing colonies or dependencies of European powers in the New World. Annexations, such as that of Texas, had been used before as a means of halting "foreign influences" and their nefarious underminings of peace and security in the neighborhood of the United States. Diplomacy and purchase were the desirable means of expansion, but annexation, by war and by conquest, was a workable alternative.

Few questioned that the annexation of Texas would mean war with Mexico and indeed, by the end of 1845, with Texas admitted to the Union, an American army was poised above the Rio Grande to do battle with a Mexican force marching north. The war with Mexico preoccupied the president, but he regarded its rewards as vastly outweighing all sacrifices: Texas was won; now he turned his attention to the other Mexican provinces north of the Rio Grande, New Mexico, and Alta California, and to the Oregon Country.

In his editorial manifesto, John Louis O'Sullivan wrote that "the day is not far distant when the Empires of the Atlantic and the Pacific would again flow together into one," and President Polk intended to fulfill this vision with his mighty one-term agenda, the most ambitious in American expansionist history: Before he left office he intended to add over 1 million square miles of territory to the United States.

3

President Polk's "whole of Oregon" inaugural credo and his avowed intention to end the joint occupancy agreement troubled the Tory government in England, then mired in colonial wars against the Maoris in New Zealand and the Sikhs in the Punjab region of India. The *Times* of London called for "resolute determination" and suggested sending a naval squadron to Oregon waters to keep the sun from setting on the British enclave in the American Northwest. Gunboat diplomats in London succeeded in having the fifty-gun warship *America* broken away from the British Pacific Squadron and dispatched to Juan de Fuca Strait under the command of Sir John Gordon, brother of British foreign secretary Lord Aberdeen. Gordon and Lieutenant William Peel, third son of Prime Minister Sir Robert Peel, traveled to Fort Vancouver in September 1845 to reassure British subjects there of the "firm protection of their rights."

In touring the Willamette valley, where the American farms and settlements were almost entirely confined, Lieutenant Peel met Jesse Applegate and observed that the immigrants, had they chosen the profession of arms, might have made "the best soldiers in the world." Applegate acknowledged that his farmer-comrades "were probably brave enough, but would never submit to discipline as soldiers." Recalling the rivalries and problems of his own overland journey, he said to Peel, "If the president himself had started across the plains to command a company, the first time he should choose a bad camp, or in any other way offend them, they would turn him out, and elect some one among themselves who should suit them better."

Bancroft believed the visit of the *America* and Peel's tour and talks with John McLoughlin, other Hudson's Bay employees and officials, and Americans in the Willamette valley averted a war between the two nations contending the Oregon Country. A decisive matter, the historian said, was McLoughlin's "joining the compact." This referred to the provisional government set up by the settlers at Champoeg after Ewing Young's death in 1841. Applegate had invited McLoughlin to participate, and since the oath of loyalty pledged to support the laws while remaining "a dutiful citizen of the United States or a subject of Great Britain," he took the pledge.

When Gordon and Peel came to Fort Vancouver, Bancroft wrote, "they expected to maintain England's hold on the north side of the Columbia River" but unexpectedly found the Hudson's Bay Company working with rather than against the Americans and "learned the fearless and resolute character of the colonists, and their rapidly increasing numbers." McLoughlin, Bancroft said, "constantly checked" any expressions of hostility toward the Americans, stating to his various visitors and "spies" (often one and the same), as he had openly averred in letters to England, that the country "was not worth a war."

Not all listened to the factor's admonitions, however, or approved of his fatalistic attitude or his generous assistance to the colonists. Chief among these disapprovers was Governor George Simpson, who regularly reported on the American invasion of Oregon to Whitehall.

At the time of the Gordon-Peel visit, Simpson and McLoughlin had been associates for over twenty years, a relationship that began eroding almost from the moment the two met in the Canadian wilderness en route to old Fort Astoria in 1824. Simpson was the ideal Hudson's Bay governor. He was brusque and ruthless, kept his eye on the ledgers, roamed about his domain in his *canot du maître,* dressed in a black suit, neck-stock, tartan-lined cloak, and tall beaver hat as he slashed staffs, closed unprofitable trading posts, and issued edicts and orders. McLoughlin, always wary of his ostentatious superior, could never keep a distance. Simpson visited Fort Vancouver frequently and when not at the fort was forever assailing the factor with correspondence and urgent memoranda.

In 1842 a rift opened between the two men that would never close. In June of that year McLoughlin received a letter from Simpson stating that John McLoughlin, Jr., had been murdered at Fort Stikine, the Hudson's Bay trade center near Wrangell, Alaska. Oldest of McLoughlin and Marguerite's four children, John Jr. had been left in charge of the remote post, which was surrounded by hostile natives and what a contemporary called "a gang of miscreant workers" and, according to Simpson's chillingly matter-of-fact letter, had died in a "drunken fray, by the hand of one of his own men." The governor said the young man's conduct at the post had been "exceedingly bad" and that when he drank he showed violence "amounting to insanity" and had driven his men to such a degree that he had been killed "under the influence of terror, as a measure of self-preservation" by one of his employees. Simpson added that any "Tribunal by which the case could be tried, would find a verdict of 'Justifiable homicide'" and advised McLoughlin not to press charges.

The White Eagle, at once devastated by the news and furious at Simpson's brutally accusatory account of the murder, decided to conduct his own investigation into the matter. He found many of his son's workers willing to testify that John Jr. rarely drank (indeed, fort records showed his liquor allowance had been scarcely touched) and that the problem with the men had erupted over Company rules discouraging liaisons with Indian women. John Jr. had quite correctly punished some men who had "scaled the Picquets" after stealing items from the post to give as gifts to their Indian paramours.

The factor also learned that the killer, a man named Heroux, after firing the shot and with his victim "writhing in the agonies of Death," had walked up and smashed in John Jr.'s head with a rifle butt. For this, Simpson coolly informed McLoughlin, the murderer had been turned over to the Russians, from whom Fort Stikine had been leased. When the Muscovites announced that they had no jurisdiction in the matter, Heroux was released from custody.

McLoughlin wrote Simpson bluntly, "Instead of conducting the examination so as to endeavor to find out what had led to the murder, you conducted it as if it had been an investigation into the moral conduct of the Deceased, and as if you were desirous to justify the conduct of the murderers."

After his findings, which he communicated to Hudson's Bay authorities, the official version of the story began to change from that reported by Simpson, so much so that a Company official wrote, "I have come to the conclusion that McLoughlin was not a habitual drunkard, that the punishments he inflicted were not of excessive severity; and that he was very vigilant and strict in keeping the men to their duty day and night."

That was the only satisfaction McLoughlin was to have in the tragedy. He requested that authorities at York Factory

send Heroux and his henchmen to England for trial but was
notified that if it were done he would have to bear the cost,
more than £10,000. He had to abandon the case.

Soon after this awful summer McLoughlin returned to the
Catholic faith of his youth and had his marriage to Marguerite sanctified.

As a result of one of George Simpson's memoranda to England in 1845, the government sent two officers out to Fort
Vancouver as "observers" to scout military sites in the event
of war and to gather information on the colonists. The men,
Lieutenant Henry J. Warre of the Fifty-fourth Regiment
and Lieutenant Mervin Vavasour of the Royal Engineers,
traveled to the fort by the transcontinental route from the
Red River to Fort Colville and reached Vancouver even before Captain Gordon and Lieutenant Peel of the Royal Navy
departed for England that fall. The officer-emissaries posed,
rather too ostentatiously, as tourists by wearing beaver hats,
figured vests, and tweed trousers, and they lounged about
the fort partaking of McLoughlin's hospitality. He knew
they were spies but had to endure them as they made notes
for their report to London.

The two gathered little information to support a military
defense of Oregon lands, particularly those south of the Columbia, but they did make damaging accusations against
Hudson's Bay's handling of the American influx, charging
McLoughlin with welcoming the colonists to the country in
such numbers that they now outnumbered British residents.
Warre and Vavasour reported that they had personally observed immigrants arriving at Vancouver who were sold
goods from the Company's stores at cheaper rates than those
offered British subjects, and said that McLoughlin was also
"overly friendly" to American missionaries. Without his aid,
they said, "not thirty American families would now have
been in the settlement."

The factor's good deeds were not to go unpunished. The two army lieutenants, and in his more moderate report, Peel of the Royal Navy, were critical of the Company's overly generous relationship with American colonists, directing them to the farmlands south of the river and assisting them with men, equipment, and transportation instead of discouraging their settlement and perhaps advising that they move on south to Mexican California. Hudson's Bay directors had repeatedly warned McLoughlin not to give more than minimal humane assistance to the Americans, their missionaries in particular. They knew, probably from Governor George Simpson's reports, that the factor not only sold the clerics all the supplies they needed to start their mission stations, but even extended the Company's protection over their little enclaves situated among unpredictable natives.

"What would you have?" McLoughlin responded. "Would you have me turn the cold shoulder to the man of God who came to do that for the Indians which the company had neglected to do?"

Yes, he had assisted the colonists and the missionaries, had assisted Americans long before their numerous arrivals in 1843, '44, and '45, he said. Yes, he had provided food for them, and boats and boatmen to transport them to the Willamette before the Columbia iced over. Yes, he had taken care of their sick and injured at the fort hospital and gave them seeds if they could not afford to buy them so they could plant a crop and stave off starvation. (These matters Bancroft called "Christ-like Deeds.") Had he and his officers refused such humanitarian succor, he said, the Company would have been "covered with obloquy."

While touching lightly on the ingratitude of those who neglected to pay their debts and the rudeness of those who made him despair for American honor, McLoughlin nonetheless defended the Americans from what he considered to be the ignorant slurs of government spies.

"They have the same right to come that I have to be here,"

he insisted, and repelled the notion that the Company was duty-bound to defend British territorial rights. His responsibility, he said, was to Hudson's Bay directors, not to colonial or military affairs. Those were in Whitehall's province, not his. And as to being in league with the colonists' rudimentary government, he produced copies of letters he had written to England in 1843 describing the potential American threat to Fort Vancouver and asking for protection he never received.

The "White Eagle of the Old Northwest" admitted that British lands had been invaded, but said pointedly, "I have found British subjects just as keen at catching at an opportunity to benefit themselves, in some instances to my cost, as these American backwoodsmen."

McLoughlin had been keen to catch such opportunities himself, having a large property interest in Oregon City, terminus of the Oregon Trail south of the Columbia, and he had been wise to invest in it. He had grown weary of his responsibilities and thankless burdens, and had become desolate over the Company's plan to quit Fort Vancouver. He had first heard of the idea during one of Governor Simpson's visits. Sir George said Hudson's Bay headquarters would likely be moved to Vancouver Island, that the old post had outlived its usefulness, that the bar of the Columbia was too dangerous and the new headquarters would be more central to the northern operations. Now, in 1845, with the fur trade in a steep decline along the Columbia, the region was no longer prized. Moreover, the Company's directors were alarmed at the numbers and aggressive nature of the American settlers in the Willamette valley and feared for the safety of its stores and property at Vancouver.

McLoughlin, seeing that his life work was to be thrown away, tendered his resignation from the Hudson's Bay Company in the fall of 1845—the year the American population of Oregon reached 5,000—and took up residence in Oregon City the following spring. He had intended to seek

American citizenship, but with the news in the spring of 1845 of the election of President Polk and the threat of war with England, he could not change his allegiance without being branded a traitor and forfeiting his retirement stipend.

He would have to await settlement of the boundary issue.

4

The Oregon boundary question had first surfaced as a diplomatic issue during the War of 1812, when Fort Astoria was sold to the North West Company. It cropped up again in 1818, when the United States negotiated with the British and fixed the Canadian-American border at the 49th parallel between Lake of the Woods and the crest of the Rocky Mountains. No boundary was established for the region west of the Rockies, and since both nations claimed the Oregon Country, in compromise negotiators decided to leave the territory "free and open" to both nations in what was termed "joint occupation."

Meantime, President James Monroe's secretary of state, John Quincy Adams, sought to pressure Spain to relinquish her claims to all territories north of the 42nd parallel, the northern border of California. Weakened by colonial revolutions, Spain dragged out the negotiations but capitulated in 1819 with the Adams-Onís Treaty, which established the 42nd parallel as the northern boundary of California and turned over to the United States all claims to the Oregon Territory.

Adams said, "the remainder of the continent should ultimately be ours," and warned that his government "considered this hemisphere closed to any new European colonial establishments." In truth, the government considered the hemisphere closed to *old* colonial establishments as well, and with Spanish claims settled, diplomatic attention turned to Russia. In the late eighteenth and early nineteenth centuries,

Russian traders had moved south of their holdings in Alaska and established outposts as far south as San Francisco Bay, but this expansionism ended in 1825. In that year, Adams negotiated a treaty with the czar's ministers providing that Russia would lay no claim to territory south of 54 degrees 40 minutes, a line eastward from the southern tip of Prince of Wales Island. The United States agreed in turn to make no claim to lands north of that line.

With only Great Britain and the United States remaining to contest the territory between the 42nd parallel and 54 degrees 40 minutes, in 1827 the joint occupation agreement between the two nations was extended indefinitely. The document carried the proviso that either power could terminate it after giving the other a year's notice.

The issue lay more or less dormant for a decade, but by the early 1840s, with the first emigrant trains entering Oregon, the boundary question again rose to prominence. Commercial interests became sensitive to the importance of establishing trade ports on the Pacific for business with the Far East, American migration to the Oregon Country was leaping forward (in 1841 there were about 500 Americans scattered throughout the region; by 1845, 5,000), and militant expansionism, the idea expressed in John O'Sullivan's "Manifest Destiny," was taking wing. The idea that Oregon should be annexed by the United States had been gaining momentum since Robert Gray discovered the mouth of the Columbia River in 1792, and after a half century, the time had arrived to settle the matter.

Britain's case for superiority over the Oregon Country rested on the Nootka Sound Convention of 1790, under which Spain relinquished its claims, the discovery voyage of Captain James Cook in 1778, various explorations such as those of Vancouver in 1792 and Alexander Mackenzie in 1793, and the establishment, beginning in 1821, of fur-trading posts controlled by the Hudson's Bay Company.

The United States pointed to its own explorations: Gray;

Lewis and Clark in 1804–06; the acquisition of Spanish rights north of the 42nd parallel via the Adams-Onís Treaty, and to the coast south of 54 degrees 40 minutes by treaty with the Russians; the fur-trading post at Astoria, established in 1811, and the first permanent settlement in Oregon; the actual occupation by American settlers, most of them in the Willamette valley; and the fact that Oregon was contiguous to American soil.

In his inaugural address President Polk had referred to America's claim to Oregon as "clear and unquestionable," but he at least nodded politely toward John Bull by saying that "every obligation imposed by treaty or conventional stipulation should be sacredly respected." He had no intention of risking war with England—he already had an impending war on his hands, with Mexico over the Texas annexation—and he wanted to resolve the matter expediently and peacefully by extending the 49th parallel west to the Pacific. Despite all the talk of "54-40 or Fight!" and the use of it as an unauthorized campaign slogan, the 54th parallel was never seriously in contention. Nor for that matter did England aspire to the whole region as far south as the California line, but early in the dispute did want to make the Columbia River, which meandered through Oregon to the sea several hundred miles south of 49 degrees, the southern border of Canada. The British, specifically its Hudson's Bay directors, believed control of the river essential to maintain hegemony over the interior fur trade. Without some adjustment to the 49th parallel, the British insisted, they would be cut off from the southern end of Vancouver Island and denied access to the Juan de Fuca Strait.

A few months after Polk's inaugural, Richard Pakenham, the British minister in Washington, was instructed to reopen negotiations of the Oregon question. He said his government was willing to accept the 49th parallel boundary but with some modifications of the line as it reached the sea and retention of rights to navigate the Columbia.

On September 12, 1845, Polk replied through his ineffectual secretary of state, James Buchanan (who, Bernard De Voto said, "had the greatest possible shrewdness but no backbone whatever"), proposing extending the 49th with all of Vancouver Island ceded to the British, but he refused to offer use of the Columbia.

Polk could not resist writing into the document a statement that the United States was making the concession even though its claims to *all* of Oregon were patently valid.

Pakenham rejected the offer without submitting it to his government and Polk, angered by this, broke off the talks.

In December, in his first message to Congress, the president placed the failure of the negotiations entirely on Britain, stating that the United States had acted in "a spirit of liberal concession" and "will be relieved of all responsibilities which may follow the failure to settle the controversy." He referred to the Monroe Doctrine, asked Congress to provide armed escorts for wagon trains heading for Oregon, and said it would be desirable to serve England a one-year notice that the joint occupancy agreement would be terminated.

Senator Thomas Hart Benton of Missouri, the most voluble expansionist in Congress and a tireless promoter of an all-American Oregon, originally supported compromising with Britain on the boundary issue, but after the failure of the opening parley he suggested that the government muster "thirty or forty thousand American rifles beyond the Rocky Mountains that will be our effective negotiator." And in the January 1846 issue of the news magazine *Niles' Register*, the editorial titled "Are We to Have Peace or War?" had to do not with war with Mexico but war with England, which the editor believed the more likely of the two; he also thought that an Anglo-American war would be precipitated by the Oregon boundary question.

In London the American president's bellicose language distressed the Peel ministry, which was juggling problems ranging from the potato famine in Ireland to colonial campaigns in New Zealand and India. Peel's foreign secretary, Lord Aberdeen, long a proponent of compromise, told the American minister in London that "the possibility of a rupture with the United States" had to be "considered."

On April 16, 1846, a resolution was introduced in the Senate to "abrogate the convention of 1827" and give notice to the British government that the United States would terminate the Oregon joint occupancy agreement.

Benton of Missouri filibustered on behalf of the measure for three days; it passed both houses, the president signed it, and on April 28 he sent the notice by special packet to the sovereign of Great Britain.

During these difficult days fortuitous news arrived in London that the Hudson's Bay Company had moved its main depot from the Columbia to Fort Victoria on Vancouver Island. Now Lord Aberdeen and other moderates in the government were able to counter the argument among their colleagues in Parliament that the Columbia River was indispensable, not only for Hudson's Bay trade but for the western provinces of Canada. Aberdeen quietly informed the American secretary of state that the 49th parallel was acceptable to England. The memorandum asked only that when the line reached saltwater it would swing through the main channel of the Strait of Georgia to Juan de Fuca Strait and westward to the Pacific.

The Oregon treaty, signed by both nations on June 15, 1846, recognized the 49th parallel as the international boundary from the Rocky Mountains to the middle of the channel between Vancouver Island and the mainland, thence along a line running southward through Juan de Fuca Strait to the Pacific. Free navigation of the channel and strait by both signatories was stipulated.

Senator Benton made a speech upon the treaty ratification, pointing out that the 49th parallel had been tendered

to Britain for nearly forty years; by Jefferson in 1807, Monroe in 1818 and 1824, Adams in 1826, Tyler in 1842, and Polk
in 1845.

When news of the settlement reached the Columbia on November 12, 1846, not all the Americans there greeted it with
approval. Some expressed dismay that Washington had
retreated from its "All of Oregon," "Fifty-Four Forty or
Fight!" battle stance; others pointed to the few American
farms located near Hudson's Bay posts north of Forty-nine,
lands now in British control.

To these malcontents H. H. Bancroft devoted one of his
finest polemics. "Man is a preposterous pig," he wrote,
"probably the greediest animal that crawls upon this planet."
He continued:

> Here were fertile lands and temperate airs; meadows, for-
> est, and mountains; bright rivers and broad ocean sea-
> board, enough of earth for half a dozen empires; and all
> for nothing—all stolen from the savages and never yet a
> struggle, never yet a dollar in return, only fevers, syphi-
> lis, and the like by way of compensation; and yet these
> colonial representatives of the great American nation
> grudge their brethren, but little later than themselves from
> Great Britain, a few squares of land round the posts which
> they had built and occupied for so long . . .

Instead of falling on their knees for the blessings bestowed
upon them, he said, "they fell to cursing; they cursed the
British, and particularly President Polk, for failing to carry
out his policy avowed before election." They had believed
in that promise, had painted "54-40" on their wagon covers, "and poverty-stricken and piggish, had wended their way
to the Pacific in the faith that they were helping to accomplish

this high destiny for the United States, this broad destiny for themselves."

The Americans had won five degrees of latitude, he said, yet, preposterous pigs that they were, wanted more.

But since they were not to get more, the colonists of the Willamette valley turned their energies toward increasing their numbers, petitioning for territorial status and what the most ambitious thought was an eventuality: statehood.

Increasing the population of the Oregon Country by encouraging and aiding new emigration was not a point of argument, but granting territorial status proved to be bitterly disputatious. The provisional government set up by Oregon settlers in 1843 had made a point of excluding slavery in the region, and when a similar ban was included in the Oregon territorial bill in 1846, pro-slavery forces in Congress defeated it, which they did again in 1847, despite support of the legislation by President Polk and Senator Benton.

The idea of instant post–boundary settlement statehood was regarded as even more of a distant dream. Even had slavery not been an issue, granting statehood to an unmapped wilderness as remote from civilization as Timbuktu seemed laughable. The matter of distance had been elaborately, amusingly, and indelibly expounded upon as far back as an 1825 Senate debate in which Senator Mahlon Dickerson of New Jersey (subsequently secretary of the navy in the Jackson and Van Buren administrations) rose with some statistics he had worked out for his colleagues.

"The whole distance from Washington to the mouth of the Columbia River is 4,650 miles," he said. "The distance, therefore, that a member of Congress of this 'state of Oregon' would be obliged to travel in coming to the seat of government and returning home, would be 9,300 miles. This at a rate of eight dollars for every twenty miles, would make his traveling expenses amount to $3,720." He said that at the rate members of Congress travel according to law, twenty miles per day, "it would require, to come to the seat of government from Oregon and return, 465 days . . . . But if he should travel at the rate of thirty miles per day, it would require 306 days. Allow for [rest on] Sundays it would amount to 350 days. This would allow the member a fortnight to rest himself at Washington, before he should commence his journey home."

The senator said, "It would be more expeditious, however, to come by water round Cape Horn, or to pass through Behring's Strait round the north coast of this continent to Baffin's Bay, thence through Davis' Straits to the Atlantic, and so on to Washington. It is true, this passage is not yet discovered, except upon our maps; but it will be as soon as Oregon shall be a state."

Actually, the impatient Oregonians did not have to wait for discovery of the west-to-east Northwest Passage before their new home was declared a territory of the United States. In fact, they had less than two years to wait.

22

The Bostonian

■

"GREAT CHANGES ARE AT HAND. . . ."

1

On June 15, 1846, the day the United States and Great Britain signed the Oregon boundary treaty, Francis Parkman rode into Fort Laramie on the North Platte below the mouth of Laramie Creek. He had departed Boston early in April on a gentlemanly "Summer's Journey Out of Bounds" to observe the Indians of the Plains and perhaps write something about them before their way of life disappeared, a casualty of the advent of the white man. In truth, he did not know precisely what he was doing on the Oregon Trail or what he would do when he returned. He was twenty-three and Harvard educated, and had the luxury of a wealthy bachelor's aimlessness.

Parkman had been a familiar, respected name in Massachusetts for a century or more when Francis was born on Boston's Beacon Hill in 1823. His grandfather had risen to become one of the city's wealthiest merchants; his father, an 1806 Harvard graduate, served as minister of the New North Church for thirty-six years; his mother was Caroline Hall of Medford and her father owned a farm bordering 3,000 acres of timberland known as the Middlesex Fells where young "Frank" hunted, trapped, and hiked.

At age twelve Parkman attended private school in Medford and demonstrated an aptitude for composition and literature; in 1840 he entered Harvard, earned a Phi Beta Kappa key, became a popular clubman, and fell in love with a girl from Keene, New Hampshire, who turned down his entreaties and married another.

He tramped alone in the Berkshires and made many excursions into the mountains and forests of New England, Montreal, and Québec; became adept at woodcraft; sharpened his rifle and horsemanship skills. "I was haunted with wilderness images day and night," he later wrote.

During his undergraduate work at Harvard and as a law student later, his health faltered. He began having heart palpitations, migraine headaches, swellings in his joints, insomnia, weakening eyesight, and the general diagnostical grab bag labeled "nervousness." His friends attributed the problems to his "Spartan life," his incessant hiking, canoeing, and camping in the back country of northern New England, sleeping under the stars in wet and cold weather, wading through frozen streams, and pushing himself to exhaustion in the college gymnasium.

In his senior year at Harvard Parkman suffered a physical collapse and since he abhorred idleness, he convalesced by sailing for Europe, then part of the education of every wealthy gentleman, well or ill. He reached Gibraltar on a barkentine out of Boston loaded with fruit, traveled on to Sicily and wandered for weeks in the island's western wilds, spent time in a Passionist Fathers retreat in Rome in hopes of gaining some insights into Catholicism, and tramped about Switzerland, France, and England.

He returned to Cambridge in June 1844 and received his degree in August, then spent eighteen more months studying law, earning his jurisprudence degree in January 1846. He never applied for admittance to the bar and seems to have given little thought to actually practicing in the profession. History and literature (they were attached in Parkman's time, great histories rising to great literature) had taken command of his imagination.

He did not have to earn a living, but since it would have been unthinkable for a Parkman not to do something constructive with his life, he began thinking of combining his literary interests with his love of the outdoors. He began by publishing articles on his trips to New Hampshire in *Knickerbocker Magazine* in New York, something his family and friends believed was more a harmless hobby than anything leading to a profession, but soon he cast about for a bigger project. When he was eighteen and at Harvard, he had made an exploration into the northern New Hampshire woods and out of the experience felt an inspiration to write a history of the last French war in America and the conquest of Canada. That great project now returned to mind: Since he had conceived a great admiration for Pontiac, the Ottawa chief who conspired against the British, perhaps he could begin a history of the French and Indian Wars with a scholarly book on Pontiac's rebellion of 1763. To do so he would have to visit many libraries, read original documents, and make voluminous notes, but he had strained his eyes studying law and his physician warned him that he must take a respite from reading and research. What to do until he could resume scholarship?

He was considering his options when a cousin, one with the perfect Bostonian name of Quincy Adams Shaw, came visiting and said he was preparing to depart for the Rocky Mountains on a hunting expedition and would Frank like to come along?

Parkman's darkening days suddenly brightened. The seasoned if somewhat insular outdoorsman had been handed the opportunity to travel west of the Mississippi with a trusted and lively companion for a season among the savages such as Herman Melville—whose first novel, *Typee,* was published in 1846—had experienced in the South Seas. Here was a chance to witness Indian life firsthand. He

realized that the Plains natives differed markedly from the
forest tribes of the Eastern Seaboard, but even the differences could be important grist for preparation of the book
he intended to title *The Conspiracy of Pontiac and the
Indian War after the Conquest of Canada.*

Parkman visited Nathaniel Wyeth of Cambridge, Oregon
Trail pioneer and one-time *bourgeois* at Fort Hall, then bid
his parents and friends farewell, and took a riverboat down
the Ohio to Saint Louis, where on April 28, 1846, he and
Shaw set out up the Missouri by riverboat to Westport
Landing.

The things he saw with his tired eyes, no matter how
lovely or awful, invigorated him and soothed, if not cured,
whatever ailed him, stimulating his ability to remember
and describe. Everything interested him, especially the
people—the emigrant farmers, the traders, soldiers, and
frontiersmen—he squinted at and who peered back at the
handsome, long-nosed Bostonian with the shock of brown
hair curling over his ears and collar who wanted nothing
more than to learn from them and jot things in his notebooks.

At Westport, Parkman and Shaw completed outfitting for
their journey and hired as guide Henry Chatillon, an intelligent, illiterate plainsman, "a natural gentleman," Parkman
said, who had spent two decades trapping and hunting in the
Rockies and, as the Bostonian delightedly learned, was married to the daughter of Bull Bear, principal chief among the
Oglala Sioux. The party was completed by the hiring of a
good-natured Canadian named Deslauriers to serve as cook,
wagon driver, mule skinner, and general factotum.

As they collected their horses and supplies to move out
on the Trail, Parkman heard the pilots shouting at the emigrant men to get their wives, children, dogs, horses, chickens, cow herds, oxen, mules, and wagons ready to begin
moving west by daybreak; watched trade wagon convoys
coming in from the Santa Fé Trail; listened to the rumors of
war with Mexico. One thing about Westport that concerned

him more than the war talk: "Whiskey," he wrote, "circulates more freely in Westport than is altogether safe in a place where every man carries a loaded pistol in his pocket."

Parkman and Shaw decided to avoid traveling with an emigrant train, too slow for their purposes, but did find themselves linking up with a party led by Captain Bill Chandler, an Irishman retired from Her Majesty's Army, out to see the West with a vast amount of superfluous baggage and a variety of arms to kill the West's animal life. With the captain were his brother Jack; three *engagés* hired as bearers, muleteers, and general handymen; and a fop named Romaine, said to be a Templar and graduate of Trinity College. This man, Bernard De Voto said, was "a faintly literary gentleman who bossed everything, knew nothing, was inept in all things, and expressed his type at the very beginning by leading them off the trail for a full week."

The ten men made their first stopover at Fort Leavenworth and there met General Stephen Watts Kearny of the First Dragoons Regiment, who was just then gathering his troops for the long march to Bent's Fort, Santa Fé, and Alta California.

2

For one setting out with only a vague idea of linking the Plains tribes with future research on Pontiac of the Ottawa, there was a weird precision in Francis Parkman's plans. Although he was trained for law, history had a hold on him, and it swirled in the wake of the steamer he took down the Ohio to the Mississippi and in the tracks of the horses he rode to Fort Laramie. Indeed, in the six weeks he took to reach that out-of-bounds place on the Laramie River, he quite literally rode into history, then made some of it himself.

This was the summer of 1846 and, only a month after the

Bostonian had departed the salons, soirées, eligible ladies, and intellectual causeries of Boston and Cambridge society, a leathery, tobacco-chewing American general named Zachary Taylor fought and won two battles against a Mexican army. These occurred on May 7 and May 9 among the cactus and chaparral at Palo Alto and Resaca de la Palma, places nobody could find on a map but that belated newspaper reports said were "just north of the Rio Grande," and they took place a week *before* the United States and Mexico were officially at war.

Then, at about the time Parkman and Shaw were chatting at the rail of the steamer taking them from Saint Louis to Westport Landing, a prosperous Illinois farmer named George Donner, age sixty-two, thrice married and with thirteen children, rode out in front of an Oregon Trail caravan bound from Independence to California. Accompanying him were his newest and last wife, Tamsen, forty-five; their five youngest children; and Donner's older brother Jacob and his family. In Springfield, Donner's neighbor James Frazier Reed, a furniture factory proprietor who had fought with Abraham Lincoln's company in the Blackhawk War, also set out for the Missouri border. With him were his wife, Margaret, their four children, and Margaret's mother, Mrs. Sarah Keyes, age seventy-five. While her husband was away attending to circuit court duties, Mary Todd Lincoln and her son Robert came out to see the Reeds' departure. James Reed had fabricated a huge "two-story" wagon fitted out with bunks and even a stove drawn by eight Durham oxen, and he had two accessory wagons stocked with "fancy goods" and liquor, plus spare draft animals and horses.

The Donner brothers had twelve yoke of oxen, five saddle horses, a small herd of milk and beef cattle, several hired hands, a dog, and a fortune of $10,000 in cash sewn into a quilt.

Parkman saw the Donner-Reed wagons corralled on the prairie beyond Fort Laramie that June as he stood on a bluff above the fort and watched other emigrant trains cross the Laramie River. He may also have encountered some of the party when he wrote of entering a log-and-mud "apartment" at the fort full of men "all more or less drunk" on Missouri whiskey apparently carried by "a company of California emigrants." These had unencumbered the liquor at great loss to the fort's traders, he said, and were getting rid of the rest of it by drinking it on the spot.

At the time he saw them, the Donner-train occupants were otherwise unremarkable, not much different from the other emigrant parties departing the frontier.

But the Donners were making mistakes at the commencement of their journey: They were getting a late start, rushing to catch up with the rear guard of the '46 migration, and they were overburdened with "fancy goods." Their gravest miscalculation lay in their decision to take an untested shortcut to California recommended in a popular guidebook written by a zealot named Lansford Warren Hastings. This Ohioan had gone out to the Mexican province in 1842 and dreamed of a flow of American pioneers and adventurers, a revolution, and perhaps himself as president of an independent republic. In his *Emigrant's Guide to Oregon and California,* published in 1845, a year before he saw the route himself, Hastings recommended that overlanders depart the Oregon Trail at Fort Bridger instead of taking the customary turnoff at Fort Hall. He advised them to travel directly across the Wasatch Range into the Salt Lake valley, thence across the Great Basin to pick up the California Trail at the Humboldt River of Nevada. The route, he said, would save 400 miles.

Nearly six months would pass before any news of the Donners reached California, and it would be many months later that Parkman would learn their fate.

3

Although Parkman, Shaw, and the others preferred to ride at their own pace, hunting and resting at their leisure and observing no timetable, they did occasionally attach to an emigrant train and sometimes made a night camp among the circled wagons. There the men gathered at the cookfires and told the "news," mostly rumor amplified in the retelling, brought in by riders from the Missouri settlements: that bands of Kaw Indians were lurking in the brush along the Kansas and Platte Rivers eager to fall upon the trains for loot and scalps; that a party of Englishmen—perhaps a reference to Captain Chandler's group—were on the move under Her Britannic Majesty's orders to incite the natives to, as Parkman wrote, "rob, murder, and annihilate" travelers on the Oregon Trail; and that thousands of "Saints"— Mormons—were gathered near the emigrant camps, armed with rifles, knives, and brass field-pieces. These people, the stories said, had blood in their eyes after being chased out of Nauvoo, their settlement in swampy Illinois country bordering the Mississippi, and then evicted from Missouri as well.

Parkman fell in with this latter fantasy, writing, "No one could predict what would be the result when large armed bodies of these fanatics should encounter the most impetuous and reckless of their old enemies on the prairies."

The few Mormons in the vicinity were, in fact, 100 miles north, near Kanesville, Iowa, and while it was true that they kept their guns loaded and eyes narrowed for the sighting of any hated Missourians—whom they called collectively "pukes"—they were not interested in the innocent "Gentile" travelers on the Oregon Trail.

Bernard De Voto said that Parkman's experiences on the Oregon Trail, and what he wrote of them, were hampered by his "Brahmin snobberies," and that he "almost felt the emigration" but "succumbed to a parochialism of his class" and failed to have the empathy for the pioneers needed to write a great work. In his unyieldingly disapproving approach to the Mormons, whom he consistently dismissed as "fanatics," Parkman mirrored a majority attitude but he missed one of the epic stories within the epic of the Oregon Trail.

The Mormons he saw that summer were the vanguard of thousands searching for a new Zion and but a year distant from finding it. They had vacated their homes in Nauvoo during the winter before Parkman saw the first of their number and eighteen months after the murder of Joseph Smith, founder of their Church of Jesus Christ of Latter-Day Saints. Smith's successor, the forty-three-year-old Vermont-born farmer-carpenter Brigham Young, had supervised the Nauvoo exodus in February 1846, leading 1,600 of his "peculiar people" across the ice-blocked Mississippi to a "Camp of Israel" at Sugar Grove, Iowa, while the others in Illinois waited to cross the river. By June, at about the time Parkman reached Fort Laramie, Young had covered the first 400 miles toward Zion by leading the Saints across Iowa to a place on the Missouri River where no town yet stood, but which became known as Kanesville and later as Council Bluffs.

In the winter, while Parkman was warming his feet at his Beacon Hill fireplace, 12,000 Mormons had established quarters at Florence, Nebraska, near Omaha, where 600 of them were to die in the snows. And in April 1847, after the first three parts of Parkman's Oregon Trail memoir had appeared in a New York magazine, Brigham Young took a "Pioneer Band" of 143 men, 3 women, and 2 children and pushed west along the north bank of the Platte (to avoid contact with emigrant Missourians on the south bank). The band had seventy-three wagons; 211 horses, mules, and oxen; six months' rations; and a small brass cannon to frighten off hostile Indians. This vanguard reached Fort Laramie and crossed South Pass in June, bore southwest to Fort Bridger, and moved on over the rugged Uinta Mountains and then across the desert into the eastern spur of the Wasatch Range.

On the last fifty miles of their journey, they followed a narrow and tortuous trail across the Wasatch that had been broken the year before by the Donners and the Reeds. On July 19, 1847, after the sixth of Parkman's twenty-one Oregon Trail memoir installments had appeared, Young's scouting party caught the sun's glint of a great silvery body of water in the distance, and on the twenty-fourth the Mormons entered the valley of the latter-day Dead Sea known as the Great Salt Lake. They were 1,400 miles from Nauvoo, "thrown like a stone from a sling," Young said, "and we have lodged in this goodly place just where the Lord wants his people to gather."

Within a month of their arrival the Saints had cleared a seven-mile wagon road to bring fir and pine logs to build a fort and frame and roof houses, and had thrown up a stockade that enclosed twenty-nine cabins, a smithy, communal storehouses, and corrals. So much was done in that month that Young and an escort were able to retrace their route to the Iowa-Nebraska frontier and point the 13,000 others waiting there toward the Mormon Trail and their new home.

Four days out on the Platte, a country Parkman, apparently infused with Stephen Long's old exploration reports, called "the Great American Desert," the party spotted a buffalo herd and made their first serious "hunt," the white man's euphemism in buffalo country for "slaughter." Parkman's horse Pontiac had not been broken to such exertions, and the Bostonian was armed with only a pistol, but these were not hindrances. Buffalo were big, dull-witted targets with poor eyesight, and they tended to bunch up: A hunter merely kept shooting into the herd until one or more fell, blood frothing at mouth and nostrils from lung-shots (their deeply buried hearts were rarely hit and bullets glanced off the plates of their skulls). The more their numbers increased, the more were killed—and wasted. Often only the tongue and a few steaks carved from the hump were taken. Parkman's guide Henry Chatillon, the only real marksman in the party, was averse to sport killing and in deference to him the Americans stopped it.

By the time Parkman's party reached the South Platte, they stopped something else: They had had enough of the Englishmen. Captain Chandler "was by no means partial to us," Parkman said, and seemed determined to retard the journey "we were anxious to quicken" by calling a halt at unreasonable hours, often when they had traveled but fifteen miles. The Americans resolved to travel on to Fort Laramie on their own, a matter Captain Chandler said was "an extraordinary proceeding, upon my word!" However, his officer-as-gentleman remonstrances did not change the decision.

Parkman reached Fort Laramie on June 15, 1846, the day of the Anglo-American treaty settling the Oregon boundary question and the day before a band of American squatters captured the town of Sonoma, raised their homemade Bear Flag Republic banner, and signaled the beginning of the conquest of Mexican California.

In 1846, Laramie was a fur-trader's oasis, a decrepit but busy log-palisaded adobe fort on the North Platte adjacent to 600 lodges and upwards of 2,000 Oglala and Brulé Sioux. The Americans arrived there just as a band of Oglala, headed by a chief named Old Smoke, rode in from their village at a watering place called Horse Creek. This event, a happening common to the habitués of the fort, proved eventful to Parkman. Chatillon, who was married to a Sioux woman, made a visit to the Indian camp and introduced his Boston friends to Old Smoke. The chief agreed to let them stay.

In the two weeks that followed that July of 1846, Parkman found the "savage adventure" of his Oregon Trail journey. The experience was not to be without cost. He had come out West to study Indians and improve his health, and he had in fact strengthened on the journey to Laramie. But once there he had contracted dysentery and was so weakened he could scarcely walk, and it was in this frail state he was given the opportunity to study the Indians and live among them.

When he and Shaw joined them, Old Smoke's people were preparing to go to war against the Shoshoni to punish some obscure outrage committed the year before, but for reasons equally obscure the war party became a buffalo hunt, a safer venue for Parkman to observe the Indians in their daily survival work. He was dangerously ill, still battling dysentery, taking six grains of opium at a dose, feeble, giddy, and often doubled over with the agony of stomach cramps. Nor did the Oglala diet help. Early in his stay with Old Smoke's band he visited the chief's lodge and was invited to stay for a meal. Outside, one of the chief's wives knocked a puppy in the head with a stone mallet, chopped the dog to pieces, singed its hair off over the fire, and threw it all, entrails included, into a stew pot. Parkman ate his share. "A dog-feast," he said, "is the greatest compliment a Dakota can offer to his guest; and, knowing that to refuse eating would be an affront, we attacked the little dog, and devoured him."

He joined the hunters even when mounting his horse exhausted his ebbing strength. "To have worn the airs of an invalid would certainly have been an indiscretion," he wrote, and in any event he felt he had to go. If he lay abed, he said, "a horse, a rifle, a pair of pistols, and a red shirt might have offered temptations too strong for aboriginal virtue." While hunting buffalo on horseback over a broken country when "he could scarcely sit upright in the saddle" was not strictly necessary for maintaining prestige, he believed "that to tame the devil it is best to take him by the horns."

He had a sharp eye for the divergence of cultures around

Fort Laramie: the Indians; the French-Canadians who married into their bands; the trappers, hunters, and guides; and
the American emigrants camped in the meadows along the
river.

Parkman knew there could be but one end to it. The Indians were a dying race and he saw the Oglala as representative of a culture that could never withstand the white
invasion. At Horse Creek he once stood with Old Smoke and
one of his young wives, who sat astride a fine mule caparisoned with whitened deerskins and held her husband's feathered lance and shield. Not far from them were other tribal
leaders, "stately figures, their white buffalo robes thrown
over their shoulders, gazing coldly upon us," and behind
them, their camp, swarming with warriors, women, children,
and dogs, and "close at hand, the wide, shallow stream was
alive with boys, girls, and young squaws, splashing, screaming, and laughing in the water." For a thousand summers
such a carefree and peaceful tableau had taken place there,
but Parkman saw something that augured the end of it. Approaching and crossing Horse Creek came a long train of
emigrant wagons, "dragging on in slow procession by the encampment of the people whom they and their descendents,
in the space of a century, are to sweep from the face of the
earth."

He tried to depict the Indians he saw with honesty: They
were at once noble and petty; they had great courage and
physical prowess; they lived in a disorderly society, rudimentary in its greatest moments; they were preoccupied
by internecine warfare; they were dogged and doomed by
such ancient traits as their inability to make a plan and
abide by it.

"Great changes are at hand," he wrote. "The buffalo will
dwindle away, and the large wandering communities who
depend on them for support must be broken and scattered.
The Indians will soon be abased by whiskey and overawed

by military posts; so that within a few years the traveller may pass in tolerable security through their country. Its dangers and its charms will have disappeared altogether."

As his stay among the Oglala lengthened Parkman became an insomniac—the warriors drummed and sang at all hours and his host had dreams that forced him to get up at midnight to join in a long song-chant. He wrote of being "hipped"—depressed—a condition that would plague him throughout his life. But when the Sioux exhausted their stock of buffalo meat and moved north toward the Black Hills, he accompanied them. Away from the camp, in the open wilderness, afoot as often as on horseback, he seemed to recoup his strength and after two weeks with Old Smoke's band was ready to return to Laramie.

He distributed his few remaining gifts among his hosts and then, with a couple of Indian companions and one of the French-Canadians in the camp, took his leave of them and returned on August 3 to Fort Laramie, where Shaw and the others had preceded him.

They decided to return to Saint Louis by a different route, a 300-mile drop straight south to the Arkansas River, east to Bent's Fort and to the Missouri frontier along the Santa Fé Trail. They joined a party of trappers and hunters and set off.

En route to Bent's they learned that the expected war with Mexico was no longer a rumor, and at a dilapidated village in Colorado called the Pueblo they picked up some details of Zachary Taylor's first victories, encountered a scattering of Mormons and learned of their desperate winter crossing of the Mississippi from Nauvoo into Iowa. Parkman continued to regard the Saints as "blind and desperate fanatics."

Bent's Fort, the great oasis on the Arkansas River, showed the effects Kearny's expedition had in passing through en route to Santa Fé, the Gila River, and California: His dragoon horses, draft animals, and cattle herd had consumed the grass around the fort.

Parkman and Shaw returned to Westport Landing, paid off Deslauriers, and, with Chatillon accompanying them, took a steamer downriver to the Mississippi, an eight-day voyage with one-third of the time spent fast aground on a sandbar. Once they reached the crowded Saint Louis levee, the Bostonians took rooms at Planter's House, sought a tailor, and bought clothing appropriate for the return home.

Henry Chatillon paid them a last visit at the hotel. "No one who met him in the streets of St. Louis," Parkman wrote, "would have taken him for a hunter fresh from the Rocky Mountains. He was very neatly and simply dressed in a suit of dark cloth; for although since his sixteenth year he had scarcely been a month together among the abodes of men, he had a native good taste which always led him to pay attention to his personal appearance." Both Bostonians had a high regard for their guide—"He had served us with a fidelity and zeal beyond all praise"—and in addition to the salary he had been paid at Westport, Shaw had given Chatillon his horse and Parkman presented him with his favorite rifle.

A fortnight later, in mid-October, they were home, and in February 1847 in *Knickerbocker Magazine* appeared the first of twenty-one installments of "A Summer's Journey Out of Bounds By a Bostonian," under the general heading "The Oregon Trail."

23

• •

Waiilatpu

■

"IS THERE ANYTHING I CAN DO TO STOP THE BLEEDING?"

1

On the Oregon Trail and its busy tributary into California, 1847 opened and closed in lamentation.

The year began with a story of a calamity in the snow-drifts of Truckee Pass in the eastern foothills of the Sierra Nevada Range. There were no details in the early reports received at John Augustus Sutter's fort on the west side of the mountains, only sketchy information on an emigrant party of Illinoisians said to have been shut out of the passes by wind and blizzard. The details, when they did become known, were terrible beyond imagination.

When Francis Parkman saw their wagons on the meadow beyond Fort Laramie in June, the Donners and the Reeds and the others making up their California-bound train were getting a late start toward reaching the Sierras before the onset of winter, but they were confident. They planned to reduce travel time by 400 miles by departing the Oregon Trail at Fort Bridger and taking the "Hastings Cut-off." This route would take them south along the Wasatch Range, past the Great Salt Lake, and across the Utah-Nevada desert to the Sierra foothills in time to cross the mountains before winter closed them out.

Their party had swollen to eighty-seven, forty-one of them children, and twenty-three sagging wagons when it set out from Bridger on the last day of July 1846. Within a few days' crawling travel, they learned the awful truth of the shortcut described in Lansford Hastings's guidebook; the Donner-Reed train took twenty-one days to make the thirty-six-mile crossing of the Wasatch Mountains.

They reached the Humboldt River on September 30, after a nightmarish crossing of the desert, which killed most of their oxen and forced abandonment of all but a few of their wagons, and they approached the Sierra Nevada foothills a month later. By now they had exhausted their rations and were eating wild onions and dabs of tallow from their tar buckets. Many of their cows and horses were stolen in a raid by Paiute Indians; they hoped to salvage the remaining animals against the prospect of a starving time before reaching the Sacramento valley.

On October 20, eleven killing weeks out of Bridger, they reached the lush meadows of the Truckee River and rested, grazing their pitifully reduced animals for five fatal days with an early winter snow falling on the mountain ridges before them. The party moved on to a big lake on the thirty-first, just beyond which lay Truckee Pass, the last major barrier between them and their destination.

But they could not cross. The blizzards, snowdrifts, and murderous winds of the pass closed the corridor. They found an old cabin, threw another one together from timber and driftwood along the lake, made lean-tos and brush shelters, and erected tepees and tents to huddle in against the snow and cold. Snowshoes were fashioned for futile attempts to cross the mountain range. The last animals, including the Reeds' dog, were killed for food. They made gruel for the babies from precious handfuls of flour; ate owls, wolves, and whatever other starving animals strayed near enough to be killed with a rifle shot; boiled hides and drank the gluey broth; and, on the day after Christmas, began roasting and eating strips of flesh from the dead.

By the time the first rescue party reached them on February 4, 1847, Jake Donner and three of his hired hands were dead; George Donner was dying from exposure, starvation, and a gashed hand turned gangrenous; and the others were reduced to wraiths, several teetering on the brink of insanity. Rescuers stumbled through snowdrifts to come upon scenes more chilling than any Sierra gale. In one appalling camp where a woman named Elizabeth Graves and her five-year-old son Franklin had died, parts of their bodies were found boiling in a pot as her infant daughter, a miraculous survivor, lay wailing near Elizabeth's carved-up corpse. Two members of the rescue team, William Eddy and William Foster, who had struggled over Truckee Pass with a few others to seek help at Sutter's Fort on the Sacramento River, returned to an unutterable horror. Each had left a young son behind at Truckee Lake in the care of others, and both boys had died. A big, well-educated German named Lewis Keseberg, who had emigrated to the United States only two years past, told Eddy and Foster that he had found the boys' bodies in the snow and eaten them. He was discovered lying beside a pot containing the liver and lungs of one of the boys and said he had subsisted entirely on human flesh despite the nearby ox quarters lying in the snow, which he claimed were "too dry for eating."

Of the eighty-nine members of the train who crossed the Wasatch Mountains, five had died before reaching Truckee Lake; thirty-six others perished in the camps below Truckee Pass or in attempting to cross it, and one died after the rescue: The toll was forty-two dead, forty-seven alive.

After her ordeal, twelve-year-old Virginia Reed, daughter of James and Margaret, all of whom had survived the ordeal without resorting to cannibalism, wrote a cousin back home, "Never take no cut ofs and hury along as fast as you can."

2

Marcus and Narcissa Whitman were not sure what they had accomplished in their eleven years in the Oregon Country. They had come out in '36, before any migration, great or small, filled with inspiration and fervent to do the Lord's work "among the heathen." They had carved out their mission station among the Cayuse people at their Place of the Rye Grass with the expectation that if they made the Bible and its message available the people would come, just as the Flatheads and Nez Percé had journeyed all the way to Saint Louis to find out about the white man's God.

They were not expecting miracles; the work would take time, supreme physical and mental effort, and forbearance, and this, they knew, would take a toll on them. But they would make progress even if as water dripping on a stone. They would convert the savages to Christianity, send the saved out to proselytize among others of their tribe and bring them in to Waiilatpu in ever-increasing numbers. They were prepared for every exigency but failure.

The sheer joy over their prospects and the daily labors building the mission house, schoolrooms, outbuildings, and mill; tilling the soil and planting; teaching and ministering to the bodies as well as the souls of those who drifted to them masked any foreboding they had after hearing Dr. John McLoughlin's early warning that the Cayuse were a "bad people," not to be trusted. At first the Whitmans could not countenance such an idea—there were no "bad" Indians, only ignorant ones awaiting the salvation the missionaries were bringing to them. But they came to see, with the passage of months and years, little evidence that their religious work was making a difference; they had made a few converts but those few seemed listless and irresolute, with none of the humble gratitude and fervor expected of the newly saved.

Whitman had made an arduous return east in the spring

of 1843 to appeal directly to the Board of Foreign Missions not to close his Waiilatpu station, Henry and Eliza Spalding's place among the Nez Percé at Lapwai, or any of the others. He made no professions of success in converting the Indians but set before the board's directors other compelling arguments: The Indians ought not to be abandoned at a time when the immigrant population was increasing almost daily; the stations were needed to provide medical aid and assistance to the emigrant trains; the Catholics were moving in in numbers and would fill any vacuum left if the Protestants departed.

He won but a small triumph: The missions could stay open but without further monetary assistance from the governing board.

He returned disconsolately to Oregon with the Gantt-Applegate train in May 1843 and learned that in his absence Narcissa had suffered indignities at the hands of the increasingly truculent Cayuse. On an October night during his absence, a man named Tamsucky, believed to have been a subchief under Tiloukaikt of the Cayuse, tried to enter her bedroom but was run off. When he heard of the incident, Archibald McKinley, the Hudson's Bay factor at Fort Walla Walla, drove a carriage to the station and insisted that she accompany him back to the fort. Subsequently she spent time with the Methodists at The Dalles, the inland port on the Columbia, and with friends in the Willamette. While she was away, the Waiilatpu grain mill was burned to the ground. Marcus heard the stories, surveyed the ruins, and became convinced that McLoughlin had been right all along.

As the only physician in an area extending from Fort Walla Walla to The Dalles, Whitman was away from Waiilatpu more often than not, riding hundreds of miles on horseback to provide medical aid to settlers and Indian villages. In the first few years of their work Narcissa accompanied him, but as the numbers of emigrants on the Oregon Trail increased, she was left alone to manage the mission and its farm, to run the school for Cayuse Indian boys she had started, to assist newcomers, and to entertain such distinguished visitors as John C. Frémont, John A. Sutter, up from his "New Helvetia" land grant in northern California, and Charles Wilkes.

After a few years of lonely work at the mission, Narcissa's letters home devolved from youthful exuberance and naïveté to despondency over the "proud, wayward" natives she had come out to serve. She was an "indefatigable instructress," T. J. Farnham said after visiting the mission in 1839, and a Wilkes expedition member reported in 1841 that she had 124 natives on the school rolls (although the average attendance was but twenty-five). She tried to teach Cayuse women to sew, knit, and spin, but with little success. She wrote a friend, "The Kayuse women are too proud to be seen usefully employed." Nor did she have better luck with the Walla Walla women, a related people.

She confided to her family that the Indians sought the "Book of Heaven" as a source of white man's power rather than for its Christian inspiration, and said that they were becoming distrustful of the missions and missionaries. Her letters were filled with her health concerns, and with an overall graveness and melancholy that worried her family.

The Whitmans' apprehension of the Cayuse began before Marcus made his Boston journey and grew apace after he returned. The Indians had always seemed indolent, selfish, and ungrateful, but these were ancient traits that simply had to be dealt with patiently. There were more ominous developments: The natives began stealing horses and cattle, sought to extract payment from the missionaries for everything from "language lessons" to use of their land for farming. They raided the gardens, stole vegetables, fruits, and grain so blatantly that William Gray, the "secular agent" who accompanied the Whitmans and the Spaldings to Oregon, decided to respond by poisoning some melons he knew would be stolen. The violently ill culprits learned no lesson from this extreme measure but they promised revenge.

"The savages of the Upper Columbia were very good men, for savages," H. H. Bancroft wrote. "It is true they were thieves, and if their natural benevolence prompted them to relieve the necessities of the white strangers, they rewarded themselves the first opportunity. Thieving was a legitimate means of securing themselves against want, and lying only a defence against discovery and loss." The mistake the missionaries made, he said, was believing that such behavior was proof of the Indians' need for spiritual guidance, "when it was, in fact, an evidence of a natural emulation, to put themselves on a footing with the superior race." In this, he said, "both teachers and pupils were deceived; the savages in expecting to acquire in a single lifetime the civilization which was the slow growth of unknown ages; the missionary in believing that he could graft on this wild stock a germ whose fruit would not be tinctured with the bitter sap of the uncultivated tree."

At the root of the mission failures, he said, lay the "characteristic covetousness of the aboriginal, and his inability to understand that he could not at once become the equal of his teacher. Here his self-love was mortified. He began to suspect that his teachers were governed by selfish and sinister motives in intruding into his country. The more white men he saw, the more this conviction grew."

At their Lapwai station, Henry and Eliza Spalding grew worried about the spreading Indian unrest, worried more for the Whitmans than for themselves. Even the Nez Percé distrusted the Cayuse people, and Henry made a point of warning emigrants coming through his mission lands to avoid them. After the boundary settlement he also began asking newcomers if the United States might be sending army dragoons to keep the peace.

The Spaldings, like the Whitmans, had initial successes at their station, with good school attendance, a sawmill and gristmill in operation, and families working in the fields, but by 1842, with the first sizable force of emigrants arriving on the Oregon Trail, they saw the crumbling of the edifice they had so laboriously built. The Indians began deserting the mission, and classroom and worship-service attendance dwindled.

Joel Palmer, among the 1845 emigrants, visited Lapwai in the spring of 1846 to buy horses, and while he admired the work done by the Spaldings, he wrote that "it is impossible for one family to counteract all the influences of bad and designing men, of whom there are not a few in the country."

The Spaldings' plight was eerily similar to that of their counterparts at Waiilatpu. The Nez Percé had their own share of dangerous renegades, not just those demanding payment for use of the wood and water on their lands and those who vandalized the mills, broke machinery and windows, cut down precious fruit trees, and disrupted the schoolrooms, but also those threatening physical violence against the white intruders. Spalding wrote in January 1847 that "At one time probably 500 people were collecting threatening to go to my house tie & whip my wife." He said the Indians were furious because Eliza had summoned a Nez Percé chief to remove from the mission premises two men "who had just presented themselves before the school naked & painted with the most horrible figures, & continued their indecent jestures till Mrs. S. was obliged to leave the house."

Elsewhere he wrote of the sad state of their religious work. "I know not there has been a conversion for the last two years," he wrote in February 1847. "The sabbath which was once very strictly observed, is now generally desecrated."

3

Eighteen forty-six ended with New Mexico conquered and Americans on the march to occupy Los Angeles. The annexation of California would take place six weeks into the new year. There were still nine months of battles to be fought deep into Mexico, but few doubted the outcome of President Polk's war.

In the Oregon Country the boundary was settled, and the Governor and Company of Adventurers Trading in Hudson's Bay had removed to their new post of Victoria on Vancouver Island. The liege lord of the Oregon Country, Dr. John McLoughlin, had retired to private life in Oregon City, and Peter Skene Ogden had taken charge of what Company business remained north of the Columbia. The Americans in the Willamette were preparing memorials to Congress seeking immediate territorial status, composing contracts to bring supplies on American merchant ships coming to the northwest coast, requesting confirmation of the settlers' land claims, and requesting a railroad, military troops, and steam tugboats and lighthouses for the Columbia estuary.

News of the boundary treaty had reached the Columbia in the winter that killed half the Donner party in the Sierra Nevada foothills, a winter that proved disastrously bitter on the Columbia as well. The Nez Percé and Cayuse people lost half their horse herds in the arctic-like days, game grew scarce, people starved, and all the while territorial talk spread along the Willamette and to the Whitmans' station. The suffering Indians were learning that the British had moved out and the Americans were now claiming sovereignty over their lands. Year after year, white men in an endless army were marching in. As yet they had not tarried in Cayuse or Nez Percé country, but how long could the Willamette valley contain them?

This simmering unrest frowned in the air like a storm cloud. The Spaldings had felt something dire spreading toward them for years and began writing to friends that they might have to move to the Willamette for the safety of their four children. The Whitmans had similar thoughts. In the spring of 1847, fearing that a rising of some kind might be in the offing, the doctor was able to scrape together the funds to purchase the vacated Methodist mission station at The

Dalles, intending to move Narcissa and the Waiilatpu furnishings there. The Dalles site was but two days by canoe to the safety of Fort Vancouver, now American property.

Yet, for all his suspicions and forebodings, Whitman hesitated. The Catholic fathers were building a mission on the Umatilla River, only thirty miles from Waiilatpu, and he could not abide the idea of his Cayuse and Walla Walla students and converts, small in number as they were, falling into the hands of the Romans. He and Narcissa had invested eleven years in their mission and soon, if they held on, an Indian agent of the United States would arrive, perhaps even a military force, and the natives would be quieted, the Protestant missions secured under a real territorial governance.

Meantime, he was moving milling machinery to his rebuilt gristmill to make flour for the new wave of immigrants. He had much to do, and Narcissa did as well. They would wait awhile.

The first wagons of the 1847 emigration crossed the Blue Mountains in late August, detoured north to the Whitman mission for a rest, and continued on to make camp at The Dalles. They brought with them news gathered on the journey, including estimates that as many as 5,000 settlers would be coming in before the year ended.

The newcomers, and those who flowed in daily in their wake, had suffered on the Trail, particularly the last few hundred miles of it, and had buried some of their number en route. They spoke of "mountain fever" as the ailment that had claimed the lives. They were much less concerned over the measles contracted by many of the children and a few adults during the journey; the measles victims ran fevers but recovered.

What followed, as wagon after wagon rolled across the Blues in the fall and winter months, was unaccountable: The measles, a particularly virulent strain it was said later, became a scourge among the Oregon tribes, obeying what Bancroft called "that inscrutable law of nature which makes it fatal to the dark races to encounter the white race." The disease spread from The Dalles to Puget Sound and before it ran its course killed thousands of Oregon's "dark races," including half of the Cayuse people.

While nothing could stop it, it became Marcus Whitman's fate to be the lone physician, and a white one, among a native populace plagued by a white man's disease. He ministered as best he could with his primitive bag of nostrums, cold compresses, and prayers, but the efforts were futile. No amount of white doctoring cured the white affliction and yet, as quickly became clear to the Indian, the white people were not dying from the disease they called "measles"; only the Indians died of it.

While Whitman worked himself to exhaustion, his efforts earned no gratitude; the Cayuse regarded him as a failed medicine man and, worse, a sorceror, pretending to help but secretly poisoning their people with his potions so that he, in league with other whites, could steal Indian lands.

In this spreading conviction the natives were assisted by a number of what Bancroft called "dissolute characters, half-breeds from the mountains to the east, hanging upon the skirts of the travellers." These men, "whose wild blood was full of the ichor of hatred of religion and civilization, and poisoned with jealousy of the white race, the worst traits only of which they had inherited," were likened to a white-hot brand being towed through the tinder of the stricken Indian villages.

Chief among these firebrands was a French-Canadian drifter with the Americanized name of Joe Lewis, who was said to have come to Oregon from Maine. He appeared at Waiilatpu in the fall of '47, destitute and with his clothing in rags. Whitman fed and outfitted him and tried to find employment for him, but Lewis seemed content to be a hanger-on and soon came to be regarded as a troublemaker. This idea was proven when the idler fastened himself to the Cayuse and became instrumental in spreading the calumny that the measles epidemic could be traced to Dr. Whitman's blueprint to steal the Indians' lands.

Lewis was said to have met with a tribal council and reported that Whitman, and Henry Spalding at the Lapwai mission, were writing to friends in the East to have fresh supplies of poison shipped in to kill the Cayuse and Nez Percé people. Lewis even reported to the council a conversation he claimed to have overheard between the two missionaries. Spalding, Lewis said, asked Whitman why he was so slow in his killings among the Cayuse and the doctor replied, "Oh, they are dying fast enough; the young ones will die off this winter, and the old ones next spring."

The source of Lewis's alleged remarks was William Craig, a forty-year-old Virginian who had come out to Oregon in 1829 after trapping in Blackfeet country with Jedediah Smith. Following a peripatetic career as a fur trader, he recrossed the Rockies and established a farm eight miles north of the Spalding mission. He was distrusted by Henry Spalding, who believed Craig the ringleader of a group of malcontents causing problems among the Nez Percé. But Craig's account of the Joe Lewis-Cayuse council conversation bore the stamp of truth despite the fact that he was the second bearer of it. The story had been told to Craig by a Cayuse who swore by it and added that Lewis told the tribal council that "unless they killed Dr. Whitman and Mr. Spalding quick, they would all die."

4

John McLoughlin's warnings, the pre-epidemic trepidations of the missionaries that the Indians might one day rise, the massive increase in emigrant traffic, and the scourge accompanying it all rushed to a fatal conclusion in November 1847.

The third week of the month began routinely when Henry
Spalding rode down to Waiilatpu with his ten-year-old
daughter Eliza (named for her mother) to put the girl in the
Whitmans' school. Accompanying the Spaldings was a
Mr. Jackson, who led a string of mules loaded with grain
to be milled. En route they paid a visit to a familiar figure
in the valley, Chief Peupeumoxmox, "Yellow Serpent," of
the Walla Wallas, whose camp lay near the river and fort
bearing the tribal name. The chief was an intelligent and
dignified man related by forebears and marriage to the
Cayuse, Yakima, and Nez Percé tribes, and he was influential among all the native people of the Oregon Country. He
had sent his son to be educated among the Methodist missionaries in the Willamette valley, but in 1844, after the
young man was murdered at Sutter's Fort, Yellow Serpent
had entertained the idea of a war against the whites, in California and even along the Willamette. He was eventually
deterred from this plan by John McLoughlin, who told the
chief that such an action would result in the extermination
of his people.

Still regarded as "friendly" to whites even after some of
his tribe died in the measles epidemic that winter, the chief
confided in Spalding that he had heard the rumors about the
Americans trying to destroy the Cayuse but said he did not
believe them.

Spalding and his daughter reached Waiilatpu on Monday,
November 22, and spent the week with the Whitmans. On
Saturday, a messenger arrived from the Cayuse camps in the
Umatilla valley, thirty miles south, asking for assistance.
The missionaries mounted up and rode out in a rainstorm.
Spalding later remembered that they talked about how they
had entered the valley in '36 along the same route they were
now riding, and about the disturbing Indian threats both
were hearing. At one point Whitman said, "But my death
will probably do as much good for Oregon as my life can."

They rode to the villages on the south edge of the

Umatilla, visited the Cayuse chiefs Five Crows and Tauitau, and ministered to some sick villagers. Then, on Sunday afternoon, November 28, they reached the lodge of a chief named Sticcas, considered a friend of the missionaries. He warned Whitman that Joe Lewis was stirring up trouble among the Cayuse and advised the doctor to leave Waiilatpu "until my people have better hearts." This alarmed Whitman enough that he decided to break his own rules against working or traveling on the Sabbath to hasten back to his mission. Spalding stayed behind for the day, and, at dawn on Monday, as he prepared to mount his horse not far from the chief's lodge, a native woman warned him to avoid the Place of the Rye Grass. This was something Spalding could not do: He had left his daughter there and so hurried on, his path leading directly from the north side of the Umatilla past the camps of Tiloukaikt, a Cayuse chief who had troubled Whitman in the past, and a younger man named Tomahas.

Whitman arrived home at near midnight on the twenty-eighth. He was exhausted from the ride but stayed up to relieve Narcissa, who was nearly as fatigued from nursing three of their adopted children, Helen Meek and Louise and Henrietta Sager, who were ill. He ate breakfast alone. Narcissa remained in her room and when one of the Sager girls took a tray of food to her, she found her sitting on a chair, sobbing into a handkerchief.

In the dawn chill Whitman went outside the mission house to supervise the butchering of a beef, then made his rounds to check on his patients at the station hospital. On that day, November 29, three more Cayuse children were discovered dead, one belonging to Chief Tiloukaikt, who had earlier lost two others to the disease. They were quickly buried, with Whitman presiding with prayers, this a depressing, daily occurrence.

School opened at nine.

The T-shaped Waiilatpu mission house lay on an east-west axis with the crossbar of the T at the west end. It consisted of a parlor, a sitting room with stairs leading to a small loft, and an "Indian Room" with sleeping quarters. At the southern end of the neck of the T was a half-completed addition to the building, and running north lay the schoolroom, bedrooms, and a spacious kitchen next to the crossbar with doors opening into the sitting room, the Indian room, and outside. The house was spacious and comfortable, warmed by three large fireplaces, and except for some low fencing, open and unprotected.

As the twenty-ninth wore on, Whitman, after two days without sleep, walked through the kitchen to the sitting room of the house and sat by the fire to read and rest. At about two o'clock in the afternoon, as he nodded there, Tiloukaikt, Tomahas, and some other Cayuse men knocked on the outside door that led into the kitchen. Narcissa answered and turned toward the sitting-room door. "Doctor, you are wanted," she said.

What occurred in the next few minutes remains, a century and half later, confused by the several survivor accounts, but it appears that Tiloukaikt demanded some medicines and, as the doctor came through the door, he tried to push him back into the sitting room. Whitman resisted, shut the door behind him, and went to the cabinet to fetch the medicines, telling Narcissa to leave the room and close the kitchen door behind her. There were two children in the kitchen, Mary Ann Bridger, Jim's daughter, adopted by the Whitmans, and, just recovering from the measles, seventeen-year-old John Sager, one of the seven Sager children whose parents had died on the Oregon Trail. The two youngsters saw Dr. Whitman hand some medicines to Tiloukaikt, saw Tomahas step behind the doctor, swing a brass tomahawk, and strike Whitman on the head, and saw the doctor crumple to the floor as one of the Indians shot at him while Tiloukaikt and Tomahas hacked at his face and head with their war axes.

WAIILATPU   447

John Sager drew a pistol but was shot before he could fire it; Mary Bridger shrieked, climbed out the kitchen window, and ran to the west end of the station house yelling, "The Indians are killing Father and John!" Whitman, blood gouting from his wounds, staggered out the kitchen door, where he was clubbed down again. Either Tiloukaikt or Tomahas jammed a rifle muzzle against his throat and pulled the trigger. Narcissa ran forward and with the help of some other women dragged Marcus back through the kitchen to a settee. She tried to stanch the blood with a towel and ashes from the fireplace, ordered the children to bolt the doors and shutters and hide in closets.

"Do you know me?" she said to her husband.

"Yes." His voice was a whisper.

"Is there anything I can do to stop the bleeding?"

"No."

Outside, the Cayuse, led by Tiloukaikt, Tomahas, and the half-breed Joe Lewis, had dropped the blankets that hid their rifles. A man named William Marsh was gunned down as he ran from the gristmill; another, Isaac Gilliland, working at his tailor's table, fought back with an ax long enough for some mission folk to escape before he was cut down; L. W. Saunders, a schoolteacher, was hacked to death while trying to climb a rail fence as his daughter watched from a school window.

Narcissa walked to the sitting-room window and saw Joe Lewis and the others running amok. "Is it you, Joe, who are doing this?" she cried out. At that moment, a young Cayuse named "Frank" Escaloom fired his rifle into the sitting room, the bullet striking Narcissa under her left arm. She fell but staggered up, helped by the others to a seat while she prayed to God to protect the children.

As the attackers broke windows and smashed at the door, an immigrant named Andrew Rodgers, wounded in the arm, got the women and children, and one other wounded man, upstairs. There Narcissa was placed on a bed, her blood soaking the blankets. No attempt was made to move Marcus, who lay unconscious on the settee below.

When the Indians broke into the sitting room Rodgers met them aiming an old rifle he had found. For a time the intruders were cowed. Then Tamsucky, the Cayuse who had attempted to break into Narcissa's bedroom five years past, promised that no harm would come to the whites if they would surrender. One of the women in the upstairs bedroom recognized Tamsucky as the man who had killed L. W. Saunders and warned the others, but they had no choice but to descend the stairs and hope for mercy.

Narcissa, weak from bleeding, was helped down to the sitting room and nearly fainted at the sight of her husband, still lying on the settee, eyes closed, hideously mutilated, breathing stertorously.

The Indians moved all the captives to the Indian room at the northwest corner of the house and there debated their fate, Tamsucky's promise forgotten. Eliza Spalding, the daughter Henry had brought only a week before to enroll in school, understood enough of their language to know they were arguing over whether or not to kill all the captives. Finally, their decision was to spare the children and all the women except Narcissa.

She was carried out on a settee, Andrew Rodgers, despite his wounded arm, lifting one end of it, and the ringleader of the attack, Joe Lewis, the other. Outdoors, Lewis dropped his end of the couch and stood back as several Cayuse opened fire, killing Rodgers and Narcissa Whitman instantly. One Indian stepped forward and slashed Narcissa's lifeless body with a whip, after which her corpse was dumped into an irrigation ditch.

Soon after these murders, Frances Sager, who had been hiding in the attic above the schoolroom, came down and was dragged outdoors by Lewis and shot to death. She was the third of four of the Sager orphans killed and the ninth white killed before nightfall.

Marcus Whitman, mercifully unconscious, died of his wounds in the sitting room.

Five other Waiilatpu residents would also die, including Helen Meek and Louise Sager, before the end of the siege on December 5.

The bodies of the Whitmans and Andrew Rodgers lay in the dirt outside the Indian room for nearly three days before the Cayuse would permit them to be buried in a common grave.

Six men escaped the massacre. One drowned in the Columbia in flight, another, W. D. Canfield, fled on foot to Lapwai, 120 miles northeast, and warned Eliza Spalding of the horrific events at Waiilatpu. She was frantic for the safety of her husband and daughter and sent two Nez Percé men to the Whitman station to do what they could to rescue them.

Henry Spalding meantime was riding toward Waiilatpu when on the thirtieth he learned of the massacre and that his daughter had survived but was a captive of the Cayuse. He pushed on toward Lapwai—and probably passed without seeing the Nez Percé his wife had sent down on the rescue effort. He rode wildly thirty miles before he fell exhausted from his horse and slept fitfully a short time, during which interval his horse wandered off and he was forced to walk, covering the last ninety miles to Lapwai in six days.

When he reached the outskirts of his mission, Spalding saw a crowd of Indian looters milling about and believed for an instant that he was gazing upon another Waiilatpu, a scene of murder and perhaps other nameless atrocities. Were either of his Elizas alive? His other children? Had any of his mission workers survived?

He was rescued from the shock of these thoughts by one of the Nez Percé faithful who told him his wife and the others were safe, that they had taken refuge at the William Craig farm eight miles north. He was reunited with them on December 7, but his mind had been "injured" by the ordeal of the past week, Bancroft states, so much so that "all his subsequent writings show a want of balance." Thereafter, when relating the events of that experience, "his forehead was covered with great drops of sweat, and his eyes had a frenzied expression."

His manner on such occasions was compared to that of Donner party survivors recollecting their winter ordeal at Truckee Lake.

At Waiilatpu, the Cayuse held captive forty-seven whites—thirty-four children, eight women, and five men. Several of the women were "taken for wives" by the Indians, and Spalding later wrote that they were compelled to cook for a large number of the savages and that his daughter Eliza had been forced to taste the food to prove it unpoisoned. The women also sewed garments from goods looted from the mission, and it was reported that the women and girls were subjected to many more "revolting brutalities."

On December 19, Peter Ogden, the Hudson's Bay Company's finest troubleshooter, a clever and forceful man not unused to or even avoiding violence when he deemed it necessary, arrived at Fort Walla Walla. He gathered the chiefs together and announced, "The company have nothing to do with your quarrel. If you wish it, on my return I will see what can be done for you; but I do not promise to prevent a war. Deliver me the prisoners to return to their friends, and I will pay you a ransom, that is all."

The ransom was too alluring to refuse, and in return for $500 worth of shirts, blankets, guns, ammunition, flints, and tobacco provided by the Company, the prisoners were handed over by the Cayuse at Waiilatpu.

Henry and Eliza Spalding arrived at Fort Walla Walla from the Craig farm on New Year's Day 1848, with an escort of fifty loyal Nez Percé, and were reunited with their daughter.

They had closed their mission, taking only a few household goods with them and an inventory for the Board of Missions to employ in making a claim for government restitution. Spalding listed eleven buildings, 100 head of cattle, thirty-nine horses, thirty-one hogs, two wagons, a carriage, two carts, a feather bed, two rocking chairs, four settees, two spinning wheels, fifty-six apple trees, four peach trees, and one pear tree.

He estimated the property and belongings to be worth $10,048.11. It worked out to $913.46 for each year the unsalaried and unappreciated missionaries had spent at Lapwai.

24

Last Trails

■

"... THE IMAGE OF AN IRREVOCABLE PAST."

1

In February 1848 Joe Meek, the big, shag-bearded, good-natured "bull buffalo" mountain man from Virginia, rode into Waiilatpu with an escort of militia men and some pack animals. He was heading out from Oregon City on a mission to deliver certain important papers to President Polk in Washington and wanted to see again the place where so many of his friends had died, and where his daughter had suffered. Helen Meek, "adopted" by the Whitmans and schooled by them at their mission, had died in December, not long after being freed by the Cayuse and delivered with the other captives to Peter Ogden at Fort Walla Walla.

The ruins of Marcus and Narcissa Whitman's eleven years of labor and hope lay before him: the burned-out shell of the T-shaped house; piles of melted adobe bricks, charred timbers, lintels, roof beams, and planking; and, littering the grounds, shards of china and pottery, snow-stained books and letters, and the rubble of household items the marauders deemed of no value. All the orchard trees had been hacked down, the fields trampled, and the wolves had been at work among the graves. Gnawed bones and rags of clothing had to be gathered up and reburied. Meek found Narcissa

Whitman's remains and snipped a lock of her hair as a keepsake before placing her in a deeper grave than before.

As he and his escort rode down to the Umatilla to pick up the Oregon Trail and head east, the Waiilatpu killers remained at large. Tiloukaikt, Tomahas, Joe Lewis, and all the others had vanished. Some said they were still lurking somewhere near their terrible handiwork, and others claimed they had fled into the Blue Mountains. Meek had to contain his great hunger for revenge; he had other work to do, and in any event, the Cayuse' days on the run were closing. The killers could not stay free long when the countryside was swarming with men hunting them down. He only wished he could be in on the kill.

He would be, but two and a half years would pass before the raiders, some of them at least, would be brought to justice.

Joe Meek, now thirty-seven and as tough, durable, and dependable as he had been in the days when he headed trapper brigades to rendezvous on the Green River of Wyoming, had been the settlers' choice to deliver an assortment of petitions and papers to Washington. He had served his offices well from the time of the pioneering governmental meetings at Champoeg in '43 when he acted as auctioneer of Ewing Young's estate. He had been the provisional government's choice for sheriff and later marshal, and for his new assignment had another advantage: He was related to the Childresses, Sara Childress Polk's people, and might thereby have an entrée to the president that was denied to others.

One memorial Meek carried was from the officers of the provisional legislature beseeching the federal government to extend to Oregon "the benefit of its laws and protection." The authors of the document were adamant: They had "called upon the government of the United States so often in vain," had received too many empty promises, and now, with legislation pending to grant territorial status to Oregon and the Whitman tragedy underscoring the limits to which the Americans there could protect themselves or punish criminals, stated, "We have the right to expect your aid, and you are in duty bound to extend it." The authors also expressed confidence in the federal government to send them "men of the best talent and most approved integrity" to serve as governor and in the courts regardless of their residency in Oregon or any office presently held. Among the other papers in Meek's saddlebag was a petition signed by 250 settlers and government officials requesting that the president, upon passage of the territorial bill, appoint Joseph Lafayette Meek United States Marshal of the new Territory of Oregon.

Meek's orders originally called for him to take a route to California, to deliver messages asking the American military government there for a requisition of arms, and to request that a warship from the United States Pacific Squadron be sent to the Columbia. The mountain man knew his mountains, however, and, to the annoyance of his dispatchers, decided he could not cross the passes into California in the winter snows and would ride east on the Oregon Trail.

He reached Saint Louis on May 17 and proceeded to Washington by steamer and rail purposely wearing his filthy trail outfit of buckskins and moccasins, presenting himself as a ragged but genuine "Envoy Extraordinary and Minister Plenipotentiary from the Republic of Oregon to the Court of the United States."

The president received Meek immediately. The normally dour Polk was lighter-hearted, enjoying the final nine months of his term. The war had been won and a treaty signed in which Mexico ceded 40 percent of its territory to the United States. With the Oregon settlement, the country had doubled in size, with 1,200,000 square miles added in three years of war and diplomacy. The paper Joe Meek brought from the place Polk had won but would never see must have seemed a pleasant diversion from the toils of his office. The president saw no obstacle in presenting to Congress the memorial Sara Polk's reeking relative delivered from the provisional government in Oregon, especially since the matter it contained was by now moot. As for the marshal's appointment, Meek was told to wait. The president had a job for him.

On August 13, 1848, Polk signed the long-awaited bill creating Oregon Territory.* There had been some division over it. South Carolina Senator McDuffie said he would not "give a pinch of snuff for the whole territory" but he was in the minority, and the bill sailed through Congress. Five days after the signing, Joe Meek was sworn as United States Marshal and on the twenty-seventh he was given the honor of delivering the governor's commission to Joseph Lane, a forty-six-year-old brigadier general and hero in the late Mexican War who had started his military career as a private in the Second Indiana Volunteers.

Meek presented the commission to Lane in Indiana, and the two started for Fort Leavenworth on September 10. They avoided the winter snows of South Pass and beyond and turned southward with ten wagons and a party of trappers, wagon masters and teamsters, and twenty-five soldiers, down the Santa Fé Trail. In the New Mexican capital, now American territory, they left the wagons and switched to pack mules as Colonel Stephen Watts Kearny had done in marching his dragoon force to California two years earlier, and followed Kearny's route down the Rio Grande valley, swinging west to Tucson and the Colorado River. In Los Angeles the Meek-Lane party caught an American warship for passage

*The Territory included what would become the states of Oregon and Washington (which gained its own territorial status in 1853) plus portions of Idaho, Wyoming, and Montana.

to San Francisco and reached the mouth of the Columbia on March 3, 1849, one day before President Polk's term expired.

The ashes of the Whitman station were still warm when the provisional government of Oregon issued proclamations and posted notices calling for volunteers to form a punitive expedition against the Cayuse. Two hundred and thirty men responded to the first call, and 500 would eventually be formed into companies of a regiment of Oregon Mounted Riflemen to take part in the campaign. They were loosely organized and poorly led, as might have been expected of a force of volunteer farmers, hunters, trappers, clerks, mill workers, drifters, and militiamen, but they had a single nine-pounder cannon contributed by Oregon City and a single-mindedness in their mission to punish the savages behind the Waiilatpu atrocities.

The "Cayuse War" consisted of a strung-out series of horseback pursuits and small scuffles from The Dalles, headquarters for the volunteers, along the Umatilla into the Snake River country, southeast into the Blue Mountains, and north beyond Fort Walla Walla, close to the juncture of the Snake and the Columbia, where the Palouse tribe harbored some of the fleeing marauders. The volunteers had no supply train and had to live off the country until returning to headquarters or reaching a farmhouse along the route. The wildest of the skirmishes lasted minutes and resulted in little more than an expenditure of precious ammunition. The war itself produced more rumors than casualties. The Nez Percé, Walla Wallas, and Yakimas were said to be in league with and harboring the outlaws. The Cayuse miscreants were sighted as far east along the Snake as Fort Hall, as far west as the Pacific coast, hiding among the Chinooks. Some suggested the culprits may have gone into Utah to seek protection among the Mormons.

Governor Lane made the difference. The year following

his arrival in Oregon, he devoted to bringing the killers to justice, negotiating with tribal elders for the voluntary delivery of the culprits for trial. He was a skillful diplomat and his work reached fruition in the spring of 1850, when he traveled to The Dalles with a military escort to receive the prisoners. There were five of them: Tiloukaikt, Tomahas, the best known of the raiders; and men named Klokamas, Isaiachakalis, and Kiamasumpkin. To the infinite regret of all, Joe Lewis had escaped capture and disappeared from Oregon and from the historical record. Some Oregonians believed he was killed in one of the punitive raids, others say he died at the hands of the Nez Percé, or, even more satisfactory, was killed by the Cayuse for sowing the seeds of their destruction.

The Cayuse prisoners were questioned closely en route to Oregon City, where they would stand trial. When offered food by Lane's escort Tiloukaikt said, "What hearts have you to offer to eat with me, whose hands are red with your brothers' blood?" and when asked why he surrendered, said, "Did not your missionaries teach us that Christ died to save his people? So we die to save our people."

The trial opened on May 22 with the Indians defended by the secretary of the Territory and three army legal officers, and prosecuted by the newly arrived district attorney. John McLoughlin, who had warned the Whitmans of the perils of trying to work among such truculent savages, appeared to testify against the condemned.

The proceeding was brief but dignified; the defendants were all convicted and sentenced to death by hanging by the trial judge, O. C. Pratt, originally of Ontario County, New York, a distinguished lawyer with, according to H. H. Bancroft, "analytic intelligence" and "fine sensibilities."

On June 3, 1850, before much of the white population of Oregon City and some who had traveled far for the witnessing, the condemned men mounted a scaffold built to hang them simultaneously. A Catholic father, who had given the men the sacraments of baptism and confirmation in their cells, attended them on the gallows with the prayer, "Onward, onward to heaven, children; into Thy hands, O Lord Jesus, I commend my spirit."

Joe Meek, United States Marshal of Oregon Territory, served as executioner and years later recalled the moment.

"I brought forth the five prisoners," he said, "and placed them on the drop. Here the chief, who had always declared his innocence, Kiamasumpkin, begged me to kill him with my knife—for an Indian fears to be hanged—but I soon put an end to his entreaties by cutting the rope which held the drop with my tomahawk. As I said, 'the Lord have mercy on your souls,' the trap fell and the five Cayuses hung in the air."

Three of the five died instantly; the other two struggled, Meek said, "the Little Chief, Tomahas, the longest. It was he who was cruel to my little girl at the time of the massacre; so I just put my foot on the knot to tighten it, and he got quiet."

Most of the surviving Cayuse people, weakened by disease and reduced to small, scattered groups, were moved to a reservation with the Umatillas in 1855; others melded into the Nez Percé, Yakima, Palouse, and other tribes.

The Cayuse had lived in the region between the Walla Walla and Umatilla Rivers for five centuries before, in Bancroft's words, the "Juggernaut of an incomprehensible civilization" under "whose wheels they were compelled to prostrate themselves to that relentless law, the survival of the fittest, before which in spite of religion or science, we all in turn go down."

2

An important postmortem to the Whitman tragedy came about when Narcissa Whitman's sister, Miss Jane Prentiss, wrote a letter in 1849 seeking an answer to the question that had caused her family such anguish: "Why did the

Indians kill my sister and her husband who had done so much for them?"

She directed her inquiry to Reverend H. K. W. Perkins, Methodist missionary at the Waskopum station at The Dalles, with whom Marcus Whitman often visited in his travels to and from the Willamette valley. Perkins had visited Waiilatpu as well, and seems to have known both Whitmans intimately, the reason, no doubt, that Jane Prentiss sought his counsel.

Perkins answered her question with great clarity, underlining words and phrases for emphasis, and with forthrightness; more of it, perhaps, than Miss Prentiss anticipated.

He said the Whitmans "were out of their proper sphere" in mission work. Marcus was "perfectly fearless and independent" but had no talent for patient talk with the Indians, "could never stop to parley," and saw no gray areas between yes and no. The Indians feared him, Perkins said, but he "never identified himself with the natives as to make their interests <u>paramount</u>." Dr. Whitman, he said, had "no sense of personal dignity—manners, I mean," presumably referring to Whitman's habitual slovenliness of dress, and was "always at work," but not necessarily at religious and educational efforts among his Indian charges. The result, he said, was that the Cayuse "began to suspect that he was more interested in the white man than in them."

Narcissa, Perkins wrote, "felt a deep interest in the welfare of the natives," but was considered by them to be "haughty" and "very proud." He concluded that she "was not adapted to savage but <u>civilized</u> life. She would have done honor to her sex in a polished & exalted sphere." Her death, he said, "was her <u>misfortune</u>, not her fault. She was adapted to a different destiny. She wanted something exalted—communion with mind. She longed for society, <u>refined society</u>."

He concluded his extraordinary analysis by saying of Narcissa, "The self-denial that took her away [from refined society] was suicidal . . . . She was not a <u>missionary</u>, but a <u>woman</u>, a highly gifted, polished American lady. And as such she died."

After the Waiilatpu massacre and the closing of their Lapwai mission, Henry and Eliza Spalding took up residence in the Willamette valley. He seemed to be searching for answers to the question Jane Prentiss posed when, with a group of Presbyterian adherents, he opened an attack on those he considered to be at the source of the tragedy: the Catholic clergy.

Spalding's letters appeared in the *Oregon American,* a small monthly paper printed in Oregon City on a handmade press. He asserted that not only the nefarious Joe Lewis but also certain Jesuits who arrived at Fort Walla Walla in September 1847 had spread the lethal lie among the Cayuse that the Americans had brought the measles plague to kill them so that their lands could be confiscated. The missionary, and others supporting his viewpoint, maintained that the Jesuit clergy had conspired with the Indians to destroy all the Protestant missions.

"All were termed Jesuits," Bancroft wrote angrily on this episode, "whether Jesuit, secular, or Oblate; and fertile imaginations, half crazed by horrors, were sown with suspicions the foulest and most unnatural."

The charges, examples of the dread of "Romanism" and "Popish designs" among the Protestant missionaries, did not reflect well upon Spalding's otherwise excellent record of work and sacrifice among the Nez Percé, Bancroft said; indeed, he wrote, "The mere intimation of such atrocity exposes the heart of those who made them." Nor did the campaign in the short-lived *Oregon American* (it lasted six issues) come to anything, least of all an investigation. "The Presbyterians blamed the Catholics, and the Catholics blamed the devil," the historian summed up, "for what the exercise of ordinary good judgment ought to have averted, but which sectarian pride and obstinacy resolved to dare rather than avoid."

When Eliza Spalding died at the age of forty-eight on January 7, 1851, the 200-word epitaph her husband composed for her tombstone told of her birth and marriage, their crossing of the Rocky Mountains with the Whitmans in 1836, Eliza and Narcissa being the first women to do so, and their devoted labors among the Indians until "Dr. and Mrs. Whitman and 12 others were cruelly massacred by the Cayuse Indians." She hoped that their mission might be resumed, the inscription went on, "but the shock of the massacre and the trial and suffering occasioned by those sad events, laid the foundation for the sickness, which finally caused her death." All this was followed by the sentence, "She always felt that the Jesuit missionaries were the leading cause of the massacre."

Henry Spalding remarried in 1853 and returned to Lapwai in 1871 at the behest of the Presbyterian Board of Foreign Missions. He was greeted enthusiastically by the Nez Percé and claimed to have baptized 1,000 Indians during his tour.

He also paid a memorial visit to the Waiilatpu ruins and saw that it had become a place of rye grass again.

At his home in Kamiah, Idaho, he baptized a Cayuse chief with the Christian name Marcus Whitman, and the chief's wife as Narcissa Whitman.

Spalding died at Lapwai on August 3, 1874, and in 1913, Eliza's remains were moved there and reburied alongside her husband's. The old accusatory tombstone had been destroyed and a new monument placed over their graves.

3

Francis Parkman's "A Summer Journey Out of Bounds by a Bostonian" began appearing serially in *Knickerbocker Magazine* in February 1847, at the time when rescuers were reaching the appalling camp of the Donner party in the

Sierra Nevada foothills, and completed its twenty-one-issue run in February 1849. By then, the Mormons had reached their Salt Lake valley Zion, the Whitmans and Waiilatpu were no more, Oregon had been declared a Territory of the United States, the War with Mexico had ended, John Jacob Astor had died,* and the argonauts were on the march to the gold diggings in California.

Parkman had returned in October 1846, and for a time he had no trails to follow other than the dimly lit paths through his Beacon Hill home, those between the furrows of his rose garden, and, when he became Harvard's first professor of horticulture, the walkway to his office in Cambridge.

The Oregon Trail adventure had not revived his failing health as he had hoped. His eyesight had worsened; impaired during his law studies, it had become permanently damaged, his physicians said, by the merciless prairie sun. His heart palpitations had returned too, and he had agonizing headaches—suspected at first to derive from a cranial tumor—and insomnia.

But while his eyes never improved, Parkman's other problems seemed intermittent. He regained his strength after periods when he had to lie abed or hobble about on two canes to tend to his garden or find his research materials for his daily writing stint, then he would lose it again. He became resigned to a life as a semi-invalid and bore it with courage and humor. Once, when a doctor remarked on his "strong constitution," he said sadly, "I'm afraid that's true."

Outwardly, at least, he seemed resigned to his handicaps and serene, and found ways to work. In writing his Oregon

---

*Having lived not only to see the settlement of the Oregon Country but to read of the great migrations to the Pacific in the 1840s, some years after the western fur trade had dwindled to near extinction and long after he switched his investments to New York real estate. He died in New York City on March 29, 1848, at age eighty-one, leaving a fortune of $30,000,000 and in his will many philanthropical bequests.

Trail series for the *Knickerbocker,* his sister and his friend
and traveling companion Quincy Shaw read his rough journal
notes to him as he convalesced. He digested them, composed
paragraphs in his head, and dictated them to his volunteer
scribes. In later years he most often wrote in semidarkness
using a contraption he devised and called a "noctograph"
consisting of a wooden frame with wires stretched across it
to support his hand and guide his pen so that he could write
with his eyes closed. There were times when headaches and
listlessness from insomnia kept him from writing more
than a half-hour in a day, times when his daily production
was as little as six lines, and times when he wrote prodi-
giously.

He remained frail all his life, his health and strength fluc-
tuating from despairing periods in bed with his writing
frame propped before him to periods when he could work
outdoors, teach at Harvard, make research voyages to Europe, and even have a social life. His students and friends
saw him as a convivial host, an uncomplaining, modest, and
friendly man.

Few of those close to Parkman in the early years following his Oregon Trail experience believed he would live to
write the books he planned in his Harvard days; indeed,
many of his close associates believed he would soon tire of
chronic invalidism and welcome death, and the journal of
his one great exploit would be his first and only book, monument enough for this courageous man.

What no one counted on was his obstinacy, his ability to
discover new passions that invigorated him and to rediscover
old ones that inspired his will to live and work.

Even so, probably no one was more surprised than Parkman that he would outlive his Oregon Trail journey by forty-
three years and write all the books, and a few others, he
aspired to write. There were to be twelve volumes under the
general title *France and England in America,* the first of
which, *History of the Conspiracy of Pontiac,* appearing in

1851, he had mentally outlined before he set out with Quincy Shaw for Fort Laramie. He wrote seven other historical books, including *Montcalm and Wolfe* generally regarded to be his finest work in 1884, *The Book of Roses,* and even a novel.

Parkman's histories were hailed as classics by Henry Adams, James Russell Lowell, Herman Melville, and Henry James, and at his death at age seventy on November 8, 1893, he was hailed as "the Herodotus of American history."

Of all his books, only *The Oregon Trail** reached a popular audience and would remain in print, to date, for 150 years. The author's youthful grit and ingenuousness, his being "haunted by wilderness images night and day," and the magic of his eye for detail contributed to its endurance. Above all, his first book was the only book he wrote from a firsthand, participatory viewpoint. The sense he had that what he was seeing had long-lasting historical importance was vastly different from the books he wrote about events whose historical importance had long been established.

"The narrator must seek to imbue himself with the life and spirit of the time," he wrote in an era when history was literature and not yet as dismal a science as economics. "He must study events in their bearings, near and remote; in the character, habits, and manners of those who took part in them. He must himself be, as it were, a sharer or a spectator of the action he describes."

Only in *The Oregon Trail* was Parkman a sharer and a spectator, accountable to no research sources, depending only upon his senses and his ability to assimilate what he experienced and to put on paper what Bernard De Voto

---

*It appeared in book form in March 1849, three months before the death of President James K. Polk, on June 15, in Nashville, at the age of fifty-three, three months and twelve days after he left office.

called "one of the exuberant masterpieces of American literature."

Parkman returned west of the Mississippi but once, a visit to Saint Louis in 1867, where in the nearby town of Carondelet he was reunited with his noble old guide, Henry Chatillon. "Time hung heavy on his hands," the Bostonian said of his "brave and truehearted" friend, "as usual with old mountain-men married and established."

They met two years before the Union Pacific and Central Pacific rails linked up at Promontory Point, Utah, at a time when a government "peace commission" was concluding treaties at Medicine Lodge Creek in Kansas, with the Arapaho, Cheyenne, Comanche, and Kiowa. These papers were to establish reservations and provide the Indian with everything he abhorred: a fixed residence, farms, schools, allowances of food and clothing, restrictions on areas he could hunt.

Among the snippets of news Parkman learned from Chatillon was the fate of Old Smoke and his people, that "band of the hated Sioux" at Horse Creek, "with whom," the Bostonian said, "I had been domesticated." The guide told him "they had nearly all been killed in fights with the white men."

Parkman kept abreast of western affairs and lamented the "Great changes" he had seen coming in '46. In 1872, in the preface for a new edition of *The Oregon Trail,* he expressed gratitude that his book had not been allowed to fall into oblivion and ascribed its extended life to the interest attached "to the record of that which has passed away never to return . . . . the image of an irrevocable past."

He recalled a time when he and Quincy Shaw rode together by the foot of Pike's Peak on their return journey from Fort Laramie. Shaw said the time would come when the plains would be transformed to a grazing country, the

buffalo giving place to cattle, farmhouses springing up along
the watercourses, and wolves, bears, and Indians "numbered
among the things that were." He and his companion knew,
Parkman wrote, that gold lurked in the seams of the
pristine mountains before them, "but we did not foresee
that it would build cities in the waste, and plant hotels and
gambling-houses among the haunts of the grizzly bear."
They knew in 1846 that the Mormons—"a few fanatical
outcasts"—were "groping their way across the plains seeking asylum from gentile persecution," but did not imagine
that "the polygamous hordes . . . would rear a swarming Je-
rusalem in the bosom of solitude itself.

"We knew that, more and more, year after year, the trains
of emigrant wagons would creep in slow procession towards
barbarous Oregon or wild and distant California," he wrote,
"but we did not dream how Commerce and Gold would
breed nations along the Pacific, the disenchanting screech
of the locomotive break the spell of weird, mysterious mountains."

Even in '46 Parkman wrote in a melancholy mood about
the dwindling of the buffalo, the end of the Indian way of
life as they became abased by liquor and harried by the military, and the disappearance of the west he saw in all "its
dangers and charms." Twenty-six years later he reflected on
these inexorable changes. The Indian, whom he tried to depict honestly in his journal, and the mountain man, whom
he saw somewhat more romantically, symbolized for Parkman the sad passage of the Old West he knew.

"The wild cavalcade that defiled with me down the gorges
of the Black Hills, with its paint and war-plumes, fluttering
trophies and savage embroidery, bows, arrows, lances, and
shields, will never be seen again," he said. "Those who
formed it have found bloody graves, or a ghastlier burial in
the maws of wolves. The Indian of to-day, armed with a re-
volver and crowned with an old hat, cased, possibly, in
trousers or muffled in a tawdry shirt, is an Indian still, but

an Indian shorn of the picturesqueness which was his most conspicuous merit."

Of the Henry Chatillons he had known, he said, "The mountain trapper is no more, and the grim romance of his wild, hard life is a memory of the past."

He said he had gone out to Fort Laramie in 1846 "in great measure as a student," without a fixed purpose and with somewhat of a youthful rashness. "My business was observation," he said, "and I was willing to pay dearly for the opportunity of exercising it."

4

After twenty-two years as chief factor at Fort Vancouver, John McLoughlin took his leave of the Hudson's Bay Company's service on January 6, 1846. The Company provided him a generous £500 salary for the first year of his retirement, to be followed by a two-year "leave of absence" at full pay, then full retirement at "half-pay," similar to the British army custom for unemployed officers waiting for a war and an active service assignment. Only in McLoughlin's case there would be no more wars, and his services were no longer sought.

He had been forced out and it disturbed him, even though he was quite aware that he had assisted significantly in his own downfall.

He had been at loggerheads with Governor Sir George Simpson almost from the beginning of their relationship, when the two came down from Canada to old Fort George in 1824. They had quarreled frequently, often rancorously, and often about the factor's tendency to bend or break Company regulations and orders or twist them to meet what he believed were immediate needs. One such episode was the time Simpson sent HMS *Beaver* to the Columbia, the first steam-powered vessel on the northwest coast. It did not

impress the factor and he ordered the removal of its engine
to run a Company sawmill.

But the worst moment in their stormy relationship, and the
one McLoughlin could never forgive, was Simpson's officious and abrupt announcement of John McLoughlin, Jr.'s
murder at Stikine in '42 and his willingness to accuse young
John of drunkenness and cruelty, and of creating the mood
of violence that ended his life.

There were other rankling matters as well: Simpson's imperious orders closing certain of the Company's trading
posts that McLoughlin had labored to open and which had
not been given time to show a profit; Simpson's overbearing
anti-American pronouncements; the accusations, both inti-
mated and bald, that the White Eagle not only disobeyed
Company policy and the policies of Whitehall, but that he
aided and abetted the American takeover of the Oregon
Country.

Then there was the matter of the spies Simpson sent to
Fort Vancouver: Peel and Gordon, Warre and Vavasour, the
latter a pair of layabouts who had accused him of encouraging American settlement. They had revealed that he had extended credit to the immigrants over the years in the amount
of about $32,000 American, a sum that Simpson said horri-
fied him and which he reported somewhat too gleefully to
London.

McLoughlin's generosity had yielded a cruel irony. For all
the help and hospitality he had extended to the Americans,
from rescuing Jedediah Smith in '28 and Hall Kelley in '32,
down through the arrival of the Protestant missionaries, the
Whitmans, the Spaldings, and others, and the starving, desperate settlers thereafter—for succoring them all he had
been rewarded with was betrayal. The Americans had wick-
edly short memories: So many of those he befriended, took
into his home, loaned or gave necessities from the Company's stores—so many of them had turned their backs on him.
They lied to the British spies, and even to their own spies

(of whom there had been many, Kelley, Bonneville, Slacum,
Wilkes, and Farnham among them), and besmirched the
Company's name, and thereby his name.

McLoughlin had property, and that too had been used
against him. In 1829 he had claimed land at a place he called
the Falls, a considerable tract south of Fort Vancouver at the
falls of the Willamette River, and built a sawmill there and
some log houses. Eventually he hired a surveyor to lay out
the town that became Oregon City, sold some lots, donated
others for churches and schools, built a gristmill and a two-
story clapboard house on the property. The house was almost
ready for occupancy when McLoughlin departed Fort Vancouver for the last time. He and his beloved Marguérite, his
widowed daughter Louisa and her children, would all enjoy
the place, and his freedom, together.

A man named Samuel R. Thurston became McLoughlin's
final nemesis and deprived the White Eagle of the peaceful
old age and family joys he sought.

Thurston was a lawyer, from Maine originally, a graduate of Bowdoin College, a Methodist, and a one-time editor
of the Burlington, Iowa, *Gazette*. He emigrated to Oregon
toward the end of 1847 and in the raw new territory aligned
his political ambition and gift for hortatory on a single issue: the Hudson's Bay Company's continued "presence" in
and possession of American lands. The perfect embodiment of the problem, in Thurston's thinking, was John
McLoughlin.

"Much has been said about the rude and violent manners
of western men in pursuit of an object," Bancroft said of the
upstart, "but Thurston was not a western man; he was supposed to be something more elevated and refined, more cool
and logical, more moral and Christian than the people beyond the Alleghenies . . . and yet in the canvass of 1849 he
introduced into Oregon the vituperative and invective style

of debate, and mingled with it a species of coarse black-guardism such as no Kentucky ox-driver or Missouri flatboatman might hope to excel."

Thurston's career had a quick and high trajectory and as sudden a collapse.

After the first official meeting of the Territorial Legislature in July 1849, just eighteen months after his arrival in Oregon City, Samuel Thurston, age forty-three, was on his way to Washington as the territory's first delegate to Congress. He fell ill when being escorted across the Columbia bar in a small boat and had not recovered during the sailing to San Francisco and on to Panama. On the Chagres River, in the crossing to the Atlantic side of the isthmus, his baggage was stolen. Despite these travails, in June 1850 he was able to propose a pioneer land bill in the House of Representatives that carried with it provisions to declare John McLoughlin's claims to his Oregon City property null and void.

Thurston wrote other members of the House that McLoughlin had taken the land illegally, forced Methodist missionaries off the tract by threatening to have Indians attack them, and held the claim by threat of violence while making huge profits by selling lots and from other business enterprises. He also accused McLoughlin of refusing to take American citizenship and holding on to the property for the benefit of the Hudson's Bay Company. Among his "infamous lies," Bancroft wrote, was Thurston's statement that the Company "has been warring against our government for forty years," that "Dr. McLoughlin has been their chief fugleman, first to cheat our government out of the whole country, and next to prevent its settlement." He stated that McLoughlin "has driven men from claims and from the country to stifle the efforts at settlement."

Thurston's work did not win the endorsement of all Oregonians or former Oregonians. Nathaniel Wyeth of Cambridge warned Senator Winthrop of Massachusetts to be cautious in reacting to the freshman congressman's diatribes, and in Oregon, McLoughlin learned that many American settlers were indeed grateful for his efforts on their behalf when fifty-six pioneers put together a memorial defending the factor against Thurston's charges.

Unfortunately the petition did not reach Washington until after the congressman's land bill, and most of his charges against McLoughlin, were received and adopted in Congress.

Thurston next prepared a sixteen-page recounting of his services in Washington on behalf of the territory—careful "to leave no possible means by which the man who had founded and fostered Oregon City could retain an interest in it," Bancroft said. He also submitted himself for reelection while the victim of his malice "began the painful and useless struggle to free himself from the toils by which his enemies had surrounded him, and from which he never escaped during the few remaining years of his life."

But Thurston died first, in April 1851, aboard the steamer *California* off Acapulco en route to Oregon from Washington. His death was attributed to "natural causes from chronic ill health." Bancroft said, "Thus while preparing boldly to vindicate his acts and do battle with his adversaries, he was forced to surrender the sword which was too sharp for its scabbard."

In 1852, after McLoughlin had completed his application for United States citizenship, the territorial assembly passed an act accepting his Oregon City property as a gift for the purposes of endowing a university but, with Thurston and his democratic party out of power, there was no movement to evict the White Eagle and his family from the land and they remained at the big whitewashed house until his death.

In his last, relatively calm, years McLoughlin was often seen walking the Oregon City streets in his brass-buttoned swallow-tail coat, ruffled shirt, and black cravat, baggy trousers stuffed into long-legged, beaded Indian moccasins, carrying the gold-headed cane he had once laid alongside the

head of Reverend Herbert Beaver and tipping his tall beaver hat to the ladies. He still looked the Laird of the Pacific
Northwest, but toward the end he became more house-bound,
suffering from diabetes, and had developed a palsy in his
hands that ended his ability to answer correspondence. As
his granddaughter wrote for him from dictation, he checked
each sheet of foolscap with his eagle's eye. If any were blot-
ted she knew she would have to make a clean copy.

In the summer of 1854, Peter Ogden fell ill and was forced
to retire from Hudson's Bay and take up residence with his
wife, daughter, and son-in-law in Oregon City. McLoughlin
visited him regularly and urged Ogden to legalize his
marriage to his Indian wife. This idea did not appeal to the
leathery brigade leader, who said their devotion to one another, and to their several children, was testimony enough
to the sanctity of their relationship.

Ogden died in Oregon City on September 27, 1854, at age
sixty.

In the summer of 1857, McLoughlin met an American lawyer named Lafayette F. Grover of Maine who, ironically, had
come to Oregon at the suggestion of Samuel Thurston. The
White Eagle told the young future district attorney, "I am an
old man and just dying, and you are a young man and will live
many years in this country. As for me, I might better have
been shot like a bull; I might better have been shot forty years
ago." He asked Grover to "give your influence, after I am
dead, to have this property go to my children. I have earned it,
as other settlers have earned theirs, and it ought to be mine
and my heirs'."

Grover promised to do all he could.

On September 3, 1857, McLoughlin's nephew, Dr. Henri
de Chesne, came to look in on his patient and greeted the
old man with his usual salutation, *"Comment allez-vous?"*
This time McLoughlin answered "A Dieu," and died at eleven
that morning, from "gangrenous diabetes," at the age of
seventy-three.

He was buried in an enclosure in the Catholic church of Oregon City and on his tombstone was inscribed the legend, "The Pioneer and Friend of Oregon; also the Founder of this City."

Marguérite McKay McLoughlin died on February 28, 1860, and was laid to rest beside her husband of forty-five years.

The Oregon legislature restored the McLoughlin property to his heirs in 1862.

Herbert Howe Bancroft, who admired McLoughlin above all the great figures in the 300-year Oregon journey, wrote the most eloquent tribute to him:

I think of him as if present; and so he is, though he were dead this quarter century and more. I never saw him, and yet I see him; I never heard him, and yet he speaks to me now; I never grasped his hand, but I feel his presence, and am the better for it. The good that a man does lives after him, saith the seer.

Epilogue

In 1844 the *American Agriculturist* of New York carried an editorial inspired by the success of the "Great Migration" the year before—the one that Horace Greeley said "wears an aspect of insanity." The magazine writer, carried aloft by the spirit if not by the eloquence of Manifest Destiny, opined that "we might as well undertake to stay the sun and moon in their course over the peaks of the Rocky Mountains, as emigration to the west by the hardy nomadic population of our country." He went further: "Who will not take the risk of being scalped by Indians, or devoured by grisley [sic] bears, to say nothing of sustaining innumerable hardships for a succession of years, and living free from all moral and civil restraints, to emigrate to the Ultima Thule . . . the El Dorado of the final borders of the great illimitable west!"

By Ultima Thule and El Dorado the writer meant Oregon, but within four years of the writing the words were being applied to California.

The first book edition of Francis Parkman's masterpiece appeared with the title *The California and Oregon Trail: Being Sketches of Prairie and Rocky Mountain Life*. The author had not authorized inserting "California" into the

title since he had made no reference to the California Trail
in the book, but the publisher clearly intended making the
most of the public fixation on the road that led to the goldfields.

Parkman may have been fuming, but George Putnam's
publishing firm knew what would boost sales.

At the time the book appeared in March 1849, over a year
had passed since the first silt-like gold and small nuggets had
been found in the race of a sawmill owned by John Augustus
Sutter on the south fork of the American River in northern
California. For a time the discovery was kept localized, but
word of it inevitably spread to San Francisco, then shot
eastward.

At the uppermost estimate, there had been 1,000 emigrants in the "Great Migration" of '43; 4,000 in 1844 and
5,000 in 1845, a very small trickle of these rolling south at
Fort Bridger or Fort Hall to the California Trail. There had
been some slight falling off in the emigrant numbers during
the Mexican War years, but by 1849, 25,000 to 30,000 people, including 1,000 children, 2,000 women, and 60,000 animals, were clogging the Oregon Trail between South Pass
and Fort Bridger, most of them bound for the goldfields—
and this represented only about a third of those being somewhat ambitiously called "argonauts." The majority chose
alternate routes: southwestern trails such as that followed by
Colonel Kearny in his march from Santa Fé to Los Angeles; deadly desert paths across Mexico; isthmian crossing of
the fever swamps of Panama and Nicaragua (six weeks from
New York to San Francisco and in 1849, $400–$500 per person); and the old Cape Horn sea route. Fully 16,000 people
reached San Francisco by sea in 1849, and 12,000 in 1850.
The average voyage from eastern ports or New Orleans via
Cape Horn took 200 days, and the cheapest ticket cost $200.

The overland argonauts followed the traditions of their Oregonian predecessors. They were struck by a cholera epidemic in western Missouri that killed 1,000 of them before

they got a fair start, and they overloaded their wagons. They learned what was essential and what was not, heaved overside expensive gold-washing machines sold to them by fast-talking entrepreneurs in Saint Louis and Independence, plus weighty tools, furniture, and similar impediments. Even wagons, some of them perfectly workable, were left behind in the rush to get to California and dip gold out of the streams and chip it off the mountains. Wagons and oxen were traded for pack animals as hopeful miners threw together a few belongings and supplies and made up a pack train or rode on across the prairies with a single horse or mule for company.

Along the south bank of the Platte the Trail was strewn with wagon hulks, the boxes, wheel-spokes and anything burnable broken up for firewood, and a detritus of other abandonments—piles of rancid bacon, yokes and horse collars, wheelbarrows, household goods, rusting machinery—as the Forty-niners fled toward their end of the rainbow.

Beyond South Pass, more than half of the gold seekers followed the well-traveled Oregon Trail routes that led south to Fort Bridger, or north to Fort Hall, from these points aiming toward the Humbolt River valley. Some struck due west across the sagey wastes between South Pass and the Green River, and others, desperately short of supplies, followed the Mormon Trail to Salt Lake City. There they swapped their bags of beans, rice, and oats for fresh vegetables and meat, and traded their wagons and oxen (at a common rate of six trail-worn and skinny animals for two fresh and fat ones). They then proceeded around the rim of the Salt Lake to trudge across the desert wastelands that would take them to the Humboldt, the place where the California trails, detours, and cutoffs merged.

When the winter of '49 closed in, there were 10,000 argonauts at the foot of, or struggling across, the Sierra Nevada passes, a potential Donner party of such staggering proportions that $100,000 was appropriated for the army in

California to mount rescue and relief work. In the end, miraculously, few lives were lost.

By 1850, the California-bound overlanders, as well as the dwindling number trekking to Oregon, were traveling light, depending upon the Trail's booming trading posts between western Missouri and the Snake or Truckee valleys for outfitting. These trailside emporia ranged from tented or brush-and-board gambling hells to hammered-up plank buildings with windows and large-lettered signs selling food, whiskey, draft and pack animals, placer gold mining equipment, repair and even mail services.

The Oregon and California Trail traveler of 1850 also found ferries in operation, with prices escalating from forty cents each for wagons crossing the Sweetwater to sixteen dollars to cross the Green.

By then there were even bridges going up across the Platte, the Laramie, the Bear, and the Portneuf below Fort Hall, although there were few similar luxuries for the Oregon-bound between Hall and the Willamette valley. Fort Boisé and Fort Walla Walla remained virtually unchanged since the days when the Hudson's Bay Company ruled the Oregon Country.

In 1850, the third year of California gold, the number of Oregon Trail travelers increased to 55,000. (At Fort Laramie, now an army post, a tally was made of the people, wagons, and livestock passing through that year: 7,472 mules; 30,616 oxen; 22,742 horses; 5,270 cows; 8,998 wagons.) Of that crush of 55,000, only about 400 were headed to Oregon.

Even Oregonians were going to California in the gold rush years, thousands of them, and only half returned. During the trial of the Whitman massacre defendants, Governor Joseph Lane, mysteriously absent, was widely rumored to be at his gold diggings on California's Tuolumne River.

California gold ended Oregon's supremacy as the Ultima Thule of westward emigration and transformed, for the rest of its history, the White Man's Great Medicine Road. The Oregon Trail served for seven or eight years as the main overland thoroughfare in the 300-year journey to the Pacific Northwest; after 1848 it became the trail that intersected the trail to California.

In 1890, an assemblage of pioneers, children and grandchildren of pioneers met in Portland. The group debated a resolution that would extend membership in the organization to those who arrived in Oregon (or Washington, which gained territorial status in 1853, statehood in 1889) on or before February 14, 1859, the date of Oregon statehood. The old bylaws had established January 1, 1855, as the terminal date for those who could be considered "pioneers."

One of the 1849 pioneers present at the meeting drew a distinction between the overlanders and those arriving on shipboard:

> The word pioneer meant foot-soldier, foot-traveler; it properly represents the condition of those who came to this country as foot-travelers, and that word prepares the way. . . . I am very much opposed to extending the time beyond 1854. A pioneer is not a pioneer when he can get on a steamship in the port of New York, pay his passage, get three good meals a day, get a berth to sleep in at night, and be landed here with all his bag and baggage, without effort on his part; he is not a pioneer in any sense of the word.

Not until 1894, at the twenty-second annual reunion of the pioneers association, was the amendment passed extending the date to 1859.

By 1869, when the transcontinental railroad was completed, something on the order of 400,000 men, women, and children had made the 2,000-mile journey from the Missouri frontier to the Pacific Coast on the Oregon Trail and fulfilled the ambition of presidents from Thomas Jefferson to James K. Polk, and visionaries from Hall Jackson Kelley to Jesse Applegate, who saw the United States stretching "from sea to shining sea."

SOURCES

The literature of the old Oregon Country and the Oregon Trail—scholarly material, first-person accounts by participants in the saga, popular works—is massive and, for any new writer of the story, rich beyond imagining.

Some illustrative examples:

• In the 1930s, Philip Ashton Rollins, a New York lawyer, followed virtually every footstep of Robert Stuart's epic journey from Astoria to Saint Louis for the purpose of editing and annotating a new edition of Stuart's journals. The result was a breathtaking work of scholarship, *Robert Stuart's Narratives of His Overland Trip Eastward from Astoria in 1812–1813* (1935), available in a recent edition from the University of Nebraska Press. The opening sixteen-page biography of Stuart has 174 footnotes.

• The eminent Nebraska historian Merrill J. Mattes (1910–1996), in writing *The Great Platte River Road,* examined over 700 eyewitness overland narratives (only about half of which had been published) and listed at least 1,000 sources for his masterwork.

• *The Plains Across: The Overland Emigrants and the Trans-Mississippi West, 1840–60* was published in 1979, three years after the tragic death from a brain tumor of its thirty-nine-year-old author, John D. Unruh, Jr., of South Dakota. His magisterial book, indispensable to any writer on the mid-century West, contains such meticulous data as the average travel time for overlanders to California in the period 1841–48 (157.7 days) and those to Oregon (169.1 days).

• Francis Parkman, a formidable scholar himself, would

have admired the work of E. N. Feltskog, whose edited
edition of Parkman's *The Oregon Trail* (1849) is a model, if
not *the* model, for reintroducing such classics to new gen-
erations of readers. The recent University of Nebraska Press
edition of Feltskog's Parkman contains a staggering 314
pages of notes and bibliography, not a line of which is unimportant.

In recounting the Astor experiment in Oregon, I have
made extensive use of Washington Irving's *Astoria, or Anecdotes of an Enterprise Beyond the Rocky Mountains* (published in 1836 in two volumes), recognizing that it was a
work-for-hire, a collaboration, said Irving authority Alfred
Powers, between "the nation's Midas and the nation's Homer,"
and therefore predictably pro-Astor. Irving was paid $5,000
by the financier to write the book, and earned another
$12,000 in royalties from its substantial sale. James Feni-
more Cooper, when he heard of the Astor-Irving alliance,
predicted that Irving would make Astor "greater than
Columbus," and H. H. Bancroft declared that the book
contained "a current of unqualified sycophancy, trickery,
sentimentality, and maudlin praise." In scattered places,
Bancroft said, Irving's language was often "strange" and
filled with "effeminate inconsistency," but, worse than that
peculiarly phrased charge, declared that "many of its most
brilliant passages are pure fiction."

Whatever the case for these accusations, Irving inter-
viewed all the central characters and had access to Astor's
correspondence and papers as well as the great nabob himself, and his book is much more trustworthy than Bancroft
would have us believe. It is ironic that Bancroft was so tren-
chantly critical of Irving and De Voto so persistently critical of Parkman, because the most eloquent of the old writers
on the old Oregon Country are Washington Irving and Herbert Howe Bancroft, Francis Parkman's is the best book on
the Oregon Trail written by a contemporary, and De Voto's
work on the entire era remains indispensable.

Of modern writers of Oregon and the Oregon Trail, David Lavender has few, if any, peers; of modern publishers, the University of Nebraska Press (through its Bison Books reprints) has contributed more to the overland epic than any other, with the University of Oklahoma Press, the Arthur H. Clark Company, and Caxton Printers of Caldwell, Idaho, all having a significant share in the imposing literature of the era.

As always, the late Dan L. Thrapp's masterly *Encyclopedia of Frontier Biography* has saved countless hours in the writing of this book. I recommend the University of Nebraska Press CD-ROM version (1995) for quick reference, and the hardbound or paperback versions for a leisurely reading and education.

BIBLIOGRAPHY

John Bakeless, *Lewis and Clark: Partners in Discovery.* New York: William Morrow, 1947.

Bancroft, Herbert Howe. *History of the Northwest Coast.* New York: The Bancroft Co., 1884; two volumes.

————. *History of the Pacific States of North America: California.* San Francisco: The History Company, 1886–1890; seven vols.

Batman, Richard. *The Outer Coast.* New York: Harcourt Brace Jovanovich, 1985.

Bergeron, Paul H. *The Presidency of James K. Polk.* Lawrence: University Press of Kansas, 1987.

Bidwell, John. *Echoes of the Past.* New York: The Citadel Press, 1962; reprint ed.

Billington, Ray Allen. *Westward Expansion: A History of the American Frontier.* New York: The Macmillan Co., 1967.

Blacker, Irwin R. *Westering.* Cleveland, Ohio: The World Publishing Co., 1958.

Blevins, Winfred. *Give Your Heart to the Hawks.* Plainview, New York: Nash Publishing Co., 1973.

Case, Robert O. *The Empire Builders.* Portland, Oregon: Binfords & Mort, 1949.

Clark, Keith, and Lowell Tiller. *Terrible Trail: The Meek Cutoff, 1845.* Bend, Oregon: Maverick Publications, 1993.

Delano, Alonzo. *Life on the Plains and* Among *the Diggings.* Auburn, New York: Miller, Orton & Mulligan, 1854.

Denton, V. L. *The Far West Coast*. Toronto: J. M. Dent & Sons, 1924.

De Voto, Bernard. *Across the Wide Missouri*. New York: Houghton Mifflin Co., 1947.

―――. *The Year of Decision: 1846*. Boston: Little, Brown, 1943.

Dickens, Charles. *American Notes*. Introduction by Christopher Lasch. Greenwich, Connecticut: Fawcett Books, 1961.

Doughty, Howard. *Francis Parkman*. New York: The Macmillan Co., 1962.

Drury, Clifford Merrill. *Marcus and Narcissa Whitman and the Opening of Old Oregon*. Glendale, California: Arthur H. Clark Co., 1973; 2 vols.

Drury, Clifford Merrill, ed. *On to Oregon: The Diaries of Mary Walker and Myra Eells*. Lincoln: University of Nebraska Press, 1998. Reprint ed.

―――. *The Mountains We Have Crossed: Diaries and Letters of the Oregon Mission, 1838*. Lincoln: University of Nebraska Press, 1999. Reprint ed.

Du Pratz, Antoine LePage. *The History of Louisiana*. London: T. Becket, 1774. (Reprinted in New Orleans by J. S. W. Harman-son, n.d.)

Egan, Ferol. *Frémont: Explorer for a Restless Nation*. New York: Doubleday, 1977.

Eggenhofer, Nick. *Wagons, Mules and Men*. New York: Hastings House, 1961.

Farragher, John Mack. *Women and Men on the Overland Trail*. New Haven: Yale University Press, 1979.

Ferris, Robert G., ed. *Soldier and Brave*. Washington, D.C.: U.S. Department of the Interior, National Park Service, 1971.

Franchère, Gabriel. A *Voyage to the Northwest Coast of America*. Chicago: R. R. Donnelley & Co., 1954. Reprint of 1854 edition.

Franzwa, Gregory M. *The Oregon Trail Revisited*. Tucson: Patrice Press, 1997.

Frémont, John C. *Memoirs of My Life*. New York: Belford, Clarke & Co., 1887; two volumes.

Gilbert, Bill. *The Trailblazers*. New York: Time-Life Books, 1973.

Gulick, Bill. *Roadside History of Oregon*. Missoula, Montana: Mountain Press, 1991.

Hafen, LeRoy R., ed. *Fur Trappers and Traders of the Far Southwest*. Logan: Utah State University Press, 1997. Reprint ed.

————. *Mountain Men and Fur Traders of the Far West*. Lincoln: University of Nebraska Press, 1982. Reprint ed.

————. *Broken Hand: The Life of Thomas Fitzpatrick: Mountain Man, Guide and Indian Agent*. Denver: Old West Publishing Co., 1973.

Hafen, LeRoy R., and Carl Coke Rister. *Western America*. Englewood Cliffs, New Jersey: Prentice-Hall, 1950.

Hawgood, John A. *America's Western Frontiers: The Exploration and Settlement of the Trans-Mississippi West*. New York: Alfred A. Knopf, 1967.

Hill, William E. *The Oregon Trail, Yesterday and Today*. Caldwell, Idaho: The Caxton Printers, 1987.

Holliday, J. S. *The World Rushed In: The California Gold Rush Experience*. New York: Simon & Schuster, 1981.

Holmes, Kenneth L., ed. *Covered Wagon Women: Diaries & Letters from the Western Trails, 1853–1854*. Lincoln: University of Nebraska Press, 1998. Six volumes, reprint ed.

Horn, Huston. *The Pioneers*. New York: Time-Life Books, 1974.

Irving, Washington. *Astoria*. Portland, Oregon: Binfords & Mort Publishers, n.d. (Original edition, 1836).

Jackson, Donald, and Mary L. Spence, eds. *The Expeditions of John Charles Frémont*. Urbana: University of Illinois Press, 1970. Two volumes.

Jackson, John C. *Children of the Fur Trade: Forgotten Metis of the Pacific Northwest*. Missoula, Montana: Mountain Press, 1995.

Johansen, Dorothy O. *Empire of the Columbia: A History of the Pacific Northwest*. New York: Harper & Row, 1967.

Lavender, David. *The Fist in the Wilderness*. Garden City, New York: Doubleday, 1964.

———. *Land of Giants: The Drive to the Pacific Northwest*. Lincoln: University of Nebraska Press, 1979.

———. *The Overland Migrations: Settlers to Oregon, California, and Utah*. Washington, D.C.: U.S. Department of the Interior, National Park Service, n.d.

———. *The Way to the Western Sea: Lewis and Clark Across the Continent*. New York: Harper & Row, 1988.

———. *Westward Vision: The Oregon Trail*. New York: McGraw-Hill, 1963.

Lyman, Horace S. *History of Oregon*. New York: The North Pacific Publishing Co., 1903. Three volumes.

McDougall, Walter A. *Let the Sea Make a Noise: A History of the North Pacific from Magellan to MacArthur*. New York: Basic Books, 1993.

McGlashin, Charles F. *History of the Donner Party*. Ann Arbor, Michigan: University Microfilms, Inc., 1966. (Original edition, 1879.)

Marks, Paula Mitchell. *Precious Dust: The American Gold Rush Era, 1848–1900*. New York: William Morrow, 1994.

Mattes, Merrill J. *The Great Platte River Road*. Lincoln: University of Nebraska Press, 1987. Reprint ed.

Morgan, Dale L. *Jedediah Smith and the Opening of the West*. Lincoln: University of Nebraska Press, 1964. Reprint ed.

Morris, Richard B. *Encyclopedia of American History*. New York: Harper & Brothers, 1961.

Morrison, Dorothy N. *The Eagle & the Fort: The Story of John McLoughlin*. New York: Atheneum, 1979.

Moulton, Candy. *Roadside History of Nebraska.* Missoula, Montana: Mountain Press, 1997.

Murphy, Virginia Reed. "Across the Plains to the Sierra Nevada with the Donner Party." *Century Magazine,* July 1891.

Nevins, Allan. *Frémont: Pathmarker of the West.* New York: Longmans, Green, 1939.

Noy, Gary, ed. *Distant Horizon: Documents from the Nineteenth Century American West.* Lincoln: University of Nebraska Press, 1999.

Parkman, Francis. *The Oregon Trail,* edited by E. N. Feltskog. Lincoln: University of Nebraska Press, 1994.

Paxon, Frederic Logan. *The Last American Frontier.* New York: The Macmillan Co., 1924.

Peavy, Linda, and Ursula Smith. *Pioneer Women: The Lives of Women on the Frontier.* Norman: University of Oklahoma Press, 1998.

Pelzer, Louis. *The Cattlemen's Frontier.* Glendale, California: Arthur H. Clark Co., 1936.

Reinfeld, Fred. *Trappers of the West.* New York, Dell Books, 1964.

Robertson, R. G. *Competitive Struggle: America's Western Fur Trading Forts,* 1764–1865. Boise, Idaho: Tamarack Books, 1999.

Ronda, James P. *Astoria and Empire.* Lincoln: University of Nebraska Press, 1990.

Rollins, Philip Ashton, ed. *The Discovery of the Oregon Trail: Robert Stuart's Narratives of His Overland Trip Eastward from Astoria in 1812–1813.* Lincoln: University of Nebraska Press, 1995. Reprint of 1935 ed.

Ross, Alexander. *Adventures of the First Settlers on the Oregon.* New York: The Citadel Press, 1969. Reprint of 1848 edition.

———. *The Fur Hunters of the Far West.* Norman: University of Oklahoma Press, 1956.

Rumer, Thomas A. *The Wagon Trains of '44.* Spokane, Washington: Arthur H. Clark Co., 1990.

Rumer, Thomas A., ed. *The Emigrating Company: The 1844 Oregon Trail Journal of Jacob Hammer.* Spokane, Washington: Arthur H. Clark Co., 1990.

Russell, Carl P. *Traps & Tools of the Mountain Men.* New York: Alfred A. Knopf, 1967.

Stegner, Wallace, et al. "The Oregon Trail," in *Trails West.* Washington, D.C.: National Geographic Society, 1979.

Stewart, George R. *The California Trail.* New York: McGraw-Hill, 1971. Reprint ed.

———. *Ordeal by Hunger: The Story of the Donner Party.* New York: Henry Holt & Co., 1936.

Stokesbury, James L. "Francis Parkman on the Oregon Trail," *American History Illustrated,* December 1973.

Sullivan, Maurice S. *Jedediah Smith: Trader and Trailbreaker.* New York: Press of the Pioneers, 1936.

Thrapp, Dan L. *Encyclopedia of Frontier Biography.* Glendale, California: Arthur H. Clark Co., 1988. Three volumes. (CD-ROM version by University of Nebraska Press, 1995.)

———. *Encyclopedia of Frontier Biography: Supplemental Volume.* Spokane, Washington: Arthur H. Clark Co., 1994.

Unger, Irwin. *These United States: The Questions of Our Past.* Englewood Cliffs, New Jersey: Prentice-Hall, 1989.

Unruh, John D., Jr. *The Plains Across: The Overland Emigrants and the Trans-Mississippi West, 1840–60.* Urbana: University of Illinois Press, 1979.

Van Orman, Richard A. *The Explorers: Nineteenth Century Expeditions in Africa and the American West.* Albuquerque: University of New Mexico Press, 1984.

Vestal, Stanley. *Joe Meek: The Merry Mountain Man.* Caldwell, Idaho: The Caxton Printers, 1952.

Victor, Francis Fuller. *The River of the West: The Adventures of Joe Meek.* (Volume I: The Mountain Years).

Missoula, Montana: Mountain Press, 1983. Reprint of the 1870 ed.

Wagner, Henry R., and Charles L. Camp. *The Plains & Rockies: A Critical Bibliography of Exploration, Adventure and Travel in the American West, 1800–1865.* San Francisco: John Howell Books, 1982.

Webber, Bert, ed. *Dr. John McLoughlin, Master of Fort Vancouver, Father of Oregon.* Medford, Oregon: Webb Research Group, 1994.

Williams, Lucia. "A Letter Home." Text and photographs by Jerry Gildemeister. *American History Illustrated,* January 1988.

Winther, Oscar Osburn. *The Old Oregon Country.* Lincoln: University of Nebraska Press, 1969. Reprint of 1950 ed.

INDEX

Aberdeen, Lord, 402, 403
Aborigines Protection Society, 296
Absaroka Indians. *See* Crow Indians
Adams, John Quincy, 180–83, 221, 409
Adams-Onís Treaty (1819), 182–84, 409
Admiralty Inlet, 307
Africa, Ledyard in, 55–56
Aiken (sailor), 111–12
Alaska
    boundary of, Russian agreement, 183, 409–10
    exploration and trade in, 26, 29, 31, 50–51, 58–64
Alexander I (czar), 183
Alta California
    capital of, 231–32
    cattle in, 302, 303–4
    Frémont's expedition in, 353–54
America, H.M.S., 402–3
American Agriculturalist, 474
American Board of Foreign Missions, 332–33, 338, 436
American Falls (of the Snake), 380
American Fur Company, 94, 216, 228
American Notes (Dickens), 341*n*
American Philosophical Society, 341*n*
American Society for Encouraging the Settlement of Oregon Territory, 226, 240
Amity (New York), 266, 268, 278
Ancient Bluff Ruins (Oregon Trail), 376
Apache Indians, 230
Applegate, Charles, 388, 390, 393
Applegate, Jesse, 386–91, 393, 402–3
Applegate, Lindsey, 388, 390. 393
Arapaho Indians, 156, 171–73, 177, 272, 273, 465
argonauts, 475–78
Arikara Indians, 88, 130–31, 204, 389
    Ashley-Henry fight with, 207–9, 214
Arkansas River. *See* Bent's Fort
Army. *See* United States Army

art, Western, 216, 281
Ash Hollow (Oregon Trail), 376
Ashley, William Henry, 193, 203–6, 214–15, 340, 389
Assiniboine Indians, 88, 204, 281
Astor, John Jacob, 51, 90, 93–97, 106, 107–8, 114, 227
    attempted reopening of Astoria by, 181–82, 187
    death of, 462, 462*n*
    Great Lakes operations of, 178, 182
    Hunt's overland sending of dispatches to, 135, 147–77
    Irving's book subsidized by, 482
    overland expedition of. *See* Fort Astoria (Oregon)—overland expedition to
    Stuart's 1813 audience with, 177–78
    Thorn and, 97, 98, 101, 102, 104, 105, 108, 109, 115
    on *Tonquin* disaster, 121
    War of 1812 and, 137
Astoria (Irving), 482
Astoria (Oregon). *See* Fort Astoria
Astrolabe (ship), 31–32

Bancroft, Hubert Howe, 25, 39, 40, 45, 51, 52, 100, 114, 115, 117, 118, 138, 141, 146, 151, 189, 190–91, 198, 200, 206, 213, 219, 222, 223, 224, 226, 230, 232, 237–39, 249–51, 257, 259, 274, 279, 282, 285, 296–97, 301, 307, 308, 310–11, 317, 324, 333, 335–38, 343, 344, 396, 403, 407, 414, 438, 442, 450, 457, 458, 460, 469, 470–71, 473, 482
Banks, Sir Joseph, 55
Bannock Indians, 207, 288
Baranov, Alexandr Andreevich, 136
Barbary Wars, 97
Barkley, Charles, 32
Barlow, Samuel, 380*n*
Barnes, Jane, 16, 141–42

Baylies, Francis, 221
Bear Flag Republic, 427
Bear Lake, 206, 211
Bear River, 158, 194, 289, 331, 354, 477
Beaver, Herbert, 16, 293, 295–96, 472
Beaver (brigantine), 135–37, 150
beaver *(Castor canadensis)*, 16, 39, 81, 84–86
    Ashley-Henry expeditions to trap, 203–14
    description of, 84–86
    plan to trap to extinction in Oregon, 191–96, 214–16
Beaver (steamship), 277, 293
Bellevue (Nebraska), 270
Benoit (mountain man), 87
Bent, William, 393*n*
Bent's Fort (Arkansas River), 322, 337, 393*n*, 421, 430
Benton, Jesse (brother of Thomas), 349
Benton, Thomas Hart, 220, 238, 349, 412–15
Bering, Vitus, 26
Bidwell, John, 320–21, 324, 327, 329–30, 331, 337
Big Horn River, 88, 89, 133, 204
Bitterroot valley (Montana), 326
Black, Arthur, 212
Blackfeet Indians, 88, 130, 160, 161, 164–65, 193, 194, 204, 213, 244, 252, 269, 272, 274, 276, 281, 326, 442
    Colter's escape from, 89–90
Blackhawk War, 422
Black Mountains, 210
Blevins, Win, 218
Bligh, William, 28
Bloomer, Amelia, 379*n*
Blue Mountains, 135, 152, 153, 193, 291–92, 316, 380, 393, 441, 453, 456
boats
    of buffalo hides (bull boats), 176, 244, 270, 284, 375–76, 391
    of Great Plains Indians, 176–77
    of Hudson's Bay Company, 198
    of Northwest Indians, 35
    of overland expedition, 128, 129, 131
    See also canoes
Bodega Bay (California), 27
Boisé River, 154, 290
Bonneville, Benjamin Louis Eulalie, 244, 246, 258, 270, 282, 316, 340, 354, 469
Boone, Daniel, 90–91, 130, 349, 384
Boone, Nathan, 345

Bordeaux, James, 377
Boston (ship), 67–71
botanists on overland expedition, 129
Botany Bay (Australia), 32, 254
bourgeois ("bushway"), 215
Boussole (ship), 31–32
Bradbury, John, 129
Bridger, James, 91, 194, 205, 209, 243, 274, 340, 379
    Whitman operates on, 216, 272
Bridger, Mary Ann, 318, 446, 447
bridges, 477
Britain
    early 19th-century tension between U.S. and, 97–99
    Nootka convention between Spain and, 65, 410
    Oregon boundary settlement between U.S. and, 412–15
    Oregon claimed by, 44, 410
    in War of 1812, 136–40
British East India Company, 95
Broken Hand. *See* Fitzpatrick, Thomas
Brownson, John, 177
Brule (Nebraska), 330
Brulé Sioux Indians, 377, 427
Brummel, Beau, 85
Bryant, Edwin, 373, 377
Bryant, William Cullen, "Thanatopsis," 40
Buchanan, James, 399, 412
buffalo
    danger to wagon trains from, 330, 369
    Parkman's "hunt" for, 426–27
    unneeded slaughtering of, 329, 369–70
buffalo chips, 284, 369
Bull Bear, Chief, 420
bullwhackers, 363
Burnett, Peter Hardeman, 365, 387, 388*n*, 390
Burton, Richard, 377
Byron, Lord, 349

Cabrillo, Juan Rodríguez, 16, 24, 56
Cache Valley (Utah), 206, 210, 214
Cadboro (schooner), 235
Calapooya Indians, 252–54
California
    annexation of, 401, 439
    as emigrant goal, 320–21, 325, 331, 475
    Farnham in, 324
    Gold Rush of, 475–78
    Greeley's trip to, 383–84
    Oregon Trail turnoff to, 380

Panama shortcut to, 359
Russia in, 26–27
Smith's expeditions to, 210–14
Spanish in, 26–27
Wilkes' prediction on, 307
See also Alta California
California (steamer), 471
California Hill (Oregon Trail), 376
California Trail, 423, 475
Canada, U.S. boundary with
    Columbia River suggested, 308, 411
    Tyler administration treaty, 313
Canadians
    in Oregon Country, 303
    See also French-Canadian trappers
Canfield, W. D., 449
cannibalism
    by Donner-Reed party, 434
    suggested, in Stuart's party, 165
canoes
    of French-Canadians, at New York
        City, 92–93
    of Northwest Indians, 29, 35–36,
        60, 113
Canton (China), 42, 44, 51, 52, 58–60,
    62, 63, 71, 94, 106, 116, 136,
    137, 140, 142
Cape Mendocino, 24–25, 41, 56
Carlos III (King of Spain), 63
Carson, Alexander, 151
Carson, Christopher "Kit," 91, 151,
    230, 310*n*
    duel between Shunar and, 216, 273
    in Frémont expeditions, 351–54,
        385
Carson Sink, 354
Carthage (Illinois), 345
Carver, Jonathan, 37–38
*Carver's Travels Through the Interior
    Parts of North America in the
    Years 1766, 1767, and 1768*,
    38–39, 40, 45
Cascade Mountains, 123, 221, 380,
    380*n*, 381
Cass, Lewis, 399
Castor canadensis. See beaver
Castor fiber, 84
Catherine II (Empress of Russia), 53
Cathlamet Indians, 177
Cathlasko Indians, 148
Catholicism, 247–48, 295, 326, 332,
    338, 361*n*, 395, 406, 418, 436,
    441, 457–58, 460–61
Catlin, George, 281
Cayuse Indians, 275, 276, 293,
    316–17, 316*n*, 318, 336, 396,
    435, 436–37, 438, 440, 441,
    446–49, 450, 452–53, 461

measles epidemic among, 442–45,
    460
"Cayuse War," 456–59
Chagres River, 359, 470
Champoeg (Oregon), 235, 301, 303,
    311, 403, 453
Chandler, Bill, 421, 424, 427
Chandler, Jack, 421
Charles II (King of England), 82
Chatham (armed tender), 44
Chatillon, Henry, 420, 427, 431, 465,
    467
Chehalem Indians, 34, 115
Chemakane (Washington), 333
Chesne, Henri de, 472
Cheyenne Indians, 329, 465
Chiles, Joseph Ballinger, 387, 392
Chimney Rock (Oregon Trail), 376,
    391
Chinook Indians, 34, 35, 44, 78, 113,
    114, 123, 125, 135, 141, 148,
    177, 180, 292, 307, 321, 456
cholera, 178, 270, 272, 313, 314, 324,
    372, 475
Christian Advocate and Journal, 248,
    256, 263
Cimarron River, 217–18
Clackama Indians, 252
Clark, William, 36, 77, 90, 130, 219
    Indians seek Christian God from,
        247–48, 263
    See also Lewis and Clark Corps of
        Discovery
Clarke, John, 150
Clatsop Indians, 20, 34, 71, 78, 113, 177
Clay, Henry, 180, 399–400
Clayoquot Sound, 42, 43, 116, 118,
    120, 123, 190
Clearwater River, 294, 332
Clive, Robert, 187
Clyman, James, 91, 209
Coeur d'Alêne Indians, 34, 277, 326
Coles, John, 110, 112
Colorado River, 196, 211, 455
Colter, John, 86, 91, 129, 130
Columbia Rediviva (ship), 41, 42, 63
Columbia River, 28, 36–37, 62, 83
    Astoria, 93–94
    bar at entrance of, 140, 408
        Gray's entry, 43–44, 110, 410
        Thorn's disaster at, 110–12
        Wilkes' loss of ship, 306–7
    Lewis and Clark on, 71, 78
    naming of, 20, 44
    Oregon Trail emigrants' passage of,
        381
    as suggested boundary between
        U.S. and Canada, 308, 411

Colville Indians, 22, 36, 123
Comanche Indians, 218, 465
Comcomly, Chief, 114, 123–25, 141
Comekela (Indian), 60, 61
Concise Account of North America (Rogers), 37
Congregational missionaries, 264–65, 266, 315
Congress, U.S.
  Frémont's *Reports* to, 352–53, 355
  Oregon Question in, 219–22, 226, 227, 238, 255–57, 305, 309, 412–13, 415–16
  Oregon Trail and, 385–85
  Thurston's anti-McLoughlin land bill in, 471
Constitution, USS, 98–99
Continental Divide, 167, 378
  first wagons to cross, 244, 271
  first white women to cross, 285
Cook, James ("Captain Cook"), 27–29, 32, 40, 45, 49, 50–51, 56, 57, 58, 59, 65, 184, 410
  death of, 29, 51, 66, 106, 108
Coos Indians, 34
Cortés, Hernán, 24
Council Bluffs (Iowa), 222, 255, 270, 374, 425
Courier (ship), 210–11
Courthouse Rock (Oregon Trail), 376
covered wagons. *See* wagons
cows on the trail, 365, 390
Craig, William, 443, 449–50
Cree Indians, 190, 293, 296
Creek Indians, 349
Crooks, Ramsey, 128, 131, 134, 135, 149, 151–52, 154, 161–64, 167, 168, 170
  later life of, 178–79
Crow Indians (Absaroka Indians), 82, 87–89, 132, 133, 155, 156, 158–60, 167, 172–73, 269
Cunningham, William H., 210
Cushing, Caleb, 256, 309, 314, 315

Daily Missouri Republican, 384
Dalles. *See* The Dalles rapids
"dark horse," first, 399
Dawson, Nicholas, 329
Day, John, 128–29, 135, 149–52
Dayton (Oregon), 396
Day with the Cow Column, A (Applegate), 390
Decatur, Stephen, 97
Democratic convention of 1844, 398–99
Derouin, François, 176

Deslauriers (general factotum), 420, 431
De Smet, Pierre-Jean, 125, 326–28
Detroit Free Press, 179
Deuteronomy (book of the Bible), 371
Devil's Gate (Oregon Trail), 378, 392
De Voto, Bernard, 206, 222, 347, 350–51, 375, 398, 412, 421, 424–25, 464, 482
Dickens, Charles, 340–43, 341*n*, 344
Dickerson, Mahlon, 221, 415
Dickson, Joseph, 86
Discovery (Cook's sloop), 27–29
Discovery (Vancouver's ship), 43, 44
disease, 372–73, 441–42. *See also* cholera
dog-feast, 428
Dolly (schooner), 125
Donner, George, 422–23, 434
Donner, Jacob, 422, 434
Donner, Tamsen, 422
Donner-Reed party, 422–24, 432–34, 440, 449–50, 461–62
Dorion, Pierre and Marguerite, 128, 131, 134, 157–58*n*
Douglas, Captain, 62, 63
Douglas, James, 292, 293
Drake, Sir Francis, 24, 25, 27, 28, 30, 34
Dryad (ship), 237
Duffin, Robert, 62

Eastham, E. L., 374
Eddy, William, 434
Edinburgh Review, 382
Eells, Cushing, 315, 333, 336
elephant, "to see the," 347, 347*n*
Elm Grove (near Independence), 335, 339, 348, 386–90, 392
emigrant, definition of, 375
Emigrant Gap (Oregon Trail), 378
Emigrant's Guide to Oregon and California (Hastings), 423, 433
Encyclopedia of Frontier Biography (Thrapp), 483
English Chief, 46
Escaloom, "Frank," 447

Farnham, Thomas Jefferson, 321–24, 437, 469
Felice (brig), 60–62
Feltskog, E. N., 482
Ferrelo, Bartolome, 24, 27, 34
ferries, 477
Ficklin, Orlando Bell, 385
"Fifty-Four Forty or Fight," 183, 411, 414

Figueroa, José, 229, 234, 235, 300–301
First Organic Laws (Oregon), 312
Fisk, Wilbur, 263
Fitzhugh's Mill (near Independence), 388
Fitzpatrick, Thomas (Broken Hand), 91, 205, 209, 216, 217, 243, 246, 271–73, 282–85, 287, 288, 325–29, 331, 335–36, 340
Five Crows, Chief, 445
Flathead Indians, 34, 79, 89, 210, 233, 247–52, 265, 267, 268, 271–73, 285, 288, 326, 389, 435
Flathead post of Hudson's Bay Company, 210
Fletcher, Francis, 29
Florence (Nebraska), 425
Floyd, Charles, 219
Floyd, John, 219–22, 224, 299
Fontenelle, Lucien, 269–71
Forsyth, John A., 300
Fort Astoria (Oregon), 93–94
    Beaver arrives at, 135–36
    building of, 114–15
    fortification of, 124
    Hunt as factor-in-chief at, 135–38
    loss of life at, 180n
    news of Tonquin massacre received at, 122–23
    North West's purchase of, 138–39, 177, 180–82
    overland expedition to, 123–24, 126–35, 152
        botanists included, 129
        missing men found, 156–57
    schooner launched by, 125
    smallpox epidemic threatened by, 124–25
    Stuart's bringing of dispatches from, 135, 147–77
    U.S. government fails to support Astor's reopening of, 181–82, 187
    War of 1812 and, 137–40
    See also Fort George
Fort Atkinson (Nebraska-Iowa border), 208
Fort Boisé (in Snake River country), 199, 290–91, 336, 380, 393, 477
    post traders at, 385
Fort Bridger, 379, 426, 476
    Hastings Cutoff of Oregon Trail at, 423, 432–33
    post traders at, 385
Fort Chipewyan (Alberta), 46, 47, 83
Fort Clatsop (Oregon), 71, 78, 115

Fort Colville (British Columbia), 277, 286, 315, 406
Fort George (Oregon; formerly Fort Astoria), 139–42
    closing of, 196–97
    McLoughlin as chief factor of, 189–91
    Simpson's 1824 visit to, 185–87
Fort Hall (on Portneuf River), 199, 200, 251, 258, 290, 301, 331, 336, 476, 477
    California recommended to emigrants by, 379–80, 392–93
    post traders at, 385
Fort Laramie (Wyoming), 271–72, 284, 331, 335, 391–92, 425
    description of, 377
    1850 tally of travelers at, 477
    Parkman in, 421, 423, 427–30
    post traders at, 385, 294
Fort Laramie National Historic Site, 15
Fort Leavenworth (Kansas), 283, 344, 347, 421, 455
Fort Mandan (North Dakota), 78
Fort Nez Percé (Fort Walla Walla, Washington), 195, 198–200, 274, 276, 289, 291–94, 317, 380, 393, 436, 450, 452, 456, 460, 477
Fort Okanogan. See Okanogan River
Fort Osage (on Missouri River), 130, 177
Fort Raymond (Manuel's Fort, Montana), 88, 89, 90
Fort Ross (California), 27, 30, 303
Fort Stikine (Alaska), 404–5, 468
Fort Vancouver (Washington), 195
    British officers' visits to, 402–3, 406–7
    chaplain at. See Beaver, Herbert
    description of, 196–98
    establishment of, 196
    Hudson's Bay Company's closing of, 408, 413
    Kelley in, 233–38
    McLoughlin as chief factor at, 196–200
    missionary party at, 292–94
    Parker at, 275–76
    Wyeth in, 236, 245
Fort Walla Walla. See Fort Nez Percé
Foster, William, 434
Fox, John, 110–11
France
    Louisiana Purchase from, 19–20, 76
    Oregon coast exploration by, 30–31

Franchère, Gabriel, 100, 121
Franklin, Benjamin, 52
Franzwa, Gregory W., *The Oregon Trail Revisited*, 15
Fraser River, 47
free land, 313–14, 318–19
Frémont, Jessie Benton, 350, 352–54
Frémont, John C., 80, 178–79, 348–55, 354*n*, 375, 380, 385, 387, 389, 437
French and Indian War, 37
French-Canadian trappers *(voyageurs)*, 82, 85–86, 139–40, 150, 178, 185, 198, 207, 247, 252, 295, 343, 351
   on overland expedition to Astoria, 127, 134
   on sea trip to Astoria, 92–93, 96, 99–104, 106, 109, 110, 113–14
French Prairie (Oregon), 311
frontiersmen. *See* mountain men; trappers
Fuca, Juan de, 26, 29, 32
fur trade, 20, 27, 29–30, 42–44, 46, 58–59
   Astor in, 51, 90, 93–96, 108
   decline along Columbia of, 408
   by Hudson's Bay Company, 82–83
   in jointly occupied Oregon, 187
   Lisa's expeditions, 204
   in Mississippi valley, 128
   Rockies and, 81–82
   Spanish-English conflict over, 63–66
   Thorn's attempt at, 116–18
   See also beaver; sea otter; trappers

Galaup, Jean de. *See* La Pérouse, Comte de
Gallatin, Albert, 182
Gantt, John, 386–89, 393*n*, 436
Gardner, Johnson, 195, 195*n*, 215
George III (King of England), 37, 44, 48, 64, 107
George IV (King of England), 197
Gervais, Joseph, 252
Gila River, 230
Gilliland, Isaac, 447
Golden Hind, 24–25
Gold Rush, 475–78
Gordon, Sir John, 402, 468
Grande Ronde River, 135, 153, 276, 393
Grand Island (Nebraska), 271
Graves, Elizabeth, 434
Graves, Franklin, 434
Gray, Robert, 41–45, 63, 65, 110, 184, 410
Gray, William H., 282, 288, 291, 316, 317, 333, 437

"Great American Desert," 80, 222, 352, 426
Great Basin, 354, 380, 423
Great Migration, 375, 384, 393, 474, 475
Great Plains, 79, 80
Great Platte River Road, The (Mattes), 481
Great Reinforcement, 257
Great Salt Desert, 211
Great Salt Lake, 194–96, 345, 354, 354*n*, 426, 432, 476
Greeley, Horace, 337, 382–84, 474
Green River, 133, 166, 193, 206, 210, 216, 269, 271, 276, 285, 287, 331
   ferries across, 477
   Sublette Cutoff at, 379
Gregg, Josiah, 218
Gros Ventre Indians, 245
Grover, Lafayette F., 472–73

Hafen, Leroy, 328
Haida Indians, 43
Hakluyt's Voyages, 25
Hamilton, Alexander, 65
Hamilton (brig), 254, 333
Hancock, Forrest, 86
Harrison, William Henry, 97, 312–13
Hartford *Times*, 341
Hastings, Lansford W., 335–36, 423, 433
Hawaii (Sandwich Islands), 44–45, 198
   Cook in, 28, 29, 51, 66
   Hunt's sojourn in, 136, 138
   Thorn in, 105–6
Heçeta, Bruno de, 37
Heine, Heinrich, 333
hemp for wagon covers, 361
Henry, Andrew, 203–6, 214, 340
Henry's Fort (Idaho), 133, 156, 163
Henry the Navigator, 75
Heroux (murderer), 405
Hill, Samuel, 70–71
Hinman, C. G., 347*n*
Hoback, John, 156–57, 156*n*
Hood's Canal, 307
Horse Creek, 427, 465
horses, 362, 365
Hudson, Henry, 82
Hudson's Bay Company, 82–83, 94–95, 134, 181, 184, 269, 411
   American missionaries in Oregon as suspect by, 298–99
   Astor and, 126
   California recommended to emigrants by, 279, 392

expeditions into U.S. by, 193–96,
        215
Kelley and, 227, 228, 233, 235–39
main depot moved to Vancouver
        Island, 408, 413, 440
North West Company merged with,
        83, 187, 188, 192
Simpson of, 185–93, 197, 215, 216,
        233, 258, 298, 308
Thurston's attacks on McLoughlin
        and, 469–72
Waiilatpu prisoners ransomed by,
        450, 452
Willamette government recognized
        by, 312, 403
Willamette valley residents'
        memorial against, 322–23
Wyeth and, 258
See also McLoughlin, John
Humboldt River, 196, 354, 423, 433,
        476
Hunt, Wilson Price, 90, 96
        as Astoria factor-in-chief, 135–36,
                138, 147, 182
        final successful voyage of, 140
        later life and death of, 339–40
        as overland-expedition commander,
                126, 129–35, 204

ice business, Wyeth in, 207, 241
Ice Slough (Oregon Trail), 378
Idaho, 347n
Illinois Monthly Magazine, 218
Imperial Eagle (ship), 32–33
Independence (Missouri), 206, 243,
        250, 256, 321, 374
        description of, 344–48
        time to reach Pacific from, 348
Independence Rock (Oregon Trail),
        170, 285, 378, 392
Indian Creek (near Independence), 348
Indians
        aged left behind by, 175
        alcohol in trade with, 205
        Christianizing of, 257, 275, 296,
                314–15, 318–19, 326–27,
                435–39
        end of way of life of, 465–67
        Gray's fights with, 41, 43
        of Great Plains, 113
        "marriages" of traders with, 296
        measles epidemic among, 441–43,
                460
        of Northwest, 34–36, 78, 113
        Palmer as Oregon superintendent
                of, 396
        scalping by, 156
        sign language of, 87, 149, 153

slaves held by, 34–35, 125
Smith's fights with, 207–9, 212–13
Stuart's encounters with, 148–49,
        158–60, 171–74, 177
wagon trains and, 371–72
in Willamette's First Organic Laws,
        312
See also specific tribes
"Indian Sweat," 161–62
Iphigenia (ship), 62, 63
Iroquois Indians, 248
Irving, Washington, 92, 95, 98, 102,
        104, 106, 107, 109, 112, 114–17,
        119–22, 126, 128, 131–35, 140,
        155–60, 161, 165, 167, 168, 171,
        173, 180–82, 344
        Astor-subsidized book by, 482
Isaac Todd (man-of-war), 138–41, 142
Isaiachakalis (Indian), 457

Jackal (ship), 45
Jackson, Andrew, 214, 300, 313,
        397–99
        Nashville gunfight of, 349–50
Jackson, David, 214, 217
Jail House Rock (Oregon Trail), 376
Japan, first U.S. ship in, 45
Jefferson, Peter, 75
Jefferson, Thomas, 20, 40, 47, 65,
        75–76, 90, 99, 129
        Ledyard and, 49, 52–56
        See also Lewis and Clark Corps of
                Discovery
Jesuit missions, 248, 325–26, 334,
        389, 460–61
Jewitt, John R., 68–71
Johnson, Richard M., 399
Jones, Benjamin, 151, 154–55,
        159–60, 164, 171
        later life of, 178
Jones, John Paul, 52
Jones, Roger, 244
Journal of an Exploring Tour Beyond
        the Rocky Mountains (Parker),
        277, 374
Journal of Captain Cook's Last
        Voyage to the Pacific, A
        (Ledyard), 51
Journal of Travels Over the Rocky
        Mountains (Palmer), 395
Juan de Fuca Strait, 26, 29, 32, 61–62,
        302, 307, 402, 411
        Canadian-U.S. boundary in, 413

Kalawatset Indians, 212–13
Kalispell Indians, 34
Kamehameha (King of Hawaii), 106,
        107

Kamiah (Idaho), 332, 461
Kanesville (Iowa), 424
Kansas City (Missouri). *See* Westport Landing
Kansas Indians, 346
Kansas River (Kaw River), 351, 388–89, 424
Kaw Indians, 347, 424
Kearny, Stephen Watts, 421, 430, 455, 475
Kelley, Hall J., 16, 222–39, 240, 249, 253, 256, 257, 263, 299, 300, 468–69
  background of, 223–24
  Oregon trip of, 227–37
Kendrick, John, 41, 42, 44–45, 63
Keseberg, Lewis, 434
Keyes, Sarah, 422
Kiamasumpkin (Indian), 457, 458
Kiowa Indians, 465
Klamath Lake, 195
Klamath River, 212
Klokamas (Indian), 457
Knickerbocker Magazine, 419, 431, 461, 462–63

Lady Washington (sloop), 41–42, 45, 63
Lafayette, Marquis de, 52, 54
Laframboise, Michel, 233–34
Lake Athabasca, 46, 83
Lake Tahoe, 353
Lamanse (Indian interpreter), 115–18, 120, 123
Lane, Joseph, 455, 456–57, 477
La Pérouse, Comte de (Jean de Galaup), 31–32
Lapwai Mission (Idaho), 294, 307, 314–15, 332–37, 435–36, 438–41, 449, 450, 461
LaRamee, Jacques, 377
Lark (ship), 136, 137, 183
Larkin, Rachel Hobson Holmes, 232
Larkin, Thomas O., 232
Lausanne (ship), 256–57, 333
Lavender, David, 222–24, 334, 388, 392
Leavenworth, Henry, 208
LeClairc, François, 151, 164–65, 167, 170, 178
Ledyard, John, 29, 49–56, 76, 107
Lee, Anne Maria Pitman, 254, 255, 255*n*
Lee, Daniel, 233, 236, 250, 322, 323
Lee, Jason, 16, 233, 249–57, 263–64, 273, 293–95, 299, 301, 302, 305, 306, 308, 323, 333, 340, 385
  annexation petition presented to Congress by, 255, 309

Lewis, James, 115, 199, 121
Lewis, Joe (French-Canadian drifter), 442–45, 447, 453, 457
Lewis, Meriwether, 77, 90, 194. *See also* Lewis and Clark Corps of Discovery
Lewis and Clark Corps of Discovery, 20, 40, 47–48, 57, 77–79, 81, 126, 184, 219, 224, 411
  Colter in, 86, 87, 91
  interpreter of, 128
  overland expedition and route of, 130
  on Pacific Coast, 71, 78
  winter quarters of, 71
Liberty (Missouri), 270, 282–83
Liguest, Pierre de Laclède, 343
Lincoln, Abraham, 398, 422
Lincoln, Mary Todd, 422
Lincoln, Robert, 422
Linn, Lewis, 238, 309–10, 314, 334, 335, 350, 384
Linnaean Society of Liverpool, 129
Lisa, Manuel, 87–89, 129–32, 204, 208, 340
Little Sandy Creek, 379
Long, Stephen Harriman, 79–81, 219, 352, 426
Longfellow, Henry Wadsworth, 349
López, Marcus, 42
Loriot (brig), 300, 302–5
Los Angeles (California), 230–31, 439, 455
Louisiana Purchase, 19–20, 76–77, 88
  in Adams-Onís Treaty, 183
Louis IX (King of France), 343
Louis XVI (King of France), 31, 65
Lovejoy, A. L., 337
Lutra enhydris marina. See sea otter
Lydia (brig), 70
Lyman, Horace S., 213*n*

Macao, 58, 59, 63
McClellan, Robert, 128, 131, 135, 148–51, 154, 161, 163–65, 167–68, 170–72
  later life of, 178
McDonald, John, 140
McDougall, Duncan
  Astor's later opinion of, 180–81
  as Astor's proxy, 95, 96, 122, 123–24
  Chinook wife of, 114, 123, 141
  in command of Astoria, 124–25, 138, 139
  as North West partner, 139–40, 180–81
  on voyage to Astoria, 100, 103–5, 114–15

McDuffie, George, 384, 455
"Macedonian Cry," 267, 267n, 332
McKay, Alexander, 47, 95, 96, 105,
    111, 115–19, 139, 190, 213n,
    296
McKay, Thomas, 212–13, 251, 289–90
Mackenzie, Donald, 95–96, 205
    at Astoria, 138, 139, 150
    on overland expedition, 127,
        129–30
Mackenzie, Sir Alexander, 45–48,
    122, 410
Mackenzie River, 46
McKinley, Archibald, 436
McLeod, Alexander, 213–14
McLoughlin, Eloisa, 200
McLoughlin, John, 16, 249
    American spy utilized by, 300–301
    Beaver the chaplain and, 295–98
    as district attorney at Oregon City,
        457
    as Fort George's chief factor,
        189–91
    as Fort Vancouver's chief factor,
        196–200, 406–8
        retirement, 408–9, 467
        Willamette government
            recognized, 312, 403
    hospitality of, 230, 233–36, 245,
        246, 252, 253, 255, 258, 275,
        292–95, 299, 323, 381, 384,
        406–8, 468
    last days and death of, 471–73
    Oregon cattle and, 303
    Oregon City life of, 408–9, 440,
        469, 470–71
    Simpson and, 404–6, 467–68
    Thurston's attacks on, 469–71
    Whitman warned about Cayuse by,
        317, 443
    wife of, 190, 293, 296, 406, 469,
        473
McLoughlin, John, Jr., murder of,
    404–5, 468
McLoughlin, Marguérite Wadin
    McKay, 190, 200
McTavish, Donald, 141–42, 180
McTavish, John George, 138–39
Madison, James, 55, 99, 137, 182
Mad River, 133, 159–60
Magellan, Ferdinand, 66
Mandan Indians, 31, 77–78, 83, 86,
    88, 131, 204, 281
Manifest Destiny, 219–20, 224, 401,
    410, 474
Manuel's Fort (Fort Raymond,
    Montana), 88, 90
Maquinna, 60–62, 65–71

Marcy, Randolph Barnes, 366
Marsh, John, 331
Marsh, William, 447
Martin, John, 110
Martin Chuzzlewit (Dickens), 341n
Mattes, Merrill J., 14, 364, 373n, 481
May Dacre (ship), 250, 252–53
Meares, John, 57–65
measles, 441–43, 460
medicine
    bleeding in, 271, 274
    cholera treatment in, 270–71
    on Oregon Trail, 373–74
Medicine Lodge Creek, 465
Meek, Helen, 318, 445, 448, 452
Meek, Joseph Lafayette, 16, 285, 288,
    311
    on mission to Polk, 452–56
    and murder of Whitmans, 452–53
    as U.S. Marshal, 454, 455, 458
Melville, Herman, 419
Mencken, Henry L., 266–67
Mengarini, Gregory, 326
Methodists, 247–49, 255, 334, 381n,
    387, 436, 444, 459
métis, 188
Mexico
    Kelley in, 229–30
    war with, 401–2, 420, 422, 430,
        439–40, 454, 475
Michaud, André, 76
Michilimackinac Island (Great
    Lakes), 128, 137, 178, 343
Miller, Alfred, 216
Miller, Joaquin, 349
Miller, Joseph, 128, 133, 156, 158,
    171, 174, 1778
missionaries
    in Oregon, 16, 201, 227–28, 233
        Catholic, 247–48, 325–27, 332,
            338, 381n, 389, 441, 457–58,
            460–61
        1842 consolidation, 332–33
        Hudson's Bay Company's
            suspicion of, 298–302
        Indians' request for, 248, 263,
            435
        self-sufficiency as ideal, 319
        Wilkes' opinion, 307, 315
        See also Lapwai Mission;
            Waiilatpu Mission; Willamette
            valley
    Spanish, 63
    women as, 253, 275
    See also Indians—Christianizing of
Missionary Herald, 267
Mississippi River, 79–80, 128, 342
    Carver's expedition on, 37–38

Missouri Fur Company, 204, 208
Missouri Gazette & Public Advertiser, 203, 205
Missouri River, 31, 77–81, 87–88, 169, 175–77, 342
  flora of, 129
  overland expedition on, 126, 129–30
  Saint Louis-Independence segment of, 346–47
  Three Forks of, 194, 326
Miwok Indians, 25
Mojave Indians, 196, 210–12, 230
monogamy, Cayuse rejection of, 276
Monroe, James, 27, 137, 180, 182, 409
Monroe Doctrine, 183, 400, 412
Montana, 347*n*
Monterey (California), 231–32, 304, 324
Montreal (Canada), 93, 95, 145, 342
Morgan, Dale L., 218
Morison, Samuel Eliot, 45
Mormons, 269, 345, 347, 354*n*, 368, 378, 379, 424–26, 456, 466
Mormon Trail, 426, 476
mosquitoes, smoldering chips for chasing away of, 369
mountain men, 86–91, 128–29, 466
  as guides, 217–18, 344, 347
  rendezvous for, 206–7, 216, 243, 272–73, 285–86
Mount Hood, 291, 381
mules, 362, 364
Museum of Westward Expansion (St. Louis), 15

nankeens, definition of, 44
Napa valley, 387
Narrative (Wilkes), 308
Narrative of the Adventures and Suffering . . . (Jewitt), 71
Nashville (Tennessee), Jackson's gunfight in, 349–50
Nauvoo (Illinois), 424–26
Nereid (ship), 295, 324
Nesmith, James M., 388*n*, 390, 393
New Albion, 25, 27, 41
New Orleans (Louisiana), Kelley in, 228
New Orleans Picayune, 384
New York City
  French-Canadian *voyageurs* at, 92–93
  Jason Lee in, 256, 257
  War of 1812 blockade feared in, 137
New York Daily Tribune, 382
New York Ethnological Journal, 40
New York Tribune, 337

Nez Percé Indians, 34, 207, 247, 248, 251, 272, 276, 277, 281–82, 285, 291, 315–18, 396, 439–40, 451, 456, 458
  language of, 288
Nicaragua, 475
Nicollet, Joseph, 351
Niger River, 55
Niles' Register, 412
Nodaway River, 130
Nookamis (subchief), 117
Nootka (ship), 58–59
Nootka Indians, 35, 36, 60–61, 65–66
  Salter and *Boston* crew killed by, 67–71, 97
Nootka Sound, 27, 29, 31, 32, 42, 44, 50–52, 57, 60
  Spanish expedition to, 62–64
Nootka Sound Convention (1790), 66, 183–84, 410
North American Review, 308, 384
North West America (schooner), 62–63
North West Company, 46–47, 83, 94–95, 122, 128, 190
  Astor and, 126, 181
  Fort Astoria purchased by, 138–39, 177–78, 180–82
  Hudson's Bay Company merged with, 83, 187, 188, 192
  Robert Stuart in, 145
  War of 1812 and, 137–39
Northwest Passage, 24, 26–29, 31, 82
Nuttall, Thomas, 129

Oblate missions, 327
Ogden, Peter Skene, 16, 192–96, 210, 215, 295, 440
  last days and death of, 472
  Waiilatpu prisoners ransomed by, 450–51, 452
Oglala Sioux Indians, 272, 377, 394–95, 420, 427–30
Okanogan River (and Fort Okanogan, British Columbia), 123, 147, 149, 150, 199
Old California Crossing (Platte River), 330
Old Smoke, Chief, 427–30, 465
Omaha (Nebraska), 270, 374, 425
Oregon, source of word, 40
Oregon American, 460
Oregon City (Oregon), 381, 381*n*, 391
  Cayuse trial and execution in, 457–58
  McLoughlin's interests in, 408–9, 440, 469, 470
  nine-pounder cannon contributed by, 456

Oregon Country
American emigration to
discouraged by Hudson's Bay
Company, 191, 200, 215
1841 population, 319
in 1847, 441
Farnham and, 321–24
proposals in Congress, 308–10
See also Willamette valley
American spy in. *See* Slacum,
William A.
British-American competition in,
191, 200–201
British claim to, 44, 410–11
British fifty-gun ship sent to, 402
cattle in, 302–3, 310
exploration of coast of, 16, 23–29,
30–33
first steamship to visit, 277, 293
first white child born in, 318
Gray's claim for U.S. of, 44
Great Reinforcement in, 257
Hudson's Bay Company in., 83,
185–200, 309
See also Fort Vancouver
joint occupation by U.S. and Britain
of, 183–84, 188, 299, 409
protests in Congress, 219–22
U.S. termination of agreement,
412–13
Kelley and colonization of, 222–39
Lewis and Clark in, 20. 71, 78–79,
411
Panama shortcut to, 359
plan to trap beaver to extinction in,
191–95, 215–16
Polk's negotiations with British on,
412–13
Polk's policy on, 399–400, 402–12
proposed U.S. military occupation
of, 220–22, 244, 412
Russian renunciation of, 183, 409–10
sailing-ship passage to, 359
southern boundary established,
183, 409–10
statehood proposed for, 415
territorial status granted to, 455,
455n
territorial status proposed for, 314,
415, 440, 453–54
U.S.-British boundary dispute over
final settlement, 412–14
history, 409–13
United States Exploring Expedition
in, 306–8
White appointed U.S. "subagent"
for, 334, 336
See also Fort Astoria

Oregon Dragoons, 321–24
Oregon Mounted Riflemen, 456
Oregon Pioneers Association, 374, 478
Oregon Spectator, 381n
"Oregon Territory," in preamble to
First Organic Laws, 312
Oregon Trail
in British press, 382
campgrounds of, 368
Cascades road constructed from,
380n
Congressional reaction to, 384–85
costs of emigrants on, 359–60
deaths on, 372, 393
description of route of, 375–81
discipline in wagon trains of,
367–68, 389–91
disease on, 372–73, 441
1844–46 number of emigrants on,
394
1849–50 argonauts on, 476–77
first American westbound party on,
245
first organized emigrant party on,
331
Frémont's exploration of, 351–52,
355, 387–88
Gantt party on, 386–93
grand total of pioneers on, 478
Greeley's dismay at stories of,
382–84
guides to, 217, 344, 348
Indian danger along, 371–72
Indian name for, 374
jettisoning of items along, 366–67,
378, 379, 476
murders and executions on, 373n
pioneers of, 220–21, 340
Polk proposes armed escorts for
wagon trains on, 412
profits of post traders on, 385–86
provisions on, 365–66
Sublette Cutoff, 379
as testing of will and endurance,
374
women on, 370–71
Oregon Trail, The. See Parkman,
Francis
Osage Indians, 230, 278
O'Sullivan, John Louis, 401, 402, 410
Oto Indians, 175–77
Otter (steamer), 243
overland expedition to Astoria. *See
under* Fort Astoria
oxen, 362–65

Pacific Fur Company, 93–96, 108, 127
Pacific Springs (Oregon Trail), 379

Pacific Trading Company, 241
Paiute Indians, 433
Pakenham, Richard, 411
Palmer, Joel, 379, 394–96, 439
Palouse Indians, 277, 456, 458
Pambrun, Pierre, 291–92, 317
Panama, shortcut to California and
    Oregon through, 359, 384, 475
Papago Indians, 230
Parker, Eliza, 16
Parker, Samuel, 16, 265–69, 272,
    273–77, 286, 287, 289–94,
    299, 374
Parkman, Francis, 16
    background of, 417–19
    later life of, 461–67
    The Oregon Trail, 14–15, 346–47,
        368, 385–86, 431, 461–62,
        464–65, 464*n*, 474–75, 481–82
    Feltskog's edited edition, 482
    trip west by, 419–31
Pawnee Indians, 175–76, 177, 371
Pawnee Mission (Iowa), 255
Peacock (sloop-of-war), 307
Pecos River, 230
Pedlar (ship), 136, 138, 140
Peel, Sir Robert, 402, 412–13
Peel, William, 402–3, 468
Pend d'Oreille Indians, 277
Perkins, H. K. W., 459–60
Peter the Great (czar), 26
Peupeumoxmox, Chief, 444
Philippines, 66
    Spanish trade with, 56
Pierre's Hole (headwaters of the
    Snake), 243, 251, 258, 274, 389
Pike, Zebulon Montgomery, 79, 80
Pilcher, Joshua, 208–9
pioneers, official definitions of, 478
Place of the Rye Grass, 314, 435. *See
    also* Waiilatpu
Plains Across, The (Unruh), 481
Platte River, 80, 87, 130, 169, 170,
    174–76, 244, 271, 283, 284,
    329–30, 352, 377, 391–92, 424
    bridges over, 477
    description of, 375
    water of, 345
Poinsett, Joel, 350
Point, Nicholas, 325–28
Poison Springs (Oregon Trail), 378
Polk, James K., 257, 397–400, 411–15,
    452
    death of, 464*n*
    Meek's mission to, 452–53
Polk, Sarah Childress, 398, 453, 455
Ponca Indians, 170, 177
Pond, Peter, 46

Portland (Oregon), 351*n*, 478
Portneuf River, 246, 251. *See also*
    Fort Hall
Potawatomie Indians, 326
potlatch, 35
Potts, John, 89–90
Powell, Oliver S., 268
"prairie schooners," 361–62. *See also*
    wagons
Prairie Traveller (Marcy), 366
Pratt, O. C., 457
Prattsburg (New York), 266, 268
Prentiss, Clarissa Ward, 266
Prentiss, Jane, 458
Prentiss, Stephen, 266
Presbyterian missionaries,
    333, 460
Preuss, Charles, 351, 353, 354, 354*n*,
    385
Prevost, Jean Baptiste, 134
Pribilof Islands, 136
Provost, Etienne, 209
Puget, Peter, 44, 302
Puget Sound, 44, 305, 307
Puritanism, Mencken on, 266–67
Putnam, George, 475
Puyallup Indians, 34
Pyramid Lake, 353

Queen Charlotte (ship), 59
Queen Charlotte Sound, 47
quicksand, 375, 391

Raccoon (sloop-of-war), 140
Red River, 80, 187
Reed, James Frazier, 422, 434
Reed, John, 129, 134, 147–49, 150,
    156–57
Reed, Margaret, 422, 434
Reed, Virginia, 434
Rees. *See* Arikara Indians Register
    Cliff (Wyoming)
Register of the Desert. *See*
    Independence Rock
rendezvous, 206–7, 216, 243, 272–73,
    285
Reports (Frémont), 352–53, 355
Resolution (ship), 27–29, 50
Reznor, Jacob, 156, 156*n*, 157
River of the West, 37, 39, 40
Robidoux Pass (Oregon Trail), 377
Robinson, Edward, 156, 156*n*, 157
Rocky Mountain Fur Company, 243,
    246, 258
Rocky Mountains, 80–83
    Ashley-Henry expeditions to,
        203–14
    mountain men in, 86–91

Shining Mountains as name for, 39, 81
See also Continental Divide; South Pass
Rodgers, Andrew, 447–48
Rogers, Robert, 37, 39
Rogue River, 254, 304
Roi, Jean Baptiste Antoine, 176
Rollins, Philip Ashton, 481
Romaine (traveling companion), 421
Rose, Edward, 132–33
Ross, Alexander, 107, 139, 180–81, 180*n*, 193
Rupert's Land, 187
Rush, Richard, 182
Russia
 fur trade of, 30, 51, 58–59
  Astor and, 126, 135–36
 Ledyard in, 53–54
 Oregon Country renounced by, 409–10
 Pacific explorations of, 27

Sacramento valley, 354
sagebrush, odor of, 289, 290
Sager, Frances, 448–49
Sager, Henrietta, 445
Sager, Henry, 318
Sager, John, 446–47
Sager, Louise, 445, 449
Sager, Naomi, 318
Saint Joseph (Missouri), 345, 374
Saint Lawrence River, 93, 95
Saint Louis (Missouri), 77, 79, 85, 87, 88, 90, 95, 126, 128, 140, 206, 243, 269, 431
 Dickens in, 340, 342–43
 history of, 343–44
 Indians seek Christian God in, 247–48, 435
 Jedediah Smith in, 202–4
 Kelley in, 226–27
 Parkman's return to, 465
 Stuart's arrival in, 177
St. Peter (ship), 26
Salem (Oregon), 255*n*, 257
Salish Indians, 34
Salmon Falls, 380
Salmon River, 194, 274, 276
Salter, John, 67–70
Salt Lake City, 384, 476
San Diego (California), 23, 56, 210, 229
San Diego (ship), 26
San Francisco (*formerly* Yerba Buena; California), 186, 199, 200, 303–4
 1849–50 number of sea arrivals in, 475

San Francisco Bay, 25, 27
San Gabriel Mission (California), 210
San Gabriel River, 230
San Joaquin River, 211, 304, 331
San José (California), 232, 304
San Juan River, 230
San Miguel Island (California), 23
San Salvador (frigate), 23–24
Santa Anna, Antonio López de, 229
Santa Fé (New Mexico), 217, 218, 230, 337, 347, 421
Santa Fé Trail, 243, 310, 322, 344, 375, 388, 420, 430, 455
Sapling Grove (near Independence), 320, 321, 348
Saunders, L. W., 447, 448
Schenectady barge, 128
Scott, Sir Walter, 340
Scott, Winfield, 350
Scotts Bluff (Nebraska), 376–77
sea beaver. *See* sea otter
sea otter (*Lutra enhydris marina*), 16, 30–32, 40, 58–59, 62, 81
 Indians' hunts for, 60
Sea Otter (ship), 58, 59
Selkirk, Fifth Earl of (Thomas Douglas), 187–88
sequoia trees, 355
Shasta Indians, 396
Shaw, Quincy Adams, 419–21, 424, 428, 431, 463, 464, 465
Shawnee Indians, 347
Shawnee Mission (Westport Landing), 387
Shewish (Indian), 117, 118
Shining Mountains, as name for Rockies, 39, 81
Shoshoni Indians (Snake Indians), 133–34, 154–58, 156*n*, 166–67, 177, 269, 288, 316
Shunar (Chouinard; Shunan; bully), 216, 273
Shuyelpi Indians, 277
Sierra Nevada, 331, 353, 354, 432, 476
 first white men across, 211
Simpson, Alexander, 323
Simpson, Sir George, 185–92, 196, 214, 215, 233, 258, 298, 308
 McLoughlin and, 403–6, 467–68
Sioux Indians, 129–30, 132, 208, 281, 336
 Brulé, 377, 427
 Oglala, 272, 377, 394–95, 420, 427–30
Siskadee River. *See* Green River
Sitka (Alaska), 26, 27, 127
 Hunt in, 135–36

Slacum, William A., 235, 256, 300–303, 305–6, 308, 469
slavery
  Indians and, 34–35, 125
  Texas annexation and, 399
  Willamette prohibition of, 312, 415
smallpox, McDougall's threat of, 125
Smet, Pierre-Jean De. See De Smet
Smith, Jedediah, 16, 91, 193, 196, 224, 299, 340, 389
  in Ashley-Henry company, 203–5, 207–14
    California expeditions, 210–14
    fight with Arikaras, 207–9, 214
  background of, 202–4
  death of, 217–18
  at Fort Vancouver, 200, 212–13, 468
  grizzly mauling of, 209
  in new partnership, 215, 217–18
Smith, Joseph, 345, 354n, 425
Smith, Samuel F., 280
Snake Indians. See Shoshoni Indians
Snake River, 36, 78, 83, 133–35, 147, 150, 152–54, 156–61, 163, 187, 192–93, 196, 199, 204–5, 215, 243, 274, 276, 290–91, 293, 294, 331, 340, 353, 371, 380, 392, 456
  Oregon Trail along, 380
  trapping beaver out at, 193–95
Soda Springs (Idaho), 290, 325, 331, 375
  description of, 379
Sonoma (California), 427
South Pass, 91, 168, 179, 209, 244, 271, 272, 285, 325, 331, 340, 377, 378, 392, 426, 455, 475–76
  Frémont expedition and, 351–53, 375, 387
Sowle, Cornelius, 135–37
Spain
  Adams-Onís Treaty (1819) with, 182–84, 409
  Nootka expedition by, 26–27, 63
  Nootka Sound Convention between Britain and, 66, 183–84, 410
  on Pacific coast, 26, 27, 56–57, 60
Spalding, Eliza (daughter), 444, 448–49, 450, 451
Spalding, Eliza Hart, 283, 284, 289, 314, 436, 438, 448–49, 450–51
  husband's epitaph for, 461
Spalding, Henry Harmon, 266, 268, 278–80, 281–83, 291, 340
  on Catholics as murderers of Whitmans, 460–61

  Lapwai Mission of, 294, 307, 314–15, 332–37, 435–36, 438–41, 449, 450, 461
  later life of, 461
  and murder of Whitmans, 449
  poisoning of Indians charged to, 442–43
Spaulding, Josiah, 332–33
Split-Lip, Chief, 316
Spokane (Washington), 192–93, 286
Spokane Indians, 34, 247, 277, 315, 333, 336
Spokane River, 36, 277
Stanislaus River, 211
status quo ante bellum, 181, 188
Stewart, Sir William Drummond, 216, 272, 288–89
Sticcas, Chief, 445
Stuart, David, 95, 101, 103, 111, 114–15, 122, 145–46
Stuart, Elizabeth Emma Sullivan, 178, 179
Stuart, John, 145
Stuart, Robert, 16, 95, 122, 340
  Astoria-St. Louis trip led by, 135, 147–77, 204
  encounters with Indians, 148–49, 158–60, 171–73, 177
  South Pass "discovered," 168, 179
  winter quarters, 170–71, 173–785
  background of, 145–47
  later life of, 178, 179
  Rollins' book on, 481
  on Tonquin cruise, 104, 147
Sublette, Milton, 243, 244, 246, 250, 284–85
Sublette, William, 214, 217, 243, 244, 245, 251, 258, 389
Sublette Cutoff, 379
Sugar Grove (Iowa), 425
Sultana (brig), 242, 245
Sumatra (ship), 254
Sutter, John Augustus, 354, 437, 475
Sutter's Fort (California), 354, 432, 434, 444
Sweetwater River, 169, 170, 243, 329, 336, 369, 378, 392
  ferries across, 477

Tamsucky (Indian), 436, 448
Taos (New Mexico), 230, 310n
Tauitau, Chief, 445
Taylor, Zachary, 422, 430
Tecumseh, 97
Teton Pass, 164
Texas, annexation of, 399–401
Thackeray, William Makepeace, 341n

"Thanatopsis" (Bryant), 40
The Dalles rapids, 35, 135, 147–48,
    150, 151, 157n, 251, 275, 292,
    323, 381, 436, 440–41, 457
  Applegate boys lost at, 393
  Cayuse prisoners held at, 457
  Waskopum Methodist station at,
    459
  Whitman's plan to move to, 442
Thomasson, A. H., 376
Thompson, David, 122
Thompson, John, 69–70
Thoreau, Henry David, 18
Thorn, James, 119
Thorn, Jonathan, 16
  background of, 97–98, 115
  coastal trading trip of, 116–18
  at Columbia mouth, 110–15
  death of, 118–21
  on voyage to Oregon, 98–110, 147
Thornton, J. Quinn, 347
Thrapp, Dan L., 483
Three Crossings (Oregon Trail), 378
thunderstorms, 330, 389, 390
Thurston, Samuel R., 469–71
Tillamook Bay, 41
Tillamook Head, 62
Tillamook Indians, 34
Tiloukaikt, Chief, 316–17, 436,
    445–47, 453, 457
Times of London, 402
tobacco, sold by the foot, 199
Tocqueville, Alexis de, 341
Tomahas (Indian), 445–47, 453, 457,
    458
Tonquin (ship), 16, 93–121,
    147, 182
  massacre of crew of, 119–21, 135,
    181n, 213n
Toronto (Canada), 342
trading posts for argonauts, 477
trappers
  American, 81–82, 86–91
  description of work of, 84–86
  "free" ("freemen"), 195, 206
  rendezvous for, 206–7, 216, 243,
    272–73, 285–86
  See also French-Canadian trappers
    (voyageurs); fur trade;
    mountain men
Travels to the Rocky Mountains
    (Farnham), 323
Treaty of Paris (1763), 83
Tres Reyes (ship), 26
Truckee Pass, 432, 433, 434
Truman, Harry S., 397
Tualatin Indians, 252
Tyler, John, 313, 337, 350–51

Umatilla Indians, 458
Umatilla River, 135, 153, 199, 441,
    444–45, 453, 456, 458
Umpqua Indians, 34, 252, 396
Umpqua River, 200, 212, 214, 232,
    254
United States Army
  Arikara battle of, 207–9
  Sierra Nevada rescue work by,
    476–77
  Topographical Engineers, 80, 219,
    349, 350, 351
United States Exploring Expedition,
    306–7
United States Magazine and
    Democratic Review, 401
United States Navy, Thorn in, 97
Unruh, John D., Jr., 481

Valerianos, Apostolos. See Fuca, Juan
    de
Vallé, André, 151, 167, 170, 179
Van Buren, Martin, 398–99
Vancouver, George, 44–45, 197, 302
Vancouver Island, 26, 27, 32, 35, 47,
    50, 56, 60, 62, 67, 115, 116
  as British in final settlement, 412,
    413
  Hudson Bay station transferred to,
    408, 413, 440
  See also Clayoquot Sound
Vavasour, Mervin, 406, 468
Victoria (ship), 23–24
Victoria (Vancouver Island), 413, 440
Vincennes (Indiana), 88
Vizcaíno, Sebastían, 26, 27
Voyages from Montreal Through the
    Continent of North America
    (Mackenzie), 46
Voyages Made in the Years 1788 and
    1789 from China to the
    Northwest Coast of America
    (Meares), 64
Voyages to the Pacific Ocean (Cook),
    58
voyageurs. See French-Canadian
    trappers

Waa-nibe (Arapaho girl), 273
wagons
  animals for, 362–65
  average distance per day covered
    by, 348
  circular encampment of, 283, 328,
    390–91, 424
  Conestoga, 327n, 360
  in crossing rivers, 361–62
  downhill descent by, 362

wagons (*Continued*)
first crossing of Continental Divide by, 244, 271
on Oregon Trail, 327
description of, 360–62
Whitman's faith in use of, 271, 282–83, 284, 291, 332, 387, 393
wagon wheels, 361
Waiilatpu Mission (Oregon), 276, 294, 316–18, 322, 331–38, 380, 387, 435–39, 441, 442, 444–49, 450, 460
Wakarusa River, 388
Waldo, William, 218
Walker, Elkanah, 315, 332, 333, 336–37
Walker, Joseph Reddeford, 91, 354–55
Walker, Mary, 332
Walker, William, 248
Walla Walla Indians, 34, 146, 152, 154, 177, 275, 396, 437, 441, 444, 456, 458
Walla Walla River, 152, 277, 294, 314, 316, 318, 322, 381
War of 1812, 137–40, 176, 177
peace agreement after, 181
Warre, Henry J., 406, 423, 468
War with Mexico, 401–2, 420, 422, 430, 439–40, 454, 475
Wasatch Range, 194, 354, 422, 426, 432–34
Washington, George, 65, 76
Washington (D.C.), disease-laden swamps of, 398
Washington (state), 347n, 478
Waterloo, battle of (1815), 389
Wayne, "Mad Anthony," 128
Weber River, 194
Webster, Daniel, 238, 337, 340, 350
Weekes, Stephen, 111, 112, 119–21
Wentworth, Richard, 38
Western Emigration Society, 320, 321, 331
Western Engineer (riverboat), 80
Westport Landing (Missouri), 321, 345, 355, 374, 387, 420
westward movement, 13, 19–20, 313–14, 334–35. 346. 382–86. *See also* Independence (Missouri)
White, Elijah, 256, 315, 316, 333–37, 339, 340, 385
White Eagle. *See* McLoughlin, John
Whitman, Alice Clarissa, 318
Whitman, Marcus, 16, 216, 263–64, 385
background of, 264–65
Bridger operated on by, 216, 272

first trip west by, 269–74
medical work in Oregon by, 436
murder of, 446–49
capture and execution of murderers, 456–58
Catholics charged with, 460–61
Perkins' analysis of reasons for, 459–60
poisoning of Indians charged to, 442–43
protest trip home and back by, 336–37, 387, 392, 435–36
on provisions for the trail, 365–66
second trip west of, 280, 281–93
Waiilatpu Mission of, 276, 294, 316–18, 322, 331–38, 380, 387, 435–39, 441, 442, 444–49, 450, 460
Whitman, Narcissa, 16
accused of flirting, 288
adopted children of, 318, 445
background of, 266–67
betrothal of, 268–69, 273, 277
Meeks takes lock of hair from remains of, 453
murder of, 447–49
capture and execution of murderers, 456–58
Catholics charged with, 460–61
Perkins' analysis of reasons for, 459–60
trip west by, 281–93
pregnancy, 289, 294, 318
at Waiilatpu mission, 318, 436–37, 445
wedding of, 280
Whittier, John Greenleaf, 349
Wicananish, Chief, 116, 117
Wilkes, Charles, 197, 306–8, 311, 312, 315, 437, 469
Willamette Cattle Company, 303, 304
Willamette valley
1839 memorial of complaints from, 322–23
emigrants in, 201, 246, 353
first organized emigrant party, 331
exploration of, 122–23
Hudson's Bay Company's fears of, 408
Lee's mission in, 252–54, 257, 293–94
Peel's 1845 tour of, 402–3
provisional government of, 310–12, 415, 440–41, 453–54, 456
removal of Indians from, 396
See also Oregon City

Williams, Joseph, 328
Willow Springs (Oregon Trail), 378
Windermere Lake, 122
Windlass Hill (Oregon Trail), 376
Wind River, 88, 133, 209
Wind River Range, 133, 155, 166–67,
        168, 272, 351, 352, 378, 392
Winnipeg (Canada), 83, 197
Wishram Indians, 34, 148–50, 151
Wisner, M. L., 372
Wood River, 176
Wyandot Indians, 248
Wyeth, Jacob, 241, 244
Wyeth, John B., 241, 244
Wyeth, Nathaniel, 16, 207, 226, 256.
        259. 299, 340, 379, 389, 420
    first trip west by, 236. 240–47
    McLoughlin defended by, 470–71
    second trip west by, 250–51,
        257–59, 275, 289
Wyoming, 455*n*

Yakima Indians, 34, 444, 456, 458
Yellowstone National Park, 89
Yellowstone Packet (keelboat),
        208
Yellowstone River, 79, 86, 88, 90, 130,
        195*n*, 204, 209, 217, 281
Yerba Buena (California). *See* San
        Francisco
York, John W., 247
York (slave), 77
York Factory (Hudson's Bay), 186,
        189, 197, 296, 405
Yosemite Valley, 355
Young, Brigham, 345, 354*n*, 368, 378,
        425
    Greeley's interview of, 384
Young, Ewing, 16, 91, 196, 230–35,
        236, 253, 257, 299–304
    death of, 310
    Young, Joaquín, 311*n*
    Yuma Indians, 230

BEAR FLAG
RISING

The Conquest of California,
1846

To Western Writers of America, Inc.

CONTENTS

Maps		518
Introduction		521
Prologue		525

PART ONE: THE COAST OF CATHAY

1	The Spaniards	535
2	The Mexicans	543
3	The Californios	550
4	Nueva Helvetia	559

PART TWO: BEAR FLAG RISING

5	The Dark Horse	569
6	Frémont	584
7	Hawk's Peak	600
8	Klamath Lake	614
9	War	627
10	Los Osos	635
11	Olómpali	651
12	Stockton	667

PART THREE: CONQUEST

13   Kearny   687
14   Santa Fé   701
15   Los Angeles   718
16   San Pascual   732
17   Mule Hill   748
18   San Gabriel   758
19   Cahuenga   772
20   Last Battle   782
21   Return   797
22   Court-martial   809

Epilogue   826
Sources   837
Bibliography   839
Index   845

Mexico can never exert any real governmental authority over such a country. . . . The Anglo-Saxon foot is already on its borders. Already the advance guard of the irresistible army of the Anglo-Saxon emigration has begun to pour down upon it, armed with the plough and the rifle. . . .

—John Louis O'Sullivan, *The United States Magazine and Democratic Review,* July–August, 1845

If I were a Mexican, I would tell you, "Have you not enough room in your own country to bury your dead men? If you come into mine, we will greet you with bloody hands and welcome you to hospitable graves."

—Sen. Thomas Corwin of Ohio, February 11, 1846

We go to war with Mexico solely for the purpose of conquering an honorable and permanent space. Whilst we intend to prosecute the war with vigor, both by land and by sea, we shall bear the olive branch in one hand and the sword in the other; and whenever she will accept the former, we shall sheathe the latter.

—James Buchanan, Secretary of State, 1846

Poor Mexico, so far from God, so near the United States.

—Mexican proverb

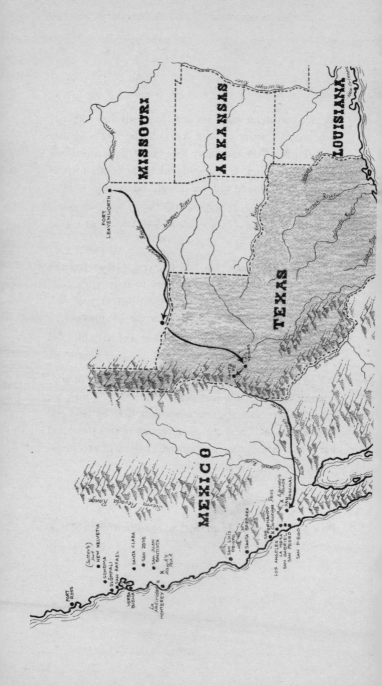

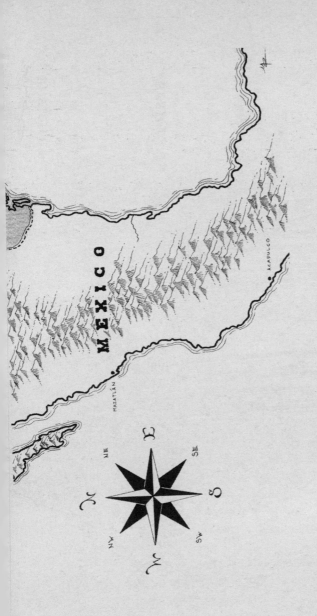

INTRODUCTION

T*he conquest* of California is representative of a concept as old and arrogant as humankind. A New York lawyer-editor named John Louis O'Sullivan called this idea "Manifest Destiny," the useful phrase printed in a summer, 1845, magazine editorial arguing in favor of the annexation of Texas by the United States. He wrote of Texas' "absorption" into the Union as "the inevitable fulfillment of the general law which is rolling our population westward," and California, he predicted, would also fall away from an "imbecile and distracted Mexico." In the minatory tones of an awakened giant, O'Sullivan said, "The Anglo-Saxon foot is already on its borders. Already the advance guard of the irresistible army of Anglo-Saxon emigration has begun to pour down upon it . . . ."

Manifest Destiny was a new phrase for an ancient abstraction that has steered and muddled every nation, primitive and civilized, since national attitudes of superiority arose.

(Substituting "Spaniard" for "Anglo-Saxon" in O'Sullivan's editorial results in a pronunciamento that might have guided Cortéz and his conquistadores when they conquered Mexico in 1520 and when his successors claimed California for Spain in 1769. At the time of the events of *Bear Flag Rising*, the British, who wrote the text on spreading Anglo-Saxon "civilization" around the globe, were warring against the Maoris in New Zealand and the Sikhs in India.)

The spirit of Manifest Destiny, the belief that it was the fate, perhaps divinely written, of the United States to rule the North American continent, was anything but an idle notion. It was a virulent force from our national beginnings, and in 1846, it swept like a rush of air into a vacuum from the Continental Divide to the Pacific, guided by what Bernard DeVoto called "the logic of geography."

Bear Flag Rising is the story of three agents of Manifest Destiny in collision with one another while on a common mission: the annexation by military force of the Mexican province of Alta California by the United States.

The event signaling the opening of the takeover occurred on June 14, 1846, when a band of backwoods malcontents raised the berry-juice-painted petticoat known as the Bear Flag over the plaza of the northern California village of Sonoma. The *process* of conquest, however, had begun six months earlier, upon the arrival in the Far West of John Charles Frémont, the first of the three linked but unbonded conquerors.

The Bear Flag is the perfect symbol of the conquest; Frémont, the highly imperfect human manifestation of it. Firmly wedged between the other two men and abraded by them, he inspired and abetted the Sonoma rising and stood at the epicenter of the thirteen-month storm that followed it. He is the looming presence of the California campaign.

He is also one of our history's enduring enigmas, a thoroughgoing man of action, easy to admire but difficult to like. A pathmarker if not a pathfinder, he is at various times an *agent provocateur,* Byronic hero, brilliant leader of men, and pathetic egoist. One of his signal characteristics is that, like the ostrich, his eye is bigger than his brain. He sees panoramas, but details, many of them urgent, confound him. What remains fixed in his character and life are his unbounded hubris and ambition, and the devotion to him of his wife, Jessie.

The second of the triad of conquerors is Robert Field Stockton, a commodore of the navy and confidant of presidents. He is wealthy, imperious, elegant, grandiloquent, and ruthless—a born satrap. He dreams of military glory, a spectacular sea fight, a great overland march to battle, some chance to prove himself, to ensure himself an eminent niche in history. He is smallish in stature and as excitable as Lord Nelson, whom he admires.

And the third figure in the story is Stephen Watts Kearny, a general of dragoons, a briary old-school martinet blooded in Indian wars. He is a master of tasks, but like his contemporary, Zachary Taylor, a primitive tactician. He is courageous in battle and, in appropriate company, courtly in manner, but he is foolish and vindictive in many critical matters, and like generals before and after his time, he surrounds himself with the like-minded and hears little in opposition to his thinking except from his enemies.

These contentious men, around whom the spectacle of the conquest tumbles and swirls like a Mojave dust devil, and the color and drama of the California conquest, preoccupy this book.

While *Bear Flag Rising* is about the California campaign from an American perspective, I have tried, at some length, to provide a picture of pre-conquest California and to do justice to the Californian "side" in the 1845–47 era, especially in recounting how leaders such as José Castro, Pío Pico, and Andrés Pico rose to oppose, as best they could with no assistance from Mexico, an event each knew was inevitable: the loss of their beloved land, and their way of life, to the interlopers.

—DALE L. WALKER
June 14, 1998

PROLOGUE

The Californios called them "Bostons."

These were the Americans who came around Cape Horn from Eastern seaports, the principal ones on the Massachusetts coast, to the Pacific Rim in the half-century before the conquest.

The first American ship to visit California was the *Otter,* out of Boston, which dropped its hook in Monterey Bay in October, 1796, en route to the Sandwich Islands and China with a cargo of sea-otter pelts. The captain of this small vessel, one Ebenezer Dorr, had several convicts aboard, escapees from the Australian penal colony at Botany Bay who had paid him to take them to the United States. Dorr asked permission of Monterey's commandante to land these "English sailors" but was politely refused. In the dark, and in the first recorded instance of the Americans wearing out their welcome, he landed them anyway.

In the dozen languorous years before the conquest, many other Bostons ventured unbidden to California. Some of them stayed, tolerated as foreign residents. One who came and returned home and wrote an influential book about his adventures was an uncommon sailor out of Cambridge, Massachusetts, named Richard Henry Dana.

His grandfather, a jurist, had been a delegate to the Continental Congress and United States minister to Russia; his father was a poet and essayist and founder of the influential literary journal, *The North American Review,* and his favorite teacher in private school was a certain serene transcendentalist and aspiring Unitarian minister, Ralph Waldo Emerson.

In 1831, at age sixteen, Dana entered Harvard but a bout with measles left his eyesight impaired and, feeling "useless, pitied, and dissatisfied," he left the college after two years to cast about for some answer to his failing health. He found it, to his family's alarm, in the port of Boston.

"There is a witchery in the sea," he later wrote, and the tall-masted ships he saw, and the carefree sailors at work on their decks, romanced him. He might have embarked as a passenger or, through his family's influence, as a merchant officer, but on August 14, 1834, he traded his frock coat, silk topper, and kid gloves for the rough duds of the ship's slop chest—a pair of baggy duck trousers, a checked pullover shirt, and a black-varnished tarpaulin hat "with half a fathom of black ribbon hanging over the left eye"—when he signed on as a common seaman on the brig *Pilgrim,* outward-bound for Cape Horn and Mexican California.

"There is not so hopeless and pitiable an object in the world as a landsman beginning a sailor's life," he said of the beginning of his two-year adventure. In fact, he had no notion of just how wretched life before the mast could be. He had swapped more than clothes: he had traded silk sheets in a warm and spacious home for a hammock slung in the crew's quarters below the *Pilgrim's* forecastle, amidst coils of rope, rigging, spare sails, stores, and the eternal stink of the bilges; he had traded sumptuous meals served at a damask-covered table for cold salt beef scummed with grease, and "scouse" (biscuits pounded into crumbs and

mixed and boiled with beef), potatoes, and pepper; he had
traded brainwork for picking oakum—old rope pieces un-
twisted and picked into shreds, then tarred for use in
caulking—and for flensing the skin off his knees in endless
days spent holystoning decks; he had traded intellectual talk
with poets and pedants for the stupefying chatter of his deck-
mates and the fearsome pronouncements of the *Pilgrim*'s
tyrannical captain, a self-described "regular down-east
johnny-cake" who promised his crew, "If you ain't careful,
I'll make a hell of heaven."

Most of the voyage to California was hellish, but not all
of it. Dana learned to love the capstan songs the sailors sang,
to delight in their effusions over the grog ration that was
passed around in bad weather; and he was filled with awe to
witness such seagoing phenomena as the weirdly beautiful
corposant—Saint Elmo's Fire—that crawled along the masts
and yards in stormy weather.

By the time the *Pilgrim* had slugged its way south in high
seas to the Falkland Islands and the coast of Patagonia, he
had learned much of sailing-ship nomenclature, writing in
his journal of the "fine breeze from the northward, topmast
and topgallant studding-sails set, and every prospect of a
speedy and pleasant passage round." He also studied
Bowditch on the voyage south and learned to identify such
navigational phenomena as the Magellen Clouds—three
small nebulae, two bright, one dim—seen just above the horizon soon after crossing the southern tropic, and, directly
overhead at Cape Horn, the four stars of the Southern Cross,
one of the brightest constellations in the heavens.

Three and a half months out, the *Pilgrim* anchored off
Juan Fernández—Robinson Crusoe's island—four hundred
miles west of Valparaiso, to fill water casks, and on January
13, 1835, sighted the California coast. It took the eighty-
six-foot Boston brig five days to beat its way one hundred
miles upcoast to its trade destination, fighting head winds
and smashing seas so unrelenting that the ship sprung its

foretopmast and was driven hundreds of miles off course.
But on January 18, the *Pilgrim* sailed past Point Pinos, the
headland entrance of the twenty-four-mile-wide Bay of
Monterey, and Dana saw the town. Before him lay a pretty
collection of whitewashed adobe buildings with red-tiled
roofs, a customshouse, and a square presidio, Mexican flag
fluttering above it, all huddled neatly on the edge of a large,
pine-wooded cove "green as nature could make it."

The bay and the town teemed with commerce. Since Monterey had the only customshouse on the coast, all trading
vessels were required to drop anchor there, enter their cargoes in the registry, undergo a haphazard inspection by harbor authorities, and receive permission to traffic in the other
ports north and south. Ships from New England threaded
through the anchorages of ships from Mexico, Central and
South America, England, France, Genoa, the Sandwich Islands, China, and Japan; on the beach and in town, trader
captains and sailors, hide droghers, shag-bearded trappers
in greasy buckskins, Kanakas, Indians, freighters, and laborers jostled with presidio soldiers and monied gentlemen in
stovepipe hats.

Since Dana spoke Spanish, the *Pilgrim*'s captain appointed him interpreter, and in the year the brig wandered
up and down the coast with its cargo of spirits, tea, coffee,
sugar, spices, raisins, molasses, hardware, tinware, crockery,
cutlery, calicoes and cottons from Lowell, boots and
shoes from Lynn, crepes, silks, shawls, scarves, jewelry,
combs, furniture—"everything that can be imagined, from
Chinese fireworks to English cartwheels"—the husky,
curly-headed New Englander kept a meticulous journal,
subsequently published as *Two Years Before the Mast*.

He loved the majesty of the Spanish language and the
beauty of its intonations among the citizenry. "Every common ruffian-looking fellow, with a slouched hat, blanket
cloak, dirty underdress, and soiled leather leggings, appeared to me to be speaking elegant Spanish," he wrote. "A

common bullock-driver, on horseback, delivering a message, seemed to speak like an ambassador at a royal audience."

He admired the dress of the Californios (the Mexican natives of California). The men, at least those of some substance, wore dark, flat-topped, broad-brimmed, silk-lined sombreros with gilt or figured bands; short, vest-like silk jackets; shirts made of broadcloth or velveteen, laced with gilt and open at the neck; pantaloons open at the sides below the knee; white stockings and Indian-made, gold-embroidered deerskin shoes; broad sashes, often blood-red, cinching the waist; dark blue or black cloaks of broadcloth with velvet trimmings; and colorful serapes slung over their shoulders.

"Every rich man looks like a grandee and every poor scamp like a broken-down gentleman," he wrote.

He saw ladies in silks, crepes, crinolines, and calicoes, all made in the European style but with short sleeves, leaving the arm bare, and loose around the waist—"corsets not being in use." They wore shoes of kid or satin, bright sashes or belts, necklaces and silver-filigreed pendant earrings, and since they wore no bonnets, their hair, loose or in long braids, was decorated and held in place by tall combs.

People of pure Spanish blood, he said, had clear "brunette" complexions. The Indians, who ran about naked except for "a small piece of cloth, kept up by a wide leather strap round his waist," were darker.

The Californios were caste-conscious, Dana recorded: "The least drop of Spanish blood, if it be only of quadroon or octoroon, is sufficient to raise one from the position of a serf, and entitle him to wear a suit of clothes—boots, hat, cloak, spurs, long knife, all complete, though coarse and dirty as it may be—and to call himself Español, and to hold property, if he can get any."

Horses—smallish, wiry animals—were prevalent in their daily lives, and it was so commonplace to see men and women on horseback that he thought of the Californios as centaurs, but he was disgusted by the neglect and downright cruelty shown to the beasts. The men may have been *caballeros,* but only insofar as the word meant "horsemen." They were not gentlemen. He wrote,

> They can hardly go from one house to another without getting on a horse, there being generally several standing tied to the doorposts of the little cottages. When they wish to show their activity, they make no use of their stirrups in mounting, but striking the horse, spring into the saddle as he starts, and sticking their longs spurs into him, go off on the full run. Their spurs are cruel things, having four or five rowels, each an inch in length, dull and rusty. The flanks of the horses are often sore from them, and I have seen men come in from chasing bullocks with their horses' hind legs and quarters covered with blood.

He said that when the people embarked on long journeys, "they rode one horse down, and catch another, throw the saddle and bridle upon him, and after riding him down, take a third, and so on to the end of the journey."

The Californios, even the "Dons," Dana wrote disdainfully, were an "idle, thriftless people" who could "make nothing for themselves." Here, he said, was a land abounding in grapes, "yet they buy, at a great price, bad wine made in Boston and brought round by us, and retail it among themselves at a *real* (twelve and a half cents) by the small wine glass." He said that cowhides, "which they value at two dollars in money, they barter for something which costs seventy-five cents in Boston; and buy shoes (as like as not made from their own hides, which have been carried twice around Cape Horn) at three and four dollars. . . ."

He told of a country where none but "Papists" could own property or even remain more than a few weeks ashore unless assigned to a trade vessel; a place with no system of credit, no banks, no investments except in cattle, no schools, and no discernible governance.

He told of a vast, bizarre, lazy and decadent land, immensely rich (if more in the potential than the tangible), whose people, other then a handful of "grandees," had no education and no initiative and seemed to be in a geographical and cultural limbo, as if apathetically awaiting conquest.

"In the hands of an enterprising people, what a country this might be!" he wrote.

Three hundred years before Dana's advent, the Spaniards, an enterprising people, had thought the same thing.

PART ONE

THE COAST OF CATHAY

■

1

The Spaniards

■

1

Juan Rodríguez Cabrillo had commanded a company of crossbowmen in the march by Hernán Cortés to the Aztec capital of Tenochitlán in 1519, and for these and other military labors, he had earned the confidence of the viceroyalty of Mexico. After two decades of service to Spain in the New World, the Portuguese-born officer was given his first command—an odd assignment for a soldier, but an important one. In June, 1542, he sailed north from the port of La Natividad, on the Pacific coast of Mexico, his flagship the caravel *San Salvador* accompanied by a smaller vessel, the *Victoria*.

Cabrillo's mission, assigned him by the viceroy, was to explore the uncharted "coast of Cathay," believed to be a large island somewhere in the north, and perhaps discover any number of fabled places: the Strait of Anián, a northwest passage between the two great oceans; or the seaport of Quivira, a land said to contain Seven Cities of Gold ruled by El Dorado, a king whose subjects dusted him with gold every morning and washed it off every night.

He might even find the island mentioned in a popular work by the Spaniard Ordóñez de Montalvo titled *Las sergas de Esplandián* ("The Deeds of Esplandián"), published in

Madrid in 1510. This tale told how the Christians in Constantinople had fought a force of black Amazons led by Queen Califía of the island of California. The island was said to be located "at the right hand of the Indies" and close to the Terrestrial Paradise, a place bounteous in gold and guarded by griffins that carried unwary intruders high into the sky and dropped them to their deaths.

Whatever he was searching for, the record of Cabrillo's voyage, written about thirteen years later, states that on "Sunday, July 2 [1542], they sighted California."

He sailed up the unknown coast, charting islands, bays, inlets, reefs and rocks, among the latter a dangerous group he named the Habre Ojos—"Watch Out." In September, he visited a "good harbor" that he named San Miguel (soon called San Diego), found ways to talk with coastal Indians, and sailed on, often far to seaward to avoid fierce winds and the terrifying crash of the ocean on the cliffs and rock-girded beaches. He sighted but did not visit a widemouthed harbor 450 miles north of San Miguel and named it Baía de los Pinos (probably Monterey Bay), and in mid-November, after sailing past a great fog-shrouded place that would become known in three hundred years as the Golden Gate, the *San Salvador* and *Victoria* anchored in a large bay about six hundred miles north of San Miguel. This anchorage was visited thirty-five years later by the English freebooter, Sir Francis Drake, and given his name.

On the return voyage, somewhere in the islands off Santa Barbara Channel on January 3, 1543, Cabrillo died of an infection caused by having broken his arm and shoulder in a shipboard fall, but he had made his mark: this Portuguese-Spaniard soldier-mariner found the land that had been named before it had been seen.

After Cabrillo's expedition, 227 years passed before the Spaniards made their first settlement there, but in the waiting, California was rediscovered many times.

Galleons from the Philippine Islands, a Spanish possession from 1564 and governed by a viceroyalty of New Spain,
built a profitable trade between Manila and Mexico and
skirted the California coast laden with cargoes of silks, damasks, spices, chinaware, wax, and other exotic goods of the
Far East. The rules of the trade called for the galleons,
outward-bound from Manila, to follow the Great Circle. This
route took them northeast toward Japan, then due east along
the forty-first parallel to the vicinity of Cape Mendocino,
westernmost point of the California coast, then south past
Baja California to Acapulco. There were at least two hundred Manila galleon voyages to Mexico and many of them,
perhaps most, touched on the California shore to fill water
casks, cut wood, and search for game.

2

Then Drake came. He and his corsairs sailed from Plymouth in November, 1577, with a fleet of six vessels led
by the hundred-ton *Golden Hind*. They ran south to the Cape
Verdes and into the Strait of Magellan, took seventeen days
to thread the hellish Horn, and, as they entered the Pacific,
endured a storm that lasted fifty-two days, destroyed some
of their ships and sent others scurrying back to England.
Now alone, a speck on the measureless ocean, Drake worried the battered *Hind* north along the gale-swept western
coast of South America, his cutthroat crew sacking Spanish
towns from Chile north to Mexico and filling the hold of the
flagship with gold and silver bullion and plate, pearls and
emeralds, and all manner of plunder. The *Hind* captured and
looted many Spanish ships as well. One of them, bound for
Panama, had the memorable name *Cacafuego* ("Shitfire")
and was grappled to the *Hind* off Lima. It was found to
contain so much booty—twenty-six tons of silver bullion,
eighty pounds of gold, plus weapons, gunpowder, clothing,

and religious artifacts—that it took three days for Drake's pinnaces to transfer the cargo to his flagship.

The master mariner sailed on and spent a month in the summer of 1579 on the California coast, careening, refitting and provisioning the *Golden Hind,* and claiming the land, which he named Nova Albion, for his patron, Elizabeth I. Drake may have entered the Golden Gate, though he made no mention of the spectacular bay that lay inside the headlands. He did trade with the Miwok Indians of the northern coast and may have journeyed as far north as the future Bodega Bay before sailing west for Mindanao, Java, the Indian Ocean, the Cape of Good Hope, and home to Plymouth in September, 1580, completing his circumnavigation of the globe in two years and nine months.

The Englishman's claim of New Albion does not seem to have greatly disturbed the Spanish crown or its viceregal authorities in the New World, but since a port was needed for the Manila galleon trade, Spain did send several expeditions to the California coast in the years following Drake's foray.

The most significant of these explorations was that of the *adelantado* (merchant-adventurer) Sebastián Vizcaíno, who set out from Acapulco with two ships in the spring of 1602. In December, he arrived off Cabrillo's Bay of San Miguel, which he renamed for his flagship *San Diego,* then moved north, bestowing names, most of them holy names, on the islands, points, and inlets he spied—Santa Catalina, Santa Barbara, Punta Concepción. At Santa Catalina, he saw many Indian canoes made of cedar and pine, their seams caulked with brea from seepages along the coast, some of them carrying fifteen men who rowed like galley slaves.

The prize discovery of Vizcaíno's expedition was the sighting of a magnificent harbor. It was, he said, "the best port that could be desired, for besides being sheltered from all the winds, it has many pines for masts and yards, and live oaks, and white oaks, and water in great quantity, all near the shore." He spoke of the bay being "excellent for shipping," sheltered from the winds, ideal to provide security and protection for ships from Manila, and a climate resembling that of Castile.

He named it for the viceroy of Mexico, the Conde de Monterey.

3

By the time the Spaniards made their first mission foothold there in 1769, the immense and still unmapped land they called California was inhabited by native peoples, perhaps 150,000 in all, in at least a hundred tribes and clans. In the north were people such as the Shasta, Modoc, Northern Paiute, the coastal Pomo, Miwok, Costanoan, and others; in the midlands were the Washo, Paiute, Shoshone, Salinan, and Yukot; in the south, the Chumash, Serrano, Diegueño, Gabrielino, Mojave, and Yuma.

They knew little of the vastness and diversity of their land for they were not nomadic and for twelve thousand years had subsisted on whatever their small domains provided.

Among many tribes, acorns provided the staple food. These were pounded and ground by mortar and pestle into a fatty, nutritious flour, winnowed by tossing in a basket, washed free of their bitter tannic acid, and rolled into a mush or unleavened cakes, seasoned with wood ashes, bits of meat or fish, and baked in earthen ovens. In the deserts, mesquite beans were a staple; in forested areas, piñon nuts. Hunters, using snares, pit traps, and arrows with obsidian points, killed deer and other small game; coastal tribes fished with nets and hooks and harpoon-like spears, gathered shellfish, and caught small fish by using buckeyes to poison pools and eddies. Mojaves and Yumas and the people of the Colorado River region grew corn, beans, and pumpkins; the more primitive tribes ate insects and grubbed for roots.

Many of the mid- and southern-California Indians lived in conical or domed huts made of poles and brush and banked with dirt; in the north, there were solid frame dwellings of redwood planks.

There were basket-makers among some of these people, clever weavers using sedge, bulrush, willow, bracken, or tule reeds, who often decorated their works with stained bird feathers. The baskets were used for gathering and winnowing, and those of finest weave were filled with water and hot stones, for cooking.

Along the coast, boats were made of tule balsa, and rafts of rushes; in the far northwest, dugout canoes were fashioned from redwood trunks.

Artisans made arrow points of obsidian, stones, and shells; made awls and pots, charms, pendants, dentalium or clam-shell beads (used for money); others made music from clap-sticks, deer hooves, turtle shells, gourds, bone whistles, and animal-skin drums.

In some places, the natives were naked; in others, they wore skirts of plant fibers or animal skins, and slept on furs and deer-hides.

Most of these disparate people were exogamous, mixing and marrying among one another; the men were polygamous, the marriages made by agreement or purchase.

Religion and medicine were guided by a shaman; sometimes drugs were a part of the religion, as in the northern San Joaquin Valley and among certain southern tribes that developed a *toloache,* or jimsonweed cult.

The Spaniards, including the missionaries, who invaded their lands were contemptuous of the Indians, describing them as lazy, filthy, immoral savages.

4

In May, 1769, a Spanish officer named Gaspar de Portolá led an expedition of fifty soldiers, servants, Christianized Indians (called "neophytes"), and missionaries from northern Baja California to the bay founded by Juan Rodríguez Cabrillo 227 years earlier.

At the head of the brown-robed Franciscan fathers in Portolá's party was a Spanish farmer's son, born on Majorca in 1713, Fray (Friar) Junípero Serra, father-president of the missions in Baja.

Portolá took possession of San Diego on July 1, established it as a presidio, and on July 16, Serra proclaimed the first mission of Alta California and named it San Diego de Alcalá.

San Diego was the earliest of twenty-one missions founded in California, each a day's journey apart and connected by a rude wagon trail called El Camino Real (the Royal Road). The northernmost of the missions, San Francisco Solano de Sonoma (Sonoma a Miwok word meaning "earth village"), was founded by Franciscans in 1823, two years after Mexico won its independence from Spain. For all its isolation from the governance of California, Sonoma became among the most prosperous of the missions. It had rich pasturage around it for herds of cattle, horses, and sheep; the grain-fields were irrigated by water piped from springs; there were grapes for wine-making, and orchards of pears and apples, pomegranates, figs, and olives.

During California's "pastoral" era (1769–1833), eighty-two thousand Indians lived, worked, and died in a feudal peonage in the missions. These neophytes were the church's slaves, given instruction in Christianity, working throughout their lives as menials in the mission fields as planters and harvesters, adobe brick-makers, and butchers of cattle for the growing hide-and-tallow industry.

In the sixty-four years that followed the founding of the San Diego mission, two-thirds of the native peoples died, most of them from the diseases brought by their conquerors: cholera, dysentery, smallpox, tuberculosis, syphilis, diphtheria, typhoid, and scarlet fever.

2

The Mexicans

∎

1

As the colony of Alta California grew, the Spanish rulers in Mexico found it increasingly difficult to garrison their remote Pacific province, or even to supply it with needed goods. Ships from Mexican ports and especially from Spain, faced long, costly, and hazardous voyages to this isolated outpost, and when the wars of independence from Spain began in 1810, these supply-ship voyages ceased entirely.

In 1821, Mexico gained its independence from Spain, and in September, 1822, California became a Mexican territory. For a time, the new mother country made an effort to exert control over its stepchild, which it promoted to a "department" in 1836. Governors were appointed from Mexico City, and a *disputación,* a sort of provincial legislature, was established. This body met only when the governor ordered, and as a result, the business of state devolved into a petty despotism, with little or no guidance from home. Mexico, preoccupied with its own perpetual inner turmoil, adopted a laissez-faire policy toward the department of California, as it did toward its New Mexico colony, allowing both to drift and find ways of maintaining themselves.

Just as California's goods, guidance, and governance were ignored by Mexico, so did matters of security languish. Many of the soldiers who were sent to the province were ex-convicts and the meanest scrapings from the streets of Mexico, unqualified for the job and as little interested in service outside their home country as were the pressed or shanghaied seamen from England and America. The Californios detested these *cholos* (half-breeds) and *borrachos* (drunks), as they called them, and Governor Juan Bautista Alvarado said of them, "The majority of these soldiers were corrupt and lustful, and so audacious that not even their officers dared to impede their mutinies and other demonstrations . . . ."

Another conflict between the central government in Mexico and the Californios had to do with the secularization of the province's missions in the period 1834–1840, converting them to parish churches and selling off their great landholdings to private individuals. This enabled the wealthy to establish large private ranches—an estate usually at least four square miles in size, some as large as thirty square miles—and haciendas, most of them over five square leagues, or twenty thousand acres, in size.

2

In the absence of shipments of goods from Mexico, trade opened in Alta California to the outside world, especially in the ports of San Diego, Monterey, and San Francisco Bay. In 1822, the first foreign trading ship, a British vessel, arrived, soon followed by a Boston trader; within months, both British and American agents were ashore and thriving.

Although the Californios had some wheat, timber, beaver and otter skins, wine, and *aguardiente* to sell, the mainstay trade in early California lay in cattle hides and tallow and, to a lesser extent, in other cattle by-products such as suet, lard, and pickled beef.

Cowhides (called "California banknotes" by the Americans), scraped, salted, and dried, fetched up to two American dollars each, and by 1846, California was producing up to eighty thousand hides annually. Tallow, packed in rawhide *botas* (bags), was valued at two dollars per *arroba* (twenty-five pounds), and twenty-five thousand *arrobas* were traded annually at peak production.

The hide-and-tallow market had its main depot at San Diego, where the hides were dumped from carts onto the beach and "droghers" cleaned and salted them, staked them in the sun to dry, folded them lengthwise, hair side in, and made great, ungainly bundles of them. These were taken by pack mules or oxcarts for transfer to small boats, then stacked into the trade ships' holds, the hides for boot and shoemaking in New England, the tallow for soap and candles.

Other anchorages for this specialized commerce were established off San Luís Rey, San Juan Capistrano, San Pedro (serving Los Angeles), Santa Barbara, San Luís Obispo, Monterey, Santa Clara, and Yerba Buena, the village that came to be San Francisco.

Trading vessels from many nations visited the California ports, paying duties that provided a $75,000-a-year income for the provinces. American ships were the most frequent and active traders and brought every conceivable commodity from the United States, from brooms to cookstoves, pianos to kegs of nails. The Californios manufactured nothing and were therefore needful of everything. As Dana recorded in his journal, even the soap and candles made from their own tallow were traded to them, as were boots and shoes and saddles made from their cowhides.

A typical cargo of trade goods out of Boston and a return shipload of hides brought a three-hundred-percent profit to the trading company.

3

In 1786, the first non-Spanish visitor since Drake made a call at the Pacific coast of North America. This was the French explorer Compte de Lapérouse, who spent ten days in Monterey Bay before sailing on to Kamchatka, the Philippines, and Australia, and to being swallowed up by the Pacific and never seen again. Neither Drake, nor Lapérouse, nor the American adventurer John Ledyard— who, in the service of the illustrious English explorer Captain James Cook, came to the north California coast in 1778—made a significant impression on the Spanish throne or its viceroys in the New World.

They continued to come, increasingly bothersome intruders: by the 1790s, Russian and British ships were in the North Pacific killing sea otters, seals, and whales—sperms, gray-backs, humpbacks, rights, and blues. By 1801, some eighteen thousand sea otters had been slaughtered in California waters, their pelts worth three hundred dollars each in Canton. By 1820, this animal, which had flourished from the Aleutians to Baja California, had been virtually extinguished.

In 1818, Monterey and San Juan Capistrano were plundered and burned by pirate patriots from two privateers sailing under the Argentine flag and commanded by a Frenchman, Hippolyte de Bouchard, a freebooter fighting against Spain in South America. So distant was the Pacific outpost from the main theaters of action in South America and Mexico that Bouchard's foray was California's only brush with the wars of independence from Spain.

Russians came to San Francisco Bay from Sitka in 1806, sent in the brigantine *Juno* by Aleksandr Baranov, head of the Russian American Fur Company, to buy supplies for his scurvy-plagued and starving colonists in Alaska and to trade cloth, agricultural implements, tools, and furniture. The

Russians, dreaming of a trans-Pacific empire, gained from Spanish authorities a temporary trading concession, and fifty miles north of San Francisco Bay they built a timber palisade and blockhouses slotted with rifle loopholes—sixty buildings in all—and armed the place, which they called Rossiya, or Fort Ross, with cannon. Soon afterward, the Russian fur traders built another post at Bodega Point, eighteen miles south of Fort Ross, and stationed eighty trapper-traders and fifty Aleut Indians there.

Even though the Spanish, and later the Mexican, authorities in California were confident that the Russians would make no advances closer to San Francisco Bay, as a precaution, the mission town of Sonoma was garrisoned and armed with nine brass cannons.

4

The original American resident of California, a genuine Boston man and merchant seaman named Thomas W. Doak, came to Monterey in 1816 on the trader *Albatross*. He may have been sent ashore to recover from some illness, or may simply have deserted his ship. Not much is known about him except that he married into a Spanish family, worked as a carpenter, and died in about 1848.

A few other Americans ventured to California in the dying years of Spanish hegemony, but most of them arrived after Mexican independence.

Jedediah Strong Smith, born in the Susquehanna Valley of southern New York, became the first American to cross into California by a land route. So respected in the mountaineer fraternity that he was called "Captain Smith" and "Mr. Smith" by men who rarely deferred to anyone, he carried a butcher's knife in his belt and a bible in his bedroll and was described as "half grizzly and half preacher" by his comrades.

In November, 1826, Smith led a party of beaver trappers across the Mojave Desert and into the San Bernardino Valley of California, completing the first overland crossing of the southwestern route to the Pacific. At the San Gabriel Mission near Pueblo de Los Angeles, he and his men were at first welcomed and treated cordially by the village *alcalde* (magistrate) but soon fell under suspicion. Fur traders were unknown in the province at the time and Smith had difficulty in explaining his purpose and profession. The Mexican authorities ended up calling him a *pescador* (fisherman) and considered imprisoning him in San Diego until they could figure out what he and his ruffian-like crew were up to. Only the intervention of the master of an American trading ship anchored in San Diego Harbor kept this from happening, but in the spring of 1827, Smith and his men were ordered to leave California.

The Yankee-trader captain took Smith north to San Pedro Bay. There he was reunited with his trapper party, equipped with new provisions and horses, and seemed to obey orders to quit the country when he retraced his route over the San Bernardino Mountains. But instead of returning east, he led his party north to the San Joaquin River Valley, which proved to be rich beaver grounds, and wintered there.

In May, 1827, after trapping along the Stanislaus River and amassing a haul of fifteen hundred pounds of furs, the captain and his men tried to cross the mountain barrier east of their trapping camp but were turned back, losing five horses along the way, by the heavy snow and ferocious winds in the passes. His main party left behind, Smith and two others made a second push and succeeded in getting through, thus becoming the first white men to cross the Sierra Nevada range.

The foray into California by Jedediah Smith and his trapper band set an ominous pattern.

In 1830, working with a seasoned mountain man named Ewing Young and a party of forty fur men, a nineteen-year-

old Kentuckian named Christopher Houston Carson made
his first expedition to California, entering the San Gabriel
Mission by Jed Smith's Mojave route. The Ewing Young
party, without sanction, trapped north as far as the Sacramento River, burned several Indian villages after a number
of their horses were stolen, then ran into trouble upon returning to Los Angeles. There, pueblo officials demanded to
know what authorization Young had to travel, trap, and kill
Indians in California. When he could provide no papers,
threats were made to jail him and his party. Kit Carson
claimed that the Mexicans tried to ply Young and his men
with liquor to make it easier to arrest them. In any event,
Young wanted to get home before his furs were confiscated
and so led his brigade out of the territory to the Colorado
River.

All this was precedent. Twenty years after Jed Smith and
fifteen years after Ewing Young left their tracks in California, the process was repeated: an American, with a band of
freebooters, Kit Carson among them, entered California uninvited, was ordered to leave, and refused.

3

The Californios

■

1

John Bidwell, a New Yorker from Chautauqua County and former schoolteacher who came to the Pacific coast in 1841, told of how a friend or stranger paid a visit to the home of a Californio and stayed overnight. All that was necessary, Bidwell said, was to bring your own blankets and a knife with which to cut meat from a common haunch. When you finished eating, you delivered your plate to your hostess and said *"Muchas grácias, Señora,"* and she would answer *"Buen provecho."*

This example of the gregariousness, generosity, and hospitality of the *gente de razón* (people of means) was echoed by many others in the dying days of Old California. Visitors wrote of being invited to picnics, lavish weddings, birthday celebrations, religious festivals, fandangos, rodeos, and amusements such as horseback grizzly-bear hunts, wild-horse roundups, and bull-and-bear baitings.

Many of the American visitors bit the hand extended to them.

In 1841, a United States Navy explorer named Charles Wilkes led a six-ship expedition to chart the Pacific coast, with particular attention given to San Francisco Bay. He had serious things to report to his superiors in Washington: he was amazed by the expanse of the bay, big enough, he said, to shelter all the world's navies, with prevailing winds that put it on sea-lanes linking ports in India, China, Japan, and Manila to the Pacific coast of North America. San Francisco was the potential key to the Orient trade, he said in his voluminous report, especially since the next significant harbor north, at Juan de Fuca Strait, was eight hundred miles distant, and San Diego Bay lay over five hundred miles to the south.

Except for a cursory look at the village of Santa Clara, at the extreme southern tip of San Francisco Bay, Wilkes himself seems rarely to have gone ashore, but others in his expedition did and kept diaries and journals on what they saw and experienced.

A party of officers from one of his ships, the sloop-of-war *Vincennes,* examined the village of Yerba Buena, a woebegone settlement consisting of a few ruined adobes and a poop-deck cabin from a wrecked sailing ship serving as somebody's home. They also visited Sonoma, the northernmost presidio of California, and were greeted by the eminent military commander of the northern frontier, Mariano Guadalupe Vallejo, whom many believed to be the most powerful man in California. The commandante led the officers on a tour of Casa Grande, the Vallejo home adjoining the garrison's barracks, and one of the Americans jotted a note describing the furnishings of the home as gaudy—in particular, certain chairs that had come from the Sandwich Islands. Colonel Vallejo was ill during the visit, but this did not diminish his hospitality and the visitors were invited to dinner. Some of the officers found the food execrable—served cold and every bite, one said, "poisoned" with red peppers and garlic.

The colonel's brother, Salvador, and three soldiers from the presidio, took the Wilkes party on a tour of the Sonoma countryside, a sportsman's Eden with thousands of ducks and geese in the marshes and deer so plentiful they were killed for their tallow. In the presidio barracks, one of the American officers counted thirteen soldiers and described them as "mere boys with enormous swords and a pair of nascent moustaches, deerskin boots and that everlasting serape or blanket with a hole in the middle for the head."

The Americans also saw an Indian village of three hundred people and left with the image of naked savages living in hovels made of tree branches, eating bullock meat and acorns.

The *Vincennes* men suffered another meal of chile and tortillas with the Vallejos and were later invited to a *baile* where they were shocked to see the ladies smoking cigarillos.

2

Most of the callers who left a record of their experience among the Californios ignored the naked Indian and his stick-and-mud hovel and the poor farmworker crowded with ten or fifteen others in a small one-room adobe. Most visitors wrote of California as the land of the Don, who, dwelling on his rancho, presided over his picturesque and spacious lands.

The Don's domain typically lay across rolling hills and creek-crossed valleys; his home was a whitewashed adobe structure with a red-tiled roof, and verandas shaded by sycamores and oaks. He might have a melon patch, grow corn, grapes, and olives for his own use. He had so many horses that he hunted and killed hundreds of them to preserve his pasturage for his cows, and let hundreds of others run free, trailing a rope for easy capture when needed.

The ranchero's source of income and his life's passion lay in his cattle. They were wide-horned, long-legged, lean, and tough animals that roamed his unfenced estate at will and required little attention until the periodic *rodeos* (roundups), in which the ranch's *vaqueros* would brand and notch the ears of the calves and record their numbers on tally-sticks— one notch per ten head.

After the rodeo, the next and final time the animals were rounded up was for the *matanza,* the slaughtering. Since the cattle were valuable to the Californios principally for their hides and their fat by-products, only a few choice haunches were kept, together with some meat to be cut into long strips, soaked in brine and dried. This black *carne seca* (which American cowboys called jerky) was carried by the *vaqueros* in their saddlebags. The rest of the hide-and-fat-stripped carcasses were left to the buzzards, wolves, and coyotes.

It never seems to have occurred to the rancheros to venture into the dairy business. "It was very common at many haciendas for the owners to say that while they had six or seven thousand head of cattle, they could not offer a traveler a glass of milk if he requested it," the Monterey customs official Antonio María Osio wrote in an 1851 memoir. "They gladly would offer him a calf, but they only used the meat they could eat at one sitting. They would dump the rest out in the same fields where they would sleep or nap while their animals grazed and rested."

That there was very little money in California seemed unimportant to the Don. He lived content in the assurance that everything he needed was available from the traders, most of them Yankees, whose ships carried foodstuffs, drygoods, hardware, guns and powder, liquors, furniture—even pianos and billiard tables—to trade for "California banknotes" and tallow.

Nor was education a matter of much consequence to him. Most of California's native-born were illiterate. No system of education, and therefore no schools, existed in the province in the 1840s or at any time before that. For one thing, the Franciscan fathers feared education, convinced that reading and writing would foment such dangerous things as rebellion and godlessness, and only a few of the many governors who came to the province attempted to change the system.

3

And so for three hundred years after Juan Rodríguez Cabrillo spied the sun-washed coast of Cathay from the quarterdeck of the *San Salvador,* Mexican California drifted, a remote, neglected satellite suspended in a governmental vacuum.

Mexico may have regarded its Pacific "department" as the inestimably precious jewel in its colonial crown and dreaded the prospect of losing it, but Californios could not remember a time when the home country had made a demonstration of any such regard. Mexico City's laissez-faire policy toward its possessions north of the Rio Grande, the product of its own incessant inner turmoil and of the two thousand miles of desert and mountain that separated it from the Pacific Rim, begat a similar policy in California. The *gente de razón* simply ceased worrying about their putative mother country. It had never seriously governed California to begin with, and the last fragile ties, those held by the church, were broken in 1834 when the missions, which had birthed such towns as San Luís Obispo, San Juan Bautista, San Juan Capistrano, and Sonoma, were secularized. Then, even the Indians were released from patronage and governance.

After nearly a quarter-century of neglect, California had evolved into a semi-autonomous colony that regarded its home country as little more than an absentee landlord, a tax collector who contributed nothing to earn his revenue. Mexico supplied a string of nominal "governors" to mind the political affairs of its cherished department, but these affairs were elementary in nature and of little interest to the average Californio.

Talk of a schism with Mexico was commonplace in the years between the 1834 secularization of the missions and 1845. Many Californios felt that a revolution would be easy, perhaps bloodless: the home country had no serious military presence there beyond four decrepit presidios along the coast, San Diego to Yerba Buena, each with a handful of slothful soldiers and some rusty cannons. In fact, in the period 1836–1845, there were four desultory revolts against Mexican authority, although none of them resulted in significant changes in the governance of California.

Some Californios remained loyal to Mexico, others favored an independent state and opposed any foreign intervention; still others leaned toward annexation by England, France, or the most prominent of the trader-nations, the United States.

By 1845, internecine rivalries and territorial jealousies characterized the politics of Mexican California. The province was unofficially divided into two regions, with San Luís Obispo the demarcation point at the approximate midcoast. South of this tiny port town to the border with Baja California lived the southern populace, the *abajeños* (those below); north of San Luís Obispo to Bodega Bay and beyond lay the country of the northerners, the *arribeños* (those above). What political guidance the province could claim was centered in the south at Pueblo de Los Angeles, an adobe village with a population of fifteen hundred, where the governor, a man named Pío Pico, resided. He had little influence among the far-flung *arribeños:* in Monterey, just four hundred miles north of Los Angeles, the senior military officer in California, General José Castro, served as quasi-governor; and in Yerba Buena and Sonoma, neither Pico nor Castro, who disliked each other and who were at odds over control of the departmental treasury and customs income, exerted any significant influence.

4

In 1845, Alta California had a population of about twenty-five thousand, of which perhaps fifteen thousand to seventeen thousand were Indians, a sad remnant, about a tenth of the number of native inhabitants there when Spain built its first mission on their lands in 1769. The eight thousand or so non-natives included as many as twelve hundred foreigners—Russians, British, Germans, Sandwich Islanders, and a smattering of other nationalities. Americans were by far the most numerous of the outlanders, numbering at least eight hundred of the twelve hundred, most of whom had settled in the northern Sacramento Valley.

What lured the Yankees there probably began with the tales told by the Bostons—the sea captains and tars such as Ebenezer Dorr and, especially, Richard Henry Dana—who came to San Diego and Monterey and San Francisco Bay and departed in wonderment at the sheer immensity of the place, its salubrious climate, its primeval beauty, hidden riches, limitless potential.

Since there is nothing like a financial disaster to create a migration, economic factors played a part in the luring. In the spring of 1837, just two months after the inauguration of Martin Van Buren as President, a panic erupted when New York banks suspended the conversion of paper money into gold and silver. The practice spread, nine hundred banks failed, there were marches by the unemployed, food riots erupted in many cities, and a six-year economic depression followed.

The Texas example also provided a precedent in propelling Americans to the Pacific.

When Mexico won its independence from Spain in 1821, several hundred Americans had been permitted—welcomed, in fact—to "colonize" the Mexican state of Texas y Coahuila, requiring only that the settlers convert to Catholicism and take Mexican citizenship. Then, with Mexico's attention diverted by internal revolutions, counterrevolutions, coups, and insurrections, the American Texans, employing the old lie of being deprived of religious and economic freedom, of being oppressed by a cruel and despotic regime, began talking of independence, of revolution. In 1836, after defeating a Mexican army sent to quell the revolt, the Texans proclaimed themselves a republic and began to work toward winning annexation by the United States.

On December 29, 1845, Texas became the twenty-eighth state of the Union.

The trails broken, the Oregon Trail in particular, were another factor in California emigration. These breakthroughs rose from the explorations of men such as Jedediah Smith, Ewing Young, Joseph Reddeford Walker, James Clyman, Tom Fitzpatrick, and army explorers such as John Charles Frémont.

The Oregon experience certainly heightened "California fever."

By 1845, the American population in Oregon territory was nearing ten thousand, an astonishing number considering that the first real overland covered-wagon migration to Oregon had taken place only four years previously when a pioneering party of seventy emigrants left Westport, Missouri, and joined up with a group of Catholic missionaries headed for the Columbia River. Within three years, these pioneers had built seventeen flour and sawmills, were raising twenty thousand head of cattle, and had harvested a hundred thousand bushels of wheat.

Congressman William Gilpin of Missouri told his congressional colleagues in 1846: "Half a dozen years ago, the Willamette was occupied by beaver and eagles; it now exhibits an American republic, with a government, agriculture, mills, and commerce."

Of that original 1841 Oregon-bound emigrant party of seventy people, thirty-two turned southward at Fort Hall on the Snake River in Idaho. This group made its way to the fertile, isolated Sacramento Valley, close to Sutter's Fort, the perfect place to be left alone.

4

Nueva Helvetia

■

1

Those who journeyed for the first time down the western foothills of the Sierra Nevada and followed the American River into Mexican California must have stopped and rubbed their eyes as they reached the slight bend in the river near its joining with the Sacramento. Before them lay a wonder of the West: an immense, tawny fortress, its adobe walls fifteen feet high and three feet thick, its corner bastions protected by twelve brass cannons, all surrounded by tilled, plantation-like fields.

Sutter's Fort, as significant a wilderness sentinel as Bent's Fort on the Arkansas, lay at the center of a much larger and even more impressive enterprise. This was John Augustus Sutter's "Nueva Helvetia"—New Switzerland—a fifty-thousand-acre empire that in peak times employed five hundred workers: Indian field hands, who were paid in special coins redeemable only at Sutter's stores, and *vaqueros*, farmers, gardeners, blacksmiths, gunsmiths, carpenters, tanners, blanket-weavers, hunters, trappers, sawyers, shepherds, millwrights, and distillers. There were even hired hands to run a launch down the Sacramento to the bays of San Pablo and San Francisco carrying loads of hides, furs, wheat, and produce, returning with lumber from the coastal redwood groves and other supplies.

The visionary, and at times improvident, lord of this spectacular domain was an amiable and hospitable entrepreneur born in Baden, Germany, of Swiss ancestry. Sutter had had a fecund marriage but an unhappy one, perhaps because of his extravagances, meager earnings, and business failures in Switzerland. Whatever the cause, he deserted his wife and five children and emigrated to the United States in 1834. He settled in St. Louis and for a time entered the Santa Fé trade and trapped beaver in the Rocky Mountains. In 1838, he removed to Oregon territory, and in July of the next year, after a circuitous voyage to Sitka in Russian Alaska, Vancouver, and the Sandwich Islands, arrived in San Francisco Bay as a self-proclaimed former captain of the Swiss Guards.

A charming, ambitious dynamo who had learned the Spanish language in his Santa Fé days, Sutter quickly became acquainted with influential provincial authorities, and in 1840 he secured from Governor Juan Bautista Alvarado permission to establish a rancho in the unsettled Sacramento Valley. He began with trapping and wild-grape brandy making, employed Indians, Kanakas, Californians, and vagabond foreign settlers, and expanded into cattle raising and wheat farming. He cleared land, built an irrigation system and a mill. In 1841, when he swore fealty to Mexico, he was granted a parcel of land eleven square leagues in size. So rapidly did he rise in wealth and influence that he was able to purchase Fort Ross on thirty thousand dollars in credit from the Russian-American Fur Company, and gained in the sale the fort's horses, cattle, and forty cannons.

Soon after acquiring the fort, with Governor Alvarado's blessing and precisely three hundred years after Cabrillo first sighted the California coast, Sutter's workers constructed a 425-by-170-foot mud-brick fort at New Helvetia, ostensibly to protect the northern boundary of California from Indian depredations and unwanted intruders.

The Swiss had earned the trust of his absentee masters.
He had become a citizen of Mexico, won a huge and spec-
tacularly productive land grant, was called "General," and
had the status of a provincial official. He was empowered to
enforce the laws of Alta California, to dispense justice,
and—a notable responsibility—to prevent Indian raids and
"the robberies committed by adventurers from the United
States."

His stature among some key Californios was diminished
by his participation, on the wrong side, in the revolt against
the last Mexican-appointed governor of the province.

Brigadier General Manuel Micheltorena, a native of Oax-
aca, was sent to San Diego in 1841 and took with him an
"army" of three hundred thugs liberated from Mexican pris-
ons and jails. These *cholos,* unpaid and undisciplined, soon
ran amok, terrorizing the *abajeños* by their drunkenness,
threats, and pillaging of shops and homes.

Micheltorena, congenial but lazy, earned the loyalty of Sutter and the Americans in the north by permitting the Swiss to
make land grants to foreign emigrants, but by the end of 1844,
the *cholo* rampages had alienated the true Californios. The
governor's predecessor, Juan Bautista Alvarado, the man who
had given Sutter permission to build New Helvetia, now organized a revolt and enlisted his friend, General José Castro of
Monterey, to lead his 220-man army of rebels.

The former governor had reason to trust Castro. In April,
1840, Alvarado had learned of a planned uprising by foreigners
intent on taking control of the province. The foreigners, it
was said, were led by one Isaac Graham, a Virginia-born
trapper who had settled at Natividad, near Monterey. Castro
captured Graham and his confederate, an Englishman named
William R. Garner, and marched them in irons to Monterey,
where they were charged with fomenting rebellion and taken
by ship to Tepic, in Baja California. There, apparently
through the influence and bribery of the British consul, they
were released and permitted to return to Monterey.

Sutter and his handful of loyalists reached Los Angeles in February, 1845, to join forces with Micheltorena. Most of his original force had evaporated, returning to their farms and homesteads in the north when it appeared that Micheltorena was doomed to failure. All that remained in Sutter's miniature army were some Walla Walla and other Indians, and a few American settlers working land near New Helvetia: Moses Carson, Kit's half-brother, a rancher in the Russian River area; Ezekial Merritt, a coarse, often whiskey-raddled trapper and frontiersman; Peter Lassen, a Dane, a blacksmith, and a naturalized Mexican citizen who owned a sawmill at Santa Cruz and a 26,000-acre land-grant rancho in the Sacramento Valley; and John Bidwell, Sutter's trusted assistant at the fort and aide-de-camp in the field.

The rebellion ended bloodlessly on February 20, 1845, in the "battle" at Cahuenga Pass near Los Angeles. Micheltorena surrendered to Alvarado and Castro and subsequently returned to Mexico.

Sutter and his men, at first taken prisoner, were soon forgiven and pardoned by Alvarado.

Pío Pico, a Californio by birth and a cavalry commander under Alvarado, replaced Micheltorena, taking office in Los Angeles. He may have sensed that he would be the last governor before his homeland was wrested from Mexico, for he seemed to advocate an alliance of some kind with the French or British to stave off the Americans, who had already made serious inroads into his country. American settlers in California he viewed as "lawless adventurers" and "avaricious strangers." He wrote,

We are threatened by hordes of Yankee emigrants; already the wagons of these perfidious people have scaled the almost inaccessible summits of the Sierra Nevadas, crossed the entire continent and penetrated the fruitful valley of the Sacramento. They are cultivating farms, establishing vineyards, erecting mills, sawing up lumber, building workshops and a thousand and one other things which seem natural to them but which Californians neglect or despise—we cannot stand alone against them.

2

Despite such words, Sutter continued to encourage emigrants, including Americans, even urging the new government to grant to foreigners two-league parcels of wilderness lands along the San Joaquin River and tributaries of it such as the Stanislaus and Merced, and offering parcels of his own grant to newcomers.

The motive behind his largesse may have been his indebtedness—Sutter owed the Russians most of the thirty thousand dollars he had agreed to pay for Fort Ross—but he was nonetheless exceedingly charitable with his money and manpower. Many times he dispatched his men across the Sierra to assist stranded or desperate emigrant parties; he was a convivial and generous host and a benefactor to the down-and-out. John Bidwell, one of the thirty-two emigrants who had come to the Sacramento Valley in 1841, said of the lord of New Helvetia, "He employed men, not because always needed or could profitably employ them, but because in the kindness of his heart it simply became a habit to employ everybody who wanted employment."

Bidwell himself worked for Sutter, serving "the General" as majordomo and bookkeeper.

Not all the Americans making their way to Sutter's Fort were farmers or others seeking gainful employment. California historian Hubert H. Bancroft said that some of the arrivals were deserters from ships visiting coastal trade ports: "Reckless, daring, and unprincipled men, with nothing to lose." He said there were also a number of men—"mere filibusters"—looking not for work, but for glory, wealth, and power under what they felt was a soon-forthcoming American takeover of the province, men who looked upon the Californios as inferior humans who had to be taught the beauties of freedom and the ways of a civilized nation.

In this, Bancroft was practically defining the spirit of expansionism defined in the summer of 1845 by John Louis O'Sullivan as "Manifest Destiny."

3

Manuel Micheltorena, early in his troubled tenure as governor, had a notable run-in with American trespassers, an affair that served as an omen, bright as a signal rocket, that the United States would be arriving soon and intended to stay.

On October 18, 1842, an American naval officer of Welsh ancestry named Thomas ap Catesby Jones arrived off Monterey in his flagship, the frigate *United States,* accompanied by a sloop-of war, the *Cyane.* Commodore Jones and a party of officers and sailors came ashore and to the astonishment of ex-governor Juan Alvarado, port officials, and townspeople, announced that he was taking possession of Monterey in the name of the government of the United States.

As it happened, Jones, commander of American naval forces in the Pacific, had been at anchor off Callao, Peru, when he received some newspaper articles and dispatches leading him to believe that the United States and Mexico were at war—apparently over the Texas dispute. Since there were no telegraphic stations in the West and all military instructions came to Pacific outposts by way of Cape Horn, the commodore concluded that in the absence of orders to the contrary, he needed to sail for California instantly and seize it. Otherwise, Mexico might do something drastic, such as ceding the province to England.

Alvarado, appalled at Catesby Jones' surrender demand, signed the proclamation dazedly. A Mexican customs official who witnessed the sudden capitulation wrote of the "true Californios, people who loved their country and were proud of their nationality," as having been forced to witness a painful ceremony in which the flag of Mexico was replaced with the Stars and Stripes: "This flag was alleged to be the symbol of liberty, but that was actually a lie. It belonged to an oppressor who displayed arrogance against the weak," the official wrote.

The comic conquest of Monterey lasted for a single day, the reversal effected by another American, Thomas O. Larkin, a Boston man who had come to California via the Sandwich Islands in 1832.

Serving as interpreter between Jones and Alvarado, Larkin showed the American some Mexican newspapers and commercial mail, all of more recent date than the material the commodore had read while off Callao, revealing that no state of war existed.

Thomas ap Catesby Jones apologized, restored the Mexican flag and province to Alvarado and his stunned subordinates, and sailed south to make his apologies to the governor.

Micheltorena meantime had issued a bombastic call to arms to repel the American invaders, and upon receiving the commodore and dining with him, presented the officer with a bill for the damages done to Monterey and its citizenry: he asked for fifteen thousand dollars in cash, sixteen hundred military uniforms, and some musical instruments.

Jones thought Micheltorena was joking but was ushered from the governor's office before he laughed out loud.

The preemptive conqueror of Monterey was recalled and temporarily relieved of his command. Washington disavowed responsibility for his actions.

Larkin took office as consul for the United States at Monterey in April, 1844.

By 1845, the American colony in northern California had become a source of grave concern to leaders such as Pío Pico and José Castro. The Graham and Jones affairs had left scars, reminders of the audacity and untrustworthiness of the American "adventurers," and with Mexico teetering on the brink of a war with the United States, the Californios decided that the flow of these intruders must be stopped.

Meantime, Sutter, ostensibly answerable to General Castro of Monterey, but with his loyalties split, said of the Americans: "Nothing can stop this migration. In case of opposition, they would fight like lions."

PART TWO

· ·

BEAR FLAG RISING

■

5

The Dark Horse

■

1

H*e has no wit,* no literature, no point of argument, no gracefulness of delivery, no elegance of language, no philosophy, no pathos, no felicitous impromptus; nothing that can constitute an orator, but confidence, fluency, and labor."

This mixed assessment of James Knox Polk was offered in 1834 by John Quincy Adams when he and Polk were opposite-aisle colleagues in Congress. The former President's remarks on the future President were perspicacious but not news to his party. Jacksonian Democrats knew more about Polk's limitations than his strengths, and when they brought him to the power of the presidency, they did so tentatively; they really did not know what to expect of him.

Born in North Carolina in 1795, he grew up in Tennessee, the son of a prosperous planter. A sickly boy from birth, at age seventeen, "Jimmy" Polk survived an operation for gallstones, a risky procedure performed with only liquor as anesthetic. He recovered slowly but never fully; fragile health shadowed his life.

He studied law at the University of North Carolina, served in the Tennessee House of Representatives, and was elected to Congress in 1825, the year after his marriage to Sarah

Childress, daughter of a plantation owner in Murfreesboro. She was a homely, lively, charming, and well-educated help-mate, a devout Presbyterian who frowned on drinking and dancing and doted on her husband, believed him to be a man of destiny, and protected him. He confided in her as in no other while he served six terms in Congress, including two years as Speaker. He was an unwavering supporter of An-drew Jackson's presidency and opponent of John Quincy Ad-ams'. Sarah was delighted when he retired from Congress to serve a term as governor of Tennessee. They had no children.

At the Democratic Party convention at the Odd Fellows' Hall in Baltimore, May 27–30, 1844, Martin Van Buren of Kinder-hook, New York, appeared to be the favorite for the nomina-tion. He had seemingly impeccable Jacksonian credentials: he had served as Old Hickory's secretary of state and vice presi-dent and had succeeded Jackson in the presidency. But as chief executive, Van Buren had fallen afoul of Southerners— the heart of Jackson's party—in opposing the annexation of Texas, which had declared its independence from Mexico in 1836. Northern politicians opposed the admission of Texas to the Union as another slave state, and Van Buren agreed with them. Democrats with long memories remembered the words of the most celebrated of the Alamo defenders, David Crock-ett, who, as a Tennessee congressman in 1835, said, "Van Bu-ren is as opposite to General Jackson as dung is to a diamond."

Van Buren's support eroded after the first ballot in Baltimore, and the other candidates—Lewis Cass of Michi-gan, Richard M. Johnson of Kentucky, and James Buchanan of Pennsylvania—did not catch on. Polk, whom some be-lieved might make a good vice president, was not in atten-dance at the convention when his name came up in the eighth ballot, and when he was nominated on the ninth, he became the original "dark horse." He accepted by letter, expressing appreciation for the endorsement of his mentor, Andrew

Jackson, and the honor bestowed on him by the delegates in Baltimore. He pledged to a one-term presidency—a tenet that Polk firmly believed was implicit in Jacksonian ideology (although Jackson served two terms)—and began the effort to defeat his Whig opponent, Henry Clay of Kentucky.

The Texas issue defeated Clay. Like Van Buren, he courted Northern favor and the abolitionist vote by his anti-annexation stance while Polk, criticized as "Jackson's puppet" and praised as "Young Hickory," stood steadfast behind the movement to admit Texas to the Union. Jackson favored the measure, and the outgoing President, John Tyler, had signed the treaty of annexation just the month before the Polk-Clay campaign opened.

Polk won the election in true dark-horse fashion. The November, 1844, results showed him nudging Clay out by 37,000 votes out of 2,600,000 cast. In electoral votes, Polk had 275, representing twenty-six states, to Clay's 105 and eleven states.

"Young Hickory," age forty-nine years and 122 days, took office as the eleventh President of the United States on March 4, 1845, three months before Andrew Jackson died in Nashville at age seventy-eight. Polk's inauguration was the first reported by telegraph.

His religion, it was said, was politics, and had been so since 1820 when he had been admitted to the bar in Tennessee. He had no discernible interests other than politics. He had no hobbies, sports, or pastimes, was neither a reader, a dreamer, a talker nor a laugher—"no wit, no literature," in John Quincy Adams' words. In a place and pursuit in which men mingled, drank and smoked and made promises, Polk did none of these things and had no intimates other than Sarah Polk.

He was lean, thin-lipped, morose, walked erectly, and dressed scrupulously. He had deep-set gray eyes and a high-browed head with graying hair brushed straight back behind his ears. To many, he gave the appearance of a formidable schoolmaster, cold, suspicious, pompous, narrow. It was believed that his distant and humorless nature was the product of his lifelong delicate health, worsened by his years in Washington. The miasmal swamps bordering the Potomac and their infestations of mosquitoes and flies gave rise to malarial and typhoid fevers, and dysentery, dangerous to a healthy man, murderous to one of such a delicate constitution as Polk's.

One attribute was granted to him by even his most vociferous opponents: James Knox Polk had *focus*, an utterly clear vision of what he intended to accomplish in his single term as President.

In his inaugural address, he spoke of the Republic of Texas and its impending annexation. "Our Union is a confederation of independent States," he said, "whose policy is peace with each other and all the world. To enlarge its limits is to extend the dominions of peace over additional territories and increasing millions." He seemed to hint that there were other lands that would benefit from annexation but said, somewhat abstrusely, that the rest of the world had nothing to fear from American military ambition and that the Texas example should be looked upon "not as the conquest of a nation seeking to extend her dominions by arms and violence, but as the peaceful acquisition . . ."

He also advocated free trade and was determined to lower taxes on imported goods, but few, other than trade-and-tariff authorities, cared about such dull matters. What Polk only hinted at in his inaugural speech was a breathtaking plan to nearly double the geographical size of the United States: he intended to preside over statehood for Texas (which included all the territory north from the Rio Grande to the Arkansas River and as far west as Santa Fé); he would push the British out of Oregon; and he would "acquire," preferably by purchase through diplomacy, Mexico's territory lying between the Continental Divide and the Pacific, with California the *ne-plus-ultra* objective.

In accomplishing all this, he hoped to avoid war, but he was willing to wage war if diplomacy failed.

2

In the expansionist 1840s, there were many "questions"—a word used in political and diplomatic circles to denote the conflict between one or more nations over some other nation's property. In Europe, the "Eastern question" had to do with England's concerns that Russia might swoop down Central Asia to Constantinople and threaten British India. This question eventually resulted in the Crimean War.

James Knox Polk, when he took office in March, 1845, had several questions to answer, the most important of them focused on Mexico. Even the "Oregon question" had a Mexican connection.

Oregon territory (including the present states of Oregon, Washington, Idaho, and parts of Montana and Wyoming west of the Continental Divide) had been under "joint occupancy" by the United States and England since Secretary of State John Quincy Adams had negotiated a treaty between the two countries in 1818. Oregon became a "question" when the first Americans, most of them Methodist missionaries, came to the Willamette Valley, south of the Columbia River, in the 1830s. This advent was followed by the "Oregon Fever" emigration a decade later, when reports of cheap land there arrived in the eastern United States. The British moved their Hudson's Bay Company headquarters to Vancouver Island, virtually conceding control to the Americans of the territory between Puget Sound south to the boundary with Mexican California.

But England still hovered over the territory, its presence an American expansionist's nightmare. British warships paid visits to the Oregon coast and were sighted as far south as Acapulco. Did the British covet California? Might they seize it from Mexico, or purchase it? And what were the Russians doing plying the sea-lanes of the northern coasts? And the French and the Prussians?

American claims on Oregon rested on the 54°-40' line of latitude, encompassing all of Vancouver Island, and one of the campaign slogans that helped Polk's election was "Fifty-four Forty or Fight!" The President, while willing to negotiate the latitude, said our "title" to Oregon was "clear and unquestionable," and one of his first moves as President was to ask Congress to give England one year's notice that the United States would assert its claim to Oregon.

A convention signed on June 15, 1846, ended the joint occupancy and Oregonians were notified that they were now American citizens.

This was the resolution of the first of Polk's objectives as President.

The "Texas question" had been hanging in the air for a decade and it was on the Texas experience, and the precedent set by it, that Polk's designs on California pivoted.

In 1821, soon after winning its independence from Spain, Mexico had welcomed several hundred American settlers to its northern province of Texas y Coahuila. These emigrants, most of them Southerners from slave states, won important concessions from Mexico—they were allowed to keep slaves, were protected from debts they had incurred in the United States—and by 1830, some thirty thousand Americans had posted notice that they were "Gone to Texas." But Mexico's internal turbulence, its changes in leadership and policy, eventually led to harsher laws, trade restrictions, and attempts to control the flow of emigrants to its Rio Grande territory. Out of Mexico's anarchy grew the Texas independence movement that culminated in the American setback at the Alamo on March 6, 1836, and Sam Houston's annihilation of the Mexican army at San Jacinto six weeks later.

Mexico never relinquished its province to the Americans, nor did it recognize the existence of the Republic of Texas. Offers by the United States to purchase the province were rebuffed. It was a certainty that the American annexation of Texas would mean war, and it was this eventuality that faced President Polk when he took office. His predecessor, John Tyler, as the last act of his administration, sponsored a resolution to annex the Republic of Texas.

In the first summer of the Polk presidency, John Louis O'Sullivan's extraordinary "Manifest Destiny" call to arms appeared in the July–August issue of his paper, *The United States Magazine and Democratic Review,* arguing in favor of the annexation of Texas. The lawyer-editor articulated the doctrine with some prescience in writing that after Texas was absorbed into the Union, "California will, probably, next fall away from the loose affiliation which, in such a country like Mexico, holds a remote province in a slight equivocal kind of dependence on the metropolis."

He said that "the Anglo-Saxon foot" was already on California's borders, and what he called "the advance guard of the irresistible army of the Anglo-Saxon emigration" was already pouring down into the province "armed with the plough and the rifle" in the first stage of a process, not far distant, "when the Empires of the Atlantic and the Pacific would again flow together into one."

3

While the phrase "Manifest Destiny" did not appear in the President's speeches, journal, or correspondence, the essence of the concept to James Knox Polk was political scripture. Oregon's boundary was in negotiation, and joint sovereignty of the territory with England would soon end;

the annexation of Texas had all but been accomplished in
the month he took office. But he knew that Mexico was unlikely to yield to diplomacy or a cash offering for its territory north of the Rio Grande and west to the Pacific—New
Mexico and, the Koh-i-noor in the crown, California.

Seventeen days after Polk took office, he had a special
meeting with his secretary of the navy, George Bancroft.
This urbane Massachusetts Democrat, a distinguished historian and author* who would soon see his dream of a naval
academy at Annapolis come true, had among other dis-
tinctions that of being as close to a confidant as the President
allowed. On March 21, 1845, as a result of their meeting,
Bancroft sent a secret message by warship around Cape
Horn to the Peruvian coastal port of Callao ordering Commodore John D. Sloat, commander of the navy's Pacific
Squadron, to proceed to the west coast of Mexico.

Sloat, age sixty-five, a New Yorker and forty-five-year veteran of the navy who had fought pirates in the West Indies
and the British in the War of 1812, moved cautiously. His
squadron consisted of the fifty-four-gun flagship *Savannah*,
the *Congress*, of sixty guns, the sloops-of-war *Warren*, *Portsmouth*, and *Levant*, each carrying twenty-four guns, the
armed schooner *Shark,* and a transport, *Erie*. One additional
ship later joined Sloat's flotilla as a reinforcement, the sloop
Cyane, which sailed from Norfolk, Virginia, that summer,
taking fifty-six days to reach Rio de Janeiro and another
fifty-three battling the Horn to Valparaiso.

The *Cyane* joined Sloat's squadron in November, and by
then the commodore had received additional orders from his
government: Bancroft's new messages said that if Sloat
learned "beyond a doubt" that the United States and
Mexico were at war, he was to sail north immediately, seize

Not to be confused with the California historian, Hubert H. Bancroft.

San Francisco Bay, and blockade or occupy other California ports as he deemed necessary. In so doing, he would "preserve, if possible, the most friendly relations with the inhabitants" of the province and be "assiduously careful to avoid any act which could be construed as an act of aggression."

Since no transcontinental telegraph system existed in 1845, nor a canal across Central America to the Pacific, Bancroft's secret orders to Commodore Sloat were carried by courier on a sailing ship and were many months in transit. Even more months passed before Sloat could provision his Pacific Squadron and make his voyage north from Callao to Mazatlán, the principal seaport on the west coast of Mexico.

In mid-June, before Bancroft's orders reached Sloat, other orders, these to the army, were carried from Washington to Fort Jesup, in the Red River Valley of Louisiana. The dispatches, from Polk's secretary of war, William Marcy, to the Fort Jesup commanding officer, Brigadier General Zachary Taylor, represented an even more overt acknowledgment of impending war than Bancroft's directive to Sloat. Taylor was instructed to move his force of about two thousand men to a camp below New Orleans, where they would embark on steamers down the Mississippi to the Gulf of Mexico, thence to another camp on Corpus Christi Bay in Texas. Taylor had commanded Fort Jesup and its euphemistically named "Army of Observation" for over a year, since, during the Tyler administration, Texas annexation had seemed imminent and with it, anticipated troubles with Mexico on the Rio Grande. The potential for such difficulties was exacerbated by the appearance in the Gulf in May, 1845, of a particularly warlike naval officer commanding the flagship *Princeton* and a small flotilla. Commodore Robert Field Stockton of New Jersey seemed to be an emissary for President Polk as he visited Galveston and spent his time assessing local attitudes toward annexation and sending urgent but unnecessary messages to Washington warning of Mexican threats if the United States interfered in Texas.

By the end of July, Stockton had returned home, the government of the Republic of Texas had approved the annexation treaty, and General Zachary Taylor had disembarked his
force—now renamed the "Army of Occupation"—at Corpus
Christi, just below the mouth of the Nueces River. By October, this army of over thirty-five hundred men had been divided into four infantry regiments, one of which was
comprised of dragoons (cavalrymen who fought dismounted
as infantry), and four of artillery. At the time, the entire standing army of the United States numbered only eight thousand,
most of whom were Indian fighters scattered around frontier
posts from the Florida swamps to the Kansas plains.

Taylor had no detailed orders or plan, no idea of the size or
whereabouts of the Mexican army; he was camped in country where firewood was scarce, the water brackish. An enormous train of camp followers trailed the army and sold liquor
to the troops, nearly half of which were Irish and German immigrants, tough fighters but owing no particular allegiance
to the United States. Desertions were commonplace.

The general and his restless army stayed put for six
months.

4

By the end of his first nine months in office, President
Polk had a squadron of warships cruising off Mazatlán
and an army camped in Texas. His War and State Departments had generated other significant missions as well, several adding to the country's war footing, one a forlorn attempt
to avert war.

In October, 1845, when reinforcements were reaching
Zachary Taylor's Army of Occupation in the Texas sand
dunes, Polk's secretary of state, James Buchanan, sent secret instructions to Thomas O. Larkin, consul for the United
States at Monterey and the most influential American in

Mexican California. Now age forty-three, Larkin had ventured to Monterey in 1832 and with a capital of five hundred
dollars, opened a small store and flour mill. From this modest
beginning grew a prosperous trade in horses, furs, lumber,
and flour with Mexico and the Sandwich Islands. Remarkably, he never took Mexican citizenship and managed to
stay aloof from provincial politics. Described as "prudent
and praiseworthy," he was tactful, practical, and honorable, a pleasant man of sound, conservative judgment. As
consul since 1842, he had from the beginning assiduously
reported his somewhat alarmist views on the activities of his
British and French counterparts.

The Buchanan dispatch, dated October 17, 1845, and
carried on the frigate *Congress* around Cape Horn to the
Sandwich Islands, reached Larkin via a merchant vessel.
It appointed him a confidential agent of the State Department at a salary of six dollars a day, and instructed him to
take advantage of any signs of unrest among the Californios, to "conciliate" them and urge their support of annexation by the United States. In these efforts he would be aided
by the American vice consul, William Leidesdorff at Yerba
Buena, the settlement in San Francisco Bay. Larkin was to
make clear to his influential contacts that the United States
could not interfere in matters between California and Mexico City, but that in the event of hostilities between Mexico
and the United States, if California asserted its independence, Washington would "render her all the kind offices in
our power as a Sister Republic." Larkin was also to spread
the word that if Californians wished to unite "their destiny
with ours, they would be received as brethren."

Larkin leaked this information to a number of American
influentials and worked to win the support of Don Mariano
Vallejo. This powerful and independent *jefe político* of
Sonoma, north of San Francisco Bay, Larkin described as
"very studious for a Californian . . . formal, stiff, pompous
and exacting . . . pleasant and condescending, anxious

for popularity and the good will of others." The consul felt
that he would be a valuable ally and would support annexation. Colonel Vallejo, whose two sisters were married to
Americans and who had many American friends, was a
wealthy man. He owned 175,000 acres of land stretching
from San Francisco Bay north to the Valley of the Moon. He
had encouraged emigration to California since, he said, he
was powerless to prevent it. He was a Californio patriot, not
a Mexican patriot, who felt that the future of California lay
with friendly relations with the United States.

In the executive mansion in May, 1845, Polk's guest list included the Senate's most impassioned expansionist, Thomas
Hart Benton of Missouri, and Benton's son-in-law, the celebrated explorer Captain John Charles Frémont, recently
returned from an army Topographical Corps expedition to
Oregon and California.

Frémont gave the President a detailed account of his journey west, spoke of the limitless potential of Oregon and
California, and of the importance of continuing the exploration of the region toward preparing accurate data and
maps. He told Polk that existing maps were not dependable
and gave as an example a map he had examined in the Library of Congress that depicted the Great Salt Lake as being linked to the Pacific by three large rivers. None of these
rivers existed, Frémont said. He had been there.

The President listened, asked questions, and in his journal
noted only that Frémont was "young" and "impulsive." But
since Mexico and its provinces of New Mexico and, especially, California preoccupied him that summer, he must
have closely questioned the explorer, who was preparing to
embark on a new westward expedition. There had been disturbing reports circulating in Washington that the British,
whose presence in Oregon was problem enough, had designs
on California and perhaps were even being welcomed there

by Mexico. Polk may have viewed the impulsive captain of topographers as an instrument to upset those plans. Frémont might be able to determine, in the event of war with Mexico, the degree of resistance the United States could face in California and how much assistance could be expected from the American settlers there.

Frémont himself later noticeably omitted mention of the President when he wrote of the meeting: "California stood out as the chief subject in the impending war; and with Mr. Benton and other governing men at Washington, it became a firm resolve to hold it for the United States. . . ."

On the evening of October 30, 1845, while Zachary Taylor and his army were waiting on the Nueces River, and as Thomas Larkin in Monterey was assimilating his secret instructions from the State Department, and Captain Frémont's new exploring party had reached the Great Salt Lake, the President made note in his diary of what became a momentous meeting with a minor military officer: "I had a confidential conversation with Lieut. Gillespie of the Marine Corps, at eight o'clock P.M., on the subject of his secret mission on which he was about to go to California. His secret instructions and the letter to Thomas O. Larkin, United States consul at Monterey, in the Department of State, will explain the object of his mission."

The marine had been selected for the assignment by Navy Secretary George Bancroft and while the details and purpose of his mission were never adequately explained, Lieutenant Archibald Hamilton Gillespie, who would soon leave Washington loaded with mysterious papers, was destined for a role in the unfolding events that was far more significant than that of courier.

A tall, red-haired career officer with a stylish, pointed beard and an air of self-importance, Gillespie was thirty-three at the time he met with the President. A native of

Pennsylvania who had been orphaned at a young age, he
enlisted in the marines at age twenty, rose to the rank of
sergeant, then received a commission upon reenlisting. His
superiors regarded him as a dependable, intelligent officer
and a natural leader. He had had seagoing experience in
the Pacific and, key to his new assignment, he spoke fluent
Spanish.

Before departing Washington, the ambitious lieutenant
wrote Secretary Bancroft: "I cannot say what I would wish
at a moment like this, setting forth on an adventurous enter-
prize, but I can assure you, you will not regret having named
me for this service."

When Gillespie boarded a commercial steamer bound for
Vera Cruz on November 16, he carried with him instructions
for Consul Larkin (which he subsequently memorized and
destroyed); orders for Commodore John Sloat of the United
States Pacific Squadron at Mazatlán; a letter to Captain Frémont of the Topographical Engineers, who had departed
five months earlier on a "surveying expedition" to California;
and a packet of letters to Frémont from his wife Jessie,
daughter of Senator Thomas Hart Benton, and from the
senator as well.

He traveled in mufti, posing as an invalid Scotch-whiskey
salesman with interests in California. He planned to cross
Mexico in a diligencia (stagecoach) to Mazatlán, rendezvous
there with Commodore Sloat, then proceed to Monterey to
meet with Larkin and to find Frémont.

The President's final duty of 1845 involved yet another
mission—a peace feeler to Mexico. To carry out this difficult if not impossible task, he appointed a former Louisiana
congressman named John Slidell to travel to Vera Cruz. As
Minister Extraordinary and Plenipotentiary, Slidell was to
attempt to negotiate a boundary between the two countries,
specifically the Rio Grande, with Mexico ceding all the

territory east and north of the river for a sum of money yet to be determined. If Mexico demonstrated a willingness to sell New Mexico and California, the United States would offer up to forty million dollars for them.

Slidell's timing was unfortunate. He arrived on the Mexican coast at the end of the year, just as one government fell and another rose. In January, 1846, the new regime, headed by the anti-Yankee army general Mariano Paredes y Arrillaga, not only refused Slidell an audience, but rejected all points of the proposed negotiation. There would be no recognition of the annexation of Texas by the United States, no boundary agreement, no sale of Mexican territory. Indeed, Paredes announced that he intended to march to the Rio Grande and defend Texas.

Eighteen forty-five thus ended. Texas was admitted to the Union on December 28, Mexico was preparing to send an army north to the Rio Grande, Zachary Taylor's army was poised to meet that army, and John Charles Frémont and his rough crew were marching into California.

6

Frémont

∎

1

When John Charles Frémont led his buccaneer's band of buckskinned mountain men, French-Canadians, and Delaware Indians down the western slope of the Sierra Nevada and into Sutter's Fort in the winter of 1845, he had been six months on trail out of St. Louis. He loved the trail and camp, loved riding with a stalwart company of frontiersmen whose loyalty he prized above all things. In the prairies, deserts, and mountain passes, he had a singleness of purpose; in remote places, he found serenity in work, none of it too routine. Finding good game, graze, wood and water for making camp became a small daily triumph. He relished such chores as ordering cook fires started and tents pitched, and assigning pickets in two-hour shifts to watch the hobbled horses and pack animals, and to listen for unfamiliar sounds. He delighted in working into the night on his papers under the flickering light of a bull's-eye lantern, and rousting the men at daybreak to cook meat and boil coffee for breakfast and to break camp. He found satisfaction in supervising the packing of mules and rolling stock for resuming the march at no later than six-thirty; he found solace in jotting, sketching, mapping, and making astronomical observations.

He was never happier than in journeying–the going there rather than the getting there. The trail brought out all his gifts. He had a cool daring in times of peril. He was decisive— pointing the way, saying yes or no. He innovated, added to his assignment, and returned to his superiors with more than they had bargained for.

Above all, he had a singular facility in commanding diverse and difficult men. He had experienced classrooms and drawing rooms, danced at balls and galas, sat in the sanctums of men of wealth and power, spoken confidently to the President of the United States. Yet he easily inspired the loyalty of men who knew nothing of social graces, were suspicious of education, wealth, and power, who could not name the President of the United States.

The men who rode with him into Sutter's Fort knew no rules or laws except the natural ones that governed the wilderness and their ability to survive in it. To all else, they were utterly independent and insubordinate, yet Frémont, time and again, led them.

The trail's end revealed another John Charles Frémont. On the journey, he could keep his balance while teetering between mountaintop and desert. But when he arrived at his destination, he resembled a sailor suddenly cast ashore, confounded by surer footing. In places shared by a citizenry and the trappings of civilization, the master of all the exigencies of the journey became a moody, directionless figure. Those he led and who enjoyed his company at the campfire and in the command tent now found him uncompanionable— peremptory, worried, humorless, quick to perceive a slight.

He was an essential adventurer and man of action, and inaction confused and braked his racing mind and turned it toward ruinous matters, such as politics and ambition.

He was an impatient man who believed that his destiny for greatness had been preordained and writ large in the celestial record. He had known for many years that his fate lay in the trackless lands west of the Mississippi and now,

riding into the Sacramento Valley in December, 1845, a
month from his thirty-third birthday, Frémont saw his destiny in finer focus. He had sensed it eighteen months ago
when he first laid eyes on Sutter's Fort.

2

Frémont's father, John Charles, Senior, whose history is
sketchy, was a royalist who fled from Napoleonic France,
took ship to Santo Domingo, was captured by the British and
spent some months in a West Indies prison before being
permitted to emigrate to the United States. In 1808, he appeared in Richmond, Virginia, and there, while teaching at
a private academy, met Anne Whiting Pryor, wife of an elderly horse-breeder and former military man. Anne and
Charles ran away together and settled in Savannah, Georgia. On January 21, 1813, their first child, John Charles, was
born and not long afterward, upon the death of Pryor, the
couple married.

After Charles Frémont died of pneumonia in 1818, Anne
took her son and her two other children to Charleston, where
she subsisted on a small inheritance and by taking in boarders. In his early teens, John attended Charleston College,
excelling in math and sciences, and although expelled at
least once for habitual absences from his classes, he earned
enough credits to land a teaching job in the city. Soon afterward, through the intervention of a family friend, Frémont,
not yet twenty, was given a post as math instructor on the
USS *Natchez,* embarking on a two-year cruise to South
America.

Frémont's patron was Joel Roberts Poinsett, a Jacksonian
politician who became the first American minister to Mexico (and the man who introduced to the United States the red
tropical flower bearing his name). In 1837, as secretary of
war in President Martin Van Buren's cabinet, Poinsett again

used his influence on Frémont's behalf and was able to obtain for his protégé a commission as a lieutenant in the newly formed U.S. Topographical Corps. This appointment, and the subsequent posting to two surveys of the territory between the Mississippi and Missouri rivers, sealed Frémont's future. In the Minnesota and Dakota Territory, he worked alongside the eminent French topographer Joseph Nicollet, a man he loved as the father he had never known and whom he characterized as his "Yale College and Harvard," and he saw his life's work lying before him like one of Nicollet's magnificent maps.

Poinsett, stirred by the young man's brilliance, manners, and natural charm, bestowed one other favor on his friend. This, the most significant gift in Frémont's life, occurred in Washington when his patron introduced the lieutenant to the man who, more than Poinsett, or even more than Nicollet, would touch and transform his life. Senator Thomas Hart Benton of Missouri was the supreme expansionist leader in Congress and the principal supporter of government-sponsored surveys and explorations of the West. Frémont began dining often at the Benton home. He was held in thrall by Benton's table talk—the huge, craggy-faced senator was a polished orator no matter the size of his audience—and by Benton's lively and beautiful teenage daughter, Jessie. She in turn fell instantly in love with the handsome, articulate, Gallic-mannered Southerner.

When Benton learned of their romance, Frémont felt the full fury of the senator's notoriously volcanic temper and saw the map of his future turn to ashes. Benton forbade any contact between his beloved daughter and the penniless upstart who had betrayed his hospitality and trust. Soon after their confrontation, Poinsett, probably at Benton's instruction, sent the lieutenant off in the summer of 1841 on an expedition to survey Iowa Territory.

His three-month exile from Washington did nothing to cool the young couple's ardor, however, and Frémont and

Jessie Benton eloped and married that October. Benton's wrath subsided after Jessie threatened to abandon him completely, and thereafter, with one future parting, the senator and his son-in-law became partners in their shared ambition to "open the West" and make it American.

3

In 1842, Benton and his expansionist political brethren muscled a thirty-thousand-dollar appropriation from Congress to survey the Oregon Trail, the growing route for emigration to the Pacific. The plan called for Joseph Nicollet to lead the expedition, but the Frenchman fell ill and Frémont, who had been assigned to serve as second in command, led the party. They journeyed to the fabled South Pass on the Continental Divide in Wyoming Territory—a saddle in the central Rocky Mountains, the great overland gateway to the Pacific—and the four-month venture inspired a detailed map and survey, and a splendid report. It also produced the first meeting between Frémont and a small, freckled, stoop-shouldered mountain man named Christopher Houston "Kit" Carson. This unprepossessing figure would eagerly share his deep and hard-won knowledge of the Western wilderness with the man he called "the Colonel" and follow Frémont—guide him, yet follow him—unstintingly in the years of adventure and conquest ahead.

Of the great inspirations in Frémont's life—his mother, Joel Poinsett, Joseph Nicollet, Thomas Hart Benton and Jessie Benton—Carson occupied a special niche. Frémont loved the little gray-eyed Kentuckian and came to regard him, and write of him, as the very apotheosis of the Western frontier, one whose name ought to be linked to those of Ulysses, Jason, Hector, Nimrod, the Norse heroes, and the knights of the Round Table.

Carson had been orphaned at a young age and had run

away from home at sixteen to work as a wrangler on the
Santa Fé Trail. Over the next decade, with the town of Taos,
the fur-trade center eighty miles northeast of Santa Fé in
Mexican New Mexico, as his *pied-à-terre,* Kit found work
as a teamster. In 1828, working with Ewing Young and his
fur brigade of forty men, he made his first expedition to California. In this venture, he was involved in a fight with
Klamath Indians as the trappers made their way north along
the Sacramento River.

Over the years before he met Frémont, Carson trapped
with such fabled frontiersmen as Jim Bridger, Joe Meek, and
Tom "Broken Hand" Fitzpatrick, fought Crow, Blackfeet,
and Comanche war parties, and traveled the rivers and
mountains from Missouri to the Pacific, from the Canadian
border to the Rio Grande. He fought a duel with a French
trapper at the Green River trappers' rendezvous in the summer of 1835 in which he "got his hair parted" and wounded
his adversary. He married an Arapaho girl and after she
died, "took up" with a Cheyenne woman. He trapped and
hunted for the Hudson's Bay Company on the Mary's River
in Nevada and on the Madison in Wyoming, traded among
the Navajo, and worked as a hunter out of Bent's Fort on the
Arkansas.

In May, 1842, on a steamer headed up the Missouri, he
met Frémont and they struck up an enduring friendship. On
the deck of the riverboat, Carson, then thirty-three, volunteered to join the explorer on the Oregon Trail journey and,
as he later remembered the moment, said, "I told him that I
had been some time in the mountains and thought I could
guide him to any point he wished to go."

Frémont made some inquiries and hired Carson as scout
and guide at a hundred dollars a month.

The Oregon Trail expedition ended in the late summer of
1842. Carson left Frémont at Fort Laramie, Wyoming, and
in January, 1843, traveled on to Bent's Fort, then to Taos. In
February, he converted to Catholicism and married María

Josefa Jaramillo, age fifteen. She was the daughter of a
prominent citizen of Taos and sister-in-law of Charles Bent,
who had opened Bent's Fort in 1833. Seventeen years earlier, Charles Bent had hired a then-sixteen-year-old runaway
named Kit Carson as a horse wrangler on a trading expedition to Santa Fé.

Frémont returned to Washington in October and worked fu-
riously with Jessie, dictating to her in numbing detail the facts
of the journey. Jessie took her husband's data and observations and transformed them into a work of literature—
lustrously written, as exciting as an adventure novel, filled
with descriptive passages, lore, colorful anecdotes, and advice to overland travelers. The report, something entirely
new among the normally labored prose of government documents, was printed in an edition of ten thousand copies
and made available to the public. The book appeared in the
spring of 1843, and despite its ponderous title, *A Report of
an Exploration of the Country Lying Between the Missouri
River and the Rocky Mountains on the Line of the Kansas
and Great Platte Rivers,* it won instant acclaim in the press.

Thomas Hart Benton, the chief Oregon Trail and westward emigration boomer in Congress, was thrilled with the
work of his son-in-law, and vindicated in having pushed him
to succeed Joseph Nicollet to lead the expedition. The senator jumped on the success of the Oregon Trail report and engineered a follow-up mission for Frémont. This time, the
exploration would continue on over the South Pass and to
the mouth of the Columbia River, in Oregon territory.

In May, 1843, Frémont organized his party in St. Louis.
Among the thirty who signed on were men who had
followed or guided him to South Pass the year before, and
others who would be notable Frémont men in years to
come. Kit Carson joined the party at Bent's Fort, and Kit's
friend Tom "Broken Hand" Fitzpatrick also came aboard.

This big Irishman had trapped and traded among Blackfeet, Crows, Arikaras, Pawnees, Cheyennes, Shoshones,
Arapahos, and Sioux since 1816, and had guided a wagon
train from Missouri to Oregon in 1841. His hair had turned
snow-white after a run-in with a Gros Ventre war party in
1832, and his left hand had been maimed in the dim past
when a firearm exploded.

Other expedition members, trusted trailsmen, included the
voyageurs Basil Lajeunesse and his brother François; Theodore Talbot, a Kentucky senator's son who became Frémont's
loyal lieutenant and second in command; and an eighteen-
year-old free black man, Jacob Dodson, one of the Benton
family's servants.

In St. Louis, Frémont obtained permission to draw some
breech-loading, smoothbore Hall muskets, carbines, and
gunpowder from the city's army arsenal. The request was approved by an officer who would reenter Frémont's life in
years to come. This was Colonel Stephen Watts Kearny,
commander of the Third Military Department. A longtime
friend of Senator Benton's, he had known Jessie since her
childhood.

When Frémont first met him at Jefferson Barracks in St.
Louis, Kearny, not yet fifty years old, was a thirty-year army
veteran whose first battle had been at Queenston Heights,
above the Niagara River in Canada, in the War of 1812. Since
1836, he had commanded one of the army's elite units, the
First Dragoon Regiment, headquartered at Fort Leavenworth, Kansas, and in 1843, in St. Louis.

He was a stiff, humorless, ploddingly unimaginative professional soldier with a reputation as a martinet. He was also
courageous and dependable, an officer whose life had followed a single path, that which connected the orders of his
superiors to his prompt and exact execution of them.

Kearny greeted Frémont cordially at Jefferson Barracks
and no doubt asked about Senator Benton, Jessie, and the
Frémonts' newly born daughter. Then he signed the

application for arms and powder and does not seem to have
questioned the request for a brass howitzer, which Frémont
thought would be useful in the event of Indian attack. The
gun, its thirty-three-inch brass barrel mounted on a large-
wheeled carriage, had been patterned after the French
cannons used by mountain troops in Algeria and the Pyre-
nees. With its range of a thousand yards, the twelve-pounder
(from the weight of the iron ball it fired) was the lightest
piece of army artillery. For a peaceful, exploratory expedition, it was an odd and cumbersome weapon to choose, but
Frémont was oblivious to the possibility that a cannon
might look warlike to the Mexicans, some of whose territory
he would need to cross, or to the British, who held Oregon
territory in a fragile joint sovereignty with the United States.
These fears did occur to those in command of the Topographical Corps and the Ordnance Department in Washington, but
no orders to return the howitzer to the armory were received
by the explorer before he and his party departed St. Louis on
May 13. The cannon, and its powder and ball, was dragged
over some three thousand miles of wilderness until abandoned many months later in a Sierra snowdrift.

Early in September, the expedition reached the Great Salt
Lake, and in November, Fort Vancouver, in Oregon territory.
There its assignment ostensibly expired, but instead of turn-
ing toward home, Frémont led his men south to explore the
Great Basin country between the Rockies and Sierra Nevada.
Then, in a move that delighted Benton and his California-
covetous colleagues, he took his party across the Sierras in
January, 1844, and into Mexican California. They reached
Sutter's Fort in the first week of March, purchased forage,
supplies, and pack animals, and rested for nearly three weeks.
Frémont and John A. Sutter met frequently over food and
wine and exchanged information and philosophical ideas.
The convivial empresario of New Helvetia made certain

that the explorer understood his dream of empire and how strongly he encouraged emigrants to his lands, particularly Americans. Sutter saw the future of California as an American province, and Frémont agreed.

The expedition resumed its journey late in the month, this time heading south down the San Joaquin Valley and into the Mojave Desert, then northeast again, through Nevada, Utah, and back to Bent's Fort on July 1.

In August, Frémont returned to St. Louis, where he was reunited with Jessie and her parents. Soon after that, the family embarked by stagecoach for Washington, where the explorer and his beloved amanuensis set to work on his new report.

4

In his absence, Frémont learned, his father-in-law had been present—and nearly killed—in an awful explosion aboard the steam frigate *Princeton* while on a Potomac cruise. The calamity had occurred on the last day of February past, at the time the explorer and his men were making their way toward Sutter's Fort.

The *Princeton* was the navy's finest steamship, the first to be driven by screw propellers instead of sidewheels, a man-of-war equipped with the most powerful gun battery afloat: twelve forty-two-pound carronades—blunt-barreled, short-range cannons—plus two monster guns, the biggest in existence, capable of firing a 225-pound iron round shot. Each of these cannons measured fifteen feet from butt to two-foot-wide muzzle, and each weighed fourteen tons.

The commanding officer of the *Princeton*, Captain Robert Field Stockton, had supervised the ship's construction in Philadelphia the year before, and in February, 1844, had taken four hundred Washington dignitaries on a Potomac cruise. Among his special guests were President John Tyler,

Tyler's son, daughter and son-in-law, cabinet members, the secretary of the navy, certain powerful members of Congress, including Senator Benton, and seventy-six-year-old Dolley Madison, widow of the fourth President of the United States.

As the frigate steamed toward Fort Washington and Mount Vernon, the ship's band playing "Hail, Columbia," Captain Stockton proudly demonstrated his guns, firing twenty-one-gun salutes with the carronades and twice ordering the firing of the Peacemaker, one of the mammoth cannons, after which the guests went below to the officers' mess for a lavish banquet and champagne toasts. When Navy Secretary Thomas W. Gilmer asked Stockton for one final demonstration of the Peacemaker, the captain went on deck to supervise it, followed by many of the *Princeton's* visitors.

Senator Benton with Senator S. S. Phelps of Vermont and other guests gathered at the starboard rail; Tyler's secretary of state, Abel Upshur, and Secretary Gilmer among others watched from the port side. As the gun crew loaded the Peacemaker with a twenty-five-pound blank powder charge, the President and his family remained below, listening to the band.

When Stockton shouted "Fire!" the great gun blew to pieces at a point about two feet from the breech, hurtling a one-ton chunk of steel backward, its shrapnel spraying the port rail and instantly killing Secretaries Upshur and Gilmer and four others.

Stockton, standing at the gun, miraculously survived, though the blast singed the hair from his head and the beard from his face.

Benton had escaped, shaken and in shock, but uninjured.

A court of inquiry later cleared the captain of any responsibility for the tragic accident and determined that the source of the gun explosion lay in a metallurgical problem.

Stockton, three months later, commanded the *Princeton*

in the Gulf of Mexico and within a year and a half was promoted to the rank of commodore. His new assignment called for him to take command of the navy's Pacific Squadron and to proceed on his new flagship *Congress* around Cape Horn to Mexican California.

With publication of his second book-length report, three times longer than the first and ten thousand copies printed and distributed, Frémont seemed to have reached the apogee of his career. Winfield Scott, commanding general of the army, had recommended him for promotion to a brevet captaincy (approved by President John Tyler just before he left office); the explorer had become a national hero, called "the Pathfinder," his name a symbol of American fortitude, adventure, and spirit. He was dashing and handsome, exuding a Gallic charm and a Childe Harold-like mystery. He had at his side the beautiful and accomplished Jessie. He was as comfortable and confident mixing with men of power in the staterooms of Washington politics as journeying into the wilderness with such peerless frontiersmen as Kit Carson—who, as a result of the munificent praise in Frémont's books, had his own fame and following.

In June, 1845, within weeks of the meeting with the President in which he had spoken of the need for accurate maps of the trans-Mississippi West, Frémont left St. Louis for Bent's Fort.

The new expedition seemed conventional work for a captain of the Army Corps of Topographical Engineers. His mission was to explore the Great Basin, the vastness of mountain and desert running north to the Columbia Plateau, south to the Mojave and sandwiched between the Rockies and the Sierra range bordering California.

In truth, he had a greater purpose. He served as westward agent for his forceful father-in-law, and he served an even more puissant master, the President of the United States, who intended making facts of the hopes and prophesies of Benton and his followers in Washington.

Frémont's ostensible duties lay in the Great Basin, with the secondary work of surveying and mapping a wagon road between Missouri and Great Salt Lake, then over the mountain passes to the Pacific. But although it was not mentioned in his official orders from the Bureau of Topographical Engineers, his real destination was California, "the road to India," "the garden of the world," as the great senator dreamily called it.

Frémont had most of his expedition members signed up by the time he reached Bent's Fort in August. Army lieutenants Theodore Talbot, James W. Abert, and William Guy Peck considered it an honor to accompany their celebrated captain, as did the civilian artist-cartographer Edward M. Kern of Philadelphia. Among the French-Canadian hunter-trappers gathered in St. Louis were Basil Lajeunesse, Raphael Prou, and Auguste Archambeau. The "free colored man," Jacob Dodson, was there, as were a gunsmith named Stepp; Denny, an Iowa half-breed; and twelve Delaware Indians recruited from a settlement near Westport Landing, on the Missouri River. The Delawares, remnants of the tribe that had been pushed ever westward since the 1750s, were led by chiefs Segundai and Swanok, who became Frémont's colorful personal bodyguards. In the East, their tribal name was Lenni-Lenape, "real men," and the explorer learned the truth behind the name in the months to come. Among Western tribes deemed enemies, the Delawares were killers and scalp-takers; at all times, they were utterly fearless and dependable trailbreakers and hunters.

"Broken Hand" Fitzpatrick had also signed the three-dollars-a-day contract, as had Lucien Maxwell, out of

Kaskaskia, Illinois, a hunter-trader among the Utes and plains tribes, plus two other mountain legends, Joseph Red-deford Walker and Alexis Godey.

Joe Walker, a forty-seven-year-old Tennessean, had been in the West since 1819, tramping and trapping from the high Rockies to the Rio Grande. During his Santa Fé Trail days, he had even been a prisoner of the Mexicans for a time. He had also served as the first sheriff of Jackson County, Missouri, and in 1833, with a party of forty free trappers, made a three-week crossing of the Sierra Nevada, and in November of the same year, discovered Yosemite Valley.

In the twelve years since his first trek to the Pacific, Walker had become a hardened California hand, leading many parties to the Mexican province to trade horses and mules, and serving as guide for California-bound parties out of Fort Bridger, on the Green River of Wyoming.

Walker had been with Frémont in '42, as had Alexis Godey, another of the explorer's prized trailsmen. Twenty-seven at the time, he came eagerly to join the new expedition. Godey had trapped with Jim Bridger in the Rockies and had made more than one trip as far west as the Mary's River in Nevada. He was a close associate and friend of Kit Carson's and earned Frémont's high praise for his dependability and cool courage. These words also applied to another Carson crony, Richard "Dick" Owens, an Ohio-born mountaineer, a proficient hunter-trapper and Indian fighter. He had a special knack for stealing horses from the Blackfeet and Shoshone, and on at least one occasion, from the Mexicans in southern California.

Frémont asserted that Carson, Godey, and Owens, had they served in Napoleon's army, would have all been field marshals. He wrote: "Carson of great courage; quick and complete perception, taking in at a glance the advantages as well as the chances for defeat; Godey, insensible to danger, of perfect coolness and stubborn resolution; Owens, equal

in courage to the others, and in coolness equal to Godey, had
the *coup d'ôeil* of a chess player, covering the whole field
with a glance that sees the best move."

Carson, when he returned to New Mexico after the 1842
expedition, had gone into partnership with Owens, and the
two set up a farming operation on the Little Cimarron River
fifty miles from Taos, where Kit built a cabin for his beloved Josefa. But he had promised Frémont that if called, he
would come, and when the message arrived from Bent's,
he and Owens sold their ranch, for about half of what they
had paid for it, Kit kissed Josefa good-bye, and the two
men rode north to the Arkansas River.

They rode northwest out of Bent's on August 16, 1845,
Frémont and his sixty-two "experienced, self-reliant"
men, heading a pack train of two hundred animals and a
two-hundred-fifty-head cattle herd. In two months, this
somewhat suspiciously overmanned and overarmed expedition crossed the Upper Colorado, trekked into the wastelands of eastern Utah, followed old Indian and trapper trails
across the Green River, traversed the Wasatch Mountains,
and arrived at the Great Salt Lake in October.

They rode across the salt plain and through gray seas of
sagebrush until, in late October, they reached the sluggish
Mary's River, which Frémont renamed the Humboldt after
the German geographer Friedrich Alexander von Humboldt.
At the camp on the river, on November 5, 1845, the explorer
split his party into two topographical units, rendezvousing
with them on November 27 at Walker Lake (named for Joe
Walker). This stunningly pristine lake, a hundred miles
northeast of the Yosemite Valley, was alive with cutthroat
trout, the fish so abundant that the men could kick them
ashore to be killed, cleaned, and roasted on the spot.

On November 29, Frémont again divided his expedition.
Most of the men, commanded by Talbot and guided by Joe

Walker, marched south along the eastern escarpment of the Sierras and crossed into the San Joaquin Valley. Talbot was to map the eastern flank of the range and its passes and rendezvous in the south after the rest of the party reached Sutter's Fort and reprovisioned. Frémont took Carson and fifteen men, including some of the Delawares, and struck out for the Truckee River. Six days were spent crossing the mountains through what later became known as Donner Pass to reach the south fork of the American River. From that point it was an easy march through the pine and manzanita country to the broad flatlands of the Sacramento Valley of Alta California.

Frémont led his men into Sutter's Fort on December 10, 1845.

7

Hawk's Peak

■

1

Frémont and his men rode into the Sacramento Valley that winter in the wake of the latest efforts to stem the flow of American settlers in the province. Just a month before the exploration party arrived, the commanding general of Alta California, José Castro, had carried out orders from Mexico City by issuing a decree ordering all American emigrants in the northern province to proceed to Sonoma. There, at Colonel Vallejo's direction, they were to swear an oath to obey Mexican laws and apply for a license to settle in the province. Those whose applications were denied would be banished from the country.

In 1845, there were about eight hundred Americans in California, most of them distributed on small farms and homesteads in the north, within a horseback ride to New Helvetia. Some of the earlier arrivals had become Mexican citizens; the more recent emigrants had not bothered to take the oath and had not been pressured to do so.

Castro's procrustean orders produced little but dissension and anger among the Americans, only twenty of them showing up in Sonoma to apply for the settler's license. The general and an escort rode north from Monterey to Sonoma to

visit Vallejo on November 11 and to reinforce the decree demanding that the Americans come forth.

Given the war clouds darkening over the Rio Grande, Castro's orders from Mexico were a wise if belated attempt to
identify the Americans who had entered California without
sanction—which meant virtually all of the newcomers—
and who might represent a threat in the event of war with
the United States.

Californios drew little distinction between them, these
Americans being sorted out, but they were a disparate lot.

William Brown Ide, a Massachusetts man, came to the
Sacramento Valley to see if he could succeed at something. He had worked as a carpenter and farmer in New
England, and even as an occasional schoolteacher in Ohio
and Illinois. None of these endeavors proved very successful and at age forty-seven, a skinny, pious teetotaler with a
wife and five children, he joined an emigrant train in Independence, Missouri, bound for Oregon. Near Fort Hall,
Idaho, Ide, a Tennessean named John Grigsby, and several
others turned their wagons south and made a harrowing
crossing of the Sierra Nevada to Sutter's lands.

Ide may have failed in the East, but he was an industrious
man, no stranger to hard work, and he soon found a tract of
rich land north of New Helvetia, built a cabin, and began
clearing and plowing.

Besides Grigsby, there were several other squatters a day
or two by horse from Ide's place. Robert "Long Bob" Semple was a six-foot-eight Kentucky dentist and printer. Granville Swift, also from Kentucky, claimed descent from
Daniel Boone and worked for the Swiss as a hunter. Peter
Lassen, the Danish blacksmith, became a trusted Sutter lieutenant and a Sacramento Valley hunter and rancher. Moses
Carson, older half-brother of Kit's, was a veteran fur trader
and Indian fighter who had become a Mexican citizen in
1836 when he settled in the Russian River area. Trappers in
the waterways off the Sacramento included Henry L. Ford

of New Hampshire, a twenty-four-year-old army deserter;
William O. "Le Gros" (Big) Fallon, a burly Irishman who
had followed beaver streams from New Mexico to California; John Neal, an Irish sailor and likely another fugitive
from justice; and Samuel J. Hensley, a Kentuckian whom
Sutter regarded as "of strong will and well-balanced mind,
generous, temperate, and brave."

Another resident in the valley, William Todd of Illinois,
had the distinction of being the nephew of Mary Todd, who
in 1842 married a Kentucky-born lawyer named Abraham
Lincoln. Todd had been in California only a few months
when, in April, 1846, he wrote home:

> If there are any persons in Sangamon who speak of cross-
> ing the Rocky Mountains to this country, tell them my
> advice is to stay at home. There you are well off. You can
> enjoy all the comforts of life—live under a good govern-
> ment and have peace and plenty around you—a country
> whose soil is not surpassed by any in the world, having
> good seasons and yielding timely crops. Here everything
> is on the other extreme: the government is tyrannical, the
> weather unseasonable, poor crops, and the necessaries of
> life not to be had except at the most extortionate prices,
> and frequently not then. . . .

He added a prescient note: "The Mexicans talk every spring
and fall of driving the foreigners out . . . . They must do it
this year or they can never do it. There will be a revolution
before long. . . . If here, I will take a hand in it."

Among the most volatile of the emigrants, one who had
shown up at Sutter's doorstep in 1841, was a big, stuttering,
excitable frontiersman with a bushy, tobacco-juice-stained
beard, a mane of graying hair, and fierce bloodshot eyes.
This specimen of a mountaineer, Ezekial Merritt by name,
had a shadowy history. He hinted that he had been with

Joseph Reddeford Walker in 1833 during the expedition
that discovered Yosemite Valley. Historian Hubert H. Bancroft described him as "a coarse-grained, loud-mouthed,
unprincipled, whiskey-drinking, quarrelsome fellow, well
adapted to the use that was made of him in promoting the
filibusters' schemes." And John Charles Frémont, who may
have known Merritt before 1845, said he was "a rugged man,
fearless and simple; taking delight in incurring risks, but
tractable and not given to asking questions when there
was something he was required to do."

Both Bancroft and Frémont were correct in their varied
descriptions of this obstreperous man. In making a point of
Merritt's unquestioning nature, the explorer was describing
the perfect Frémont man, and as events to come were to
prove, Merritt became just that.

2

On December 10, 1845, Frémont and Kit Carson led fifteen men, including some of Chief Segundai's Delawares, into New Helvetia and camped on the American
River three miles above Sutter's Fort. Frémont had made
vague arrangements to rendezvous in a month or two with
Ted Talbot, Joe Walker, and the bulk of the party, nearly fifty
men, in the San Joaquin Valley east of Monterey. The Talbot contingent was slowed by their mapping assignment on
the eastern flank of the Sierra Nevada, and in the waiting,
Frémont had to gather pack animals and provisions before
making his way south.

The explorer grew restless. He had arrived at one destination and needed to move on. He had business in Monterey, an
expedition to re-form and its work to finish. California, for
all its isolation and putative independence, was Mexican,
and perhaps, given the war fever that had been gripping

Washington six months ago when he had met with the new President, he might soon find himself in enemy territory. Although it seems never to have daunted him, he was a military officer already in enemy territory, with a small, well-armed army and subject to internment.

At the fort, Frémont learned that Sutter had departed on a business trip to Yerba Buena. In his absence, John Bidwell, the faithful majordomo, dealt with the impatient explorer and the two were quickly at odds. Bidwell, a twenty-five-year-old farmer who had come to the Sacramento Valley in 1841 with a pioneer train, was a somewhat prim, utterly honest factotum whom Sutter trusted to manage his affairs. He greeted Frémont and his men affably and listened as the explorer demanded to buy sixteen pack mules, six pack-saddles, and provisions. Bidwell explained that the fort's foodstuffs and animals were in short supply. He could not provide the mules but had some good horses and said he could make the packsaddles and come up with some flour and other edibles.

Frémont was annoyed by the man's inability to meet his demands and rode off in a huff. He had figured out why he did not get what he requested: he represented one government, Sutter and Bidwell another, and the two governments were having "difficulties." There was some truth in this. Sutter had a foot in both the Mexican and American camps and was having problems keeping his balance.

In a few days, the problems were solved. Bidwell rode out to the explorer's camp, needlessly apologized and explained that he was only an employee following instructions. Soon thereafter, Sutter returned to the fort and Frémont had fourteen of the sixteen mules he wanted, plus the packsaddles and supplies, and even a few head of cattle to provide beef for his men. The Swiss also gave the captain use of his schooner *Sacramento* to sail down to San Francisco Bay and to Yerba Buena to visit the American vice consul, William Leidesdorff.

Frémont moved his camp several times, from the American River to tributaries of the San Joaquin—colorful streams such as the Calaveras, Merced, and the poppy-covered banks of Mariposa Creek, the marshes loud with ducks and geese, rich with elk and antelope—before heading south in late January for the rendezvous with Talbot. He led his men in at least three Indian raids against the Miwoks and other "horsethief tribes" in the valley. These swift and merciless strikes were in retribution for ancient thefts of white men's horses dating back to Ewing Young's trapping expedition in 1830, in which Carson had been learning the mountain trades. The Delawares were particularly adept at the raids, and took scalps. The killing of these natives rated little more attention in the memoirs of Frémont and his men than did the shooting of geese or elk. Lucien Maxwell, Dick Owens, and Kit Carson are mentioned as "deftly shooting" Indians; Carson would later say: "We came on a party of Indians, killed five of them, and continued on to the Fort."

In January, 1846, six weeks after he entered California, Frémont and his men crossed the San Joaquin Valley to Monterey. The old capital, on the headland south of the bay seen by Cabrillo in 1542, was a cosmopolitan place by California standards, a seaport, a hub of commerce. Its whitewashed and red-roofed adobes were nestled between green hills and a white ribbon of beach lapped by ocean waters running from dark blue to turquoise and green as the sun set. On January 27, Frémont paid a visit to one of the most beautiful of Monterey's dwellings, the two-story, New England-style home of Thomas O. Larkin, and sat with the consul on a veranda overlooking the pine-circled bay.

They were a study in contrasts even though such a mix of men was common to Monterey, its path and byways a-jostle with wealthy Californios, traders, sea captains, merchant sailors, government men, Mexican soldiers, street urchins, and Indians. Even so, it must have been amusing for the urbane, mutton-chopped Larkin, in starched shirt, coat, collar, and cravat, to sit face-to-face with the scraggy-bearded explorer wearing a wide-brimmed sombrero, trail-worn boots, grimy buckskins decorated with beads and porcupine quills.

There is no record of their meeting, but it is clear that they discussed the worsening relations between their native country and Mexico and their duties should news of war arrive on the Pacific coast. Frémont told of his expedition and its purpose and asked Larkin for a loan, to be billed to the Topographical Corps headquarters in Washington, to buy supplies. The consul agreed to supply the money and took Frémont to visit two of Monterey's leading dignitaries, Commandante José Castro, and the town's prefect, Manuel Castro. Frémont told these wary men of his peaceful mission, assured them that his party was not military but comprised of civilian explorers, mapmakers, and guides under the command of army officers. He asked the commandante for permission to buy supplies and to "winter in the valley of San Joaquin." Castro, probably out of respect for Larkin, agreed to these requests with the proviso that Frémont and his men stay inland, outside the settled coastal areas.

3

By mid-February, Frémont had rejoined Talbot, Walker, Ed Kern, and the others who had crossed the Sierra Nevada farther south. Now, with his full sixty-two-man complement, he moved the party north toward the southern extremity of San Francisco Bay and camped in a meadow about fifteen miles from the San José Mission, where almost immediately he ran into trouble.

Sebastián Peralta, who owned a large rancho outside the village of Santa Clara, a short distance from the mission, registered a complaint with the *alcalde* of San José. Peralta said that some of his horses were missing and had turned up in the herd being kept by the Americans. He said he had ridden out to the American camp to claim his animals and had been ordered away. On February 20, he had addressed a letter to the leader, Frémont, and had received an antagonistic response. The explorer, Peralta reported, claimed that all his animals had been purchased and paid for, and that Peralta "should have been well satisfied to escape without a severe horse-whipping" for having the temerity to attempt to gain horses that did not belong to him.

Peralta, vastly insulted by the American officer, showed the *alcalde* Frémont's letter and fulminated over the arrogance of it. The letter ended: "Any further communication on this subject will not, therefore, receive attention. You will readily understand that my duties will not permit me to appear before magistrates of your towns on the complaint of every straggling vagabond who may chance to visit my camp."

Before this incident could be resolved, Frémont ensured that there would be trouble with Mexican authorities by moving his camp to the outskirts of the coastal town of Santa Cruz, on the north edge of Monterey Bay. Then, on March 5, the exploring party moved again, to a camp on the Salinas River, even closer to Monterey.

During this period when Frémont blatantly broke his pledge to keep his party inland and away from coastal settlements, some of his men were further testing the patience of Mexican officials. The Monterey customs official, Antonio María Osio, wrote in his 1851 memoir of the incident that ended all tolerance of the Americans.

Osio told of three of Frémont's "soldiers" who invaded a rancho near San Juan Bautista, a short distance from the

American camp. The ranch was owned by Don Ángel Castro,* who reported that one of the drunken men held a gun at his head while another tried to rape his daughter. Don Ángel, a tough former soldier, resisted, even at the risk of death, and succeeded in wrestling the gun away and chasing the *Americanos* out of his home.

This act, Osio said, had infuriated General José Castro and convinced the commandante that Frémont and his "army" were purposely inciting a confrontation. The general reacted to the outrage by notifying Consul Larkin of his decision to expel the Americans—at least from the Monterey area—and by sending a courier to Frémont's camp to deliver the message demanding that he and his men leave Monterey forthwith. Castro wrote:

> This morning at seven, information reached this office that you and your party have entered the settlements of this department; and this being prohibited by our laws, I find myself obliged to notify you that on receipt of this, you must immediately retire beyond the limits of the department . . . it being understood that if you do not do this, this prefecture will adopt the necessary measures to make you respect this determination.

Frémont received the message in his customary high dudgeon and dismissed it and the courier, whom he considered offensively brusque, with a wave of his hand. He did not respond. Afterward, he wrote, "I peremptorily refused compliance to an order insulting to my government and

---

There were many Castros in California. Ángel Castro, a former presidio soldier, was a judge and distinguished citizen of San Juan Bautista and uncle of General José Castro. The prefect at Monterey, Manuel Castro, does not appear to have been directly related to General José Castro.

myself"—thus assuming an attitude that was later cheered by Senator Thomas Hart Benton as a courageous act.

On March 5, Frémont and his men broke camp on the Salinas River and moved north a short distance to a wooded hill known locally as Gavilán (Hawk) Peak, just thirty miles from Monterey and overlooking the Salinas Valley and San Juan Bautista. The captain flouted Castro's orders by having his men chop trees and throw up a crude log fort, complete with earthworks, as if expecting a siege. A stripped sapling served as a staff from which the American flag flapped in the breeze.

From this hawk's eyrie, Frémont heatedly scribbled a note to be delivered under cover of darkness to Larkin. It was an extraordinary declaration for a man ostensibly leading a peaceful mission of exploration into a foreign country.

Frémont wrote the consul that "if we are unjustly attacked, we will fight to extremity and refuse quarter, trusting our country to avenge our death." He proceeded with a statement that Larkin, a salaried secret agent of the United States, must have found laughable: "We have in no wise done wrong to the people, or the authorities of the country, and if we are hemmed in and assaulted here, we will die, every man of us, under the flag of our country."

Unmoved by the captain's bravado, Larkin dispatched a return message patiently explaining Castro's order, what it meant and why it had been written. The consul also tried to placate the commandante, urging a more tempered approach to the Frémont problem and even suggesting that the two men meet and reach some kind of accord.

Castro was having none of this, and at San Juan Bautista on March 8, he called on the citizenry to assist him in expelling the "band of robbers commanded by a captain of the United States Army, J.C. Frémont." The leader and his "highwaymen," he said, had made their camp nearby, "from which he sallies forth committing depredations, and making scandalous skirmishes." He asked for volunteers to place themselves under his immediate orders to "prepare to lance the ulcer" that would "destroy our liberties and independence."

Castro, whom Frémont later admitted had "a fair amount of brains," put together a cavalry force of nearly two hundred men, regulars and volunteers, including a handful of local Indians, believed to have been plied with liquor, to engage the Americans. The general deployed his horsemen in plain view below Frémont's position and ordered three brass cannon dragged into the brush beneath the hill and aimed at the summit.

On Hawk's Peak, Frémont anxiously watched all this activity through his spyglass. He had practically begged for a confrontation and now had one, was outnumbered three to one and unsure of what to do next. He had a log fort and primitive siegeworks, a good high defensive position, plenty of wood, water, powder, and shot, and men—especially his Delawares, who had already smeared paint on their faces—anxious for a fight.

But what business did he have in fighting the Mexicans? Or in provoking a fight? He did not know that on the day after he occupied Hawk's Peak, Polk's minister extraordinary to Mexico, John Slidell, had reached Jalapa and was denied an audience with the government in Mexico City. He did not know that on the day General Castro issued his "band of robbers" proclamation, General Zachary Taylor had moved his army across the Nueces River in Texas, headed for the Rio Grande. He did not know as he watched Castro's cavalrymen through his glass that Polk's other secret agent, Lieutenant Archibald Gillespie, had reached Honolulu en route to rendezvous with Commodore Sloat, Consul Larkin, and Captain Frémont, and bearing important messages for each.

All Frémont knew in the three tense March days he occupied Hawk's Peak was that he had gotten into something
that far superseded his authority and that was potentially
quite dangerous. He had learned that General Castro was not
to be trifled with and that the Mexicans, despite talk of their
indolence and cowardly obsequiousness, seemed willing to
defend their country and capable of doing so.

The closest the two forces came to a fight occurred
when the Americans spotted a cavalry patrol winding its
way through the trees and brush toward the peak, apparently reconnoitering the position. Frémont gathered forty of
his men and started down the trail to engage the Californians. They waited off-trail to ambush the patrol, heard the
men's voices and saw them approach and stop, holding
some kind of consultation. Then the patrol rode back down
the slope.

Larkin meantime got messages to the explorer that he
must abandon any plans to oppose Castro, and on March 9,
Frémont led his men off Hawk's Peak and aimed them north
toward Sutter's Fort. He wrote Jessie that he left the hill
"slowly and growlingly" and he inflated the number of Castro's cavalry to "three or four hundred men."

Joe Walker, a faithful Frémont man up to the Hawk's Peak
retreat, wanted a fight and was so disgusted at the turn of
events that he quit the expedition. The Tennessean, mountain legend, and discoverer of Yosemite Valley, would later
call his old chief "morally and physically . . . the most complete coward I ever knew . . . timid as a woman if it were not
casting unmerited reproach on that sex."

In Washington, Thomas Hart Benton saw no cowardice
or timidity in his son-in-law's performance. "To my mind,"
he later wrote, "the noble resolution which they took to die,
if attacked, under the flag of their country, four thousand
miles distant from their homes, was an act of the highest
heroism, worthy to be recorded by Xenophon."

4

News of Frémont's exploit in the Gavilán Mountains preceded him upcountry. John Marsh, a Harvard-educated physician who had a cattle ranch near Mount Diablo in the northern San Joaquin Valley, was in the Monterey area during the March dust-up between Castro and the Americans and sent a courier to Sutter's Fort with the news. Marsh was a veteran of the Blackhawk War in the Midwest, a one-time post surgeon and trader in the Sioux country of Minnesota who had grown wealthy among the Californios and saw the province as a Texas in the making. He wrote letters back East encouraging emigration to California. He may have seen Frémont as the vanguard of an American takeover—which he favored—but the *filibustero* appearance of the explorer's ruffian-like band disturbed him.

Not so James Clyman, a Virginia-born mountaineer of the Joe Walker stripe. Clyman had fought Arikaras with Jedediah Smith and Tom Fitzpatrick while Frémont was still in knee pants in Savannah. Now the frontiersman, newly arrived at California and hearing of the Americans' "defense" of Hawk's Peak, wrote the explorer a letter offering him a company of emigrant volunteers to help fight the Mexicans. Frémont answered Clyman's inquiry:

> I have received information to the effect that a declaration of war between our government and Mexico is probable, but so far this news has not been confirmed. . . . If peace is observed, I have no right or business here; if war ensues, I shall be outnumbered ten to one, and be compelled to make good my retreat, pressed by a pursuing enemy. . . . Under these circumstances, I must make my way back home, and gratefully decline your offer of a company of hardy warriors.

Frémont and his men, after camping among the lupin, poppies, and oaks of the San Joaquin Valley, moved north to the American River. On March 21, 1846, he reached Sutter's Fort to refit his expedition to continue north to the Oregon Territory and, perhaps, to turn east for home.

8

Klamath Lake

∎

1

In June, 1845, Commodore John Sloat, the elderly, cautious commander of the United States Pacific Squadron, received orders from the Navy Department to proceed from the Peruvian coast to Mexican waters. Aboard his sixty-gun flagship *Savannah,* after delays in provisioning, he led his seven-vessel squadron northwest and in November was joined off Mazatlán by the sloop-of-war *Cyane,* which carried more recent instructions.

Sloat's orders were a reflection of the Polk administration's belief, reinforced by Larkin, Leidesdorff, and other Americans in California, that the citizens there were friendlier to the United States than to their home country. The commodore was thus instructed that if he learned with certainty that war had begun between Mexico and the United States, he was to seize San Francisco Bay and blockade the other California ports, while attempting to preserve friendly relations with the people.

In an odd choice of words to send to an officer assigned to blockade and seize foreign territory, Sloat was told to be "assiduously careful to avoid any act which could be construed as an act of aggression."

Larkin in particular had advocated that a deft and delicate touch would be necessary to win over the Californios, and Frémont's ham-handed little drama at Hawk's Peak had greatly upset him. So much so, in fact, that he sent a panicky message to Sloat, then poised off Mazatlán, asking that one of his ships be dispatched to Monterey. Even after Frémont had abandoned Hawk's Peak and disappeared into the San Joaquin Valley, Larkin apparently feared that the explorer's defiance of General Castro might lead to bloodshed.

Sloat responded to the consul's request by sending Commander John B. Montgomery's twenty-four-gun sloop *Portsmouth* to Monterey Bay, ostensibly to discover "the designs of the English and French" in California—an old bugaboo given credence by Larkin's worried messages to Washington. More important, Sloat wanted Montgomery to discover "the temper of the inhabitants" and to demonstrate the "friendly regard" for them held by the Americans. In a more overt act, one that might have been seen as openly fomenting rebellion, the *Portsmouth* skipper was also to distribute among the people of Monterey copies of the constitutions of the United States and the new State of Texas, translated into Spanish.

The *Portsmouth* anchored in Monterey Bay on April 21, 1846, four days after Larkin had had a long, private conversation with a young marine lieutenant named Archibald Gillespie. This emissary, sent by Navy Secretary George Bancroft, had made his way overland from Vera Cruz to Mazatlán bearing important messages from Washington.

Another of the consul's visitors on this eve of war was Lieutenant Charles Warren Revere, patriot Paul Revere's grandson, who had transferred from the *Cyane* to Montgomery's *Portsmouth*. He had permission from Larkin and local authorities to take horseback rides around the Monterey hills, hunting and sightseeing, and was captivated by the place. He predicted that the land "will yet prove one of the brightest stars in the American galaxy."

Sloat and his squadron were patrolling between Mazat-lán and the Sandwich Islands; the impetuous Frémont, who had come close to starting a war from his eyrie in the Gavi-lán Mountains, was still in the province, up in the north with sixty well-armed and restless men; and now an American warship lay at anchor off Monterey. Three weeks passed before war was declared against Mexico, and several more weeks went by before news of the war reached the Pacific rim, but Washington had already placed its agents in California on a war footing.

2

After buying supplies at Sutter's stores, Frémont led his men north, following the Feather River to a horse-and-cattle ranch on Butte Creek run by Samuel Neal, a black-smith who had served with Frémont in '43 and who had asked for his discharge at New Helvetia. On March 30, the Americans reached Peter Lassen's Rancho Bosquejo on Deer Creek, some two hundred miles north of Sutter's. Las-sen, also a blacksmith by trade, was a forty-five-year-old Dane who had come west with a fur brigade in 1839. He had traveled from Vancouver Island to Sutter's lands and in 1841 built a sawmill at Santa Cruz, become a Mexican citizen, and received the twenty-six-thousand-acre Deer Creek land grant in 1843. Except for the Indians he hired to work his horses and cattle, he lived in isolation and at the time Frémont arrived, had not seen a white man for seven months.

Lassen was a hospitable man and he and Frémont became good friends; the explorer and his men rested in camp on the Dane's land for a week before moving on again, this time toward the western flank of the Cascades. There the tentative plan was to map a route across the Great Basin to link with the Oregon Trail and then head home.

The American settlers who saw or heard about Frémont's exploring party regarded it as a miniature army, perhaps presaging a full-scale military invasion of California. That spring of 1846 had brought threatening news, especially for the squatters in the Sacramento Valley who had ignored the requirement to report to Colonel Vallejo in Sonoma. This disobedience of orders from Mexico City, and Frémont's defiance at Hawk's Peak, seemed to have energized General José Castro.

At the end of March, three weeks after the Americans skulked off the mountain, Castro called a military *consejo* (council) in Monterey to formulate a strategy to answer the insults of Frémont and his men. In attendance were the most powerful leaders in the province: Castro, Vallejo of Sonoma, the newly appointed governor Pío Pico, who came north from Los Angeles, and former governor Juan Bautista Alvarado

News of the *consejo,* carried north by mocassin telegraph, gave rise to fresh rumors: Castro was arming Indian tribes to help expel the illegal emigrants; he was courting French and British officials to assist in the event of war with the United States.

On April 17, a *bando* (proclamation) was issued in Monterey that confirmed the settlers' worst fears: unnaturalized foreigners would no longer be permitted to hold or work land in California and were subject to expulsion.

By the time Lieutenant Archibald Gillespie met with Larkin in Monterey on April 17, 1846, many of the confidential messages entrusted to him had been memorized and destroyed. Instead of making his way to California by the common routes around Cape Horn or a portage across the Isthmus of Panama, he had spent five nerve-racking months traveling across Mexico in a stagecoach under the guise of a whiskey salesman. The overland journey had a purpose, and Gillespie was a resourceful and intelligent officer. He was fluent in the Spanish language; he read, listened, watched, and absorbed everything he could in a country seething with political chaos; he saw firsthand examples of the hatred of Americans over the annexation of Texas, and the preparations for war.

After meetings with President Polk, Secretary of State Buchanan, Navy Secretary Bancroft, Senator Thomas Hart Benton, and Jessie Frémont, Gillespie had departed Washington the previous November 16 and traveled to Vera Cruz by commercial steamer. He reached Mexico City by *diligencia* and spent a month there while one government fell and another, led by a military man, took its place. He read of the mission of the American minister John Slidell, who was coming to Mexico to attempt to buy the country's provinces north of the Rio Grande.

By the time he was able to leave the Mexican capital, his ears rang with *"¡Dios y Libertad!"* and *"¡Viva, Mexico!"* and anti-American speeches; his brain teemed with newspaper stories about the United States' attack on Mexico's honor and scenes of soldiers on the march.

He had reached Mazatlán in April, gotten word to Commodore Sloat, and after delivering oral messages and briefing the officer on his mission, had boarded the *Cyane* for a voyage to Honolulu, thence to Monterey.

Gillespie met with Larkin and upon learning of the Hawk's Peak incident and Frémont's probable whereabouts north of Sutter's Fort, he prepared to move upcountry to intercept the explorer. On the evening before his departure, he was invited to a ball at the home of former Governor Alvarado. The marine's mufti did not seem to fool the Mexican officials in attendance. Colonel Vallejo eyed the American with undisguised suspicion, and Commandante Castro seemed overly attentive, plying Gillespie with brandy and asking difficult questions.

With a servant and two horses provided by Larkin, Gillespie made his way north. At Yerba Buena, he visited Vice Consul Leidesdorff, then proceeded north to New Helvetia. Sutter recognized the lieutenant—they had met in Honolulu some years before when the marine had been assigned to the Pacific Squadron—and the Swiss knew that this man was no whiskey salesman.

On May 8, 1846, Frémont learned that a military man carrying some kind of dispatches was riding north to intercept him. Sam Neal brought the news from his Butte Creek ranch to the explorer's camp, sprawled among a stand of cedars in a meadow at Upper Klamath Lake in Oregon territory, a few miles above the northern limits of Mexican California. Neal said that the officer was about a day behind.

The next morning, Frémont gathered ten men—Kit Carson, Alexis Godey, Lucien Maxwell, Dick Owens, Basil Lajeunesse, Denny the Iowa half-breed, Bill Stepp the gunsmith, and the Delawares Segundai, Swanok, and Crane—and by sunset, after a thirty-mile ride, found Gillespie. He, Peter Lassen, and a few other men from Sutter's Fort were camped at the lower end of the lake.

Although neither man left a detailed record of their meeting on the wilderness shore of Klamath Lake, Frémont's normally chilly demeanor must have been put to the test. It had been eleven months since he had seen Jessie and his baby daughter Elizabeth—little Lily—eight months since he and his party had ridden out of Bent's Fort. He was news-famished, had had no contact with any American fresh from the East, had heard no news since his visit with Larkin in Monterey the past January. He was supposed to be heading home, but war was imminent and he could not yet abandon California. He desperately needed orders, news, something to guide his movements, and now there were possible answers, carried by this military man who had come across

Mexico bearing letters, perhaps instructions, and certainly news.

Gillespie must have been similarly anxious as he was greeted by a trail-weary gallant in buckskins who turned out to be John Charles Frémont, the celebrated Pathfinder, explorer, author, husband of Jessie Benton. And the others! Kit Carson, the shy little gray-eyed man Frémont had hailed in his famous reports as the very embodiment of the intrepid Western frontiersman; and the French-Canadians, sons of *voyageurs* and *couriers du bois,* and the grimly silent Delawares who seemed to be the captain's bodyguard.

The marine even saw a small delegation of Klamath Indians as they hesitantly visited the camp and gave Frémont's men some salmon from their strings. The Klamath chief personally handed one of the fish to Gillespie.

After a meal of salmon cooked over the roaring fire built to ward off the winter wind hurtling off the lake, the marine and explorer talked into the night. In his tent under hurricane-lantern light, with the men rolled in their frosty blankets beneath the cedars as the wind whistled, Frémont read the mail and messages Gillespie presented in an oilskin packet. There were letters from Jessie; a note from Secretary of State Buchanan dated November 1, 1845, introducing the lieutenant; cryptic letters from Senator Benton, and miscellaneous newspaper articles.

Gillespie had committed to memory certain confidential messages from President Polk, Senator Benton, and Larkin. It is certain that Benton and the President had something to say about the British navy's presence off California, a matter Larkin had reported to Washington in the winter of '45; something was relayed about the imminence of war with Mexico, and Gillespie certainly talked at length about his journey from Vera Cruz to Mazatlán, his month in tumultuous Mexico City, and what he had learned from Sloat and Larkin.

In his memoirs published forty years afterward, Frémont remarked only on the messages from Benton that Gillespie carried, these on the old John Bull fear, subsequently proven groundless, that the British were concocting some scheme to "steal" California from the Americans. "The letter of Senator Benton," he wrote, "was a trumpet of no uncertain note. Read by the light of many conversations and discussions with himself and other governing men in Washington, it clearly made me know that I was required by the Government to find out any foreign schemes in relation to California, and to counteract them so far as was in my power. His letters made me know distinctly that at last the time had come when England must not get a foothold; that *we must be first.* I was to *act,* discreetly but positively."

In a peculiar anachronism in his memoir, Frémont wrote that he learned from Gillespie that "my country was at war." He could not have learned this from the marine since their meeting at Klamath Lake occurred on May 9, 1846, four days before the war against Mexico was officially declared.

Years later in his own memoirs, Kit Carson also remembered learning of the war before it could have been possible for him to have heard of it: "A few days after we left [Lassen's rancho, on April 24], information was received from California that war was declared. . . . Lieutenant Gillespie, U.S. Marines, and six men were sent after us to have us come back."

Clearly, it was not the actual news of war that turned Frémont south again; it was the certainty of war as borne out by Gillespie's experiences and the intelligence he had picked up in Mazatlán and Monterey. The explorer was a trailsman too experienced not to have known of the impossibility of crossing the Cascade range in winter. He knew that winter snows blocked the passes, that game was scarce, his animals in poor shape. Common sense demanded that if he did return east, he would need to do so from a southern route. In a letter to Benton from Klamath Lake, he had laid the groundwork for returning to California, writing that "snow was falling steadily and heavily in the mountains," that "in the east, and north, and west, barriers absolutely impassable barred our road; we had no provisions; our animals were already feeble."

(Benton later added to the confusion as to why his son-in-law turned back to California when he wrote that it was "in the midst of such dangers, and such occupations as these, and in the wildest regions of the Farthest West, that Mr. Frémont was pursuing science and shunning war, when the arrival of Lieutenant Gillespie, and his communications from Washington, suddenly changed all his plans, turned him back from Oregon, and opened a new and splendid field of operations in California itself. . . .")

The truth seems to be that Frémont's movements north of Sutter's Fort comprised a calculated delaying tactic and that he fully intended to return to New Helvetia, there to bide his time and learn what he could. If war was averted through some eleventh-hour diplomatic legerdemain, he would head his men for Walker's Pass and a southern route home.

3

That night of his meeting on Klamath Lake with Frémont gave Archibald Gillespie his first taste of combat since he had entered the Marine Corps in 1832.

Kit Carson remembered the long day's ride on May 9 and falling exhausted into his bedroll on "the only night in all our travels, except the one night on the island in the Salt Lake, that we failed to keep guard." He said that since Gillespie and his companions had strengthened their party, they anticipated no Indian attack and that "the Colonel," as he called Frémont, posted no night watch and sat up late talking with Gillespie.

"Owens and I were sleeping together," Carson wrote, "and we were waked at the same time by the licks of the axe that killed our men. . . ."

Deep into the night, the scout had heard a noise and wakened suddenly. He called out to Basil Lajeunesse, sleeping nearby: "What's the matter there? What's the fuss?" There was no answer. Lajeunesse was dead—"his head had been cut in, in his sleep," Carson said. Instantly, the camp had come alive with men scrambling for their weapons amid the yelping of the attackers—a Klamath band—and the frenzied stamping and snorting of hobbled horses.

As the Klamaths fell on the camp, the four Delawares sprang up, and one of them, Crane, who had failed to load his carbine, flailed at the attackers with the gun until he fell, bristling with arrows. The half-breed Denny was also killed in the first few seconds of the melee. Frémont burst from his tent and joined Maxwell, Godey, and Stepp, all of them running toward the Delawares at the center of the fight.

Carson, who found his rifle useless because of a broken cap-nipple, sprinted toward the others, firing his pistol.

"I don't know who fired and who didn't," the scout said later, "but I think it was Stepp's shot that killed the Tlamath chief; for it was at the crack of Stepp's gun that he fell . . . . When the Tlamaths saw him fall, they ran . . . ."

Maddened at seeing his friend Lajeunesse's head split open, Carson had taken an ax to the fallen Klamath chief's skull, after which Segundai's knife sliced expertly and he popped the scalp off.

Frémont recalled that his party had encountered some of the Klamaths the day before and that the slain leader, who had given a salmon to Gillespie, had worn an "English half-axe" hanging from his wrist. "Carson seized this and knocked his head to pieces with it," the explorer said. The arrows in the chief's quiver were "all headed with a lancet-like piece of iron or steel—probably obtained from the Hudson's Bay Company's traders on the Umpqua—and were poisoned for about six inches. They could be driven that depth into a pine tree."

The quick fight was over, "but we lay," Carson said, "every man with his rifle cocked, until daylight, expecting another attack."

None came and at daylight, the bodies of Lajeunesse, Denny, and Crane were wrapped in their blankets and buried in a laurel grove before Frémont gathered his men for a retaliatory strike.

On May 12, Carson and ten men found a Klamath village of fifty lodges and charged in, Frémont and the others following. Within minutes, fourteen Indians lay dead, the lodges and huts and stores of dried fish on scaffolds torched, the canoes smashed to kindling. The Delawares, determined to avenge the slaying of Crane, did particularly close work with knives and axes.

Carson, who commanded the raid, recalled, "Their houses were built of flag [a lakeshore plant with sword-shaped leaves], beautifully woven. They had been fishing and had in their houses some ten wagon loads of fish they had caught. All their fishing tackle, camp equipage, etc., was there. I wished to do them as much damage as I could, so I directed their houses be set on fire. The flag being dry, it was a beautiful sight."

Gillespie, goggle-eyed at the bloodshed, opined, "By heaven, this is rough work," and promised that his superiors in Washington would learn of the gallantry of Frémont and his men.

Before they returned to California, there were several isolated incidents when Indian arrows whispered out of the trees at them. On one occasion, Carson fell off his horse as an arrow missed him by inches. Frémont spurred his big mount, El Toro de Sacramento, into a gallop and ran the lone Indian down. Segundai finished the job and took the hair.

The Klamaths were suspected of being recruited, along with Modocs and other tribes, by General Castro to harass the Americans. Carson said merely that "The Indians had commenced the war with us without cause and I thought they should be chastized in a summary manner. And they were severely punished." Frémont's view was somewhat different, writing that the reason for his brutal raids on the natives was to "anticipate" Indian problems and strike first to make them realize that "Castro was far and I near."

They reached Peter Lassen's ranch on May 24 and there learned that the sloop-of-war *Portsmouth* had anchored at Sausalito, on the northern headland of the Golden Gate. Gillespie, who had put himself under Frémont's command, was sent down to request supplies from Captain John B. Montgomery—rifle lead, percussion caps, gunpowder, and foodstuffs—and to ride on south to Monterey with a letter to Larkin assuring him that while Frémont and his expedition were back in California, they were heading home.

Writing almost a hundred years later, Bernard DeVoto asserted that Frémont returned from Oregon "to seize California for the United States and wrap Old Glory round him, to give a deed to the greatness in him." The historian maintained that the explorer needed honor and glory, "to seize the hour, take fortune at the full . . . to trust that the war which was certain to come would transform an act of brigandage into an act of patriotism, would transform the actor from a military adventurer, a freebooter, a filibuster, into a hero."

Frémont had written home that "The nature of my instructions and the peaceful nature of our operations do not contemplate any active hostility on my part, even in the event of war between the two countries." But forty-five years later, he contradicted himself, writing in his memoirs that he "knew the hour had come" before he turned south from Klamath Lake, even though he made a pretense of heading "home." He said he was "but a pawn, and like a pawn, I had been pushed forward to the front at the opening of the game."

9

War

■

1

When Gillespie and Frémont rendezvoused at Klamath Lake on May 9, 1846, four days remained before the United States and Mexico went to war, yet cannon smoke had already settled on one battlefield and was rising on another.

In Mexico City, Gillespie had witnessed the country's furious reaction to America's annexation of Texas and attempts to buy the provinces of New Mexico and California. Mexico's President José Herrera, after refusing to meet with the United States' special envoy John Slidell, ordered his top military man, General Mariano Paredes y Arrillaga, to organize an army and march north to subdue the Texans and reclaim the annexed territory. A rabid anti-American, Paredes stepped up his orders: he turned the army against Herrera, seized the government, and installed himself as president. His first act thereafter was to send a five-thousand-man army to Matamoros on the Rio Grande, and on April 23, 1846—while Frémont was heading his men north out of Sutter's Fort—he declared a "defensive war" against the United States.

The army Paredes sent north, commanded by General

Mariano Arista, had some of Mexico's most experienced light-infantrymen and sixteen hundred lancers under a celebrated cavalry general, Anastasio Torrejón. When the commanding general of this Army of the North arrived at Matamoros on April 24, his American counterpart, General Zachary Taylor, had been waiting with his expeditionary force of three thousand men for nearly a month. When Arista sent a lancer patrol across the Rio Grande twenty-four miles upstream from Matamoros and dispatched a polite message to the American camp that "hostilities have commenced," Taylor welcomed it and sent his own patrol of dragoons to meet Arista's lancers.

On April 25, the as yet undeclared war began.

2

The President chose Zachary Taylor to "defend the Rio Grande" because Taylor, as commanding general at Fort Jesup in Louisiana, was closer to the river than any other of the army's senior officers. Ever the political man, Polk the Democrat despised Taylor's Whig politics but hated even more the idea of appointing the army's top general, Winfield Scott, to command the expeditionary force. Polk considered Scott, also a Whig, a political intriguer and a man who, when not preening in his spotless blue uniform with its braided gold epaulettes and yellow sash, was preparing for a run at the presidency. Moreover, Scott wanted to take time to train and equip an army before moving it into battle. The President had no interest in such time-consuming matters. Quickness interested him—quick victories if diplomacy failed, a war ended quickly.

Scott was sixty-one, six-foot-four in height, a wounded veteran of Lundy's Lane in 1814, a scholar of war, and a tireless, inspirational officer always in the thick of a fight. But because of his politics, his insistence that men should be trained before sent into battle, and his well-known vanity (his men bestowed the "Old Fuss and Feathers" sobriquet on him), he was temporarily left in the capital. There, while waiting the appointment he knew would eventually come to him, he said sagacious, presidential-sounding things such as, "I do not desire to place myself in the most perilous of all positions, a fire upon my rear from Washington and the fire in front from the Mexicans."

Meantime, it was left to Zachary Taylor to start the ball, and no officer in the army stood in sharper contrast to the impeccable Scott than "Old Rough and Ready." Born in Virginia and raised on the Kentucky frontier, he had a rudimentary wilderness education, but in his nearly forty years in the army, he had fought in the War of 1812, in the Blackhawk War in the Midwest in 1832, and against the Seminoles in Florida. He was sixty-one, short, solid, and as powerful as a bullock, with a face furrowed with deep lines, unruly gray hair, and big knotty hands. In the field, he commonly wore a filthy oilskin or straw hat mashed on his head, a long, mud-spattered linen duster, rumpled shirt, and baggy trousers. He was often taken to be a camp follower or sutler as he sat under a shade tree, an ammunition box for desk, gnawing a lump of salt pork or chewing a huge quid of tobacco.

He hated pomp, was quickly bored with paperwork—Scott thought him "slow" of pen and speech—and knew little of strategy or tactics. He had a perfect correlative in the British army, General Hugh Gough, a Tipperary Irishman who was fighting Sikhs in the Punjab region of northern India while Taylor was fighting Mexicans on the Rio Grande. Like Taylor, Gough knew little of grand designs in war. Once, on a battlefield against the Sikhs, he was informed that his artillerymen were running low on powder and shot. "Thank God," Gough said. "Now I can be at them with the bayonet!"

Zachary Taylor and a certain dragoon general-to-be, Stephen Watts Kearny, had the same battle philosophy.

Taylor's officers loved to tell stories of his perfect calm in battle, of how he slouched on his horse "Old Whitey," chewing and spitting and growling orders amid musket balls, round shot, shrapnel, and cannon smoke. His men loved him.

Taylor brought his expeditionary force to the Rio Grande on March 28, 1846, and raised the Stars and Stripes on the bank of a horseshoe bend of the river. There he ordered the building of a fort from which his gunners could rake Matamoros with artillery fire. This pentagonal structure, its walls nine feet high and fifteen feet thick, with a bastion at each corner holding a cannon battery, was completed by the time General Arista came north to command the Mexican army of five thousand men opposing Taylor's three thousand.

The fighting began on April 25 when an American patrol marched through the chaparral to some abandoned ranch buildings twenty-five miles upriver from their fort opposite Matamoros. In a skirmish with Mexican lancers, sixteen Americans were killed, several others wounded and taken prisoner.

Taylor sent a message by courier to Washington, two weeks away from the Rio Grande: "American blood has been spilled."

More was due to be spilled before the President received the intelligence. On May 8, as the Americans were returning to their besieged fort from their supply base at Port Isabel on the Gulf Coast, Taylor met Arista's army, spread out in the saw grass on the treeless prairie, blocking the road at a place called Palo Alto. The Mexican cannons opened fire at two-thirty that afternoon, their range too short, the round shot bouncing and ricocheting like croquet balls and rolling into the American lines so slowly that the ranks opened to let them pass. Taylor's own big guns, eighteen-pounders loaded with grapeshot, were better manned and more accurate, and his "flying batteries" of small brass six-pounders and cast-iron twelves did murderous service among Torrejón's advancing lancers.

The artillery duel ended at nightfall, and as the cook fires were lit and the surgeons in their bloody aprons sawed, cauterized, and wound dressings around stumps and torn flesh, the casualties were counted: Taylor had lost five dead, forty-three wounded; Arista, over thirty killed.

The next day, the day Gillespie and Frémont met at Klamath Lake, Arista's battered army made a stand in a shallow ravine that formed an arc facing the road from Port Isabel to Matamoros. This roadway, called Resaca de la Palma, required more than cannon-shot to vanquish the enemy, and Taylor warned his infantry, Gough-like, that their "main dependence must be upon the bayonet." His flying battery advanced on the road, his infantry plunged through the tangle of chaparral, and as enemy grape and canister shot raked them, his dragoons charged Arista's cannons with Taylor shouting through the din, "Take those guns, and by God, keep them!"

The Fourth and Fifth Infantries charged into the Mexican line and after firing their muskets once, and with no time to reload, began the furious hand-to-hand bayonet killing the old general had predicted would be necessary.

The attack routed Arista's troops; they fell back south toward the river, leaving four hundred wounded behind.

The Americans lost thirty-three dead and eighty-nine wounded at Resaca de la Palma, but Taylor's army had won the first two battles of the war with Mexico, the first battles against non-Indian forces since 1815.

On May 18, the army was ferried across the Rio Grande and after occupying Matamoros, Taylor began laying plans to move deeper into Mexico.

3

President Polk received the general's "blood has been spilled" message on May 9, and with his *casus belli* in hand, sent his own message to Congress two days later. He asked that the legislators acknowledge that a state of war existed and provide "the means for prosecuting the war with vigor, thus hastening the restoration of peace." He asserted that "the cup of forbearance had been exhausted" and that Mexico, by entering Texas, had invaded American territory and opened hostilities.

Despite Whig opposition, in which Polk was accused of fomenting war by sending Taylor to the Rio Grande in the first place, a war bill passed empowering the President to raise fifty thousand troops to serve for the duration of the war—said troops to furnish their own uniforms and horses—and appropriating ten million dollars to bring the "existing war" to conclusion.

On May 13, 1846, the war became official by a vote of 42 to 2 in the Senate, 174 to 14 in the House. The declaration was filled with high-minded words but many, especially Polk's Whig opposition, saw the war as a plot by Southerners to spread the evil of slavery into the West. Others saw it as blatant aggression and a landgrab. In a Senate debate, Senator Thomas Corwin of Ohio said that greed alone had created the war. "If I were a Mexican," he said, "I would tell you, 'Have you not enough room in your own country to bury your dead men? If you come into mine, we will greet you with bloody hands and welcome you to hospitable graves.'"

In the House of Representatives, Abraham Lincoln, the young Illinois Whig, called the President "a bewildered, confounded, and miserably perplexed man" and spent much of his single term demanding that Polk prove his allegations that the Mexicans had provoked the war by attacking Americans on American soil.

But in the *Brooklyn Eagle,* poet Walt Whitman spoke for the political expansionists of the Polk and Benton stripe, and for a sizable portion of American citizenry, as he echoed the doctrine of Manifest Destiny in writing: "Let our arms now be carried with a spirit which shall teach the world that, while we are not forward for a quarrel, America knows how to crush, as well as how to expand."

Soon enough, General Winfield Scott would plan and command the campaign to the Halls of Montezuma. In November, 1846, the President reluctantly appointed the man he considered "rather scientific and visionary in his view" to command the Vera Cruz expedition. Scott assembled his army at Tampico, engineered an amphibious landing at Vera Cruz, and captured the city in May, 1847. Then, without a dependable supply line, he led fourteen thousand men against superior forces into the mountainous gateway to Mexico City, emerged from the passes, and stormed Chapúltepec Castle, said to be impregnable, on September 14, 1847, to crown one of the most brilliant campaigns in American military annals.

(In the process of trying to identify a Democrat who could lead the army into Mexico, Polk had been visited by Thomas Hart Benton of Missouri. The senator, who had no military experience whatever, had offered to command the American force if the President would appoint him lieutenant general—then the highest rank in the army, held by only one man: Winfield Scott. The President let this preposterous idea die.)

The seventeen months of warfare cost thirteen thousand American lives (seventeen hundred were killed in battle or died of wounds, the balance dying of "other causes," mainly disease). It cost a hundred million dollars and changed the map of the United States more radically than any event after the Louisiana Purchase.

On the day of the war's declaration, while Captain Frémont and his men were riding south from above the forty-second parallel and seeking out Klamath Indian villages to burn, the War Department made its first overt move toward capturing the biggest prize of the war. On May 13, 1846, War Secretary William Marcy sent orders to Colonel Stephen Watts Kearny, commanding the First Dragoon Regiment at Fort Leavenworth, Kansas. Kearny was to prepare to march west, conquer and occupy the province of New Mexico and its capital at Santa Fé, and continue on to California.

10

Los Osos

■

1

A *week after* the war officially opened, Frémont and his
men, with the marine courier Lieutenant Archibald
Gillespie and his escort riding with them, were camped in
the low hills known as the Buttes, sixty miles north of Sutter's Fort. During the ride down from the Oregon border, still
smoldering over the murder of Basil Lajeunesse and the others in the Klamath attack, the Americans had fallen on several small Indian villages, burning lodges and scattering the
inhabitants. "The number killed I cannot say," Kit Carson
wrote later. "It was perfect butchery. Those not killed fled
in all directions. . . ."

At Peter Lassen's place and beyond, Frémont heard gossip
and settlers' tales claiming that the attack on his men on
Klamath Lake was but a precursor of planned massacres and
burnings of fields. This strategy, it was said, had been authored by General Castro and other Californios to drive the
Americans from the valley. Furthermore, it was rumored,
Castro was issuing *bandos,* arming the Indians, and organizing a huge army that would soon march north from Monterey.

The settlers were banding and they looked to Frémont, the
man who had defied Castro at Hawk's Peak, for guidance.

Everything came together, and fell apart, in June.

In the first week of the month, Frémont appears to have thrown in with the squatters while managing to keep up a pretense of neutrality. During that week, he later said, he had "decided on the course which I would pursue," but as late as June 16, he wrote to Commander Montgomery of the sloop-of-war *Portsmouth:* "It is therefore my present intention to abandon the further prosecution of our exploration and pro-ceed immediately across the mountainous country to the eastward . . . and thence to the frontier of Missouri." Mont-gomery must have thought it remarkable that this return home would require the supplies Frémont requested through his emissary to the *Portsmouth,* Lieutenant Gillespie: eight thousand percussion caps, three hundred pounds of rifle lead and a keg of powder, along with flour, coffee, tea, tobacco, salt pork, and similar ordinary provisions.

What triggered Frémont's decision to join the Sacramento Valley rebels, however furtively at first, is not clear. One im-portant factor was the request by Kit Carson and others in his party to release them from service so that they could join the "Osos," the name the rebels had adopted, inspired by the grizzly bears in the area whose "fighting spirit" they much admired. The explorer had instructions of some kind. He had them when he left St. Louis with his men and others had been brought to him by Gillespie. War, he knew—from Gillespie's experiences and from information Benton and others had relayed to him—was a virtual certainty. The Californios were attempting to expel American emigrants from the province, and these settlers were rising. He could not leave California, could not overtly lead the rebels, but he could encourage and advise them in a silent partnership until his path became better defined.

He wavered, waited, talked with Sutter and listened to the couriers and news- and rumor-bearers who beat a path in and out of New Helvetia.

Sutter himself was in a vise. The pinch was not so much

a matter of divided loyalties—he was Swiss, not American—as his trying to find a footing amid the tremors of war between an impending American takeover and his loyalty to those who had trusted him. He was a Mexican citizen, had been given an enormous, profitable land grant, and the trust, to the degree that any foreigner was trusted, of Mexican authorities. He had been warranted as a departmental official. He had encouraged American emigration, employed many of the Americans who had made their way to the Sacramento Valley, and he foresaw the end of Mexican California and the old way of life, knowing that he had had a hand in ending it.

In June, 1846, the twilight of his loyalty to Mexico and, more specifically, to his immediate superior, José Castro, Sutter, in one last act of loyalty to his adopted country, notified the general that the whiskey salesman named Gillespie was in fact an American military officer carrying secret dispatches and urged Castro to consider sending a "respectable garrison" north in the event of trouble with the settlers.

Frémont, while enjoying Sutter's hospitality and depending on him for supplies and mounts, did not trust him, knew of the empresario's divided loyalties, but also knew where the teetering man would fall when California fell.

The man none of the Americans could gauge, the most influential personage in northern California, and to Frémont's thinking, the most dangerous, was Don Mariano Guadalupe Vallejo of Sonoma. This thirty-eight-year-old aristocrat, former commanding general of California, had the peculiar distinction of being at once a respected Californio patriot and a man known to favor the United States' intervention in California. At least he favored it over Mexico's ruinous rule, and over other rumored contenders for annexation such as England.

Born in Monterey in 1808, Vallejo had earned the respect of Californios, north and south, and of men such as Sutter,

the consuls Larkin and Leidesdorff, and the occasional
visitors to his home in Sonoma and his rancho, named
Lachryma Montis (Tears of the Mountain) after the springs
in the surrounding hillsides. He was a portly, handsome,
well-educated, somewhat fatalistic man, frustrated in his
administrative duties by Mexico City's neglect of his beloved land, and especially of its northernmost outpost.

He was also a man with a keen sense of justice, a trait illustrated in a story told by a contemporary Californio, Antonio María Osio of Monterey, who knew Vallejo well.

At Yerba Buena in the 1830s, a soldier named Francisco
Rubio was condemned to die for raping and killing two small
children. This man, holding a crucifix, said at his execution,
"I shall presently account for my actions to this Divine
Redeemer I hold in my hands. I tell you—He is my witness—
that it was not I who killed Ignacio Olivas's children. Some-
day you will realize this. But I have committed other
offenses, and I should resign myself to the decrees of Providence."

Vallejo, who was *ayudante de plaza* (adjutant of the town),
refused to take charge of the execution detail, although he
witnessed Rubio's death. He was apparently convinced that
the soldier had told the truth—"virtually all the inhabitants
of that area believed that Rubio was not guilty," Osio said.

Vallejo decided to inquire into the case and kept the
investigation going for six or seven years, during which
time he was appointed a commandante and moved to Sonoma.

Eventually he received convincing information that an
Indian named Román, from Mission San Rafael, was the
actual killer of the Olivas children. "When he had verified
this," Osio said, ". . . he ordered Sergeant Lázaro Piña to go
there [Mission San Rafael] with a detachment of soldiers. He
ordered Piña to shoot the Indian four times as soon as he
found him, to leave the Indian lying there on the ground, and

to return straightaway to report that he had fulfilled his duty. Two days later, the order was carried out."

Larkin, who described Vallejo as "stiff, pompous and exacting . . . pleasant and condescending," believed this *jefe político* would support American annexation if for no other reason than because neither Mexico nor Alta California could prevent it.

But others were not so trusting of Don Mariano, especially after it was learned that Castro had visited Vallejo at Lachryma Montis on June 5, 1846. The general, it was widely believed, had sought the eminent Sonoman's assistance in enforcing the new restrictions on American emigrants and in preventing any new flow of them into the Sacramento Valley. Castro also had collected horses and supplies for his men from Vallejo's rancho.

Three days after this meeting, William Ide, the Massachusetts carpenter who farmed north of Sutter's Fort, was visited by another American of the area, William Knight, a Marylander who operated a ferry on the Sacramento. Knight reported that "armed Spaniards on horseback" had been seen in the valley burning homes, destroying crops, and driving off horses and cattle. Ide grabbed his carbine, said good-bye to his wife and children, and mounted up, riding with Knight to Frémont's camp north of New Helvetia. When the two men arrived, they found others already talking to the captain, among them Ezekial "Stuttering" Merritt, and Henry Ford, the New Hampshireman and army deserter who worked for Sutter as a trapper.

The tale Knight had reported had no foundation in fact, but as it happened, a real Castro matter was being reported to Frémont. A Lieutenant Francisco Arce, Castro's secretary, and a militia officer named José María Alviso, with an armed squad of eight men, had crossed the Sacramento near Sutter's with a herd of 170 horses, said to have been obtained from Colonel Vallejo in Sonoma. Arce, it was reported, was taking the herd to Santa Clara, near the southern shore of San Francisco Bay, where General Castro was organizing a cavalry force to drive the American settlers out of California.

On June 10, Merritt, Ford, "Long Bob" Semple the Kentucky giant, and sharpshooter Granville Swift, descendant of Daniel Boone ("in a fight, worth a dozen men," Frémont said of him), took six volunteers, picked up four more en route, and rode out to intercept Arce. They surprised the lieutenant in his camp on the Cosumnes River south of Sutter's Fort, forced his surrender and seized the horse herd. The Americans returned the swords to the two officers and left one horse each to Arce, Aviso, and their men. Arce was told to deliver to his commander the message that if he wanted the rest of the *caballada*, he would have to come get them.

The Americans drove the herd north to the Buttes camp the next day.

Frémont's role in this escapade is not known, although there is evidence that he encouraged the raid, if not actually directed it. One of his men, a twenty-two-year-old Tennessean named Thomas Martin, later claimed that the captain "called us together and told us that we were going to take the country and called for volunteers to go and capture this band of horses." But William Ide's recollection differed. He said that Frémont "in my hearing, expressly declared that he was not at liberty to afford us the least aid or assistance; nor would he suffer any of his men to do so . . . that he was able, of his own party, to fight and whip Castro if he chose, but that he should not do so unless first assaulted by him. . . ."

H. H. Bancroft, four decades after the fact, wrote that Frémont "instigated and planned" the horse raid as a continuation of the insolence he had demonstrated at Hawk's Peak and that the explorer "spoke guardedly" to the Sacramento Valley settlers, "inciting them indirectly to revolt, but cautiously avoiding remarks and promises which might in certain contingencies be used to his disadvantage later."

Thomas Hart Benton gave an orotund rationale to the press for his son-in-law's behavior, saying that Frémont had found his progress north in the Klamath Lake area "completely barred by the double obstacle of hostile Indians, which Castro had excited against him, and the lofty mountains covered with deep and falling snow." He said that General Castro had been assembling troops "with the avowed object of attacking both Frémont's party and all the American settlers." The formidable Missourian, known for bellowing "The *facts*—what are the *facts*?" in the halls of Congress, said: "I could add much more to prove that Captain Frémont's private views and feelings were in unison with his ostensible mission—that the passion of his soul was the pursuit of science and that he looked with dread and aversion upon every possible collision either with the Indians, Mexicans, or British, that could turn him aside from his cherished pursuit."

Benton's "facts" notwithstanding, before the June 10 horse raid, the Sacramento Valley settlers were looking for a leader; after it, they seemed to have found one.

2

For a few days following the capture of the horses, Frémont managed to remain in the shadows. He could not be identified as the leader of the Osos and their now open rebellion. He was an army officer with an ostensible scientific mission, as yet uncertain that California had become enemy territory. His act of belligerency the past March, from which he had narrowly escaped, had produced a modicum of caution. He had to walk heel to toe like an acrobat on a swaying wire, advising and directing while giving the impression—to whom, it is not clear since no one was fooled—of his neutrality.

Zeke Merritt, who appears to have been Frémont's hand-picked leader, had gathered a dozen new volunteers in his ride back from the horse raid and had thirty eager Osos in the Buttes camp when the next stage of the miniature revolution began. This step, a far more ambitious and potentially dangerous scheme than a mere horse raid, was directed against the most powerful man in northern California and the seat of his governance. The strategy was to seize the town of Sonoma, force the surrender of Colonel Vallejo and his military garrison, and thus forestall General Castro's plans to harry the settlers and force them from the country.

This plan, which many thought in the aftermath was designed and directed by Frémont, had little of military thinking behind it, but at least it depended on more than blind luck. Sonoma's primitive defenses were no secret to anyone who passed through the village, and no one doubted that even a tiny armed force could occupy the town without bloodshed.

On June 13, one month after war was declared against Mexico, Ezekial Merritt and thirty-three men rode southwest from the Buttes, crossed the Sacramento River, and headed for Sonoma, thirty-five miles north of San Francisco Bay. In the party were William Ide, John Grigsby, Bob Semple, Henry Ford, William Todd, Le Gros Fallon, William Knight, Granville Swift, and three recently arrived settlers, Sam Kelsey, Thomas Cowie, and George Fowler.

Frémont himself did not saddle up, nor would he allow any of his men to take part in the raid, although many of them, notably Kit Carson and his friend Dick Owens, were anxious to join the Osos.

The village of San Francisco Solano de Sonoma was squalid and flyblown, its spacious plaza littered with rubbish and the bones of slaughtered cattle and surrounded by caved-in *jacales* and weed patches. More important to the Osos, the town's defenses, never remarkable, had deteriorated to ruin since the time they were set up by Colonel Vallejo in 1835 as protection against possible incursions by Russians out of Fort Ross. These defenses consisted of a *cuartel,* a windowed wooden barracks on the north side of the town's central plaza adjoining Vallejo's two-story Casa Grande home; a *torreon,* a four-story adobe tower with loopholes for riflemen; nine brass cannons stationed around the plaza; and an armory, located in the barracks building, holding 250 muskets, some lead ball and iron shot, and a hundred pounds of gunpowder.

But even the *cuartel* was a sham. Sonoma had no garrison, no one to lay the cannons or load the muskets. The soldiery had been removed during the Micheltorena troubles in '45 and never replaced. Mexico City had been of no help—the home country insisting that all its colonies be self-supporting—nor was Governor Pico in Los Angeles of any assistance; he provided no finances for a Sonoma garrison despite the problem of the unauthorized settlers in the north.

These matters were known to the Osos as they clattered across the bridge between the Napa and Sonoma valleys at dawn on June 14, entered the town from the north, rode past the Misión San Francisco de Solano, reined up in front of Vallejo's Casa Grande, and banged gun butts on the door.

Don Mariano came to the door in his nightshirt. Arrayed before him, bathed in the yellow lantern light, some still on horseback, some afoot, stood a crew that might have come north from San Pablo Bay off a ship flying the Jolly Roger. This motley nightmare consisted of "about as rough looking a set of men as one could well imagine," Kentuckian Robert Semple later said. Some wore bandannas, pirate-fashion, on their heads, others coon, fox, and coyote-skin caps; most favored buckskin hunting shirts and trousers, and Indian moccasins. All were armed—rifles, muskets, pepper-box pistols, tomahawks, hunting knives—and all were tired and agitated.

After a few words at the door, Vallejo invited the ringleaders into his *sala*. As they lounged on his mahogany furniture and eyed the piano and paintings, the colonel dressed. His wife Doña Francisca begged him to escape from these banditti through the back of the house, but he rejected this idea; he would not desert her and their six children. He sent a servant to fetch his brother-in-law, the Ohio-born merchant Jacob Leese, to serve as translator.

"To what happy circumstances shall I attribute the visit of so many exalted personages?" Vallejo asked Merritt with a witty irony lost on the ruffian with the tobacco-juice beard.

"We mean to establish our own government in California, an independent republic, and are under arms to support it. You are under arrest, General, as the responsible head of the Mexicans hereabouts," Merritt stuttered. He added a point, useful and perhaps even true, asserting that he and his men were acting under orders from Captain Frémont of the United States Army.

Frémont's name must have convinced Vallejo that these "white Indians," as he later called them, were not mere bandits. He handed over the keys to the town arsenal and offered the men food and brandy. One eyewitness reported that after hearing of their mission, he went to his room and, "following the usages of war," retrieved his ceremonial sword, which he offered to his captors. None of the Osos seemed to know what to do with it and so Don Mariano returned it to his room.

After sunrise, Vallejo's brother, Salvador, a captain in the Mexican army, and the colonel's secretary, a French emigré named Victor Prudon, came to Casa Grande and were also placed under arrest. Now, the buckskinned Osos and their prisoners enjoyed the repast the general's servants brought into the *sala*. William Ide later recalled that the "generous spirits gave proof of his [Vallejo's] usual hospitality as the richest wines and brandies sparkled in the glasses, and those who had thus unceremoniously met soon became merry companions. . . . The bottles well nigh vanquished the captors."

Meantime, with the town now awake, the rebels still lounging outside Casa Grande were growing restless. They had found a few villagers willing to sell them food and wine but were tired of the waiting, and some of them drunkenly surveyed shops and homes with looters' eyes. John Grigsby volunteered to find out about the delay and disappeared into the casa. William Ide followed some time later.

At last documents were drafted by Robert Semple, written in both English and Spanish, in which Vallejo agreed to surrender Sonoma to the Americans with the provision that the townspeople would not be molested and personal properties would be respected.

Three hours had passed since Merritt and the others had entered Vallejo's home. Those outside listened as the capitulation paper was read aloud. To several of the Osos, primed with *aguardiente,* everything was too easy—no fight, no booty, no reward for their efforts—and there was loud talk of abandoning the revolt. Grigsby, under the clear impression that Captain Frémont had ordered the capture of Sonoma and its leading citizens, said he would resign and back out of the scrape." Others talked of tearing down Casa Grande and ransacking it and the town before riding back to the Buttes.

Semple was furious over such talk and threatened to shoot any man who tried to turn the revolution into a "looting expedition," and was backed up by Grigsby and Sam Kelsey.

It fell to the schoolteacher-farmer William Ide to bring the rabble under control. In a theatrical speech to his fellow insurgents, he said, "Saddle no horse for me. I will lay my bones here before I will take upon myself the ignominy of commencing an honorable work, and then flee like cowards, like thieves, when no enemy is in sight. In vain will you say you had honorable motives. Who will believe it? Flee this day, and the longest life cannot wear off your disgrace!"

He closed his peroration by shouting like a backwoods Bible-thumper: "Choose ye this day what you will be! We are robbers, or we *must* be conquerors!"

The exhortation had its effect. Twenty-four Osos voted to stand with Ide and elected him their leader and spokesman.

The raiders "seized and held in trust for the public benefit" the armory, the nine cannons and 250 "stands of arms," shot and powder, estimated to be worth twelve hundred American dollars, and 140 horses that were handed over to the Americans by Vallejo and Leese.

Next, ten men, Semple, Grigsby, and Merritt among them, were selected to escort the prisoners—Vallejo, his brother Salvador, and Victor Prudon, with Leese as interpreter—to the American camp on the Sacramento, eighty miles northeast. Ide apparently confirmed to Don Mariano that Captain Frémont had ordered the raid, and Vallejo was relieved to learn it. He felt that he would be treated justly by an officer of the Army of the United States.

Ide and twenty-five Osos controlled Sonoma. The still-terrified Doña Francisca and her six children remained at Casa Grande under guard.

The escort and prisoners spent a night on the trail and arrived at Frémont's camp at noon on June 16. Vallejo's hope of cordiality and fairness from the explorer was quickly dashed. Frémont denied responsibility for the raid, denied even that the colonel was his prisoner, yet lectured the stunned Californio on the complaints of the Americans in the Sacramento Valley. Vallejo shrewdly assessed the captain as having "a very elastic conscience."

Merritt and the others, with Frémont's approval, removed

the prisoners to Sutter's Fort, where the empresario treated them with kindness, leaving them unguarded, sharing meals with them, and permitting them walks outside their quarters to escape the stifling heat. (Frémont, when he visited the fort sometime later, sternly reprimanded Sutter for trying to make Vallejo's cell more comfortable.) The prisoners' cubicles were infested with mosquitoes rising from a slough behind the fort, and the colonel soon developed malarial symptoms, lost weight, and presented a haggard appearance. This disturbed Sutter and after he sent a message to Montgomery of the *Portsmouth,* anchored off Yerba Buena, a ship's surgeon came to the fort, escorted by Lieutenant Charles Warren Revere, to treat the prisoners.

By the time he was released from captivity on August 1, Vallejo's frayed and shabby clothing hung on his six-foot frame as on a bone rack. After being reunited with his wife and children, he toured his Lachryma Montis estate and sadly estimated that during his six-week imprisonment, more than a thousand head of cattle and six hundred horses had been stolen from his lands. His entire untended wheat crop was also lost.

During his absence, Doña Francisca treated the Americans with Californio courtesy and hospitality and earned their respect and admiration. The surgeon from the *Portsmouth,* who tended her husband and visited her at Casa Grande, described her affectionately as *"muy gorda* [very fat], but still has the evidence of much beauty. She seems to be femininely passive and voluptuous, contented and happy."

Months after the event, Thomas Hart Benton reported on the "capture" of Sonoma to his Senate colleagues. He treated the event as a military enterprise of considerable tactical effort and gave the impression that a siege had been required to force the surrender of the town, which he described as "a fortified, well-garrisoned presidio." He based his information on letters received from his son-in-law, on the scene.

In truth, of course, the decrepit, soldierless village had been conquered by dint of a rifle rap on the door of Colonel Valle-jo's home by a coonskinned company of Frémont-inspired freebooters. Sonoma, as Bernard DeVoto put it, "could have been captured by Tom Sawyer and Huck Finn."

Even so, the buckskin rising needed a symbol, and the duty to come up with one fell to William L. Todd (whose aunt Mary in Illinois, just four years past, had married a frontier lawyer named Abraham Lincoln). With the help of Ben Dewell, an Ohio saddler, and rebel Thomas Cowie, Todd fashioned a flag—a white field with a red-flannel stripe at the bottom—from a petticoat and chemise contributed by the wives of the Osos. On the white material, using a chewed stick as a brush, Todd daubed a figure of a passant grizzly bear (someone said it looked more like a "big fat Berkshire") and a large, red five-pointed star above the words "California Republic," lettered, DeVoto says, "in pokeberry juice."

This rude banner was fixed to the flagpole in the Sonoma plaza and raised on June 14 to the cheers of the gathered rebels. One shrewd observer, Antonio María Osio, said of the Osos and the occasion, ". . . they decided to camouflage the flag of stars and stripes with a temporary flag which de-picted a brown bear on a white field. . . ."

3

Two days after the capture of the town, John Montgom-ery of the *Portsmouth,* now anchored off Sausalito, sent a small landing party up to Sonoma. The commander's sixteen-year-old son accompanied the sailors and officers and recorded later that "on arriving we found a party of 24 men, mostly dressed in Buckskins . . . [led] by a plain man about 5o years old in his Shirt Sleeves . . . Capt. Ide wel-comed us to Sonoma."

Ide was actually sixty years old as he performed his first acts as commander in chief of the California Republic. With the Bear Flag newly snapping in the breeze above the Sonoma plaza, he reappointed José Berreyesa, the town's *alcalde,* to continue as local magistrate under the "new regime." He also organized his three dozen men somewhat ambitiously into two military units, designated the First Artillery (presumably in charge of the six captured cannons) and the First Rifles.

Another duty all revolutionary leaders must perform, the drafting of a grandiloquent proclamation, Ide zestfully accomplished. On June 15, he issued his, declaring that the aim of the rising was to overthrow "a military despotism" that "shamefully oppressed the laboring people in California." He and the Osos promised that all Californians who surrendered their arms would "not be disturbed in their persons, their property or social relations." The arduously phrased document declared the rebels' intent to establish a "republican government" that would ensure "civil and religious liberty . . . encourage industry, virtue and literature . . . leave unshackled by fetters commerce, agriculture and mechanism."

As this Bear Flag manifesto, mostly by word of mouth, made its way south, Americans everywhere who learned of it flocked to Sonoma, swelling the Bear Flagger ranks to over a hundred men within a week, many of them sunshine patriots attracted by the prospect of the square league of land offered as an enlistment enticement.

Of Ide's effusion, H. H. Bancroft said sourly, "As a whole, in truthfulness and consistency, as in orthography and literary merit, it was below the plane of Castro's and Pico's proclamations. In respect to bombast and general absurdity, it stood about midway between the two. . . . As a product of filibusterism, pure and simple, it deserves praise not to be awarded from any other standpoint."

Castro and Pico did not delay in issuing responses to the Osos' declaration. On June 17, from his headquarters in Santa Clara, the general condemned "the contemptible

policy of the agents of the government of the United States,"
which he said had induced a number of "adventurers" to invade
the province and capture Sonoma. And in Santa Barbara,
Governor Pico declared that "a gang of North American adventurers, with the blackest treason that the spirit of evil
could invent, have invaded the town of Sonoma, raising their
flag, and carrying off as prisoners four Mexican citizens."

11

Olómpali

■

1

On *June 14*, the day the Bear Flag was raised in Sonoma plaza, Frémont and his band, as yet knowing nothing of the outcome of the raid, rode into Sutter's. Lieutenant Gillespie and sailors from the *Portsmouth* were waiting for him on the American River with a launch loaded with the gunpowder and supplies the explorer had requested. Among the bags, boxes, and barrels was a gift from Commander Montgomery, a hogshead of whiskey, which the men fell upon with a will.

On the sixteenth, Merritt, Semple, and Grigsby rode into the fort with Colonel Vallejo and the other prisoners, turned them over to Sutter, their reluctant jailer, and provided endless embroidered details of the capture of Sonoma.

Nearly a month passed before Frémont learned with certainty that the United States and Mexico were at war, but he seemed to regard Merritt's news as the act requiring him to exert his leadership. He began signing his letters "Military Commander of U.S. Forces in California" and proceeded to alienate John Sutter by commandeering his supplies. Ned Kern, the civilian artist-cartographer from Philadelphia,

who got along well with Sutter, was placed in command of
the fort and its prisoners.

In Sonoma meantime, Captain William Ide of the Republic of California's hundred-man army sent William Todd on
a mission to the *Portsmouth* to notify its skipper of the horse
raid, the surrender of Colonel Vallejo and the town, and, in
effect, of the Osos' independent declaration of war. Unlike
Frémont, Ide was hesitant to ask Montgomery for gunpowder. and supplies since the naval officer, with no assurance
that his country was at war, could not legally arm and provision a rebel force. Instead, Todd was given a second assignment and, with another man, rode north toward Bodega
Bay to find American settlers who had stores of arms and
powder. Ide also dispatched two other Osos toward the Russian River below Fort Ross for the same purpose. These
men, Thomas Cowie and George Fowler, were to locate Moses Carson, who could help them find arms and gunpowder.
Carson had been a Mexican citizen since 1836 and now
served as majordomo at the Sotoyomi rancho owned by
Henry D. Fitch, a former trade-ship master from New Bed-
ford, Massachusetts.

Two days passed and when the parties failed to return
from the short ride north, Ide's chief lieutenant, Henry L.
Ford, organized an eighteen-man search team to comb the
countryside between Sonoma and the Russian River. Moses
Carson reported that he had seen neither Cowie nor Fowler,
but during the return to Sonoma, Ford and his party spotted
a small body of Californio soldiers and after exchanging a
few gunshots, captured a man who told them of the awful
fate of the two Osos.

The prisoner, one Bernardino "Four-Fingered Jack" García, whom Vallejo described as "the wickedest man that
California had produced up to that time," said that the two
Americans had been captured near Santa Rosa by a patrol
of "irregulars" led by Castro lieutenants Juan Padilla, a
barber, and Ramón Carrillo, brother of Francisca Vallejo.

García, who was present during the horrors he described, and probably participated in, said that Cowie and Fowler were tortured for two days—tied to trees, stoned, mutilated with knives, and disembowled—before being shot.

(Writing in the *New York Evening Post* in October, 1856, the faithful Frémont man Alexis Godey, who saw the corpses, said ". . . their bodies presented a most shocking spectacle, bearing the marks of horrible mutilation, their throats cut, and their bowels ripped open; other indignities were perpetrated of a nature too disgusting and obscene to relate." He said that Cowie "was well known to many of our men, with whom he was a favorite, and the sight that his lifeless remains presented, created in the breasts of many of his old friends a feeling of stern and bitter revenge. . . .")

After delivering García to the *calabozo* in Sonoma and giving Ide the details of the murders, Henry Ford and Granville Swift gathered eighteen volunteers and, on the morning of June 23, rode northwest toward Santa Rosa. They hoped to pick up the trail of Padilla and his irregulars and determine the fate of the still-missing Bill Todd and his companion.

Near the village of San Antonio, Ford's men captured four Californios and after camping the night and acting on information the prisoners provided, the searchers turned south on a trail toward San Rafael. At mid-morning, near the mouth of the Petaluma River, they found a corral of horses at a place known locally as Olómpali, named after a Miwok Indian village that had been visited by Drake's freebooters in 1579. It was also known as Camilo's Rancho for its owner, Camilo Ynita, an Indian wheat grower and one-time business partner of Colonel Vallejo's.

Ford and his men dismounted after spotting a number of uniformed Californio lancers milling around Ynita's adobe ranchhouse eating a late breakfast. The horsemen, about fifty in number, were commanded by Captain Joaquín de la Torre, a veteran officer from Monterey. He had been sent north by Castro after the American attack on Sonoma, and with him at the rancho was the Cowie-Fowler culprit, Juan Padilla.

The Californios ran for their horses after Ford's men opened fire on them from the brush and trees bordering the rancho. They managed to make a ragged cavalry charge toward the brush, but the American volley fire killed one lancer, wounded one, and scattered the others, forcing them to kick their mounts out of rifle range. After some desultory firing on both sides, De la Torre and his men, Padilla among them, escaped downtrail toward San Rafael.

During the volley from Ford's men, William Todd and his gunpowder-searching partner, both captured by De la Torre some days earlier, ran from the ranchhouse to the American line and reached it unscathed. Todd said he was saved from execution by the Californios by telling his captors that if they killed him and his partner, the Americans would execute *their* prisoners—presumably alluding to Vallejo and the others in Sutter's cells.

Ford did not pursue the lancers. None of his men had been scratched in the encounter, he had rescued the two missing Osos, and he feared that his tiny force might ride into a trap if he chased De la Torre's already superior numbers, so he gathered his men and rode on to Sonoma to report to Captain Ide.

The "Battle of Olómpali" was the only fight of the Bear Flag Republic.

2

Frémont, in camp with his ninety men near Sutter's, learned of the fate of Cowie and Fowler, and of Ford's patrol, from an express dispatched from Bear Flag headquarters in Sonoma. Days earlier, he had learned from various Sutter men that General Castro had called for a *levée en*

masse and had sent a force of lancers north from Mission
Santa Clara preparatory, it was believed, to an attack on Sonoma. The informants said that Castro was determined to
chase the rebels out of Sonoma, but considered it his real
duty to rid California of all Americans—Frémont and his
men first among them.

On June 25, the explorer and his men (among them a new
recruit named James Marshall, a thirty-five-year-old New
Jersey wheelwright and carriage-maker), with Archibald
Gillespie, Kit Carson, Segundai, and his Delawares in the
van, rode into Sonoma, where they learned of the skirmish
at Olómpali. The next morning, joined by Lieutenant Ford
and a detachment of Osos, Frémont rode out of Sonoma
south to San Rafael, hoping to intercept De la Torre and Padilla. Upon reaching the village and discovering that the
Californios had vanished, the Americans set up camp at the
old mission, situated on a hill overlooking San Pablo Bay.
In the waiting, scouting parties fanned out toward Sausalito
to see if there was any activity among Castro's forces.

Across San Francisco Bay, Castro had yet to learn the
whereabouts of his lancer patrol, and on June 28, he sent a
boat into San Pablo Bay with a message to Captain De la
Torre. In the small launch were an oarsman and three others: the twin brothers Francisco and Ramón de Haro, age
twenty, of Yerba Buena, and their uncle, José de los Reyes
Berreyesa, father of the *alcalde* of Sonoma, who hoped to
visit his son, whom he believed had been taken prisoner by
the Americans.

From his perch on the mission hill above San Rafael, Frémont trained his telescope on the launch as it crawled across
the bay toward the landing at Point San Pablo and ordered
three of his men, Kit Carson, Granville Swift, and the Pennsylvania blacksmith Sam Neal, to ride down to the beach
and ascertain the business of the boatmen.

Precisely what occurred after the oarsman rowed across
the bay and the old man and the twin brothers slogged ashore

with their saddles and gear is not known, but it is indisput-
able that the three, apparently unarmed, were murdered in
cold blood.

In his memoirs, Frémont dismissed the incident in a few
lines and seemed to forget whom he had sent to intercept the
boat—or perhaps he wished to protect Carson, Swift, and
Neal—especially Carson—from blame. He also reduced the
number of murders by one, neglecting to mention there were
two De Haros killed. "Both the settlers and the men of my
command were excited against the Californians by the recent murder of the two Americans [Cowie and Fowler]," he
wrote, "and not by the murder only, but by the brutal circumstances attending it. My scouts, mainly Delawares,
influenced by these feelings, made sharp retaliation and
killed Berreyesa and de Haro, who were bearers of inter-
cepted letters."

A man named Jasper O'Farrell, an Irish resident of San
Rafael at the time, reported in the *Los Angeles Star* in September, 1856, that he was in the village when Captain Frémont and his "troops" arrived and when the boat landed the
three men at the Point San Pablo estuary. O'Farrell wrote
that Kit Carson and two other men were detailed to intercept the boat and that Carson soon returned to where Frémont was standing in the corridor of the mission "in company
with Gillespie, myself, and others, and said, 'Captain, shall
I take those men prisoners?' In response, Frémont waved his
hand and said: 'I have got no room for prisoners.'" Then,
according to O'Farrell's account, Carson and the others "advanced to within fifty yards of the three unfortunate and
unarmed Californians, alighted from their horses, and de-
liberately shot them."

In a highly improbable postscript to the story, the Irishman claimed to have talked with Carson in 1853 about the
incident, "and he assured me," O'Farrell said, "that then and
since he regretted to be compelled to shoot those men, but
Frémont was bloodthirsty enough to order otherwise, and he

further remarked that it was not the only brutal act he was compelled to commit while under his command."

O'Farrell concluded, "I must always look upon [Frémont] with contempt and consider [him] as a murderer and a coward."

Many years later, Archibald Gillespie, by then alienated from the man he once considered his hero, placed responsibility for the murders on his former chief. In Gillespie's recollection, when Carson returned from the estuary, Frémont asked, "Where are your prisoners?" And when Carson said, "They lay out yonder," the captain replied, "It is well."

(Bernard DeVoto's version of the incident, lifted from O'Farrell's with customary sarcasm added, was that "Kit reported to Napoleon and asked for instructions. The Conqueror's mind·swarmed with enemies, this was war, and he must be stern. 'I have no room for prisoners,' he said, possibly thinking of biographers unborn. So Kit Carson and his corporal's guard killed them.")

Alexis Godey, in the *New York Evening Post* story in which he described the savage mutilations of Cowie and Fowler, claimed that Berreyesa and the De Haros were "carrying letters to the commander of the enemy's force" and that they "resisted efforts to seize them as prisoners." Godey said, "Had they submitted, and not attempted to escape, they would have received no harm, but they furnished a pretext which, to the friends of Tom Cowie, was, perhaps, not unwelcome."

Bancroft called the incident "cowardly vengeance," the time when "the only blood of Frémont's campaign was spilled, and that under such circumstances as to leave a stain of dishonor upon the commander and some of his men."

Ten years after the event, José S. Berreyesa, the Sonoma *alcalde,* recounted in a Los Angeles newspaper a sad footnote to the murder of his father. After the capture of Sonoma and his imprisonment before being reinstated as magistrate, Berreyesa said that Don José had embarked from Santa Clara for San Pablo to determine his son's condition and fate. The *alcalde* said that on the day after the event at the estuary, as he was held prisoner in a room in Sonoma, he saw a soldier pass by with a serape that had belonged to his father. He made a request of Frémont: "I told him that I believed my father had been killed by his orders and begged that he would do me the favor to have the article restored to me that I might give it to my mother . . . to this, Col. Frémont replied that he could not order its restoration as the serape belonged to the soldier who had it, and then he retired without giving me any further reply. I then endeavored to obtain it from the soldier, who asked me $25 for it, which I paid, and in this manner I obtained it."

3

After the estuary murders, Frémont moved his camp from San Rafael south to Sausalito, still hoping to encounter Captain De la Torre and his lancer patrol and prevent them from rejoining General Castro in Santa Clara. (De la Torre, meantime, had escaped; he and his men had been ferried from the southern shore of the Marin Peninsula across the strait to Yerba Buena some days before.)

At the end of June, the merchant barkentine *Moscow*, which had made a run around Cape Horn from Worcester, Massachusetts, anchored off Sausalito and its master, Captain William D. Phelps, a veteran in the California trade, paid Frémont a visit. Phelps described the celebrated explorer as a "slender and well-proportioned man, of sedate, but pleasing, countenance," and said that the captain was dressed in a blue, open-collared flannel shirt covered by a deerskin hunting jacket, blue cloth pantaloons, moccasins, and a cotton handkerchief tied around his head. Phelps said the outfit "might not appear very fashionable in the White House or be presentable at a Queen's levee; but to my eye it was an admirable rig to scud under or fight in."

The two men struck up a friendship, and on July 1, Phelps provided passage on the *Moscow* to Frémont, Gillespie, Carson, and several other of the explorer's men for a small venture. The bark ferried the party from Sausalito across the strait—which Frémont felicitously named "the Golden Gate"—to Castillo de San Joaquín, just south of the entrance to San Francisco Bay. This vacant, horseshoe-shaped fort, built in 1794, had ten rusty cannons on its battlements that Frémont believed could be used by the Californios to harass American ships attempting to enter the bay. Bill Stepp, a blacksmith and an old wilderness hand, had come along on the mission to end even the remote possibility that the cannons could be used. With a maul and a handful of rattail files, Stepp plugged the cannons' touchholes with the iron shafts and snapped them off.

The next day, Long Bob Semple and a small force of Osos crossed the Golden Gate to Yerba Buena, took a few Mexican officials prisoner, and occupied the village without resistance.

On Independence Day, 1846, with new volunteers arriving every day, the Bear Flaggers held a celebration in Sonoma. The Declaration of Independence was read loudly in the town plaza, cannons banged salutes, whole beeves were roasted, tubs of tamales and chiles, and bottles, jugs, demijohns, and kegs of wine, brandy, and whiskey were consumed. The festivities ended on the night of the Fourth with a fandango held in Salvador Vallejo's big adobe home, now serving as Frémont's headquarters, with waltzes and quadrilles, mountainmen stomps, and Delaware war dances performed to whoops and loud chatter, and the music of fiddles, guitars, mouth harps, and concertinas.

The next day, Captains Frémont and Ide and their officers
met to discuss new strategy. Ide's rebels now numbered
nearly three hundred men, but it seemed clear that the Bear
Flaggers' day was ending. Although explicit news that the
United States and Mexico were at war had yet to arrive in
Sonoma, few doubted it would be long in coming. Frémont
hedged and contradicted himself, telling the group he was
determined to find and defeat Castro and his forces but that
until war was a certainty, he was not aiming at conquering
all of California. He pledged support of the Osos and said
he would supply them from stores he had commandeered at
Sutter's Fort. In return, he asked the Bears to pledge to "conduct the Revolution honorably," to "abstain from the violation
of the chastity of women" and to "obey properly consti-
tuted officers."

He also announced, to the confusion of all, that the time
had come to form a disciplined army, which he volunteered
to command, to meet the exigencies of real war; a force that
could march south, engage Castro and any other force of
Californios, and conquer the entire province in the name of
the Government of the United States. The Osos did not resist this move; Ide, ever the orderly minded, practical leader,
even seems to have anticipated it: he resented Frémont's
usurpation of his command (and wrote vehemently of it in
the years to come), but knew that his Bear Flaggers had
started something they could not finish.

Frémont set out to organize what he came to call the "California Battalion," with Gillespie as his adjutant. His original
exploring party served as the veteran core of the force, and
over two hundred of Ide's rebels, Sutter workers, and a
handful of local Indians signed pledges to serve. In all, Frémont had close to three hundred men, whom he organized
into four companies. Dick Owens, the Rocky Mountain trapper, Indian-fighter, and friend of Kit Carson's, was named
captain of Frémont's men; John Grigsby, Granville Swift,
and Henry L. Ford were named to lead the other three

companies. Grigsby and fifty men remained in Sonoma; the rest of the battalion marched out with Frémont on July 6 for the American River camp near Sutter's. There they planned the campaign against Castro and the Californios fifty-five days after the war against Mexico had been officially declared, twenty-nine days after the official news of the war had reached California, and three days before the official news of the war reached Frémont.

Commodore John D. Sloat and his Pacific Squadron had been patrolling between the Sandwich Islands and Mazatlán, on Mexico's west coast, for many months, awaiting a message from the Navy Department on the war. Sloat had spent a lifetime at sea, an eternity awaiting orders from Navy Secretary George Bancroft. He was sixty-five years old, ill, and dreaming of retirement; indeed, in early May, he had requested that he be replaced in his command. While he waited for that eventuality, he had no orders and no initiative. For months after he reached Mexican waters, he knew only that when he learned "beyond a doubt" that the war was on, he was to sail north, seize San Francisco Bay, blockade the other main California ports, and "preserve, if possible, the most friendly relations with the inhabitants" of the province.

On May 18, after detailed news of General Zachary Taylor's army fighting on the Rio Grande reached him, Sloat sent the *Cyane,* under Captain William Mervine, to Monterey to inform Consul Larkin of the increasing rumors of war, and Commander John B. Montgomery's *Portsmouth* to San Francisco Bay to be in a position to occupy the harbor. With Mervine, the commodore sent a confidential letter to Larkin in which he revealed his tentativeness. Despite admitting to Larkin "it appears certain that hostilities have commenced on the north bank of the Rio Grande," he said it was his "intention to visit your place immediately, and from the instructions I have received from my government, I am led to hope that you will be prepared to put me in possession of the necessary information, and to consult and advise with me on the course of operations I may be disposed to make on the coast of California."

After asking a civilian for guidance in his anticipated military operations, the commodore dallied at Mazatlán. He may have mistrusted the information he had received on May 18 from overland travelers, and may have been given contradictory information. But on May 31, he received reports that he knew were trustworthy, telling of Taylor's battles at Palo Alto and Resaca de la Palma and the capture of Matamoros.

But was there a war? On June 6, he wrote at length to Secretary Bancroft that he had, "upon more mature reflection," concluded that in the absence of news of an actual declaration of war, he felt no justification in "taking possession of any part of California, or any hostile measures against Mexico (notwithstanding their attack upon our troops)." In referring to his original orders, he advised Bancroft that he would "be careful to avoid any act of aggression" and would proceed to California "to await further intelligence." He said that the "want of communication" from Washington "renders my situation anything but pleasant; indeed it is humiliating and mortifying in the extreme, as by my order I cannot act, while it appears to the world that we are actually at war on the other coast."

By the time the secretary received this message, all had been rendered moot, but on August 13, Bancroft reacted with barely restrained fury: "The department willingly believes in the purity of your intentions," he wrote, "but your anxiety not to do wrong has led you into a more unfortunate and unwarranted inactivity." The secretary, referring to Sloat's request to be replaced, and "other reasons," which were unnamed, relieved the commodore of his command.

While his fatal letter to Bancroft was en route by courier

to Washington, Sloat had sailed north from Mazatlán on the
Savannah on June 8, a day after he received news that an
American squadron had blockaded Vera Cruz. He reached
Monterey harbor on July 1, seventeen days after the Bear
Flag had been raised in Sonoma. The *Cyane* and *Levant* had
preceded him and were awaiting orders.

He remained in a funk; instead of being inspired by the
news of Taylor's battles and the Vera Cruz blockade—in
effect, a war confirmation—he seemed inert with uncer-
tainty. What to do now? Spread out between Mazatlán, the
Sandwich Islands, Monterey, and San Francisco Bay, he had
six warships, an armed schooner, and a transport vessel.
Mexico had no warships in California waters, and the
British were the only potentially hostile foreign power
Sloat had sighted in all his months in the Pacific. Admiral
Sir George Seymour's flagship *Collingwood* was, in fact, a
nettlesome presence in its seemingly aimless patrolling of
the Mexican coast from Mazatlán to San Francisco Bay.
Moreover, there was a persistent fear among the Americans
in California that the Mexican populace favored British in-
tervention and that England had designs on the province.

And Larkin, ever cautious, influenced the dithering Sloat
with his ideas that Pico and Castro would eventually raise
the Stars and Stripes voluntarily if courted with fine diplomacy rather than insulted by the rash tactics of Captain Frémont and the Bear Flaggers.

And finally, the commodore allowed himself to be haunted
by the mistake of 1842, when Captain Thomas ap Catesby
Jones had "captured" Monterey because he acted on false information.

Sloat took his gig ashore on July 4 and met at length with
Larkin to hear the consul express his hope that California
could be annexed to the United States without bloodshed.
During this meeting, the officer bared his muddled state of
mind to Larkin when he exclaimed, "I shall be blamed for
doing too little or too much—I prefer the latter."

Still he delayed in occupying Monterey, and might have
wavered longer had he not received a message from Commander Montgomery in San Francisco Bay telling of the
developments in Sonoma and Frémont's involvement with the
Bear Flaggers. The news galvanized the ailing commodore.
Frémont's actions *must* have been sanctioned by Washington,
he must be acting on *orders,* something Sloat desperately
sought. His return message said he was "very anxious to
know if Captain Frémont will cooperate with us," and he told
Montgomery: "If you consider you have sufficient force or if
Frémont will join you, you will hoist the flag . . . at Yerba
Buena . . . and take possession . . . you will secure the bay of
San Francisco as soon as possible."

On July 6, he summoned Larkin aboard the *Savannah* and
spent the day with the consul preparing dispatches to Washington, messages to his officers, and a lengthy and carefully
worded proclamation.

The next morning he sent a party ashore under Captain
Mervine to demand the surrender of Monterey. In his yellow stone presidio headquarters, Captain Mariano Silva, an
artillery officer in command of the virtually nonexistent garrison, told Mervine he was not "authorized to surrender the
town." Silva was let off the hook and kept under guard.

At mid-morning, after reading orders to his sailors on the
conduct expected of them, Sloat sent boats from the *Savannah, Levant,* and *Cyane* and landed 225 sailors and marines
on the beach. Within minutes of the landing, the American
flag was hoisted over the two-story frame customshouse, and
after a twenty-one-gun salute from the three warships offshore, Sloat's expert, conciliatory proclamation was read. It
announced the existence of war and the annexation of Monterey and the department of Alta California to the United
States: "I declare to the inhabitants of California that, although I come in arms with a powerful force, I do not come
among them as an enemy to California; on the contrary, I
come as their best friend, as henceforward California will

be a portion of the United States, and its peaceful inhabitants will enjoy the same rights and privileges as the citizens of any other portion of that territory. . . ."

He promised a fair and permanent government, improved commerce, reasonable duties, guarantee of titles to real estate, payment for provisions and supplies, no confiscation of property or goods. He touched on such familiar grievances as governmental neglect, corruption among officials, high prices for imports, and high duties on exports.

Messages from Sloat and Larkin were sent to General Castro, then located at San Juan Bautista, notifying him of the surrender of Monterey and asking him to a parley. Castro responded on the ninth: he intended to spare no sacrifice in defending his country and said he would consult with Governor Pico to plan this defense. The general added some lines condemning the activities of Frémont and his "gang of adventurers" and demanded to know whether these men were part of Sloat's invading force.

Sloat also dispatched a message to Pico in Los Angeles: "I beg your Excellency to feel assured that although I come in arms with a powerful force, I come as the best friend of California; and I invite your Excellency to meet me at Monterey, that I may satisfy you and the people of that fact."

By July 12, Sloat had three hundred officers and men ashore, had armed the presidio with two eighteen-pound carronades (short-barreled, muzzle-loading cannons that sailors called "smashers") mounted on trunnions as fieldpieces, and had ordered construction of a stockade and blockhouse.

Captain Mervine, appointed commander of the American garrison in Monterey, took up office in the customshouse and established a curfew, closed stores and shops for two days, and forbade the sale of liquor. He organized a company of horsemen to patrol the countryside and to confiscate arms.

There were no untoward incidents; not a shot had been fired accidentally or in anger. Larkin was overjoyed at the

wise proclamation authored by Sloat and the gentlemanly ease with which the war had come to his beloved
California.

Sloat himself could now relax. He had begun the annexation of this vast and priceless land for the United States and
had done it fairly, democratically, and without violence. His
dispatches on the occupation of Monterey and San Francisco
Bay were en route to Washington, and his replacement in
command of the Pacific Squadron, Commodore Robert Field
Stockton, was due in Monterey within the week.

He had made a mighty capstone for his military career, a
thing for which he would be remembered in history.

12

· ·

Stockton

■

1

Lieutenant *Charles Warren Revere* had been commissioned a midshipman in the navy in 1828 at age sixteen.
Promotion and command were the stuff of dreams in the
peacetime navy, but his assignment to the Pacific Squadron
in the summer of 1845 seemed to offer a rare opportunity:
wartime service. He had shipped aboard the *Cyane* out of
Norfolk, Virginia, made the passage around the Horn, and
joined Commodore Sloat's squadron off Mazatlán in November. He had been assigned to Commander John B.
Montgomery's sloop-of-war *Portsmouth* in time for its visit
to Monterey in April, come to know Consul Larkin, and
taken horseback rides into the piney hills above the bay. He
fell in love with California and predicted that it would become "one of the brightest stars in the American galaxy."

When Sloat had ordered the *Portsmouth* north in May, Revere had resumed his horseback outings, visiting San José
village and the old Santa Clara Mission, near which General Castro would later have temporary headquarters. After
the capture of Sonoma on June 14, he had visited the town,
met the Oso leaders, and escorted the ship's surgeon to Sutter's Fort to attend to the ailing General Vallejo.

He was the senior lieutenant on the *Portsmouth* and now, on July 9, 1846, two days after Monterey's forced surrender, he had the honor of claiming San Francisco Bay for the United States.

At eight that Thursday morning, the handsome, gregarious Revere led a landing party of seventy sailors and marines ashore at Yerba Buena and raised the American flag—twenty-seven stars (Texas too new to be included)—over the customshouse. After a twenty-one-gun salute offshore, he read Commodore Sloat's proclamation, with Vice Consul Leidesdorff translating it into Spanish. There was not a single Mexican official in Yerba Buena to surrender the town.

Later in the day, Lieutenant Revere carried out his second flag-raising duty. In Sonoma plaza, before a gathering of cheering Osos and warily silent townsfolk, he again read Sloat's words and had them posted in both English and Spanish. Afterward, the grandson of Paul Revere watched as the passant grizzly banner, fashioned by the nephew of Abraham Lincoln, was lowered and the Stars and Stripes raised in its place.*

The twenty-five-day Bear Flag Republic had ended.

On July 10, in his camp on the American River, Frémont was visited by the purser of the *Portsmouth* carrying a message from Montgomery on the navy's occupation of Monterey and Yerba Buena. Now, at last, there was a war on and the word had spread that General Castro had retreated south to Los Angeles, seat of Pío Pico's government and of whatever resistance the Californios would muster

---

Revere is said to have tucked the original Bear Flag in his pocket. Years later, it was donated to the Society of California Pioneers in San Francisco but was destroyed in the earthquake and fire in 1906. The flag design became the official state emblem in 1911.

against the Americans. Even the British, whose warships Sloat had seen patrolling the sea-lanes between Mazatlán and Monterey, seemed to know something was brewing. The sloop *Juno* had sailed past the Golden Gate on July 11 and the HMS *Collingwood,* Rear Admiral Sir George F. Seymour commanding, arrived on July 16. These visitors caused Montgomery to take some steps to defend Yerba Buena, but after courtesy calls by Seymour and his officers, the Americans became convinced that the British were mere observers and posed no threat.

On July 12—With the American flag now run up at Monterey, Yerba Buena, Sonoma, Sutter's Fort, and Bodega Bay on the coast north of the Russian River—Frémont, with his original exploration party, and the Bear Flaggers who had followed him from Sonoma, rode into New Helvetia. A letter from Sloat was awaiting him there, giving details of the capture of Monterey. The commodore said he expected General Castro to surrender but asked Frémont to bring in at least a hundred "well mounted" men to prevent Indian depredations against the Californios in the area.

The request seemed specious to the explorer, but he had received orders from a superior officer and prepared to march. He sent Gillespie ahead and after provisioning his hundred and sixty men and requisitioning cattle, horses, pack mules, and two small fieldpieces at Sutter's, he led his battalion down the Sacramento Valley. He expected that his meeting with Sloat would include plans to pursue Castro to Los Angeles.

The Americans reached San Juan Bautista on July 16, raised the flag there, and entered Monterey three days later.

The placid and picturesque town, accustomed to strangers strolling its pathways and bayfront trading posts, had seen nothing in its history like the entrance of the Americans

that bright July day, and the citizenry, Californio and out-
lander alike, lined up to witness it.

The Americans were preceded by their beef herd and
horses and mules, three hundred animals kicking up an immense cloud of dust. Some yards behind them rode Frémont
and his praetorian guard of Lenni-Lenape "real men," the
Delaware Indians, their faces painted, hair braided and
strung with feathers, their big skinning-knives strapped at
their waists, heavy muskets held across their saddle pommels.
Next, two by two, rode Kit Carson, Alexis Godey, Lucien
Maxwell, Dick Owens, Jacob Dodson, gunsmith Stepp, the
French-Canadians, army lieutenants Talbot, Abert, and
Peck, former Bear Flaggers Ide, Swift, Merritt, Ford, Semple, and others, most of them sunbaked, trail-fouled, bearded
apparitions in grimy deer-skin trousers and coats, and high
moccasin-like boots lashed with rawhide thongs.

Admiral Seymour's *Collingwood* had preceded Frémont's battalion to Monterey, and his officers and sailors
were ashore to watch the spectacle. The British were
particularly interested in catching a glimpse of Kit Carson,
whose name and exploits were almost as legendary in England as Horatio Nelson's. Frémont, too, was an object of
special interest by the British seamen. One midshipman
wrote of him as "a middle-sized man with an aquiline nose,
very piercing eyes and hair parted amidships." Another officer described him as a "spare, active-looking man, with
such an eye! He was dressed in blouse and leggings, and
wore a felt hat." The middies viewed the Delawares admir-
ingly, likening them to characters from a James Fenimore
Cooper novel.

A copse of fir trees on the outskirts of town served as a
camp. Once the animals were secured and under watch,
the men were free to visit the town, to pass their time,
one unimpressed observer recalled, "in drunkenness and
debauchery."

2

A navy launch took Frémont and his adjutant, Gillespie, out to the *Savannah* at midday on July 19 and Sloat greeted them cordially, questioning the explorer at length on his role in the rebellion in Sonoma and his subsequent actions. Sloat particularly wanted to know by whose orders Frémont and his men had aided the rebels, imprisoned General Vallejo, spiked the guns at Castillo de San Joaquín, and organized the force he now had camped at Monterey. After a month of inertia, Sloat had taken Monterey only after he had learned of Frémont's work among the Bear Flaggers in the north, and he now needed to know the source of the explorer's authority. Had Lieutenant Gillespie brought orders from Washington? From Secretary of War Marcy? From President Polk himself?

When Frémont casually explained that he had acted on his own authority to assist the settlers who were facing a fight with Castro and expulsion from the province, Sloat paled and retired to his cabin.

Frémont was livid. He had expected to talk to this officer about amalgamating his men into official service, thereby receiving a sort of ex post facto sanction for all his filibustering work over the past four months—Hawk's Peak, his encouragement of the Bear Flaggers, the imprisonment of Vallejo, the murders at San Pablo estuary, his commandeering of Sutter's Fort. He also had hoped to talk to the commodore about pursuing Castro south to San Luís Obispo, Santa Barbara, and Los Angeles. Instead, he learned that the navy had no shore operations planned other than holding actions, and that the highest-ranking American officer in California was old, ill, and timid.

What Frémont did not know was that his rescuer, Commodore Robert Field Stockton, had arrived in Monterey

Bay. He had sailed for California from Norfolk, voyaging the customary route—the Horn, Valparaiso, Chile; Callao, Peru, and the Sandwich Islands—and on July 15, 1846, made his way into Monterey roads from Honolulu on the sixty-gun frigate *Congress*.

Stockton's sealed orders were dated October 17, 1845, the precise date of Secretary of State James Buchanan's orders to Thomas O. Larkin appointing him a "confidential agent" and instructing him to "conciliate" the Californios and urge them to support annexation.

Bernard DeVoto calls Stockton the d'Artagnan of the conquest of California, and there are similarities. Both the commodore and the swashbuckling Gascon were ambitious, vain, bombastic, and excitable, and both hungered for glory. But in contrast to the Dumas character, who rode penniless into Paris on a yellow pony, Stockton was a fifty-one-year-old blueblood who had arrived in Monterey on the biggest warship of the Pacific Squadron to the shrilling of a bosun's pipe and a cannon salute.

Born in Princeton, New Jersey, his grandfather had been among the signers of the Declaration of Independence, his father a lawyer and politician, serving in both houses of the Congress of the United States. Robert attended Princeton briefly but in 1811, at age sixteen, a perfect time for active service in far-flung stations, he earned a warrant as a midshipman in the navy.

He served in the war of 1812 on the frigates *President* and *Gurriere* at Chesapeake Bay, the defenses of Baltimore, Washington, and Fort McHenry. As a schooner lieutenant in the Mediterranean, he took part in the capture of Algerian warships, which brought an end to the Barbary Wars. In 1821, on the schooner *Alligator* off the West African coast, he directed the capture of four French slavers, and on the return voyage from Liberia, fought a successful engagement with a Portuguese pirate vessel. In the West Indies in 1822, the *Alligator* destroyed three pirate ships and captured their loot.

Stockton had retired from the navy in 1828 upon the death of his father and his inheritance of the family estate in Princeton. For ten years, he concentrated on improving the family's already substantial fortune in New Jersey railroads and ship canals. He married, became a celebrated horse-breeder, traveled in Europe, and dabbled in politics, first as a supporter of John Quincy Adams, later as an ardent backer of Andrew Jackson and John Tyler.

Upon reentering the navy in 1838, he was promoted to captain of the warship *Ohio* and studied naval architecture and marine engineering in England, where he became a disciple of John Ericcson, the steam-and-screw propulsion pioneer. When he returned to the United States, he promoted the idea of a screw-driven warship and used his wealth and political influence in supervising construction of the Ericcson-designed man-of-war *Princeton*. It was this ship, Stockton in command, that in February, 1844, had taken President John Tyler and four hundred Washington dignitaries—including Senator Thomas Hart Benton—on a cruise of the Potomac. The pleasure cruise had ended in unutterable tragedy when, during an ordnance demonstration, one of the *Princeton*'s massive guns, ironically called the Peacemaker, exploded, killing Tyler's secretary of state, secretary of the navy, and four other onlookers.

Stockton, who had been burned by the gun explosion, was cleared of any responsibility for the catastrophe. The next year, President Polk ordered the captain and a small squadron, including the *Princeton,* from the Mediterranean to patrol in the Gulf of Mexico and prevent any Mexican intervention during negotiations over the annexation of Texas. Stockton overstepped his authority in conducting talks with Texas officials and whipping up the idea of military intervention in Mexico, but since this notion was not unknown in the White House, its main tenant did not censure the officer for his arrogance. In fact, soon after his Texas coast duties, he was promoted to the rank of commodore and given command of the Pacific Squadron with orders to proceed to California.

He had not changed much in character over the thirty-five years since he entered the navy. His natural impertinence and tactlessness had flowered as he climbed the command ladder. He was obedient to his superiors as long as they remained in Washington and he far removed; he gave orders with alacrity, took them reluctantly, was protective of his rank and command, brooking no dissenting opinions among his officers.

He was also zealous, patriotic, and energetic. He did not avoid decision-making, did not let his rank interfere with his love of a fight.

He was a smallish, handsome man, long-nosed, dark-haired, clean-shaven, with piercing dark eyes and a cutlass slash of a mouth.

He had so much in common with John Charles Frémont that the two became fast friends at once.

The two commodores met for the first time on July 15 when Sloat took the preliminary step toward retirement by naming Stockton commander in chief of all the land forces in California.

Frémont and Gillespie, meantime, had also met with the new commodore and were greatly encouraged by Stockton's eagerness to pursue Castro and finish the conquest of California with land forces—including Frémont's 160 men.

On July 23, Stockton mustered the former Bear Flaggers and Frémont's men into the military service of the United States as the "Naval Battalion of Mounted Volunteer Riflemen"—soon known as the California Battalion—with Frémont as major in command, Gillespie as captain and second. Within a few weeks following, some 428 other volunteers were engaged, most of them at Sonoma and Sutter's Fort, to be paid twenty-five dollars a month. Fifty Walla Walla Indians from Oregon enlisted at Sutter's.

Commodore Sloat transfered his pennant to the *Levant* on July 29 and headed home. Among his last acts before turning the Pacific Squadron command over to Stockton was the ordering of the release of General Vallejo and the other prisoners at Sutter's Fort.

On the day of Sloat's departure and before sailing south to San Pedro on the *Congress,* Stockton issued a hammering proclamation annexing California to the United States, vowing to drive Castro and all Mexicans opposing the measure out of the province. He said he would march "against these boasting and abusive chiefs" who had "violated every principle of international law and national hospitality by hunting and pursuing with several hundred soldiers, and with wicked intent, Capt. Frémont of the U.S. Army, who came here to refresh his men, about forty in number, after a perilous journey across the mountains, on a scientific survey." The document named Castro as a "usurper" who "has been guilty of great offenses, has impoverished and drained the country of almost its last dollar, and has deserted his post now when most needed." Stockton wrote that "reports from the interior" told of "rapine, blood and murder" at the hands of the Mexican general and his soldiers. He went on, "I must therefore, and will as soon as I can, adopt such measures as may seem best calculated to bring these criminals to justice, and to bestow peace and good order to the country."

H. H. Bancroft called Stockton's declaration a "pronunciamento filibustero," found the remarks on Castro's "hunting and pursuing" Frémont particularly amusing, and said of it as a whole, "The paper was made up of falsehood, or irrelevant issues, and of bombastic ranting in about equal parts, the tone being offensive and impolitic even in those inconsiderable portions which were true and legitimate. . . . It should have borne the signatures of Frémont and Gillespie, who managed to gain for the time being complete control over the commodore. . . ."

Commodore Sloat, who took a copy of the proclamation with him on the *Levant,* wrote to the secretary of the navy, "It does not contain my reasons for taking possession of, or my views or intentions toward that country; consequently it does not meet my approbation."

3

Following Stockton's manifesto, General Castro, in Santa Clara, began his move south to Los Angeles to join forces, such as they were, with his old rival, Governor Pío Pico. At the time of the Olómpali skirmish with the Osos, Castro had close to two hundred men in his command, mostly local militiamen; now, with many of them deserting, drifting toward home rather than abandoning their families for a real and potentially deadly campaign against the Americans, his force had dwindled to about a hundred. He hoped—but probably knew the impossibility of it—to raise an army to "rise en masse irresistible and just" to crush the invaders and announced, "Duty leads me to death or victory. I am a Mexican soldier and I will be free and independent or die with pleasure for those inestimable blessings."

Governor Pico, doting on classical references, was even more emotional in his response to the Monterey takeover and subsequent American flag-raisings. "Fly, Mexicans, in all haste in pursuit of the treacherous foe," he wrote in his message to the populace. "Follow him to the farthest wilderness; punish his audacity; and in case we fail, let us form a cemetery where posterity may remember to the glory of Mexican history the heroism of her sons, as is remembered the glory won by death of that little band of citizens posted at the Pass of Thermopylae under General Leonidas."

On July 16, as Frémont and his men were en route to Monterey, Pico issued a more formal proclamation on the American invasion. He promised to "make every possible effort to repel this the most unjust aggression" and issued a conscription order for all Mexican citizens of the department of California between the ages of fifteen and sixty to "defend the country when as now the national independence is in danger." The governor called a special meeting of his legislators and gave the assembly a report on the invasion. "He and the others," historian Bancroft said, "made patriotic speeches."

But the speeches rang leadenly: the legislators were apathetic, and few among the citizenry saw any hope in defending California—neglected by its motherland throughout its history and now, in war, utterly abandoned—against so mighty a foe as the United States. There was no money to finance an army, no appreciable stock of weapons to arm it. Further, many influential Californios welcomed the American invasion and many others were secretly sympathetic to it. Thus few flew to pursue the treacherous foe; Pico's hope of raising a force with his conscription order produced about a hundred men to combine with Castro's hundred from the north.

Stockton knew nothing of the precise numbers opposing him when he determined to mass his men at Los Angeles to locate, confront, and defeat Castro in battle. On July 26, he ordered Frémont and his battalion from Monterey down-coast on the *Cyane* to San Diego, there to gather cattle, oxen, horses, and a pack train of mules, preparatory to a march north to the capital. Stockton, meantime, planned to land his force from the *Congress* at San Pedro, thirty-five miles south of Los Angeles, and rendezvous with the explorer.

The California Battalion, about 120 weak-kneed, seasick men, landed at San Diego on July 29 and raised the flag there without opposition. A week-long search produced only a few horses and pack animals.

On his move south, Stockton dropped off a small garrison at Santa Barbara, and on August 1, the *Congress* dropped anchor in San Pedro Bay and landed the commodore and his 360 sailors and marines armed with muskets, pistols, cutlasses and boarding pikes, and four six-pounder cannons.

Thomas Larkin, who had accompanied Stockton on the *Congress,* came ashore at San Pedro with hopes high that he might negotiate a peaceful annexation of California. These hopes rose even higher on the day after the landing when two representatives from Castro arrived at Stockton's camp. The commissioners, Pablo de la Guerra and Captain José María Flores, delivered a letter to the commodore in which the Mexican general expressed a willingness to negotiate for peace provided that "all hostile movements be suspended by both forces."

This gentlemanly proffer seemed eminently reasonable to Larkin but not to Stockton, who did not believe negotiations with Castro would be valid without sanction from Mexico City and so rejected the terms of the letter out of hand. His return message to the general, dated August 7, said, "I do not wish to war against California or her people; but as she is a department of Mexico, I must war against her until she ceases to be a part of the Mexican territory. This is my plain duty." He ended the letter with a proposal he knew would be rejected: ". . . if, therefore, you will agree to hoist the American flag in California, I will stop my forces and negotiate the treaty."

Castro eloquently and indignantly rejected this proposal. "Never, never, never!" he proclaimed, and called the commodore's ultimatum "humiliating," "shameful," and "insidious." "Never will I consent that [California] commit so base an act . . . And what would be her liberty with that protection offered at the cannon's mouth?"

Two days after Stockton's truce-ending message was written, Castro held a war council at La Mesa, just south of Los Angeles, and dispatched a letter to Governor Pico. He said that he had been able to muster only a hundred men and these "badly armed, worse supplied, and discontented by reason of the misery they suffer." He notified the governor, "I have reason to fear that not even these few men will fight when the necessity arises." He had resolved, he said, to journey to Sonora, there to report to the supreme government in Mexico City the plight of their people in California, and he invited Pico to join him. He included in the letter his farewell address to the people of California, in which he said, "With my heart full of the most cruel grief, I take leave of you. I leave the country of my birth, but with the hope of returning to destroy the slavery in which I leave you; for the day will come when our unfortunate fatherland can punish this usurpation, as rapacious as unjust, and in the face of the world, exact satisfaction for its grievances."

Pico read Castro's messages to the legislature in Los Angeles. He announced that he agreed with Castro that it would be impossible to defend the department against the American invaders and told of his intention to join the general in leaving California to notify Mexico City of the latest occurrences. He proposed that the assembly adjourn *sine die,* and this was done.

"My friends, farewell!" Pico wrote in an open letter, an echo of Castro's, upon departing Los Angeles. "I abandon the country of my birth, my family, property, and whatever else is most grateful to man, all to save the national honor. But I go with the sweet satisfaction that you will not second the deceitful views of the astute enemy; that your loyalty and firmness will prove an inexpungable barrier to the machinations of the invader. In any event, guard your honor, and observe that the eyes of the world are fixed upon you."

On the night of July 10, Castro and Pico left Los Angeles separately. The general and twenty men rode toward the Colorado River. With him was his secretary, Francisco Arce, who precisely one month earlier had lost a horse herd after encountering Ezekial Merritt and other Bear Flaggers on the Cosumnes River. Early in September, Castro and his party reached Sonora, where he sent dispatches to Mexico City explaining his flight and urging that forces be marched to the defense of California.

Pico hid out with friends in San Juan Capistrano for a month before making his way to Mulegé on the eastern Baja California coast, thence across the Gulf of California to Guaymas and subsequently to Hermosillo, the Sonoran capital. He too urged, unavailingly, the Mexican government to defend its Pacific department.

4

On the day these two highest-ranking political officers departed the capital, Thomas O. Larkin rode into Los Angeles, sent ahead by Stockton with messages, now undeliverable, to General Castro. On August 13, with the news that Castro had fled, the commodore rode into the town of fifteen hundred inhabitants, a clamorous brass band from the *Congress* in the vanguard, followed by the trudging force of marines and sailors, the baggage train, bullock carts, and ox teams pulling the ponderous artillery caissons. Stockton's force was followed by Major Frémont and his scary, scruffy California Battalion of mountaineers, Indians, and former Osos.

The invaders were unopposed; the ship's band attracted many cheering Angelinos to the procession route.

At La Mesa, on the way to the capital, ten pieces of artillery were found at Castro's abandoned camp, only four of the guns spiked.

On August 17, Stockton, by this time referring to himself as "Commander-in-Chief and Governor of the Territory of California," issued a new proclamation, announcing that California was now a part of the United States, the people of California American citizens. He promised that a civil government would soon be established and that elections would be held. The document imposed a 10:00 P.M.-to-sunrise curfew, and warned that any person found armed outside his home during those hours without permission would be treated as an enemy and subject to deportation. Thieves would be punished, life and property would be protected.

This proclamation read and posted in two languages, Stockton ebulliently reported to Secretary of State Bancroft on August 22 that "The Flag of the United States is now flying from every commanding position in the Territory, and California is entirely free from Mexican dominion." In a burst of fantasy, he said that in under a month he had "chased the Mexican army more than 300 miles along the coast, pursued them 30 miles into the interior of their own country, routed and dispersed them, and secured the Territory to the United States, ended the war, restored peace and harmony among the people, and put a civil government into successful operation."

The commodore deemed the conquest at an end, and it had been a bitter disappointment. He was a man of action, seeking the exhilaration, the promise, of glory—and promotion— that "active service" offered. These emoluments had been denied him since 1812, the Barbary Wars, the pirate pursuits off the African coast and in the West Indies. The California command had been a bright hope, but in a month he had seen little more than the ashes of the enemy's campfires. He had grown tired of writing proclamations, was anxious to remove his sailors and marines from the now-conquered

territory—"to leave the desk and camp and take to the ship
and sea"—and find something worthy of his energy and
talents.

One matter beckoned. Stockton had studied his maps and
begun to fear the possibility of attacks on American commercial vessels in the Pacific by Mexican privateers based
in Acapulco. He had alerted American ship captains on the
availability of San Francisco Bay as a sanctuary harbor, and
he began making plans to sail south to put an end to the privateer menace. Acapulco, he reasoned, would give him a
base of operations for an even more ambitious plan that
would put his name on the forefront of the war's heroes: he
would raise a force of a thousand men and make an overland march "to shake hands with General Taylor at the Gates
of Mexico."

Stockton took Frémont into his confidence on his scheme
and said that upon his departure from California, the explorer would assume the governorship of the territory.

On September 2, 1846, the commodore divided California into three military districts. A few days earlier, he had
named Frémont military commandant of the new territory
and had installed Gillespie as *alcalde* of Los Angeles. He
assigned the marine a garrison of fifty men and issued instructions that until further notice, Gillespie would continue
imposing martial law, enforcing the curfews, and oversee-
ing the other regulations that had been imposed.

Stockton also authorized Frémont to enlarge the California Battalion to three hundred men to provide both a mo-
bile field force and garrisons for the main California
settlements. The two officers made arrangements to meet at
Yerba Buena on October 25 to make further plans for the
governance and protection of the territory.

Among his last duties before departing Pueblo de los Ángeles on September 2, 1846, Stockton ordered Kit Carson
to Washington with a full report to President Polk and Secretary Bancroft on the conquest. Letters to Jessie Frémont

and Senator Benton were included in the dispatch pouch, and Carson was authorized to take a pack train of mules and handpick fifteen men to ride with him. Kit estimated that he could get the job done in sixty days—and that included a brief visit with his wife Josefa in Taos, New Mexico.

On September 5, the commodore ordered his sailors and marines back aboard the *Congress* at San Pedro and set sail for Monterey. There, as Frémont and his men were making their way north toward the Sacramento Valley, the commodore had time to further study his grand scheme to shake hands with Zachary Taylor in Mexico City. He decided that he needed more men and sent word ahead to Frémont to raise seven hundred volunteers in the north to join him.

Finally, he sailed and arrived in San Francisco Bay in the last week of September. At Yerba Buena, where an official greeting had been arranged for him by Colonel Mariano Vallejo, Stockton— resplendent in full uniform—came ashore in a barge to meet the erstwhile Bear Flagger prisoner, himself elegantly arrayed and wearing his medals. A large welcoming committee lined the wharf to see the conqueror of California and to follow his procession along the rutted streets of the village. The parade ended at the home of Vice Consul Leidesdorff, where a speech was made by William "Owl" Russell, a Kentuckian, veteran of Seminole battles in Florida, former U.S. Marshal, Frémont crony, and major of artillery in the California Battalion. He spoke generously of the commodore's illustrious career.

But Stockton had only a few days in which to enjoy the accolades. His plans to meet with Frémont, recruit men for his overland march, and sail for Acapulo were abruptly halted on October 1 with the arrival in Yerba Buena of a courier named John Brown. This man, known as "Juan Flaco" (Skinny John) had made the ride from Los Angeles—a distance of five hundred miles—in six days to carry the news that a force of armed Californios had risen in the capital and was besieging Gillespie's garrison.

Stockton treated the news dubiously but ordered Captain Mervine to sail for San Pedro on the *Savannah* and dispatched an express to Frémont's camp near Sutter's Fort ordering the explorer to bring his men down to Yerba Buena.

His plans gone awry, the commodore told his officers that if harm came to Gillespie or his men, he would "wade knee-deep in blood to avenge it."

PART THREE

CONQUEST

■

13

Kearny

∎

1

On the Congress, the conqueror of California pored over his sea charts and maps. At last he had time to perfect his plan to make a sensational sortie against privateers off the Pacific coast of Mexico and an overland march to the enemy capital. He would take a thousand men—a full regiment of marines, sailors, and volunteers—down Baja California, sail around Cabo San Lucas, take on supplies at Mazatlán, and proceed south by southeast around the elbow of Mexico, past San Blas and Manzanillo to Acapulco. There he would disembark his men and lead them the two hundred and fifty miles north to Mexico City. The idea of merging his force with Zachary Taylor's for a march into the ancient heart of Mexico—it was something a lesser man might find too daunting to contemplate.

Robert Field Stockton dreamt of a glorious apogee to his career as his flagship butted through blue-green Pacific swells on that splendidly clear September day of 1846. The *Congress* made its passage north from San Pablo roads to San Francisco leisurely. The commodore was at ease, if not at peace, thinking of what the future held for him, while outside his comfortable cabin, momentous events were unfolding in Mexico, New Mexico, and, just behind him, in Los Angeles.

Between September 20 and 25, as the *Congress* neared the Golden Gate, General Zachary Taylor's army of six thousand was fighting a Mexican army of similar strength in Monterrey* just two hundred miles south of the Rio Grande. It would be a full year before General Winfield Scott, leading a force of fourteen thousand, reached Mexico City.

In Los Angeles, meantime, Lieutenant Archibald Gillespie and his fifty-man garrison were under attack by an unorganized, angry band of Californios who had quite suddenly decided not to yield to conquest as docilely as expected.

And in the province of New Mexico, another military officer had begun a march down the valley of the Rio Grande, a thousand miles out of Fort Leavenworth, leading three hundred dragoons and an enormous wagon and pack-animal train, headed south to the Gila River.

Of the triumvirate of conquerors of California, Stephen Watts Kearny was the last to arrive at the seat of conquest. Frémont had entered Sutter's Fort in December, 1845; Stockton had sailed into Monterey Bay in July, 1846; but it was Kearney's fate to be the first of the three to engage in battle on California soil and to throw a handful of grit into the well-oiled machinery set running by his predecessors. Between the time he arrived in California in December, 1846, and left six months later, Kearny annexed and secured the territory for the United States once and for all and placed his own reputation and career, and those of Frémont and Stockton, in peril.

Ninety-five years after Kearny's California adventure,

Spelled with two r's in Mexico, one in California. Either way, it means King's Mountain.

Bernard DeVoto said of him: "In the vaudeville show of swollen egoism, vanity, treachery, incompetence, rhetoric, stupidity, and electioneering which the great generals of the Mexican War display to the pensive mind, Kearny stands out as a gentleman, a soldier, a commander, a diplomat, a statesman, and a master of his job, whose only superior was Winfield Scott."

A newly appointed brigadier general with thirty-three years of army service at the time he led his dragoons toward the Gila, Kearny was the youngest of thirteen children of a prominent lawyer and landowner in Newark, New Jersey. As a lieutenant in the Thirteenth Infantry, he had fought his first (and until California, only) battle on October 13, 1812, at Queenston Heights on the Niagara frontier, where he was wounded and taken prisoner by the British. In 1819, then a captain, he had joined a regiment in Iowa and begun his long tenure in the Western territories—Council Bluffs, Iowa; Fort Smith, Arkansas; Fort Atkinson, Nebraska; St. Louis—with brief service in Detroit and in Baton Rouge, Louisiana, and expeditions across the Missouri River to the Yellowstone.

Except for minor skirmishes against Winnebagos in Wisconsin, Poncas and Mandans on the Missouri River, and Choctaws on the Texas border, he had seen nothing of the "active service" career that officers had pined for since 1812. In 1836, however, he did receive an important promotion, to the colonelcy and command of the First Dragoon Regiment at Jefferson Barracks in St. Louis.

He knew the great city on the Mississippi, had been assigned there before, and had married there. His bride was a lively eighteen-year-old named Mary Radford Clark, and Kearny had fallen in love with her the instant they were introduced. She was the stepdaughter of the great soldier-explorer William Clark, who with Meriwether Lewis had led the first expedition across the trans-Mississippi west to the Pacific in 1804. They were married in September, 1830, at Clark's Beaver Pond estate, just outside St. Louis.

In 1842, Kearny had been elevated to command of the Third Military Department of the Army, headquartered in St. Louis, and made responsible for guarding a thousand miles of frontier with little more than six hundred infantry and cavalry to patrol it. His duties were to keep the tribes at peace, inspect the reservations, and oversee escorts, patrols, and expeditions into troubled areas. In St. Louis, he came to know Missouri's foremost citizen, Senator Thomas Hart Benton, his vivacious teenage daughter Jessie, and in May, 1843, Jessie's husband, John Charles Frémont of the army's Topographical Corps. Colonel Kearny, probably out of his friendship with Benton and Jessie, had magnanimously authorized the issuance of some Hall carbines and a twelve-pounder brass cannon to the young lieutenant, then en route to Oregon on his second expedition into the far West. He never saw the gun again, but he would see the explorer later, under the most trying of circumstances, in California.

In 1845, Kearny took five companies of the First Dragoons on an expedition along the Oregon Trail to the South Pass of Wyoming, holding a council with the Lakota tribes near Fort Laramie and returning to Fort Leavenworth by way of Bent's Fort and the Arkansas River.

The expedition had been particularly timely, giving his dragoons a long march, experience in the daily travails of the wilderness, and familiarity with the Santa Fé Trail. In under a year, he and his heavy cavalry would retrace the trail to Bent's great rest-and-outfitting oasis on the Arkansas.

On May 13, 1846, on the day President Polk declared hostilities against Mexico, Secretary of War William Marcy ordered Kearny to ready his three hundred First Dragoons for travel and be prepared to accept a thousand volunteers for the purpose of organizing an Army of the West. This army was to march to Santa Fé, capture the capital, and annex the province of New Mexico to the United States.

Kearny, soon to receive his brigadier general's star, had earned it and the command. Bernard DeVoto's assertion that he was "not only a practised frontier commander but one of the most skillful and dependable officers in the army" would be sorely tested in California—and his skill, at least, called into question.

Now age fifty-two, his physical appearance had not changed much since the time he had courted Mary Clark in St. Louis. He had a long, noble head with a fine crown of reddish-brown hair shot through with gray and combed forward, Roman-like, at the temples. His blue eyes retained their fire—his officers were often withered by his stare. He was clean-shaven, slim, and walked and sat erect—"tall, straight, bronzed, lean as a sea cusk," a contemporary described him.

In over three decades of army service, he had evolved into the prototypical "by-the-book" soldier and had a reputation as a martinet, this perhaps having had its origin among the volunteers in his army. These men, many of them hardscrabble farmers and ungovernable wanderers, could not abide Kearny's standard that they receive the same exacting discipline that kept his regular troops in order. One of his officers said of Kearny's iron disciplinary policies: "During the whole time he commanded the First Dragoons, no soldier ever received a blow [from flogging] except by the sentence of a general court-martial for the infamous crime of desertion . . . though the strictest disciplinarian in the service, there was less punishment in his corps than any other." And Ulysses S. Grant, who as a young lieutenant saw the dragoon commander in St. Louis in the early 1840s, called him "one of the ablest officers of the day" and said that his disciplinary measures were "kept at a high standard but without vexatious rules or regulations."

But while Kearny's twenty-five years on the windswept prairies of the Western frontier had browned and toughened him, it had also scoured him clean of humor and afflicted him with a certain plodding grimness like that of a blindered plow horse in a furrow. Kearny knew survival in lands

unrelentingly hostile to humans; he was a gritty, demanding commander and had a righteous sense of duty. But his
imagination, whatever there had been of it, had eroded, and
occasional Indian skirmishes had not educated him in the
skills of war.

And as a proconsul-in-the-making in New Mexico and
California, he demonstrated considerable adeptness in dealing with conquered people when operating without specific
direction from his superiors. But in an arena that required
political delicacies among peers who held differing views,
he saw no nuances, wielded his authority sullenly, and entertained no argument.

2

Kearny's original May 13, 1846, orders from Secretary
of War Marcy were supplemented on June 3 to make
clear the objective of the Western campaign: "It has been decided by the President to be of the greatest importance, in
the pending War with Mexico, to take the earliest possession of Upper California," Marcy wrote. He advised Kearny
that "in case you conquer Santa Fé," it was expected that
New Mexico would be garrisoned before the march continued to California. Kearny was to have "a large discretionary power" in conducting the campaign: choosing the route
to the Pacific, taking on volunteers, organizing supplies, and
procuring animals to carry them. Marcy said that the President was desirous "that the expedition should reach California this season" but should the President be "disappointed
in his cherished hope," Kearny was assured that he would
be "left unembarrassed by any specific directions in this
matter."

Significantly, Marcy's "Confidential Instructions," written
one month before Commodore Sloat occupied Monterey,
contained the news that "it is expected that the naval forces

of the United States which now, or will soon be, in the Pacific, will be in possession of all the towns on the sea coast, and will co-operate with you in the conquest of California." In addition to making clear who would "cooperate" with whom, the secretary added, "Should you conquer and take possession of New Mexico and Upper California, or considerable places in either, you will establish temporary civil governments therein. . . ."

Kearny was notified that his promotion to brigadier general would take effect "as soon as you commence your movement towards California."

The secretary's "instructions" were similar in vagueness to those sent to Commodores Sloat and Stockton in California. The War Department's knowledge of New Mexico was sketchy—there were no dependable maps of it—and critical questions were unanswerable in Washington or anywhere else. It seemed unlikely that Mexico would deliver without a fight a province of a hundred thousand square miles that had been held for three centuries, but how defiantly would the Mexicans defend New Mexico? What manpower and arms lay awaiting an invading force?

At least it was clear to Kearny that he would command the entire conquest of Mexico's western territory and that the navy would cooperate with him as he took charge of all military and political efforts once he reached the Pacific.

Kearny's organization of his Army of the West turned out to be a logistical masterpiece. Working with the quartermaster general in St. Louis, arms, munitions, 1,556 wagons, 459 horses, over four thousand mules, and fifteen thousand head of cattle and oxen were massed at Fort Leavenworth. Supplies were sent ahead in small pack trains to Bent's Fort, rendezvous point for the invasion of New Mexico.

Answering the call sent out into Missouri and along the Santa Fé Trail to Bent's, volunteers began pouring off

Missouri River steamboats and into the fort in the first week of June. The First Regiment of Missouri Mounted Volunteers came in under the command of Colonel Alexander W. Doniphan, a handsome six-foot-four Clay County lawyer. He had his ragged assemblage of 860 shag-bearded farmers, hunters, and drifters under control—a fact not lost on the discipline-minded Kearny, who overlooked the Missourians' tendency to call him "Ol' Hoss" to his face. Soon after the arrival of Doniphan's force, the Laclede Rangers, 107 men who would be attached to the First Dragoons, arrived, followed by two companies of volunteer infantry and two of artillery, all from St. Louis. Two additional companies of regular First Dragoons rode in from northern outposts.

An odd addition to Kearny's gathering army came from the Mormon colony, camped at Council Bluffs, Iowa. In February, 1846, Brigham Young, the prophet and leader of the Church of Jesus Christ of Latter-day Saints, had led sixteen thousand of his people from Nauvoo, Illinois, across the ice-clogged Mississippi. In five harrowing months, during which six hundred "Saints" died, the congregation reached Council Bluffs on the Missouri River en route to founding the church's new "Zion" somewhere in the Western wilderness. The Mormons were offered a chance to enlist in Kearny's army and assured of quick discharges once they reached California. The "Mormon Battalion," while having no direct role in the conquest of California, accomplished an epic march that would rival Kearny's own.

With his army and supply train growing massively by the day, on June 6, Kearny sent two companies of the First Dragoons ahead on the trail southeast toward Bent's Fort, 537 miles distant, and parceled out other units on the trail over the following three weeks. Doniphan's eight companies of First Missourians departed Leavenworth between June 22 and 28; the bullock-drawn trade and supply wagons and eight hundred head of cattle followed along with them. On June

28, the balance of the six troops of First Dragoons moved out, together with a 150-man battalion of infantry, two companies of light artillery, the latter 250 men commanded by Major Meriwether Lewis Clark, General William Clark's son, who also happened to be Mary Kearny's stepbrother and former suitor.

The fragmenting of his force was Kearny's plan to conserve the enormous amount of firewood and forage required to fuel the Army of the West.

By June 29, the colonel notified his superiors in St. Louis: "I have started fifteen hundred and twenty men from here on the Santa Fé Trail. I will leave tomorrow to overtake them and will concentrate the whole near the crossing of the Arkansas." Then, on the morning of the thirtieth, he hugged his wife and children on the steps of his bungalow, mounted his bay horse, and rode with his staff officers out of Fort Leavenworth to rendezvous with his army.

In all, he commanded a force of over seventeen hundred men, counting a hundred or so civilian hunters and teamsters, sutlers, Santa Fé traders, and Delaware and Shawnee scouts. He had a contract surgeon, a remarkable Virginian named John S. Griffin, who kept a meticulous diary of the march; a small topographical corps headed by Lieutenant William H. Emory of Queen Anne's County, Maryland, a West Pointer and former artilleryman; and an interpreter, Antoine Robidoux, a naturalized Mexican citizen who had until recently operated a trading post in the desolate Uinta River region of Utah.

Kearny's ordnance train consisted of four twelve-pounder and twelve six-pounder brass field howitzers.

The dragoons, Kearny's and the army's pride, rode as confidently, if less splendidly accoutred, as the British "heavies" under General George Yorke Scarlett at Balaclava ten years hence. They were big men on big horses—grizzled, squint-eyed veterans of the sun and wind of the Western plains. They wore blue-flannel shirts and trousers, broad-brimmed hats, huge skinning knives in sheaths cinched around their waists together with braces of cap-and-ball pistols, and carbines in leather boots strapped to their saddles. Except for their weaponry and ammunition pouches, the dragoons traveled light: all they needed—spare blouses, mess tin and utensils—they carried wrapped in a blanket roll behind their saddles.

3

Kearny and his officers swiftly caught up with the main body of the army, and despite the ponderous string of ox wagons, horse- and mule-drawn carts, and gun caissons—a dust-clouded tail miles long wagging the dog of the soldiery afoot and on horseback—managed to push an exhausting pace of twenty to thirty miles a day in the broiling summer heat. The column was slowed only in the tedious crossing of the Kansas River.

On July 7, while Commodore Sloat was forcing the surrender of Monterey, Kearny's army, a hundred miles out of Leavenworth, reached Council Grove, the Santa Fé Trail gateway. The trail, already a fabled trader's route, in its busy twenty-year history had never carried a multitude, military or civilian, close to the numbers of Kearny's army.

Over the years, traffic on the trail had nearly denuded the countryside around it of timber, and game was scarce enough to force the civilian hunters hired to accompany the army to travel far afield to find meat. Kearny forbade the slaughter of any of the army's beef herd as long as his hunters were able to bring in deer and buffalo to add to the meager rations each man carried.

At Pawnee Rock, after a march of 250 miles, hunters riding several hours ahead of the force found a buffalo herd, an undulating brown blanket of half a million animals spread out for miles before them, and solved the meat problem for the rest of the march to Bent's Fort. The buffalo also supplied tinder for cook fires as troopers learned the value of dried *bois de vache* (buffalo chips) and how to skewer them with their ramrods without dismounting.

Water plagued the army in both its scarcity and abundance. Torrential rains burst on the crawling column with little warning, and those lasting a half-day turned the trail into a black porridge, burying the heavy wagons to their wheel hubs, balking mules and bullocks and filling the air with the crack of bullwhips, the shouted curses of the freightmen and the bellowing of the animals struggling forward. But often the rains were harmless cloudbursts that did little more than settle the dust plumes and add a steaminess to the day's heat, frequently a hundred ten degrees and higher.

On July 22, three weeks out of Fort Leavenworth, a landmark came into view far to the northwest, shrouded by thunderheads. The Spanish Peaks, the Wah-to-yah (Breasts of the World) of the Indians, signaled to the jaded army that they were nearing the end of the first leg of their journey, nearing an outpost of civilization in the midst of the eternal plains, a place as fabled among Western travelers as Sutter's New Helvetia—Bent's Fort.

This outpost, built in 1833 by the fur-trading partners Charles Bent and his brother William of Virginia, and Cerán St. Vrain of Missouri, lay twelve miles upstream from the junction of the Arkansas and Purgatoire rivers of Colorado. The fort, called the "Big Lodge" by the Indians who frequented it and camped along the river nearby, had the configuration of a rough rectangle about 180 by 130 feet in size. Its yard-thick walls rose fourteen feet high, and at opposite corners of the square were two crenellated, martello-like towers, the battlements equipped with small field cannons. On the north side of the packed-adobe fort were two-story buildings, their roofs providing wide walkways to the ramparts. Above the gateway into Bent's, a great iron bell was housed in a belfry above which the proprietors kept an American flag flapping in the breeze.

Inside the compound there were shady arcades of trading rooms, cooper, carpenter, and joiner shops, a wagon park, blacksmith's forge, hide presses, water wells, warehouses, corrals, kitchens, apartments, the proprietor's home—even an icehouse and a billiard room. Built expressly to take advantage of the growing Santa Fé trade, the fort was the only permanent post between the Missouri River and the New Mexico capital and commanded the trade routes north and south along the Platte River and east and west along the Santa Fé Trail.

Bent's traded in everything—furs, livestock, buffalo robes, blankets, nails, guns, galena, powder, spirits, knives and axes, wagon parts, saddlery, foodstuffs—and services for the broken wagon, the shoe-worn horse, the tired, hungry, and thirsty Indian, trapper, trader, and ordinary traveler.

On July 29, 1846, the day in which Commodore Stockton was issuing his first bellicose proclamation as conqueror of California, Thomas "Broken Hand" Fitzpatrick rode up from Bent's and joined Colonel Kearny and his officers for the last leg of their march to the fort. The colonel and this white-haired native of County Caven, Ireland, were well acquainted. Just a year past, Fitzpatrick had guided Kearny and five companies of his First Dragoons along the Oregon Trail to the South Pass of Wyoming and back to the Arkansas. They had developed a mutual respect. Kearny knew that no man had better scouting credentials—not even Kit Carson—than this steadfast mountaineer who for more than twenty years had roamed the rivers, mountains, passes, and landmarks of the far West, from Missouri to the Pacific and from the disputed northern border with Canada down through Mexican lands to the Gila River.

Fitzpatrick brought the news circulating at the fort that Governor Armijo had called a war council in Santa Fé and was amassing a force to defend New Mexico.

The next day, July 30, Kearny and the vanguard of the Army of the West arrived on the Arkansas within sight of the great adobe walls of Bent's Fort. As the teamsters and their ox wagons and pack mules straggled in, the tents of the big camp bloomed along the river east of the fort; Major Meriwether Lewis Clark set up his ordnance park, and Colonel Alexander Doniphan ordered the horses and pack animals to be turned loose to graze.

Captain Benjamin D. Moore, who commanded the advance party of dragoons in scouting the campsite, reported to Kearny the capture of four Mexican "spies" who admitted they had been sent up from Santa Fé to gather information on the advancing American army. The men were brought to Kearny's command tent and questioned. The colonel shrewdly ordered they be given a tour of the massive camp— Major Lewis's twelve howitzers were especially impressed on them—before being freed to return across Ratón Pass to report to Governor Armijo what they had seen.

Kearny was anxious to press on. At Bent's on the last day of July, he issued a proclamation to the people of New Mexico, stamped from the same template as that written by Sloat in California. "The undersigned enters New Mexico with a large military force," Kearny wrote, "for the purpose of seeking union with and ameliorating the conditions of its inhabitants." He "enjoined the citizens of New Mexico" to "remain quietly in their homes and pursue their peaceful avocations" and said that as long as they did this, they would not be "interfered with by the American army," but he warned that those who took up arms against him "will be regarded as enemies and will be treated accordingly."

The freed spies carried copies of the proclamation to Armijo.

Meantime, an important courier arrived at the fort with

messages for Kearny from President Polk and Secretary of War Marcy. This was James Wiley Magoffin of Kentucky, an eminent figure in Mexico who had been trading north and south of the Rio Grande since 1825. He had served as United States consul at Saltillo and Ciudad Chihuahua, married into a prominent Mexican family, spoke fluent Spanish, and had a wide circle of influential friends, including Senator Thomas Hart Benton of Missouri. It was Benton, in fact, who had pressed on the President the idea of sending Magoffin from Washington to intercept Kearny at Bent's Fort. The messages delivered, which Kearny probably divined before reading them, urged him to do whatever was necessary to persuade Armijo to surrender New Mexico peaceably and said that Magoffin was to serve as emissary to the governor-general.

On August 1, Kearny assigned one of his favorite officers, Captain Philip St. George Cooke of Leesburg, Virginia, a thirty-seven-year-old West Point graduate and Black Hawk War veteran, with twelve dragoons to escort Magoffin to Santa Fé bearing a letter for Governor Armijo. The letter bluntly said that the United States Army was on the march to annex all of New Mexico north and east of the Rio Grande and that if Armijo and his people presented no opposition, their lives, property, and religious practices would be honored and protected.

Magoffin, Cooke, and the dragoon escort, carrying a truce flag, entered the capital on August 12. Armijo read Kearny's message and said he would not surrender.

14

Santa Fé

■

1

In 1846, *Santa Fé* stood as isolated as the Australian outback and had once been as forbidden to outsiders as Mecca and Timbuktu. The town was founded as La Villa Real de la Santa Fé (The Royal City of the Holy Faith) in 1610 and lay on an abandoned Tanoan Indian village in the foothills of the Sangre de Cristos. Conscripted Pueblo Indians had built the mission-presidio there, and for 120 years it lay virtually unknown to the rest of the world, even to the Spanish authorities who governed it from fifteen hundred miles south in Mexico City. The mission-presidio population grew slowly and quietly in a vacuum of time and space as Franciscan fathers went about their work of converting the Indians of the region to Christianity and reducing the converts to the same agricultural serfdom as those in California.

Miscellaneous outsiders trickled into Santa Fé as the decades passed but were generally treated harshly—jailed, their possessions appropriated, ordered out of the province on instructions from the viceroy in Mexico City. Such a greeting met the explorer-soldier Zebulon Montgomery Pike. In an exploration of the lower Louisiana Territory, he set out from Belle Fontaine, Missouri, in July, 1806, with

twenty-one men ("a Dam'd set of Rascals but very proper
for such an expedition," he said of them), explored the Republican River and the headwaters of the Arkansas, then
moved south to present-day Colorado and built a stockade
on the Rio Grande. In February, 1807, a patrol of one hundred Spanish soldiers took Pike and his men into custody
and marched them to Santa Fé, where the expedition's papers were confiscated. Pike was escorted to Chihuahua for
questioning, then escorted back to United States territory
near Natchitoches, Louisiana, after five months as a prisoner of the Spanish.

Not until 1821 was an American, by happenstance, welcomed to Santa Fé.

William Becknell, a thirty-three-year-old veteran of the
War of 1812, migrated to Franklin, in far-western Missouri
Territory, from his native Amherst County, Virginia. In September, 1821, he and four partners ventured westward on a
somewhat daring expedition to trade among the Comanches.
The party crossed the Little Osage and Verdigris rivers,
picked up the Arkansas, and followed it across Kansas and
into Colorado.

At some point in their journey, Becknell and his trading
company learned, perhaps from trappers, buffalo hunters, or
a Mexican patrol, that the "gates of Santa Fé" were open—
Mexico had won its independence from Spain—and so
changed directions, heading south across Ratón Pass and
into the fabled town. He fully expected to be jailed there
and his goods taken, but he and his partners were welcomed
and treated cordially. Clearly, the new authorities in New
Mexico were eager to make contact with Americans, particularly those who came to trade. Josiah Gregg, a chronicler
of the Santa Fé Trail, said that up to Becknell's time, the
province had received all its goods and supplies from the
internal provinces of Mexico and at such exorbitant
prices "that common calicoes, and even bleached and brown

domestic goods, sold as high as two and three dollars per *vara* (a Spanish yard of thirty-three inches)."

Becknell returned to Franklin in January, 1822, with his saddlebags full of Mexican silver.

There was but a single route from Missouri to the capital during the first year or so after Mexican independence and that over the treacherous Ratón Pass. The trail presented an obstacle for the heavy, wide-tracked and big-wheeled Murphy wagons, which became the conveyance of choice in the Santa Fé trade, some of them carrying three thousand pounds of goods. They could not negotiate the steep and narrow trail Becknell had blazed with pack animals and so, armed with a pocket compass and the stars to guide him, he traced an alternate route, crossing the water-scarce and searing (120° in summer being common) Cimarron Desert to the headwaters of the Cimarron River. Ignorance of the hardships of the route nearly cost Becknell and his party their lives: a few days into the desert, their canteen water ran out and the traders were reduced to killing their dogs and scoring the ears of their mules for blood, a measure that only added to the madness of their thirst. Close to the Cimarron, the men found a wandering buffalo, its belly distended with water, killed it and drank from its stomach. Now sustained and having found the river, the party reached Santa Fé without further incident.

Although always perilous—heat, thirst, and raiding Indians foremost among the dangers—Becknell's new route, called the Cimarron Cutoff, was shorter and flatter, and by 1824, when traders began traveling in caravans, it became favored over the Ratón Pass route.

The caravan system virtually eliminated the incidence of Indian attack and enabled traders to carry sufficient water and provisions to cross safely the fifty miles of the Cimarron Desert. Elimination of this hazard was aided by a Congressional bill sponsored in 1825 by Senator Benton that appropriated twenty thousand dollars from the Treasury to negotiate a treaty with the Osage and Kansas tribes for right-of-way through their lands and another ten thousand dollars to conduct a survey of the trail.

By the 1830s, caravans as large as one hundred wagons and two hundred men were wending westward out of Missouri to cross the prairies, mountains, and deserts to the New Mexican capital. They carried goods similar in their eccentric variety to the trade ships soon to be visiting the California coast: knives, axes, traps, kegs of nails, farm implements, glassware, thread, buttons, spoons, scissors, bolts of bright cloth, clothing, hats, spices, rifles, whiskey—all seemingly commonplace items such as were avidly sought in Santa Fé. Goods worth $35,000 were commonly traded for $200,000 in gold, silver, furs, horses, and mules.

The town also naturally changed. From a somnolent mission of under a thousand priests, soldiers, and *Indios* in 1820, after Mexican independence and the opening of trade, Santa Fé grew to a thriving commercial center. Shadowed by the snowcapped Sangre de Cristos, it was gathered around a 250-foot-square plaza of packed dirt, had a scattering of cottonwood trees, and an *acequia* (irrigation ditch) ran along two sides of it. The plaza was dominated by the governor's *palacio*. This unprepossessing building was constructed of the same adobe as all the other town dwellings and places of business but roofed with pine and spruce logs. It formed part of a presidio that enclosed a garrison barracks, drill ground, chapel, and *calabozo*.

The plaza of Santa Fé also offered access to the great cathedral and several other smaller churches, a customshouse, a hotel, houses and shops of whitewashed adobe, and the La Fonda Inn. The latter did a thriving business in liquor, gambling, and "painted women" (who were actually painted—wearing a white flour paste on their arms and faces as protection against sunburn) who smoked corn-shuck *cigarillos* and lounged in the shade of the *portales* (arcades).

By 1830, the sleepy plaza had been transformed into a great open bazaar, a raucous, odoriferous square seething with horses, mules, oxen, wagons, babbling traders and buyers (*"Los Americanos! Los carros! La entrada de la caravana!"* the Mexicans greeted the American traders and their trains of wagons), gamblers with tables for faro, monte, and dice games, beggars, Pueblo Indians selling pots and blankets, watchful Mexican soldiers and town authorities, kids playing under the cottonwoods, and women cooking and baking in open-air ovens. At night, there were the *bailes*— fandangos and other dances to the accompaniment of fiddle, guitar, and drum; on Sundays and feast days, there were cockfights, and *vaqueros* chasing bulls in a wild game called the *coleo,* in which the horseman attempted to overturn a running bull by seizing it by its tail.

For a decade, Americans with their goods and money were welcome in the teeming capital and no frontiersman who visited the place in "the earlies"—before the war with Mexico—ever forgot the experience. In 1826, when he was seventeen, Kit Carson had run away from home and work in Franklin, Missouri, to join a Santa Fé trade train as a "cavvy"—horse wrangler. As he rode with his employers into the town for the first time, the Mexicans shouted at the small and frail figure, *"Un muchacho Americano! Mira!"*—"Look at the American boy!" He loved the town, and New Mexico, as no other place in his life of wanderings.

With its newfound prosperity and flow of American and Canadian traders, mountain men down from the Rockies, mule drivers and bull-whackers, business agents, speculators, smugglers, gamblers, and outlaws, Santa Fé's monied citizenry came to resent the raucous intruders in their once-placid, remote, church-oriented community. It naturally followed that the Americans began finding their own reasons for resentment, particularly over the fickle method of levying tariffs on trade goods brought into the town. In general terms, the Mexican method was to charge what the traffic would bear, send as little as possible to the ruling government in Mexico City, and pocket the balance.

One particular nemesis of the *gringos* in Santa Fé was Manuel Armijo, thrice governor and a man the Americans called "His Obesity." He was a huge, brusque, rapacious character, a former sheep-rustler who had clawed his way from obscurity, who wore a spectacular self-designed uniform with gold epaulets and a helmet with a white ostrich plume as he traveled about his town in a gilded coach. When afoot, he had a propensity for caning any citizen who failed to doff his hat quickly enough in the imperial presence.

Never averse to taking a bribe, Armijo levied outrageous tariffs—often a flat five-hundred-dollar tax on each wagonload, large and small, of trade goods—and grew rich in the process.

As in the pattern of Texas and California, the Americans, at first welcomed in New Mexico, became worrisome in their numbers and defiant independence, and Mexico City, racked by its own internal tumult, gave scarce attention to its old, remote province and the encroaching dangers it faced.

And now, in the summer of 1846, Governor Armijo, commandante-general of New Mexico, faced the same crisis as his California brethren, José Castro and Pío Pico: the Americans were on the march and there was little he could do but plan his escape.

2

Doniphan's Missourians cleared their camp on August 1 and proceeded south in advance of the main army to the Purgatoire River, first leg of the hundred-mile march to Ratón Pass, gateway to Santa Fé. Kearny led the balance of the force past the walls of Bent's Fort the next day.

All made slow progress in the suffocating heat, which rose

on several days to 120° as horses, pack animals, and wagon bullocks lumbered along the waterless trail through mesquite and prickly pear, a hot wind carrying a pumice-fine dust that scoured eyes and clogged noses and throats. Some of the animals collapsed, wagons overturned, and gun limbers fell off the trail, to be labored aright by cursing teamsters and soldiers, many of whom themselves fell, prostrated by heat and exhaustion.

As each sweltering day waned, water and forage parties fanned out into the scrub to find likely campsites; cook fires were lit, half-rations and half-cups of tepid water from dwindling casks were doled out, and sentries posted. At nightfall, the Army of the West fell into a fatigued sleep wrapped in their blankets in the welcome night chill. The wolves and coyotes, after following the army from afar during the day, came closer, brushes up, sniffing the edges of the camp, howling into the starry night, awaiting the time when they could scramble and scavenge among the scraps left behind.

A hundred hard miles out of Bent's, the army made its ascent of Ratón Pass, the rarified air at seventy-five hundred feet and the narrow, unstable trail slowing the march to as little as a mile a day. From the summit could be seen a brilliant panorama: the Wah-to-Yah to the northwest, and beyond it the peak named for its discoverer, Zebulon Pike; the white-capped Sangre de Cristos (Blood of Christ) mountains on the southwest; and directly below, where the pass debouched, piney hills, fields of wildflowers and corn, a sluggish stream or two winding through red earthbanks, and, visible through the officers' telescopes, the heat-shimmered, mirage-like outlines of old adobe villages.

The descent of the pass, only slightly less painstaking and dangerous than the climb, was accomplished on August 14, and on that day a Mexican officer and an escort of three lancers rode into Kearny's camp to deliver a message from the governor-general of New Mexico. Armijo acknowledged

having received the colonel's demand for surrender but said
he intended leading his people in arms to resist the invasion
and suggested that he and Kearny meet in the village of Las
Vegas to discuss there vital matters.

Kearny asked the officer to convey a message to the governor: "The road to Santa Fé is now as free to you as to myself. Say to General Armijo I shall soon meet him, and I
hope it will be as friends."

They were never to meet.

All manner of rumor—none of it dependable—had reached
Kearny from the time he departed Bent's Fort to his march
south to Las Vegas, sixteen miles from the foot of Ratón
Pass. There were stories that two thousand Pueblo Indians
were being armed to help defend Santa Fé—very reminiscent of the rumors of General Castro's enlisting Indians in
California. Other tales said that the citizenry of the entire
province was rushing to assist in repelling the American
invaders, that Mexico had dispatched a force of dragoons to
reinforce Armijo's garrison, that the Americans would have
to fight for every inch of ground on the road to the capital.
The warnings became so alarming that several of Kearny's
officers who had been left behind at Bent's rushed out to
intercept him and offer their services. (One of them brought
news of Kearny's official promotion to brigadier general.)

In fact, Armijo, who appealed to the military commanders of Chihuahua and Durango for reinforcements and was
promised assistance, received none; as well, most of the citizenry of about sixty thousand—as in California—were either ignorant of the invasion because of their remoteness
from the seat of government in Santa Fé, apathetic about it,
or in favor of American intervention.

In Las Vegas, Kearny issued a blunt proclamation that was
posted in two languages at every village on his route of
march to the capital. "I have come amongst you by the

orders of my government, to take possession of your country and extend over it the laws of the United States," he said. "We come amongst you as friends—not as enemies; as protectors—not as conquerors."

He "absolved" the citizenry of all allegiance to Mexico and General Armijo and announced that he, Stephen Watts Kearny, was now governor of the new United States territory of New Mexico. He promised religious freedom, protection against thievery and misconduct by his army and from Indian depredations, and pledged safety for all who did not take up arms against him and execution by hanging for all who did.

Captain Philip St. George Cooke, who had escorted James Magoffin to Santa Fé on August 1 to deliver the American ultimatum to Armijo, rejoined Kearny's force on August 15. He reported that the governor and his ninety-man bodyguard had fled the capital into Chihuahua, but, Cooke said, the militia Armijo had raised to defend the province was reported ready to oppose the Americans at Apache Canyon, twelve miles from the capital.

This defense never materialized, and on the morning of August 18, a man named Nicholas Quintaro rode into Kearny's camp astride a mule and shouted, "Armijo and his troops have gone to Hell and the canyon is all clear!" Quintaro, secretary of state in the new government, carried a letter from Acting Governor Juan Bautista Vigil y Alarid welcoming the Americans to New Mexico.

3

On August 18, 1846, fifty days and 850 miles from Fort Leavenworth and in a sudden squall of rain, Lieutenant Thomas C. Hammond of the First Dragoons led the vanguard of the Army of the West into Santa Fé.

The town, with its jumble of low, flat-roofed adobe *jacales*, seemed to fit the "more a prairie-dog village than a capital" description. A few townspeople gathered along the route to the governor's palace to witness the arrival of the Americans, the army and its train of equipage strung out for miles behind Hammond's advance guard. If the townspeople were awed by the spectacle, they made no outward expression of it. Except for the clop and snort of horses and the screech of wagon wheels on ungreased axles, the army rode in silence through the pelting rain.

At the one-story adobe Palace of the Governors, Vigil y Alarid had arranged a thirteen-gun salute to welcome General Kearny and his army and the raising of the American flag over the plaza. After the courtesies and *abrazos,* and wine and brandy served the general and his officers, Kearny read a notice to the governor, his staff, and the townspeople gathered at the entrance to the palace. In it, in proper monotone, he instructed the people of New Mexico to "deliver their arms and surrender absolutely to the government of the United States" and promised protection to the "persons, lives and property" of those who did so, "and in this manner I take this province of New Mexico for the benefit of the United States."

The governor responded, "In the name of the entire department, I swear obedience to the Northern Republic and I tender my respect to its laws and authority."

Kearny was eager to proceed to California but he had duties to perform as the first American governor of New Mexico, and five anxious weeks passed before he could gather his force for the march south and west. He ordered construction of a fort, named Fort Marcy for the secretary of war, above the Santa Fé plaza. He attended mass (he was an Episcopalian) in the St. Francis Cathedral. He conferred with the governor and his staff and met often with his own officers to plan the security of the vast province after he left it. He visited the sick troops at Dr. Griffin's improvised

hospital. He pored over the primitive maps of Mexican
territory, planning his forthcoming march. He attended to a
vast correspondence, keeping his Washington superiors informed of his every plan and pronouncement. He sponsored
a public fandango at the palace in which five hundred people attended, dancing what one American described as "a
kind of swinging gallopade waltz," and feasting and drinking until dawn.

On August 22, the day another American conqueror,
Commodore Robert F. Stockton, was setting up his civil
government in California, Kearny issued a more formal
proclamation. He declared New Mexico a territory of the
United States, repeated his warnings to those who would
oppose him and his promises to those who did not. Alexander Doniphan's lawyerly skills were put to work drafting a
legal code and bill of rights for the newly annexed region.

Between September 2 and 11, the general, with an ostentatious seven-hundred-man escort, toured the southern
settlements—the *Río Abajo*—of New Mexico. In the villages of Bernalillo, Albuquerque, Peralta, San Tomé, and
others, he reiterated to local *alcaldes* and *jefes políticos* that
he and his army came "as friends, protectors, not as conquerors," and that no one would be molested who tended his
fields and herds and did not take up arms. "Not a pepper,
not an onion, shall be disturbed or taken by my troops without pay or by the consent of the owner," he said, adding the
grave warning, "But listen! He who promises to be quiet, and
is found in arms against me, I will hang!"

Last arrangements were made. Garrisons were set up in
Santa Fé and several other towns; patrols were sent out to protect New Mexicans from predatory Indians; Charles Bent, a
Taos lawyer and one of the founders of Bent's Fort, was selected to serve as the first civilian governor of the territory.

Two of Kearny's support forces—a second regiment of Missouri volunteers commanded by Colonel Sterling Price, and the Mormon Battalion under Captain James Allen— were en route to Santa Fé as the general prepared to leave the capital. He had promised to send surplus troops to Chihuahua to join Brigadier General John E. Wool's force two hundred miles south of the Rio Grande, and he picked Colonel Doniphan to lead the Second Missourians to a rendezvous with Wool. Another favorite officer, Philip St. George Cooke, stayed behind to take command of the Mormon Battalion and march the five hundred volunteers to California. Colonel Price, a well-connected, Virginia-born Missourian who had resigned his seat in the House of Representatives to serve in the war, was designated military governor of New Mexico.

(Three weeks after Kearny departed, Cooke marched his battalion out of Santa Fé with a dozen wagons and oxcarts and moved down the Rio Grande. He led his force along a route considerably south of Kearny's and reached Tucson on December 14 to find that the Mexican garrison there had abandoned the town. With replenished supplies, the Mormons marched north along the Santa Cruz River and in late December, struck the Gila. They struggled into San Diego in the last days of January, 1847, nearly naked and shoeless, but with most of their wagons.)

4

The general departed Santa Fé on September 25, 1846, with three hundred of the First Dragoons, now mounted on mules—he believed them better adapted to the southwestern desert terrain than horses, surer to make what Captain Cooke described as "a leap in the dark of a thousand miles of wild plain and mountain." With Tom Fitzpatrick as guide, the troopers and their pack train moved down the east bank of the Rio Grande to Albuquerque, then crossed to the west bank as they neared the town of Socorro.

The dragoon column made good progress in cool weather down the Rio Grande Valley despite the tendency of the mules to wander off into the lush cornfields and the time taken to haggle with wary villagers in buying food, forage, and spare pack animals. A band of Navajo marauders had recently raided some of the pueblos on the line of march and Kearny sent a patrol ahead to locate them, but to no avail.

On October 6, two hundred miles south of Santa Fé and ten miles below the village of Socorro, there occurred an astonishing coincidence, one that Kearny's biographer said recalled Clotho, Lachesis, and Atropos, the Greek Fates who spun, determined the length, and cut the tread of human destiny.

Kearny, several of his officers, and Fitzpatrick, riding ahead of the column, spotted what appeared to be a large dust devil in the distance, then heard a shout and watched as a band of horsemen galloped toward them. Broken Hand instantly recognized the lead rider as his old comrade of trapping days in the mountains, Kit Carson.

Thirty days earlier, with fifteen men, including six of Frémont's Delawares, and a small pack train, Carson had ridden out of Los Angeles, bound for Washington with dispatches from Commodore Stockton announcing the capture of California. The scout had estimated that the journey would take sixty days, and his "express" party had traveled eight hundred miles over dim or nonexistent trails through hostile country when it spied the dust cloud of Kearny's column.

The meeting between the general and the scout was to be fateful for each, far beyond the coincidental timing of their encounter below Socorro.

Kearny read the dispatches Carson carried and the news stunned him: California had fallen to Stockton and his

naval force and Frémont's volunteers. The Mexican governor and commandante-general had fled the province. A
civil government under Frémont was in the making. The
war in the West was over.

This was crushing news, but Kearny recovered from it in
old-army fashion: he had orders and he intended to follow
through on them. Four months earlier, the War Department
of the United States had instructed him that he was to have
"a large discretionary power" in commanding the Army of
the West, and that while it was expected that American naval forces would soon be in possession of the coastal towns
of California, Secretary Marcy had been clear that the navy
would "co-operate with you in the conquest of California."
The secretary had stated unequivocally what he expected of
the general: "Should you conquer and take possession of
New Mexico and Upper California, or considerable places
in either, you will establish temporary civil governments
therein. . . ."

Half of that assignment had been accomplished. He had
conquered New Mexico and organized the rudiments of a
new civil governance under Charles Bent. Carson's news did
not alter his essential plan to proceed to California to attend
to the other half of his orders, to assume governmental responsibilities there. True, since Stockton and Frémont had
already pacified the province, certain adjustments would have
to be made, and in his command tent in a cottonwood grove
on the Rio Grande, Kearny worked out the details.

He now needed only a modest escort to proceed to California. With fewer men, he could travel faster and worry less
about finding game, water, and forage en route. Carson
warned that the southern route into Los Angeles lay across
harsh, arid terrain, pitiless to man and animal alike, and that
heavy wagons could not negotiate the primitive trails.

Kearny trusted Carson's information and cut his force by
two-thirds, sending two hundred of his dragoons back to

Santa Fé to join Doniphan's force preparing to march into Chihuahua. He retained two companies, C and K, of the First Dragoons, a hundred men under Captain Benjamin D. Moore and Lieutenant Thomas C. Hammond, and two mule-drawn mountain howitzers. The supply and baggage wagons were sent back to Santa Fé, and the officers returning there carried orders that packsaddles and additional mules were to be brought down to join the line of march.

Kearny also ordered Kit Carson to guide him and his foreshortened dragoon force back to California. This order made perfect sense: Carson knew the lay of the land between the Rio Grande and Los Angeles, was familiar with it from times past, had, in fact, just traveled it. He knew the water, game, and forage sources, knew the hazards, knew the dangers of moving through Apache lands. What better guide than Kit Carson, who only a month ago had departed California, had been intimately involved in its conquest, knew the Californios and their vast province from Klamath Lake on the north to San Diego on the south?

Kearny had no dependable maps; he needed the maps, and the experience, in Carson's brain.

But the issue was weightier than these practical elements. In ordering Carson to guide him, the general made the first overt assertion that he commanded all the American military forces in the Mexican territories of the West. He had orders and believed they were explicit on this. Those orders did not mention Stockton or Frémont, or any other officer superior to or superseding him.

Nor did he give a moment's pause in nullifying Stockton's orders to Carson to carry dispatches to Washington. The answer to that was simple: Tom Fitzpatrick could deliver the papers to the capital.

Carson must have wished he had taken a slightly more northern route out of Los Angeles, thereby bypassing the Army of the West entirely. He had come eight hundred miles

through lean and dry country, he and his men at the edge
of starvation, subsisting on parched corn, before striking
the Rio Grande Valley. He was 250 miles from his home in
Taos, from seeing his wife, Josefa, and his children, for the
first time in fourteen months since he left her to join Frémont at Bent's Fort for the California expedition. He had
intended to take his men to Taos for rest and recuperation
before continuing on east. Now he was ordered to go west
again.

He protested to Kearny, but while the general later admitted that Carson was "at first very unwilling to turn
back," he said that the scout, after being told that Fitzpatrick would carry the dispatches, "was perfectly satisfied
with that and so told me." John S. Griffin, the dragoon surgeon, recorded in his journal that Kearny's force turned
west "with merry hearts & light packs on our long march—
Carson as guide, every man feeling renewed confidence in
consequence of having such a guide." Captain Abraham
Johnston, regimental adjutant, commented in his diary: "It
requires a brave man to give up his private feelings thus for
the public good; but Carson was one such! Honor to him
for it."

If he was angry, which is likely, Carson left no evidence of it in his own dictated recollections. He was
never much of a protester even as a civilian attached to
the army, when he might have given notice and simply
quit when inconvenienced. In truth, when it came to the
military, Kit was a born follower and now, as an officer of
the California Battalion and officially mustered into the
service, he could scarcely disobey the orders of a general.
He said, "On the 6th of October, '46, I met General
Kearny on his march to California. He ordered me to join
him as guide. I done so and Fitzpatrick continued on with
the dispatches."

On October 15, after Fitzpatrick and most of Carson's express party had headed east, the scout rode west with the

general, his officers, and dragoons from the cottonwood-grove bivouac below Socorro. With the small force and pack train, the journey, for all the difficulties of the trail, would be swift. Everyone knew that California, like New Mexico, had been conquered and was at peace, but the general had his orders: he had work to do and was anxious to get it done.

15

- -

Los Angeles

■

1

A month passed before Kearny heard news of it, but as he led his dragoons west from Socorro, a counterrevolt in California had stalled the conquest. At the time Kit Carson and his express party had departed Pueblo de los Ángeles in early September, the reports he carried had assured President Polk and the War Department that the province had been annexed and pacified, and it had been on this intelligence that the general had reduced his Army of the West by two-thirds.

The pacification had lasted five weeks, from August 17, when Commodore Stockton read his proclamation declaring California a territory of the United States, until September 23, the day Kearny marched south out of Santa Fé with three hundred dragoons. On that day, a tiny band of insurgents had besieged the American garrison in Los Angeles.

At the root of the problem lay Stockton's insensitivity and inattention. California had fallen far too easily to the restless commodore and his lethargic predecessor, John D. Sloat. Calling the annexation a "conquest" was certainly hyperbolic; there had been no war, no battle, no "campaign" to win the land. Sailing up and down the coast, raising flags, firing salutes, and reading proclamations to the dumbfounded citizenry did not comprise an ambitious officer's idea of military glory. Stockton had quickly tired of California; he had no interest in serving as its military governor and he turned his attention to his splendid scheme of raising a thousand volunteers and marching to Mexico City.

Nor did the commodore attempt to understand the Californios. Unlike Sloat, whose public pronouncements were unthreatening and studiously diplomatic, and who listened to men such as Thomas O. Larkin, who knew the land and its people, Stockton's approach was that of an impatient patriarch toward unruly children. He sought no counsel, issued belligerent statements and harsh orders, and while paying lip service to the "rights" of the new American citizens, plainly regarded them simply as a conquered people meekly willing to toe whatever line he drew for them. He seemed ignorant of the essential key to their contentment: the Californios had no loyalty to Mexico and its age-old policy of benign neglect, and while Los Angeles was the center of what little anti-American feeling existed in the province, it was at best a lukewarm hotbed. There existed what H. H. Bancroft called a "turbulent, lawless, and hitherto uncontrollable" element among the *abajeños* but little interest in the internecine rivalry between their *jefes políticos* and those in the north. In general, the Californios were willing to abide American annexation—indeed, many influentials openly championed it—provided their way of life could proceed unchallenged by unnecessary American rules.

Stockton had assured that this simple requirement would be denied when he assigned Marine Brevet Captain Archibald H. Gillespie to succeed Frémont as military commandant of Los Angeles.

The career marine had qualities that attracted Stockton as they had Frémont, who had been impressed with Gillespie from the moment they had first met at Klamath Lake in May,

1846, and who had subsequently selected him as adjutant of the California Battalion. He had been the perfect courier for President Polk and the Secretary of the Navy. He was courageous and imaginative in carrying dispatches and orders across hostile Mexico to Mazatlán, Monterey, and to Frémont in northern California. He had fought Indians alongside Frémont's men, and had been successful in the several missions entrusted to him. He was fluent in Spanish.

Now age forty-three, with fifteen years of service and still only a lieutenant of marines, Gillespie's weaknesses emerged fully when he was left in command of Los Angeles with a garrison of forty-eight men. The taste of power seemed to infuse him with the Marine Corps spirit, which a century later was described as "gung ho." He took control with a will, became imperious, quick-tempered, and tactless. He regarded Mexicans in general as a cowardly, inferior people, and his ill-concealed contempt for the Californios fit perfectly the attitudes of Frémont and his men, and of Stockton and his. Gillespie, now commanding men who had served with both Frémont and Stockton, was as drunk on power as the men were drunk on *aguardiente*.

The instructions he had received were simple: he was to "maintain military rule" in accordance with the commodore's proclamation and to be lenient with citizens "well-disposed" toward the United States, exempting them from the burdensome rules directed at the more recalcitrant populace. But Gillespie ignored these niceties and from his Government House headquarters, wrote orders like a man accustomed only to taking orders. He issued directives on enforcing curfews, closing shops at sundown, searching homes for weapons, outlawing gatherings in private homes, forbidding even family reunions in homes. He made it illegal for liquor to be sold without his permission, illegal for two people to walk in the streets together, illegal to gallop a horse across the plaza. He ordered the breaking up of fandangos—which he apparently felt were opportunities for the gathering of malcontents. He presided over and decided petty lawbreaking cases instead of leaving them to local magistrates. He freely used the word "rebel" in his adjudications, imposed fines, jailed perceived offenders without hearings.

After five weeks of obnoxious regulations and frivolous arrests, Gillespie's satrapy succeeded in igniting the damp tinder of revolt in Los Angeles.

2

Rumors of an insurrection in the planning reached the marine and his men weeks before the first overt sign of it. A militia captain named Cérbulo Varela, described by Bancroft as "a wild and unmanageable young fellow, though not a bad man at heart," gathered around him a number of like-minded "irresponsible fellows" and announced that he and his friends would not submit to the American's police-like rules. Varela and his street toughs seem to have harassed Gillespie's enforcers, yet remained out of range of capture while stirring discontent among the Angelinos.

In mid-September, in response to the burgeoning trouble, Gillespie made a fatal mistake. He divided his meager force by sending a detachment of nineteen men under Ezekial Merritt to San Diego, which had been left ungarrisoned. Merritt and his men had been gone a week when, before dawn on September 23, 1846, Varela and twenty of his ruffians made a noisy assault on the barracks building housing the remainder of Gillespie's men. The insurgents were apparently hoping that by firing a few shots in the air, beating drums, and shouting, they could roust the Americans and force their surrender. The ploy did not work and Varela and his rebels were chased off with a rifle volley. When the smoke cleared, however, the comic attack on the barracks had produced the result Varela hoped for: a swelling of the rebel ranks from among the numerous Californios who had held their tempers in check during the weeks of what they considered a suffocating governance. People began digging up the guns they had buried, and within days of his first sortie Varela had three hundred men in his ragged command, divided into bands, each with a "captain" in charge, several of these veteran officers officially "under parole" and pledged not to serve against the Americans.

The growing rebel force gathered at La Mesa, one of José Castro's old camps east of the village, and soon other leaders emerged. Captain José María Flores, an intelligent, professional military man, was elected *mayor general* of the insurgent force; Flores' second in command was José Antonio Carrillo, former *alcalde* of Los Angeles and a veteran intriguer against several governors of the province; and a third man, destined to loom larger than the others in the events to follow, was Captain Andrés Pico, now *commandante de escuadrón* (squadron commander), age thirty-six and the younger brother of the departed Governor Pío Pico.

On September 24, the insurgents issued their own proclamation, addressed to the "Citizenry" of California and signed by Varela and over three hundred others. The rebels said that "we see ourselves subjugated and oppressed by an insignificant force of adventurers from the U.S. of N. America, who, putting us in a condition worse than that of slaves, are dictating to us despotic and arbitrary laws. . . ." The manifesto, redolent of Pico's exit oratory and somewhat more portentous than those written by Stockton and Gillespie, called for freedom from "the heavy chains of slavery" and warned that the American oppressors intended "barbarous servitude" for native Californians. "Shall we wait to see our wives violated, our innocent children beaten by the American whip, our property sacked, our temples profaned, to drag out a life full of shame and disgrace? No! A thousand times no!"

A call to arms followed, asking all citizens from age fifteen to sixty to join in repelling the invaders and branding as traitors those who did not take up the fight.

The issuance of this document was accompanied by a demand that the Americans surrender. Gillespie now busied his men with unspiking four old cannons they had captured in August and in gathering what ammunition and powder he could find while awaiting developments from among the rebels.

On September 24, Gillespie dispatched John "Juan Flaco" Brown to Monterey with urgent messages scribbled on cigarette papers that were balled up and placed in the express rider's hair. Brown stopped at Santa Barbara to warn Lieutenant Theodore Talbot of the trouble brewing in Los Angeles, then proceeded to Yerba Buena with Gillespie's message to Stockton that Los Angeles was under siege.

The Americans held their position for several days after slipping out of Government House to the nearby gun emplacements at Fort Hill, an unreconnoitered position that was found to be waterless. Meantime, General Flores renewed his surrender demands and generously offered to permit Gillespie and his men to march out of town unmolested, taking their small arms with them, and proceed to San Pedro Bay, where they could board a merchant ship to remove them from California waters.

On about September 29, Gillespie accepted Flores' offer and surrendered. Five days later, he embarked with his force on the merchant vessel *Vandalia*.

In Santa Barbara, a small band that had split off the growing insurgent force in Los Angeles demanded the surrender of Theodore Talbot and his nine-man garrison. The lieutenant, one of Frémont's trusted adjutants and original exploration-party members, escaped with his men and lurked in the mountains within sight of the town for a week, hoping that an American man-of-war might arrive to rescue them. When none appeared, they crossed into the interior valley and pushed on to Monterey, a patrol of Californios snapping at their heels. They arrived there exhausted, starving, their clothes in rags, on November 8 and rejoined Frémont and his men, who had entered the town a few days before on the American trader *Sterling.*

In the old hide-and-tallow depot of San Diego, Zeke Merritt and his dozen men were joined by Sutter's majordomo John Bidwell and a handful of other American sympathizers. They fled the town upon the arrival of a party of fifty of General Flores' insurgents and boarded the commercial whaler *Stonington,* at anchor in the bay.

3

Stockton's Acapulco–Mexico City scheme evaporated on October 1. That day, Skinny John Brown, after a ride of five hundred miles in seven days, reached Yerba Buena on the last of a string of blown horses and delivered the news of the impending fall of Los Angeles. The commodore, poring over his charts in the cabin of the *Congress,* received Brown's report dubiously but cleared his table and called his officers to a war council. He dispatched Captain William Mervine of the *Savannah* to reinforce the Los Angeles garrison; he also sent a courier to Frémont's camp near Sutter's Fort ordering the explorer to bring his California Battalion down to San Francisco Bay.

The *Savannah* reached San Pedro Bay on October 6 and found Gillespie and his men still aboard the *Vandalia* awaiting rescue. The next day, Mervine landed 350 sailors and marines on the beach, was joined there by Gillespie and his men, and began the march north toward Los Angeles. The expedition was poorly planned and ill-equipped, Mervine apparently having been infected with the prevailing belief that the Californios would run for the hills upon the approach of an American force. The sailors were armed with an assortment of muskets, cutlasses, belaying pins, and boarding pikes; no cannons had been taken from the *Savannah,* although several light, manageable ones were available. Mervine had no horses, no ambulance wagons, no supply train, and knew nothing of the terrain or the numbers and deployment of the rebel force. Gillespie later said that the captain was "without reason," and indeed, the two officers were at instant odds, Mervine accusing the marine of unprofessional, even criminal, conduct in surrendering his garrison.

After a few hours' march from the beach, the Americans began spotting mounted men in the distance, watching their advance. A few random shots were exchanged but Mervine and his force reached the Domínguez rancho, an outpost about fifteen miles from Los Angeles, without serious incident.

General José Flores had been able to mount about two hundred men in the week since Gillespie's surrender and had taken a wise precaution in herding all horses and cattle inland to deprive the Americans of them. While his force, equipped with lances, swords, skinning knives, and old muskets and pistols buried or hidden during the American takeover, was nearly as poorly armed as Mervine's, it did have a cannon. This ancient brass four-pounder, used for ceremonial salutes, had been buried in the garden of one Inocencia Reyes, exhumed, and mounted on a makeshift, horse-drawn limber. Flores and his second in command, Colonel José Carrillo, rode out with an advance guard to harass the American advance, and on October 8, 1846, just north of Rancho Domínguez, the engagement known as the "Battle of the Old Woman's Gun" took place.

The rebel tactics were simple and effective: the four-pounder was placed athwart the road on which the Americans had to advance; long ropes were lashed to the limber by which the gun could be pulled into the brush for reloading. Flores and Carillo deployed their horsemen at a safe distance from the roadway on the flanks of the approaching enemy.

Mervine's force advanced in close columns on the narrow trail, with Gillespie and his men serving as skirmishers on the flanks, all the men bunched up and vulnerable, with no reconnaissance to determine the enemy number and whereabouts. When they came within four hundred yards of the rebel position, the old fieldpiece was fired and quickly yanked back into the brush, followed by a ragged volley of musket fire from Flores' flankers.

The first several cannon shots were ineffective because of the weak homemade powder used, but inevitably, with the Americans clotted along the trail, the four-pound balls did some damage, as did the rebels' musketry. Mervine, who had placed his troops in square formation—the classic defense against cavalry—was helpless with his men afoot against a virtually unseen and uncounted enemy. With a dozen serious casualties, no place to hide, and no chance to advance on Los Angeles, he turned his force back to San Pedro Bay and reboarded the *Savannah*. After a few days, the warship sailed north to Monterey.

The "battle" had lasted less than an hour; four of the twelve Americans struck by ball and bullet died of their wounds and were buried on a little island in San Pedro Bay, perfectly named Isla de los Muertos (Island of the Dead).

Frémont meantime had gathered his 170 men and reported to Stockton at Yerba Buena. Many of the men were afoot. Horses were becoming scarce in the north and both officers counted on finding mounts once they reached Santa Barbara, seventy miles upcoast from Los Angeles.

Stockton needed to get to sea and retake what Gillespie had lost, and on October 12, the day after Frémont arrived, he took the *Congress* out through the Golden Gate, Frémont and his men following on the chartered trader *Sterling.* But a day out and in a heavy fog, the *Sterling* lost sight of the flagship and all plans went awry. Stockton went on to Monterey, learned that the small garrison there feared a rebel attack, and left reinforcements. He proceeded to San Pedro and reached the bay on October 23. Mervine had returned there on the *Savannah* a few days earlier and Stockton learned the details of the recent encounter with Flores' rebels. Over the next couple of days, eight hundred sailors, marines, and Gillespie's volunteers were landed at San Pedro. Stockton then moved on to San Diego to set up a base of operations for the campaign against Flores, to drill and train his sailors, and to scour the countryside and send patrols into Baja California to locate horses and livestock.

(Antonio María Osio of Monterey said that Stockton's efforts in San Diego were abetted by "corrupt Californios and some Mexican traitors" who offered supplies to the commodore "so that he could increase his ranks and resources in the war he was fighting against the men whom they should have regarded as their brothers." Osio said that these turncoats were blinded by ambition and that "if those men had been Americans, Señor Stockton, a patriotic and upright man, would have hanged them like bunches of grapes from every yardarm of his frigate's main mast.")

4

After the false start, Frémont and his men proceeded toward Santa Barbara on the *Sterling,* but en route met the *Vandalia,* the merchant ship on which Gillespie and his men had taken refuge upon surrendering the Los Angeles garrison. After learning from the merchant skipper of Mervine's failure to retake Los Angeles and that the rebels had run all horses and cattle inland, Frémont ordered the

Sterling to reverse course for Monterey. There he hoped to gather horses and increase his volunteer force for an overland march to Los Angeles to join with Stockton, whose exact whereabouts for the moment were unknown.

Frémont's return to Monterey on October 27 and the three weeks he tarried there removed him and his men from the theater of operations between San Diego and Los Angeles, but he did not waste the time. Mervine's experience against Flores proved that the insurgents were perhaps more numerous than anybody had estimated.

From his headquarters in Monterey, Frémont, who received word there of his promotion to the brevet rank of lieutenant colonel of the army, sent express riders north with letters to Captain Montgomery of the *Portsmouth* in San Francisco Bay and to Ned Kern at Sutter's Fort. These messages requested that volunteers and horses be massed and made ready to join Frémont's force in Monterey. This recruiting effort, with Sutter's as the main depot, and with the efforts of Kern and Lieutenant Revere in Sonoma, produced nearly two hundred men, including a number of Paiute and Walla Walla Indians. These mounted volunteers and a remuda of spare horses and mules came south to Frémont toward the end of November.

While the explorer awaited reinforcements, Ezekial Merritt, John Bidwell, and two dozen men were landed from the whaler *Stonington* a short distance from San Diego and wrestled the three small cannons appropriated from the ship to the outskirts of the town. Flores' men discovered them and set up a desultory fire, but after the pieces banged a few times, the rebels vanished into the brush and Merritt and his tiny force reoccupied San Diego. They raised the flag in the town plaza and nervously held their position until the end of October, when Stockton and Mervine arrived in the bay with their warships and the town was secured once and for all.

The commodore's main order of business was to find horses, saddle-rigging, mules, and cattle; armed patrols fanned out into the countryside and others shipped to the Baja California coast to gather the animals and equipage. One of these expeditions succeeded in gathering a hundred forty head of horses and five hundred of cattle, but did not return until late December.

While Stockton was establishing his base in San Diego and preparing to march north and Frémont was gathering his force in Monterey for a march south, General José Flores was also regrouping. At an assembly convened in Los Angeles, he had been elected governor and military commander of California, but the added power did nothing to alleviate his problems. He had no funds with which to pay his men— regulars and unenthusiastic volunteers, about four hundred in all; he was running low on powder and ammunition and had to operate with an inadequate supply train. He had also divided his force into thin units, a hundred men under General José Castro at San Luís Obispo, between Monterey and Santa Barbara, to watch for the advance of Frémont's force, another hundred under Captain Andrés Pico to guard the eastern approaches to San Diego, and the remainder of the men—less than two hundred—in Flores' own command, camped near Los Angeles to counter, as best they could, either Stockton or Frémont, or both.

One significant encounter between the Americans and Californios occurred during this November regrouping period and involved the United States consul in Monterey, Thomas O. Larkin. He rode out of Monterey for Yerba Buena after receiving news that his four-year-old daughter Adeline was seriously ill there. He was aware of the danger of the journey, knew that he might be taken prisoner in retaliation for General Vallejo's capture in Sonoma, and during the night of November 15, while staying with friends in San Juan Bautista, his worst fears were realized. He was captured by

Castro's troops and taken to the general's camp on the Salinas River, within view of Frémont's old battlements on Hawk's Peak.

As these events unfolded, there arrived in San Juan a force of California Battalion men out of Sutter's Fort, bringing five hundred head of horses and mules to Colonel Frémont in Monterey. As the advance guard of the battalion advanced toward the Salinas and reached a rancho called La Natividad, they were met by a patrol of 130 Californians—with their prisoner Larkin among them. The melee that ensued, later called the "Battle of La Natividad," cost the lives of five to seven Americans, two Californians, and several wounded on each side. Larkin was unhurt but was not released from captivity for a month. In that period, Adeline Larkin died in Yerba Buena.

Frémont got news of the skirmish as he prepared to depart Monterey; he took his men north the thirty miles to the San Juan Bautista outskirts to gather his new recruits and the horses and mules they had herded. He spent two weeks there as reinforcements continued to arrive from the Sacramento Valley, bringing with them more horses and pack animals.

At last, on November 30, in a thunderstorm that instantly turned the dirt trail into a muddy swamp, he was ready to strike out toward Los Angeles. He led an army of 430 men, three artillery pieces, and nearly two thousand horses and mules.

Frémont and his cumbersome force were still slogging down the Salinas River Valley, three days out of San Juan Bautista, when Commodore Stockton, in San Diego, received a letter, brought in by an express rider, from Brigadier General S.W. Kearny of the United States Army. The general informed the commodore that he was approaching the city from the east and asked about the state of affairs in California.

Stockton sent for Gillespie, gave him quick orders to select a number of good horsemen and ride out to meet Kearny and his men. Gillespie led his patrol out of San Diego in the early evening of December 3, 1846.

16

San Pascual

■

1

Stephen Watts Kearny received the news that California had been annexed with his customary stoicism, but it shocked him. The miraculous convergence of his path down the Rio Grande Valley with that of Kit Carson and his escort on October 6, a month out of Los Angeles, seemed a wicked trick of fate. He had come a thousand cruel miles at the head of an army and raised the flag of the United States over the old province of New Mexico. Now, the second half of his objective had been snatched from him by the navy, a gang of topographical explorers, and a handful of malcontents calling themselves Bear Flaggers.

Carson could be trusted. He told of the capture of Sonoma and the subsequent surrender of Monterey, of the occupation of San Francisco Bay and Los Angeles, matter-of-factly. The Californians had folded pitifully. Carson said they were cowardly, had no means to resist and, worse, no will.

Carson's news dictated a new course of action. The general still had responsibilities in California, now political rather than military. His orders were to take over command there, and with the navy's cooperation, establish a civil government and serve as proconsul. The War Department was shipping another army unit around Cape Horn to California, commanded by Richard B. Mason, colonel of the First Dragoons, and Mason would succeed Kearny as military governor when the general was satisfied that the entire territory had been pacified.

He now needed only an armed escort to travel through Indian country and so sent back to Santa Fé two hundred of his three hundred dragoons and all but two fieldpieces, and cut his supply train to the bone, trading his wagons for packsaddles. He retained only the First Dragoon companies, under Captain Benjamin D. Moore and Lieutenant Thomas C. Hammond, the latter married to Moore's sister. His other officers were Captain Henry Smith Turner, acting assistant adjutant general; Captain Abraham R. Johnston, aide-de-camp; Major Thomas Swords, quartermaster; lieutenants William H. Emory and William H. Warner, topographical engineers; Lieutenant John W. Davidson, in charge of the two mountain howitzers; and assistant surgeon John S. Griffin. A dozen assistants and servants were selected to accompany the escort, and the French-Canadian Antoine Robidoux, a veteran tracker, remained the principal guide, with Kit Carson his associate.

On October 15, Robidoux and Carson led Kearny and his escort, most of them mounted on mules, and the pack train southwest toward the Santa Rita del Cobre country, inhabited by Mimbreño Apaches. The trail was an ancient one, used by Spaniards and Mexicans traveling to and from California, and it cut through wilderness both weirdly beautiful and forbidding: in the first few days, a lushly green country of oaks, ash, and walnut trees, and aspens on the higher ground, the Mimbres range and other mountains to the north; then rock-strewn desert, countless bone-dry arroyos, great canyons, mesas disappearing into the horizon, yucca and Joshua trees and all manner of cactus, some hugging the ground with tentacles spread seeking moisture, others squat and fat and decorated with gorgeous flowers, still others tall and stately, like sentinels with arms pointing skyward, their hides pocked with bird holes. There were occasional grassy stretches along the old roadway, and small streams and rivulets and great cottonwood copses, but these were rare, and water and forage were daily problems for man and beast.

On October 20, five days out of the Socorro camp, the Americans crossed the Continental Divide and reached the southernmost branch of the Gila River, where they made camp, and watered their stock. Before starting out the next morning, Kearny and his officers were startled when a band of twenty Apaches—Mimbres men led by their great chief Mangas Coloradas (Red Sleeves)—rode into the camp. Through sign language and what Apache-Spanish Kearny's officers could understand, Mangas said that his visit was peaceful and assured them they could pass through his country unmolested. He knew that Kearny had captured Santa Fé and he was delighted—the Apaches and Mexicans were ancient enemies, slaughtering each other since conquistador times—suggesting to the general that he join forces with the Apaches and conquer all of northern Mexico. Kearny politely declined and after many hours of bartering with the band for a few mules, the march was resumed and Mangas led his men south into the hills.

In early November, the trail threaded through scattered villages of the Pima and Maricopa tribes, some of them with irrigated patches of land growing corn, wheat, beans, melons, and squash. The Pimas were especially friendly and when Carson tried to barter with a chief, he was told that "bread is to eat, not to sell; take what you want." But there were no horses or cattle available and the Americans were able to gain only a few bony mules, these from a Coyotero Apache band.

They rode on, twenty or thirty miles a day, depending on water and graze and the state of fatigue of the men and ani-

mals, fording streams and arroyos—dismantling the guns
and their carriages each time—climbing rocky hills, trudging across miles of deep sand that bogged the heavily laden
mules and fieldpieces. Each day, men in advance of the main
column searched for water, grass, and suitable campsites,
and each night, after the animals were fed and picketed,
the men ate their frugal meal and fell exhausted into their
bedrolls.

The tedium of the march was broken on November 22
when the column reached a point ten miles from the confluence of the Gila and Colorado rivers. The advance guard had
discovered near a pueblo ruins fresh remains of an abandoned camp. The size of the camp and the countless hoof-
prints around it seemed to indicate that a large number of
horses had been there, tended by a few men.

After the two mountain guns were brought forward, Kearny dispatched Lieutenant Emory and a detail of riders to
investigate, and ten miles downtrail, they discovered a dust
cloud caused by a *caballada* of at least five hundred animals. Emory and his men took four Mexican herders prisoner with no resistance and brought them to Kearny's camp
to be questioned. "Each gave a different account of the
ownership and destination of the horses," Emory wrote, and
while it appears that the animals were headed from California to Sonora to be sold, many of the dragoon officers
were convinced that the horse herd belonged to General
José Castro.

Of far more importance than the captured horses was the
alarming news related by one of the Mexican prisoners that
there had been a revolution in Los Angeles and the pueblo
had been taken back from the Americans. This astonishing
story was substantiated the next day when Emory captured
a courier carrying dispatches to Castro in the Sonoran capital. The papers were unsealed, found to be dated October 15
and containing details of a counterrevolt that had "thrown
off the detestable Anglo-Yankee yoke." Castro was informed

that Pueblo de Los Ángeles, Santa Barbara, and other towns in the southern province were again in the hands of the Californians and that General Flores had defeated the American naval officer Mervine at San Pedro.

The news in the captured dispatches was five weeks old and Kearny had no idea of what might have happened in the interim, but one thing seemed clear: the Californians had been misjudged.

2

Kearny had no intention of taking prisoners and did not need five hundred wild horses. The captured dispatches had transformed his hundred-man dragoon force into a flying column and he was restless, fretting over every hour spent off the trail, desperate to discover the state of affairs in California. He freed the horse herders, even resealing and returning the dispatches to the courier, and in a gentlemanly and unwarlike gesture, purchased twenty-five of the tamest animals and a few mules and gave the Mexicans some tea, coffee, and sugar from his meager stores.

On November 25, the dragoons found a suitable ford on the Colorado, a place where the river, nearly a half-mile wide, ran less than four feet deep. Because Carson had advised that the grass and mesquite thinned out a short distance from the river, the mules were loaded with forage and bags of mesquite pods after the laborious crossing. Ahead lay desert country and within two days of the Colorado crossing, Kearny's men were digging deep into the sand in dry streambeds looking for water seepage. The four-day crossing of the desert cost the lives of several of the 250 mules and horses in the expedition, but the dragoons found water and graze at Carrizo Creek, struggled through a gap in the foothills of the Vallecitos Mountains, and in the mid-afternoon of December 2, reached Warner's

Ranch, fifty miles northeast of San Diego, the first trace of civilization the Americans had seen since leaving the Rio Grande Valley on their "thousand-mile leap" fifty days ago.

The ranch and nearby springs lay on the Agua Caliente land grant awarded in 1844 to Jonathan Trumbull Warner of Lyme, Connecticut, who had served with Jedediah Smith's 1831 trading expedition to New Mexico (during which Smith was killed by Comanches). Warner was a naturalized citizen of Mexican California and had a fifteen-year history in the province. Carson knew "Juan Largo" Warner (Long John stood six-foot-three), and Kearny was anxious to meet the proprietor of the remote way station, but Warner was away on business when the dragoons reached the springs. There they were greeted by Juan Largo's factotum, an American named Marshall. With men and animals watered and fed and the camp made, Marshall told Kearny and his officers all he knew: the Californians had taken control of much of the southern province; the Americans still held the ports of San Francisco, Monterey, and San Diego. A neighboring Englishman, a former sea captain named Edward Stokes, came to the Warner ranchhouse and confirmed this information. He said he was on his way to San Diego and offered to carry with him any messages Kearny wished delivered to Commodore Stockton.

On December 2, Kearny wrote to Stockton from "Headquarters, Army of the West, camp at Warner's":

Sir: I this afternoon reached here, escorted by a party of 1st regiment dragoons. I came by order of the pres. of the U.S. We left Santa Fe on the 25th Sept., having taken possession of N. Mex., annexed it to the U.S., established a civil govt in that territory, and secured order, peace and quietness there. If you can send a party to open communication with us on the route to this place, and to inform me of the state of affairs in Cal., I wish you would do so,

and as quickly as possible. The fear of this letter falling
into Mexican hands prevents me from writing more. Your
express by Mr Carson was met on the Del Norte; and your
mail must have reached Washington at least 10 days
since. . . . Very respectfully . . .

Kearny's letter, in announcing that his arrival was upon
direct orders of the President of the United States, contained the hint that he now commanded the American
forces in California. He made no mention of the strength
of his "party," of the fact that he had given Stockton's dispatches to Tom Fitzpatrick "on the Del Norte," or that he had
ordered Carson to turn back and guide the Army of the
West to California.

Stockton's reply, dated on the evening of the third and
reaching Kearny on December 5, said that Captain Gillespie, a detachment of mounted riflemen, and a fieldpiece
were proceeding "without delay" to intercept the general
and his force and that "Capt. G. is well informed in relation to the present state of things in Cal., and will give you
all needful information." The note contained its own hint
of who was in charge: it was signed "Robt. Stockton,
commander-in-chief and governor of the territory of California, etc."

Kearny and his dragoons made their way south from Warner's ranch in a flogging rain on December 4, taking the
entire day to snail along the swampy roadway the fifteen
miles to Stokes' Santa Ysabel property, where a hot dinner
was prepared for them by the Englishman's majordomo and
Indian workers.

The thunderstorm had not abated the next morning
when the march resumed toward some rugged hills in the
west and the Indian village of San Pascual, but after a few

hours on the trail, Stockton's promise was fulfilled: the
dragoons, making their way through an oak grove, met
outriders from Archibald Gillespie's detachment of thirty-
five sailors, marines, and volunteers from the *Congress*
and the California Battalion. The two American columns
merged and camped—a short distance apart, as if Stockton,
or Gillespie, wanted Kearny to be mindful of separate
commands.*

As Kit Carson and Alexis Godey celebrated their reunion,
Captain Gillespie and his two officers, Navy Lieutenant
Edward F. Beale and Midshipman James M. Duncan, met
with Kearny and his staff and Gillespie announced the
most critical news: a force of lancers, perhaps a hundred
men under Captain Andrés Pico, was posted at San Pascual
village, about ten miles ahead on the direct route to San
Diego. Stockton, who had learned of the insurgents' position from two captured deserters, suggested, via messages
carried by Gillespie, that Kearny attack Pico and "beat up
the camp if the general thought it advisable" in order to
continue the march without harassment. One of the deserters, an Indian named Rafael Machado, had been sent along
with Gillespie's party.

At a war council that night, Captain Benjamin Moore, one
of Kearny's ablest officers, asked to lead a raid on Pico's
camp and the general appears to have given this idea serious consideration. But he decided instead to send a patrol
out under Lieutenant Thomas Hammond to reconnoiter the
enemy position and return with as much detailed information as could be gathered in the dark of night. Moore opposed this decision, saying that a horseback reconnaissance
might be discovered and thereby ruin the element of sur-

---

*These camps were near the modern town of Ramona, a few miles
from the San Pascual battlefield, today a state historic park lying
eight miles southeast of Escondido on California Route 78.*

prise. He preferred a full-blown night attack that would find
Pico's men unmounted and unprepared—"To dismount them
is to whip them," he said.

The captain was overruled, and on the night of December 5 Hammond, the deserter Machado, and six dragoons
rode out in a sleety rain to find Pico and his insurgents.

3

Thomas Clark Hammond of Fort McHenry, Maryland,
West Point class of '42, was age twenty-seven when he
led the patrol that night. The second lieutenant had been
married two years; his wife was the daughter of a prominent
Platte County, Missouri, judge, and he was the father of a
one-year-old son. He was a dedicated career officer, tough,
uncomplaining, ambitious, eager for a fight. Kearny would
not have entrusted the mission to a lesser man.

The patrol located San Pascual village with no difficulty,
and as the dragoons huddled against the biting cold and nee-
dling rain in the brush at the foot of a hill, Hammond sent
Machado into the scattering of huts to "bring an Indian out"
who could tell of the strength of Pico's force. Gillespie, in
recounting the events later, said, "Rafael went into the midst
of the Enemy where they were sleeping, pulled out an Indian and ascertained that Andrés Pico was there with one
hundred men." Lieutenant Edward Beale explained the ease
by which Machado gained the critical information: "The Indians are very inimical to the Californians and always
ready to betray them."

After waiting some anxious minutes for Machado's return, Hammond, fretting lest the Indian had run into trouble, led his dragoons to the outskirts of the village. According
to Gillespie, the clank of the dragoons' sabers alerted Pico's
sentries and instantly dogs began barking and the Califor-

nians, thrown awake, began shouting *"Viva California!"* *"Abajo los Americanos!"* and "a great variety of abuse."

Pico, it appears, could not at first credit that the intruders were Americans. The insurgents' spy network in San Diego, rudimentary but effective, had notified him of the hated Gillespie's departure from the town on December 3 with a small party of horsemen, riding east. Apparently no mention had been made of the brass cannon being pulled along at the rear of the American party, for Pico believed that the marine officer was merely leading a foraging expedition to find horses and stray cattle. He had taken his lancers—probably about a hundred men*—to San Pascual to keep an eye on Gillespie and did not know of Kearny's arrival nearby. He could not believe that a small foraging patrol would be so audacious as to challenge him and seemed to resist the idea that Gillespie was not alone in the area, even when a sentry showed him a dragoon jacket and a blanket stamped with the letters "U.S." that had been dropped on the trail. When Pico ordered his lancers to gather their horses, he did not know what to expect—a skirmish with the marine and his foraging party still seemed unlikely.

Not until dawn, when he saw Kearny's army for the first time, did he realize that he faced a full-fledged battle.

Hammond and his horsemen returned to Kearny's camp at two on the morning of December 6 and the lieutenant reported Machado's information and the unfortunate fact that Pico and his men had been alerted to the American presence. The general's reaction to the latter news is not recorded but his fury, and that of Captain Moore, who had warned of this danger in the reconnaissance, cannot be doubted. Gillespie, who was not present to witness it, placed

---

Some sources put the number as high as 160.

the blame for the fiasco directly on the patrol commander: "Thus the Californians were warned of the proximity of the Americans. The blunder by Hammond lost for Kearny the powerful advantage of surprise."

Kearny had no time to lecture; he ordered the camp be awakened and the men mounted; he sent Alexis Godey and Lieutenant Beale to Gillespie with orders for the marine to gather his men and join the dragoons on the trail to San Pascual village.

The advance began before dawn on December 6. The rain had stopped, but in the bitter cold the men had to wrestle themselves from their frozen blankets and saddle up in the moonlight with no time for breakfast rations. They were exhausted and hungry, as were their animals, as they plodded along a cart trail in a thick fog toward San Pascual.

Combined with Gillespie's small force, Kearny's Army of the West now numbered about 150 men. Twelve dragoons under Abraham Johnston led the army, with Kit Carson riding with them, followed by Kearny, Lieutenant Emory, and the engineers. Next in the column rode Captain Moore, Lieutenant Hammond, and fifty dragoons, most of them mounted on mules, followed by Gillespie with twenty men of the California Battalion, and Lieutenant John Davidson with two mountain howitzers and the crew to serve them. In the rear, the balance of the force, fifty or sixty men under the quartermaster, Major Thomas Swords, rode with the baggage train and Gillespie's brass four-pounder. The army was strung out, two columns wide, for nearly a mile along the brushy trail.

As the Indian huts of San Pascual came into view, lying at the east end of a flat valley, Kearny stopped his column in a narrow ravine that followed the valley floor into the village and there he gave some final orders to his officers. Precisely what these orders were is unknown, but he appears to have given a version of Lord Nelson's oft-used admonition that "every man is expected to do his duty" and urged his officers not to depend upon musketry (much of the army's powder had been dampened in the rain), but in true dragoon custom to rely upon the point of the saber. He had no real idea of the enemy numbers or of their deployment, or of the terrain, shrouded by the ground fog, and therefore he had no tactic. He said something about surrounding the village and taking as many prisoners as possible.

Ahead, gathered around the Indian huts, Andrés Pico and his horsemen waited, wrapped in bright serapes and leather cuirasses, their seven-foot-long, needle-pointed, fire-hardened, ashwood lances couched. Pico, with poorer firearms and powder than the Americans, had but a single order for his men: "One shot and the lance!"

4

The battle began by mistake, its opening move like a miniature version of the charge of the Light Brigade at Balaclava. Kearny's order to "Trot!" was apparently misheard by Abraham Johnston, who suddenly yelled something, unsheathed his saber, and spurred his horse down the valley, followed by Kit Carson and the twelve dragoons who led the American column. Captain Johnston's charge toward the village, three-quarters of a mile away, was so startling that gaps began opening in the line of march as Kearny, Benjamin Moore, and others yelled orders to follow. Those in the front of the column were able to spur their horses and mules, most of them weak and blown already, but minutes passed before those in the rear even realized that the army was on the move.

In the gray dawning, Johnston and the vanguard reached San Pascual fatal minutes ahead of Moore and the fifty dragoons who had followed closest behind, and Pico's horsemen were awaiting them in a gully on the eastern edge of the village. The Californians fired what few carbines they had, then wheeled to uncouch their lances. Johnston was killed by one of the first shots fired—struck in the forehead—and rolled off his horse; another bullet hit Carson's horse and the guide went down, his carbine flung from his grasp, and rolled off the path as the others thundered past. He retrieved his rifle but found it smashed, took a carbine and cartridge box from a wounded dragoon, and scrambled ahead on foot until finding a sniper's roost in the rocks bordering the gully.

Pico had by now realized the number of Americans opposing him, and after meeting the initial charge with a volley, the lancers fell back momentarily to a level stretch of ground a half-mile away on the west of the village. This maneuver was interpreted by Moore—commanding the main body of dragoons—as a retreat, and he led a charge against Pico's force with all the men who by now had reached the battle zone. The horses and mules picked their way forward through the brush and rocks until they came upon Pico and his men, who had in the meantime re-formed and now turned, leveling carbines and lances, and countercharged. Moore, some yards ahead of his men, rode directly at Pico. He fired his pistol, then slashed at the Mexican captain with his saber. The blow was parried as two of Pico's men rushed up, lances leveled, and speared Moore from his horse. The American was shot as he lay wounded on the ground, then killed by lance thrusts. Later, when his body was recovered, Moore was found still grasping his broken sword, his body torn by sixteen lance wounds.

As Moore fell from his horse, his brother-in-law, Lieutenant Thomas Hammond, rode up yelling to those behind him, "For God's sake, men, come up!" and was also lanced and unhorsed. He died in agony several hours later.

Within seconds, the fight devolved into a furious hand-to-hand combat, gun butts and sabers against gun butts and lances, engaging Pico's men both on the flat and in and around San Pascual village, where Kearny and the others were fighting. The Californians were not only skilled horsemen ("the very best riders in the world," Kearny later said), but adept with the *reata,* managing to drop their loops over several of the mule-mounted Americans and jerk them from their saddles.

Gillespie arrived in the midst of the fight, the artillery pieces in tow, but was thrown from his horse and gashed so deeply in the chest by a lance thrust that his lung was exposed. Afoot and yelling "Rally! Rally! Face them!" he fended off six other attackers, then was literally nailed to the ground by a lance. Incredibly, he managed to pull the spear free and struggle over to one of the howitzers. He fumbled with flint and steel and was able to light the *machero* (a wick in a box used to light the gun's fuse) before being knocked to the ground again, this time by a jabbing lance that split his lip and broke off a front tooth.

Kearny, too, was in the midst of the fight, slashing with his saber and trying to stay on his mount. At one point, he was surrounded by lancers, and before Lieutenant Emory and Captain Henry Turner could come to his aid, took two lance wounds, one in the upper arm, the other in the buttock. Emory, who dug in his spurs and forced his way forward, probably saving Kearny's life by slashing at the attackers with his saber, later said, "The old general [he was but fifty-two] defended himself valiantly and was as calm as a clock."

Gillespie, weak from loss of blood, now found the second of Kearny's howitzers and managed to light the *machero* with his flint and steel. After he handed it to one of the gunners and heard the flat bang of the gun, he fainted. Navy Lieutenant Edward Beale, Gillespie's second, then took over the gun and also managed to find the Sutter four-pounder and bring it into position. The gunners loaded both guns with grapeshot and fired each once toward the Californians. Pico was unwilling to put his lancers against the guns and wisely withdrew, leaving the field and dragging with *reatas* one of Kearny's howitzers—the one Gillespie had failed to fire—whose mule team had bolted into the enemy lines.

Beale's cannon shots ended the battle. It had lasted no more than thirty minutes, ten of them in the desperate hand-to-hand fighting that followed Johnston's first engagement with Pico's lancers and Moore's charge that followed.

San Pascual village was deserted, and as the Americans fell into it, exhausted, famished, and thirsty, their animals done in, the dragoon surgeon John Griffin used it as a dressing station. He had much bloody work to do. In all, three officers—captains Johnston and Moore, and Lieutenant Hammond—and nineteen men of the Army of the West had been killed in the battle and another eighteen wounded, among them Kearny, Gillespie, Lieutenant Warner of the Engineers, who suffered three wounds, and Robidoux, the guide. Only two men—Johnston and one dragoon—had been killed by musketry, the others by lance.

The casualties among the Californians was never dependably recorded. Pico claimed to have lost only eleven wounded. He also reported that he had defeated a force of two hundred Americans, killing over thirty, including the "despicable Gillespie." He made no mention of the one Californian taken prisoner by the Americans. Ironically, he said he suffered most of his casualties after retiring from the San Pascual field when he lost eleven men in an attack by a band of Luiseño Indians.

Kearny's report, written a week after the battle, was at least as exaggerated as Pico's. He wrote that he had defeated 160 Californians, that six dead were left on the field, the rest of the dead and wounded carried away by Pico's men.

During the battle, the general had brushed off Griffin's ministrations and ordered the doctor to attend to the more seriously wounded. Then, like Gillespie, he fainted from blood loss. The gashes in his forearm and buttock were deep and since he was not sure he could mount a horse, he turned over temporary command of the army to his adjutant, Captain Henry Turner, a Virginian and West Pointer who had served with Kearny since 1835.

With Kit Carson supervising the detail, the dead were buried on the night of the battle under a willow tree east of the San Pascual camp as wolves howled in the moonglow. Of the graves dug in the frost-covered ground, Emory wrote: "They were put to rest together forever, a band of brave and heroic men."

17

Mule Hill

■

1

For the moment, pursuit of Pico's horsemen was impossible and the Americans—"the most tattered and ill-fed detachment of men that ever the United States mustered under her colors," William Emory called them—spent the rest of the day of San Pascual in their sodden camp while Surgeon Griffin tended the casualties. There were no wagons for the wounded and some of the men fashioned travois by lashing buffalo robes between willow poles to be dragged behind mules. For the present, the men and animals were too fatigued to move on. The Indian village produced little food and the rations the dragoons had carried were but a memory.

As the day wore on, cold and gray-skied, fires were built and Captain Henry Turner, in temporary command of the army while the wounded Kearny was gathering his strength, wrote a letter to Stockton. He briefly described the fight, said that Pico's force was still hovering nearby, and asked for reinforcements, supplies, and carts for the wounded. Kearny approved the message, and Alexis Godey, a lieutenant with Frémont's California Battalion, was selected to make his way past Pico's outposts to deliver it to the commodore in San Diego, forty miles distant.

Before daybreak on December 7, accompanied by California Battalion volunteer Thomas Burgess and an Indian sheepherder, Godey and the others mounted the choicest mules available and set out for San Diego through the low hills south of San Pascual.

At mid-morning, Kearny decided he could mount a horse despite his painful arm and buttock wounds and resumed command of the battered force, now consolidated into a single dragoon company under Captain Turner's command. The general announced to his officers that he needed to move on toward San Diego and join whatever relief force and provisions Stockton had sent out—assuming that Godey reached the commodore safely with Turner's letter.

By early afternoon, the Americans were on trail down the San Pascual Valley. They crossed a dry streambed and after several hours, the mule-drawn travois slowing the march to a crawl, reached a deserted rancho known locally as San Bernardo. Kearny's outriders had found a few head of stray cattle on the route and some chickens were captured on the property. After a brief respite at the rancho, during which the wounded were fed and their dressings changed, the column moved on to the San Bernardo riverbed, on the lookout for forage for the animals and for any enemy patrols in the vicinity.

When they reached the foot of a low hill that overlooked the streambed, a detachment of Pico's lancers burst from the brush and, at a distance too far for accuracy, opened fire on the dragoons. In the panicky seconds following the sudden gunfire, Emory and eight men scattered the Californians, then wheeled and scrambled through the tangle of cactus and thorny brush up the hill while Kearny and his officers led the balance of the army toward the summit on the other side. A number—Emory said forty—of Pico's horsemen rode up the hill to intercept the Americans but were chased off by Emory's men, and in minutes the Army of the West occupied the position with their two fieldpieces and the travois. The brief skirmish had cost no American casualties; Kearny reported five killed and wounded among the Californians.*

The hill, while an excellent defensive position, could not long sustain a large force, but the general determined to camp his army among a battlement of boulders and cactus for the night. Holes were dug by a patrol venturing down to the San Bernardo bed and this resulted in a small seepage of muddy water. During the brief fight, the few head of cattle that had been driven in front of the dragoons ran off, and several of the mules had to be slaughtered, the meat roasted over brushwood fires and the scraps boiled to a broth in pots of muddy water. The men quickly dubbed their high ground "Mule Hill."

On the morning of the eighth, the siege of Mule Hill was interrupted briefly by the arrival of a courier, riding under a truce flag, with a message from Pico. The courier carried a bag of sugar and tea and a request for an exchange of prisoners. Kearny's men had taken one Californian under guard from the San Pascual battlefield and the general was startled to learn that Pico had captured Alexis Godey, Thomas Burgess, and the Indian guide, the men who were to deliver Captain Turner's message to Stockton in San Diego. Lieutenant Emory escorted the Californian prisoner on the ride back with Pico's man and made the exchange, returning to the hill with Burgess. This man had disappointing news: he and his partners had delivered Turner's message to Stockton and had been captured near the San Bernardo while making their way back with packsaddles of food and clothing. Burgess said that Stockton's responding message had been cached in a tree to prevent it from falling into the hands

---

*Historian H. H. Bancroft treats this figure with an "(!)."

of the enemy but that he knew its content: the commodore had said that he would be delayed in sending reinforcements until after sufficient horses were gathered, and that he had no carts or wagons for the wounded.

As the daylight dwindled, Pico, in a gentlemanly gesture, sent the captured packsaddles to Mule Hill but kept Godey and the Indian under guard and the hill patrolled by his lancers. Kearny held another war council with his officers and Gillespie's, the result of which was the writing of a second message to Stockton, to be carried to San Diego by Navy Lieutenant Edward Beale of the California Battalion. Beale asked Kearny for Kit Carson to serve as guide and at first the general resisted this. He said he needed Carson's skills in the event the reinforcements did not arrive and the army had to fight its way off the hill and make its way west. Beale suggested that the scout's presence would greatly improve the chances for the success of the mission, and Carson opined that while he considered the plan a "forlorn hope" (the old British army term for a suicide mission), especially since they had to travel afoot through Pico's cordon of lancers, he hated to see the "boy"—meaning Beale—go alone. Kearny relented, and at dusk on December 8, Beale, Carson, and an Indian volunteer from among Gillespie's men crept down the hill on their bellies to an oak grove where they split up, intending to reunite after a safe distance from the Californians.

2

Kearny waited two days on Mule Hill, during which time one of his dragoon sergeants wounded at San Pascual died. In addition, Antoine Robidoux, who had taken a lance wound in the back during the battle, suffered greatly in the night freeze on the hill and was thought to be dying. He had served Kearny as interpreter among the Indians and, with Kit Carson, had led the Army of the West on its Gila River journey to California. The general thought highly of him, as did Lieutenant Emory, who tried to comfort him by bringing him a steaming cup of coffee to help ward off the cold. Emory later recalled that Robidoux seemed to rally and in gratitude gave him a sort of cake, an emergency ration that Emory described as "made of brown flour, almost black with dirt," that he said had "for greater security, been hidden in the clothes of his Mexican servant, a man who scorned ablutions." The lieutenant ate more than half of the cake "without inspection." Then, upon breaking off another piece, he said, "The bodies of the most loathsome insects were exposed to my view. My hunger, however, overcame my fastidiousness."

On December 10, as the Americans' horses and mules were allowed to nibble on the withered grass at the foot of Mule Hill, Pico's lancers drove a small band of horses into the grazing animals, intended to stampede them. Somehow, a number of dragoons scrambled down the hill in time to thwart this plan; a warning shot was fired from the Sutter cannon, and the general's sharpshooters even managed to kill two of Pico's horses, adding the meat to their near-empty larder.

Kearny was determined that his force would fight its way off the hill the next morning and issued orders that everything that could not be carried be burned. He doubted that the three-man express party had reached San Diego and he could not continue to hold Mule Hill while awaiting reinforcements.

Beale, Carson, and the Indian apparently never regrouped after splitting up at the beginning of their mission, for the Indian—whose name, according to one of Stockton's men, was Che-muc-tah—arrived in San Diego first, at about six in the evening of December 9. Beale followed the next morning, so exhausted by the journey and affected by exposure that he collapsed and was said to be "mentally deranged" for several days thereafter. Carson, who had taken a more circuitous route to the town, arrived on the eleventh, limping on torn and bleeding feet. By then, a relief expedition had already reached Mule Hill.

An hour or two before dawn on December 11, as Kearny's men slept fitfully among the brush and rocks of their encampment, sentries spotted movement below and shouted "Who goes there?" "Americans!" came the reply as Stockton's aide-de-camp from the *Congress,* Lieutenant Andrew F. V. Gray, appeared in the moonlight at the San Bernardo riverbed leading a force of 215 sailors and marines.

The Army of the West and the relief force celebrated for hours among the hill's breastworks. Gray's men had brought coffee, tobacco, jerked beef, hardtack, and clothing; Kearny's men offered steaming mule soup and long accounts of what had happened at San Pascual and their survival in the five days since the battle. Everyone managed to sleep an hour or two before dawn, at which time Kearny intended to resume the march.

The advent of Lieutenant Gray's tars and marines ended whatever plans Andrés Pico had to prevent Kearny from entering San Diego. The Californians had received their own reinforcements since San Pascual, over a hundred men sent from Los Angeles by General José Flores, but Pico, his strength presently at least 250 "effectives," made no use of them. By the time the Army of the West, now numbering about 350 with Gray's men, returned to the San Bernardo rancho at daybreak on December 11, Pico had abandoned the field, reporting to General Flores that the "want of horses" prevented him from pursuing the Americans any further. H. H. Bancroft provided another unsatisfactory explanation for Pico's action, or lack of it, writing that "the

Californians had a pardonable aversion to charging on horseback up a hill to meet cannon-balls and rifle-bullets." In fact, it is impossible to believe that Pico ever contemplated an "attack" either before or after Gray's arrival, and least of all, up Mule Hill. He was too intelligent an officer to charge into the muzzles of the American howitzers. His "want of horses" explanation to his commander in chief was no more than a euphemism for his pardonable aversion to sacrificing his lancers to superior numbers and guns. With the addition of the hundred men from Los Angeles, he might have made it difficult for the Americans to continue to San Diego, but he could not have stopped them.

In their haste to quit the field, the Californians left their small cattle herd behind and it was captured by Kearny's men and driven ahead of the column. Camp was made at another abandoned rancho on the night of December 11, where the army was well fed for the first time in many days and fortified with confiscated wine by the time it resumed the march the next morning.

At four in the next afternoon, Kearny led the advance guard of dragoons into the nondescript adobe village of San Diego, ending a thousand-mile march that had begun at Fort Leavenworth six months less four days past.

Stockton and his officers from the *Congress* met the general on the eastern edge of the village and rode with him to the commodore's quarters, which were graciously offered to the haggard Kearny, still tortured by his wounds.

3

"It is difficult to regard the affair at San Pascual otherwise than as a stupid blunder on the part of Kearny, or to resist the conclusion that the official report of the so-called 'victory' was a deliberate misrepresentation of the facts." So wrote H. H. Bancroft forty years after the battle, when some of the participants (though not Kearny) were still living. The historian allowed that while the Americans had possession of the battlefield after Pico's lancers fled, "this fact by no means sufficed to make of defeat a victory. . . ." There was no reason for the attack on Pico at San Pascual, especially with a small force of exhausted men, Bancroft insisted, asserting that Kearny could have joined Stockton in San Diego "without risk or opposition" and proceeded as commander in chief to devise plans to recapture the lost towns and complete the conquest of California. Instead, as the historian wrote:

Coming in sight of the enemy, he orders a charge and permits a use of his men, benumbed with cold, their firearms wet and useless, their sabres rusted fast in the scabbards, mounted on stupid, worn-out mules and half-broken horses, to rush in confusion upon the California lances, presenting a temptation to slaughter which the enemy—even if they are as cowardly as their assailants believe—cannot resist.

"Individually, the Americans fought most bravely; nothing more can be said in praise," Bancroft said, but "many lives are recklessly and uselessly sacrificed. An irresponsible guerrillero chief would be disgraced by such an attack on Indians armed with bows and arrows." But Kearny was no guerrillero chief, he was a brigadier general commanding regular troops of the United States and, said the historian, "Success would have brought him no glory; defeat would have brought him disgrace."

Apart from the lack of evidence that Kearny actually ordered a charge, the assertion that there would have been no glory had the attack been a success, and the ludicrous "rusted sabre" image (no dragoon would ever let his saber rust: it was his principal weapon and he oiled and sharpened it religiously), there is much that is undeniable in

Bancroft's polemic, much that is inexplicable in Kearny's conduct.

Why did he move, with men and animals decrepit from their fatiguing march, against an enemy force about which he was utterly ignorant? He did not know the number in Pico's force, what arms they carried (he did not even know they were lancers), or what artillery might be supporting them. Of the deployment of the enemy and the ground over which it was deployed, he knew only what tidbits were told him by Lieutenant Hammond and the Indian spy when they returned from the disastrous reconnaissance patrol.

Bancroft and others made much of Kearny's dependence on the word of Kit Carson and Archibald Gillespie about the "cowardice" of the Californians, but no officer of Kearny's experience would have regarded such opinion as more than campfire badinage. He had heard of the "cowardice" of the British who had wounded him and taken him prisoner at Queenston Heights in 1812, and of the "cowardice" of the Poncas, Mandans, and Comanches he had fought as an officer of dragoons on the Western frontier.

Did Stockton's message urging him to attack Pico and "beat up the camp if the general thought it advisable" cause Kearny to act so precipitously? Did he hope to impress Stockton by some glorious result at San Pascual? This too seems unrealistic. Bancroft reluctantly states that "we may charitably suppose that he [Stockton] did not realize the condition of Kearny's force," but in truth, Kearny had no need to impress a naval officer who would become his subordinate, and in any event, he was not the kind of officer who fought to make an impression on anybody but the enemy.

His own biographer, Dwight Clarke, states that "General Kearny's tactics on the night of December 5–6 were at fault. 'Blunder' is one word applied to them with reason." But, Clarke argues, the chief blunder occurred when Hammond's troopers alarmed Pico's camp; the battle of San Pascual turned upon that happenstance and upon the overruling of Captain Benjamin Moore's argument to attack the Californians while they slept.

As would be expected, Kearny reported San Pascual as a "victory," as did Gillespie, whose lance wounds attested to his being in the forefront of the fight.

To Bancroft, San Pascual was a "criminally blundering" defeat for the Americans.

Kearny's biographer calls the fighting around San Pascual village a "check that came perilously close to defeat" and admits that the result was "a Pyrrhic victory" for the Americans.

Based on the "conduct" of the thirty-minute battle by the Americans, the negligible gains in ground and advantage, and the resulting casualties of the two sides—twenty-two dead (including three officers) and eighteen wounded among Kearny's force, perhaps a dozen wounded among Pico's—the word "victory" must have given Kearny pause in the writing. But he could say no less; nor could Andrés Pico say the truth about why he left the field to the Americans after the fight.

18

San Gabriel

∎

1

For the first several days after reaching San Diego, Kearny was content to rest and let his wounds heal. He wrote his official account of San Pascual and sent soothing letters to his wife Mary in St. Louis, assuring her of his good health and of his fondest wish: that he could be home with her and their seven children with the Christmas holidays drawing close.

He had, pro forma, presented his War Department orders to Commodore Stockton but had not discussed the issue of command. In his thinking, there was little to discuss: when he could do so, he would assume both military and civil authority as his orders demanded. For the present, he would not interfere with the scheme of things.

Neither, at first, did Robert Field Stockton give attention to the command matter. The entry of the wounded, sick, starved, and weary dragoons into San Diego had delayed his plans to pursue and force the surrender of the rebels. He had five hundred sailors, marines, and a gang of volunteers drilling daily in the scrub near his presidio headquarters; he had search parties in the countryside, and in Baja California, gathering horses, mules, and cattle; he had

Frémont, now somewhere in the Monterey vicinity, adding
recruits to his California Battalion and also searching for
horses in preparation to march south. He had a firm grip on
the helm, knew the course his ship was headed, and would
soon correct the unfortunate but "temporary interruption"
caused by the seizure of Los Angeles by the California
mob of malcontents.

Although Stockton's position had something in it of a patrician military officer's blind certitude of correctness, he
had the history of the past five months of a sort of eminent
domain at his advantage. His predecessor, Commodore
Sloat, had raised the flag at Monterey on July 7—while
Kearny was still en route from Fort Leavenworth to Bent's
Fort. Stockton had taken command of the Pacific Squadron
on July 22, a month before Kearny had reached Santa Fé.
Moreover, he had five hundred men in his command; Kearny had only about sixty "effectives" who could join the
march to Los Angeles.

The commodore did not question Kearny's orders, dated
June 3, 1846, and did not see them as superseding his own
orders from the navy secretary, dated eighteen days later.
The War Department had directed the general of dragoons
that "Should you conquer and take possession of N. Mex.
and Cal., or considerable places in either, you will establish
temporary civil governments therein. . . ." The general had
fulfilled only the first part of these tentative "should you"
orders. He had taken possession of New Mexico. But in the
matter of California, the issue now at hand, Stockton had
stolen the march five months earlier.

During the sixteen-day lull between the advent of the Army
of the West in San Diego and the beginning of the 150-mile
march to Los Angeles on December 28, both officers
seemed certain in their knowledge of whose authority was
paramount. Even so, as they prepared to march, each man

made certain gentlemanly gestures. Stockton suggested that the general take command of the combined army and offered himself as aide-de-camp; Kearny declined, said the commodore should lead the force with himself, Kearny, as aide-de-camp. Stockton repeated his offer before the march began, and again Kearny declined.

H. H. Bancroft's explanation for Kearny's strange reluctance to take the command he assumed belonged to him by his seniority of rank and War Department order is that he felt he owed Stockton a favor. After the disaster of San Pascual, which Bancroft said "reflected no credit on his ability as an officer," he had entered San Diego under "peculiar circumstances, wounded, like so many of his men, deprived of his best officers who had been killed, his whole command perhaps saved from destruction by the commodore's aid." The delicacy of Kearny's position and the fact that Stockton was actively engaged in organizing an expedition against the enemy, the historian wrote, "prompted the general not only to abstain from demanding the chief command, but to decline it when proffered by Stockton."

The breech in the amenities opened on December 22 after Stockton described his plans to Kearny: he would advance to the coastal town of San Luís Rey, forty miles north of San Diego, and there determine the whereabouts of Colonel Frémont and the deployment of the enemy. Failing to join with Frémont, he said, might dictate a course of falling back to San Diego.

Kearny's soldierly brain could see no benefit in such a tentative movement, especially one that might leave Frémont and his California Battalion, the strength and location of which were unknown, in limbo. He said as much to Stockton in a letter counseling a quick march to Los Angeles via San Luís Rey and stating, "I shall be happy to . . . give you any aid either of head or hand of which I may be capable."

Stockton's reaction to this sensible suggestion was inex-

plicably harsh and filled with demonstrably false suggestions. The commodore asserted that the Californians might
be fielding a more numerous army than his and Kearny's
combined force of six hundred men, and that this phantom
army "might get in my rear and cut off my communication
with San Diego," and even put his ships off the California
shore at hazard.

This exchange of ideas on the conduct of the Los Angeles campaign seems to have tipped the scale for Kearny. A
few days before the march, he met with Stockton and said
that in the national interest in completing the annexation of
California, he needed to command the army.

In a later report to the War Department, he said that the
command "was reluctantly granted to me by Commodore
Stockton on my urgent advice that he should not leave Colonel Frémont unsupported to fight a battle on which the fate
of California might for a long time depend."

Stockton's view differed. In his subsequent testimony in
Washington, he said that Kearny "gave me to understand he
would like to command and after a conversation I agreed to
appoint him . . . but I retained my own position as commander in chief."

Kearny seemed to admit that while he had the immediate
command, Stockton's authority was preeminent when he
wrote that "during our march, his authority and command,
though it did not extend over me, or over troops which he
had himself given me, extended far beyond where we were
moving. It extended to the volunteers stationed at Nueva Helvetia, Sonoma, Monterey and I think some few in San Francisco and over the California Battalion of mounted riflemen
under Colonel Frémont's command which I had not then
claimed."

The Stockton-Kearny army thus set out for Los Angeles
on December 29, 1846, with the band from the *Congress*
leading the force of forty-four officers, fifty-seven First

Dragoons under Captain Henry Turner, and five hundred
sailors, marines, and volunteer riflemen, the latter, the only
men on horseback, commanded by Captain Archibald
Gillespie. The column was armed with muskets, carbines,
boarding axes, and six artillery pieces, followed by ten oxcarts of supplies, the bullocks so feeble that the men had to
help drag the fieldpieces and stores wagons. They moved
slowly, covering only thirty miles in the first three days on
the route Kearny had taken into San Diego, and on New
Year's Eve, they camped at the San Bernardo rancho.

"Our men were badly clothed, and their shoes generally
made by themselves out of canvas," Stockton wrote; yet, as
he perhaps thought befitted a commander in chief, he slept
in a lavish tent suite complete with night tables and a bed
with a mattress, while Kearny slept on the ground wrapped
in a bearskin.

2

At about the time Kearny and his battered veterans of
San Pascual first reached San Diego, Lieutenant Colonel Frémont had brought his California Battalion down the
boggy trails from Monterey to San Luís Obispo. His call for
volunteers had been answered and his battalion had grown
to a demi-regiment made up of his old exploring company,
immigrants newly arrived at New Helvetia, a company of
Walla Wallas and a miscellany of California Indians, some
sailors and marines detached from warship duty in San
Francisco Bay, and the Bear Flaggers of the Sonoma garrison under Captain John Grigsby. He had 428 men in buckskins and moccasins and all manner of cobbled-together
outfits, three fieldpieces, ammunition and stores wagons, and
an enormous herd of nearly two thousand horses and mules,
plus a small collection of cattle. All, men and animals, had
been gathered and on the march in the space of two months.

It had taken nearly a month for his cumbersome party, moving in rain squalls along eroded mud paths, to reach San Luís Obispo, and when Frémont set up his camp in the mountain foothills above the mission village on the night of December 14, he had no idea what resistance the Californians might throw against him. He was operating in a vacuum three hundred miles from San Diego: he did not know of Kearny's fight at San Pascual, nor of the whereabouts of Stockton and his men, who were presumably coming north toward Los Angeles.

The San Luís Obispo Mission was surrounded and occupied quickly with no resistance. Frémont's men captured several local influentials, including José de Jesús Pico, a cousin of Andrés and Pío Pico, and thirty-five of his rebels who had fought Frémont's men at La Natividad in October. José Pico had surrendered to the Americans months before and had been granted "parole"—freedom under the promise that he would not bear arms or engage in any insurgent activities. However, a search of his quarters turned up letters and documents showing that he was in regular contact with General Flores, commander of the Californians. Amazingly, Frémont, supposed to be on the march toward the critical recapture of Los Angeles, decided to hold a court-martial to punish the captured officer for violating his parole. This was done on December 16 and Pico was sentenced to death by firing squad the next morning.

He was rescued minutes before he was to stand blindfolded before his executioners. After paying a visit to the condemned man, Frémont granted an audience to Pico's wife, a woman described by those who knew her as "striking." She was dressed in black and brought her children and knelt before the colonel to beg for her husband's life. Frémont raised her to her feet and promised he would consider her entreaties. He had the prisoner brought to him, later describing him as "calm and brave . . . a handsome man, within a few years of forty, with black eyes and black hair," and told him his life had been spared and for this, he should thank Señora Pico.

In his memoirs, Frémont said that Pico made the sign of the cross and said, "I was to die—I had lost the life God gave me—you have given me another life. I devote the new life to you."

In truth, Frémont may have intended sparing Pico's life all along; several of the California Battalion officers had come forward with the suggestion. It turned out to be a wise decision, as was the freeing of the other captives taken in the mission town. Pico volunteered to accompany the expedition to Los Angeles, and those freed from captivity—reluctant and unpaid volunteers to begin with—passed the word that the Americans had overwhelming numbers and it was futile to resist them.

The march was resumed on December 17 with Santa Barbara, a hundred miles south of San Luís Obispo, the next significant town en route to Los Angeles. Frémont led his battalion inland toward the western slopes of the Santa Ynez Mountains, traveling over country until recently stricken by drought. The new rains had produced only sparse grass, and the horses and pack train grew jaded and weak as the days wore on, each day ending with little more than fifteen miles of progress for the weary force.

On Christmas Eve, the Americans crossed San Marcos Pass, a few miles northwest of Santa Barbara, in a freezing mountain rainstorm. The trail, which virtually disappeared in the flash floods, caused a hundred pack animals to loose their footing and dump their packsaddles and baggage "like the trail of a defeated army," as Frémont put it. The battalion camped in the mud, ate cold rations since cook fires were impossible, crossed ravines choked with uprooted trees and dense brush, watched helplessly as mules and horses buried themselves in mud, and were hurtled into the rocks by winds so strong they could snatch a man off his feet. They struggled into the town in the afternoon of

December 27 so trail-worn, hungry, and fatigued that it took a week for the men and animals to recover sufficiently to resume the march.

Fortunately for Frémont and his prostrate army, Santa Barbara, its shops closed and streets deserted, offered no resistance and no prisoners to worry about, and the flag was raised in the central plaza with no onlookers. The Americans themselves were too tired to cheer.

The six-hundred-man Stockton-Kearny force approached the vineyards of San Luís Rey Mission on January 4, 1847, and there the commodore exercised his authority as commander in chief. A party of three men arrived in the American camp under a truce flag, bringing a message dated January 1 from now-Governor José Flores, who proposed a suspension of hostilities. Rumors were abroad that Mexico and the United States were negotiating a peace settlement, Flores wrote, and further bloodshed should be avoided until these reports were verified.

Stockton, without consulting Kearny, angrily rejected the proposal, ridiculing Flores' claim to be governor of California and declaring to the couriers that the Mexican officer had broken parole and would be executed if captured.

As the combined army moved on from San Luís Rey to San Juan Capistrano, Stockton received a report that Frémont and his men had reached Santa Barbara. Upon reading this, the commodore sent Captain George Hamley, master of the whaler *Stonington,* to deliver a message to the colonel warning him of the near presence of the Californians, and of their belligerence after defeating Gillespie and Mervine—and Kearny at San Pascual. Hamley rode back to San Diego, then took passage upcoast on a trader to intercept Frémont.

By the time he reached the explorer, the last battle in the conquest of California had ended.

3

From his headquarters at San Fernando, north of Los Angeles, Governor-General José Flores had reached his wit's end. He had hoped to harass the Americans with hit-and-run guerrilla tactics, buying time until Mexico either sent him reinforcements—which he knew was little more than a dream—or signed a peace with the United States. He had close to five hundred men but they were unpaid, ill-equipped, and disgruntled. The American Frémont and his buckskinned battalion were heading south out of Santa Barbara, and the American Stockton, who had rejected the New Year's Day cease-fire proposal, was on the march north out of San Diego. The surrender of Gillespie and his garrison in Los Angeles three months past and the subsequent defeat of the Americans at San Pascual had inspired the Californians with renewed patriotic zeal. But the euphoria had been short-lived: the Americans were on the march from the north and south, with larger numbers than ever before, and they would converge on Los Angeles.

During the first days of the new year, Flores expected it would be Frémont he would first meet in battle. This expectation changed after his scouts brought news of Stockton's rapid advance, and on January 7, the Californian moved his force into camp on a steep bluff overlooking a ford of the San Gabriel River, twelve miles northeast of Los Angeles. It was an advantageous place amid willows and mustard brush on the American line of march, perhaps a perfect place for an ambush.

Stockton's scouts located Flores' potential ambuscade during the night and reported the enemy position. The commodore ordered a crossing of the river on a lower ford than originally planned and halted his force about a quarter-mile from the river at around two in the afternoon of the eighth, the anniversary of Andrew Jackson's 1815 victory at New Orleans.

The Californians watched the American advance and Flores stationed sharpshooters, Andrés Pico's lancers and two other squadrons of horsemen, all strung out along the fifty-foot-high-bluff four hundred yards west of the stream. He placed a large force of horsemen and his two nine-pounder cannons at the crossing ford.

Upon reaching the San Gabriel bank, Stockton's skirmishers exchanged rifle fire with the Californians, and by the time the crossing began in earnest, Flores' cannons were pelting the water with grape and round shot. The river, about a hundred yards wide and knee-deep, had a quicksand bed that slowed the crossing and gave the Californians fish-in-a-barrel targets from their positions on the bluff. But Flores' powder was of poor quality and there were few casualties.

As the main force of Americans reached the riverbank, Kearny ordered two nine-pounders brought forward to counter the Californian artillery, but Stockton, who had no experience in land fighting, countermanded the order and insisted that the guns not be unlimbered until after they had crossed the river. The cannons were pulled by flailing mule teams and manhandled with guy ropes across the spongy streambed under a hail of rifle and cannon fire. At one point, seeing one of the nine-pounders stalled and sinking, Stockton rode to it, grabbed a rope, and shouted at the desperate gunners, "Quicksand be damned, come on, boys!"

Incredibly, they managed to get the guns over and unlimbered as Stockton, who did have experience in laying guns at sea, took command of the pieces, yelling, "Steady, boys, don't waste a shot!" Meantime, his main force splashed across the San Gabriel, finding shelter under what Lieutenant William Emory called "a natural banquette, breast-high" while being deployed. Kearny directed the deployment, sending his dragoons, Gillespie's volunteers, and the tars from Stockton's ships up and downstream as the balance of the force continued the crossing under the galling musket fire from the bluff. The carts of the baggage train foundered in the sand and the terrified mules and horses were belabored to shore by the ropes and whips of the teamsters and the flat blades of dragoon sabers.

Stockton was too busy to notice the chaos in the stream. He took command of one of the nine-pounders, laid it so accurately toward Flores' guns on the bluff that the first shot smashed the carriage of one of the enemy cannons to splinters, rendering the piece useless.

Kearny now had most of his men deployed to his satisfaction and stood, big dragoon pistol in each hand, shouting to Stockton, "I am now ready for the charge!" The commodore nodded and yelled to the sailors and marines in front of him, "Forward, my Jacks! Charge!" They scrambled up the hill, bayonets fixed and shouting "New Orleans!" as Stockton's gun crews flogged their mule teams up at the same time.

Near the top of the bluff, Kearny's party swerved to the right, and the left wing of the Californians fell back after firing their weapons, abandoning their disabled cannon. But some of Flores' mounted troops circled the Kearny column as if to attack its flank and rear guard, and the general quickly ordered his men into a square formation. Faced with the hedgerow of bayonets, the Californians retreated out of range.

On Kearny's left, Stockton met a feeble charge by Flores' horsemen, but as the commodore later wrote, "finding so warm a reception . . . they changed their purpose and retired, when a discharge of artillery told upon their ranks."

By the time the Americans reached the top of the bluff, the enemy had disappeared, only the dust raised by their rear-guard horsemen marking their retreat.

The battle at the San Gabriel, from the first skirmisher's shots through the contested river crossing and the climbing of the heights, had lasted less than two hours. Two American sailors had been killed, eight men were wounded. The Californian casualties were never authenticated. H. H. Bancroft asserts that they were "probably the same in killed. . . . Each party as usual greatly overrated the enemy's loss."

With the animals too spent in the day's work to give chase, Stockton and Kearny made camp on the bluff. On the night of January 8, Flores' campfires could be seen flickering in the distant hills athwart the road to Los Angeles and a few desultory shots were exchanged in the darkness. In the morning, as Stockton ordered the march to continue, the Californians had again vanished.

Before leaving the bluffs on the morning of January 9, a courier rode into the American camp under a white truce flag, bringing news that Frémont and his men were now in San Fernando, about twenty-five miles north of Los Angeles. Stockton sent a message back urging the colonel to bring the force into the pueblo quickly and join his command. Presumably he told Frémont of the fight on the San Gabriel and that he and Kearny would enter Los Angeles later in the day.

The Americans detoured off the main road at noon after reports reached Stockton that Flores had regrouped what remained of his force—many of his men had deserted—and was drawn up in a horseshoe-shaped formation on an open plain on a mesa about six miles from the San Gabriel. Kearny again placed his men in a hollow square, the pack animals and provision and baggage carts in the center, and ordered that there would be no stragglers or breaking of ranks, that every man needed to keep his post and pace to thwart any cavalry charge by the enemy.

As Stockton's naval bandsmen played "Hail, Columbia" and the infantry square, dragoons, and skirmishers advanced toward the mouth of Flores' horseshoe, the Californian cannons opened fire and sent round shot bouncing harmlessly toward the American flanks. Stockton halted his army, brought his own fieldpieces forward and answered the fire. The exchange lasted for a quarter-hour before Flores ordered his lancers to charge the front of the enemy square—a fool-hardy decision that, as contemporary militarists like to say, "defied all the rules of war."

The lancers, ten horsemen wide and three rows deep, thun-dered toward the square, their long, needle-tipped lances tucked under their armpits. Kearny held his two front ranks of dragoons and marines in check, shouting "Steady! Pick your men, boys!" Then, when the horsemen approached to within a hundred paces, he roared "Fire!" The rifles in the first rank cracked and produced a plume of smoke; instantly Kearny ordered "Front rank, kneel! Rear rank, fire!" The front rank fell to its knees, each man's bayonet at the ready to meet any horseman attempting to break the square, as the second rank rose, took aim, and fired. The volleys staggered the careening lancers; horses and men tumbled to the ground, upsetting oth-ers behind, and by the time the musket smoke cleared, the Californians and several riderless horses were fleeing back toward Flores' main force.

Kearny ordered the square forward, and as it lumbered across the mesa, the Californians again charged, this time on the left and right flanks simultaneously. Kearny ordered "Steady! Keep your ranks! Give 'em Hell!" and again the first two ranks on each of the square's sides volley-fired against the enemy horsemen, broke their order, and sent them reeling. A smaller attempt at the rear of the square was similarly repulsed while Stockton, expertly directing his cannoneers, sent such a shower of grapeshot after the retreat-ing horsemen that Flores retired his entire force into the low hills surrounding the mesa.

For such a furious little engagement, the two-and-a-half-hour "Battle of the Mesa" produced few casualties. Among the Americans, there were only five wounded men (Gillespie was one of them, suffering a slight contusion from a spent bullet); Flores had at least one man killed and between twenty and forty wounded.

On the evening of January 9, Stockton and Kearny took their men across the Los Angeles River and set up camp three miles below the town.

19

. . . .

Cahuenga

■

1

O*n the morning* of January 10, three men approached the Stockton-Kearny camp on the Los Angeles River, the delegation sent as representatives of the town to say that no resistance would be made toward the Americans. Stockton promised that if this were true, there would be no reprisals and the peaceable citizenry would be protected.

At noon that day, the two officers led their men into the pueblo and dispersed them through all its principal streets and byways, converging on the central plaza to the drumbeat and martial airs of the navy band. Hundreds of Angelinos lined the streets and overlooking hills to watch the pageant, and there were some touchy moments along the route when, as Stockton wrote, his men were "slightly molested by a few drunken fellows who remained about the town." Several shots had to be fired to scatter the drunks, and two artillery pieces were hauled to the crest of a hill as a warning, but Gillespie was able to raise the flag over his old headquarters, abandoned four months earlier, without incident.

With sentries posted and horsemen patrolling the fringes of the village to watch for any sign of Flores' men, Stockton wrote his account of the San Gabriel "campaign" for the War Department. He extended a minimum of credit to Kearny and made no mention of the general's command of the square that had fended off the charges by the Californian lancers. The commodore said he had been "aided by General Stephen W. Kearny with a detachment of sixty men on foot from the First Regiment of U.S. Dragoons and by Captain A. H. Gillespie with sixty mounted riflemen." Subsequently, at a court-martial proceeding in Washington, he narrowed the credit even further, making certain that the government realized that he, Stockton, "was wholly and solely responsible for the success of the expedition" and that the campaign had merely been "sustained" by the "gallant and good conduct of General Kearny and all the officers and men under his command."

The commodore's pronouncements to his men for their "brilliant victories" and "steady courage," his proclamations to the Angelinos assuring them of peace and protection, and his reports to Washington, were the mortar holding together the shaky framework of his command. He needed to make sure there would be no question about who had conquered California and who, now that it had been accomplished, was in control.

At first seemingly oblivious to Stockton's maneuvering, Kearny went about his business. He was comfortable with the knowledge that as the senior officer in the field, armed with what he fancied as explicit War Department orders, he was the military commander in chief in California and would soon assume control of its governance. More immediately, he needed to bring Frémont in. Just before the San Gabriel fight, Stockton had received a courier's message saying that the California Battalion had reached San Fernando, a short distance northwest of the pueblo. If Kearny was nettled by the lieutenant colonel's failure to join his and

Stockton's force earlier, he made no hint of it in the message he dispatched to Frémont on the afternoon of January 10: "We are in possession of this place, with a force of marines and sailors, having marched into it this morning. Join us as soon as you can, or let me know if you want us to march to your assistance; avoid charging the enemy; their force does not exceed 400, perhaps not more than 300. Please acknowledge receipt of this, and dispatch the bearer at once."

These were orders from the superior officer. There could be no question of who was in command.

On January 12, with no response from San Fernando, Kearny wrote another note, and on January 13, two more, asking the battalion's whereabouts, and sent a note to Stockton expressing the fear that Frémont, if ignorant of the recapture of Los Angeles, might "capitulate and retire to the north." He offered to take a force out to find the missing battalion but this proved unnecessary when an express rider from Frémont arrived with startling news.

2

The fight at the Mesa had ended and the Americans were within a day of recapturing Los Angeles when George Hamley, master of the whaler *Stonington,* found Frémont a few miles east of San Fernando. He handed over Stockton's six-day-old message warning of the Californians' growing belligerence and urging caution in moving the battalion south.

The explorer had been cautious from the moment he had led his men out of Monterey in mid-December. He did not underestimate the threat posed by Flores' army after the fall of San Diego. He had the fight at La Natividad in mind and had learned of Kearny's battle at San Pascual. He had no idea of the Californian strength, armament, or whereabouts. His

men were volunteers, untrained, undisciplined, and unpredictable. He was an officer of topographical engineers and
had no experience in warfare, but he was no fool and saw
his duty as bringing his men and animals safely to the con-
joining with Stockton's army. The commodore's letter had
confirmed the wisdom of his caution: "If there is one single
chance for you," Stockton had written, "you had better not
fight the rebels until I get up to aid you, or you can join me
on the road to the pueblo [Los Angeles]."

More messages arrived. On January 11, as the battalion
reached the summit of San Fernando Pass, two friendly Californios brought the news to Frémont of the fights at the
San Gabriel and the Mesa and of the American reoccupation of Los Angeles. Another courier brought the "join us as
soon as you can" note from General Kearny, dated January
10, urging the colonel to "avoid charging the enemy" and
asking if he needed assistance in continuing on to the pueblo.
A day later, more Kearny notes arrived, ordering Frémont
to report to him at his headquarters and asking for an acknowledgment of the order and a time when he would reach
Los Angeles. The notes made no mention of Stockton, a fact
that might have given Frémont pause.

The explorer put the notes aside; he would answer soon,
but for the present he was concentrating on a peace negotiation. José de Jesús Pico, who had been captured at San Luís
Obispo, was a key figure in the effort. He had faced a firing
squad for breaking his parole, his life had been spared by
Frémont, and he now regarded the American officer not only
as his savior, but as his friend. H. H. Bancroft said of Pico:
"He was a man of some influence, came to men who had no
fixed plans, dwelt with enthusiasm on the treatment he had
received, and without much difficulty persuaded his countrymen that they had nothing to lose and perhaps much to
gain by negotiating with Frémont instead of Stockton."

On January 11, Pico completed his talks with General
Flores and Manuel Castro at their camps at San Pascual and

a rancho nearby called Los Verdugos. By the end of the day, Flores turned over command of the Californians to Andrés Pico and, with his escort, rode toward Sonora. The next morning, as Frémont issued a proclamation at the San Fernando mission calling for a meeting to end all hostilities, Don José brought two of Andrés Pico's officers to Frémont's headquarters to "treat for peace."

The treaty and armistice were written and signed on January 12 at a deserted rancho on the north end of Cahuenga Pass,* between San Fernando and the northern outskirts of Pueblo de los Ángeles.

Antonio María Osio, the Monterey influential who apparently received a detailed description of the meeting at Cahuenga Pass, said of it: "When the two *jefes* encountered each other . . . Señor Frémont was recognized for his military expertise, and he correctly esteemed the courage of his opponents. Because he also was a shrewd man, he was convinced that these courageous Mexicans would be of use to the territory after it became a state . . . . With this in mind, Frémont proposed terms for a surrender to Señor Pico."

The document, its seven articles written by Theodore Talbot in both English and Spanish, was signed by Frémont and Andrés Pico. It forgave all past hostilities and allowed all Californian officers and volunteers to return home on parole after surrendering their arms and promising not to resume hostilities. It absolved them of taking an oath of allegiance until after a treaty between the United States and Mexico came into effect and guaranteed them the protection and equal rights of all American citizens. And it permitted any person who wished it the right to leave the territory.

The terms were exceedingly liberal and Frémont knew they might be questioned. But he did not seem to entertain the

---

The site is commemorated by a historical marker on Lankershim Boulevard, in North Hollywood.

critical question: why make a treaty at all? He was being bombarded with increasingly petulant messages from Kearny and Stockton urging him to proceed to Los Angeles; he knew that both men were of superior rank, were a half-day distant, and either one more appropriate, even more "legal," for treaty-making than he.

H. H. Bancroft's answer to this question bore the pervasive cynicism that typified his treatment of the man he called a "filibustero chieftain": "Frémont's motive was simply a desire to make himself prominent and to acquire popularity among the Californians, over whom he expected to rule as governor. It was better to adopt conciliatory methods late than never."

The generosity of the treaty's terms was to Frémont entirely defensible. Exacting punishment—perhaps even execution—for the Californian officers and draconian measures for the populace might have resulted in a rising similar to that which had ousted Gillespie's garrison from San Diego. Such an approach might have created guerrilla bands of angry citizens who would strike and run and prolong the fighting for months. The battles had been fought, Los Angeles was retaken, all the principal towns and ports were in American hands, the Californians had surrendered, their commanding general had escaped to Sonora, their best field commander was now cooperating in the armistice. Frémont expected the governorship of the new territory of California. What was to be gained by alienating the people he would govern?

In addition, he and his men had missed all the fighting. There was little glory left. Pico had turned over to him the howitzer captured from Kearny's dragoons at San Pascual and at least he could lead his battalion into Los Angeles with the cannon and with a paper that he later said "put an end to the war and to the feelings of war." The Cahuenga treaty, he said, "tranquilized the country, and gave safety to every American from the day of its conclusion."

In a dispatch to Stockton and Kearny, he wrote of the surrender of Pico and his men, of the recovered San Pascual gun, and of his imminent arrival in Los Angeles. He entrusted the letter and a copy of the treaty to Lieutenant William H. "Owl" Russell of the California Battalion to deliver to the American headquarters.

3

Since his arrival in Los Angeles, Stockton had received details on the suppression of a small rising in the north that bore some similarity to what had occurred to Captain Gillespie's garrison in San Diego. On December 8 past, at the time Stockton was learning of the San Pascual fight, a small band of Californians, reacting to what they considered unnecessarily harsh treatment by the Americans, had seized the acting *alcalde* of Yerba Buena, a Lieutenant Washington A. Bartlett. The rebels announced that they wished to trade this captive for another officer, Captain Charles Weber, whose behavior was said to be particularly oppressive and insulting. In late December, Marine Captain Ward Marston had set out with a party of marines and sailors for Santa Clara, where the rebels were camped. On January 2, Marston found a force of about 120 Californios under Francisco Sánchez, the former military commander at Yerba Buena. The skirmish that ensued cost the Californios four dead and five wounded, the Americans, two wounded. The next morning, Sánchez agreed to a cease-fire and on January 6, to an unconditional surrender.

Now, with the news of Pico's surrender at Cahuenga, the war was certainly over.

But the treaty pleased neither commander. Who was Frémont to write and sign such a document? Stockton was furious over the liberal terms of the surrender and shared

Kearny's concern that a mere lieutenant colonel of volunteers would assume such a responsibility when his superior officers were within hailing distance.

Owl Russell was witness to the reactions of the commanders and, although leaving no precise record of it, must have been confused at what he heard, especially after Stockton, when finished ranting over the paper, told Russell he intended naming Frémont governor. The signals became further mixed in Kearny's headquarters, where Russell, who had known the general in Missouri, spent the night of January 13. Kearny seemed less concerned about the paper than Stockton did. True, the treaty had been written in haste by one not authorized to negotiate a peace, but the terms of it were in accord with what Washington wanted. Kearny agreed with Stockton that Frémont should be given the governorship.

The commodore, despite strong reservations over the treaty, gave it reluctant approval when he wrote to Navy Secretary Bancroft on January 15, "Not being able to negotiate with me, and having lost the battles of the 8th and 9th, the Californians met Colonel Frémont on the 12th instant on his way here, who, not knowing what had occurred, entered into the capitulation with them, which I now send to you; and although I refused to do it myself, still I have thought it best to approve it."

The California Battalion entered Los Angeles in a rainstorm on the afternoon of January 14, 1847. Riding with his beloved, war-painted Delaware bodyguard in front of his four hundred men, pack animals, baggage train, and mule teams pulling six artillery pieces through the muddy streets, Frémont sat his horse straight as a lath. He was tanned and bearded, wore an open-collared, blue-flannel shirt, deerskin hunting jacket, blue-canvas trousers, moccasins, a buccaneer's bandanna on his head, covered by a slouchy, wide-brimmed hat. The men who followed him looked more like a huge fur brigade riding to a mountain rendezvous than an authorized military force. They were a sunburned, trail-ragged, mud-caked, grizzle-bearded lot—farmers, frontiersmen, hunters, trappers, wanderers, sailors—in their favored buckskins and sun-faded shirts and big floppy hats, carrying huge knives, sidearms, and all manner of carbines, musketoons, and long rifles.

Owl Russell rode out five miles from the pueblo and gave his colonel the news of the reactions to the treaty. Russell reported that he thought Kearny more amenable to it than Stockton, and he probably also gave Frémont his impressions of the rivalry between Kearny and Stockton and of the commodore's claiming credit for the battles of San Gabriel and the Mesa and for having rescued Kearny at San Pascual.

Frémont thus had a sense of the political problems rising in Los Angeles, but he had no idea of their gravity until he found himself enmeshed in them.

Since he had no doubt of which officer was the superior in California, he paid a visit first to Stockton. This was the man who had commissioned him in the navy (despite the fact that Frémont had no right to accept the commission since he was already an officer of the army's Topographical Corps and had not resigned), the man who had rescued Kearny at San Pascual, the man Russell said had offered to turn over to Kearny command of American military forces in California and had been refused.

The meeting was brief and polite. Stockton was not comfortable with the treaty and was prepared to write an additional article or two before sanctioning it, but he expressed no displeasure with his lieutenant colonel's actions.

The meeting with Kearny was similarly cordial. The two had not met since May, 1843, when, at Jefferson Barracks in St. Louis, Colonel Kearny, then in charge of the army's Third Military Department, had granted Frémont's request to be issued a brass fieldpiece, powder, and shot to take with him on his expedition to Oregon. That gun had been abandoned,

but now the son-in-law of his friend Tom Benton of Missouri
was "returning" another, the one lost at San Pascual. The
general did not need to be reminded of this. He must also
have disliked Frémont's unmilitary appearance and im-
proper tendency to talk as if he alone had won the peace in
California.

But Kearny allowed the man some latitude. He did not
view Frémont as a military man—a topographical engineer
was to a general of dragoons only nominally "army" to begin with, and the officer was young, ambitious, with a splendid wife and influential in-laws, and had accomplished
much in his explorations. Soon after their initial meeting,
Kearny wrote Senator Benton that Frémont had arrived in
Los Angeles, fit and well. He asked, "Will you please in my
name congratulate Mrs. Frémont upon the honor and credit
gained by the Colonel and with my best wishes for her and
all your family."

It was a kind thing to do and demonstrated Kearny's confidence that Frémont would serve well under his command.

20

Last Battle

■

1

Owl Russell had warned Frémont that there were two camps in Los Angeles and a wide gulf between them, that big trouble was brewing between Commodore Stockton and the army's senior officer in California, Brigadier General Kearny. Owl had earned his nickname—he saw things and heard things—and was an utterly dependable and loyal Frémonter. The explorer believed what Russell said but when he marched into the village in mid-January, 1847, he naively thought that he stood outside and aloof from the problems of the two senior officers.

He had the Cahuenga treaty in his saddlebag, had confidence that the commanders would work out their differences and that he, a mere lieutenant colonel, had no role in their conflict. He had been in California for thirteen months and under Stockton's command for six of them. Kearny had a mere six weeks in the country and it was common knowledge that he had bungled one battle, had to be rescued by the commodore's men under Archibald Gillespie, and had turned over land operations to Stockton at San Gabriel and the Mesa.

To Frémont, the chain of command was not disputable:

Stockton had led in the conquest of California, had recovered Los Angeles, and remained in command now.

But, trapped between the colliding forces, he learned that nothing was so simple: his arrival in Los Angeles with his four-hundred-man California Battalion served as a long-awaited signal to Kearny to assert his command over all American forces and all civil governance in California.

The source of difficulty between the two senior officers was as old as war: ambiguous orders from a government far removed from the battlefield, orders written inexplicitly because of the time that would lapse between the issuance and receipt of them, orders rendered moot and unworkable by the time they reached their destination.

Kearny had marched to California with orders from President Polk dated June 3, 1846—six months before he arrived there—to subdue the country and take control of it, and these orders contained the ruinous ". . . should you conquer" equivocation.

Stockton's orders from the Navy Department were similar and dated nineteen days after Kearny's orders. But the commodore had been the senior officer *in situ* during most of the actual conquest and he maintained that he had already conquered California before Kearny arrived on the scene and that therefore the general's orders were nullified. Moreover, he said, Kearny did not have a sufficient force to win any battle and had had to be supplemented by the navy's sailors and marines and Frémont's volunteers. In Washington, he would later say, with a certain vagueness of his own, "My right to establish the civil government was incident to the conquest, and I formed the government under the law of nations."

Frémont saw all this as irrefutable, and of his partnership with the commodore, H. H. Bancroft said, "Notwithstanding the blunders and braggadocio and filibusterism of Frémont and Stockton, really the greatest obstacles to the conquest, these officers might plausibly claim to be conquerors. . . ."

The real obstacle, which Stockton did not mention but that did the greatest injury to his position in the argument, was the September 23 revolt in Los Angeles.

Had there been no revolt, President Polk and his entire government would have accepted Stockton's precedence without question. But the Los Angeles rising and Gillespie's surrender tainted and clouded the conquest thereafter. Stockton's attitude that California had been won by the time Kearny reached Warner's Ranch on December 3, 1846, overlooked the fact that with the exception of San Diego, all of southern California had to be re-won in three battles, in all of which Kearny played a role and Frémont none.

Bancroft said of Stockton-as-conqueror: "He had shown a creditable degree of energy and skill in overcoming obstacles for the most part of his own creation, in putting down a revolt that but for his own folly would have had no existence. No more can be honestly said in praise of the commodore's acts and policy in California." The historian gave Kearny credit for realizing he was in no position to supersede the commodore upon entering San Diego, and Kearny later said that he had acquiesced to Stockton's role as commander out of "respect for his [Stockton's] situation," but that he fully intended to supersede this junior officer "as soon as my command was increased."

Ironically, a month before Kearny entered California, clarifying orders had been dispatched west by the army's senior general, Winfield Scott, soon to command the Vera Cruz expedition against Mexico. Scott wrote to Kearny on November 3, 1846: "After occupying with our forces all necessary points in Upper California, and establishing a temporary civil government therein, as well as assuring yourself of its internal tranquillity . . . you may charge Col. Mason . . . or the land officer next in rank to your own, with your several duties, and return yourself to St. Louis."

He also ordered that Frémont's volunteers be mustered into the regular army service retrospective to May 13.

These orders were entrusted to Colonel Richard Mason of the First Dragoons, to be carried over the Isthmus of Panama and to California by warship.

Unfortunately, the orders did not arrive before the storm broke.

2

On January 14, Stockton, ready to sail south to Mazatlán and find some action along the Mexican coast, and still nettled over the unauthorized treaty his subordinate had written, fulfilled a promise by tendering to Frémont the appointment as governor of California. In his proclamation, the commodore took care to permit no question of his authority to make such an appointment; indeed, he seemed to have written it expressly for the eyes of his bête noire, Kearny.

> Having, by authority of the President and Congress of the United States of North America, and by right of conquest, taken possession of that portion of territory heretofore know as upper California; and having declared the same to be territory of the United States, under the name of the territory of California; and having established laws for the government of the said territory, I, Robert F. Stockton, governor and commander-in-chief of the same, do, in virtue of the authority in me vested, and in obedience to the aforementioned laws, appoint J. C. Frémont, esq., governor and commander-in-chief of the territory of California, until the President of the United States shall otherwise direct.

Kearny, as Stockton must have expected, reacted with barely contained fury and in a letter written on January

16, questioned Stockton's authority, asserting that such appointments were his, Kearny's, specific domain and that if the commodore had such authority from the President, or from "any other channel of the president's," he asked to see "certified copies" of the documents. "If you do not have such authority," the general wrote, "I then demand that you cease all further proceedings relating to the formation of a civil government for this territory, as I cannot recognize in you any right in assuming to perform the duties confided to me by the president."

The Frémont appointment, the ensuing Kearny letter, and Stockton's bitter response occurred with orchestrated timing. The commodore answered the general with alacrity and hid a round shot in his return note. He repeated his assertion that California had been conquered before Kearny entered it and that he had communicated to the President the details of the civil government he had formed before Kearny's arrival. Then he appended acidly: "I will only add that I cannot do anything, nor desist from doing anything, or alter anything on your demand; which I will submit to the president and ask for your recall. In the meantime you will consider yourself suspended from the command of the United States forces in this place."

Frémont was caught in the no-man's-land of this letter shrapnel from the outset. Stockton had appointed him governor on January 14; two days later, Kearny had written his objection to the commodore and the commodore had returned his blistering response; now, on January 17, Kearny summoned Frémont to his headquarters in an adobe building near the town plaza: "Dear Colonel, I wish to see you on business," the note said.

The explorer knew the subject of this meeting. Kearny, on the day he had voiced his objection to Stockton's appointment, had sent his adjutant, Lieutenant William Emory, with instructions for Frémont. Kearny said that the explorer was to maintain his command of the California Battalion, not to turn it over to Gillespie—which Stockton had ordered—and to remain in that position until notified otherwise. These orders, undermining Stockton's authority, were clearly the "business" at hand.

Before reporting to Kearny's headquarters, Frémont hastily wrote a letter to the general and left instructions that it be delivered by Kit Carson to Kearny's office as soon as it was copied.

The letter and its author arrived at the general's office almost simultaneously. Frémont reread it, signed it, and handed it over to Kearny. After a polite introductory, the letter got to the point:

> I found Commodore Stockton in possession of the country, exercising the functions of military commandant and civil governor, as early as July of last year; and shortly thereafter, I received from him the commission of military commandant, the duties of which I immediately entered upon, and have continued to exercise to the present moment. . . . I feel myself, therefore, with great deference to your professional and personal character, constrained to say that, until you and Commodore Stockton adjust between yourselves the question of rank, where I respectfully think the difficulty belongs, I shall have to report and receive orders, as heretofore, from the Commodore.

He signed the letter "Lieutenant Colonel, United States Army and Military Commandant of the Territory of California."

In all his career, since he was commissioned a first lieutenant in the 13th Infantry in 1813, Kearny had never heard, much less seen written down, such an astonishing case of disobedience of a lawful command of a superior officer, such an instance of prejudice of good order and military discipline—such a clearly defined example of *mutiny*.

Yet he made allowances that he would never have permitted any other officer in similar circumstances. Frémont was an explorer and topographer, scarcely "army," and doubtlessly unaware of the gravity of what he had written; he was the son-in-law of one of the most powerful of American political figures, Thomas Hart Benton, who was a Kearny friend, as was Benton's daughter Jessie, Frémont's wife, toward whom the general had a genuine affection.

The letter was a grievous mistake, Kearny counseled. He urged Frémont to destroy it and said that if he would do so, there would be no consequences, provided there would be no questioning the general's orders thereafter. On the matter of the governorship, Kearny said he intended to return to St. Louis within a month and implied a willingness to appoint Frémont to replace him as governor at that time. He called upon his long friendship with Senator Benton and Mrs. Frémont and urged that the colonel not destroy his career and embroil others in the consequences of his disobedience.

This momentous scene was unwitnessed and neither man left a satisfactory record of it. There were two extraordinary features of it: Kearny's uncharacteristic willingness to counsel his subordinate on the evils of his letter, and Frémont's failure to ask questions about the command controversy and seek Kearny's advice—even his assistance—on the matter of how he could serve two masters without alienating either. Kearny, probably because of his regard, if not his fear,* of

---

*Brevet Major Henry S. Turner of the First Dragoons kept a journal of his experiences with Kearny on the march from Forth Leavenworth to California. He wrote that the reason Kearny failed to place Frémont in irons for mutiny was that the general "is afraid of giving offense to Benton." Turner was disgusted with his chief for his inaction in the matter and for not dealing decisively with Stockton, whom Turner characterized as "a low, trifling, truckling politician."

Benton, seemed willing to help, but Frémont did not take advantage of the offer; instead, he seems to have said something about his decision having Commodore Stockton's support, then saluted and walked out of the room.

(A year later, in Washington, Frémont pointed out that Kearny, in suggesting he rescind the letter, was in effect willing to "break the rules of the service and of war." H. H. Bancroft's devastating rejoinder to this was that "dishonor in such cases pertains not to the officer who shows such leniency but to the recipient who uses it against him.")

Bancroft wrote further: "Against Kearny's position in the dispute, nothing can be urged, and against his conduct—his blunder at San Pascual affecting only himself and his men—nothing more than a savor of sharp practice in certain minor proceedings indicating a lack of confidence in the real strength of his position, or perhaps an excess of personal bitterness against his rival."

And of Frémont: "His action in disobeying Kearny's order, or rather in leaving the two chiefs to settle their own quarrel, must I think be approved; that is, compared to the only alternative. Like Stockton, he merits no praise for earlier proceedings. He had perhaps done even more than the commodore to retard the conquest. His mishaps as a political adventurer call for no sympathy. . . . There is, or should be, honor even among filibusters."

3

Kearny had no choice but to bide his time. Addressing Stockton as "Acting Governor of California," he wrote, "I must for the purpose of preventing collision between us, and possibly a civil war in consequence of it, remain silent for the present, leaving with you the great responsibility of doing that for which you have no authority, and preventing me from complying with the president's orders."

To Secretary of War William Marcy he sent a dispatch
stating that Stockton had prevented him from carrying out
the President's orders "and as I have no troops in the country under my authority, excepting a few dragoons, I have no
power of enforcing them." He included copies of his orders
to Frémont on continuing in command of the California
Battalion, Frémont's fatal letter, and his own exchange of
letters with Stockton.

At about this time, he had made up his mind to arrest Frémont when they reached Fort Leavenworth, and see him
court-martialed.

Stockton too wrote to Washington, addressing his remarks
to the secretary of the navy on February 4, recounting his
troubles with Kearny and demanding the recall of the general to "prevent the evil consequences that may grow out of
such a temper and such a head!"

The Stockton-Kearny-Frémont imbroglio could not be
kept secret. Even a newcomer such as twenty-seven-year-old
artilleryman Lieutenant William Tecumseh Sherman, who
arrived in California on the warship *Lexington* after a
voyage around Cape Horn, saw the confusion, heard the arguments, and asked, "Who the devil is the governor of
California?"

As he promised, Kearny distanced himself from Stockton.
On January 18, after sending Lieutenant William Emory
east via Panama with dispatches on the command impasse,
he gathered the remnant of the Army of the West—fifty
reasonably able-bodied dragoons—and rode south to San
Diego.

Within two weeks of his departure from Los Angeles, the
descending star of his brigadiership began to rise; his ener-
vating experiences with Stockton and Frémont were replaced
by the exhilarating confirmation of his role as generalissimo

of American military forces in California and head of its civil government.

The first of three arrivals in the abrupt turnabout of Kearny's fortunes was that at Warner's rancho of the Mormon Battalion of 350 volunteers led by Kearny favorite Lieutenant Colonel Philip St. George Cooke of Leesburg, Virginia, a West Pointer (class of '27), veteran of the War of 1812 battles and the Black Hawk War, and a fifteen-year veteran of the First Dragoons.

Kearny had explained to the War Department that he temporarily deferred to Stockton's leadership because, especially after San Pascual, he had too few fighting men under his immediate command to argue about it. He had depended upon adding Frémont's volunteers to his dwindled regulars to assert his right to the command in chief, but Frémont's disobedience had confounded that plan. Now the arrival of Cooke's battalion gave the general the manpower he needed to seize the military and civil supremacy the President had directed.

Cooke brought his haggard battalion into San Diego on January 29 and Kearny posted them at San Luís Rey to rest, recuperate, and await further orders while he and his staff sailed on the *Cyane* to Monterey. There, where Commodore John Sloat had first raised the American flag over California and launched the conquest six months earlier, Kearny intended to set up his headquarters. Consul Thomas Larkin, now a Kearny ally, had generously offered his home for the purposes.

Monterey, the general had decided, would be the capital of American California during his governorship.

With an uncanny interdicting precision, while the general and his officers were making a leisurely eight-day voyage upcoast from San Diego, there arrived in Monterey Bay the naval officer sent to take over command from Robert F. Stockton of the Pacific Squadron.

Commodore William Branford Shubrick was a solid, stolid, fifty-seven-year-old salt from Bull's Island, South Carolina, and from a family of navy men. His older brother, John Templar Shubrick, had been a hero of the War of 1812 and was lost at sea in 1815. William Branford Shubrick, commissioned a midshipman in 1806, had, like Stockton, served in 1812, in the Mediterranean, West Africa, and the West Indies. There the similarities ended. He had none of Stockton's flamboyance and vainglory, no wealth, no political connections, and, as it quickly became evident, no use for Robert Field Stockton.

Shubrick arrived in Monterey on the razee—a refitted frigate—*Independence* in late January, and when the *Cyane* sailed into the harbor, the new commodore ordered a thirteen-gun salute in Kearny's honor. At dinner aboard his flagship, Shubrick got a lengthy briefing on the command question, took one look at the general's orders from President Polk and instantly concurred with them. He notified Kearny that new and clarifying orders would soon be arriving from Washington and wrote the Navy Department that "I have recognized in General Kearny the senior officer of the army in California; have consulted and shall cooperate with him as such. . . ." Stockton's civil government measures, Shubrick said, "have been, in my opinion, prematurely taken . . . and an appointment of governor made of a gentleman who I am led to believe is not acceptable to the people of California."

Frémont, on February 7, wrote to Shubrick to explain the difficulty of his position. "The conquest of California was undertaken and completed by the joint effort of Commodore Stockton and myself," he said, "in obedience to what we regarded paramount duties from us to our government." Once the surrender of the province had been accomplished, a civil government was organized, "designed to maintain the conquest by the exercise of mild and wholesome civil restraints over the people, rather than by the iron rule of military

force." The results of his and Stockton's labors "were precisely what was contemplated by the instructions of General
Kearny," and the record of the Stockton-Frémont conquest
had been communicated to the President by express but no
response had yet been received. "General Kearny's instructions being, therefore, to the letter fully anticipated by others, I did not feel myself at liberty to yield a position so
important to the interests of my country until, after a full
understanding of all the grounds, it should be the pleasure
of my government that I should do so."

This sensible explanation, which might have illuminated
the controversy for Shubrick, seems to have made no impression on the commodore but would resurface a year later in
a courtroom in Washington.

The next arrival in California proved the most significant
of all in Kearny's—and Frémont's—future.

The warship *Erie* came through the Golden Gate on
February 12 and Kearny traveled north to confer with its
highest-ranking army passenger, Colonel Richard Barnes
Mason of the First Dragoons, lately Kearny's second and
successor as colonel of the regiment. He was pale and sick
from the rough sea voyage from Panama when he stepped
ashore at Yerba Buena.

The scion of distinguished Fairfax, Virginia, forebears,
Mason had spent thirty of his fifty years in the army and had
compiled an excellent record of service. In 1824, he had
commanded a keelboat on a Kearny-led expedition to the
mouth of the Yellowstone River; in 1832, he took part in the
Battle of Bad Axe, which terminated the Black Hawk War,
and a year later, at Fort Gibson, Indian Territory, he was
promoted major of the newly created First Dragoons.

He was a primary Kearny crony and a Kearny-like, no-
nonsense professional soldier with a reputation as a duelist.

At Yerba Buena, Mason handed over to his chief orders

from General of the Army Winfield Scott dated November
3, 1846, giving Kearny command of all land operations in
California and the office as governor of California until such
time as a civil government could be appointed. Scott also
ordered Kearny to muster Frémont's California Battalion
into the army and instructed that when the general could be
confident of the safety and tranquillity of the country, he was
to turn over all duties to Colonel Mason and return with a
troop escort to St. Louis.

By the time Kearny and Mason returned to Monterey on
February 23, the question of authority in California seemed
to be settled. In his diary, Colonel Philip St. George Cooke
gave a biting view of the matter: "Gen. Kearny is supreme—
somewhere up the coast; Col. Frémont supreme at Pueblo
de los Angles; Com. Stockton is 'commander-in-chief' at
San Diego; Com. Shubrick, the same at Monterey; and I, at
San Luís Rey; and we are all supremely poor, the government having no money and no credit, and we hold the territory because Mexico is poorest of all."

And in Washington, President Polk took note in his diary
of the "unfortunate collision" in California between General
Kearny and Commodore Stockton "in regard to precedence
in rank" and said, "I think General Kearny was right. It appears that Lieut. Colonel Frémont refused to obey General
Kearny and obeyed Commodore Stockton and in this he
was wrong. . . ."

4

In Los Angeles, unaware of the fateful comings and goings at Monterey and Yerba Buena that February, Frémont
was trying to run a government with no money. With Stockton at sea off Baja California, he was reduced to writing desperate letters to Kearny and Shubrick begging for financial
aid to keep the primitive military administration running.

He needed money to pay the volunteers, to purchase equipment, supplies, horses, saddles, arms, and livestock, and to pay for the appropriated goods and resultant bills incurred during the conquest of California. He proposed that six hundred thousand dollars would settle the accounts—a sum that benumbed Shubrick, who refused to authorize any funds and notified Frémont in a curious non sequitur that until he, Commodore Shubrick, heard from Commodore Stockton, Kearny was the senior commanding army officer in California.

Frémont borrowed money over his personal signature, including one personal debt of five thousand dollars to purchase Bird Island (later named Alcatraz) to prevent its sale by its owner to a foreign power that could have used it to control the entrance to San Francisco Bay. On February 25, he sent Kit Carson, Lieutenant Edward Beale, Ted Talbot, Stepp the gunsmith, and others as a delegation to Washington with urgent dispatchs to Senator Benton and President Polk on the desperately impecunious and debt-burdened state of affairs in California.

By the time the California party departed overland, Kearny had returned to Monterey, where he and Shubrick began issuing a series of orders and proclamations defining the roles of the two services, placing the army in control ashore and limiting naval duties to customs and port regulations. Other public declarations assured Californians that their religious rights would be held sacrosanct, that they would be protected from enemies, foreign and domestic, that present laws would continue in force, that local magistrates and similar officials would retain their posts after taking oaths of allegiance to the United States, and that any losses realized in the American annexation would be reimbursed.

These preludes to Kearny's ascendancy ended on March 1 with a notice to the people of California that Brigadier General Stephen W. Kearny had assumed the governorship and had selected Monterey as the seat of his government.

Frémont's fifty days as governor ended with this announcement and with orders from Kearny dated March 1.
Lieutenant Colonel Cooke would relieve Archibald Gillespie
as military commander in Los Angeles, and Frémont would
report to military headquarters in Monterey and bring with
him all the California Battalion records and property, this
preparatory to mustering out the volunteers and reenlisting
those who wished to serve in the regular army. The orders
were signed "S. W. Kearny, Brig. Gen., and Governor of California."

21

Return

■

1

No *Kearny man* had any use for John Charles Frémont. Among the dragoon officers, he was regarded as an arrogant parvenu, jumped up by his political connections, an amateur "soldier" who should have been clapped in irons for his mutinous defiance of the general's orders. Now, with the Kearny star risen at last, it was time for the new governor to take the usurper to task.

The first of the several agents to essay this work was Philip St. George Cooke, the smart, capable, former commander of the Mormon Battalion. In mid-March, he took over as military chief of the "Southern District"—principally Los Angeles—sent his predecessor, Archibald Gillespie, packing, and called upon Frémont.

There is no detailed record of their meeting, only its aftermath, but it was an unpleasant one for both men. Frémont told Cooke that once mustered out, the men of the California Battalion would not enlist in the army, and because of alarming rumors of a possible rising against American authority, he could not turn over any military property—not even the howitzer that had been captured by the Californians at San Pascual. Men, arms, and materiél, he said, might be needed to defend Los Angeles.

Frémont also made known his intention to journey to Monterey to report on the unrest and other critical matters directly to General Kearny.

Cooke's immediate reaction to these announcements is unknown, but his wrath spilled over in his later report on the confrontation: "I denounce this treason, or this mutiny, which jeopardizes the safety of the country and defies me in my legal command and duties. . . ."

A hundred years after the Cooke-Frémont encounter, Bernard DeVoto wrote that the rumor of a native revolt in Los Angeles was the product of a Frémont "whoop up," mere bluster and oration, one ploy among many in the explorer's continuing "acts of treason" designed, the historian said, for the purpose of making a record for use later, when "he could play his ace, the support of his father-in-law." But there is no evidence of such a sinister and cynical design. The rumors were real: reports claiming that Californians were massing and arming in Baja California, their strength increased by the arrival of Mexican army regulars, and were intent on retaking their lost territory. Other reports reached Frémont stating that he would be "deposed by violence" because of the nonpayment of debts that Americans had incurred during their presence in California and because of proclamations issued in Stockton's absence that were, as Frémont put it, "incompatible with the capitulation of Cowenga."

This "commotion," as he called it, genuinely alarmed him. Gillespie's lamentable experience in Los Angeles proved what an ardent and armed mob of nationalists and a handful of trained officers could do against a small military garrison. The California Battalion was tenfold larger than Gillespie's pitiful force, but Frémont had no information on the extent of the army rumored to be massing against him. For all he knew, José Castro, José María Flores, Andrés Pico, and all the other Mexican commanders who had decamped to Sonora were putting together a huge army in Baja California and preparing to march on San Diego and points north.

He determined to ride to Monterey and report to Kearny in person, and on March 22, 1847, he set out with Jacob Dodson, his black manservant and an expert wrangler who minded six extra unsalted horses, and José de Jesús Pico, who had been instrumental in the surrender at Cahuenga Pass. Pico's role in the ride north is unclear but Frémont may have intended that he would confirm the reports and rumors of a brewing counterrevolt.

Principally due to Senator Benton's extolling of it in Congress, the 420-mile ride from Los Angeles to Monterey was later described as "epic." One of Frémont's most protective biographers called it "theatrical" and "unnecessary." At the least, the ride was remarkable: after brief rests at Santa Barbara and San Luís Obispo and a near-miss bear attack in their night camp, the three men reached the outskirts of Monterey at dusk on March 25, covering the 420 miles in three days and ten hours.

Frémont left Dodson and Pico to set up camp about a mile outside the town and rode his lathered horse to Kearny's headquarters at Thomas Larkin's home. The consul escorted him to the general's office, but the explorer's epic ride clearly did not impress the busy new proconsul, who announced that he would meet with Frémont the next morning.

That night, Lieutenant William T. Sherman, now a Kearny aide, paid the explorer a "courtesy call." He wrote later that, "feeling a natural curiosity to see Frémont . . . I rode out to his camp and found him in a conical tent with one Capt. [Dick] Owens . . . I spent an hour or so with F. in his tent, took some tea with him, and left without being impressed with him." It seems likely that Sherman, at this time as much a Kearny toady as Cooke or Mason, paid the visit to test the explorer's temperament and to obtain as much information as he could to report to the general in preparation for the next day's interview.

From the outset, the March 26 meeting was ruinous for Frémont. He was angry. He had worn out three horses getting to Monterey to deliver crucial information, only to be told he must wait the night to see the general. He had been rudely informed that he was relieved as governor and as commander of the California Battalion. His confrontation with Lieutenant Colonel Cooke still rankled. He had been rubbed raw between two senior officers in a command dispute that any ensign and second lieutenant could have settled amicably. He needed to present his case to Kearny in a frank, open dialogue. But when he was ushered into the general's office, he found that the meeting would not be private. Soon after their disastrous January 17 confrontation in Los Angeles, Kearny had determined that once they returned to Fort Leavenworth, he would place Frémont under arrest on charges of mutiny and disobedience of lawful orders and request that a court-martial be convened. Five months would pass before the explorer learned of this plan and realized why, on the morning of March 26, he was not meeting with Kearny alone.

Seated with the general in his headquarters office was Colonel Richard B. Mason. Frémont did not know the man or his mission but objected to his presence and suggested to the general that it was perhaps to witness some "unguarded remark." Kearny regarded this as an insult and the meeting, which dragged on over two days, corroborated for him the justice of his plans for the explorer and confirmed for Frémont that the general and his gang of lickspittles were more his enemy than the Californians had ever been.

Kearny did not appear concerned over the rumors and reports of a potential revolt among the Californians in the southern province, nor did he rise to Frémont's pointed question about whether the new civil government would assume the debts of the conquest. (In Washington subsequently, Kearny could remember neither the question nor his reply, although he said he "should have answered in the negative.")

Frémont said that he would resign his army commission, but Kearny refused to accept the proposition.

The meeting culminated with Kearny asking Frémont if he intended obeying his order to hand over the California Battalion and its records. The general, with Mason hanging on to every word, cautioned the explorer to take care in responding to the question and gave him a day to think it over.

In the end, Frémont agreed to obey and was ordered to return to Los Angeles to gather the battalion and accompany it back to Monterey, together with its supplies and papers.

After the explorer departed with Dodson and Pico, Kearny dispatched Colonel Mason to Los Angeles with a letter giving him full authority to oversee the battalion's debarkation at San Pedro and to order Frémont to report to Monterey no more than twelve days after the battalion sailed.

2

Mason arrived in Los Angeles on April 5 and set up his office in the home of Nathaniel M. Pryor, a Kentucky-born silversmith and clockmaker who had lived in the pueblo since 1830. Once established there, the colonel sent for Frémont.

Neither man was apt to be holding an olive branch, but any chance of a reasonably friendly encounter disappeared when Frémont saw that Mason, following the lead of his general, had a witness present. Lieutenant Colonel St. George Cooke may have smiled when the explorer entered the room; he was as eager as any Kearny man to witness the fall of this mutinous subordinate.

Mason repeated Kearny's orders and asked Frémont to join him the next day at Mission San Gabriel to visit the

battalion and ascertain which of the volunteers wished to
stay in the service.

The muster followed its commander's prediction. Mason
announced to the gathered men that they were to be disbanded but that all who wished to continue to serve would
be sworn into the regular army. When none stepped forward,
Mason directed his anger at Frémont, ordered the battalion
to be discharged immediately, the naval personnel among
them to be sent north on the sloop-of-war *Warren*. He instructed the explorer to gather his original Topographical
Corps party and march it to Monterey, there to report to
Governor-General Kearny, and to turn over to the appropriate
officer of the First Dragoons all horses, mules, arms,
ammunition, and supplies.

Frémont, unhumbled in the stripping of his command,
had, or contrived to have, a final encounter with the man he
considered a Kearny chauvinist. The issue centered on a sizable horse herd that Frémont had gathered for "service in
Mexico." He informed Mason by letter that he intended leading a regiment into Mexico for service with Zachary Taylor,
an option given him in correspondence to Kearny from War
Secretary William Marcy.

Mason curtly dismissed this idea as contrary to new orders from the general and sent an orderly to Frémont's
quarters demanding that the horses be surrendered to the
government forthwith.

The clash between the contemptuous colonel and the refractory lieutenant colonel switched from a paper duel to the
threat of the real field of honor when, on April 14, Frémont
was summoned to Mason's office. There would be no further dispute or discussion of the horse issue, or of any other
issue, Mason said heatedly, and when the explorer objected
to the tone of the admonition, Mason exploded, "None of
your insolence, or I will put you in irons!" In his version of
the event, Frémont took the threat calmly, saying to the choleric Kearny agent, "You cannot make an official matter of

a personal one, sir; as a man, do you hold yourself personally responsible for what you have just said?"

Whether Frémont walked out of the meeting or Mason terminated it is not clear, but within an hour of its end, the explorer sent a note to Mason demanding a written apology for his "insult" and making a threat of his own: failure to offer the apology would be translated as an "official challenge." Then, when Mason, perhaps calculatedly, did not respond, Frémont threw down the last gauntlet, making the challenge official by letter and inviting his opponent to choose his weapon.

His folly in defying Kearny had cost him his career; his recklessness in challenging Mason came close to costing him his life: the colonel of dragoons, who was believed to be familiar with dueling and was certainly familiar with bird-hunting, chose shotguns—double-barreled and buckshot-loaded. Frémont had never fired such an arm in his life and had to send an aide to locate one.

He was saved from certain death by the blind good fortune that often follows the foolhardy: the day after the challenge, the dragoon colonel sent his second to Frémont's quarters to say that the duel would have to be delayed until after they reached Monterey. A few days later, upon hearing of the pending confrontation, Kearny intervened, writing to his lieutenant colonel: "It becomes my duty to inform you that the good of the Public Service, the necessity of preserving tranquillity in California . . . require that the meeting above referred to should not take place at this time, and in this country, and you are hereby officially directed by me to proceed no further in this matter. A similar communication has been addressed to Colonel Mason."*

In 1850, Mason, having returned from his service as governor of California, wrote to his old adversary in Washington offering to fight the duel if Frémont would come to St. Louis. Frémont wisely chose not to answer the letter. The quarrel ended with Mason's death that year at the age of fifty-three.

In the end, Frémont grudgingly obeyed orders: the horse herd was surrendered, the California Battalion was mustered out on April 19, Mason sailed to Monterey to assume command of the Tenth Military District—now the official army name for California—and soon afterward, the explorer followed with what remained of his original topographical party.

On May 13, Kearny notified the adjutant general of the army in Washington that he would soon be returning to the East with Lieutenant Colonel Frémont, whose conduct in California, he said, "has been such that I shall be compelled on arriving in Missouri to arrest him and send him under charges to report to you." He did not say that Frémont had yet to be informed of the impending action against him.

Toward the end of May, at about the time he learned from Washington dispatches that General Scott had captured Vera Cruz and was marching on Mexico City, Kearny met with Frémont and the Topographical Corps men and had orders read that they were to proceed east under his command on May 31 and that any who sought to be discharged from the service would be permitted to remain in California.

Frémont had several requests to make of the general. He asked for time to locate two of his original expedition men, Ned Kern, the artist and one-time officer in charge at Sutter's Fort, and Henry King, a veteran of the explorer's western treks. This was refused. He asked if Kearny would authorize payment of financial obligations that Frémont had incurred as governor and was told no. He asked that members of the California Battalion who did not join the army receive back pay due them and this was denied. He asked permission to return to St. Louis, even if at his own expense, by either the Gila River in the south or the Salt Lake in the north and the answer was no. He asked for time to gather up

his geological and botanical specimens and scientific instruments left in Yerba Buena, and this too was denied.

He was required to turn over what surveying equipment
he had to Kearny aide Lieutenant Henry W. Halleck, and in
a particularly galling order, was instructed to camp outside
Monterey with his men while awaiting the return home.

3

On May 31, 1847, General Kearny, with Colonel Cooke
and sixty-two men plus a mule pack train and small
horse herd, marched out of Monterey, capital of the new
United States Territory of California, on the trail north to
New Helvetia. Six months had passed since he and Kit
Carson had led his small, trail-weary dragoon force into
Warner's Ranch.

Among those in the Kearny column were Lieutenant Colonel Frémont and nineteen of his original topographical
force, including his Delaware escort. Eighteen months had
passed since he had led his small and exhausted exploring
party into Sutter's Fort.

Frémont and his men were posted a mile or two in the
rear, as if in quarantine, "compelled to trail eastward at the
chariot wheels of the General," as the explorer's biographer,
Allan Nevins, put it.

The collection of indignities devised by Kearny for the pa-
riah in his assemblage were numerous and uniformly petty.
When the group arrived at Sutter's outpost on June 13, the
hospitable Swiss greeted the general with a salute from
the fort's cannon and invited him and his officers to a dinner he had prepared in their honor. Frémont was not invited,
a circumstance entirely agreeable to Sutter, who still smarted
over the explorer's commandeering of his fort during the
Bear Flag revolt and over the jailing of General Vallejo and
the other prisoners there.

Another calculated insult arose when the company departed New Helvetia for the long journey east and it was learned that Kearny had hired Le Gros Fallon as his guide through country well known to Frémont and any number of his veteran explorers.

As the final irony in the journey home, Commodore Stockton and his party of fifty officers (including Archibald Gillespie), sailors, and marines departed from Sonoma about a month behind the Kearny column. Thus, with Kearny in the lead and Stockton in the rear, Frémont was once again sandwiched between the rival conquerors of California.

The single memorable event on the return journey was the arrival at Truckee Lake on June 22, where Kearny and his company saw the pitiful remains of the Donner party, a rubble of bones, remnants of wagons, scattered goods and clothing and shattered crockery, rickety, fire-blackened cabins and lean-tos. The essentials of what had happened to the emigrants during the past winter were known, and Sutter, among others, told the story often about how the Missouri farmers George and Jacob Donner and their emigrant train had reached this place at the end of October, 1846, four months out of Independence.

They had abandoned the proven California Trail after being told of a shortcut to the Sierra foothills, and by the time they reached the Humboldt River in September and Truckee Lake a month later, the Sierra winter had locked them in. They had rested for five fatal days before attempting to cross the mountains, allowing their surviving livestock to wander and become buried in snow. They had not gathered sufficient firewood; there was no game. They camped in cabins on the lake and in tents and brushwood arbors and huts at Alder Creek. There were eighty-seven of them, nearly half small children, and they were reduced to eating brush mice, powdered bone, bark and twigs, and boiled rawhide. A group of fifteen of them started on December 16 from the lake camp to cross the Sierras on makeshift snowshoes with six days' rations. Their travail lasted thirty-two days. Eight of them died in the snow and two Indian guides were shot. The corpses were eaten by the survivors. The dead were also cannibalized at Truckee Lake. Once word finally reached Sutter's Fort and ranches around New Helvetia, relief parties were sent out through the snowbound passes to rescue the survivors. Of the eighty-seven Donner party emigrants, forty-eight reached California.

Kearny's and Frémont's men buried what bones they found and burned the remains of the cabins, then moved on to the Truckee River, the Humboldt Sink, the Humboldt River, across the Snake and on to the Oregon Trail. South Pass was reached on July 24 and Fort Leavenworth on August 22, ending a sixty-six-day march of nearly two thousand miles.

Frémont had no time to enjoy the journey's end; indeed, he barely had time to find billets for his men and smack the trail dust from his hat before being summoned to the office of Lieutenant Colonel Clifton Wharton, the post commander. There he found Kearny waiting in the ominously familiar arrangement of having a witness on hand. In Wharton's presence, the general read a document instructing the explorer to turn over all horses, mules, and other public property to the Leavenworth quartermaster, to arrange for the accounts of his nineteen men to be paid, and "having performed the above duty," Kearny intoned, Lieutenant Colonel Frémont "will consider himself under arrest, and will then repair to Washington City, and report himself to the adjutant general of the army."

Although he certainly suspected that he faced some kind of official reprimand—his exile at the rear of Kearny's party and similar affronts signaled that—the pronouncement of August 22 was the first that Frémont knew of Kearny's plan, formulated six months before, to place him under arrest. And he had enough familiarity with the procedures of military justice to know that "arrest" was but a step removed from court-martial.*

Frémont claimed that after news of his arrest spread, none of the officers at the post would speak to him or extend to him or his men any of the courtesies that were normally commonplace. He said that when he brought the horses and mules up for delivery to the post quartermaster, he, his men, and the animals were forced to wait in the sun five hours before they were officially received.

Stockton, Gillespie, and the commodore's party arrived at Fort Leavenworth a few days after Kearny, and in the last week of August, Frémont boarded the steamer *Martha* for the short voyage south on the Missouri to Westport Landing, where Jessie waited.

Twenty-seven months had passed since they were last together; Lily was just a baby when he had left. Jessie noted the graying of her husband's beard and was delighted at his garish Californio outfit of broad hat, fancy trousers, and red sash.

The Frémonts took the *Martha* downriver for a reunion with Senator Benton before moving on to Washington.

Kearny preceded them and by the time they reached St. Louis, the general was en route to Washington for a meeting with President Polk.

---

*Dwight L. Clarke, Kearny's biographer, in attempting to mitigate the six-month delay in informing Frémont of his fate, provides an inadvertent indictment of the dragoon officers the explorer regarded as lackeys. "The Lieutenant Colonel should have been very grateful that his arrest had been so long delayed,"Clarke says, adding the telling comment that had the explorer been arrested when Kearny first decided on it and a court-martial convened then, "What chance would John C. Frémont have stood with a court composed in part of Mason, Cooke, Swords, Turner and Sherman?"

22

Court-martial

■

1

Frémont *returned to* St. Louis a conquering hero. A mob of well-wishers hoping to catch a glimpse of him and the always-luminous Jessie greeted the *Martha* at the pier-head and clamored for a speech; invitations poured in from the city's social and political elite. But the explorer made only a few innocuous remarks referring to his California adventures and attended no parties. He could not linger in St. Louis; he needed to move on to Washington to clear his name of the grave charges Kearny had leveled against him. What time he had he spent with his family, giving Jessie, and especially her father, the history that had led to his arrest, from the fatal January 17 meeting with the general in Los Angeles to the August 22 arrival at Fort Leavenworth, where he had been placed under arrest.

Benton and Jessie had learned some of the story before the *Martha* docked and their hero stepped ashore. Frémont himself, in the infrequent letters he wrote home, had told of the Stockton-Kearny feud and his ordeal between the two men, and there had been other sources of information out of California as well.

In June, Major William "Owl" Russell, the explorer's close friend and, during his brief governorship, his secretary of state, came through St. Louis. He brought the unsettling news of Kearny's assumption of power in California and was carrying to Washington petitions signed by many influentials in the southern part of the Territory beseeching federal authorities to reinstall Frémont as governor.

(Neither Russell nor the explorer knew it at the time, but anti-Frémont petitions and letters were also arriving in the capital, said to have been gathered by disgruntled former California Battalion volunteers "clamorous for their pay." Other letters opposing Frémont were written by his mortal enemy, Richard Mason, by Thomas Larkin, and by certain arribeños who had not forgotten the murders of José Berreyesa and the De Haro brothers at San Rafael in June 1846.)

Newspapers were another source of information, mostly dubious, on the controversy. The New Orleans *Picayune,* Louisville *Journal,* and St. Louis *Republican,* among others, carried peculiarly skewed reports and first-person "columns" giving readers the scenario that Kearny was the honorable professional soldier trying to do his duty, thwarted at every step by the power-hungry amateurs, Stockton and Frémont. Since some of the unsigned newspaper work contained details known only among Kearny's intimate circle of officers, the authors were suspected to be Colonel Richard Mason, Lieutenant Colonel Philip St. George Cooke, and Lieutenant William Emory.

Kit Carson, Edward Beale, and Alexis Godey had also preceded the explorer to St. Louis and brought news to Senator Benton of the dire events in California—Kearny's seizing of the command primacy in Stockton's absence, his usurpation of the governorship, his humiliating initiatives against Frémont.

Carson had arrived in St. Louis in May and told what he knew. Benton, his always volatile temperament by now roiling over his son-in-law's predicament, took Kit and Jessie with him to Washington to make a personal visit to the President.

On June 7, 1847, at the time Frémont and his nineteen men were camped in exile at Sutter's Fort awaiting the departure east, Jessie escorted the celebrated frontiersman to the President's office. Polk was charmed by Carson and they chatted at length, the President acknowledging the scout's services in the war by awarding him a commission as a second lieutenant "of Mounted Rifles" at a monthly pay of $33.–33 plus $24 for rations, $16 for forage for two horses, and a servant at $16.50—a total of $89.83 a month. Kit thus happily left the capital to return home to Taos and his wife Josefa.

Jessie held Polk in much less thrall. He listened with as much patience as he could summon, giving her the same courtesy he extended to her powerful father, whose several visits on behalf of the California intrigues had taxed the presidential patience. The man who, with his cabinet secretaries, had created the command commotion in California, noted in his diary, "Mrs Frémont seemed anxious to elicit from me some expression of approbation for her husband's conduct, but I evaded. In truth, I consider Colonel Frémont was greatly in the wrong when he refused to obey the orders issued to him by General Kearny. I think General Kearny was right also in his controversy with Commodore Stockton."

On September 16, three days after General Winfield Scott's victory at Chapúltepec, the final battle of the war in Mexico, Frémont arrived in Washington and reported to Adjutant General of the Army Roger Jones. He asked for a thirty-day delay in his trial in order to amass his papers, make a study of newspaper reports, and await Commodore Stockton's arrival in the capital.

"I wish a full trial, and a speedy one," he wrote in a letter for the record to General Jones. "The charges against me by Brigadier General Kearny, and subsidiary accusations made against me in all the departments of my conduct (military, civil, political, and moral) while in California, if true, would subject me to be cashiered and shot, under the rules and articles of war, and to infamy in the public opinion." He said it was his intention to "meet these charges in all their extent and for that purpose to ask a trial upon every point of allegation or insinuation against me, waiving all objections to forms and technicalities, and allow the widest range to all possible testimony."

Frémont, aware that Kearny had preceded him to Washington and had been closeted with high-ranking army officers, the War Department, and the President, made certain that the adjutant general understood the indignities he had suffered before charges were made against him, as well as the circumstances of his arrest. He said bitterly, "Brought home by General Kearny, and marched in his rear, I did not know of his design to arrest me until the moment of its execution at Fort Leavenworth. He then informed me that among the charges which he had referred were mutiny, disobedience of orders, assumption of powers, etc. . . ."

In late October, a few days before the court-martial was to open, Benton paid a final visit to the President and, in a fireplace lecture, made a virulent argument against his one-time friend, Stephen Watts Kearny. Polk, true to his custom, was exasperatingly noncommittal. The President considered Kearny "a good officer and an intelligent gentleman" and, after a visit with the general on September 11, recorded in his journal that neither man had talked about the "difficulties" in California. "I did not introduce the subject and I was glad that he did not," Polk noted.

As to Benton's importunities, the President wrote, "I have

always been on good terms with Senator Benton but he is a
man of violent passions and I should not be surprised if he
became my enemy because all his wishes are not grati-
fied. . . ."

2

After a day of preliminaries, the trial opened on the
overcast Indian-summer Wednesday of November 3,
1847, at the Washington Arsenal, a shabby wooden building dimly lit by sunlight filtering through windows up near
the high-domed roof. The court consisted of fourteen
officers—three colonels, five lieutenant colonels, and four
majors—led by Brevet Brigadier General G. M. Brooke of
the Fifth Infantry and Major John Fitzgerald Lee, judge advocate. Eleven of the fourteen officers had thirty or more
years of army service; four were graduates of the military
academy at West Point.

In the audience there were newspapermen, congressmen,
a miscellany of Washington bureaucrats and hangers-on, and
Frémont faithfuls such as Alexis Godey and Dick Owens
(Kit Carson had returned to California). Jessie was there,
dressed in a lovely wine-colored dress, her striking oval face
shaded by a burgundy-velvet bonnet, and her sister Eliza, in
a gay blue ensemble. Eliza had suggested they dress in black
for the occasion, but Jessie rejected the idea as too funereal.

Frémont sat with his advisors. At the prosecutor's table
were General Kearny; his Army of the West second in command, Captain Henry S. Turner; and Major Lee, the judge
advocate.

After the administering of oaths, the explorer requested
of the court permission to have his brother-in-law, William
Carey Jones, an attorney married to Jessie's older sister
Eliza, and Senator Thomas Hart Benton as counsel at his defense table. This was granted under military rules, which

permitted civilian attorneys to serve in advisory roles but did not allow them to cross-examine witnesses. In this, Frémont would have to serve as his own defense lawyer.

Following various courtesies and questions, the hushed audience heard the judge advocate read the charges against John Charles Frémont.

The first and weightiest of these was the charge of mutiny, the allegation that Frémont had refused to obey orders of his superior, Brigadier General Stephen Watts Kearny, beginning on January 17, 1847, when he declared that he would continue to "report and receive orders, as heretofore, from the Commodore [Stockton]" and that he would continue, against contrary orders, as "Military Commandant of the Territory of California," which title he had employed in signing his letter to Kearny.

There were eleven specifications under the mutiny charge, with documents supporting them dating between January 17 and May 9, 1847, the latter date approximating the dispute with Colonel Mason in Los Angeles.

The second charge, "Disobedience of the Lawful Command of his Superior Officer," contained seven specifications between the same dates, and the third, "Conduct to the Prejudice of Good Order and Military Discipline," carried five specific charges.

In the course of the trial, Frémont characterized the charges as a "comedy of three errors," the first being "the faulty order sent out from this place [Washington]; next, in the unjustifiable pretensions of General Kearny; thirdly, in the conduct of the government in sustaining these pretensions." The last of these, he said, was the greatest of the three.

He pleaded not guilty to each of the twenty-three specifications.

His defense strategy centered on the struggle for command between Kearny and Stockton, this having at its source the circumstances he had explained in his February

7, 1847, letter to Commodore Branford Shubrick, who had
been sent out to Monterey to relieve Stockton of command
of the Pacific Squadron. Frémont had written Shubrick that
"The conquest of California was undertaken and completed
by the joint effort of Commodore Stockton and myself in
obedience to what we regarded paramount duties from us to
our government" and that this conquest was complete and a
civil government had been established before Kearny's arrival in California.

The explorer was also able to demonstrate that the charges
against him derived from this rivalry and from Kearny's vin-
dictiveness and temper, attributes shared by a circle of sy-
cophants such as Commodore Shubrick, colonels Richard
Mason and Henry Turner, Lieutenant Colonel Philip St.
George Cooke, and Lieutenant William H. Emory. And he
was permitted to place into the record all the affronts he had
suffered during the contretemps between his superior officers, especially those inflicted by Kearny during the march
home, the keeping of the charges against him secret for six
months, the outrageous manner of his arrest, and the subsequent demeaning treatment at Leavenworth.

Of the great latitude the court extended the defense, Bernard DeVoto said that the court, in permitting extraneous
testimony and records, allowed the explorer and his counsel
"to turn a military trial into a political circus," and characterized it as a "creature of oratory and newsprint."

But Frémont proved to be a formidable advocate,
especially relentless when, referring to himself in third
person, he questioned his accuser. Their first exchange did
not reflect well on the general.

"At what time did you form the design to arrest Lieutenant Colonel Frémont?" Frémont asked.

"I formed the design shortly after receiving his letter of
January 17. That word 'shortly' would not imply immediately. It may have been a week."

The explorer then bored in on another critical matter.

Kearny, in mid-February, 1847, had received orders from General Winfield Scott, carried to California by Colonel Richard Mason. These orders gave Kearny command of all land operations in the province and the office of military governor and authorized him to muster the California Battalion into the army.

Why, Frémont asked, had Kearny not informed Lieutenant Colonel Frémont of these orders—which would have ended all debate on the command issue?

Kearny answered haughtily, "I am not in the habit of communicating to my juniors the instructions I receive from my seniors, unless required to do so in those instructions."

(Frémont biographer Allan Nevins calls this response "a very lame excuse for a base act.")

Kearny made a poor start and was a poor witness overall. His chief weakness lay in his inexplicable memory lapses—or, as the defense had it, his highly "selective" memory. He claimed he could not remember that Frémont had made his ride from Los Angeles to Monterey for the purpose of warning about the rumors of an armed Californian force planning to recapture the southern province; he could not remember that it was Kit Carson who had delivered Frémont's letter to his office on January 17; he claimed never to have heard of the conquest debts Frémont had begged his assistance in paying; nor did he remember Frémont's attempt to resign from the army. He could not remember who had recovered the cannon he had lost in the San Pascual battle, could not remember Lieutenant Archibald Gillespie or Lieutenant Edward Beale, two of the officers who had led the Stockton relief force of sailors, marines, and California Battalion volunteers who had joined him on the eve of the battle.

One thing the general did remember clearly was that Lieutenant Colonel Frémont had attempted "bargaining" for the governorship of California.

"He asked me if I would appoint him governor," Kearny said from the witness stand. "I told him I expected shortly to leave California for Missouri . . . that as soon as the country was quieted I should, most probably, organize a civil government in California; and that I, at that time, knew of no objections to my appointing him as the governor."

He then accused Frémont of stating that he intended to see Stockton to demand the governorship, and failing to get it, he would no longer obey the commodore's orders.

Few with any knowledge of the events in California believed Kearny's account of the January 17 conversation. Frémont himself vehemently denied it in court, saying that he had received appointments from three Presidents, Jackson, Tyler, and Polk, but that he had never begged or bargained for one in his life. Furthermore, there was ample record that both Stockton and Kearny had offered him the governorship and that Stockton actually gave him the appointment on January 14, the day he rode into Los Angeles and delivered the Cahuenga treaty to the commodore.

Through his direct questions and lengthy diversions disguised as questions, Frémont was able to dwell on Secretary of War Marcy's June 3, 1846, orders to Kearny, the "Should you conquer and take possession of New Mexico and California" orders. He declared that Kearny and his Army of the West had not taken possession of anything in California, that the conquering and possessing had been done by Stockton and Frémont and that Kearny had been in no shape to possess or conquer anything; indeed, he had had to be rescued from Mule Hill after the San Pascual fight by 215 of Stockton's sailors and marines.

Kearny was forced to make damaging admissions. He had addressed official correspondence to Stockton as "His Excellency, R. F. Stockton, Governor of California," which gave a tacit concession that Stockton had superseded him in setting up a civil government. And on the charge of mutiny, he admitted that he had not imprisoned or placed Frémont in irons despite the fact that mutiny was a capital offense in wartime.

The defense was getting high scores in newspaper reports, and it was pointed out that Robert F. Stockton, a key figure in the entire controversy, had yet to take the stand.

3

Philip St. George Cooke testified for a week with no great consequence for Frémont. The judge advocate chose not to call William H. Emory as witness, but Frémont managed to reveal his role as probable author of a letter in the New Orleans *Picayune* that extolled Kearny as the hero of the conquest of California, told of the rivalry between Kearny and Stockton, and said that the commodore had drawn Frémont "on his side."

At last, on December 6, the first anniversary of the Battle of San Pascual, Stockton was sworn in as a witness. From the start, he proved a great disappointment for the defense and a source of frustration for the court, which grew far more impatient at his extemporizations than at Kearny's memory lapses. Self-confident and abnormally self-possessed, accustomed to talking more than listening, the commodore gave a windy, rambling history of the war in California but seemed uncertain about specifics and vague in answering the questions both Frémont and Major Lee posed.

He tried to be helpful to the defense, and his meandering testimony contained some coherent statements that to some extent mitigated Frémont's actions. He said that the conquest of California had been "interrupted" by the events in Los Angeles in September, 1846, when the pueblo had temporarily surrendered to the insurgents. Peace was soon restored, he said, "and therefore there was nothing for me to do in relation to the establishment of a civil government, except to hand to Lieutenant Colonel Frémont the commission as governor, which I had pledged my word to do; which I had informed the government I would do, and which I probably would have done, on the 25th day of October [1846], if the insurrection had not broken out."

As to what he called "the position of the parties"—meaning himself, Kearny, and Frémont—he said, "in my judgment and opinion . . . General Kearny had laid aside, for the time being, his commission as brigadier general, and was serving as a volunteer under my command." He asserted that after the San Gabriel battle, as their combined forces marched to Los Angeles, the troops placed by his orders under the command of General Kearny were the dragoons, sailors, and marines and Captain Gillespie's two companies of the California Battalion, "and no other." As to the disposition of the battalion after reaching Los Angeles, Stockton said, "On the arrival of Lieutenant Colonel Frémont, he reported to me; and I did not give, nor did I intend to give, General Kearny any control or command over that part of the California Battalion. It was under my own immediate command." He testified that he had appointed Captain Gillespie to take command of the battalion after he appointed Frémont governor, and said, "If I understand the matter before this court, the disobedience of orders charged against the accused, whilst I was commander-in-chief, is, that he would not obey an order which required him not to recognize my appointment of Captain Gillespie as a major of the battalion."

At one point in the questioning by Major Lee, a significant point was made for Kearny when Stockton admitted that he had no specific orders to form a civil government in California. "I formed the government under the law of nations," he said, without defining a law that apparently existed only in his mind.

Archibald Gillespie testified on Frémont's behalf, as did Lieutenant Andrew F. V. Gray and Owl Russell. Gray, the

naval officer who had led the force Stockton sent to relieve
Kearny and his dragoons on Mule Hill, said he witnessed
Kearny's offer to serve as Stockton's second in command
in the march to Los Angeles. Owl Russell supported this
testimony and added, "I remember distinctly that he [Ke-
arny] spoke of his intention of appointing Colonel Frémont
governor."

At the beginning of the trial, newspaper coverage of it was
extensive, with editors such as James Gordon Bennett of the
influential New York *Herald* regarding it as the *cause célè-
bre* of the era. But as the proceedings rolled on six days a
week through December and January, the tedium of dull and
repetitive testimony had a palling effect. There were signs
of ebbing editorial support for the defense and a growing
sympathy for the old soldier Kearny, belabored at such length
by defense witnesses and the relentless interrogations by the
accused.

Kearny returned to the stand on January 5, 1848, the
first session of the new year, and three days later provided
a startling moment in his testimony when he asked the
court permission to read a statement he had prepared. The
courtroom was silent as the general read in an obviously
troubled voice:

> "I consider it due to the dignity of the court, and the high
> respect I entertain for it, that I should here state that, on my
> last appearance before this court, the senior counsel for the
> accused, Thomas H. Benton, of Missouri, sat in his place
> making mouths and grimaces at me, which I considered
> were intended to offend, to insult, and to overawe me. I ask
> of this court no action on it, so far as I am concerned. I am
> fully capable of taking care of my own honor."

This astonishing statement shocked the court and audience momentarily; General G. M. Brooke, president of the
court, nervously said that he had not observed any offensive

facial expressions of the senator's and proceeded to read from the Articles of War the caution against "menacing" words or gestures in a court-martial proceeding.

Then Benton, towering, smoldering, stood and ignoring admonitions that he had no right to speak at the trial, launched into a booming response, saying that in earlier testimony, Kearny had made certain insinuations and "fixed his eyes upon Colonel Frémont . . . insultingly and fiendishly." He went on:

"When General Kearny fixed his eyes upon Colonel Frémont, I determined if he should attempt again to look down a prisoner, I would look at him. I did this day; and the look of today was the consequence of the looks in this court before. I did today look at General Kearny when he looked at Colonel Frémont, and I looked at him till his eyes fell—'til they fell upon the floor."

The president of the court cooled the senator's ardor by asserting that he had observed Kearny looking with "kindness" toward Colonel Frémont, and General Brooke permitted Kearny the last word on the subject: "I have never offered the slightest insult to Colonel Frémont, either here as a prisoner . . . or anywhere, or under any circumstances whatsoever."

4

"My acts in California have all been with high motives, and a desire for public service," Frémont said on January 27, 1848, standing before his accusers and judges to end the summary of his defense. "My scientific labors did something to open California to the knowledge of my countrymen; its geography had been a sealed book."

In the grim, gray Washington armory courtroom, he appeared anything but the vainglorious filibustero chieftain, the self promoting frontier Napoleon—and the mutineer—his opponents styled him. Nor, for that matter, did his appearance give a hint of the truer man.

It was difficult to credit that this man, described in newspaper columns as "slight," "trim," "erect," "olive-skinned," "dark-eyed," "sad of countenance," "handsome," and—often—"Gallic," was the celebrated explorer whose name was as synonymous with the great unknown West as Lewis and Clark's. He did not appear to be the same Frémont whose books revealed a man who found his greatest comfort among the Kit Carsons of the mountains. Was this slight, well-spoken, neatly dressed, lawyer-like figure the same man who killed Indians who opposed him, smoked pipes of willow-bark shavings, and thumbed "trapper's butter" from the cracked bones of a fresh-killed brute buffalo among Indians who befriended him?

His self-defense, if overlong and tedious in its drumming counter-accusations against General Kearny and his minions, had been brilliant for a man so out of his element. But as the trial lumbered to its close, Frémont, as if perceiving the inevitable outcome of it, grew more defensive, betraying, some said, the narcissism that was his fatal flaw.

"My military operations were conquests without bloodshed," he said untruthfully. "My civil administration was for the public good. I offer California, during my administration, for comparison with the most tranquil portions of the United States. I offer it in contrast to the condition of New Mexico during the same time."*

*The reference was directed at the aftermath of Kearny's conquest of New Mexico. In Taos in January, 1847, at the time of the Kearny-Frémont-Stockton dispute in California, Governor Charles Bent, whom Kearny had selected to serve as the first civilian governor of the territory, was killed with six others by Pueblo Indians believed

He ended his final statement with strength: "I prevented civil war against Governor Stockton, by refusing to join General Kearny against him; I arrested civil war against myself, by consenting to be deposed—offering at the same time to resign my place of lieutenant colonel in the army."

Then, as he placed his papers on the defense table, he said, "I have been brought as a prisoner and a criminal from that country . . . I am now ready to receive the sentence of the court."

The court deliberated three days and delivered its verdict on Monday, January 31, 1848.

Frémont was found guilty on all charges and every specification under each charge, and the court sentenced him to be dismissed from the service.

Six of the twelve sitting members of the court recommended that President Polk grant clemency, issuing a statement laden with irony:

Under the circumstances in which Lieutenant Colonel Frémont was placed between two officers of superior rank, each claiming to command-in-chief in California— circumstances in their nature calculated to embarrass the mind and excite the doubts of officers of greater experience than the accused—and in consideration of the

---

under orders from Mexican conspirators. Kit Carson's wife Josefa and her sister, Bent's wife, were unharmed but had to remain over a day in the house with the governor's scalped corpse. Colonel Sterling Price of Missouri led 353 men and four howitzers through deep snowdrifts to Taos, reaching the town on February 3. Fifty-one insurgents were killed; Price lost seven killed and forty-five wounded in ending the revolt. Much of Carson's later enmity toward Kearny was traceable to the fact that if he had not been ordered to guide the general and his dragoons back to California, he might have foreseen the dangers of the unrest and been able to protect his family.

important professional services rendered by him previous to the occurrence of those acts for which he has been
tried, the undersigned members of the court, respectfully
commend Lieutenant Colonel Frémont to the lenient consideration of the President of the United States.

The six signatories, in admitting that the explorer had
been caught between feuding commanders and in circumstances that would have daunted a veteran officer, had borrowed the main leaf from the Frémont defense book.

James Gordon Bennett's *New York Herald* expressed no
surprise at the verdict, seeing "during the progress of the as-
sizes . . . evidences of hostility on the part of members of
the court against Lieutenant-Colonel Frémont . . . a greater,
though a younger man, than a majority of his triers."

On February 16, the President responded to the recommendation of clemency and surprised the court by dismissing
the more serious charge against Frémont by writing, "Upon
an inspection of the record, I am not satisfied that the facts
proved in this case constitute the military crime of 'mutiny.'" He sustained the other charges and convictions but
wrote:

. . . in consideration of the peculiar circumstances of the
case, of the previous meritorious and valuable services of
Lieutenant Colonel Frémont, and of the foregoing recommendations of a majority of the members of the court, the
penalty of dismissal from the service is remitted. Lieutenant Colonel Frémont will accordingly be released from
arrest, will resume his sword, and report for duty.

Despite the urgings of Senator Benton that he accept
the President's offer to reinstate him, Frémont resigned the
army on February 19, 1848. He was not guilty of any of the
charges against him, he said, and to accept Polk's remission
of his sentence was tantamount to admitting guilt.

As he saw it, it was a matter of honor: he had been in California before the conquest began, had had a role in starting it, had seen it unfold, had seen it botched to near ruination by two warring officers, had won the surrender treaty at Cahuenga Pass, and suffered the consequences of being forced to choose between the two lesser men who were his superior officers.

Ten days before the court's verdict, Frémont had passed his thirty-fifth birthday.

He had time for other conquests.

Epilogue

1

On January 24, 1848, a week before the court-martial verdict, gold was discovered at a sawmill owned by John A. Sutter on the South Fork of the American River. The man who first saw the gleam in the millrace was James Marshall, the eccentric New Jersey wheelwright who had ridden with Frémont, Segundai, Gillespie, and Kit Carson into Sonoma after the skirmish at Olómpali.

On February 2, 1848, two days after the verdict, the war officially ended with the signing of the Treaty of Guadalupe Hidalgo. The pen strokes made just outside its capital city divested Mexico of forty percent of its territory. Five hundred and thirty thousand square miles, including all of present-day New Mexico, Nevada, Utah, Arizona, and California, plus parts of Colorado, Idaho, and Wyoming, were ceded to the United States, with the Rio Grande established as the boundary between the two nations.

In return, President Polk agreed to pay $3.25 million in indemnities owed by Mexico, plus $12 million for its annexed lands north of the river.

The 1846 settlement with England had already added lands that became known as Washington and Oregon, and most of Idaho, to the Union.

Between the Mexican War and the Oregon settlement, the United States nearly doubled in size, adding 1,200,000 square miles of territory, with the country now stretching "from sea to shining sea."

2

Following the Frémont trial, Stephen Watts Kearny joined Winfield Scott's army of occupation in Mexico and served briefly as military commander at Vera Cruz. He contracted yellow fever and came home an invalid in July, 1848. That month he was nominated by the army for promotion to major general for "gallant conduct at San Pascual and for meritorious conduct in California and New Mexico." Senator Thomas Hart Benton filibustered in the Senate for thirteen days against the promotion, repeating most of the testimony against Kearny that had emerged in the court-martial. "After the conspiracy of Catiline, Cicero had a theme for his life; since this conspiracy against Frémont, and these rewards and honors lavished upon all that plotted against his life and character, I have also a theme for my life." This "ludicrous overshooting of the mark," as H. H. Bancroft said of the tirade, had no effect. Kearny won the major generalcy but did not live to enjoy its benefits. He died in St. Louis on October 31, 1848, of the effects of the fever he had contracted in Mexico.

James Knox Polk accomplished all he had set out to do in his presidency, from the annexation of Texas to the settlement of the "Oregon question" to the extension of the Union to the Pacific. He had announced early his intention to retire at the end of a single term and happily turned the presidency over to Zachary Taylor on March 5, 1849. In his diary, Polk wrote, "I am sure I shall be a happier man in my retirement than I have been during the four years I have filled the highest office in the gift of my countrymen." He enjoyed his retirement for only three months. After the inauguration of his successor, he took a month-long summer tour along the Atlantic seaboard and the gulf states and spent his final weeks working on his papers at his home in Nashville. He had fallen ill during his tour, possibly from a cholera outbreak in New Orleans. On June 15, 1849, he died at age fifty-three.

Both Senator Benton and Thomas O. Larkin, the latter the consul at Monterey and "confidential agent" during the conquest of California, died in 1858.

General José Castro returned to Californian in 1848 and lived as a private citizen in Monterey until 1853, when he was appointed military chief and *jefe político* along the border of Baja California and American California. In 1860, he was killed, Bancroft says, "in a drunken brawl—or, as some say, assassinated."

Robert Field Stockton resigned from the navy in 1850 and served in the United States Senate, representing his home state of New Jersey from 1851 to 1853, during which time he introduced a successful bill to abolish flogging as a punishment in the navy. In 1861, he served in a peace commission promoted by former President John Tyler in an effort to avert the impending Civil War, then became president of the Delaware and Raritan Canal Company. He devoted his retirement years to importing race horses from England. He died at Princeton on October 7, 1866.

José María Flores, who directed the last Californio resistance against the Americans, remained in Mexico after the war and rose to a generalcy in the Mexican army. He died in 1866.

John Drake Sloat died in New York in 1867. He was the original "conqueror" of California who raised the American flag at Monterey on July 7, 1846, and served as Stockton's predecessor as commander of the Pacific Squadron.

Christopher Houston "Kit" Carson returned to New
Mexico in 1849, often leaving his beloved Josefa to serve as
a military scout and guide in Apache country. In 1861, he
reentered the army as a colonel of the First New Mexico
Volunteer Regiment and saw action on February 21, 1862,
at the Battle of Valverde on the Rio Grande, after which
he received the brevet rank of brigadier general. He was
then ordered to western New Mexico and Arizona to war
against the Navajo, one of the tribes terrorizing New Mexican settlers. With a force of four hundred men, he led a
scorched-earth campaign, burning villages and crops,
killing cattle, driving the Indians to starvation, and in the
summer of 1864, he invaded their stronghold in the Canyon
de Chelly in northeastern Arizona. There he forced the surrender of some eight thousand Navajos who were subsequently
marched to Fort Sumner, New Mexico, for internment.

Carson's last Indian campaign took place in November,
1864, when he led an expedition of 335 men and seventy-
five Ute and Apache scouts against marauding Kiowas and
Comanches on the Canadian River in the Texas Panhandle.

A colonel in the regular army after the Indian wars,
Carson took command at Fort Garland, Colorado Territory,
in July, 1866, and was released from military service the
next year.

Now, at age fifty-eight and after forty-two years of stren-
uous living, his health began to fail. He suffered from chronic
bronchitis, noticed a weakening of his legs, and had persistent neck and chest pains that seemed to signal a faltering
heart. With Josefa and their six children, he settled at Boggs-
ville, near present-day Las Animas, Colorado. There a physician visited him and diagnosed an aneurysm of the aorta
so large it was destined to be fatal.

Despite his weakened state and Josefa's nearing delivery
of their seventh child, he made a last journey in February,
1868. As superintendent of Indian Affairs for Colorado Territory, he led a delegation of Utes to Washington to press

for a treaty guaranteeing the tribe exclusive hunting rights to lands on the Western Slope. In the capital, he met his old comrade, John C. Frémont, who was so distressed at his friend's haggard appearance and obvious suffering that he called upon some eminent doctors to examine the frail scout. The aneurysm diagnosis was confirmed.

Carson returned home in April to the great tragedy of his life. On April 13, his wife gave birth to their seventh child, a daughter, and ten days later, Josefa Jaramillo Carson died.

He lasted a month after that. He was moved to Fort Lyon, Colorado, where, at his insistence, he slept on the floor of the post surgeon's quarters under a big buffalo robe. He made his will, leaving his estate to the care and benefit of his children, and on the afternoon of May 23, 1868, he called out, "Doctor, *compadre*—adios." Blood gushed from his mouth as the aneurysm burst and he died.

Archibald Gillespie, the courier who found Frémont at Klamath Lake on May 9, 1846, and who surrendered Los Angeles to Californian insurgents the following September, died at age sixty in San Francisco in 1873.

Andrés Pico, who commanded the Californians in the battle at San Pascual on December 6, 1846, and later negotiated the treaty of Cahuenga with Frémont, served in the California assembly and state senate after the war. He died in 1876.

John Augustus Sutter, the lord of New Helvetia, became a delegate to the convention that in 1849 drafted California's state constitution. The discovery of gold on his lands, rather than making him rich, ruined him, and by 1852 he was bankrupt. He was granted a pension by the California legislature, moved to Lancaster County, Pennsylvania, and died there on June 18, 1880.

Richard Henry Dana, Jr., whose 1840 book, *Two Years Before the Mast*, gave Americans their first real glimpse into life in California before the conquest, died in Rome in 1882.

His best-selling memoir had made the Boston patrician famous, so much so that Charles Dickens, upon first visiting the United States in 1842, asked to meet the young author. In his law practice, Dana specialized in maritime matters, especially the plight of the common sailor. "The truth is," he said, "I was made for the sea. My life on shore is a mistake." In 1859, he returned to California—by sea—and paid a visit to the Frémonts and Colonel Vallejo. He spent the last decade of his life traveling in Europe and studying international law.

Don Mariano Vallejo, arrested by the Bear Flaggers in June, 1846, like Sutter, served in the constitutional convention in 1849. He became a state senator and a leading proponent of cooperation with American authorities in his homeland. He died at his Lachryma Montis estate in Sonoma on January 18, 1890.

Pío Pico was the longest-lived of all the principal Californios. Born at the San Gabriel Mission in 1801, he saw his home country ruled by Spaniards, Mexicans, and Americans. His career as political partisan, most often in opposition to the governors Mexico sent to their far-western province, had begun in 1831, his opposition to American incursions in the early 1840s, and he served as the last Mexican governor before the American takeover. He returned to California in 1848 and took up residence near San Luís Obispo. He lost his extensive land holdings—sixty thousand acres—to an American swindler and was left a pauper. He died at his daughter's home on September 11, 1894. Bancroft judged Pico to have been a man "abused far beyond his just deserts; a man of ordinary intelligence and limited education; of generous, jovial disposition, reckless and indolent; with a weakness for cards and women; disposed to be fair and honorable in his transactions, but [unable to] avoid being made the tool of knaves; patriotic without being able to do much for his country."

3

In a wise assessment of John Charles Frémont, Irving Stone said, "In his every success there was contained the germ of his next defeat; in every defeat, the seed of his next victory."

He lived forty-three years after the conquest of California, remaining a Child of Fortune—"He was essentially a lucky fellow," Bancroft said—to the end of his days.

But his fortune was not always good and his luck did not always hold out.

In the winter of 1848, he led his fourth expedition west, into the San Juan Mountains of southern Colorado, exploring a railroad route to California. The venture ended in disaster: ten of his thirty-three men were trapped in the mountains by heavy snows and perished.

In 1853, on his fifth and last exploration, he successfully crossed the San Juans—in the winter.

He became a millionaire when gold was found on the Las Mariposas lands he had purchased for three thousand dollars in the Sierra foothills, near Yosemite Valley. He acquired real estate in San Francisco, for several years lived in affluence with Jessie and their children in Monterey, and in 1850 was elected one of California's first senators, serving through a single year of Congress, giving up his seat to return to his Las Mariposas mines.

In 1856, he was nominated the first presidential candidate of the new Republican Party ("Free Speech, Free Press, Free Soil, Free Men, Frémont and Victory!") but lost to James Buchanan in the era's most disgraceful political campaign. Frémont, accused of being anti-Catholic, a mountebank, a drunkard, a bastard, a foreigner, and a convicted mutineer, managed to carry eleven states to Buchanan's seventeen and received 1,341,264 popular votes to Buchanan's 1,838,169.

During the Civil War he resumed his army commission

and was sent to St. Louis as a major general and commander of the army's Western Department. He was obliged to work without funds, arms, or supplies, and had to organize an army in a slave state that had a strong and vocal core of secessionists. He imposed martial law and worked indefatigably to make the city safe for the Union—even issuing his own emancipation proclamation—but was removed by President Lincoln after a controversial one-hundred-day command.

In 1864, he was endorsed as candidate for president by the radical wing of the Republican Party but withdrew for the sake of party unity.

He lost his Maricopa lands and fortune in unprofitable railroad ventures.

He served as territorial governor of Arizona from 1878–1881, after which undistinguished and absentee tenure, he was granted a pension by Congress.

In 1890, while visiting Washington, Congress restored him to a major generalcy and awarded him a six-thousand-dollar annual pension, but on July 13 that year, he died at age seventy-seven of peritonitis from a burst appendix in a New York City hotel at 49 West Twenty-fifth Street. His only son, John Charles, Jr., was at his bedside and placed in his hand a locket containing a miniature portrait of Jessie. She had remained in their modest Los Angeles home, unable to afford the trip east with her husband.

Kit Carson told his biographer in 1856, "I was with Frémont from 1842 to 1847. The hardships through which we passed I find it impossible to describe and the credit to which he deserves I am incapable to do him justice in writing. But his services to his country have been left to the judgment of impartial freemen and all agree in saying that his services were great and have redounded to his honor and that of his country."

Carson paid special tribute to how Frémont "cheerfully suffered with his men when undergoing the severest of

hardships" and said, "His perseverance and willingness
to participate in all that was undertaken, no matter
whether the duty was rough or easy, is the main cause of
his success."

Jessie's epitaph for her husband: "From the ashes of his
campfires have sprung cities."

The second of Senator Benton's six children, Jessie had
married Frémont on October 18, 1841, when she was
eighteen, a bright, pretty, boisterous tomboy, and he twenty-
eight, a solemn, ardently ambitious, handsome, and gallant
suitor. She was pregnant with their first child when he departed in May, 1842, to explore the Oregon Trail to the South
Pass in the Wyoming Rockies, and thereafter she transformed the raw data of his oral narrative and notes into
memorable books.

She was also pregnant during her husband's trial, and the
couple lost the baby three months after its birth.

She argued with Lincoln on her husband's conduct in Missouri in 1861—so forcefully that the exasperated President
called her, after she left his office, "a female politician."

When their fortune disappeared in bad speculative investments, Jessie, now fifty, had to take up her pen and write
reminiscences and children's stories to earn a subsistence
wage.

But even in Frémont's brooding and bitter last years, when
he went east without her, she wrote, "Love me in memory
of the old times, when I was so dear to you," and assured
him that their advancing age and uncertain future changed
nothing. "I love you now much more than I did then," she
said.

After her husband's death, Jessie and her daughter Lily
lived in an eight-room cottage in Los Angeles given them
by the Women of California Club. In her parlor, sitting near
the Gutzon Borglum portrait of her hero, she received

occasional visitors and eked out an income by writing magazine articles. She eventually received a two-thousand-dollar annual widow's pension, and to the end of her twelve-year widowhood, sheltered the flame of her "Jason of California."

She died in her sleep at age seventy-eight on December 27, 1902, and was buried beside her husband at Piermont, New York, overlooking the Hudson River.

SOURCES

Hubert Howe Bancroft came to California in 1853, following his father, a forty-niner with a claim on the Sacramento River. He opened his book-selling and publishing company in San Francisco in 1856, amassed a sixteen-thousand-volume library (sixty thousand by 1905), and launched publication of his histories in 1874. In all, there are thirty-nine volumes in his series, *The Native Races of the Pacific States* and *The History of the Pacific States*. Of the twenty-eight volumes in the latter, the seven volumes devoted to California appeared between 1886 and 1890.

No one is certain of how much of Bancroft's work was written by Bancroft himself. He certainly could not have written the histories alone, although he is listed as sole author, and the personal pronoun can be found frequently in the voluminous footnotes in the books.

It is known that he employed many capable "assistants," as he called them, and the names of several of these researchers, editors, and writers are known.

Whatever the weight of his contribution as author, it is to H. H. Bancroft and his band of unsung heroes that I owe my greatest debt. By preserving most of the significant documents of the era, and in citing them, often fully quoting them, his California volumes have become quite priceless, providing a narrative of inestimable value to any writer interested in the conquest, or in any other episode in Pacific Coast history.

And, for so massive and scholarly an undertaking, they

are a delight to read, as I hope the material I have quoted directly demonstrates.

Of the three principals in the story of the Bear Flaggers and the conquest of California, Frémont, as one might expect, has been the biographers' favorite. The best among these books, in my belief, is Ferol Egan's thorough, eminently fair, and spiritedly written *Frémont: Explorer for a Restless Nation.* The explorer's own *Memoirs* is invaluable if used carefully.

Dwight Clarke's *Stephen Watts Kearny: Soldier of the West* is a keen defense of the dragoon general, meticulously researched and an apt example of the author's assertion that "It is essential to a good biography that its author show some partiality for his subject." I agree, and this is the principal reason I like Egan's *Frémont.*

There is no modern biography of Stockton, a curious omission for a figure of such magnitude in the era of Manifest Destiny. Bancroft provides a wonderfully irascible portrait of this irascible figure, and fortunately there are good, dispassionate essays on him in Spiller and similar military references, and in the histories of the U.S.–Mexican War.

Bernard DeVoto's *The Year of Decision, 1846* is indispensable as an endlessly entertaining, personal, polemical *view* of the era. As a source on the conquest of California, it is quotable but erratic, and the author's anti-Frémont bias makes even Bancroft's attacks on the explorer pale by comparison.

As always, I am indebted to my late friend, Dan L. Thrapp, for his *Encyclopedia of Frontier Biography,* a monument to the history of the American West.

BIBLIOGRAPHY

American Guide Series. *California: A Guide to the Golden State*. New York: Hastings House, 1939.

Bancroft, Hubert Howe. *History of Arizona and New Mexico, 1530–1888*. San Francisco: The History Company, 1883–1888; three vols.

———. *History of the Pacific States of North America: California*. San Francisco: The History Company, 1886–1890; seven vols.

Bashford, Herbert and Harr Wagner. *A Man Unafraid: The Story of John Charles Frémont*. San Francisco: Wagner Publishing Co., 1927.

Bauer, K. Jack. *The Mexican War, 1846–1848*. Lincoln: University of Nebraska Press, 1992. (Originally published 1974.)

Bean, Walton and James J. Rawls. *California: An Interpretive History*. New York: McGraw-Hill, 1983.

Beck, Warren A. and Ynez D. Haase. *Historical Atlas of California*. Norman: University of Oklahoma Press, 1974.

Bergeron, Paul H. *The Presidency of James K. Polk*. Lawrence: University Press of Kansas, 1987.

Bidwell, Gen. John. *Echoes of the Past*. New York: Citadel Press, 1962. (Originally published 1900.)

Blackwelder, Bernice. *Great Westerner: The Story of Kit Carson*. Caldwell, Idaho: Caxton Printers, 1962.

Blevins, Winfred. *Give Your Heart to the Hawks*. Plainview, New York: Nash Publishing Co., 1973.

Burdett, Charles. *Life of Kit Carson*. New York: A. L. Burt, 1902.

Caughey, John W. *California : A Remarkable State's Life History*. Englewood Cliffs, N.J.: Prentice-Hall, Inc., 1970.

Clarke, Dwight L. *Stephen Watts Kearny: Soldier of the West*. Norman: University of Oklahoma Press, 1961.

Cleland, Robert Glass. *Californian Pageant: The Story of Four Centuries*. New York: Alfred A. Knopf, 1946.

Connor, Seymour V. and Odie B. Faulk. *North America Divided: The Mexican War, 1846–1848*. New York: Oxford University Press, 1971.

Dana, Richard Henry, Jr. *Two Years Before the Mast*. Pleasantville, N.Y.: Reader's Digest Association, 1995. (Originally published in 1840, this edition contains Dana's full narrative plus his "Twenty-Four Years Later" memoir and the essay, "Richard Henry Dana, Jr.'s Endless Voyage" by Thomas Fleming.)

DeVoto, Bernard. *The Year of Decision, 1846*. New York: Houghton Mifflin, 1989. (Originally published 1941.)

Dillon, Richard. *Humbugs and Heroes: A Gallery of California Pioneers*. Garden City, N.Y.: Doubleday, 1970.

Egan, Ferol. *Frémont: Explorer for a Restless Nation*. New York: Doubleday, 1977.

Eisenhower, John S. D. *So Far From God: The U.S. War With Mexico, 1846–1848*. New York: Random House, 1989.

Frémont, John C. "Conquest of California," *The Century Magazine*, April, 1891.

———. *Memoirs of My Life*. New York: Belford, Clarke & Co., 1887; two vols.

Gilbert, Bil. *The Trailblazers*. New York: Time-Life Books, 1973.

Grant, Blanche C., ed. *Kit Carson's Own Story of His Life*. Taos, N. M.: Kit Carson Memorial Foundation, Inc., 1955.

Hafen, LeRoy R. and Carl Coke Rister. *Western America*. Englewood Cliffs, N.J.: Prentice-Hall, 1950.

————and W. J. Ghent. *Broken Hand: Life of Thomas Fitzpatrick, Chief of the Mountain Men.* Denver: Old West Publishing, 1931.

Hansen, Harvey J. and Jeanne Thurlow Miller. *Wild Oats in Eden: Sonoma County in the 19th Century.* Santa Rosa, Calif., n.p., 1962.

Hawgood, John A. *America's Western Frontiers: The Exploration and Settlement of the Trans-Mississippi West.* New York: Alfred A. Knopf, 1967.

Henry, Robert S. *The Story of the Mexican War.* Indianapolis: Bobbs Merrill, 1950.

Herr, Pamela and Mary Lee Spence, eds. *The Letters of Jessie Benton Frémont.* Urbana: University of Illinois Press, 1993.

Jackson, Donald and Mary L. Spence, eds. *The Expeditions of John Charles Frémont.* Urbana: University of Illinois Press, 1970; two vols.

Johannsen, Robert W. *To the Halls of the Montezumas: The Mexican War in the American Imagination.* New York: Oxford University Press, 1985.

Lavender, David. *Bent's Fort.* Garden City, N.Y.: Doubleday, 1954.

Lynch, Robert M. *The Sonoma Valley Story.* Sonoma, Calif.: The Sonoma Index-Tribune, 1997.

Marks, Paula Mitchell. *Precious Dust: The American Gold Rush Era, 1848–1900.* New York: William Morrow, 1994.

Marti, Werner H. *Messenger of Destiny: The California Adventures of Archibald Gillespie, 1846–1847.* San Francisco: John Howell, 1961.

McCaffrey, James M. *Army of Manifest Destiny: The American Soldier in the Mexican War, 1846–1848.* New York: New York University Press, 1992.

Morison, Samuel Eliot. *The European Discovery of America: The Southern Voyages, 1492–1616.* New York: Oxford University Press, 1974.

————*The Oxford History of the American People.* New York: Oxford University Press, 1965.

Nevin, David. *The Mexican War.* Alexandria, Va.: Time-Life Books, 1978.

Nevins, Allan. *Frémont: Pathmarker of the West.* New York: Longmans, Green, 1939.

Osio, Antonio María. *The History of Alta California: A Memoir of Mexican California.* Madison: University of Wisconsin Press, 1996.

Papp, Richard Paul. *Bear Flag Country.* San Francisco:, n.p., 1996.

Parkman, Francis. *The Oregon Trail,* ed. by E. N. Feltskog. Lincoln, Neb.: University of Nebraska Press, 1994. (Annotated new edition of the 1849 original.)

Paul, Rodman. *California Gold.* Lincoln: University of Nebraska Press, 1969.

Pittman, Ruth. *The Roadside History of California.* Missoula, Mont.: Mountain Press, 1995.

Proceedings of the Court-Martial of Lieutenant Colonel John C. Frémont. Washington: 30th Congress, Executive Document 33, n.d. [1848].

Richman, Irving B. *California Under Spain and Mexico.* Boston: n.p., 1911.

Rogers, Fred B. *William Brown Ide: Bear Flagger.* San Francisco: John Howell, 1962.

Rolle, Andrew. *John Charles Frémont: Character as Destiny.* Norman: University of Oklahoma Press, 1993.

Rosenus, Alan. *General M. G. Vallejo and the Advent of the Americans.* Albuquerque: University of New Mexico Press, 1995.

Royce, Josiah, "Montgomery and Frémont," *The Century Magazine,* March, 1891.

Sabin, Edwin L. *Kit Carson Days, 1809–1868.* Lincoln: University of Nebraska Press, 1995 (originally published 1935); three vols.

Singletary, Otis A. *The Mexican War.* Chicago: University of Chicago Press, 1960.

Smith, Justin H. *The War With Mexico.* New York: Macmillan, 1919; two vols.

Spiller, Roger J., ed. *Dictionary of American Military Biography.* Westport, Conn.: Greenwood Press, 1984; three vols.

Stone, Irving. *They Also Ran.* New York: Doubleday & Co., 1943.

Thrapp, Dan L. *Encyclopedia of Frontier Biography.* Glendale, Calif.: The Arthur H. Clark Co., 1988, 1994; four vols.

Vestal, Stanley [Walter Stanley Campbell]. *Kit Carson: The Happy Warrior of the Old West.* Boston: Houghton Mifflin, 1928.

Weems, John Edward. *To Conquer a Peace: The War Between the United States and Mexico.* Garden City, N.Y.: Doubleday, 1974.

Woodward, Arthur. *Lances at San Pascual.* San Francisco: California Historical Society, 1948.

INDEX

Abert, James W., 596, 670

Acapulco, Mexico, 537, 538, 573, 682, 687

Adams, John Quincy, 569, 570, 573, 673

Agua Caliente, 737

Albatross (ship), 547

Albuquerque, 713

Allen, James, 712

Alvarado, Governor Juan Bautista, 544, 560, 561, 564, 617, 618

Aviso, José María, 639, 640

American River, 559, 599, 603, 613, 651, 661, 668

Americans
land grants to, 563
perceived threat from, to Californio way of life, 562–63
required to take oath of Mexican citizenship, 560, 600–601, 617
residents in Mexican California, 556, 563–64
trade with California, 544–45

Apache Indians, 733–34

Arce, Francisco, 639–40, 680

Archambeau, Auguste, 596

Arista, General Mariano, 627–28, 630–31

Armijo, Governor Manuel, 699–700, 706, 707–8

Baja California, 537, 541, 680, 727, 729, 758, 794, 799

Bancroft, George, 576–77, 581, 615, 618, 661, 662, 681, 682, 779

Bancroft, Hubert H., 564, 603, 640–41, 649, 657, 675, 719, 721, 753–55, 760, 769, 775, 777, 783, 789, 827, 831
historical value of work, 837–38

Baranov, Aleksandr, 546

Bartlett, Washington A., 778

"Battle of La Natividad," 730

"Battle of the Mesa," 769–71

"Battle of the Old Woman's Gun," 725–76

battles, other. *See locale of battle*

Beale, Edward F., 739, 740, 742, 745–46, 751, 752–53, 795, 810, 816

Bear Flag
fashioning and flying of, 648, 668
final fate of, 668n

Bear Flag Revolt, 635–50

Becknell, William, 702–3

Bennett, James Gordon, 820, 824

Bent, Charles, 590, 697, 711, 714, 822n

Bent, William, 697

Benton, Senator Thomas Hart, 582, 590, 594, 609, 618, 622, 633, 636, 673, 683, 690, 700, 703, 781, 788–89, 788n, 795, 808, 809, 810–11, 824, 827, 828
at Frémont's trial, 813, 820–21
expansionist policy, 588
support for Frémont, 580–81, 611, 641, 647, 799, 812–13

Bent's Fort, 697–98

Berreyesa, José de los Reyes, murder of, 655–56, 810

Berreyesa, José S., 649, 657–58

Bidwell, John, 550, 562, 563, 604, 724, 728

Bird Island (Alcatraz), 795

Bodega Bay, 538, 652, 669

Bodega Point, 547

"Bostons" (American immigrants to early California), 525–28

Bouchard, Hippolyte de, 546

Bridger, Jim, 589, 597

British
California said to be threatened to be seized by, 562, 565, 573–74, 580–81, 615, 620–21, 663
expansion of Empire, in 19th century, 521–22
and Oregon Territory claim, 572, 573–74
patrolling California waters, 663, 669
trade with California, 544
whaling industry, 546

Brooke, G. M., 813, 820–21

Brown, John ("Juan Flaco," Skinny John), 683–84, 723, 724
Buchanan, James, 570, 578–79, 618, 620, 672, 832
Burgess, Thomas, 749, 750
Butte Creek, 616
Buttes, the, 635, 640, 642

Cabrillo, Juan Rodríguez, 535–36
Cacafuego (ship), 537
Cahuenga Pass
  battle of (1845), 562
  treaty of (1847), 776–77, 776n
California
  American designs on, 521, 572, 575–76
  American immigrants to, 557–58, 579, 600–601, 637, 640
  annexation, attempted in 1842, 564–65
  annexation of, 664, 675, 681, 732
  armies, in the Mexican era, 561
  Californios' resistance to annexation, 718–31
  commerce and external trade, in the Mexican period, 528, 530, 544–45
  early Anglo-American visitors to, 525–28, 543–44, 554–58
  foreign population of, in the Mexican period, 556
  Mexican governors of, 543, 554–55
  Mexican period of rule, 525–28, 543–44, 554–58
  origin of the name, 536
  politics, in the Mexican era, 554–55
  revolts against Mexico, 555, 560
Californios
  dress and fashion, 529
  manners and lifestyles, 529–30, 550–54
Callao, Peru, 564, 565, 577
Camilo Rancho, 653
Camino Real, El, 541
Cape Horn, 537
Cape Mendocino, 537
Cape Verdes, 537
Carrillo, José Antonio, 722, 725
Carrillo, Ramón, 652
Carson, Josefa, née Jaramillo, 590, 598, 683, 811, 822n, 829–30
Carson, Kit (Christopher Houston), 590, 619, 620, 636, 642, 655, 659, 670, 733, 736, 737–38, 747, 751–52, 756, 787, 822, 822n, 833–34
  (1830) first exploring visit to California, 549

  (1842–43) with Frémont on first and second Western expeditions, 589–91
  (1845) with Frémont on third Western expedition to California, 597–98
  (1845) with Frémont in California, 619, 620, 636, 642, 655
  (1846) assists at the murders of Berreyesa and two Haro brothers, 655–56
  (1846) ordered by Stockton to report to Washington, D.C., 682–83, 713–14
  (1846) ordered by Kearny to escort him back to California, 715–16, 732–33
  (1846) at the battle of San Pascual, 742–44
  (1846) arrives in San Diego, 753
  (1847) leaves California, 795
  (1847) reports to Polk in Washington, and returns to Taos, 810–11
  biography, 588–89, 705
  character and appearance, 588–89, 670
  as Indian fighter, 605, 622–24, 635
  later career of, 829–30
  marriage and residence in Taos, 598
  memoirs of, 621
  on the trail, 597
Carson, Moses, 562, 601, 652
Cascade Range, 621
Cass, Lewis, 570
Castillo de San Joaquín, 659
Castro, Angel, 608, 608n
Castro, General José, 523, 566, 608n, 618, 635, 637, 660–61, 663, 671, 674, 675, 729, 735
  (1840) rebels against Micheltorena, 561
  (1845) requires American residents to take oath of Mexican citizenship, 600–601
  (1846) meets Frémont, 606
  (1846) confronts Frémont about actions of his men, 607–11
  (1846) denounces the Americans after the taking of Sonoma, 649–50
  (1846) military actions against Americans, 653, 654–55, 658
  (1846) declines Frémont's offer to parley, 665
  (1846) withdraws to Los Angeles, 668

(1846) military maneuvers around Los Angeles, 676–77
(1846) response to Stockton's declaration, 678–79
(1846) abandons Los Angeles, 680
attempted actions against American immigrants, 617, 640
later career, 828
power of, 555
suspected of fomenting Indians against the Americans, 625
Castro, Manuel, 606, 608*n*, 775
Cathay, search for passage to, 535
cattle, 552–53
Chapúltepec Castle, 633
Che-muc-tah (an Indian), 752
Childress, Sarah, 569–70
Chumash Indians, 539
Clark, Mary Radford, 689
Clark, Meriwether Lewis, 695, 699
Clark, William, 689
Clarke, Dwight L., 756–57, 808*n*, 838
Clay, Henry, 571
Clyman, James, 557, 612
Collingwood (ship), 663, 669, 670
commerce, in early California, 528, 530, 544–45
Congress (ship), 576, 579, 595, 672, 675, 677–78, 683, 724, 727, 739, 754
Cook, James, 546
Cooke, Philip St. George, 700, 709, 712, 791, 794, 796, 801, 805, 810, 815, 818
Corwin, Thomas, 632
Costanoan Indians, 539
Cosumnes River, 680
Cowie, Thomas, 642, 648, 652–53, 656, 657
Crane (a Delaware Indian), 619, 623, 624
Crockett, David, 570
Cyane (ship), 564, 576, 614, 618, 661, 663, 664, 667, 677, 791, 792

Dana, Richard Henry, 830–31
description of early California, 528–31, 556
sea voyage to California, 526–28
Davidson, John W., 733, 742
Deer Creek, 616
De Haro, Francisco and Ramón, murder of, 655–56, 810
De la Guerra, Pablo, 678
De la Torre, Captain Joaquín, 653–55, 658
Delaware Indians (Frémont's), 596,

603, 605, 610, 619, 620, 623, 624, 655, 656, 670, 779, 805
Democrats, 569, 570–71, 628
Denny (halfbreed), 596, 619, 623, 624
De Voto, Bernard, 625, 648, 657, 689, 798, 815, 837
Dewell, Ben, 648
Diegueño Indians, 539
disputación (legislature), 543
Doak, Thomas W., 547
Dodson, Jacob, 596, 670, 799, 801
Domínguez rancho, 725
Doniphan, Alexander W., 694, 699, 706, 711, 712, 715
Donner party, 806–7
Dorr, Ebenezer, 525, 556
Drake, Sir Francis, 537–38, 546
dress and fashion, of the Californios, 528–29
Duncan, James M., 739

Egan, Ferol, 837
Emory, William H., 695, 733, 735, 742, 745, 747, 748, 749–50, 752, 767, 786–87, 790, 810, 815, 818
Ericsson, John, 673
Erie (ship), 576, 793

Fallon, William O. "Le Gros," 601–2, 642, 806
Feather River, 616
filibusters, 564, 612, 649, 675
Fitch, Henry D., 652
Fitzpatrick, Thomas "Broken Hand," 557, 589, 590–91, 596, 698–99, 712–13, 715, 738
flags
   Bear Flag, 648, 668, 668*n*
   of United States, 565, 668
Flores, José María, 678, 722, 723, 725, 727, 728, 729, 753, 763, 765, 766, 767, 768–69, 775–76, 828
Ford, Henry L., 601, 639, 642, 652–54, 660–61, 670
Fort Hill, 723
Fort Ross, 547, 560, 563, 643
Fowler, George, 642, 652–53, 656, 657
Franciscan fathers, 541, 553–54
Frémont, Jessie, née Benton, 582, 595, 618, 620, 682–83, 690, 788, 808, 809, 811, 813
   final years, 834–35
   helps John Charles Frémont write his public reports on his western journeys, 590
   marriage, 588

Frémont, John Charles, Sr. (the
    explorer's father), 586
Frémont, John Charles (the explorer),
    603, 664, 665, 668, 674, 675,
    684, 690, 719, 724, 726, 729,
    759, 760, 761, 769, 794, 801–2,
    804–5, 830
  (1842) first western exploration of
    the Oregon Trail, 588
  (1843) second western exploration
    of the Oregon Trail, 590–71
  (1845) meets Polk, 580–81
  (1845) third western exploration
    from St. Louis to Californian,
    595–99
  (1845) arrives in California, 603–5
  (1846) visits Monterey to meet
    Larkin, 605–6
  (1846) on Gavilán (Hawk) Peak,
    609–11, 615
  (1846) at Klamath Lake camp,
    616–26
  (1846) joins in Bear Flag revolt,
    635–50
  (1846) forms the California
    Battalion, 660
  (1846) orders or instigates murder
    of Berreyesa and the Haros,
    655–58
  (1846) spiking of old guns at Yerba
    Buena, 659, 671
  (1846) enters Monterey, 669–70
  (1846) forces of, integrated with
    Stockton's U.S. forces, 675
  (1846) sent to San Diego, 677
  (1846) occupies Los Angeles,
    680–81
  (1846) promised governorship of
    California, 682
  (1846) returns to Monterey to get
    reinforcements, 727–28
  (1846) commands troops marching
    on Los Angeles, 762–63
  (1847) ordered to join forces with
    Kearny, 773–74
  (1847) negotiates treaty of
    Cahuenga Pass, 776–78
  (1847) caught between conflicting
    orders of Kearny and Stockton,
    780, 786–88, 792–93
  (1847) appointed by Stockton
    governor of California, 785
  (1847) letter to Kearny rejecting his
    authority, 787–88
  (1847) rides to Monterey to warn
    Kearny of possible new
    uprising of Californios, 798–800
  (1847) formal meeting with Kearny,
    800–801
  (1847) challenges Mason to a duel,
    802–3, 803n
  (1847) disbands the California
    Battalion, 804
  (1847) escorted from California to
    St. Louis, 805–8
  (1847) arrested in St. Louis,
    807–8
  (1847–1848) court-martial of, in
    Washington, D.C., 811–24
  (1847–1848) pro-and anti-factions,
    re his court-martial, 809–10
  (1848) convicted, but clemency
    offered to and granted by Polk,
    823–24
  (1848) resigns commission, 824
  biographers of, 837
  capture of California, 714
  character and appearance, 522–23,
    584–85, 658–59, 797, 832–34
  courts and marries Jessie Benton,
    587–88
  early career, 586–87
  explorations of, 557
  later career, 832–34
  orders to, in event of war, 582
Frémont, John Charles, Jr. (the
    explorer's son), 834
Frémont, Lily, 619, 834
French, proposed alliance of
    California with, 562

Gabrielino Indians, 539
García, Bernardino "Four-Fingered
    Jack," 652–53
Garner, William R., 561
Gavilán (Hawk's) Peak, 609–11, 615,
    616
Gillespie, Archibald H., 627, 636, 651,
    655, 659, 671, 674, 676, 731, 738,
    740–41, 742, 751, 756, 757,
    770–71, 773, 787, 796, 797, 798,
    806, 808, 816, 819, 819
  (1845) secret mission through
    Mexico to California, 581–82,
    610, 637
  (1845) arrives from Mexico with
    orders to various persons in
    California, 615, 618–26
  (1846) serves with Frémont, 660,
    669
  (1846) present at Berreyesa and
    Haro murders, 657
  (1846) named alcalde of Los
    Angeles, 682, 720–21

(1846) besieged in Los Angeles, 684, 688
(1846) loses Los Angeles, 724–25, 784
(1846) meets Kearny on the trail, 739
(1846) wounded at battle of San Pascual, 745
(1846) commands troops marching on Los Angeles, 761
(1847) recaptures Los Angeles, 772
character of, 581–82, 719–20
later career, 830
Gilmer, Thomas W., 594
Gilpin, William, 557–58
Godey, Alexis, 597–98, 619, 623, 653, 657, 670, 739, 742, 748–49, 750–51, 810, 813
gold, discovery of, 826
Golden Gate (mouth of San Francisco Bay), 536, 538, 659
Golden Hind (ship), 537–38
Graham, Isaac, 561
Gray, Andrew F. V., 753, 819–20
Great Basin, 595
Great Britain. *See* British
Gregg, Josiah, 702
Griffin, John S., 695, 716, 733, 746, 748
Grigsby, John, 601, 642, 645, 651, 660–61, 762
Guaymas, Mexico, 680
Guerra, Pablo de la, 678

Halleck, Henry W., 805
Hamley, George, 765, 774–75
Hammond, Thomas Clark, 709–10, 715, 733, 740–41, 742, 744, 746, 756
Haro, Francisco and Ramón de, murder of, 655–56, 810
Hawk's Peak, 730
Hensley, Samuel J., 602
Hermosillo, Mexico, 680
Herrera, José, 627
hides, trade in, 544–45, 553
horses and horsemanship, 529–30, 552
Houston, Sam, 574
Hudson's Bay Company, 573
Humboldt River, 806, 807
Humboldt Sink, 807

Ide, William Brown, 601, 639, 640, 642, 644–46, 648–49, 654, 660, 670
Independence (ship), 792

Indians, of California, 539–42
attacks by, on whites, 623, 635
decline of, 542, 556
life and customs, 538, 539–40, 552
massacres of, by whites, 605, 624–25, 635
their hatred of Californios, 740
Indians, other. *See individual tribes, e.g.,* Navajo; Pueblo
Isla de los Muertos, 726

Jackson, Andrew, 570–71, 673, 817
Johnson, Richard M., 570
Johnston, Abraham R., 716, 733, 742, 743, 746
Jones, Eliza Benton, 813
Jones, Roger, 811–12
Jones, Thomas ap Catesby, 564–65, 663
Jones, William Carey, 813
Juno (ship), 546, 669

Kearny, Mary, 758
Kearny, Stephen Watts, 591–92, 630, 730–32, 748, 750–51, 775, 777, 779, 801, 802, 803, 808, 812, 813–14
(1846) ordered to proceed overland to California and take possession, 634, 692
(1846) march to Santa Fé, 706–7
(1846) en route to California, learns of Californios' revolt, 735–36
(1846) wounded at battle of San Pascual, 745–46
(1846) reaches Los Angeles, 758
(1847) orders Frémont to join him, 773–74
(1847) question of who is in command of California, 758–62, 767–71, 773–86, 788n, 789–94, 819
(1847) confirmed as in command in California, 794
(1847) meeting with Frémont in Monterey, 799–801
(1847) plans to arrest Frémont, 800, 804
(1847) arrests Frémont in St. Louis, 807–8, 808n
(1847) at Frémont's trial, 816
biographers of, 808n, 837
career, 688–92
character of, 523, 591–92, 689
later career, 827
Kelsey, Andrew, 645
Kelsey, Sam, 642

Kern, Edward M., 596, 606, 651–52, 728, 804
King, Henry, 804
Klamath Indians, 589, 620, 623–25
Klamath Lake, 619
Knight, William, 639, 642

Lachryma Montis rancho, 638, 639, 647, 831
Lajeunesse, Basil, 591, 596, 619, 623, 624
Lajeunesse, François, 591
La Mesa, 679, 681, 722
La Natividad, Mexican port, 535, 763
La Natividad rancho, battle at, 730
Lapérouse, Compte de, 546
Larkin, Adeline, 729, 730
Larkin, Thomas O., 608, 625, 638, 639, 667, 672, 680, 719, 799, 810, 828
    (1845) secret instructions to, in event of war, 582, 618
    (1846) meets Frémont, 605–6
    (1846) attempts to placate Frémont in his actions toward Castro, 609, 610, 611
    (1846) aids Sloat in taking possession of California, 661–66
    (1846) captured by Californios, 729–30
    (1847) sides with Kearny, 791
    activities of, in Monterey, prior to annexation, 565–66
    advice re dealing with Californios, 614–15
    as American consul, 578–79
    character of, 579
Lassen, Peter, 562, 601, 616, 619, 625, 635
Ledyard, John, 546
Lee, John Fitzgerald, 813, 819
Leese, Jacob, 644, 646
Leidesdorff, William, 579, 604, 614, 619, 638, 668, 683
Levant (ship), 576, 663, 664, 675
Lewis, Meriwether, 689
Lexington (ship), 790
Lincoln, Abraham, 632–33, 648, 834
Los Angeles, 665, 668, 671, 676, 713, 754, 759, 769, 777–78, 780, 798
    (1846) abandoned by Castro, 679
    (1846) occupied by Americans commanded by Gillespie, 680–81, 682, 720–21
    (1846) Californio revolt in, 684

    (1846) American loss of, 718–31, 735, 784
    (1847) recapture of, 772, 777
    (1847) governed by Frémont, 794–95
    early American visitors to, 548
    history of, 561–62
    Mexican government in, 555
Los Angeles River, 772
Los Verdugos, 776
Luiseño Indians, 746

Machado, Rafael, 739, 740
Magoffin, James Wiley, 700, 709
Mangas Coloradas (Red Sleeves), Chief, 734
Manifest Destiny, 521, 564, 575
Manila, 537
Marcy, William, 577, 634, 690, 692–93, 700, 714, 790, 802, 817
Maricopa Indians, 734
Marin Peninsula, 550
Marsh, John, 612
Marshall, James, 655, 737, 826
Marston, Ward, 778
Martha (ship), 808, 809
Martin, Thomas, 640
Mason, Richard Barnes, 733, 784, 785, 793–94, 801–4, 803*n*, 810, 814, 816
Matamoros, Mexico, 627–31, 662
Maxwell, Lucien, 596–97, 605, 619, 623, 670
Mazatlán, Mexico, 577, 582, 614, 615, 616, 618, 661, 662, 663, 667
Meek, Joe, 589
Merced River, 563
Merritt, Ezekial, 562, 602–3, 639, 642, 644, 646, 651, 670, 680, 721, 724, 728
Mervine, William, 661, 664, 665, 684, 724–25, 736
Mexican-American War, 621, 627–34, 688
    end of, 826
Mexico
    Aztec, Spanish conquest of, 535
    hostility toward U.S., 618
    independence from Spain, 543
    oaths of fealty to, by Americans, 560, 600–601, 617
    peace overtures to, prior to war, 582
    policy toward its California territory, 543–44, 554–58
    threat of war with, 564–65
    U.S. relations with, 573, 582–83
Mexico City, 618, 633, 687

Micheltorena, Governor Manual,
    561–62, 564–65
missions, 541
    secularization of, 544, 554
Miwok Indians, 538, 539, 541, 605,
    653
Modoc Indians, 539, 625
Mojave Desert, 548, 593
Mojave Indians, 539, 540
Monterey (city), 582, 600–601, 603,
    617, 625, 669–70, 683, 723, 724,
    726, 727, 728, 737, 759, 791, 794,
    801, 802, 804, 805
    (1842) one-day American conquest
        of, 564–65
    (1846) taken possession of by the
        Americans, 664
    (1847) Kearny's capital, 791, 795
    customshouse at, 528
    described, 528, 605
    history of, 546, 561
    Mexican government in, 555
    trade with, 544, 545
Monterey Bay, 525, 528, 536, 538–39,
    546, 564, 615, 663, 791
Monterrey, Mexico, 688
Montgomery, Commander John B.,
    615, 625, 636, 647, 648, 651, 661,
    664, 667, 669, 728
Moore, Benjamin D., 699, 715, 733,
    739–40, 741, 743, 744, 757
Mormon Battalion, 694, 712, 791
Moscow (ship), 658
Mount Diablo, 612
Mulegé, 680
Mule Hill, siege of, 750–51

Napa Valley, 643
Natividad, 561
nautical life, en route to California,
    526–27
Navajo Indians, 713, 829
Neal, John, 602
Neal, Samuel, 616, 619, 655–56
Nevins, Allan, 805, 816
New Helvetia, 603, 619, 669, 762, 805
New Mexico, 688, 690, 692, 822,
    822n
    American conquest of, 701–12
    Mexico's policy toward, 543
Nicollet, Joseph, 587, 591
Northern Paiute Indians, 539
"Nova Albion" (California), 538
Nueva Helvetia, 559–63

O'Farrell, Jasper, 656–57
Olivas murder case, 638
Olómpali, skirmish at, 653–54

Ordóñez de Montalvo (Spanish
    author), 535–36
Oregon Territory, 557, 560, 572
    annexation of, 573–74, 827
Oregon Trail, 557, 588, 589–90
Osio, Antonio María, 553, 607–8,
    638, 648, 727, 776
"Osos" (Bear Flag rebels), 635–50
    dress and appearance of, 643, 670
O'Sullivan, John Louis, 521, 563, 575
Otter (ship), 525
Owens, Dick, 597, 598, 605, 619, 623,
    642, 660, 670, 799, 813

Pacific trade route to the Far East,
    537–39
Padilla, Juan, 652, 653–55
Paiute Indians, 539, 728
Palo Alto, 662
Panic of 1837, 556
Paredes y Arrillaga, Mariano, 583,
    627
Peck, William Guy, 596, 670
Peralta, Sebastián, 607
Petaluma River, 653
Phelps, Captain William D., 658–59
Phelps, S. S., 594
Philippine Islands, 537
Pico, Andrés, 523, 722, 729, 739–41,
    743, 744, 746, 749, 750–51,
    753–54, 755, 757, 767, 775–76,
    830
Pico, Governor Pío, 523, 555, 562–63,
    566, 617, 643, 650, 663, 665,
    676–77, 831
    leaves Los Angeles, 679–80
Pico, José de Jesús, 763–64, 775, 799,
    801
Pike, Zebulon Montgomery, 701–2
Pilgrim (ship), 526–28
Pima Indians, 734
Poinsett, Joel Robert, 586–87
Point Pinos, 528
Polk, President James K., 569–83,
    618, 700, 792, 795, 808, 812–13,
    817
    character of, 571–72
    declares war, 632
    expansionist policy of, 572
    grants clemency to Frémont,
        823–24
    later career, 826, 827–28
    meets Kit Carson, 810–11
    and Mexican war, 628
    opinion about Kearny-Stockton
        conflict, 794, 811
Pomo Indians, 539
Portolá, Gaspar de, 541

Portsmouth (ship), 576, 615, 625, 636, 647, 648, 651, 652, 661, 667–68, 728
Price, Sterling, 712, 288*n*
Princeton (ship), 577, 673
 explosion on, 593–95
Prou, Raphael, 596
Prudon, Victor, 644, 646
Pryor, Anne Whiting, 586
Pryor, Nathaniel M., 801
Pueblo Indians, 701, 713
Punta Concepción, 538

Quintaro, Nicholas, 709

Rancho Bosquejo, 616
ranchos and haciendas, 544, 552–53
Republican Party, 832, 833
Revere, Lieutenant Charles Warren, 615, 647, 667–68, 728
Reyes, Inocencia, 725
Robidoux, Antoine, 695, 733, 746, 751–52
Román (an Indian), 638
Rubio, Francisco, 638
Russell, William H. "Owl," 683, 778, 779, 780, 782, 810, 819, 820
Russian American Fur Company, 546, 560
Russians
 settlements in California, 547, 643
 whaling industry, 546

Sacramento (ship), 604
Sacramento River, 559, 639, 642, 646
Sacramento Valley, 558, 560, 562, 586, 599, 647, 669, 683, 730
St. Vrain, Cerán, 697
Salinan Indians, 539
Salinas River, 607, 609
Salinas Valley, 609
San Bernardino Valley, 548
San Bernardo, 749, 750, 753, 762
Sánchez, Francisco, 778
San Diego (city), 712, 721, 737, 741, 749, 752, 754, 758, 761, 784, 790, 791, 794
 (1846) recapture of, 727, 728–29, 753, 754
 early American visitors to, 548
 founding of, 541
 history of, 561
 occupied by Americans, 677–78
San Diego (ship), 538
San Diego Bay, 536, 538, 551
San Diego mission, 541–42
Sandwich Islands, 579, 616, 661

San Fernando, 766, 769, 773–74, 775, 776
San Francisco. *See* Yerba Buena
San Francisco Bay, 544, 547, 550–51, 559, 577, 579–80, 604, 614, 669, 682, 683, 728, 737
San Francisco de Solano mission, 642–43
San Gabriel, Battle of, 766–71
San Gabriel mission, 548, 549, 801
San Gabriel River, 766
San Joaquin River, 563, 605
San Joaquin Valley, 548, 593, 599, 603, 612
San José, 667
San José mission, 606
San Juan Bautista, 607, 609, 665, 669, 729
San Juan Capistrano, 545, 546, 680, 765
San Luís Obispo, 546, 554, 671, 729, 762, 763, 764, 775, 799
San Luís Rey, 546, 760, 791, 794
San Luís Rey mission, 765
San Marcos Pass, 764
San Pablo, 687
San Pablo Bay, 559, 655
San Pascual, 738, 740–41, 747, 748, 775
 battle of, 739*n*, 742–47, 754–57, 777, 778, 817
San Pedro, 545, 675, 677, 683, 684, 727, 735
San Pedro Bay, 548, 723, 724
San Rafael, 653, 654, 655
San Rafael mission, 638
San Salvador (ship), 535–36
Santa Barbara, 538, 545, 650, 671, 678, 723, 726, 736, 764–65, 766, 799
Santa Barbara Channel, 536
Santa Catalina, 538
Santa Clara, 545, 551, 607, 640, 649, 658, 676, 778
Santa Clara mission, 655, 667
Santa Cruz, 562, 607, 616
Santa Fé, 690, 692
 campaign at, 701–17
 described, 701–6
Santa Fé trade, 560
Santa Fé Trail, 696
Santa Rosa, 653
Santa Ynez Mountains, 764
Santa Ysabel, 738
Sausalito, 625, 655, 658, 659
Savannah (ship), 576, 614, 663, 664, 671, 684, 724–25, 726

Scott, Winfield, 595, 628–29, 633, 689, 784, 794, 804, 816
sea routes to California, 525–27, 537–39
Segundai (a Delaware Indian), 596, 619, 623, 625, 655
Semple, "Long Bob," 601, 640, 642, 643, 645, 646, 651, 659, 670
Serra, Fray Junípero, 541
Serrano Indians, 539
Seymour, Rear Admiral Sir George F., 663, 669, 671
Shark (ship), 576
Shasta Indians, 539
Sherman, William Tecumseh, 790, 799
Shoshone Indians, 539
Shubrick, William Branford, 792–93, 794, 795, 815
Sierra Nevada range, 548, 559
Silva, Captain Mariano, 664
slavery issue, 570–71
Slidell, John, 582–83, 610, 618
Sloat, Commodore John D., 610, 667, 669, 675, 676, 759, 828
  (1845) orders to, in event of war, 576–77, 582, 618
  (1845) patrols California waters, 614–16
  (1846) takes possession of California, with some hesitation, 661–66
  governorship of California, 718–19
  interrogates Frémont, 671
Smith, Jedediah Strong, 547–48, 557, 737
Sonoma (city), 547, 551, 555, 600, 617, 639, 654, 655, 657–58, 659–60, 667, 668, 675, 728, 762, 806
  described, 642–43
  seizure of, 642–50
Sonoma mission, 541, 643
Sonoma Valley, 643
Sonora, Mexico, 680
Sotoyomi rancho, 652
Spain
  conquest of Mexico, 537
  discovery of California, 535–42
  loss of American colonies, 543
Spanish language, 528–29
Stanislaus River, 548, 563
Stepp, Bill, 596, 619, 623, 659, 670, 795
Sterling (ship), 724, 727
Stockton, Commodore Robert Field, 666, 723, 728, 729, 730–31, 737–38, 748, 751, 758–59, 775, 777, 778–79, 788n, 789, 791–93, 794, 806, 808, 811
  (1844) and explosion on the *Princeton*, 593, 594–85
  (1845) in Texas waters, 577
  (1846) arrives in California, 671–72
  (1846) annexes California, 677–81, 713–14
  (1846) plans to join attack on Mexico, 682, 785
  (1846) attempts to recapture Los Angeles, 726–27
  (1846) meets Kearny, 755
  (1847) question of who is in command of California, 758–62, 767–71, 773–86, 789–94, 819
  (1847) at Frémont's trial, 818–19
  biographers of, 837
  character and appearance of, 523, 672
  later career, 828
Stokes, Edward, 737, 738
Stone, Irving, 832
Stonington (ship), 724, 728, 774
Strait of Magellan, 537
Sutter, John Augustus, 604, 619, 639, 647, 651–52, 805
  character of, 559–63
  divided loyalties of, 566, 636–37
  hospitality of, 592–93
  later career, 826, 830
Sutter's Fort, 586, 592, 599, 613, 616, 667, 669, 675, 728, 805
  (1846) commandeered by Frémont, 651–52, 660
  (1846) Sonoma prisoners held at, 647
  as American center, 558
  described, 558–59
Swanok (a Delaware Indian), 596, 619
Swift, Granville, 601, 649, 642, 653, 655–56, 660–61, 670
Swords, Thomas, 733, 742

Talbot, Theodore, 591, 596, 598–89, 603, 606, 670, 723, 724, 776, 795
tallow, trade in, 545, 553
Tampico, 633
Taos, 589, 598, 822n
Taylor, Zachary, 523, 577–78, 610, 628–32, 661, 662, 687, 688, 802, 827
  character of, 629
Tepic, Baja California, 561

Texas
  American aims on, 521, 564
  annexation of, 557, 570–71, 572,
    574–75, 577–78, 583, 627, 673
  independence of, 557, 575
  Mexican policy toward, 574–75
Thrapp, Dan L., 837
Todd, Mary, 648
Todd, William L., 602, 642, 648, 652,
  653, 654
Torre, Captain Joaquín de la, 653–55,
  658
Torrejón, Anastasio, 628
Treaty of Guadalupe Hidalgo, 826
Truckee River, 599, 807
Turner, Henry Smith, 733, 745, 747,
  749, 750, 762, 788n, 813, 815
Tyler, John, 571, 575, 577–78, 593–94,
  595, 673, 817, 828

United States, relations with Mexico,
  573, 582–83
United States (ship), 564
Upshur, Abel, 594
Ute Indians, 829

Vallejo, Francisca, 644, 646, 647
Vallejo, Mariano Guadalupe, 579–80,
  600, 617, 618, 637–39, 652, 654,
  667, 675, 683, 831
  capture of, 642–50
  character of, 638
  hospitality of, 551
Vallejo, Salvador, 551–52, 644, 646
Valley of the Moon, 580
Van Buren, Martin, 556, 570–71, 586
Vandalia (ship), 723, 724, 727
Varela, Cérbulo, 721–22
Vera Cruz, Mexico, 582, 618, 633,
  663, 804, 827

Victoria (ship), 535–36
Vigil y Alarid, Governor Juan
  Bautista, 710
Vincennes (ship), 551
Vizcaíno, Sebastián, 538–39

Walker, Joseph Reddeford, 557, 597,
  598–99, 603, 606, 611
Walla Walla Indians, 562, 675, 728,
  762
Warner, Jonathan Trumbull, 737, 746
Warner, William H., 733
Warner's Ranch, 736–37, 791, 805
War of 1812, 672
Warren (ship), 576, 802
Washo Indians, 539
Weber, Captain Charles, 778
whaling industry, 546
Wharton, Clifton, 807
Whigs, 570, 628, 632
Whitman, Walt, 633
Wilkes, Charles, 550–52
Willamette Valley, 573
Wool, John E., 712

Yerba Buena (later San Francisco),
  604, 619, 647, 659, 664, 682, 723,
  724, 726, 729, 778, 793
  (1846) American flag raised
    at, 668
  American representation in, 579
  described, 551
  Mexican government in, 555
  trade with, 545
Ynita, Camilo, 653
Yosemite Valley, 597, 603
Young, Brigham, 694
Young, Ewing, 549, 557, 589, 605
Yukot Indians, 539
Yuma Indians, 539, 540